Iraq

The ancient sites
& Iraqi Kurdistan

the Bradt Travel Guide

**Geoff Hann Karen Dabrowska
Tina Townsend-Greaves**

edition
2

www.bradtguides.com

Bradt Travel Guides Ltd, UK
The Globe Pequot Press Inc, USA

D0844042

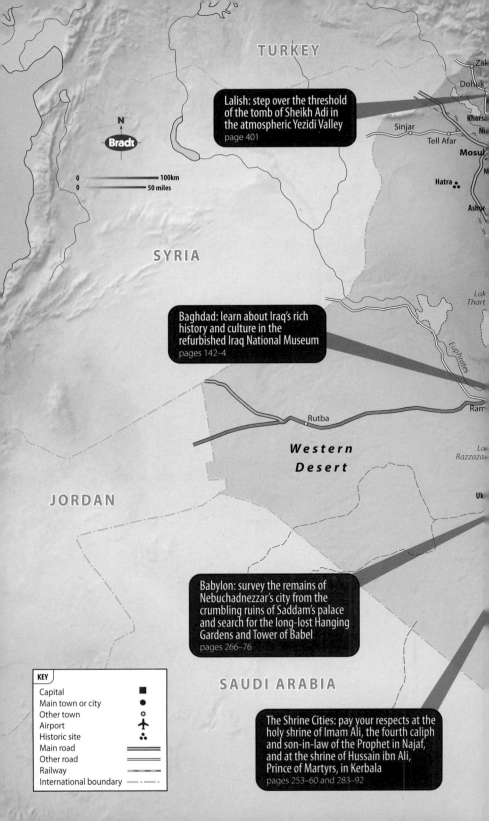

TURKEY

Zak
Dohuk
Khorsa
Lalish: step over the threshold
of the tomb of Sheikh Adi in
the atmospheric Yezidi Valley
page 401

Sinjar
Ni
Tell Afar
Mosul

N

Bradt

Hatra

Ashur

0   100km
0   50 miles

SYRIA

Lak
Thart

Baghdad: learn about Iraq's rich
history and culture in the
refurbished Iraq National Museum
pages 142–4

Euphrates

Ram

Rutba

*Western
Desert*

La
Razzaza

JORDAN

Uk

Babylon: survey the remains of
Nebuchadnezzar's city from the
crumbling ruins of Saddam's palace
and search for the long-lost Hanging
Gardens and Tower of Babel
pages 266–76

SAUDI ARABIA

The Shrine Cities: pay your respects at the
holy shrine of Imam Ali, the fourth caliph
and son-in-law of the Prophet in Najaf,
and at the shrine of Hussain ibn Ali,
Prince of Martyrs, in Kerbala
pages 253–60 and 283–92

KEY

Capital
Main town or city
Other town
Airport
Historic site
Main road
Other road
Railway
International boundary

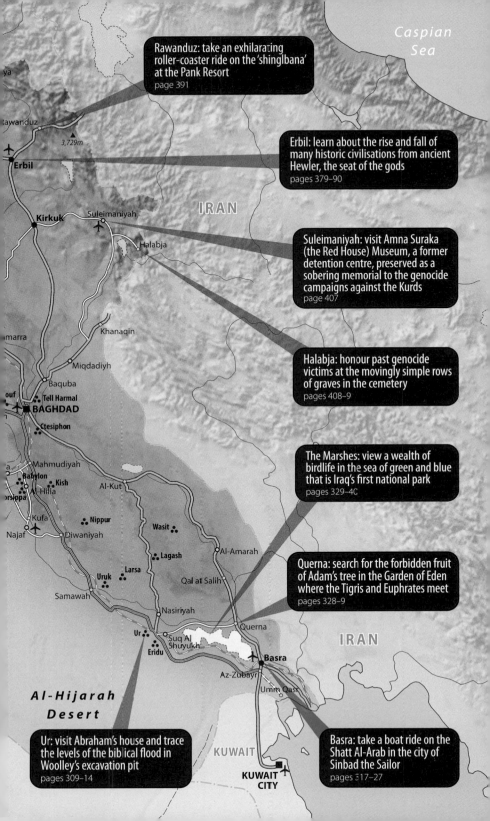

Rawanduz: take an exhilarating roller-coaster ride on the 'shinglbana' at the Pank Resort
page 391

Erbil: learn about the rise and fall of many historic civilisations from ancient Hewler, the seat of the gods
pages 379–90

Suleimaniyah: visit Amna Suraka (the Red House) Museum, a former detention centre, preserved as a sobering memorial to the genocide campaigns against the Kurds
page 407

Halabja: honour past genocide victims at the movingly simple rows of graves in the cemetery
pages 408–9

The Marshes: view a wealth of birdlife in the sea of green and blue that is Iraq's first national park
pages 329–40

Querna: search for the forbidden fruit of Adam's tree in the Garden of Eden where the Tigris and Euphrates meet
pages 328–9

Ur: visit Abraham's house and trace the levels of the biblical flood in Woolley's excavation pit
pages 309–14

Basra: take a boat ride on the Shatt Al-Arab in the city of Sinbad the Sailor
pages 317–27

Caspian Sea

Rawanduz

3,729m

Erbil

Kirkuk

Suleimaniyah

Halabja

IRAN

marra

Khanaqin

Miqdadiyh

Baquba

ouf

Tell Harmal

BAGHDAD

Ctesiphon

Mahmudiyah

a

Babylon

Kish

orsippa

Al-Hilla

Al-Kut

Kufa

Nippur

Najaf

Diwaniyah

Wasit

Uruk

Larsa

Lagash

Al-Amarah

Samawah

Qal at Salih

Nasiriyah

Querna

IRAN

Ur

Suq Al Shuyukh

Eridu

Basra

Az-Zubayr

Al-Hijarah Desert

Umm Qasr

KUWAIT

KUWAIT CITY

Iraq
in colour...

The Marshes
The lifestyle of the Marsh Arabs dates back 5,000 years
(RA) pages 329–40

Baghdad
Evening celebrations in Baghdad are starting to become more common
(RA) page 138

Ancient sites
The Arch of Ctesiphon is the largest single-span brick arch in the world (OL) pages 163–6

The Shrine Cities
Every year millions of pilgrims visit the Holy Shrine of Imam Ali at Najaf (RA) pages 287–8

Erbil
Erbil's Citadel is currently out of bounds to visitors while renovation work continues
(EL) page 388

above   Baghdad lies at the heart of the Tigris–Euphrates valley (RA) pages 119–56

left   The suburbs of Baghdad don't seem to have changed much for hundreds of years, but look carefully and you can spot 21st-century satellite dishes (s/S) page 110

below left   Baghdad was the capital of the Muslim empire AD750–1258 (RA) pages 147–9

below right   The Iraq National Museum reopened to the public in February 2015 (RA) pages 142–4

above   Celebrations in Kerbala mark the birth of Imam Hussain (RA) pages 253–60

above right   The security forces are a highly visible aspect of Iraqi life (RA) page 90

right   Kurdish cuisine is heavily influenced by Turkish and Iranian dishes (EL) pages 371–3

below   Children enjoying a cool break in the Baghdad sun (RA)

top Visitors to Babylon will see a mixture of the surviving remains of the ancient site and extensive modern reconstruction (RA) pages 266–72

above left The Temple of Mithras at the UNESCO-listed ruins of Hatra (RA) pages 241–3

above right Ur has been excavated by a succession of archaeologists since 1854 (RA) pages 309–14

below The military exploits of the Assyrians were immortalised in magnificent reliefs (khd/S) page 41

above Huge crowds gather in the Shrine of Hussain ibn Ali at Kerbala (TK/S) page 260

right Inaugurated in 2007, the Jalil Khayat mosque in Erbil holds up to 2,000 people (EL)

below Intricate tile work is typical of Iraqi mosques (RA)

left   Mar Matti Monastery, one of the most significant Christian sites in Iraq, is renowned for its dramatic location (OL) pages 219–20

below   The Hamilton Road stretches through the mountains and gorges of Kurdistan to the Iranian border (SS) page 364

bottom   A traditional village in the heart of the Marshes (SS) pages 329–40

your route to IRAQ

IKB Travel & Tours Ltd specialise in arranging travel to Iraq for our corporate clients. Our dedicated team have excellent local knowledge and the ability to arrange any method of transport to and from Iraq.

↳ GSA for many Iraqi Carriers
↳ Private/VIP Jet
↳ Cargo to and from Iraq
↳ Premium/Budget Insurance
↳ Scheduled Airline Travel

↳ Visa Service
↳ Transport in/out of Green Zones
↳ Group Travel
↳ Business Travel
↳ Flights to Iraq

A lifetime of travel has taught me one thing above all others: that to get the true measure of a country you need to listen to the opinions of the local people. To travel is to realise how much we are dependent on second-hand views and how different the reality is when we talk to the vendor in the market, or our taxi driver or local guide and learn about their every-day concerns. Bradt guides make a point of setting the tourist information against a background of history and cultural identity, and we have always tried to let the people speak for themselves, rather than impose our own political views. This aim has never been more important than in Iraq, a country on which everyone has an opinion but very few have first-hand experience. Karen Dabrowska, Geoff Hann and Tina Townsend-Greaves not only know Iraq intimately, but their love of the country and its people persuaded us to publish their first guide to Iraq in 2002. Yes, just a few months before the war.

Whatever your view on the events that have led to the current situation, there is no doubting that the Iraq that inspired us to commission the original guide has gone. A new Iraq has emerged, well documented by war correspondents and news commentators, but the focus has, inevitably, been on the aftermath of the war and the threat of ISIS. This new edition attempts to redress the balance, taking the original background information about the country and its people, and incorporating the present-day reality that restricts tourism to the few safe areas, which only a tour operator as experienced as Geoff Hann can know about.

The day will come when all of Iraq is again peaceful and safe for tourism. At present that day seems far away, but I remember saying that of Vietnam, Mozambique, Rwanda... In more than 40 years in travel publishing I have learnt that the people of these turbulent countries are magnificent in their stoicism and desire for peace. It will happen. Meanwhile learn what you can about this wonderful country, even if you are not planning a visit.

Second edition published August 2015
First published 2002
Bradt Travel Guides Ltd
IDC House, The Vale, Chalfont St Peter, Bucks SL9 9RZ, England
www.bradtguides.com
Print edition published in the USA by The Globe Pequot Press Inc,
PO Box 480, Guilford, Connecticut 06437-0480

Text copyright © 2015 Geoff Hann and Karen Dabrowska
Maps copyright © 2015 Bradt Travel Guides Ltd
Some town plan maps include data © OpenStreetMaps contributors
Photographs copyright © 2015 Individual photographers (see below)
Project Manager: Claire Strange
Cover research: Pepi Bluck, Perfect Picture
Index: Jonathan Derrick
Arabic language: Maria Oleynik

ISBN: 978 1 84162 488 4 (print)
e-ISBN: 978 1 84162 785 4 (e-pub)
e-ISBN: 978 1 84162 686 4 (mobi)

British Library Cataloguing in Publication Data
A catalogue record for this book is available from the British Library

Photographs
Rasoul Ali (RA); Eric Lafforgue (EL); Oliver Lee (OL); Shutterstock.com: khd (khd/S),
Tomas Koch (TK/S), sydcinema (s/S); SuperStock: www.superstock.com (SS)
Front cover Samarra Minaret (Images & Stories/Alamy)
Back cover Kurdish man (EL); Assyrian relief (RA)
Title page Minaret of Imam Abbas, Kerbala (RA); prayer beads (RA); Caliph's
palace, Samarra (SS)
Page 117 Baghdad mosque (RA)
Page 349 Statue of Ahmed Ibn al Mustawfi at Erbil Citadel (EL)

Maps David McCutcheon FBCart.S; colour map base by Nick Rowland FRGS;
Typeset by Ian Spick
Production managed by Jellyfish Print Solutions; printed in India
Digital conversion by www.dataworks.co.in

Contents

GEOFF HANN Born in High Wycombe and founder/ Director of the Adventure companies Hann Overland and Hinterland Travel, Geoff Hann is an experienced overland traveller and adventurer. Since the mid 1960s he has travelled extensively in the Middle East and Asia taking many groups from London to Kathmandu. More recently he has led groups to Afghanistan, India, Pakistan and Iraq.

His love of history and taste for exploring little-known routes has led him to travel extensively in Iraq, and during the Iraq-Iran conflict his groups were often the only travellers there. In 2000, he re-established his archaeological/historical tours, which continued until the outbreak of war again. In 2003 he paid a fleeting personal visit as war ended, and then led a rather famous post-war Iraq tour. Then sadly this open window closed. In 2007 he operated two tours of Iraqi Kurdistan and waited for southern Iraq to open again. Patience was rewarded and from 2009 through to 2014 he has been able to travel throughout all of Iraq. However, 2015 has seen an interruption to this, and at the moment owing to the situation with ISIS, only Baghdad and the south of Iraq can be travelled in relative safety. He expects this will change again, however, in the near future.

AUTHOR'S STORY   *Geoff Hann*

After the Second Gulf War, I was determined to revisit Baghdad. My friends were there – how had they coped? What damage had been done? Could we run tours again? What was the future for Iraq? I travelled to Baghdad alone. There were scary moments, once hurriedly leaving a restaurant to bursts of Kalashnikov fire. But the Baghdadis' enthusiasm for freedom after Saddam's constrictive regime was very infectious and apart from looting, there was little damage to the city. So with outrageous enthusiasm I embarked on my post-war tour of Iraq in October 2003, accompanied by people almost as crazy as I was. It was a wonderful experience. There were no restrictions and we totally bemused the military. How could tourists be travelling past their checkpoints as they were hunkered down over their machine guns? The general air of relaxation extended to us mingling with the Pilgrims in Najaf and Kerbala, and being welcomed into the Great Mosque at Kufa. However, this freedom to travel did not last beyond early 2004.

I consoled myself with exploring Kurdistan Iraq, a region difficult to visit under Saddam. In 2007 I arranged two tours. I was delighted to discover the Bavian Gorge with its Assyrian Reliefs. But there came a burst of reality when attempting to locate the site of Jarmo, a Neolithic village excavated in 1958, known for its pottery sequence dating back to 6000BC. Saddam had destroyed the local village and mosque, and we could see little of the site. Returning, we were suddenly stopped and arrested with brutal and fear-inducing efficiency. Our drivers were bound and we were driven at great speed to a police station. Four hours later, following a hilarious interrogation in German between a local interpreter and our German lady client of over 80 years, we were released. Surreal! The Chief of Police offered a guard for another visit, but I politely declined.

A visit to Iraq will always be an adventure. The delights of meeting new people and exploring are always there.

KAREN DABROWSKA Karen Dabrowska was born in Wellington, New Zealand in 1956. She worked as a journalist on the *Evening Post* in Wellington before emigrating to the UK in 1985 where she graduated with an MA in international journalism. Her Arab class mates introduced her to the Middle East and her fascination with the region led to a career writing about it. She was editor of *New Horizon* a Middle Eastern/Islamic publication dealing mainly with the politics and culture of the Islamic world, and helped
set up a number of publications for the Iraqi opposition to Saddam Hussein, including *Iraq Update* and *Baghdad*. When *New Horizon,* closed she worked as London correspondent for JANA News Agency and contributed articles on a freelance basis to *The Middle East, The Guardian, Islamic Tourism* and other publications. She joined the Sudanese National Council, a medical charity, as development officer in August 2011 and is a board member of the Kurdish Aid Foundation.

Her books include: *Addis Ababa: A guide to the country and its people, The Libyan Revolution: Diary of Qadhafi's Newsgirl in London, Into the Abyss: Human Rights Violations in Bahrain and the Suppression of the Popular Movement for Change,* as well as a collection of short stories: *Melancholy Memories: Foreign Dreams.*

In the course of her work she has visited over 30 countries including Afghanistan, Australia, Fiji, Oman, Syria, Libya, Palestine, Morocco, Tunisia, Iraq, Jordan, Western Sahara, Ethiopia, USA, Iran, Yemen, St Lucia, North Cyprus, Turkey, Canada, Poland, Ukraine, Kenya and Tanzania.

AUTHOR'S STORY   *Karen Dabrowska*

When I was working on the first Bradt guide with Geoff Hann many people advised me that the book was premature. 'Wait until the situation improves,' they said. But I soon realised that waiting for the new dawn in Iraq is like waiting for Godot. In 2003 I set up a good news website *Another Iraq* to highlight positive developments in the country and I hope and pray that the Iraqi people will not allow the extremists to win the battle for the soul of Iraq. As this book was being prepared the world witnessed the ransacking of the Mosul Museum, an attack on the 2,000-year-old city of Hatra with bulldozers, and an assault on the ancient Assyrian city of Nimrud. But rather than cursing the darkness, the guide sheds light on Iraq's beauty and heritage. The Iraqi people could once be compared to a necklace where the thread of nationality united a variety of unique and colourful beads. Let us hope the mud can be removed from this necklace and its jewels will sparkle once again.

TINA TOWNSEND-GREAVES Born in Huddersfield, Tina Townsend-Greaves, a career civil servant, has travelled very extensively throughout the Middle East and Afghanistan and has visited Iraq many times in recent years.

A lifelong enthusiast for learning, her degrees in Law and Security Management have often come in useful on her travels.

AUTHOR'S STORY
Tina Townsend-Greaves

Having avidly read the adventures of Gertrude Bell, H V Morton, Agatha Christie, Freya Stark and dreamed, alas too late, of travelling across the Syrian Desert on a Nairn Coach, I couldn't wait to actually visit Iraq. I got my chance in 2009, when I joined the first group of tourists to visit Iraq 'proper'.

Although much changed from the genteel, slow-paced country of a hundred years ago that I had read so much about, it was still a joy to be there and to visit places resonant with history – Babylon, Ur, Uruk.

What amazed me most was the interest our visit generated in Iraq and across the world. Suddenly everywhere we went there were journalists, cameras and film crews. On our final day in Baghdad our hotel was besieged by the media. Suddenly everyone wanted to know 'Why Iraq?'

Why Iraq? Because it's there. Because, despite everything, it still has beauty. To wander over 6,000 years of history, the pots of people long gone crunching under your feet. To see where the Hanging Gardens once grew, where the flood washed away the layers of civilisation, where the tree of life once flourished in the Garden of Eden. To walk in the bustling souks and see the faces of the people as they realise you are not a soldier, not an NGO; you are a tourist, a traveller visiting their country because you want to, because you can, bringing a small measure of normality back to the country and to their lives.

Why Iraq? Why *not* Iraq!

FOLLOW BRADT

For the latest news, special offers and competitions, subscribe to the Bradt newsletter via the website www.bradtguides.com and follow Bradt on:

- ⓕ www.facebook.com/BradtTravelGuides
- 🐦 @BradtGuides
- 📷 @bradtguides
- ⓟ www.pinterest.com/bradtguides

Acknowledgements

GEOFF HANN Firstly I would like to thank the ordinary people of Iraq. They come to my mind when I wish to acknowledge my passion for their country. For so diverse a nation, many of them transcend the divisions of religion, culture and life experiences. Special thanks must go to the Ministry of Tourism; the Director, the guides, the drivers and all those security personnel who have become friends. Special thanks need to be given to my fellow collaborator Tina. Tina's training and Iraq experiences have contributed to this book immeasurably, and this book could not have been written without her. Finally, I would like to thank all my friends and all the travellers who have been my companions in Iraq. They know what it is like to be obsessed with travel and they gracefully accept my comings, goings and reminiscences.

KAREN DABROWSKA For their assistance with information and comments, I would like to thank Fran Hazelton and Lamia Al-Gailani. For their support and inspiration, my thanks to Sifu Gary Wragg and members of WU'S TAI CHI CHUAN Academy, London.

TINA TOWNSEND-GREAVES I would like to thank Geoff, Karen and Bradt for inviting me to help write this book and to my friends and colleagues for their support. Also Mr Gorton, my school teacher, in the hope this book will go some way to showing that people caught reading magazines under the desk in English lessons do occasionally make good!

FEEDBACK REQUEST AND UPDATES WEBSITE

At Bradt Travel Guides we're aware that guidebooks start to go out of date on the day they're published – and that you, our readers, are out there in the field doing research of your own. You'll find out before us when a fine new family-run hotel opens or a favourite restaurant changes hands and goes downhill. So why not write and tell us about your experiences? Contact us on ☏ 01753 893444 or e info@bradtguides.com. We will forward emails to the author who may post updates on the Bradt website at www.bradtupdates.com/iraq. Alternatively you can add a review of the book to www.bradtguides.com or Amazon.

Introduction

Iraq, the land between the two rivers, the Tigris and the Euphrates, is a jigsaw puzzle with three main pieces: the mountainous snow-clad north and northeast making up about 20% of the country, the desert representing 59%, and the southern lowland alluvial plain making up the remainder.

The history of Iraq has often been a history of conflict and bloodshed, but during periods of serenity, splendid civilisations have emerged to make numerous indisputable contributions to the history of mankind: it is the land where writing began, where zero was introduced into mathematics, and where the tales of *The Thousand and One Nights* were first told. Iraq was the home of the famous Hanging Gardens of Babylon and the mythical Tower of Babel. Querna is reputed to be the site of the biblical Garden of Eden. Splendid mosques and palaces were built by rulers who insisted on nothing but the most magnificent. Through trade, Iraq absorbed the best of what its neighbours had to offer and incorporated the innovations of others into its own unique civilisation.

In the 20th century Arab nationalism was nourished in Iraq – it was the first independent Middle Eastern state and developed a strong Arab identity. Art was encouraged and Baghdad became the venue for many international cultural festivals.

But the 20th century was also the time of the Iran-Iraq War, the Iraqi invasion of Kuwait and the subsequent war. The Iraqi people also suffered from some of the most stringent economic sanctions ever imposed by the United Nations, and from Saddam Hussein's totalitarian regime.

The dream of a better future after the 2003 war, when the US-led Coalition toppled Saddam, soon turned sour and there began years of sectarianism, insurgency and sheer misery for the ordinary Iraqi. Much of the budget originally allocated by the USA for a massive rebuilding programme was diverted into maintaining security.

However, with the departure of the US occupying forces in 2007 and the establishment of Iraqi rule and with good, free elections in 2014, the country was beginning to stand on its own two feet. Iraqis are a resilient people. The mistakes are theirs, the triumphs are theirs, the future is theirs.

But how could anyone have envisaged the advent of ISIS (Daesh) in June 2014 and the rapid and almost total collapse of the Iraq forces and the invasion of Iraq, the taking of Mosul, Barji and Tikrit, the advance on Baghdad and the taking control of the desert lands of Anbar Province by the so-called Islamic Caliphate based in Raqqa in Syria.

It has taken some months for the Baghdad government to recover, to replace its ministers for a fresh approach to combat its own sectarianism, which has encouraged support for ISIS in some communities, notably in the north of Iraq, and for the outside world to also realise the consequences of what this could mean within the region. The resultant chaos and fleeing of vast numbers of people, both inside and outside of its borders, in response to the atrocities of ISIS, destruction of their homes and the fighting back of Kurdish forces and the Iraqi army against this invasion, has been immense. It has also exacerbated the divisions between the Kurdish regional government and the Iraqi government in Baghdad.

Both Bradt and the authors have thought hard about the wisdom of publishing a travel guide at this time. But Iraq – Mesopotamia – the land between the two rivers – is also the heritage of the world. Its civilisations, the ancient and historical sites, and the advances of knowledge that took place at these sites over thousands of years, have changed all our lives. Despite present restrictions visitors can still travel in many of the places described in this book and we look forward to the day, hopefully soon, when access to all areas of Iraq is possible. As we have said, the Iraqis are resilient people and with a little help from their friends, the country will recover.

In the words of Gavin Young, author of *Iraq: Land of Two Rivers*:

'If the oil should ever run out, the twin rivers will still uncoil like giant pythons from their lairs in High Armenia across the northern plains, will still edge teasingly closer near Baghdad, still sway apart lower down, still combine finally at the site – who knows for sure that it was not? – of the Garden of Eden, and flow commingled through silent date-forests to the Gulf. Whatever happens, the rivers – the life-giving twin rivers for which Abraham, Nebuchadnezzar, Sennacherib, Alexander the Great, Trajan, Harun Al Rashid and a billion other dwellers in Mesopotamia must have raised thanks to their gods – will continue to give life to other generations.'

KEY TO SYMBOLS

——·—·	International boundary		♦	Statue/monument
	Road (town plans)		$	Bank
═══════	Main road (regional maps)		⊠	Post office
═══════	Other road (regional maps)		⊞	Hospital/health centre, etc
======	Track (regional maps)		⌂	Hotel
═══	Railway		✕	Restaurant
▭	Railway station		✝	Church/cathedral
(A110)	Road numbers		◻	Cemetery
✈	Airport		⊄	Mosque
⛟	Bus station		❀	Gardens
⛴	Boat launch		⚘	Historic (archaeological) site
℗	Car park		•	Other place of interest
⚏	Tourist information office		▲	Summit (height in metres)
❸	Embassy		♣	Woodland feature
⍨	Museum/art gallery		✕—✕	Entrance barrier
▣	Theatre/cinema		(✹)	Stadium
⊞	Important/historic building			Marsh
▙	Castle/fortification			Urban park
🏛	Tomb			Shopping centre

As our previous book *Iraq Then and Now* reached the end of its life we began researching and writing this current, purely guide book to Iraq, in 2014, just as ISIS was expanding its territory in Syria, with the intention of publishing it in 2014/2015. Iraqi tourism had been buoyant over the previous years and so it seemed an appropriate time to do so.

Like the governments and the ordinary Iraqis we were shocked at the emergence of ISIS, an organisation capable of invading Iraq, taking the major city of Mosul and the towns of Barji and Tikrit, besiege the town of Samarra and head for Baghdad. The collapse of the conventional Iraqi army was also a great shock and the subsequent atrocities and destruction of historical sites, totally alarming.

However, with the knowledge that constant change is taking place we are intent on publishing for all to read, knowing that Iraq, its people and its culture are all enduring and the history of the country is still unfolding.

Please see the map in *Chapter 2* (page 67) and safety advice in *Chapter 4* (pages 98–9) for additional information.

HOW TO USE THIS BOOK

NOTE ABOUT MAPS Map research for this guide has proved problematic because of the security situation and unfortunately the detail on the mapping may not be as up to date as we would like. However, we have included the maps and site plans as we believe that they still give good geographical context and other information that will be useful for readers.

NOTE ABOUT PRICES
Accommodation price codes The price codes used in this guide indicate the approximate price of a standard double room with breakfast per night in US$. Note that many hotels in Iraq offer a wide variety of room permutations and rates, so this can only serve as a rough guide. The number of rooms has been listed where possible.

Luxury	**$$$$**	More than US$200
Upmarket	**$$$**	US$100–200
Mid-range	**$$**	US$50–100
Budget/Shoestring	**$**	Less than US$50

Restaurant prices The price of a three-course meal in a local city restaurant will cost about US$15–20 per person; however, in one of the better hotels the price will probably be double that.

Part One

GENERAL INFORMATION

GEOGRAPHY
Size/Area 441,839km^2
Location Middle East
Bordering countries Iran, Jordan, Kuwait, Saudi Arabia, Syria, Turkey
Capital Baghdad
Main towns Basra, Mosul, Kirkuk
Climate Mild to cool winters; hot, cloudless summers
Average temperature Varies from 48°C in July/August to 0°C in January
Terrain Desert, steppe, mountain forest and alpine regions
Vegetation Mainly desert: the country has few trees
Natural resources Oil, natural gas, sulphur, phosphates, petroleum, plus small deposits of coal, salt and gypsum
Main exports Main revenue from oil
National Parks Mesopotamia Marshland National Park

HUMAN STATISTICS
Population 33,929,316 (2014)
Life expectancy Average of 70.9 years (men 69.4 years; women 72.4) (2014)
Religion 95% Muslim; Christian minorities mainly in villages around Mosul; religious sects: Sabaeans, Yezidis
Ethnic divisions Arab 75–80%, Kurdish 15–20%, Turkmen, Assyrian or other 5%
Official language Arabic (Kurdish in Iraqi Kurdistan)
GDP US$242.5bn (2012)

POLITICS/ADMINISTRATION
Government Republic
Ruling party Elections were held in 2014 and the beleaguered Shia-dominated government of Prime Minister Nuri al Maliki was replaced by a more broad-based government led by Haider al Abadi. The government is facing severe challenges from ISIS, which controls a third of the country and from disputes with the Kurdish Regional Government over revenue sharing from oil sales.
President Fuad Masum
Prime Minister Haider al Abadi
Flag Three bands, red over white over black, with the words *Allah u Akbar* (God is great) written in Arabic on the white stripe
Governorates The country is divided into 18 governorates: Anbar, At Tamim, Babil, Baghdad, Basra, Dhi Qar, Diyala, Dohuk, Erbil, Kerbala, Maysan, Muthanna, Najaf, Nineveh, Qadisiya, Salahuddin, Suleimaniyah and Wasit

PRACTICAL DETAILS
Time GMT +3
Currency Iraqi dinars (IQD) (IQD1 = 1,000 fils). US dollars are also in circulation and are widely accepted
Electrical voltage 220V
International telephone country code +964
National airline Iraqi Airways

1

Background Information

GEOGRAPHY AND CLIMATE

GEOGRAPHY Except for the narrow strip of land providing access to the Arabian Gulf (also referred to as the Persian Gulf or The Gulf) known as the Shatt Al-Arab, Iraq is landlocked, with Iran to the east, Kuwait and Saudi Arabia to the south, Jordan and Syria to the west and Turkey to the north. With an area of 441,839km², it is slightly larger than Sweden. Iraq's landscape is dominated by two rivers, the Tigris (1,850km long, of which 1,418km are in Iraq) and the Euphrates (2,350km long, of which 1,213km are in Iraq). The two rivers are separated from each other by 400km of open plain when they emerge from Turkey's Taurus Mountains and flow into Iraq. The Tigris flows southwards, the Euphrates to the southeast. Near Baghdad they are separated by a mere 32km. At Querna in southern Iraq, reputed to be the site of the Garden of Eden, their waters join the Shatt Al-Arab.

For centuries the silt of the rivers, deposited in the valleys through which they flow, has ensured the fertility of the soil. The rivers' waters are also essential for irrigation. Floods, most common in March, April and May, have caused serious problems for centuries, as Sumerian legends and the biblical story of the flood tell us. In 1954 Baghdad was devastated by a flood that killed thousands and resulted in an estimated US$50 million worth of damage.

Iraq is made up of the snow-clad mountains of the north and northeast (which account for 20% of the land area); the desert (which accounts for 59%); and the flat lowland alluvial plain in the south, famous for its unique swamps and marshlands. This area was once the home of some 250,000 Marsh Arabs, also known as the Madan, whose unique lifestyle dated back to 3000BC, the time of the Sumerians. Today, the Marsh Arabs are returning to their traditional way of life as Saddam's drainage of the marshes is being reversed.

The Kurds, meanwhile, inhabit the mountainous region, a thin crescent around the upper rim of the country extending from Dohuk to Erbil and Suleimaniyah, with magnificent snow-clad peaks ranging from 1,000m to more than 3,600m near the Iranian and Turkish borders. The mountains of Kurdistan Iraq form a natural barrier between Turkey and Iran and are a traditional area of refuge from the heat of the plains. On the lower slopes the temperate climate and plentiful rainfall make the growing of fruit, vegetables, grain and tobacco possible. The rest of the country's population is concentrated along the Tigris and Euphrates, whose waters are the lifeblood of the country.

Finally, the desert, where Bedouin live off their herds of camels, goats and sheep, has been described in a geography textbook as *'an area so desolate and uninviting that even a rattlesnake would feel lonely there'*.

CLIMATE Iraq not only has two seasons, hot and cool, but also two climatic areas: the hot lowlands where crops require irrigation and the much wetter northeast

3

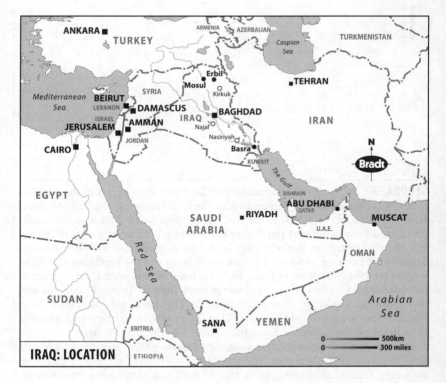

IRAQ: LOCATION

where the mountains produce cooler temperatures and precipitation for crop cultivation. In the lowlands (mostly southern and central Iraq), there are two seasons, summer and winter. The summer, which lasts from May to October, has high temperatures ranging from 20°C to over 40°C. In Baghdad, temperatures can reach over 50°C at their highest, but 40°C+ is more usual. There is usually no rain between June and September. The winter of December to February is mild with temperatures ranging from 2°C to 15°C. Rain occurs between November and April, with an annual mean of 100–180mm. In the northeast, the summer lasts from June to September and is usually dry and hot, but with temperatures usually up to 6°C cooler than the lowlands.

Rainfall is mostly in the winter period. The winter here lasts longer and is colder, with mountain temperatures of -4°C to +5°C, but slightly warmer in the uplands or foothills with temperatures ranging up to 12°C. Annual rainfall up to 550mm is typical, but is higher in the actual mountains themselves.

The summer months in Iraq are affected by southern and southeasterly hot and dry winds, which often bring with them destructive dust storms. These occur from April to early June and again from late September to November. However, from mid-June to mid-September the steady wind from the north and northwest called the 'Shamal' brings very dry air, which results in little cloud cover and which, in turn, causes the land to be intensely heated by the sun; the wind does have a slight cooling effect.

Other extremes to be noted are the range of temperatures that occur in the desert regions, such as the western desert, from below freezing at night to 45°C at the peak of day. Note that during the summer period the Basra region and the marshes suffer extreme humidity approaching 100%.

FLORA Four vegetation zones are recognised in Iraq: the desert, the steppe, the mountain forest and the alpine regions. Low rainfall plays a dominant role in the formation of the short-lived herbaceous plants in the latter two. Arboreal types are practically absent in the steppe and deserts of Iraq. The northern part of the country, with its mountains and available rainfall, sustains virgin forests, cultivated forests, and a large number of crop plants and their wild relatives. Over cutting and overgrazing in the Zagros Mountains have reduced some of Iraq's oak forests to scrub lands, although stands of other trees (maple, hawthorn and pistachio, for example) remain. Alpine plants that can survive harsh weather appear at higher elevations. Indigenous plant and animal life in Iraq is under increasing threat from the impact of development. Overgrazing and mismanagement have led to the loss of natural plant cover. Deforestation is now a major concern in the northern highlands and mountains. Reeds, box thorns, buttercups, rushes and salt bush still grow in the plains and marshes however, and date palms thrive in many parts of the country. Occasionally poplars and willows are found in the plains.

In Kurdistan the scenery is magnificent, sometimes wooded and watered by turbulent streams, sometimes gaunt and bare, but always dramatic and often awe-inspiring, with bright dazzling colours of tulips, roses, hyacinths, gladioli and daffodils. The main crops are wheat and barley grown on the plains of Erbil.

DATE PRODUCTION IN DECLINE

Finding a date in Iraq never used to be a problem – in the 1960s and 1970s there were over 30 million date trees in the country, with around 450 different varieties. Indeed, Iraq was known as the land that first produced date palms, and it was not possible to discuss agriculture in Iraq without mentioning dates and the palm trees that produced them. The trunk of the date palm grows to a height of up to 18m and a female tree can bear 200–1,000 dates each season. A cluster of dates weighs up to 12kg and the annual yield of a single tree may reach 270kg. The tree begins to bear fruit in its eighth year, reaches maturity at 30 years, and begins to decline at about 100 years.

Before the Iran-Iraq War (1980–88) Iraq was one of the world's leading producers of top-quality dates, supplying over 60% of the world's crop, but the decades of wars, diseases, droughts, dredging operations and construction projects that the country has witnessed in the past 40 years have seen agricultural production in Iraq slashed, with date palms being one of the worst-affected crops. A sharp decline in production of this valued fruit means that today only around 6 million trees remain.

The decline has mostly affected the southern Iraqi city of Basra where more than half of the expansive date-palm groves have been damaged owing to war and high salinity levels in water. But exports dwindled following the 1991 Gulf War. Water shortages, high levels of salinity, and desertification have also had an impact on the production of dates in the country. As a result of these conditions, most of Iraq's dry and yellow date-palm trees are now being cut down in the area stretching along the Shatt Al-Arab waterway, once famous for its large crop yields. Many of the city's date factories were also shut down, and those that were operating saw their production levels decrease.

Suleimaniyah is a traditional tobacco-producing region. Fruits such as apples, cherries, plums and pomegranates are also grown in Iraqi Kurdistan.

WILDLIFE Centuries of human settlement have depleted Iraq's wildlife and conservation has not been a priority. Creatures once native to the country, such as fallow deer, ostrich, wild goat and antelope, were extinct by the turn of the 20th century, owing in no small part to indiscriminate hunting from cars. The threat to wildlife was made worse through the destruction of their habitats, particularly deforestation: Iraq lost at least 10% of its natural forest during the 1980s. Surviving mammals include bats, rats, jackals, hyenas and wildcats, with wild pig and gazelle found in more remote parts. Reptiles are numerous and include lizards, snakes and tortoises. Among Iraq's domesticated animals are camels, oxen, water buffalo and horses. Northern Iraqis raise large flocks of sheep and goats for their milk, meat, wool and skin. More than 40 different types of fish are found in the rivers and streams of Kurdistan and the mountains were once popular hunting grounds for wild boars, bears, hyenas, ibexes and hares. The last lion was reported killed around 1910.

BIRDS There is a distinct hierarchy among the birds: eagles, vultures, kites and other birds of prey make a meal of smaller birds. Water birds include pelicans, geese, ducks and herons. Storks were once a common sight throughout the country. They build their nests on trees, roofs and domes. The hoopoe is a legendary creature,

IRAQ'S FIRST NATIONAL PARK

In a historic first, Iraq announced the creation of its first national park, Mesopotamia Marshland National Park, in July 2013.

The Mesopotamia Marshland National Park is a unique wetlands complex rich in wildlife. Located in southern Iraq, the park is considered to provide an ecological bridge between the Africa region (termed the Arabic region of the African plate) and the Eurasian region. It is an important resting and feeding site for millions of migratory birds. With its unique confluence of water and land plus the sheer size of the wetlands, it has a richness of birds and other wildlife, as well as a high ecological value. Endemic birds include the Basra reed warbler (*Acrocephalus griseldis*) and Iraq babbler (*Turdoides altirostris*), the Iraqi subspecies of the little grebe (*Tachybaptus ruficollis iraquensis*) and the African darter (*Anhinga rufa chantrei*). Mammals found in the park include the smooth-coated otter (*Lutra perspicillata maxwelli*) and Bunn's short-tailed bandicoot rat (*Erythronesokia bunnii*). The park also contains endemic fish, such as bunnei (*Barbus sharpeyi*).

The marsh area around the National Park is also home to indigenous tribes with rich cultures and traditions. Still practising their customs today, they hand down their knowledge of the use of traditional, natural resources to new generations. Although their heritage is strongly supported by the park, owing in part to draining of the Marshes in the 1990s, there are fewer villages actually located within it than in the past.

In addition to the above, more than 60 archaeological sites have been documented throughout the area. Although these are still unexplored, they add to its historical importance and attraction for tourism.

Despite this richness and diversity, the new park still faces a number of challenges, including uncontrolled hunting and fishing, the use of dangerous which sheltered the Prophet Mohammed with its wings when he fell asleep in the desert. In gratitude the bird was offered a gift and the vain creature chose its glorious crown. The sand grouse, which resembles a pigeon, nests in the desert in temperatures higher than 38°C. Water is brought to the young on the breast feathers of their parents, who shelter them with their wings.

ECOLOGICAL DAMAGE Iraq's Marshes once stretched over 20,000km^2, interconnecting shallow and deep-water lakes, mudflats, reed marshes, seasonal lagoons, and salt-tolerant scrub. Believed by many to be the site of the Garden of Eden, this large wetland ecosystem formed a crucial stop for many millions of migratory birds travelling between Siberia and Africa and provided nursery grounds for economically important Persian Gulf fish and shrimp, as well as other marine and freshwater species, making the Marshes a vital area of biodiversity. However, in recent decades the ecosystem of the Marshes has been repeatedly shaped and reshaped by conflict. The Iran/Iraq border runs directly through the Marshes, and they were a main battleground of the 1980s war between those two countries. Both sides used the waters strategically; building dikes, draining some areas to facilitate their own troop movements and flooding others to stop the enemy.

The real ecological disaster, though, struck in the early 1990s when Saddam Hussein's regime drained the Marshes in response to the Shia uprising that spread through southern Iraq following the Gulf War. By the year 2000, a series of dikes and channels had reduced the Marshes to less than 10% of their original size,

chemicals in the area, the introduction of exotic species, uncontrolled reed harvesting, buffalo breeding and development of settlements and infrastructure, as well as damage and looting of archaeological sites. To address these, the park's management has set out five main objectives:

- to secure and maintain the habitat conditions necessary to protect significant species, groups of species, biotic communities or physical features of the environment where these require specific human manipulation for optimum management;
- to facilitate scientific research and environmental monitoring as primary activities associated with sustainable resource management;
- to develop limited areas for public education and appreciation of the characteristics of the habitats concerned and of the work of wildlife management;
- to eliminate and thereafter prevent exploitation or occupation inimical to the purposes of designation; and
- to deliver such benefits to people living within the designated area as are consistent with the other objectives of management.

After the draining of the Marshes in the 1990s, water, vegetation and wildlife are steadily starting to return. As it continues to address local and regional conservation and development challenges, Mesopotamia Marshland National Park not only represents history as Iraq's first national protected area, but also serves as an inspiring solution for people and nature in an area once devastated by conflict.

1

transforming the landscape into a parched desert covered by salt crusts over a metre deep in some areas. Local temperatures increased by 5°C, siltation damaged coral reefs in the Persian Gulf and dust storms plagued the land. Several species endemic to the Marshes (such as the smooth-coated otter, the bandicoot rat, the long-fingered bat, and a species of barbel fish) were driven to extinction. Dozens more bird species were placed in danger of disappearing forever and Persian Gulf fish and shrimp catches declined.

With the ousting of Saddam Hussein in 2003, the tide turned. International and Iraqi organisations supported by local people began to reclaim the Marshes and to restore the ecosystem. By the end of 2005, 40% of the Marshes' former area had been re-inundated and substantial regrowth of reeds had begun. As native vegetation returned, wildlife followed. Bird surveys have found that 72 species of birds, including 10 regionally or globally threatened species, have returned and several endemic species, including the Basra reed warbler and the Iraq babbler, are thriving. In 2013 the Mesopotamia Marshland National Park opened, crowning the rebirth of the Marshes and securing their future protection. Generally speaking, this war's effect on the environment in the Marshes has been positive.

Elsewhere, however, the future is hardly certain. Despite the shutdown, albeit temporary, of nearly 200 industrial plants pouring effluent into the Tigris and Euphrates, high soil salinity and stagnant water may limit the possibilities for restoration in some areas. A series of dams upstream (both the Tigris and the Euphrates originate in Turkey) has diminished the flow of these two rivers over decades, and reduced the amount of spring snow melt that previously nourished the land between the rivers with nutrients and alluvial soil.

GOVERNMENT AND POLITICS

Iraq is nominally a representative democratic republic comprising of 18 governorates. The government of Iraq takes place in the framework of a federal parliament, made up of executive, legislative and judicial branches. Legislative power is vested in the Council of Representatives. Executive power is exercised by the prime minister and the Council of Ministers (of whom he is the head). Iraq has a multi-party political system, with ministerial posts divided between the major ethnic and religious groups, with Shias, Sunnis, Kurds and other minority groups each holding a proportion of the posts. The central government is dominated by the Shia majority who currently make up about 60% of the total population. (See pages 19–20 for an explanation of the Sunni-Shia schism.) Iraq's Kurdish minority enjoys a strong autonomy in the north of the country with its own government and security forces. Although the government of Iraq is nominally secular, as in most Muslim countries Islam bears influence on the laws and regulations it enacts.

The **president of Iraq** is the head of state. His role is to safeguard the commitment to the Iraqi constitution and preserve Iraq's independence, sovereignty, unity and the security of its territories in accordance with the provisions of the Constitution. He is elected by a two-thirds majority by the Council of Representatives and is limited to two four-year terms. His job is to ratify the treaties and laws passed by the Council of Representatives, issue pardons (on the recommendation of the prime minister) and to perform duties relating to the higher command of the armed forces in relation to ceremonial and honorary functions.

The **prime minister** is the head of the government. Originally it was an appointed role subordinate to that of the president, and only nominally leader of the Iraqi parliament. However as part of the changes made to the constitution following 2003, the prime minister is now Iraq's major executive authority. The prime minister (and his deputies) are nominated by the president and must be approved by a majority of members of the Council of Representatives.

The **Council of Representatives** is Iraq's sole legislative body, with the power to enact, amend and repeal laws. It is currently composed of 325 seats and at least one-quarter of its members must be female. Its duties include enacting federal laws, monitoring the executive branch, electing the prime minister and approving the Council of Ministers appointed by him. The council serves a four-year term.

The **Council of Ministers** (also known as the cabinet) comprises the prime minister, three deputy prime ministers and 30 cabinet ministers, it is the executive branch of the government. Appointed by the prime minister and approved by the Council of Representatives, its function is to act as the cabinet of the government. It serves a four-year term, concurrent with that of the Council of Representatives.

Iraq's judicial branch is composed of the Higher Judicial Council, Federal Supreme Court, Court of Cassation, Public Prosecution Department, Judiciary Oversight Commission, and other federal courts. The Higher Judicial Council supervises the affairs of the federal judiciary. The Federal Supreme Court has limited jurisdiction related to intra-governmental disputes and constitutional issues. The appellate courts appeal up to the Court of Cassation, the highest court of appeal. The establishment of the federal courts, their types, and methods for judicial appointments are set forth by laws enacted by the Council of Representatives.

The first Iraqi parliament was formed in 1925 following the establishment of a constitutional monarchy under Faisal I. Ten elections took place between 1925 and the coup of 1958, which saw the end of the monarchy and the abolition of parliament. In 1970 a constitutional republic was formed with an elected National Assembly (al-Majlis al-Watani); however, elections for this did not take place until 1980, when these were called by Iraq's new military president, Saddam Hussein. Under Saddam and the Baathist Party rule, the posts of president, prime minister and chair of the Revolutionary Command Council were all rolled into one and occupied by him. The remaining important government posts were allocated to Sunnis who made up his inner circle, meaning that the Assembly was largely a figurehead which rubber-stamped his decrees. Although several elections took place between 1989 and 2003, these were not considered free and fair by the international community as only members of the Baath Party were ever elected.

Between 2003 and 2011, under the American-led administration, Iraq completed a transition from the dictatorship of Saddam Hussein to a plural political system in which varying sects and ideological and political factions compete in elections. A series of elections began in 2005 followed by a seven-month interim period of Iraqi self-governance that gave each community a share of power and prestige in an effort to promote co-operation and unity. However, disputes over the relative claims of each to power and economic resources permeated every part of the government and were never fully resolved. These disputes continued after the parliamentary elections held in March 2010, and along with disputes over vote counting, legal interpretations and alliance negotiations, led to more than eight months of political deadlock as no one party or bloc was able to command a majority. The Iraqi National Movement (Sunni) led by former interim prime minister Ayad Allawi won 91 seats and the State of Law Coalition (Shia) led by Nuri al Maliki won 89 seats. Parliament began its deliberations in June 2010 and an agreement on the formation of a National Unity government (which turned out to be neither) was reached in November with al Maliki as prime minister, but serious disagreements and tensions continued to cause friction between the two major blocs.

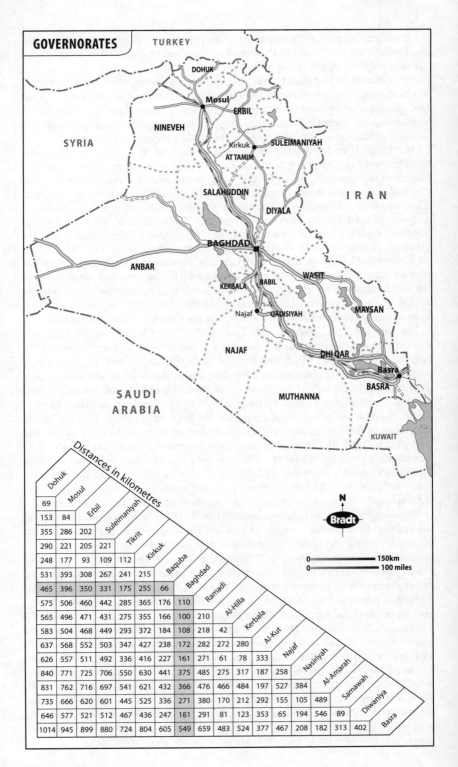

GOVERNORATES

TURKEY

DOHUK

Mosul

ERBIL

NINEVEH

SYRIA

Kirkuk   SULEIMANIYAH

AT TAMIM

SALAHUDDIN

DIYALA

I R A N

BAGHDAD

ANBAR

WASIT

KERBALA   BABIL

Najaf   QADISIYAH

MAYSAN

NAJAF

DHI QAR

Basra

SAUDI
ARABIA

MUTHANNA

BASRA

KUWAIT

N

Bradt

| 0 | | 150km |
| 0 | | 100 miles |

Distances in kilometres

Dohuk																
69	Mosul															
153	84	Erbil														
355	286	202	Suleimaniyah													
290	221	205	221	Tikrit												
248	177	93	109	112	Kirkuk											
531	393	308	267	241	215	Baquba										
465	396	350	331	175	255	66	Baghdad									
575	506	460	442	285	365	176	110	Ramadi								
565	496	471	431	275	355	166	100	210	Al-Hilla							
583	504	468	449	293	372	184	108	218	42	Kerbala						
637	568	552	503	347	427	238	172	282	272	280	Al-Kut					
626	557	511	492	336	416	227	161	271	61	78	333	Najaf				
840	771	725	706	550	630	441	375	485	275	317	187	258	Nasiriyah			
831	762	716	697	541	621	432	366	476	466	484	197	527	384	Al-Amarah		
735	666	620	601	445	525	336	271	380	170	212	292	155	105	489	Samawah	
646	577	521	512	467	436	247	181	291	81	123	353	65	194	546	89	Diwaniya
1014	945	899	880	724	804	605	549	659	483	524	377	467	208	182	313	402	Basra

One year later, in December 2011, US troops pulled out of Iraq and full state sovereignty was transferred back into the hands of Iraqi authorities. Following this, these unresolved political differences re-emerged, and 2012 saw a return to sectarian divisions and Sunni-Shia allegiances dominating the political environment. There is still no political consensus on what the post-Saddam government should look like. Most Kurds advocate a federal state (and many wouldn't mind seceding from the Arabs altogether if given a chance), joined by some Sunnis who want autonomy from the Shia-led central government. Many Shia politicians living in oil-rich provinces could also live without the interference from Baghdad. On the other side of the debate are the nationalists, both Sunni and Shiites, who advocate a unified Iraq with a strong central government.

Prime Minister Nuri al Maliki's State of Law Coalition won 92 seats in the April 2014 elections. Smaller parties headed by State of Law members who ran under separate electoral lists secured another eight seats. Sunni parties performed poorly in the election as they ran during a time of deep internal divisions. The leading Sunni Mutahidoun list, headed by parliamentary speaker Osama al Nujaifi, won only 23 seats across the country.

However, there was widespread dissatisfaction with al Maliki and pressure was building inside his State of Law coalition to oust him. Factions led by Haydar al Abbadi of the Dawa Party and Hussein al Shahristani, the current Deputy Prime Minister broke with al Maliki, along with a total of 38 Dawa MPs and 12 members of the Shahristani bloc, leaving him with the backing of only around 45 members of the original 95-member State of Law bloc. The Shia National Alliance presented Haydar al Abbadi of the Dawa Party as their candidate for prime minister and he was charged by President Fuad Masum to replace al Maliki and to form the next government.

The greatest threat to the Iraqi government comes from ISIS a powerful, extremist, Sunni militant group based in Syria which has been seizing towns and embarking on a reign of terror since mid-2014 (see pages 66–8). It has formed alliances with other radical Sunni militant groups, but its barbaric killings have alienated some who were hostile to al Maliki's government and Sunni militant groups have clashed with ISIS forces. As this book went to press roughly one third of Iraq was controlled by ISIS, including Mosul, which was captured in June 2014.

ECONOMY

Despite a stifling bureaucracy – it can take more than two years to sell a building – rampant corruption, bombings and continuing security problems, Iraq is emerging as a country of opportunities. It is the second largest oil producer in OPEC behind Saudi Arabia and production of 3.5 million barrels per day (bpd) in 2015 seems feasible. The oil sector provides more than 90% of government revenue and 80% of foreign exchange earnings. If Baghdad allows Kurdish oil exports they could amount to 250,000 bpd. Several oil fields started producing and in 2015 the economy may well benefit from the country's largest budget of US$150 billion – if the government agrees to pass it.

Foreign oil companies – BP, Exxon Mobil, Royal Dutch Shell and Eni have been active in the fields of Rumalia, West Qurna-1 and Zubair since 2010 when they signed service contracts with Baghdad. As the Iraqi Kurdish publication, *Rudaw*, pointed out: 'The lifting of Chapter 7 sanctions in mid 2013 can be considered one of Iraq's biggest achievements since the ousting of Saddam Hussein a decade ago, allowing Baghdad to regain control over its own currency, oil and economy.

Chapter 7, imposed on Iraq by the UN Security Council after Saddam's invasion of Kuwait in 1991, froze all Iraqi assets in international banks, ordering they be used to compensate victims of the aggression. Besides placing limits on the use of its wealth, the sanctions also placed limits on the Iraqi military. One of the biggest advantages of the lifting of the sanctions is the return of all frozen assets to the Iraqi government, estimated at US$82 billion, according to Central Bank data. The return of the oil companies will not only revitalise the economy, it will strengthen the value of the Iraqi dinar and increase its purchasing power.'

More than ten years after the American-led invasion the economy is slowly rebuilding and there are predictions that, with the help of crude oil prices, it will be the fastest growing on earth. According to the Wall Street Bank, Iraq was the only country which showed double-digit growth in 2012 with a 10.5% improvement in GDP. Foreign investors showed their optimism by spending US$55.67 billion in the country in 2011 – a 40% increase on 2010. Chinese investment was valued at more than US$3 billion. Iraq's National Investment Commission reported that foreign investment is set to drop significantly to US$35 billion as potential investors, including Gulf neighbours, are deterred by regional tensions and political insecurity.

The Economist Intelligence Unit (EIU) said 'We expect Iraq's economy to grow by a robust 9% on average during 2013–17, driven primarily by rising oil production. Bouts of violence, especially in central areas around Baghdad, will continue to disrupt the economy but improvement overall in the security situation should aid economic activity in some of Iraq's more ethnically and religiously homogeneous southern and western provinces, leading to increased wholesale and retail trade. The private sector is also expected to chip in with oil companies driving growth and boosting infrastructure development, housing, transportation and communications.'

There have also been positive developments in banking. After the 2003 war to oust Saddam Hussein, foreign banks could not operate at first in Iraq. Today there are 15 international banks with a presence in Iraq, in addition to 7 state banks, 23 private lenders and 9 other banks that operate under Islamic law.

Iraq is diversifying its exports into Asian markets. A new pipeline to carry crude from southern Iraq across Jordan to the port of Aqaba on the Red Sea, primarily to Asian markets, is being built. Iran is becoming an increasingly important trading partner. The value of trade between the two countries exceeded US$10 billion in 2013 and Iran will start supplying natural gas to Iraq. Before the oil industry can develop to its full potential a number of challenges will have to be overcome, among them investment in infrastructure, institutional reform, the finalisation of the hydrocarbon law and rebuilding the capacity of the central bank. One of the most intractable problems – the long-standing dispute with the Kurdistan Regional Government – has been resolved. Investment by oil companies in the Kurdish region, without the approval of the central government brought Iraq to the brink of a civil war at the end of 2012. Companies operating in Kurdistan were not paid and for some time the Kurds stopped pumping their share of oil exports.

With the support of the international community, debt has been brought down to sustainable levels and inflation has been reduced to single digits. The government allocated US$450 million to reduce unemployment which stands at 23%. The oil sector is unable to alleviate the problem as it is capital-intensive. Over the next three years the World Bank Group support for Iraq (US$900 million) will focus on job creation, social inclusion and building stronger institutions. Most Iraqis still see the government as a source of employment and 30% of the government's US$100 billion budget is spent on salaries and pensions.

The weak financial system and its limited role within the economy, are making development of a much-needed dynamic private sector extremely difficult. Political and economic tensions between Baghdad and local governments have led some provincial councils to use their budgets to independently promote and facilitate investment at the local level. According to the Social Watch Report 2013, political disputes and security challenges have put development on the back burner even though the government announced a poverty-reduction strategy in 2009. The report states: 'Quality of life has fallen: poverty stays firmly, the education system draws back and women are becoming more and more vulnerable. The inequities persist between cities and rural areas and between men and women. To get on the right track the Iraqi government must conduct a census that has been delayed since 2007, to collect reliable information for the design of comprehensive, effective and appropriately funded development plans.'

Migration of professionals and skilled labourers continues to be a problem and could result in an oil-revenue rich Iraq that Iraqis continue to flee from and that remains under-developed.

The agricultural and manufacturing sectors have stagnated since imports were liberalised following the 2003 invasion. In his paper *The economy of Iraq since 2003 – a follow up,* Yousif Bassam pointed out that that the agricultural sector has found it difficult to compete, especially with subsidised cereals produced in the West, while manufacturing has been particularly hard hit by the loss of electrical capacity resulting from sanctions and the US invasion. The Saudis have expressed an interest in the agricultural sector but no contracts have been signed yet. The main farming area is in the region of the country's two major rivers, the Tigris and Euphrates. Of Iraq's total land area, 77% is not viable for agriculture. Less than 0.4% consists of forest and woodlands situated along the Turkish and Iranian borders. The remaining 22% (about 9.5 million ha) is used for agricultural activities, including seasonal grazing of goats and sheep, tree crops (figs, grapes, olives and dates), field crops such as cereals, pulses, fruit and vegetables, and grains, mostly wheat and barley. The fishing industry is small and centred around freshwater species.

Because of the largely inactive manufacturing sector – many of the country's 240 factories were looted after the 2003 war – the range of imports is large and includes food, fuels, medicines and manufactured goods. There has been little government support for moribund small and medium-sized private industries. It is not possible for them to compete against cheap imports and thousands of Iraqi manufacturers who used to manufacture everything from food to fabrics, metal and plastics have either sold or moth-balled their factories, or turned them into storage sites. The government is trying to assist the manufacturing sector through the introduction of import tariff protection for local products and anti-monopoly laws. Contracts have been awarded to rehabilitate the Kerbala cement factory and a cement factory in Anbar.

The Iraq Britain Business Council (IBBC, see ad on inside back cover) is an organisation that brings together business, trade and investment, for the benefit of the Republic of Iraq and its members. It is a powerful network of important global corporations as well ask key Iraqi and British companies and trade chambers. It runs twice-yearly conferences in London, and frequent missions and business events in Iraq. In a triumph of hope over experience the Iraqi Tourism Board maintains a staff of 2,500 and 14 regional offices throughout the country.

The EIU concluded that despite the challenges on many fronts, the economy is enjoying a revival which could raise the standard of living of many Iraqis and bring them into the middle class, which would secure domestic growth, rather than depending on oil exports.

ETHNIC GROUPS The Iraqi people were once like a necklace, where the thread of nationality united a variety of unique and colourful beads. Today the thread holding the necklace together is becoming increasing fragile as ethnic and religious conflicts continue to claim more and more lives. The Arabs are in the majority, making up at least 75% of the population, while 18% are Kurds and the remaining 7% consists of Turkmen, Assyrians, and other, smaller minorities. Many of Iraq's minorities, which consist of some of the oldest communities in the world, have fled because of the violence unleashed against them. Before 2003 there were 30,000 Mandaeans in Iraq. Today there are maybe only 5,000. The figures for the Turkmen are 800,000 in 2003, now down to perhaps 200,000; the Jewish community from a few hundred to less than a handful, maybe none; Palestinians from 35,000 to 10,000 or less. The Yezidis are said to number 550,000.

Arabs Iraq's dominant ethnic group are the Iraqi or Mesopotamian Arabs. They are a fusion of old Mesopotamian, Arabian, Iranian, and other populations who now speak Mesopotamian Arabic.

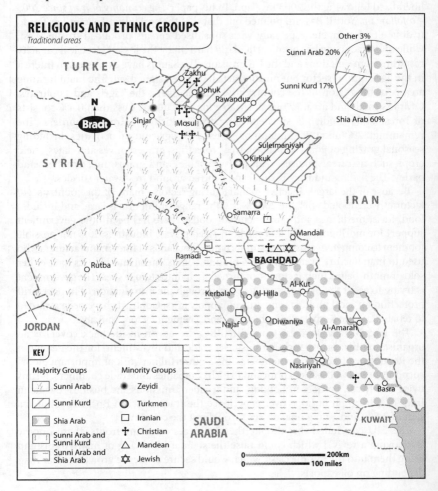

Kurds The Kurds are people of Indo-European origin who live mainly in the mountains and uplands of the Kurdistan region where Iraq borders Turkey and Iran. Ethnically and linguistically they are most closely related to Iranians and have existed in Iraq since before the Arab-Islamic conquest. They are possibly descended from the ancient region of Corduene which was centred near the modern-day city of Van in Turkey.

Turkmen This minority group is mainly found in the northeast of Iraq along the border between the Kurdish and Arab regions in an arc of towns and villages stretching from west of Mosul to Khaniqin. Descendants of the Turkish-speaking Oguz tribes from Central Asia, Turkmen migrated to Mesopotamia over several hundred years starting in the 7th century AD. Following the collapse of the Abbasid Empire a number of Turkmen states were founded in Iraq, the Ottomans encouraging the Turkmen to settle at the entrances of valleys that provided access to Kurdish areas and to repel raids. Many Turkmen families are probably descended from Turkic soldiers or fugitives from early Ottoman control, although they claim to be descendants of the earlier Seljuk Turks. It is thought that the term 'Turkmen' for Iraqi Turks originated during discussions on the Mosul issue in the 1930s in order to isolate the Iraqi Turks from Turkey, and it was used as a factor during the negotiations to join the oil-rich Mosul province with the newly founded Kingdom of Iraq.

Assyrians Also known as Chaldeans or Syriacs, the Assyrians are an indigenous people of Iraq, descendants of the ancient Mesopotamians who ruled ancient Assyria, Akkad and Babylonia, and the Aramaean tribes who intermarried with them. There are only an estimated 800,000 Assyrians remaining in Iraq today, many having fled persecution in the 1980s and again in the wake of the 2003 war.

Yezidis This group is mostly Kurd (although some believe they have a degree of Assyrian heritage). Most of the Yezidis in Iraq live in the Kurdistan Region, around the town of Ain Sifni, near to their religious centre, the Temple of Lalish. The Yezidis have established strong links with the Kurds over the years, although they consider themselves a separate ethnic group. Most speak Kurdish, but some speak Arabic. Yezidi society is well organised with the chief sheikh as the religious figurehead and an Emir as the secular head. During the days of the Ottoman Empire the Yezidis were persecuted and at least 20 major massacres occurred between 1640 and 1910 when they refused to convert to orthodox Islam. Attempts have also been made to replace their Kurdish identity with that of the Arabs, and they have been referred to as Umayyad Arabs by both the Syrian and Iraqi governments. The Yezidis, as ethnic Kurds, were doubly persecuted by Saddam's regime which regarded them as heathens. During the Arabisation programme they were forced out of their villages, denied national identity cards and prevented from holding jobs and visiting the temple at Lalish. After the establishment of the Kurdistan Regional Government (KRG) the 50,000 or so Yezidis living in the KRG began to enjoy new freedoms, although today they are still the victims of sectarian violence and persecution.

Mandaeans Also known as Subbi and Sabians, Mandaeans (like the Assyrians) are also indigenous ancient Mesopotamians who speak their own dialect of Aramaic known as Mandiac. Prior to the 2003 war, the Iraqi Mandaean community was the most important in the world with around half of the population of Mandaeans worldwide living in the area around the Tigris and Euphrates rivers. They are one of the smallest ethnic and religious groups in the world with only about 70,000 followers in total. The Mandaeans used to live in the Marshes, where they earned a reputation as the best canoe-makers and most talented carpenters. But the majority left for Baghdad during the 1950s, where they became Iraq's renowned silversmiths and goldsmiths who, in the words of the legendary British explorer Wilfred Thesiger, 'were satisfied with no less than perfection in their work.' Several hundred Iraqi Mandaeans migrated to the USA and Canada during the Iran-Iraq War in the 1980s. There were thought to have been about 40,000 Mandaeans in Iraq prior to the 2003 war, during which the vast majority of Baghdadi Mandaeans left Baghdad for Jordan or Syria or the West. Mandaean communities of southern Iraq are mostly secure, and today, of the 30,000 members who remain in Iraq, most are in Nasiriyah, Basra, Querna, Al-Amarah and Suq-esh-Shiuk. Mandaeans, although an ethnic and religious minority, consider themselves Iraqi and have supported the Iraqi nation patriotically, serving in the army during various conflicts.

Armenians Although the traditional Armenian homeland is immediately north of Iraq, it contains the uppermost parts of the Tigris and Euphrates rivers and so Armenians have a long history of association with Mesopotamia, dating back over 2,000 years. Estimated to number around 50,000, most Iraqi Armenians are to be found in Baghdad, Basra or Mosul where they have strong links with the Iraqi Assyrian community.

Shabaks The Shabak are an ethnic and religious minority living mainly in the villages of Ali Rash, Khazna, Yangidja and Tallara in Nineveh Province, who have retained their own distinct pre-Islamic religion. An Indo-European (Aryan) people, they speak Shakaki, an Indo-European language with elements of Turkish and Arabic infused. Despite having their own language and culture unique from other groups, Kurdish authorities have attempted to Kurdify the Shabaks by designating them 'Kurdish Shabaks' and there have been clashes with the Democratic Shabak Coalition, a group which wants separate representation for the Shabak community. There are estimated to be about 40,000 Shabaks in Iraq.

Minority groups There are a small number of Iraqis with African ancestry living around Basra. These **Afro-Iraqis** are descendants of sailors or slaves from East Africa brought to Iraq over a thousand years ago to work in the date and sugarcane plantations. Records show that some of these slaves took part in a series of uprisings known as the Zanj Rebellion (Zanj being the name used by medieval Arab geographers to refer to part of Africa's Swahili Coast and its Bantu occupants) in Basra between AD869 and 883. Today, although Arabic-speaking Muslims, they retain some cultural and religious traditions from their ancestral homeland relating to weddings, funerals and healing, and elements of Swahili.

A small **Palestinian** population lives in the Baghdadi neighbourhood of Al-Baladiya, some of whom have been residing there since they were forced to flee their homeland in 1948. **Kawliya** (Qawliya or Kowawlah) are Iraq's gypsies or Roma people (*qawliya* means gypsy in Arabic), a nomadic people whose traditional home was the village of Qawliya, located about 70km southeast of Baghdad. As an ethnic minority they were treated as second-class citizens under Baath party rule. Although historically significant, the **Jewish** community of Iraq today numbers a mere handful of people. The vast majority of Iraqi Jews emigrated to Israel in the early 1950s in Operation Ezra and Nehemiah. Iraq also has a **Bedouin** minority. **Marsh Arabs** are also sometimes regarded as a separate ethnic group; however this is more to do with their culture than any proven ethnic characteristics.

LANGUAGE

Arabic in its various forms is the official language of Iraq and is spoken and understood by almost the entire population. Baghdadi Arabic, the dialect spoken in Baghdad, has become the universal language of Iraq and is the language of commerce and education. Baghdadi Arabic has three distinct dialects: Muslim, Jewish and Christian. Muslim Baghdadi belong to a group called the Gelet dialects, while Jewish and Christian Baghdadi belong to the Qeltu dialect. Baghdadi Gelet Arabic, which is considered the standard Baghdadi Arabic, shares many features with Gulf Arabic and is of Bedouin provenance, unlike Christian and Jewish Baghdadi, which are believed to be descendants of medieval Iraqi Arabic. During the first decades of the 20th century, when the population of Baghdad was less than a million, some inner city quarters still had their own distinctive pidgin version of Arabic. Containing a large number of words borrowed from English, Turkish, Persian and Kurdish it had been used in small enclaves of the city for generations and it continued to be spoken until the 1950s. From about the 1960s, with the population movement within the city and the influx of large numbers of people hailing mainly from the south, Baghdadi Arabic has become more standardised, incorporating some rural and Bedouin features, and has evolved into modern standard Arabic.

Modern Baghdadi Arabic is a sub-variety of the southern (Gelet) Tigris dialect cluster of Iraqi or Mesopotamian Arabic which is a continuum of the mutually intelligible variety of Arabic spoken in the Mesopotamian basin of Iraq south of Baghdad as well as in neighbouring Iran and eastern Syria. As with Baghdadi Arabic, Iraqi Arabic has two major groupings, Gelet and Qeltu, and borrows extensively from Aramaic, Akkadian, Persian, Kurdish and Turkish. As well as the Tigris dialect cluster, the southern (Gelet) group includes a Euphrates dialect cluster, known as Furati (Euphrates Arabic). The northern (Qeltu) group includes the north Tigris dialect cluster, also known as North Mesopotamian Arabic Maslawi (Mosul) Arabic as well as both Jewish and Christian sectarian dialects such as Baghdadi Jewish Arabic. English is widely understood, especially in urban areas.

Many other languages are spoken by a variety of ethnic groups, most notably Kurdish which is the largest minority language. There are two dialects of Kurdish spoken in the Kurdish Region, Kurmanji (spoken mainly in Dohuk and environs) and Sorani (spoken mainly in Erbil, Suleimaniyah and environs). Sorani is the second official language of Iraq and is referred to in official documents simply as Kurdish. It has regional language status in Kurdistan. In contrast with Kurmanji (which is usually written using Latin script) Sorani has a modified Perso-Arabic script; however, during the past few years official TV in Iraqi Kurdistan has started to use Latin script for Sorani. The Shabaks in Kurdistan historically speak a distinct dialect of Kurdish, although in recent years they have linguistically assimilated into the language practice of Sorani speakers in the area in which they live.

Unlike in the West, in Iraq, Christianity is a cultural identity as much as a faith, denominations being marked by subtly different cultural and social behaviours as well as religious practices. Nowhere is this more outwardly apparent than in the languages spoken by the various Christian denominations. For example, Chaldaeans and Syriac Catholics in the main speak Arabic in everyday life, whereas Assyrians and Syrian Orthodox Christians speak a modern version of Syriac, a member of the Eastern Aramaic sub-family, which is the liturgical language of many Christian denominations throughout the Middle East. And while both use traditional Syriac, the language originally used in the Assyrian and Babylonian empires, as their liturgical language, the Assyrians speak a differently accented version of it and have their own written script which differs from that used by the Uniate churches, reflecting their eastern and western divergence.

Mandaeans speak their own dialect of Aramaic known as Mandiac. Classical Mandiac (a Semitic language which is another member of the Eastern Aramaic sub-family closely related to the language of the Aramaic portions of the Babylonian Talmud), is used by a section of the Mandaean community in liturgical rites and is related to Syriac. Speakers of Classic Mandiac (a variety of Aramaic notable for its use of vowel letters and the striking amount of Persian influence in its lexicon) can still be found in southern Iraq. Its script is related to Nabataean writing and is used for the incantation texts and on the Aramaic incantation bowls found throughout Mesopotamia. Since the 1990s the use of neo-Syriac in northern Iraq has undergone a renaissance, with an increasing number of modern publications using it and its use in schools and the media of the Christian communities.

Some Turkmen have been able to preserve their language (despite a strong linguistic Arabisation policy by Saddam Hussein) and still converse in a Turkish dialect. Azerbaijani is spoken in pockets of northern Iraq and Persian is spoken in pockets of southern Iraq. The Shabak speak Shabaki, an Indo-Iranian language with elements of Turkish and Arabic infused.

RELIGION

The major religion of the country is Islam and is followed by 97% of the population, while the remaining 3% is made up of Christianity, Mandaeism, Yezidis and others. Northern Iraq, in particular the areas around Mosul and Kirkuk, are places of total fascination for anyone interested in how religion has changed history and influenced communities right up until the present day.

ISLAM Islam is the religion of the majority of Iraqis who belong to either the Sunni or Shia sect. Iraq is one of the few Arab countries where the Shia sect constitutes a majority. Estimates of the number of Shias vary from 54% to 70% (of Iraqi Muslims). The beliefs of Sunnis and Shias do not differ greatly: both sects believe in the five pillars of Islam (the profession of faith that there is no God but Allah, to pray five times a day, to fast during the month of Ramadan when the Koran was revealed to the Prophet Mohammed, to give alms to the poor and to make a pilgrimage to Mecca). Both Shias and Sunnis believe that the Mahdi will return to save the Earth, when there will be a battle between the forces of good and evil followed by a thousand-year reign of peace and then the end of the world, the only difference being that the Shias believe the Mahdi is the son of the 11th Imam al Askari whereas for the Sunnis the identity of the Mahdi is not fixed.

Religious differences centre around the Shias' veneration of the family of the Prophet Mohammed and his descendants, and their veneration of the 12 Imams, whom they see as the rightful successors to the Prophet. Major Shia holidays mourn the martyrdom of Imam Ali and Imam Hussain. The main Shia holiday is Ashura, marking the martyrdom of Hussain and his followers outside the city of Kerbala in 680. It is commemorated with a procession to Kerbala, a passion play re-enacting the martyrdom and, in some cases, self-flagellation. The Sunnis look with disdain upon the veneration of Hussain and Ali, accusing the Shias of a violation of monotheism, and extremist Sunni groups, like al-Qaida and ISIS, view Shias as *kafirs* (unbelievers), who must be killed. The Shias also have a more centralised and hierarchical clergy, in which they normally follow the advice of an *ayatollah* on the interpretation of the Koran and Islamic law (*sharia*).

The Sunni-Shia (orthodox–heterodox) schism dates back to the first half of the 7th century and arose due to disagreement over who should lead the Islamic community following the Prophet Mohammed's death in Medina in 632. The Sunnis believed that any faithful Muslim could become leader of the faithful; the Shias believed that the leader should come from the Prophet's family. As the Prophet died without leaving any instructions regarding his successor, his followers elected Abu Bakr, his father-in-law and long-time companion and trusted advisor as leader. He adopted the title of Caliph which means successor. However, Ali ibn abi Talib, the Prophet's cousin, son-in-law and close intimate had not been present at this election and did not take the oath of loyalty until six months later. Old and frail when he became the caliph on 23 August 634 Abu Bakr died and Umar ibn al Khattab became the second caliph. He ruled for ten years before he was murdered by a former Persian slave in 644. Before his death, however, he summoned a selection committee to appoint his successor. It soon became apparent that only Ali and Othman ibn Affan were serious candidates. By the fourth morning of the selection process relations between the factions of Ali and Othman had become tense. Finally, all agreed to abide by the decision of Abdul Rahman, who had himself refused to stand for election. He chose Othman, a genial man of 70 years to be the third caliph in November 644. Now with a weak caliph under the influence of disruptive factions, coupled with the need to control what had now grown into a large empire, events gradually slipped out of control. Mutinous armies marched on Medina. On 17 June 656 a screaming mob of mutineers burst into Othman's room and hacked the caliph to death. Four leaders of the Muslims had been in Medina at the time of his murder, but they had done little or nothing to save his life. Five days later Ali was acclaimed as the fourth caliph and the mutineers returned to their garrisons.

However, Muawiya, the Umayyad governor of Syria, refused to acknowledge Ali as caliph until the murderers were punished. But Ali took no action, pleading the need for restoration of discipline before the offenders could be brought to book so Muawiya replied by charging Ali with complicity in the murder. The standard of revolt was raised in Basra, but Ali proved the victor at the Battle of the Camel (over Talha and Zubair who had been supported by Aisha the Prophet's widow) and the revolt was quelled. Ali then set up his capital at Kufa. But the conflict was not finished and Ali had to fight again in July 657 against the Syrian army. A truce was called, and a mutinous movement began in the army of Ali. The malcontents, who became known as Kharijites or 'outsiders', were extreme puritan egalitarians. Sickened by the rivalries of their leaders they demanded a theocracy, ruled only by God.

On 20 January 661 a fanatical Kharijite, Mohammed ibn Muljam, assassinated Ali at the door of the mosque in Kufa. The death of Ali left the field clear for his Umayyad rival Muawiya, who became caliph in July 661 after persuading Hassan, Ali's eldest son, to renounce his claim to the caliphate. Muawiya died in April 680 and his son Yazid was acclaimed in Damascus as caliph. But it was soon apparent that all was not well. Arabs have never entirely accepted the hereditary right to succession, and Yazid's position was logically weak. If his right to the caliphate was based on heredity, the previous caliphs had all left sons who had as much right as he. If, on the other hand, the post should go to the most suitable candidate, then many were obviously better qualified than Yazid. His most formidable competitor was Hussain ibn Ali, who was not only the son of Ali, the fourth caliph, but also the grandson of the Prophet through his daughter Fatima. Moreover Hussain was pious, serious and virtuous, in contrast to the frivolous Yazid.

At this critical moment letters reached Hussain from Kufa inviting him to come and assume leadership in Iraq. After much hesitation, he decided to leave Mecca and cross the Arabian deserts to Kufa, without an army, accompanied only by his family. This departure caused great alarm in Damascus, and Ubaidullah was appointed governor of Kufa by Yazid. In a few days the new governor had arrested and executed Hussain's principal supporters and completely established his own authority. When Hussain's little convoy approached Kufa, it was met and surrounded by a large troop of cavalry and was forced to halt in the desert at a place without water called Kerbala. Hussain claimed that he had done nothing wrong and was willing to go and confront Yazid in Damascus. Ubaidullah, however, insisted on unconditional surrender. As the stalemate continued, entreaties for a little water for the women and children fell on deaf ears. At length, on 10 October 680 the cavalry closed in. Hussain drew up his 72 relatives and retainers for battle. The cavalry were 4,000 strong. For several hours Hussain's little party were subjected to constant sniping by archers till all his men, and several of his children had been killed. At length Hussain, bleeding from many wounds stood at bay, alone except for the women crouching in the tents behind him. At the command of an officer called Shamir, Sinan bin Anas bin Amr cut off the head of Hussain. The day of his death is known as 'ashura' and is commemorated every year by Shias on the tenth day of the month of Muharram. The martyrdom of Hussain divided the Muslim world into two parts. The Shias lost the struggle for leadership of the Muslims, resulting in their minority status within global Islam.

It took until the 18th century before Shia Islam again flourished in Iraq. Following the capture of Esfahan by the Sunni Afghans, the Shia centres of learning moved from Persia to Kerbala and Najaf, where the Persian language was widely used, swiftly followed by the Persian *ulama* (religious scholars) and their students. During the 1860s Indians from the Shia state of Awadh, prompted by the British annexation of the Awadh kingdom and the Indian Mutiny, flocked to these cities. The religious activities of these cities had a profound influence on the surrounding rural tribes whose large-scale conversion from Sunni to Shia Islam took place during the 19th century when they changed from nomads to a more settled existence which disrupted their traditional tribal structure leaving them in need of a new identity. As Shias their status increased in the eyes of the townspeople. Conversion to Shi'ism was also a way of escaping conscription. Although the Shias have outnumbered the Sunnis in Iraq since this time, the Sunnis have maintained their hold on political and religious power. It wasn't until 2005 that Iraq emerged as a major Shia government when Shia candidates achieved political dominance in the elections for the first time.

Islam in Kurdistan The majority of Kurds are Sunni Muslims, with Shia and Alevi Muslim minorities. In the Kurdistan religion and pagan superstition go hand in hand. Allied to the different ethnic origins from the regions' past conflicts, there is a great awareness of the invisible realm in everyday life, and blessings and spontaneous prayers are part of normal vocabulary. Although the Kurdish form of Islam contains many mystical elements associated with Sufism, this is fractured, with the Suleimaniyah region for example, heavily influenced by the Qadiriya (a widespread Sufi order) and the Naqshbandiya (a Dervish order

THE CHRISTIAN CHURCH IN IRAQ

The churches in Iraq at the beginning of the 21st century (before the collapse of the Baathist regime) can be categorised as follows:

Churches of the East
1 The Ancient Church of the East
2 Assyrian Church of the East

Oriental Orthodox Churches
1 The Syrian Orthodox Church
2 The Armenian Orthodox Church
3 The Greek Orthodox Church (al-Rum al-Orthodox)

Catholic Churches
1 Chaldean
2 Syrian Catholic
3 Armenian Catholic
4 Latin
5 Greek Catholic (al-Rum al-Cathulik)

The Protestant Churches
1 National Evangelical Church
2 Assyrian Evangelical Church
3 Armenian Evangelical Church
4 Jehovah's Witnesses
5 Seventh-day Adventists

The Coptic Church
Once there were over 2 million Christians in Iraq, but their number has more than halved in the last few years. Church leaders are extremely concerned that the ancient Christian faith and heritage in Iraq will disappear altogether in the face of the onslaught of the majority Shia and persecution by groups such as ISIS.

founded in the 14th century) Islamic Brotherhoods. Dr Michiel Leesienberg of the University of Amsterdam has written about and described some of the ethnic groups of Muslims scattered along the fringes of Kurdistan. These include the Shebash, the Bajalon, the Sarli, the Kakais and the Yezidis (although most people would deny that they are Muslims). Some of these communities are hidden away in small valleys, marked out only by their different dialects, Gorani or Maclo. These groups resemble orthodox Sufi orders and all have a hereditary class of religious leaders. Their religious beliefs and practices form a mixture of heterodox Islam with pre-Islamic elements.

CHRISTIANS The origins of Christianity in Iraq are ancient and hark back to apostolic days. According to Dr Sebastian Brock of the Oriental Institute, Oxford University, 'most people are unaware that Christianity was already in Iraq well before it reached Britain and that it continues to be a significant cultural and religious influence in the country right up to the present day'. A variety of churches emerged in Iraq, including the Nestorians (now known as the Church of the East) and the Syrian Orthodox Church, which resulted from doctrinal decisions made at the Councils of Ephesus and Chalcedon in 431 and 451 respectively. By the 7th century evangelists from Iraq had brought Christianity to China, Central Asia and India, and between the 9th and 13th centuries the diocese of the Church of the East rivalled in scale that of the Latin Church and was looked upon by many as the 'Third Branch of Christianity'. However, the prominent position of Christianity in Iraq on the world stage ended after sizeable parts of the country were laid waste by Timur in the 14th century, after which the Church of the East and the Syrian Orthodox Church were sidelined to enclaves in northern Iraq. Despite this, these two churches still remained the major Christian denominations in Iraq until the arrival of Roman Catholic missionaries in the 16th century, and schisms developed, leading to the formation of the Uniate churches – the Chaldaean and the Syrian Catholic – both of which continue to have adherents in Iraq today as the scattered churches and monasteries of north Iraq, many still with monks and priests, testify. Chaldaeans are Eastern-rite Catholics whose hierarchy operates somewhat autonomously from the Vatican but still recognises the pope's authority. In many of the Chaldean churches in Iraq, services are recited in the ancient Aramaic, the language of Jesus.

Day-to-day difficulties in the face of persecution have led to the mass exodus of many Christians from Iraq. According to Human Rights Watch, two-thirds of Iraq's Christians have fled their homes, and estimates are that Iraq's Christian population has halved since the ousting of Saddam Hussein. Christians made up less than 5% of Iraq's population when the war began (being about 1 million in number), however they now constitute an estimated 10% of internally displaced Iraqis and 20% of Iraqi refugees in neighbouring countries, according to a report in the *Christian Science Monitor*, with many of those remaining relocating to Kurdistan. In the wake of the attack on the Our Lady of Salvation Chaldaean Catholic church in Baghdad in 2010, the president of the Kurdish regional government, Massoud Bagani, offered Christians protection and refuge. Today as Christians (and other minorities) are persecuted for reasons of religion, the indigenous Christian Church in Iraq faces a threat as serious as any it has had to face in the past, with many of the Christians who remain planning on how they too are going to leave Iraq. Their displacement not only threatens to end Christianity's 2,000-year history in Iraq, it also deprives the country of a huge swath of middle-class professionals at a critical time. Since no Christian was able to have a government job under Saddam Hussein, university graduates became lawyers, doctors and engineers. Crucial to Iraq's recovery, they are now scattered, afraid to return. 'The scale of the problem is total, and it has created an existential crisis,' says Michael Youash of the Iraq Sustainable Democracy Project, who campaigns on behalf of Iraqi Christians. 'It may be that in 20 years there could be no more Christians in Iraq.'

ASSYRIANS Assyrians began to convert to Christianity in the 1st and 2nd centuries formerly having followed the ancient Sumerian-Akkadian religion (also known as Ashurism). For a time some were Manicheans, following the religion created by the Iranian prophet, Mani. Assyrian Christians are found mainly in Dohuk and Chaldean Christians are concentrated in Shaqlawa and Erbil. The Christian quarter of Suleimaniyah (in the eastern part of the city) has three churches and most Christians in Suleimaniyah belong to the Chaldean Church, which is linked to the Church of Rome.

JEWS The origins of Judaism in Iraq is a debatable subject. Traditionally it is said that the Tribe of Benjamin first settled in Kurdistan after the Assyrian conquest of the Kingdom of Israel during the 8th century BC. Historically, Jews in Mesopotamia can be traced back to c586BC when Nebuchadnezzar captured Jerusalem and took a number of Jews (including the prophet Ezekiel) captive back to Babylonia. Following the fall of Babylon to the Persian King Cyrus some 50 years later, some of the exiles returned to Judea, but others remained and from this point until the rise of the Islamic caliphate in the 7th century AD, the Jewish community of Babylon thrived as the centre of Jewish learning and many Jewish communities grew up in the ancient towns and cities of Iraq. During the Mongol invasions most of the pre-existing Jewish community either died or fled, and Islamic discrimination in the Middle Ages further contributed to its decline. In the following centuries though, Jewish people began emigrating from surrounding countries such as Syria and forming settlements in Iraq. Under the Ottomans the Jewish community thrived, and in the 20th century, Iraqi Jews played an important role in the early days of Iraq's independence. The Iraqi Jewish community decreased drastically after the 1948 Arab-Israeli War, and in the early 1950s 120,000 Jews (around 75%) were evacuated to Israel. Although it is unknown if there are still any Jews in Iraq today, in parts of Kurdistan there still remain traditional Jewish songs and verse, relics of the Jewish community. For more information on Judaism in Iraq, see page 122.

MANDAEANS Historically speaking, Mandaeism is one of the ancient religions of Mesopotamia and one of the earlier-known monotheistic religions, along with Abrahamic faiths and Zoroastrianism. The name Mandaean is Aramaic for knowledge, referred to in Greek as *gnosis*, and Mandaeans are the last practitioners of Gnosticism, a major religion in the Middle East during the first centuries after the birth of Christ. Their knowledge of astronomy has prompted speculation that the three wise men who visited Jesus were Mandaeans. In Arabic they are called baptisers (*Sabaeans*). Present-day Mandaeans also refer to themselves as observants (*nasorayye*). John the Baptist is an important religious figure in Mandaeism and the Mandaeans have also been called Christians of St John (running water is seen as the source of life and members of the sect try to live near a river). The religion is a combination of beliefs drawn from Babylonian, pre-Islamic, Persian and Christian sources.

Tore Kjeilen, writing in the *Encyclopaedia of the Orient*, summarises the Mandaean beliefs as a view of the cosmos made up of two forces, the world of light, located to the north, and the world of darkness, located to the south. There is a ruler in both surrounded by smaller gods and kings. The two forces came into conflict and their infighting created the world. Man was a product of the forces of darkness, but the soul (*adam*) has its origin in the world of light. Death is the day of deliverance when the soul leaves the body and starts on a dangerous journey to the realms of light. The Mandaean holy book, *The Treasure* (*ginza*), deals with mythological, cosmological and moral treatises, and hymns and songs that focus on the fate of the soul.

According to Erica Hunter's entry in *The Dictionary of Religion*: 'Mandaean literature relates little about history; but the Scroll of the Divine Revelation suggests that the community emigrated in the second centuryAD from Jerusalem to northern Mesopotamia as a result of persecution by orthodox Jews. Later pressure from the Byzantine Church resulted in their movement to southern Mesopotamia, the area with which they have become traditionally associated'. Given the peaceful ethos of

Mandaeans and lack of missionary movement within the faith, they traditionally formed a successful community with their Sunni, Shia and Christian neighbours and were considered 'People of The Book' which Islamically speaking allowed them to practise religion and integrate into Iraqi society even though technically this is incorrect as they are neither Jews nor Christians. According to the Sabian Mandean Association in Australia (SMAA), attacks by Muslims against Mandaeans have been prompted by the declaration of the late Ayatollah al Hakim, head of the Supreme Islamic Council, that Mandaeans are not People of The Book, meaning they can be forced to convert to Islam or be killed if they do not, and this religious classification has led them to become outcasts, making it difficult for them to find work or live in an Iraqi society which is becoming more Islamicised.

Although Mandaeans can occasionally still be found on the banks of the Tigris and Euphrates practising their ancient rituals (brides standing knee-deep in freezing water as a barefoot priest wielding a long stick splashes icy water on their faces, hands and chests), Mandaeans are threatened with extinction: converts are not allowed and one is only considered a Mandaean if both one's parents are Mandaeans. Recruitment to the priesthood is difficult and the sect is having trouble maintaining its traditions as many of the priests have little knowledge of the old language and scriptures.

ZOROASTRIANISM Also called Mazdaism, Zoroastrianism rose to prominence when Iraq was part of the Persian, Parthian and Sassanian empires. Today it is the smallest of the major religions in the number of its followers; however, it is one of the most interesting and important from a historical viewpoint. Its roots are in the proto-Indo-European spirituality that also produced the esoteric religions of India. It was the first of the world's religions to be founded by an inspired prophetic reformer, the Persian Zoroaster (or Zarathushtra, which means Shining Light). Opinions vary greatly as to Zoroaster's date of birth, ranging from 6,000 years before the death of Plato (c6350BC) to 258 years before Alexander (c600BC). Most scholars place Zoroaster's birth between 1500BC and 1200BC. Zoroastrianism was influential on Mahayana Buddhism and the Abrahamic religions of Judaism, Christianity and Islam. To the latter three, Zoroastrianism bequeathed such concepts as a cosmic struggle between right and wrong, the primacy of ethical choice in human life, monotheism, a celestial hierarchy of spiritual beings (angels and archangels) that mediate between God and humanity, a judgment for each individual after death, the coming of a Messiah at the end of this creation and an apocalypse culminating in the final triumph of Good at the end of the historical cycle.

Zoroastrianism is an organised faith with a highly developed ethical code, the tenets of which are set out in the sacred writings of the *Zend-Avest* (written in the ancient language Avestan, which is closely related to the Sanskrit of the ancient Vedic hymns) and in later Persian commentaries. In Zoroastrian cosmology, the head of the manifested universe is Ahura Mazda, the wise and universal lord who is the source of all life. Behind Ahura Mazda is Zarvan Akarana, the boundless time and space and un-manifested absolute from which Ahura Mazda, as the word incarnate, emerged. Ahura Mazda appears in Zoroastrian scriptures as a kind of trinity – 'Ahura Mazda, threefold before other creations' along with the twin spirits of Spenta Mainyu (the holy or bountiful spirit) and Angra Mainyu (the destructive or opposing spirit), two principles that represent all the opposites of life, who came forth from him. Along with this trinity there are seven divine realities called the Amesha Spentas. Sometimes thought of as archangels and sometimes as manifestations of Ahura Mazda himself, these seven are also guardians of various kingdoms of nature. The principal beliefs of Zoroastrianism are the existence of the supreme deity and the continuous struggle between good and evil – not only between Spenta Mainyu and Angra Mainyu, but also the cosmic struggle between Ahura Mazda and his arch enemy, Ahriman, the spirit of evil and darkness.

Zoroastrianism places great emphasis on purity and not defiling any of the elements; earth, water, air or fire. For that reason traditionally Zoroastrians were neither buried nor cremated, instead, their bodies were taken to a Tower of Silence and laid out under the sun for vultures to devour them. Fire is highly symbolic, being the supreme symbol of God and divine life, and has a central role in religious ceremonies. Zoroastrian places of worship, called Fire Temples, have an eternal flame which is kept burning within them. The first fire is said to have been brought down from heaven by Zoroaster with a rod.

There are still a small number of followers in the Kurdish region today. In line with the beliefs of Zoroastrianism, Kurdish women are careful when pouring hot liquid into an empty container as a spirit (*jinn*) could be harmed. Angels are seen as God's messengers who can bring rewards or punishments. Amulets for protection against the evil eye are common throughout the area. Zoroastrians do not proselytise, they are born to the faith through their fathers only. If a woman marries outside the religion her children cannot be Zoroastrians.

YEZIDIS In Iraq Yezidis are found mainly in Kurdistan, in the town of Sinjar, on the slopes of the Sinjar Mountains and in the Dohuk region, where they live intermingled with the other religious communities. The Kurdish word for Yezidis is 'Ezdisd', meaning 'those who are close to God'. They are an esoteric sect, whose beliefs are drawn from paganism, Zoroastrianism, Christianity and Islam. The chief divine figure is Malak Taus, the peacock angel who rules the universe with six other angels, all subordinate to the supreme God who has taken no direct interest in the universe since he created it. The Yezidis believe that when the devil repented of the sin of pride, he was pardoned and reinstated by God to his previous position as chief of the angels. This has earned them the undeserved reputation of being devil worshippers. They observe a number of religious taboos, including the forbidding of the wearing of the colour blue and eating lettuce and olives. Yezidi society is well organised with the chief sheikh as the religious figurehead and an Emir as the secular head. Their main religious text is the *Black Book* (*Meshaf I Resh*). Sheikhi, who is said to have been a reincarnation of Malak Taus, was the author of a 500-word scripture known as *Revelation* (*Khiwa*).

The burial place of Sheikh Adi in the valley of Lalish is a Yezidi shrine and has a magical atmosphere. The entrance to the tomb is adorned with a black stone snake and inside fires burn. The temple complex has cave formations with water pools and dates back to 512BC. All Yezidis are required to visit the temple once in their life and to pray five times a day. They celebrate New Year in April and their holy day is Wednesday. Lam, which consists of a seven-day feast, is the most important celebration for Yezidis and during the festivities worshippers are shown the bird icon called the Anzal of Malak Taus. Yezidis may have up to seven wives, but they cannot marry outside their religion as they fear they will lose their identity. However, this policy may be revised as their numbers are rapidly decreasing.

SHABAKS Shabaks claim to be the descendants of the Qizilbash, the red-capped warriors who founded the Safavid Dynasty. Founded in the 16th century among poor and disempowered villagers, Shabak religious beliefs contain elements from both Islam and Christianity. Shabaks comprise of three different *taifs* or sects: the

Bajalan, Dawoody and Zengana and the Shabak proper. About 70% of Shabaks are Shia and the rest are Sunni. Shabaks combine elements of Sufism with their own interpretation of divine reality, which according to them, is more advanced than the literal interpretation of the Koran or Sharia law.

There is a close affinity between the Shabak and the Yezidis, and Shabaks perform pilgrimage to Yezidi shrines. Shabak spiritual guides (*pirs*) are individuals well versed in the prayers and rituals of the sect. *Pirs* themselves are under the leadership of the Supreme Head or Baba, and act as mediators between Divine power and ordinary Shabaks. Their beliefs form a syncretic system with such features as private and public confession and allowing the consumption of alcohol. The beliefs of the Shabak closely resemble those of the Yarsan, a syncretic religion founded by Sultan Sahak in Persian in the late 14th century.

OTHER MINORITY RELIGIONS The majority of Turkmen are Muslim but they are not divided along sectarian lines. Approximately 60% of Turkmen are Sunnis, while the remainder are Ithnaashari or other Shia. Shia Turkmen tend to live in the more southerly and rural areas. Tiny extreme Shia communities (for example, Sarliyya and Ibrahimiya) exist in Tuz Khurmatu, Tauq, Qara Tapa, Taza Khurmatu, Bashir and Tisin, and Tell Afar. There are also about 30,000 Christian 'Catholic' Turks living in Iraq. One of the most important historical places in the city of Tuz Khurmatu to visit is the Gawer Kalasi, which means 'Christian castle' in the Turkmen language. We should also briefly mention the cult of Angels, Alevism, Nusayrim and Yarsanism, all of which are small religious communities in Kurdistan that make no attempt to be Muslim and are therefore ready targets for abuse by their Muslim neighbours today. It says much for past community tolerance that they still exist at all.

EDUCATION

Growing oil revenues during the 1970s enabled Iraq to develop a modern education system which was one of the best in the Middle East and North African region in the 1980s. Primary school enrolment was close to 100% and there was an effective literacy programme. Had Iraq progressed at the same rate as other Middle Eastern countries, primary school enrolment for both boys and girls would be 100% today according to the UN Children's Fund (UNICEF), but decades of war and sanctions have dealt a devastating blow to the country's education system. The decline in educational standards, school enrolments and literacy began with the Iran-Iraq War (1980–88) when the squeeze on resources began. During the years of sanctions there was a 10% drop in primary school enrolment rates from 90.8% in 1990 to 80.3% in 2000.

The widespread looting during the 2003 war had a drastic effect on education: 3,000 schools were looted and libraries and colleges were burned. One of the spin-offs of the De-Baathification programme was a brain drain from the universities. More than 400 Iraqi academics have been assassinated by death squads between 2003 and 2010 leading to a brain drain as thousands of teachers and scholars fled the country. During the most intense period of the civil war (between 2006 and 2007) the government estimated that only 33% of children attended school regularly.

Women's education was acutely affected as parents were reluctant to send their daughters to school due to security concerns.

Today there are more than six million illiterate people in Iraq, most of them women according to the parliamentary committee on education. One in five Iraqis between the ages of 10 and 49 cannot read or write a simple statement related to daily life. Illiteracy jumped to 20% in 2010. Illiteracy among women is 24% – more than double that of men. The Iraqi Liaison for the international NGO Mercy Corps drew attention to the fact that 'there are some locations – particularly rural locations – where illiteracy rates are actually much higher and in some communities half of the women may not be able to read.' In June 2013, the Iraqi authorities decided to establish more than 500 literacy centres, after the Ministry of Education, led by Sunni politician Mohammad Tamim, acknowledged that the illiteracy rate in Iraq had risen to 22%.

Meanwhile, in Kurdistan since 2005 education has improved at all educational levels. Numerous educational establishments have been opened all over Kurdistan, including international universities and colleges. Public universities have been founded and the people of Kurdistan have been given the opportunities to improve their education. American universities and colleges have greatly assisted in the establishment of courses for students in Kurdistan particularly in the study of the English language and IT skills, and the American University of Iraq in Suleimaniyah which opened its doors in 2007, now offers a truly comprehensive American-style education. The Kurds have been quick to seize the opportunity to develop a modern educational system and this investment will eventually show great results.

Suleimaniyah is the cultural centre of the Sorani-speaking Kurds. The first school for Kurdish girls was founded here in 1915. The actual University of Suleimaniyah was founded in 1968 and is the oldest institution of higher education in northern Iraq. Currently there are approximately 10,000 students studying there, over half of whom are women.

CULTURE

Culturally Iraq has a very rich heritage and today, despite Iraq's political hardships, literary and artistic pursuits flourish, especially in Baghdad, where Western artistic traditions (including ballet, theatre and modern art) are juxtaposed with more traditional Middle Eastern forms of artistic expression. Music and cinema are again becoming popular. The country is known for its poets and poetry still thrives in Iraq with 20th-century Iraqi poets, such as Muhammad Mahdi al Jawahiri, Nazik al Malaika (one of the Arab world's most prominent woman poets), Badr Shakir al Sayyab, and Abd al Wahhab al Bayati, renowned throughout the Arabic-speaking world. Iraqi painters and sculptors are among the best in the Middle East, and some of them, such as Ismail Fattah Turk, Khalid al Rahhal, and Muhammad Ghani, have become world renowned. Iraq is known for producing fine handicrafts and the government is endeavouring to preserve traditional arts and crafts such as leather and copper work. The architecture of Iraq is seen in the sprawling metropolis of Baghdad, where the construction is mostly new, with some islands of exquisite old buildings and compounds, and elsewhere in thousands of ancient and modern sites across Iraq.

MUSIC Music is important to Iraqis. Traditional Iraqi music is informal and largely improvised, the life of a song being marked by the changes introduced by succeeding generations. The ability to improvise and embellish a melody still constitutes one of the standards by which a performer is judged. Well-known traditional instruments include the *oud* (similar to a lute), the *rebab* (similar to a violin), the *riqq* (a type of tambourine) and the *darbuka* (a hand drum). Famous *oud* players include Munir Bashir, Salem Abdul Karim, Nasir Shamaa, Ali Emam and Riad Hoshabr.

Traditional music Iraqi *maqamat* (a system of melodic modes used in traditional Arabic music) dates back to Abbasid times. Its modern form descends from the 19th century Turkmen composer Rahmat Allah Shiltegh (1798–1872). The *pesteh*, a light song which concluded a *maqamat* performance, was popularised in the later 20th century. Arabic folksongs in Iraq can be classified into Bedouin songs, Bedouin-rural songs, the songs of southern Iraq and the songs of the towns. Bedouin songs can further be subdivided into heroic or love poems (which are usually sung to the accompaniment of the one-string *rebab*), sung poetry (which usually accompanies the march of the camel caravan), war songs and women's songs. A new society, half Bedouin, half rural, was created by the tribes who settled on the banks of the river and cultivated the land. They performed Bedouin songs and also developed dance songs with different patterns of rhymes. The songs of southern Iraq are based on four-line stanzas. The singer is accompanied by a drum, clapping, clicking fingers, large cans or trays! The towns are the places for folk songs. The singer typically sings the whole stanza and the chorus repeats the last word of the refrain.

Traditional Kurdish music, which influenced that of Iran and Turkey, tends to be melancholic and a reflection on the trials and tribulations of life. In Iraq, these days Kurdish music has been influenced by the fast, joyous tempo of Arabic music. Kurdish folk songs, or story songs with heroic, amorous, religious and political themes, are stories told to the accompaniment of music. Travelling Kurdish balladeers once sang about the achievements of epic heroes.

20th century At the beginning of the 20th century Iraq's most prominent musicians were Jewish. In the early 1920s, Iraq's most famous composer was Ezra Aharon, an *oud* player, and its most prominent instrumentalist was Duwad el-Kuwaiti. Iraq Radio, established in 1936, had an ensemble made up entirely of Jewish musicians, except for the percussion players. The most famous singer of the 1930s and 1940s was Salima Pasha, who was highly respected both in the Arab world and in Israel. Salima was married to another very famous Iraqi, singer and actor Nazem al Ghazali, and even after the bulk of Iraqi Jews left Iraq, Salima continued to live there until her death in 1974.

Many orchestras and companies have gradually disbanded over the years as artists have emigrated. Despite this the Iraqi National Symphony Orchestra continues to perform more or less regularly, even abroad. All their concerts are free, thanks to Government support. Karim Wasfi, chief conductor of the orchestra considers that in a sense they represent a collective achievement for the country. His mission is to make the orchestra open to every part of Iraqi society, and indeed every sect is represented in it – Christians, Shias, Sunnis and Kurds – men and women. Karim has launched a youth orchestra and even pays disadvantaged children to come to concerts.

Contemporary performers Western music has always been popular with younger Iraqis and before the 2003 war there were no shortage of discos in Baghdad, the lighting and sound in which was most definitely not subdued. The most popular radio station keeping young people up to date with Western trends was 'Voice of Youth FM' owned by Saddam's oldest son Uday. From the 1970s onwards a number of bands in Iraq played Western music in clubs. Ilham el Madfaii adapted some traditional tunes and composed new ones with Iraqi Baghdadi characteristics to be player on electric guitars and keyboards by rock bands. Acrassicauda (Black Scorpion), formed in 2001, is often credited as being the first heavy metal group to emerge from Iraq. The original band consisted of three Arab members and one Assyrian. Born out of a basement rehearsal space in Baghdad and inspired by Western bands like Metallica, Slayer, and Slipknot, Acrassicauda played only three live shows in Iraq before the country began to disintegrate around them. Eventually after carrying cans of diesel along with guitars to power the generators needed for their equipment, then having the rehearsal studio and equipment blown up by a bomb missile, it became impossible to find any venue where they could perform safely. The death threats from Islamic militants, who thought that the band was worshipping Satan, coupled with the increasing violence in Baghdad, left the members of the band – Marwan Hussein, Faisal Talal, Firas al Lateef and Tony Aziz – with no option but to flee, first to Syria, then Turkey before being granted refugee status in the United States of America, where they recorded and toured. Although no longer running the risk of being killed for playing heavy metal, some of their fans have been killed for listening to it. Although it is not safe for them to return to Iraq, they refuse to let their dreams die and in 2014 Acrassicauda announced their 'Kickstarter Campaign' to fund their first full-length album recording.

In the past Iraqi musicians played at weddings and parties and used to be picked up from the street, literally. But recently music was declared *haram* (sinful) for Muslims by the Islamic fundamentalists. Music has begun to disappear from the streets and many music shops are closed under threat of violence. What is left on the shelves are mainly Arabic artists, of which very few are Iraqi musicians. The most famous Iraqi singer today is arguably Kazem al Saher, whose mournful songs about life in the good old days, juxtaposed with lyrics describing the state of Iraq today, are incredibly popular. He has become one of the most successful singers in the Arab world, having sold more than 30 million albums since the start of his career. Ranging from big romantic ballads to more political work, from pop to Arab classical, he has covered the spectrum of music with the kind of success not seen since the heyday of the Egyptian songstress Umm Kalthum.

ARTS AND CRAFTS The story of Iraqi art starts with the splendid Mesopotamian civilisation and its Sumerian glazed-brick architecture with colourful designs dating back to 4500BC. Throughout the centuries, art has reflected the values and taste of the society from which it has emerged. When the Assyrian kings of ancient times ruled in 1400BC, art was an official profession that ensured the rulers' exploits were glorified and immortalised. The 'professional' Assyrian artists created statues of winged bulls that once guarded the palace portals and city gates, and recorded the life of their kings in magnificent, larger-than-life murals depicting hunting, wars and battles. In the words of one of the most famous 20th-century Iraqi artists, Jewad Selim:

'Art in Mesopotamia has always been like its people, who have been the product of the land and the climate. They have never reached decadence and never achieved perfection: for them perfection of craftsmanship has been a limitation on their self-expression. Their work has been crude but inventive, has had a vigour and boldness which would not have been possible with a more refined technique. The artist has always been free to express himself, even amid the state art of Assyria'.

Islamic art During the Abbasid period (AD750–1258), Islamic art with a unique spiritual dimension emerged. It was enhanced rather than stifled by the prohibition on portraying living forms. Calligraphy, script embellishment, floral and geometric designs and miniature painting characterised Islamic art, which was also influenced by Chinese ceramics, paintings and textiles brought back to Iraq by traders.

The first Islamic art school was established in Baghdad in the 12th century, where artisan and craft guilds flourished.

Kings, aristocrats and intellectuals generously rewarded calligraphers who decorated their houses and palaces with ornamental designs based on Arabic letters. Mubarak al Makki perfected the Kufic (square block) lettering style, while Yahya al Wasiti was the most famous figure in 13th-century book illustrations: his drawings provide a rich source of historical information. Architecture, furnishings, weapons and national costumes were all depicted.

Throughout the Abbasid period, Baghdad was the intellectual centre of the Islamic world, where art, science and philosophy flourished. When Baghdad was sacked by the Mongols, art was dealt a devastating blow. It did not fully recover until the beginning of the 20th century when an amalgam of the ancient and the contemporary became a recurring theme.

Modern art The first generation of painters, the 'early pioneer artists' – Abdul Qadir al Rassam, Mohammed Salih Zeki, Asim Hafidh and Haj Mohammed Selim – belonged to a class of officers or officials of the Ottoman Empire who saw a promise of regeneration in European culture and science in the early years of the 20th century. In tune with the disaffection towards the old regime of the Young Turks and Kemal Ataturk, they also nurtured an avid patriotism towards their homeland. It was men like these, claiming a rational, scientific perspective to guide the hands of the future, who first breached the traditions and forms of identity. Significantly, the early pioneers were the only ones who portrayed what they saw: landscapes both urban and rural, images of people in daily social contexts, portraits and self-portraits. During World War II the military once again made a contribution to Iraqi art when a group of Polish officers who came to Baghdad with the Allied troops, joined the country's cultural life. One Iraqi artist commented that after discussions with the Poles he came to know what colour was and how it should be employed.

The post-war years launched a generation on scholarships abroad, among them a handful of talented young artists collectively known as al-Ruwad (the pioneers or the Fifties generation), including Faiq Hassan, Jewad Selim, Ismail al Sheikhli, Kamil Chadirji and Nadhim Ramzi, who bridged the gap between modernity and heritage. Al-Ruwad were a mixture of art school graduates and self-taught artists who left their studios to paint scenes from the country and city streets. They were led by Faik Hassan, the father of Iraq's modern art movement. After graduating from the Academie Nationale des Beaux Arts in Paris he became a teacher at the Institute of Fine Arts in Baghdad. In 1951 Jewad Salim (1921–61) formed the Baghdad Group of Modern Art, eager to establish an Iraqi artistic identity. He believed that a new trend in painting would solve the artistic identity problem in the contemporary awakening by following in the footsteps of the 13th-century Iraqi painters. After gaining an appreciation of the aesthetic values of ancient art while working at the Directorate of Antiquities in Baghdad, Salim studied in Rome and England before abandoning painting to concentrate on sculpture. His most famous work is the Freedom Monument in Baghdad (see page 150). The Impressionists emerged in 1953 and gravitated around Hafid al Drubi, who opened the first independent painting studio in Baghdad. After training at Goldsmith's College in London, he turned to Impressionism and Cubism, which he used to depict landscapes and city scenes.

Two artist groups captured the spirit of the decade that would define the Sixties generation. They were Al-Mujadidin (the Innovationists) 1965, and included Ali Talib, Salim al Dabbagh, Salman Abbas, Amer al Obaidi, Salih al Jumaie, Faiq Hussain, Nida

DIJLA ART GALLERY

I have been in the art milieu for many years. To remain vital, I surround myself with exciting, stimulating art and seek challenges.
Zainab Mahdi

Dijla Art Gallery is a prominent gallery in Baghdad specialising in contemporary Iraqi art. It is dedicated to the encouragement and promotion of Iraqi art pioneers as well as emerging and established artists, working primarily in painting, sculpture, graphic and ceramic art. Established in 1997, the gallery is situated in the heart of Baghdad's art district on Abu Nawas Street overlooking the river Tigris (Dijla) and based in an old family home built in 1932. Its owner, Zainab Mahdi, has succeeded in creating an intellectually stimulating atmosphere with art that generates great interest and encourages creativity. She says:

'The realisation of this gallery had always been my dream. It took a long time to come true. The first tangible spark was in December 1993 when the Red Cross of Iraq requested my aid in creating a mural representing the birth of their organisation. The mural had to be 9x3m so I needed spaces and help of other artists. Immediately, I thought of the old family home as the rooms are large enough and the atmosphere is so inspiring for the creation of this project. I could there conduct this art work and have the opportunity to once again sense the antiquity of the place while reminiscing.

Having spent about two months working on the mural, I became deeply attached to my home once again. Although the thought of refurbishing the large deserted home was immensely overwhelming, it was easier to bear than the thought of locking the doors once again. Finally, I have started the big task. It took a very long time as the circumstances were very difficult. Eventually, it was all over and was first inaugurated on the 7th of July, 1997. From that time on, we have succeeded in presenting exclusive art works and organising many exhibitions in which some of them were very distinguished. I have realised that with the help and encouragement of friends, family and artists, namely the late Ismaeel al Shaikli, Jamil Hammoudi, Dr Khalid al Qassab, Dr Nouri Bahjat, Nazeeha Salim, Nouri al Rawi and the late Nazar al Hindawi, thanks to whom, did I live to enjoy the fulfilment of my dream.'

As a result of Zainab's endeavours, visitors now have the opportunity to participate in an aesthetic experience and complete the dialogue that was started by the artist.

Kadhim and Talib Makki. Al-Ruyah al-Jadida (the New Vision) 1968 included Ismail Fattah, Mohammed Muhridden, Hashim al Samarchi, Salih al Jumaie, Rafa al Nasiri and Dia Azzawi. They exhibited a distinct individualism; an essential component of the artist's identity. The Arab identity in the works of some of these artists dealt with issues such as the shock of the Six Days War of 1967, the Palestinian cause and the Lebanese civil war, which inspired a creative response of powerful empathy, such as in al Jumaie's 1967 work *Bullet Trace*. The 1960s began with the establishment of the Institute of Higher Education which became the Art College.

The prosperous decades of the 1970s and 1980s were the years of 'cultural exports' and the staging of numerous international art exhibitions, festivals and symposia in Iraq. Iraqi artists took their work to North Africa, Egypt, Syria and

Lebanon. Iraq hosted the first international arts gathering, the Al-Wasiti Festival in 1972. Then came the meeting of the First Congress of Arab Artists, which led to the formation of the Union of Arab Artists. Exhibitions in Baghdad included the Arab Graphic Art Exhibition and the Baghdad International Exhibition of Posters. The cult surrounding Saddam Hussein resulted in the 'art of veneration' which became a pervasive art form in Iraqi society while Saddam was in power. He was portrayed as a benevolent 'uncle' in a variety of costumes and was depicted on numerous posters throughout the country. The Saddam Arts Centre opened in 1986 and featured the work of artists from across the world. In 1988 it was the venue for an International Calligraphy Festival. The Babylon Festival became an international cultural event, which has not been revived in post-Saddam Iraq. The works of the 1980s, especially the eight years of the Iran-Iraq War (1980–88) were characterised by challenge and cynicism. There was a marked shift in the work of the Eighties generation towards a form of abstractism.

The lack of security and deteriorating living standards in the years following the 1991 Gulf War led to a mass exodus of Iraqi intellectuals and artists who now live and work in the diaspora, their work influenced by the situation in their home country. During the Saddam era there were six art galleries in Abu Nawas Street alone. Today there are probably no more than six in the whole of Baghdad. In 1992 against the general trend Qasim Sabti founded the Hewar Art Gallery in Baghdad, which become an important and active oasis for Iraqi artists. The Dijla Art Gallery was established in 1997 by Zainab Mahdi to encourage and promote emerging and established Iraqi artists and to provide a venue for cultural activities such as lectures, open debates and musical performances. The Madarat Gallery was opened in Baghdad in January 2006 by Attitudes SAC (an NGO which promotes culture in Iraq) to host cultural events such as exhibitions, music concerts and cultural sessions.

The Iraqi Museum of Modern Art in Baghdad, which contained thousands of works spanning the period from the 19th century, was damaged by fire and looting in 2003. Today rebadged as the National Museum of Modern Art, it has been rehoused in the same building as the Ministry of Culture. It is home to a collection of more than 19,000 artworks representing the art history of the Iraqi people, their traditions and heritage. As well as making these works accessible to visitors, the museum also runs educational workshops about Iraqi arts, and promotes cultural ties within Iraq and with other countries and cultures.

CINEMA The first Iraqi films were shown in the Al-Shafa House on the banks of the Tigris in 1909. But nobody knew where these films or 'magic tricks' as they were termed by the Baghdadis had come from. After the screening of the first eight films, which included *Leopard Hunting*; *The Agitated Sea*; *The Industrialist* and *The Funeral of Edward VII*, the daily papers urged everyone to see the 'magic tricks' for themselves. The first attempt at making local films failed miserably; in 1938 Hafidh al Qadhi dispatched his brother to England to import the necessary equipment and materials to start producing a film. This proved over-ambitious and beyond the capabilities of the new 'industry'. Until financiers and war-profiteers started setting up film companies such as the Baghdad Company for Film Production, licensed in 1942, the Iraqis could only manage to appear in Egyptian films as extras. In 1946 an Iraqi-Egyptian company produced *Son of the East*, in which a number of Iraqi actors and actresses made their debut and the film industry was born. Shortly after its inception the industry suffered from an acute attack of sluggishness which lasted until the Arts World Company brought it out of the doldrums in 1953 with the production of *Fetna and Hassan*. A number of poor quality, amateurish films followed, namely *Who is Responsible?*, *The Watchman* and *Saied Effendy*, filmed on the streets of Baghdad.

The State appeared on the scene during the 1960s and commenced its feature film production with *The Collector*. The most sophisticated equipment was made available to the film industry, which excelled in documentaries and prompted Iraq to take part in international film festivals. The productions included *The Long Days*, a highly propagandist account of Saddam Hussein's life, *Another Day*, a film about feudal life and the *Battle of Al Qadisiya* (fought in AD636 and at which the Arabs defeated the Persians). Egyptian films, especially romances, were very popular in Iraq, as were Indian films. During the years of sanctions the production of Iraqi films virtually stopped.

Film and photography These two fields of creative activity developed after 2003. As the security situation worsened, foreign filmmakers and photographers became rather thin on the ground. A mixture of NGO and individual funding allowed Iraqis to find expression and documentation and has opened up new opportunities and markets. Though much of the imagery reaching Western audiences is seen as news footage, there have been works of an artistic nature as young Iraqi filmmakers concentrate on documentaries. One of the first was Uday Rashid's *Underexposure*, filmed with out-of-date Kodak film stock (hence its name) between October 2003 and April 2004. The film poignantly captures the feeling of a city under occupation. Hadi Mahood's film *The Office* deals with Saddam's security office where thousands of people were tortured. Two young Iraqi filmmakers have made a film about the history of Iraqi cinema as seen through the eyes of two young filmmakers.

In 2005 Baghdad staged the First International Iraq Short Film Festival. In the previous year, the Independent Film and Television College was set up in Baghdad by filmmakers Kasim Abid and Maysoon Pachachi to provide free intensive short courses in film and television techniques, theory and production. It has trained Iraqi filmmakers and also supported the Iraqi film industry by providing production facilities and information about funding and further training. Films made by its students have been shown at various international film festivals. Although it was forced to close in 2006 after explosions nearby caused major damage to its structure, it has reopened, offering a series of one-, two- and three-month courses for 20–25 students. On each course at least 25% will be women and half will be students from outside Baghdad.

In the past Baghdad had numerous small and not so small cinemas showing a variety of films, local and international. However, recent years have seen the closing down of most cinemas which have been turned into commercial outlets. An erratic electricity supply made it difficult to screen films and pressure from Islamists made it hard for small cinemas to remain in business. Sadly, all cinemas are closed at the moment in Iraq (2015).

LITERATURE Throughout the Middle East, poetry is held in high esteem. In Iraq, poetry was very important in pre-Islamic times, with poets acting as historians, soothsayers and propagandists. The early poems started to be collected in the 8th century and were referred to as Muallaqat, or hung poems, as they were hung in the most sacred place in Islam, the Kaaba – the large cuboidal structure in the al-Masjid al-Haram Mosque in Mecca. The Abbasids introduced the preoccupations of court into poetic themes. Arab poetry was influenced by Persian civilisation, as seen in romantic and heroic epics and poems with mystical themes, while Sufism

(Islam's mystical tradition) is characterised by unique verse written to induce a state of ecstasy.

At the turn of the 20th century, Iraqi poetry followed traditional form and restricted itself to verses for formal occasions such as weddings and poems venerating the Prophet and high ranking religious and tribal leaders. The two pioneers of modern Iraqi verse are Ar-Rasafi (1875–1945) and Az-Zahawi (1863–1936). They worked on the principle that content was much more important than form and they used language to inform; social and political topics replaced idealised Bedouin themes such as courage. During World War I poetry became charged with patriotic emotion and the revival of Arab heritage started in the Shia city of Najaf, a traditional centre of Islamic scholarship. By World War II, however, Iraqi poetry was becoming influenced by Western forms, among them the works of T S Eliot, and extending the patriotic themes to those of rebellion; the Iraqi poets of the 1940s and 1950s experimented with new, untried forms. Poets such as Buland al Haidari, Mahmoud al Brekan, Nazik Almakaeka, Badr Shakir al Sayyab and Saadi Yousif are regarded in the Middle East as the soul and conscience of the Arab world.

Today Iraqi poets are no longer obliged to praise the 'great leader Saddam'. Religious poetry commemorating the martyrdom of Imam Hussain is making a comeback. Themes of violence and loss still abound. Popular poets inside Iraq include Kazim al Hajaj, Muwafak Mohammed, Hasan Sheikh Jafar, Hussain Abdulatif, Alfrid Saman, Sami Mahdi, Abdul Razzaq, Abdul Wahid and the late Yousof Alsayg. Today's poetry is often written in local dialect rather than literary Arabic and is published by hundreds of writers who make extensive use of internet sites.

SPORT A wide variety of sports are played and followed in Iraq.

Football By far the most popular sport, football is Iraq's national passion and is considered a uniting factor, following the years of war and unrest. The Iraqi Football Association (IFA) is the governing body of football in Iraq, controlling the Iraq National Football Team and the Iraq Super League (Dawn Al-Nokba). Under the Baath Party, sports were highly politicised and Uday, Saddam's eldest son, was the president of the Iraqi Football Federation.

The Iraqi national team is commonly known as Usood Al-Rafidain, the Lions of Mesopotamia. The national sport reached its peak in the 1970s and 1980s with Iraq qualifying for the 1986 World Cup held in Mexico. They are one of the most successful national teams in the Arab League, having won a record total of four Arab Nations Cups. On the Asian level, Iraq is one of the premier teams, having won the AFC Asian Cup in 2007, the Gold Medal of the Asian Games in 1982, three Gulf Cups of Nations (in 1979, 1984 and 1988) and the West Asia Championship in 2002. They have also been awarded the AFC National Team of the Year Award twice in 2003 and 2007. In the 2004 summer Olympics held in Athens, Iraq finish in fourth place behind the Italian team by virtue of a single goal. In 2006 the national football team participated in the Asian Cup finals for the first time in more than two decades defeating South Korea and ending the tournament as runners-up. They went one better in 2007 when they won the title AFC Asian Cup Champions.

Iraq played their home games on neutral territory in the 1980s due to the Iran-Iraq War. After 2003 they were again forced to do so for security reasons, with fixtures being held in Jordan, Syria, Qatar and the United Arab Emirates. In 2009

FIFA ended its ban on Iraq hosting official matches, allowing them to resume playing home matches on home soil. They celebrated in July of that year by beating Palestine 3–0 in a friendly in the Franso Hariri Stadium in Erbil. Playing the same opponents three days later in the Al-Shaab Stadium in Baghdad, they won 4–0 in front of a crowd of more than 50,000. In 2011, Iraq played their FIFA World Cup qualifier against Jordan on home ground for the first time in many years in front of a crowd of 24,000. Despite no longer being allowed to host international friendlies because of nationwide violence, Al-Shaab Stadium remains a popular venue and throngs of Iraqis wait outside the gates even after the stadium has filled. Millions more watch via television throughout the country.

The current Iraq Super League champions are Al-Shorta (the Police Club), one of the most successful clubs in the history of Iraq. Other big clubs include Al-Quwa Al-Jawiya, Al-Zawraa, Erbil SC, Al Talaba and Najaf FC.

The Olympics The Iraqi National Olympic Committee (INOC) was formed in 1948 and later that year the country made its Olympic début in London. Following this, Iraq missed the 1952 games and boycotted the 1956 games as a result of their opposition to the Anglo-French-Israeli Suez attack. They returned to Olympic competition again in 1960 at the summer games in Rome, when they won their first medal, a bronze in weightlifting. They participated in the next three games but once again did not appear in the 1972 and 1976 games in boycott of apartheid South Africa (in joining the boycott, Iraq became only the second non-African state to do so, the other being Guyana). Since 1980, Iraqi competitors have appeared in every summer games despite the Iraq wars, though they have not competed at the winter games.

Uday Hussain became the chairman of the INOC in 1984 under the Saddam regime, when Iraq was suspended from the Olympic Council of Asia (OCA) after the OCA president was killed by Iraqi troops during the Persian Gulf War. Iraq did not attend the Pan-Arab Games in 1992 and 1997, with Kuwait and Saudi Arabia at times boycotting games in which Iraq participated. In 2003 the INOC building in Baghdad was looted and burnt, however Iraq's Olympic programme recovered in time to compete in the games in Athens in the following year.

Basketball There are two major basketball leagues in Iraq, the Iraqi Basketball Association, the country's professional organisation, which runs a number of adult and youth leagues, and the Iraqi Premier League, which is for elite players. The Iraqi National Basketball Team represents Iraq in international competitions.

Iraq also has one of the strongest wheelchair basketball teams in Asia with 15 years' experience of the sport.

Other sports Swimming, weightlifting, body-building, taekwondo and tennis are all popular. Iraq has a kick-boxing world champion, Riyafh al Azzawi, who became the 2008 World Kick-boxing Network (WKN) World Champion after a fight against three-times world champion Tomasz Borowiec in the 91kg category, becoming the first-ever Arab World Champion in heavyweight kick-boxing with a record 34–0 at the time. Boxer Najah Ali qualified for the 2004 Olympics in Athens, earning a wild-card spot. Competing at light flyweight, Ali hoped to become Iraq's first Olympic boxing medallist, and second medallist overall. He won his first bout against a North Korean by a healthy margin of 21–7, but was defeated in his second by Armenian Aleksan Nalbandyan.

IRAQI SPORTSWOMEN

Female students at Iraqi colleges of physical education are frustrated that they cannot put what they learn into practical use owing to the conservative values of Iraqi society. The social environment in present-day Iraq is not conducive to girls engaging in outdoor sports activities and even physical education students have to do these within the confines of their college or at home. This conservative outlook is also visible in the courses, which are overwhelmingly theoretical, with a minimum of actual physical training and exercise. Furthermore getting the chance to use the skills that they have acquired outside college is virtually impossible owing to the lack of sports facilities for women.

However, Dr Mudhaffar Abdullah Shafiq, chairman of the Iraqi Association of Sports and Exercise Medicine, considers that sports and exercise in general are alien to Iraqi women, who he says also have bad eating habits. He said that a tremendous awareness campaign is required about the physical and psychological benefits of sport and exercise to women, including the favourable impact on their looks as well as stamina for working women, in order to change the situation.

Thuraya Najim, a member of the Parliamentary Youth and Sports Committee, considers that sports education starts both at home and school. She urges the government to make sports compulsory, as many schools skip physical education in favour of other subjects because they view exercise as unimportant for girls.

Fawziya al Attiya, a professor of sociology at Baghdad University, adds that traditional customs and values restrict the chances of women engaging in sport throughout the Arab world and Iraq is no exception. She recalled that the situation was better in the 1960s and 1970s, when attention was paid to sports at school, and clubs had sportswomen as swimmers, gymnasts, tennis players, etc. But wars, international sanctions and insurgent violence have conspired to disrupt this trend. Al Attiya hopes that stability, modern education, better economic conditions and higher living standards will eventually contribute to encouraging women to re-engage in sport.

IRAQ ONLINE

For additional online content, articles, photos and more on Iraq, why not visit www.bradtguides.com/iraq.

2

History

EARLY MESOPOTAMIA

Recorded history began at Sumer, a city state in ancient Iraq, but long before the first cities made their appearance in 4000BC Mesopotamia, the land between the two rivers, which we now know as Iraq, was the home of prehistoric man. Among the world's oldest human remains is a campsite, estimated to be 120,000 years old. It was found in 1949 by Dr Naji al Asil, the Director General of the Iraqi Department of Antiquities. The discovery was made at Barda-Balka, between the northern Iraqi cities of Kirkuk and Suleimaniyah. Four skeletons – one 60,000 years old and the others 45,000 years old – were also discovered in northern Iraq, in Shanidar Cave near the town of Rawanduz.

The great agricultural revolution – when man stopped his wandering existence based on hunting wild beasts and gathering plants and began to domesticate animals and cultivate crops – took place in Mesopotamia around 10,000 years ago. Primitive settlements grew into towns and villages, which eventually evolved into

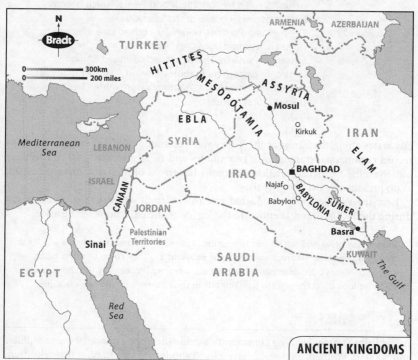

ANCIENT KINGDOMS

CHRONOLOGY

6000–4000BC	Eridu, perhaps the first city as we know it.
4000–3000BC	The ancient kingdoms of Sumer and Akkad were the first civilisations developed on the banks of the Tigris and Euphrates.
1900BC	Babylon emerged from the union of the Sumerian Akkadian kingdoms. Hammurabi developed his famous code of Law.
1700–1400BC	The Kassite Kingdom
1400BC	Rise of Assyria, a kingdom that conquered more than 40 nations. The Assyrians founded the largest empire of their time and built great cities such as Ashur, Nineveh and Nimrud.
606–539BC	Neo-Babylonians. One of the most famous rulers during this period was Nebuchadnezzar, who built a magnificent summer palace and the Hanging Gardens of Babylon.
539–330BC	Achaemenian Persians. Cyrus the Great, founder of the Achaemenian Dynasty, ascended the Persian throne. He was at first welcomed by the Babylonians, who were the victims of a series of inefficient rulers.
336–323BC	Alexander the Great conquered the Persian Empire, establishing Greek monarchies from Greece to India, marking the beginning of the Hellenistic period. He took Babylon as one of his capitals.
331–129BC	Seleucid Greeks. Seleucius I, one of Alexander the Great's generals, ruled Mesopotamia and Persia, which became known as the kingdom of the Seleucids.
130BC–AD226	The Parthian Persians, originally a mixed race of nomads, ruled ancient Iraq from Ctesiphon.
AD227–636	Sassanian Persians. This dynasty challenged Roman control of eastern trade routes. During their rule many of the ancient cities of Mesopotamia were buried beneath the sand of the desert.

city states along the banks of the Tigris and Euphrates. Writing was developed to record commercial transactions; ceremonies and rituals became part of everyday life. Even the British coronation ceremony has traces of Mesopotamian practices, as do present-day baptism rituals.

Leonard Woolley, who conducted extensive excavations at Ur's royal cemetery during the 1930s, draws attention to the legacy of ancient Iraq when he asks:

'How many of us realise that our superstitious impulse to turn back when a black cat crosses our path stems from the people of Babylon? Do they come to mind when we look at the twelve divisions on our watch-face, when we buy eggs by the shock (sixty), when we look up at the stars to read our fate in their movement and conjunctions?'

BEFORE SUMER

Ancient Iraq's early farming communities made their appearance between 9000BC and 5000BC. Women, anxious to have a fixed abode in which to raise their children,

The *Epic of Gilgamesh* is one of the oldest written stories on earth, predating Homer by many centuries. Originating in Ancient Sumeria the poem, which tells the story of Gilgamesh, a historical king of Uruk, was originally written on 12 clay tablets in cuneiform script, which were found at Nineveh in the library of Assyrian King Ashurbanipal. It relates Gilgamesh's adventures on his journey in search of the Babylonian Noah and the secret of eternal life following the death of his friend Enkidu.

influenced the decision to abandon the nomadic hunter-gatherer lifestyle, as did a decline in edible plants and animals. **Jarmo**, founded in 6500BC in the foothills of the Kurdish Zagros Mountains, is one of the oldest known permanent settlements. Its inhabitants lived in mud houses, weaved flax and used tools such as sickles made of obsidian.

People from the **Hassuna** culture, which dates back to 6000BC, introduced irrigation, were accomplished potters and embarked on trade from the Persian Gulf to the Mediterranean. Some of the world's finest ceramics were produced during the Halaf (north Mesopotamia) period (5000BC) that followed. The villages now had cobbled streets and animals grazed in the surrounding fields.

In south Mesopotamia during the **Ubaid** period (also c5000BC), the settlements along the Tigris and Euphrates, including Eridu, Ur, Lagash, Nippur and Kish (the forerunners of the Sumerian city states) were built around a shrine. The primitive irrigation system was augmented with small canals and reservoirs, and historians have commented on the division of labour that became evident in society.

The **Uruk** period (3800–3200BC) was a time of rapid urbanisation. As many as 45,000 people lived in the city of Uruk itself. A collection of temples were dedicated to the goddess Inanna, queen of heaven and earth. The temples became a hive of commercial activity where craftsmen plied their trade. The first pictographs (symbols representing objects) were developed here, as trade could not be conducted without written records, and so writing began. Cylinder seals (devices used for establishing ownership or recording an agreement with personal pictorial marks carved on a small cylinder as a signature) were also an invention of the people of Uruk. The increased size of the strip-system of agriculture that was developed in Uruk transformed its agricultural wealth. Not only did superior potters' wheels become a feature, but wheels for carts were developed and used for the first time here.

The **Jemdat Nasr** period (3200–2900BC) built on the achievements of Uruk. The story of the flood, another Mesopotamian myth that has striking parallels to the biblical story of Noah, is believed to date back to this period. Floods were a common occurrence in Mesopotamian life, but it seems that there was one great flood, which is written about in the *Epic of Gilgamesh*.

THE SUMERIANS

The seeds of Sumerian culture sown in Iraq's prehistory germinated during the Hassuna, Halaf, Ubaid, Uruk and Jemdat Nasr periods and blossomed in the city states of the 3rd millennium BC, among them Sippar, Kish, Akshak, Larak, Nippur, Adab, Umma, Lagash, Bad-tibira, Uruk, Larsa, Ur and Eridu. The cities began as simple agricultural settlements on the fertile banks of the Tigris and Euphrates. Regular supplies of fish and birds could be relied on if there was a problem with crops. Floods, however, were unpredictable, building materials had to be imported, and the inhabitants of Mesopotamia fought three main battles: the battle against nature, the battle against other cities who wanted to expand their boundaries, and the battle against foreign invaders. After their phenomenal expansion the empires were plagued by internal disputes and were frequently dealt a death blow by their neighbours. Some conquerors assimilated the culture and wisdom of the vanquished, while others were only interested in pillage and destruction.

The walled cities produced security and stability. Primary allegiance shifted from the family to the group, and unity was fostered by faith in personal gods who protected every settlement and city. The civil service and political institutions could function and develop, and there was time to engage in cultural and leisure pursuits.

However, the growth of cities with fixed boundaries resulted in boundary disputes, a recurrent theme in the history of the Middle East. Each city relied on a section of irrigated land for its survival and the history of Mesopotamia is largely the history of wars and disputes between various city states.

The early settlements were fledgling democracies governed by assemblies appointed by the citizens. But in the face of military threats the citizens felt they needed a leader to ensure their victory in boundary disputes. The term 'big man' (*lugal*) was used to refer to the first leaders, who were only appointed for the duration of a particular conflict. But as the conflicts became more frequent, the leaders became permanent and the institution of kingship developed.

The city states were united in the 24th century BC by Sargon, King of Akkad. His city, known as **Agade** (which has yet to be discovered), lay to the northwest of the Sumerian kingdoms. Akkadian was adopted as the language of diplomacy and Sargon's empire sprawled into Persia, Syria and along the Mediterranean coast into Lebanon.

After the death of Sargon's son, eastern barbarians known as the Guti destroyed the empire and wiped Agade, Sargon's capital, off the map. Utuhegal, the ruler of Uruk, drove out the invaders only to be deposed by one of his generals, Ur-Nammu, who founded the 3rd dynasty of **Ur** (2113–2006BC). The kingdoms of Sumer and Ur were united once more. But the unity was more of a partnership in which Ur, with its temple to the moon goddess and 80m ziggurat, was the senior partner. Despite his usurpation of power, Ur-Nammu presided over the Sumerian renaissance, a time of increased prosperity during which the arts were given a new lease of life. Ur-Nammu continued the tradition of concern for fairness and justice and inscribed the first law code on cuneiform tablets, three centuries before the creation of Hammurabi's renowned 2.4m stele of black diorite, with its 282 laws. The Sumerian renaissance continued under Ur-Nammu's son, Shulgi.

Ur fell after an attack by the Amorites (Semitic nomads from the deserts of Syria and Arabia) and the Elamites (from an ancient kingdom east of the Tigris). The attack was a watershed in the history of ancient Iraq: city states were replaced by small kingdoms and kings rented out land. A society in which the temples were the focus of economic activity was replaced by a society of farmers, citizens and traders.

BABYLON AND HAMMURABI

After the Amorite conquest, warfare plagued the region as power shifted between rival princes, but in 1780BC, Hammurabi, sixth King of Babylon, once again united Mesopotamia. For him unity meant a centralised administration, backed up by the rule of law and an efficient system of justice implemented by magistrates under his control. Hammurabi was a man of patience and foresight. Before embarking on his empire-building he spent 25 years cementing military and political alliances. His empire, with Babylon as its capital, extended northward from the Persian Gulf through the Tigris and Euphrates river valleys, and westward to the coast of the Mediterranean Sea. Roads were improved to facilitate trade and to enable troops to move quickly and execute their orders. Fifty-five of Hammurabi's official letters to local governors have been discovered. Even ordinary citizens wrote to their ruler. Messengers ensured the efficient flow of correspondence. Even after Babylon's political significance was eclipsed it was respected as an enlightened cultural centre.

THE ASSYRIANS

Early in the 10th century BC the Assyrians perfected the art of war and conquest and, overthrowing the Elamites, succeeded in establishing their grip on nearly all of the Near East. They came from the state of Assyria in the north which was centred on three cities: Ashur, Nimrud and Nineveh. At the height of their power Egypt was nothing more than an Assyrian province. The Assyrian Empire stretched for 1,600km, from the Nile Valley in Egypt to the mountains of Armenia. Their conquests had a religious dimension: the enemies of the king were also the enemies of the god Ashur. Just as Ashur stood at the head of the religious hierarchy, his man on earth, the King of Assyria, had to stand at the head of all other rulers, and battles were seen as crusades. Conquests went hand in hand with the brutal slaying of the inhabitants of cities that had been subdued. Victory was the Assyrians' *raison d'être*, war was a way of life, and the spreading of terror was their speciality. Military exploits were immortalised in magnificent works of art. The Assyrians are remembered mainly for their reliefs, which depict winged bull-men and lion-men who look down from the gates of palaces. The walls of palaces were decorated with war scenes sculpted in limestone. The sculptures also served as propaganda: remain subservient to the conquerors or perish. Art was no longer a medium for glorifying the gods: it now depicted the exploits of kings and armies.

The Assyrian Empire was dealt a swift death-blow in 612BC when the Babylonian King Nabopolassar joined forces with the Elamites and the **Medes** (a young and little-known people of the Iranian Plateau from whom the Kurds are said to be descended), and led a combined attack against Nineveh. The disintegration of the Sumerian city states was lamented, the downfall of Babylon was mourned, but no-one shed a tear at the collapse of the hated Assyrian giant.

BABYLON REVISITED

The Neo-Babylonians ended Assyrian supremacy and resurrected Babylon to its former glory through a dazzling renaissance of Mesopotamia, presided over by Nebuchadnezzar II. It was essentially a religious revival accompanied by an extensive building programme, which focused on the restoration of religious shrines to long-revered Babylonian gods. Babylon was also the home of the Tower of Babel, a 90m ziggurat, and 1,179 temples, which once again became the focal point of economic activity. The Neo-Babylonians had slaves, as well as a class of people who laboured for the clergy in return for food and lodgings. When the city was threatened by foreign invaders, the people flocked to the temples seeking the protection of the gods.

Nebuchadnezzar's architectural boom included the reconstruction of Sumer and Akkad. But the greatest attention was devoted to the rebuilding of Babylon, a city of 100,000 inhabitants that could accommodate a quarter of a million. The city's 16km

After the collapse of their massive empire, which had lasted for almost 14 centuries, the Assyrians became ethnic groups of people living at the mercy of their overlords in widely scattered lands in the Middle Eastern region. They embraced Christianity in the 1st century and today are followers of the ancient church of the East, the Syrian Orthodox Church of Antioch, the Chaldean Catholic Church and various Protestant denominations.

Until the cultural renaissance in the middle of the 19th century, the Assyrians almost lost their ethnic identity when numerous atrocities befell them because of their religious beliefs and origins. Like the Yezidis and Armenians they were the victims of Ottoman massacres. In 1915, the Turks drove them out of the Hakkari Mountains where they were living as a semi-independent people and they joined their brethren in the Urmia and Salams districts of Iran.

World War I proved disastrous, as their support was enlisted by the allied forces (British and Russian) at dreadful cost. In 1918, just before the war ended, they were forced to retreat from Urmia. More than one-third of the entire Assyrian population perished during the trek to join the British forces in Baghdad. They were settled in camps in Baquba and used to protect the newly installed government of Iraq and British air bases.

Like the Kurds, the Assyrians were promised help by the allies. In Iraq they were offered a special position in the Mosul district, a promise that proved unacceptable to the other interested parties (namely the Turks and Kurds), and that was not kept. In 1933, betrayed by British promises regarding their personal safety, over 600 were massacred in Simeil and 2,000 in the surrounding villages by their Kurdish neighbours.

Since 1960 hundreds of Assyrian villages have been destroyed by Iraqi forces in the north of the country. Churches and monasteries have been levelled and the Assyrians have been denied the right to practise their religion and preserve their culture and language.

The toppling of Saddam's regime led to the recognition of the Assyrians as a distinct entity for the first time in the Iraqi constitution but the status of the community is so treacherous that this recognition is of little practical assistance.

Since 2003 the Assyrian community has been under siege. In 2003 more than 25 churches were attacked and bombed by terrorists. Priests have been abducted and beheaded, and Christian women have been beheaded for refusing to wear the veil, purportedly by al-Qaida terrorists. Sunni jihadist and Kurdist Separatists in Mosul and Kirkuk have bombed churches, killed thousands of Assyrians and expelled them from their homes. In the autumn of 2008, 2,500 Assyrian families fled from Mosul after a vicious campaign of terror: some to Syria, the well qualified to the West and the rest to Iraqi Kurdistan or the Nineveh Plains.

The Kurdistan Regional Government is also turning the Assyrians into second-class citizens. They are forced to sign pledges of support in return for food and substandard housing in disparate areas. To receive health care or education they must identify themselves either as Arabs or Kurds, the old Saddam rules.

The Nineveh Plains Project to resettle the Assyrians may prompt their expulsion from the rest of Iraq. Above all they need to be recognised as citizens of Iraq, and not be treated as a ghettoised minority (see page 15).

outer wall was wide enough for two chariots of four horses to ride abreast. Festival Avenue, with a magnificent gate known as Ishtar Gate, led to the royal palace of Nebuchadnezzar.

PERSIAN CONQUEST

The splendour of Babylon was of no great benefit to the ordinary people who could not make ends meet on their meagre wages and banking families made a fortune by charging 20–30% interest. The death of the Babylonian Empire came slowly in the form of a gradual decline and disintegration. While the Babylonians were feasting, the armies of Cyrus the Great diverted the waters of the Euphrates into a trench and marched along the dry river bed into the city. For the first time in history the land of the two rivers, the cradle of civilisation, lost its independence and was annexed to a foreign empire. Cyrus proved that empire building could be accomplished with a minimum of destruction. He respected his subjects, and life returned to normal along the banks of the Tigris and Euphrates, until the power-hungry Xerxes levelled a crippling tax on the people of Babylon to finance his military exploits. The Persians also monopolised trade with India and the East through the Royal Road from Sardis to Susa, which bypassed Babylon. The people revolted and the empire began to crumble. Magnificent buildings were left to decay, the canals silted up and much of the land reverted to desert.

ALEXANDER THE GREAT

From 334BC, Alexander the Great, pupil of Aristotle and army commander from the age of 16, inflicted a series of defeats on the Persians, and conquered their empire. Alexander the Great heralded a new age in which the world was bent on extensive commercial intercourse, bursting with curiosity, eager to reappraise most of its religious, moral, scientific and artistic values. Seleucus, one of Alexander's generals, succeeded him as ruler of Mesopotamia and Persia, then known as the kingdom of the Seleucids, which had its power centre at Seleucia on the Tigris, 32km south of modern Baghdad. Two hundred years later the Seleucids were challenged by new powers to the north, the Parthian Persians of nomadic origin, who competed with the Romans for control of the region. During the Parthian period (126BC–AD227) the city of Hatra was constructed 80km south of Mosul, and prospered as a great caravan centre of trade.

The history of the region then became the history of a series of wars between Western armies and the Persians. By the mid 7th century the Sassanids and the Romans were exhausted by their struggles and the Sassanian Empire was reduced to a number of small states. The region was ripe for conquest by Arab invaders who had recently converted to Islam, a new monotheistic religion inspired by the teachings of the Prophet Mohammed that were spread by both the book and the sword.

THE UMAYYADS

The Muslim conquests were successful largely because the people they sought to bring under their control resented the oppression and heavy taxation of their former rulers. In AD637 the Muslims ended Persian (Sassanid) rule in Iraq at the Battle of Qadisiya. The gem-laden, panther-skin banner of the enemy was captured. In Ctesiphon the Muslims discovered remarkable treasures, but resisted the temptation to attack Persia. The Arab troops, largely nomadic Bedouin, were

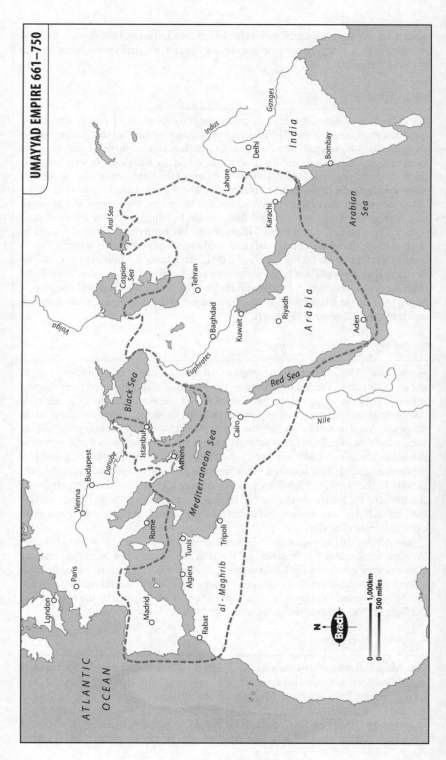

UMAYYAD EMPIRE 661–750

London

Paris

ATLANTIC OCEAN

Madrid

Rabat

al - Maghrib

Algiers

Tunis

Rome

Vienna

Budapest

Danube

Tripoli

Mediterranean Sea

Athens

Istanbul

Black Sea

Volga

Caspian Sea

Aral Sea

Baghdad

Euphrates

Kuwait

Riyadh

Arabia

Red Sea

Aden

Tehran

Nile

Cairo

India

Ganges

Indus

Delhi

Lahore

Karachi

Bombay

Arabian Sea

N

0   1,000km
0   500 miles

Bradt

stationed at two military garrisons: Basra and Kufa. They soon grew into large towns, which became the hotbeds of rebellion.

The Umayyads were responsible for many long-lasting social changes: they changed the caliphate into an empire, they made Arabic the language of the state, minted their own coins, and built a number of great mosques including the Dome of the Rock in Jerusalem, the Umayyad mosque in Damascus and the great mosque of Qairawan in present-day Tunisia. The mosques assumed the architectural features of the country: in Syria they were modelled on a square stone watch-tower, whereas in Iraq the mosque took a more traditional Arab form until, at a later date, under the Abassids, the spiral form of minaret originated, inspired by the earlier ziggurats. A regular postal service, schools, hospitals and charities for the sick were also established, as was a navy. Basra became an important port for the Islamic Empire, and ships sailed for Sind in Pakistan, East Africa and China. Stories of Sinbad the Sailor also became popular at around this time (see box, pages 318–19).

UMAYYADS, ABBASIDS, MONGOLS AND OTTOMANS

CHRONOLOGY – AD

570	Birth of the Prophet Mohammed in Mecca. Emergence of Islam, the third of the monotheistic religions.
632	Death of the Prophet Mohammed in Medina.
637	Defeat of the Persians by Arab forces at the Battle of Qadasiyah.
661–750	Umayyad caliphs in Damascus. The second caliph, Abu Bakr (successor to Prophet Mohammed) subjugated Mesopotamia. The time of the greatest expansion of the Muslim Empire. Rebellious Arabs were slaughtered in their thousands at Kufa and a series of brutal governors was installed to keep them in a state of subjugation.
680	Battle of Kerbala led to Sunni-Shia divide in Islam.
750–1258	The Abbasid caliphs in Baghdad. Baghdad replaced Damascus as the capital of the Muslim Empire. The golden age of wealth and learning (transmission of Greco-Roman philosophy to the Western world) the rulers promoted medicine, chemistry, geometry, mathematics, astronomy and poetry.
836	Capital of Abbasid Caliphate move to Samarra for 56 years.
1258–1356	The sacking of Baghdad by Hulagu, the grandson of Genghis Khan and the founding of the Ilkhanid Dynasty.
1261	Caliphate moved from Baghdad to Cairo.
1356–1410	Jalayrid Dynasty. The Jalayr kingdom was set up by the family of Amir Hussain Jalayr. They were capable rulers and Baghdad once again became an important town.
1408	The sacking of Baghdad by Timur.
1410–1509	Turkmen tribes began gaining influence.
1509–1533	Safavid Persians. Ismail Shah, founder of the Persian Safavid Dynasty, conquered Iraq, and forced many to convert to the Shia faith.
1534–1918	Ottoman period. Iraq was divided into three provinces (Baghdad, Mosul and Basra) by its Turkish rulers. Ottoman rule was characterised by centuries of neglect and poverty. Mosul and Basra were important commercial centres.

Umayyad society was divided into four classes: Arabs, who formed the aristocracy; the neo-Muslims, or converts; the *dhimmis* (non-Muslims in an Islamic state, ie: Christians, Jews, Zoroastrians and Berbers); and finally, slaves. The first Arab Empire was a politically, culturally and economically self-contained unit. The world was divided into the House of Islam (Dar Al Islam) and the House of War (Dar Al Harb). Peace came when the enemies surrendered and converted to Islam. There was little time or need for diplomacy: opponents were quickly subdued and incorporated into the House of Islam. The Iraqis in Basra and Kufa proved to be a continual thorn in the side of the Umayyad rulers. They resented the fact that Umayyad rule meant Syrian rule, they were excluded from government, and treated as non-Arab Muslims (*mawali*), who had to pay higher taxes. They also felt the taxes they paid should be spent to develop the areas from which they were collected. Nor did the local people benefit from the land reclamation projects. Their spiritual allegiance was to Ali, the cousin of the Prophet Mohammed, and they were aggrieved by the events at the battle of Kerbala, when Ali's son was killed by the Umayyad ruler Yazid. (See pages 19–20 for an explanation of the Sunni-Shia schism.)

The governors sent to Iraqi areas ruled by a combination of carrot-and-stick and resettlement. Al Mughira bin Shuba al Thaqafi, one of Kufa's first governors, converted to Islam, which annulled all past misdeeds. He adopted a policy of benign oversight as long as his authority was not threatened, and allowed the residents to keep the revenues of some districts. However, one of the most brutal governors was Hajjaj bin Yusuf al Thaqafi, who was in charge of both Basra and Kufa. He leapt onto the pulpit (*minbar*) in Kufa and made a speech famous in Arabic literature: 'People of Kufa, I see that your heads are ripe for cutting. You are always making mischief but this time you have made too much of it; there must be an end to it. Believe me, an end will be made, and my sword will make it.' Some historians claim the massacre resulted in 100,000 deaths.

Internal conflicts plagued the Umayyad Dynasty, which alienated many of its former supporters and could not provide the leadership expected of Muslim rulers, who became increasingly preoccupied with affairs of state. Corruption set in: one of the governors of Iraq accused of embezzling on a massive scale. The Abbasids, descendants of Abbas, the uncle of the Prophet Mohammed, invoked religious legitimacy. They organised themselves into an effective force, which relied heavily on the Persians for civil government and administration, and Abu-l-Abbas, the great-great grandson of the Prophet's uncle, led a rebellion that toppled the Umayyads in 750. Arab hegemony over the Islamic Empire was brought to an end, the various conquered populations slowly moved up in the social hierarchy and a new society evolved.

THE ABBASIDS

The Abbasids emphasised the equality of all Muslims. Persians played an influential role in the political and cultural life of the empire and as the Persians were not Arabs, appeals to Arab nationalism could no longer be made. The Abbasids campaigned for the return of power to the family of the Prophet Mohammed and descent from an uncle of the Prophet helped legitimise their religious credentials. But despite the emphasis on equality and an end to discrimination between Arab and non-Arab Muslims, a ruling elite soon developed and the caliph, surrounded by a vast court, lost touch with his subjects and became an absolute ruler, abandoning the traditional Arab notion of a leader chosen by a council of his peers. The palaces were massive institutions with a complex network of servants and secretaries. The caliph was assisted by a *vizier* (a high-ranking adviser). Muslim judges (*qadis*) were appointed

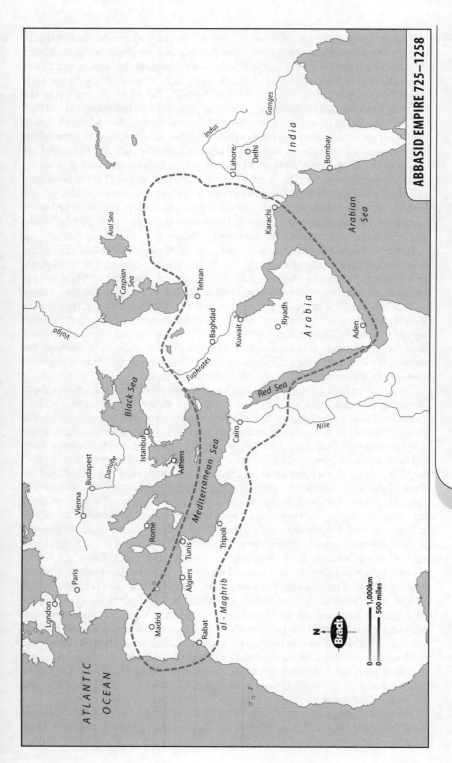

ABBASID EMPIRE 725–1258

by the central government. Ministers and senior military officers were in charge of a wage-earning bureaucracy and an army. Academics were greatly respected. Next in the pecking order came merchants, followed by farmers, herdsmen and slaves, who ceased to be social outcasts. A magnificent cultural renaissance spanned the reigns of the dynasty's first seven rulers (750–842), the most famous being the reigns of Mansour (754–75), Harun al Rashid (786–806) and Mamum (813–33).

Kufa was the first capital of the Abbasid Empire, but Caliph Mansour began the construction of a purpose-built capital, Baghdad, which served as a model for many towns and cities, including Cairo. Baghdad soon became the cosmopolitan centre of the Islamic medieval world and its richest city, blessed as it was with a plentiful supply of water. The rivers were an important means of communication and there was no malaria. It was a round city with three concentric enclosures, one for the ruler, one for the army and one for the people. Caliph Mansour died a few years after the completion of his capital. He ordered 100 graves to be dug for him to ensure that no-one could find his tomb and desecrate it.

Harun al Rashid presided over Baghdad in its heyday, established diplomatic relations with Byzantium and sent the Frankish Emperor Charlemagne an elephant as a present. Prosperity, though, led to ridiculous extravagance. When he was forced to seek shelter in a peasant's hut on the Euphrates the bill for lodgings came to 500 dirhams. The caliph inadvertently gave him a warrant on the treasury for 500,000 and insisted this amount was paid. Zubaida, Harun's wife, only allowed vessels of gold or silver studded with gems at her table; al Amin, one of Harun's sons, had boats made in the shapes of animals at a cost of millions of dirhams. But towards the end of his reign the legendary caliph lost interest in affairs of state and allowed the Barmakid family to exercise power in his name.

Social life centred around parties and hunts, chess, intellectual discussions about literature, philosophy, or religion, and poetry and literary symposiums. Outdoor games included polo, fencing, hawking (hunting with a bird of prey) and horse racing. The poet Abu Nuwas provided extensive details about court life. The Abbasid caliphs combined iron-fisted rule with impressive administrative skills and a sharp intellect. Once in power they embraced Sunni Islam and disavowed any support for Shia beliefs. This led to numerous conflicts and widespread bloodshed, and the flight of many Shias to the Maghreb. Long periods of stability proved conducive to cultural and intellectual pursuits, the arts were patronised and learning of every sort was encouraged. Classics from many languages were translated into Arabic at the House of Knowledge, erected near the Baghdad observatory. Science and philosophy were studied in the House of Wisdom. Advanced irrigation systems enabled the introduction of crops such as oranges and sugar. Paper, a Chinese invention, was popularised and assisted academic pursuits. Basra was famous for its glass and soap production, Kufa for its silk, especially silk handkerchiefs.

Abu Bakr Muhammad ibn Zakariya al Razi, the chief physician of a hospital in Baghdad, has been acknowledged as one of history's greatest physicians. The philosopher Muhammad Ibn Yarkhan Abu Nasr al Farabi wrote about an ideal state and was referred to as 'the second teacher', the first being Aristotle. Muhammad Ibn Musa al Khwarizmi compiled the first book on algebra and the Arabs were the first people to devote attention to alchemy, the mother of modern chemistry. Ibn Sina became an authority on medicine and philosophy for both the Muslim and European world, and his book on the law of medicine was used as a textbook until the 16th century.

The seed which grew into a forest of thorns and strangled the Abbasids was sown by al Mutasim (822–42), who allowed his Turkish bodyguards, numbering some 4,000, to rise to the rank of officers. They slowly wormed their way into positions

CHRONOLOGY – AD

16th century	Iranians converted to Shiism in large numbers.
18th century	Southern Iraq became a magnet for Persian religious scholars and their students after the Sunni Afghans captured Isfahan in Persia.
1737	Kerbala replaced Isfahan as the main centre of Shia scholarship.
1801	Kerbala sacked by Wahhabis.
1803	Construction of Hindiyya canal alleviated Najaf's water problems.
1805	Wahhabis laid siege to Najaf.
1843	Najib Pasha occupied Kerbala and returned it to Ottoman control.
1860s	Indians from Awadh migrated to Najaf and Kerbala in large numbers.
1875	Iranians accorded special status under a law that made them answerable to the Iranian consul and exempted them from paying taxes. Famous Shia *mujtahid* (Islamic scholar) Muhammad Hasan Shirazi, left Najaf for Samarra, increasing that city's status as a Shia religious centre.
20th century	Large-scale conversion of Iraqi tribes to Shiism, most of whom settled down and started farming.

of control and towards the end of their reign, the once feared and revered Abbasid caliphs became nothing more than tools in the hands of strong Turkish generals, the next masters of the Arab world.

THE MONGOLS

The years of peace, and the Abbasid Empire itself, were ended by the wanton destruction of the Mongols. Hulagu, a grandson of Genghis Khan, destroyed Diyarbakr, in present-day Turkey, and spent the next two years preparing for the siege of Baghdad with weapons such as fire-arrows, in which naphtha was used. The city surrendered on 10 February 1258 and 800,000 of its inhabitants were slaughtered, along with the caliph and his family. Books from the famous libraries were thrown into the river, the treasures were looted and the palaces and gardens were laid to waste.

After the Hulagu Dynasty (1258–1336) came the relative calm of the Jalayrids (1336–1432), a Mongol tribal dynasty that ruled Iraq and Azerbaijan, and made Baghdad their capital. Under this dynasty a flowering of Mongol art took place in Iraq, encompassing poetry, painting and calligraphy, and under the Jalayrid Sultan Ahmed (1382–1409) many architectural projects were undertaken in Baghdad. However, Tamerlane, a descendent of Genghis Khan, expanded his empire with even more savagery than Hulagu, and ravaged Baghdad. In 1401, when that city revolted against him, he slaughtered its inhabitants and made a pyramid of their skulls. Sultan Ahmed re-established his rule in 1405, when Tamerlane died. He was assisted in this by Kara Yusaf, a chief of the Black Sheep Turkmen from the Kara-Koyunlu principality of Anatolia. Peace did not last long, however, and in 1409 the two quarrelled and Yusaf killed the Sultan and took Baghdad for himself.

In 1466 the White Sheep Turkmen (another Anatolian tribe from Diyarbakr) under Hassan the Long defeated the Black Sheep Turkmen and took control of the country. But soon Iraq became a battleground between the two main expanding regional powers of the time, the Persians (the Safavids) and the Turks (the Ottomans). It also became a battleground between Sunni and Shia as the Ottomans were Sunni Muslims as were most Turkmen at that time after converting centuries before. The new Safavid Persian Empire was based in Azerbaijan with Tabriz as its capital. Shah Ismail I was proclaimed as its first shah or king, and having been tutored at a very early age into the Shia faith, he enforced this branch of Islam on his mainly Turkman subjects. In 1508 the White Sheep Turkmen ruling in Iraq were deposed by the Persian Ismail Shah, who then made a pilgrimage to Iraq's Shia shrines and destroyed the tombs of a number of Sunni saints and executed prominent religious Sunni leaders. However, the Ottomans were convinced for both political and religious reasons that the power and influence of the Persians had to be curbed.

THE OTTOMANS

In 1534 the Ottoman Sultan Suleiman the Magnificent took Baghdad and Iraq was integrated into the Ottoman Empire, which extended over present-day Hungary, Serbia, Albania, Greece, Bulgaria, Romania, the Ukraine, the Crimea, Turkey, Iran, Iraq, Syria, Lebanon, Jordan, Egypt, Libya, Tunisia and Algeria. The Persians, however, did not give up easily. They re-took Baghdad in 1623 and the repression of the Sunnis began anew under Shah Abbas. Few buildings from the times of the Abbasids were left standing. But the Ottomans, under Sultan Murad IV, once again ousted the invaders in 1638. This time a peace treaty was signed to demarcate the borders between the Persian Safavid Empire and the Ottomans. Sunni shrines were rebuilt, as were bazaars. Gardens were planted and attempts were made to beautify the city.

The later Ottoman administration, though, was largely corrupt and most of the governors were only concerned with extracting as much revenue as possible for their masters. It was a time of stagnation and poverty. Internal resistance came from the Shias in the towns and the tribes. Between 1620 and 1700, Basra was governed by a local ruler. Tribes such as the Aniza, Shammar, Dhafir, Muntafiq, Chaab, Bani Lam, Zubaid and others dominated the countryside, were hostile to the Ottomans and often engaged in 'highway' robberies. The Ottomans employed Christian slaves (Mamluks) from the Caucasus who converted to Islam and were trained in a special school and then assigned military and administrative duties as civil servants in Iraq. Their competent administration led to an economic revival during the 18th and 19th centuries. They cleared the canals, developed industries and permitted the establishment of a British Trade Agency – the Basra office of the East India Company. Between 1747 and 1831 the Mamluk officers became autonomous from the court of the Ottoman Empire and ruled Iraq.

Mamluk rule was brought to an end by a fatal combination of disease and flood in 1831. Baghdad was devastated by bubonic plague, with 2,000–3,000 people dying every day. The healthy fled, the administration collapsed and robbers plundered anything worth stealing. The Tigris burst its banks and destroyed hundreds of houses. The population of the city, which had risen to 150,000 during the prosperous rule of Daud Pasha, the last of the Mamluks, was reduced to 50,000. As Turkish influence declined, European influence increased. Steam boats started appearing on the Tigris and Euphrates, followed by telegraph lines, a newspaper, military factories, a hospital, schools and administrative councils.

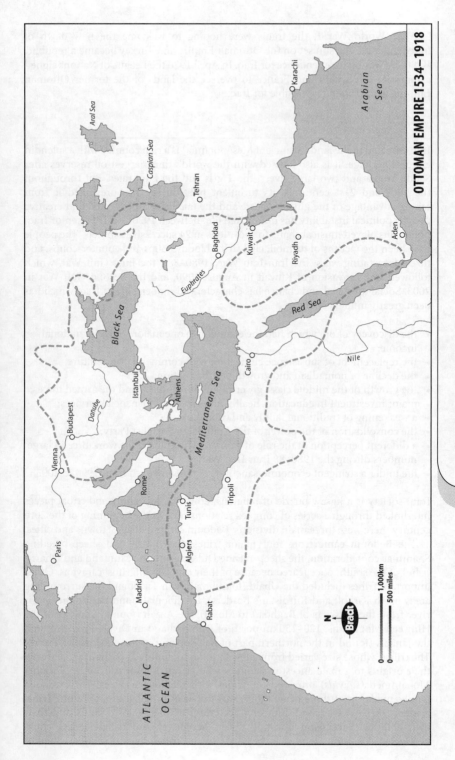

OTTOMAN EMPIRE 1534–1918

ATLANTIC OCEAN

Paris

Madrid

Rabat

Algiers

Tunis

Rome

Tripoli

Vienna

Budapest

Danube

Athens

Istanbul

Black Sea

Mediterranean Sea

Nile

Cairo

Red Sea

Aral Sea

Caspian Sea

Tehran

Baghdad

Euphrates

Kuwait

Riyadh

Aden

Karachi

Arabian Sea

N

0   1,000km
0   500 miles

Bradt

After World War I, the Iraqis were hoping to welcome the new dawn of independence. The sun set on the Ottoman Empire and Turkey became a republic. But there was no independence for Iraq. In April 1920 the League of Nations signed a mandate for Britain and France to oversee the lands of the former Ottoman Empire, with Britain responsible for Iraq.

MODERN TIMES

Iraq (situated in the lands of ancient Mesopotamia) is a rich country with a splendid cultural heritage. It is also blessed with the world's third-largest oil reserves after Saudi Arabia and two large rivers, the Tigris and the Euphrates. But throughout the 20th and 21st centuries, its turbulent political life has prevented it from taking advantage of the gifts of nature and the talents of an educated and creative people; political instability has dominated life. Between 1920 and 1958 senior Iraqi politicians played musical chairs for positions in 24 successive cabinets. The people have been the victims of turmoil, civil strife, bloody coups and counter-coups, and three devastating wars: the Iran-Iraq War (1980–88), the First Gulf War, which followed Iraq's invasion of Kuwait in August 1990, and the Second Gulf War in 2003. Social upheaval and change has characterised modern life in Iraq, which has been greatly influenced by:

- the discovery of oil, which tied the economy to one major source of national income;
- the replacement of subsistence cultivation with commercial agriculture;
- the decline of nomadism and growth of urbanisation;
- the growth of the middle class, government bureaucracy and the armed forces;
- major investment in education, health, housing and other social services;
- a weakening of traditional family and tribal links;
- the consolidation of the power of the Arab Baath Socialist Party;
- a different perception of the role of women, who entered the workforce in large numbers during the 1980–88 Iran-Iraq War;
- life under a stringent economic-sanctions regime imposed from 1990 to 2003.

Iraqi society is a jigsaw puzzle of religious, ethnic, class, family and tribal pieces interlinked through a series of complex relationships. At the beginning of the 20th century there were three main divisions: Bedouin camps; villages; towns and cities.

The Bedouin came from four major tribes: the camel- and sheep-breeding Shammar confederation, the sheep-raising Dulaym, and the Muntafiq and Dharfir tribes of the south, once feared because of their raids on pilgrims' caravans. Other important tribes included the Ubaid (found mainly in Tikrit and the surrounding areas up to Kirkuk and Kurdistan's borders), the Jibour (found beside the Tigris river from the outskirts of Baghdad to Mosul), the Azzah (found mainly near the Himreen Mountains, 120–150km north of Baghdad and in Diyala Province) and the Janabis (found in the northern part of Babylon and in the outskirts of Tikrit). The tribes, whose size varied from a few families to hundreds of thousands, traced their origins to a male ancestor. Families who claimed descent from the Prophet Mohammed (*sayyids*) provided the tribes with religious services. The extended family, made up of three generations, was the basis of tribal organisation. Tribal leaders (*sheikhs*) exercised authority according to their family status and their own abilities. Succession was not always hereditary and tribal leaders could be elected. Decisions tended to be made in the tribal council (*majlis*). Sheikhs

CHRONOLOGY

1918	Religious scholars filled power vacuum created by the departure of the Ottomans and the end of World War I.
1919	The Treaty of Versailles ended World War I.
1920	British mandate established, which led to the modern state of Iraq.
1921	Kingdom of Iraq founded under King Faisal I.
1924	*Fatwa* issued against any Muslims who took part in the elections to the constituent assembly.
1927	Oil discovered.
1932	Kingdom of Iraq formally granted independence and admitted to the League of Nations. Iraq also became the centre of Arab nationalism and active resistance to Zionism.
1933	King Faisal died. Succeeded by his son Ghazi.
1935	Shia lawyers in Baghdad and *mujtahids* presented a manifesto to the government calling for greater participation in parliament, government and civil service, and greater investment in Shia areas.
1936	General Bakr Sidqi, a Kurd, overthrew the government in the Arab world's first military coup.
1937	Sidqi assassinated by army officers. Six coups followed.
1939	King Ghazi died in a car accident. Succeeded by his infant son Faisal II. World War II declared in September.
1940s & 50s	Shias increased their demands to secure government civil service posts.
1941	Government of National Defence headed by the pro-German Rashid Ali Kailani formed. Fighting broke out between British forces and Iraqi army. Kailani escaped to Iran.
1946	Leadership of the Shias shifted from the southern Iraqi city of Najaf to the Iranian city of Qom after the death of Abu al Hassan Ishahani.
1958	'Free Officers' overthrew the monarchy. King Faisal II killed; pro-British politicians eliminated. Brigadier Abdul Karim Qasim became prime minister.
1959	Half a million people demonstrated for communist representation in government.
1963	Prime Minister Qasim was overthrown in a Baathist coup. General Abd al-Salam Aref overthrew first Baathist regime.
1968	Second Baathist coup.
1972	Iraqi Petroleum Company nationalised.
1970s	Thousands of Shias expelled to Iran under the pretext of their Iranian origin.

traditionally settled family disputes, consented to marriages and divorces, and assumed responsibility for the tribe's welfare – and warfare! As the authority of the central government extended into tribal areas, they also became responsible for tax collection. Business advisers were sometimes appointed to liaise between the tribes and the central government, which put a stop to raiding. The nomads were gradually absorbed into sedentary life and turned to farming or employment in industry, including the oil industry. Between 1957 and 1965 the nomadic Bedouin population decreased by 50%. Today it is estimated at 100,000.

THE BRITISH MANDATE As a largely neglected province of the Ottoman Empire, Iraq was catapulted into the 20th century and provided with a modern state structure under British guidance during the 12-year mandate period following World War I (1920–32). Britain had established a presence in Iraq as early as 1798, when its permanent agent took up residence. The East India Company had an office in Baghdad in 1783. Britain's decision to invade Iraq at the start of World War I was prompted by the Ottoman Empire's alliance with Germany, the need to safeguard British oil production in Persia, and fears for the security of India, which in 1914 was the most important part of the British Empire. The Turks did not give up without a fight, and in 1916 the British lost 10,000 men at Kut. However, Baghdad was occupied a year later. Sensing a British victory the Turks started looting the capital. While the citizens hid in their houses, shops and bazaars were ransacked.

In March 1917 British forces, under the command of General Stanley Maude, captured Baghdad. A British mandate on Iraq was conferred at a meeting of the Allied powers in the Italian town of San Remo in 1920. For its new governors, Iraq proved to be a hornets' nest, with numerous unresolved conflicts: urban dwellers wanted protection against the tribes, and the tribal sheikhs expected the government to confirm their titles to land and give them new land. They also fought among themselves. Merchants demanded legal protection from the courts and the people expected welfare services such as health and education. Canals and roads had to be built and upgraded and agriculture developed. But the British treasury was not a very generous benefactor and attempts were made to keep the administrative costs of the mandate to a minimum. Nationalist sentiments, originally directed against the Turks, were soon directed towards the British. In 1920 a four-month rebellion, commonly referred to as the Great Iraqi Revolution, which united Sunnis and Shias, tribesmen and urban dwellers, against a common enemy, resulted in 10,000 casualties, cost the British £40 million, and was only quashed when reinforcements arrived from India.

It became obvious that the Iraqis would no longer tolerate a military regime imposed by the British, or indeed by any foreign nation. The time had come to repay Hussein ibn Ali, the Sharif of Mecca, for his assistance during the Arab Revolt of 1916, when he helped the British in their campaigns against the Turks in Arabia. Hussein's son, Faisal, was enthroned on 23 August 1921 after a carefully contrived referendum in which he was 'chosen' by around 96% of the Iraqi people. The king was kept stronger than any one tribe, but could be challenged by a coalition of tribes. This enabled the British to pursue their divide and rule policy and act as arbitrators in local disputes. In 1924 an elected constituent assembly met for the first time. It was a foreign attempt to introduce democracy in which the ordinary people did not participate. The land-owning elites competed with the families in the cities, Ottoman-trained army officers and bureaucrats. Britain's legacy in Iraq included the establishment of a Basra–Baghdad–Kirkuk–Mosul railway, a new route that linked Baghdad with Damascus and Beirut and eventually Aleppo and Istanbul; an indigenous Iraqi army in which the Sunnis dominated the higher ranks; the installation of a system of law courts and a modern police force; an overhaul of the Turkish land-revenue system; and the introduction of sterling-based Iraqi currency. Economic assistance was offered through European banks and the setting up of small-scale industries, such as brick making, cotton ginning, cigarette making, soap making and tanning was encouraged. Oil exploitation began.

The Iraqis were keen to be rid of British influence, but Britain took a step-by-step approach towards independence through four Anglo-Iraqi treaties: 1922, 1926, 1927 and 1930. Iraq was formally admitted to the League of Nations on 3 October 1932; the mandate was over and a new country had joined the international community.

INDEPENDENCE: THE FIRST 26 YEARS King Faisal died in 1933 and was succeeded by his son Ghazi I, who remained in power until 1939, when he died in a car crash, attributed by Arab conspiracy theorists to Britain's hidden hand. The next king was Ghazi's infant son, Faisal II. Ghazi's first cousin, Amir Abd al Illah, was made regent. With Nuri Said, the most prominent politician during the emergence of post-Ottoman Iraq, he changed the political orientation of the monarchy. He was murdered by a mob in Baghdad when the revolution of July 1958 overthrew the monarchy.

The military entered Iraqi politics in 1933. Disenchanted with their failure to secure a region in which they could set up a nation state, the Assyrians, the largest Christian minority group, living mostly in the north of Iraq, insisted that their patriarch be given some temporal authority. When this was refused some 800 Assyrians headed for the Syrian border. They were denied entry and returned to Iraq, where General Bakr Sidqi, a Kurd, permitted his men to kill about 600 Assyrians in the village of Simeil (see box, page 42). Following this incident, the army became embroiled in a series of coups and counter-coups, which began in 1936 when General Sidqi overthrew the government in the Arab world's first military coup. He allied himself with the reform-oriented Ahali group, but it was an alliance doomed to fail due to Sidqi's ruthless crushing of a tribal revolt (which alienated the Shias), his encouragement of the Kurds to join the army (which alienated the nationalist military elements) and his attack on the liberals and socialists (which outraged the Ahali leaders). Sidqi was murdered in 1937 by an army faction that had turned against him. His death was followed by six successive army coups. The seventh culminated in the setting up of a government of National Defence in 1941, headed by Rashid Ali Kailani, the prominent politician and Iraqi nationalist who had been Prime Minister in 1933, 1940 and finally in 1941. Its pro-German stance was motivated by anti-imperialist and anti-British sentiments. Pro-British politicians fled from Iraq. Meanwhile, Kailani tried to modify the terms of the 1941 Anglo-Iraqi Treaty and placed conditions on Britain's request for troop landings in Iraq. The British response was swift and decisive: 2,250 troops landed at Basra and the country was occupied for a second time. On 30 May 1941 an armistice was signed: Amir Abd al Illah was re-imposed as regent and his right-hand man Nuri Said became a dominant figure in Iraqi politics until the revolution of 1958. Kailani and the pro-German generals fled. They were tried *in absentia* and sentenced to death.

During World War II Iraq became a base for the military occupation of Iran, Syria and Lebanon. In 1945 it was a founding member of the Arab League. In the same year it joined the United Nations. In 1955 Iraq signed the Baghdad Pact, a mutual defence treaty with Turkey that later included the UK, Pakistan and Iran. Grievances with the British-installed monarchy and Nuri Said mounted, largely due to foreign policy rather than domestic issues. Iraq's membership of the Baghdad Pact was not widely supported. In 1948 the Portsmouth Treaty, which called for a board of Iraqis and British representatives to decide on defence matters of mutual interest, led to a major uprising, which resulted in the treaty's repudiation. During one of Nuri Said's stints as Prime Minister in 1954 (in all, he held some 47 cabinet posts during his career), he banned political parties, which he believed were made up largely of opportunists. Newspapers were suspended and a curfew imposed. The period was characterised by rising inflation, poverty among the city dwellers and the salaried middle classes, corruption in government circles and the enrichment of the elite while the Baghdad slums grew. Widespread discontent was contained by repression and a stifling control over the political process.

THE 1958 REVOLUTION AND ITS AFTERMATH The revolution of 14 July 1958, which toppled the monarchy, was one of the greatest watersheds in modern Iraqi politics. The depth of hatred for the British-installed rulers was illustrated by the killing of King Faisal and his supporters. The body of Nuri Said, the main British protagonist, was run over by buses. Faisal Street in Baghdad became Jamal Abdul Nasser Street. A request for assistance from the Iraqi military from King Hussein of Jordan, who feared that an anti-Western revolt in Lebanon could spill over into his kingdom, prompted a battalion led by Abdul Karim Qasim (founder of the Free Officers movement, a group dedicated to Iraq Nationalism, with a central committee of 14 members) and Colonel Abdul al Salam Aref, to move into Baghdad instead of Jordan. The day after the coup, Qasim issued a public statement in which he proclaimed the liberation of the country from the domination of a corrupt group that was installed by imperialism, announced the formation of an Iraqi republic that would preserve Iraqi unity, and called for brotherly ties with other Arab countries.

Unlike the pro-British government, the revolution made dramatic changes to Iraq's social structure: the power of big landed sheikhs and the merchant class was drastically reduced during an extensive land reform programme. The urban centres, Baghdad and Basra especially, grew at a phenomenal rate, with urban dwellers almost tripling between 1958 and 1987. The middle class also grew during the 1950s and 1960s as education became increasingly accessible to the people and prepared them for civil occupations. The numbers of merchants, shopkeepers, craftsmen, and professional and government officials began to increase steadily. Qasim believed passionately in bettering the lot of the poor – the urban slum dwellers and the exploited peasants – but not at the expense of the wealthy. A slum reform programme was instituted in Baghdad, political prisoners were released, trade and peasant unions were recognised, rents went down along with food prices, and spending on health, education and housing increased. The Communist Party, once suppressed by Nuri Said and forced to remain underground during the monarchist era, became an important force in Iraqi politics. Relations with the Soviet Union were re-established and economic co-operation, along with arms sales, began.

In March 1959 army officers from conservative, Sunni backgrounds who objected to Qasim's strong links with the communists attempted to overthrow him. Qasim and his allies mobilised 250,000 supporters in Mosul and a massacre of nationalists and leading Mosul families followed. This was not the only attempt to topple the government. Saddam Hussein, Iraq's future president took part in an assassination attempt in which Qasim was injured. Abd al Salam Aref, the man who had been so instrumental in Qasim's coup, also tried to overthrow Qasim after he was relieved of his post as Deputy Prime Minister following disagreements about his pro-Nasser stance. Despite its attempts at genuine reform, though, Qasim's government was plagued with many problems, both domestic and foreign. For one, the communists were getting too powerful. In Kirkuk one of their rallies resulted in a battle with the Turkmen, and Qasim decided it was time for a crackdown. Iraqi Communist Party (ICP) members were removed from sensitive government positions, union activities were curtailed and communist newspapers were shut down.

The Kurds, who supported the 1958 revolution, soon found themselves at odds with the government, as the new constitution – which clearly stated that they would be equal partners in Iraq's development – was only a paper promise. In 1961

Kurdish *peshmerga* (guerrillas) were involved in extensive fighting with the Iraqi army, who were not as effective as the *peshmerga* in the rugged mountain terrain. Qasim left power just as he had gained it – through a military coup. It took place on 8 February 1963. He was executed the next day. The coup was carried out by the Arab Baath Socialist Party with the assistance of the army. One of its main instigators was Abd al Salam Aref. This time he was successful in toppling Qasim.

BAATH RULE   After seizing power the Baathists set up the Revolutionary Command Council as their highest policy-making body. Ahmad Hassan al Bakr became Prime Minister and Aref President. But the party was not united and did not have any clear policies. It was dominated by cliques from the same village, town or tribe, and relied on the paramilitary National Guard to counter the lack of support in the regular army. The Baathists were sharply divided between the hardliners and the pragmatic, more moderate left wing. They too were unable to quell the Kurdish unrest in the north and they only stayed in power for nine months, before being overthrown by military officers in a bloodless coup in November 1963. Following this coup, Abd al Salam Aref assumed more effective power, dissolved the National Guard and remained President until 1966.

After the death of Abd al Salam Aref in a helicopter crash in 1966, his brother, Major General Abd ar Rahman Aref, took his place. The Kurdish insurgency sapped the government's strength and Aref's freedom of movement was limited by the dominance of the officers who put him in power. The Kurds were pacified by promises of control over the municipal administration in the north and allowing the use of the Kurdish language. But the army, fearing its power would be curtailed, opposed the rapprochement. Colonel Abd ar Razzaq an Nayif and Ibrahim Daud, two disenchanted Aref supporters, staged a successful coup but lacked grass-roots support to hold on to power. They were quickly outmanoeuvred by the well organised Baathists, who again took over the government in 1968. They had learnt from their previous mistakes and this time they were here to stay.

THE RISE AND FALL OF SADDAM HUSSEIN   An estimated three million citizens were killed during the Baath regime's tenure of power from 1968 to 2003, while approximately four to five million Iraqis (around 15% of the population) were living in exile. After seizing power the Baathists were determined to establish their credentials as exponents of Arab nationalism. They adopted an uncompromising position on the Palestinian issue. At the beginning of 1969 a public spectacle was made of the hanging of nine Jews and others for spying. When the Egyptian President Anwar Sadat signed the Camp David Accords with Israel in 1978, Saddam Hussein cherished Egypt's isolation in the Arab world and was eager for Iraq to replace Egypt as a leading regional power. An attempt was made by the Baathists to fully integrate the Kurds into society and the state of emergency imposed since 1958 in Kurdish areas was lifted. In March 1970 a 15-article peace plan was announced. It stated that the Kurds should participate fully in government, Kurdish officials would be appointed in northern Iraq, and Kurdish would be the official language alongside Arabic. These positive measures were accompanied by the forced relocation of Kurds to other areas, the settlement of Arabs in northern Iraq and the destruction of Kurdish villages along the 1,300km border with Iran. This carrot-and-stick approach did not work and the guerrilla war began again. However, the Kurdish resistance collapsed in 1975 when Iran and Iraq signed an agreement to end their border dispute at an OPEC meeting in Algiers, and Iranian assistance to the Kurdish rebels ceased.

SADDAM'S RISE TO POWER During the 1970s Saddam Hussein worked tirelessly to consolidate his power base. Despite Baath Party attempts to institutionalise its rule, real power remained in the hands of a narrowly based elite united by loose family and tribal ties. By 1977 the most powerful men in the Baath Party were all somehow related to the triumvirate of Saddam Hussein, Ahmed Hassan al Bakr, and General Adnan Khayrallah Talfah, Saddam Hussein's brother-in-law. All were members of the party, its ruling Revolutionary Command Council and the cabinet, and all were members of the Talfah family of Tikrit, headed by Khayrallah Talfah. Surnames were abolished to disguise the rule of a single clan: ID cards and birth certificates only recorded the child's first name and the name of the father. But Baathist rule did not go unchallenged. In 1973 the Security Chief, Nazim Kazzar, planned a coup against the military faction of the Baath Party. The attempted coup failed, Kazzar was executed and this led to an amendment of the constitution to give the president more power, and to the formation of a National Front consisting of the Baath Party and the Iraqi Communist Party. Despite their socialist rhetoric, however, the Baathists had many capitalist tendencies. During the mid-1970s the private sector trebled, and by 1980 there were hundreds of multi-millionaires in Iraq, most with connections to the Baath Party.

Some efforts were made to employ the country's oil revenues for the benefit of the people, especially through investment in the education and health sectors. Legislation was passed giving women equal pay. The number of students in technical fields increased by 300% between 1976 and 1986 to more than 120,090. In the mid-1980s Iraq also made substantial progress in controlling malaria, trachoma, influenza, measles, whooping cough and tuberculosis. But much of the country's revenue went into the pockets of the ruling elite.

The capitalist tendency did not mean a pro-Western foreign policy, and relations with the West, especially America, remained poor. A number of foreigners were expelled for spying. Relations with the Soviet Union were warm, and the Soviets kept the Iraqis supplied with weapons. On 16 July 1979 Saddam Hussein finally realised his ambition. President Bakr was ousted and he became President of the Republic, Secretary General of the Baath Party Regional Command, Chairman of the Revolutionary Command Council and Commander-in-Chief of the armed forces. Iraq was now Saddam's Iraq, a country ruled with an iron fist and an 'octopus-like' security apparatus that extended its tentacles into every sphere of life.

THE IRAN-IRAQ WAR Saddam was not content to stamp his imprint on one country: conquest was on his mind and in 1980 oil revenues of US$21.3 billion made him confident he could easily bankroll his political adventures. In the same year, he started the Iran-Iraq War. He was secretly encouraged by leading American, British, French and Russian politicians and industrialists, who not only saw the political advantages but also the financial benefits in keeping Iran, with its spreading religious influence, to its own side of the Gulf. Iraq invaded Iran on 22 September 1980. Prior to the invasion two leading Iraqi Shia personalities, Ayatollah Baqr al Sadr and his sister Bint al Huda, were hanged and 97 members of the leading Islamic Dawa Party were executed.

The eight-year war (1980–88) can be divided into several stages: the Iraqi invasion, Iraqi retreats, the war of attrition, the tanker war and the war of the cities. When a truce finally came into effect on 20 August 1988 neither country had lost much territory and both countries were still being ruled by the same leaders. Iran consolidated its Islamic revolution and Iraq was now the most

CHRONOLOGY

1979	Saddam Hussein became President. Some 500 top-ranking Baathists were executed.
1980	Execution of renowned Shia scholar Muhammad Baqir al Sadr and his sister Bint al Huda.
1980–88	Iran-Iraq War.
1990	Iraq invaded Kuwait and sanctions imposed on Iraq.
1991	Gulf War started. Popular uprising in 14 out of 18 Iraqi governorates brutally crushed by the army.
1992	No-fly zone declared south of the 32nd parallel and north of the 36th parallel.
1995	Oil-for-food programme allowed Iraq to sell up to US$2 billion worth of oil in a 180-day period and use the revenue to buy food, medicine and other basic necessities, but Saddam never fully implemented this for the Iraqi people.
1997	Iraq's demand for a timetable for the end of sanctions was denied.
1998	Iraq ended co-operation with UN Special Commission to oversee the destruction of weapons of mass destruction. Bombing campaign 'Operation Desert Fox' to destroy Iraq's nuclear, chemical and biological weapons programmes launched by US and UK.
	Assassination of Ayatollah Ali al Gharavi.
1999	Assassination of Mohammed Sadiq Sadr. UN Monitoring, Verification and Inspection Commission (UNMOVIC) set up to Replace Unscom.
2000	Hans von Sponeck, the UN Senior Representative in Baghdad responsible for co-ordinating humanitarian aid, resigned because he believed the sanctions were unfairly harming the civilian population.
2001	Britain and USA carried out bombing raids to disable Iraq's air defence network. Saddam Hussein celebrated his 64th birthday. Iraqi exiles estimated the celebrations cost US$8 million.
2002	UN weapons inspectors returned to Iraq backed by a UN resolution which threatened serious consequences if Iraq was in material breach of its terms.
2003	Chief weapons inspector Hans Blix reported Iraq accelerated its co-operation but said inspectors needed more time to verify Iraq's compliance. UK's ambassador to the UN said the diplomatic process on Iraq has ended. US-led invasion toppled Saddam Hussein.
	Thousands of Shia pilgrims celebrated Ashura in Kerbala, the performance of rituals previously banned by Saddam's regime.

powerful state in the region. The cost in terms of human life and resources was phenomenal: 194,931 Iranians and an estimated 160,000–240,000 Iraqis lost their lives. The war cost Iran US$74–91 billion and military imports amounted to US$11.26 billion. Iraq spent US$94–112 billion on the war. Military imports totalled US$102 billion.

THE INVASION OF KUWAIT At the end of the Iran-Iraq War Saddam pretended to launch an Iraqi *perestroika* with promises of a new constitution, a multi-party political system and a free press. But just two years after the war with Iran the Iraqi people were once again dragged into another conflict. At the end of July 1990 Iraq and Kuwait held talks that failed: the Iraqis accused the Kuwaitis of not wanting to rectify the harm they had done to Iraq by depressing oil prices in mid-July, which they had achieved by increasing their daily oil production at the behest of the West's industrial nations. On 2 August 1990 Iraq invaded Kuwait. The response of the international community was swift: on 6 August sanctions were imposed and by 29 November the UN Security Council had adopted Resolution 678, authorising 'all necessary means', including the use of force, to restore international peace and security in the area. A number of diplomatic initiatives to resolve the crisis peacefully failed. On 14 January 1991 the Iraqi parliament decided to go to war rather than withdraw, and two days later the air campaign began. By late February the US-led coalition composed of 28 UN member states had flown a total of 91,000 air missions over Iraq and Kuwait. On 3 March Iraq accepted ceasefire terms outlined during a meeting of its military commanders and the commander of the multinational force, General Norman Schwarzkopf of the US army. A popular uprising, concentrated largely in the north and south of the country, followed the Gulf War.

Despite the rhetoric of Western leaders, who advocated the overthrow of the Iraqi regime and the establishment of a democratic state, the multinational force did not intervene to support the southern Iraqi people in their attempt to overthrow the regime. At the beginning of the war the UN consensus, which included Arab nations, did not extend to the break-up of Iraq as an independent state, once victory was achieved. So Saddam survived once again. More than two million Kurdish people fled to the mountains after the uprising failed. They were dying at the rate of 450 to 750 a day because of diarrhoea, acute respiratory infections and trauma. This catastrophe prompted the setting up of a 'safe-haven' for the Kurds in northern Iraq. In October 1991, the Iraqi government withdrew all services from Iraqi Kurdistan, and the Iraqi Kurdistan Front (IKF) later held elections for a 105-member Kurdish National Assembly: a de facto Kurdish state had been established and it is now run by the Kurdistan Regional Government. But no similar assistance was offered to the people of the south who were brutally suppressed.

Throughout the Iran-Iraq War the Baathist regime adopted a policy of guns and butter to ensure the civilians did not suffer undue hardships. But the civilians were the main victims of the 1991 Gulf War. This time there were no generous allowances for the parents and relatives of war heroes. The country had been bombed out of the 20th century. Estimates of the numbers of Iraqi soldiers killed in the conflict vary between 30,000 and 100,000. Between 3,000 and 5,000 civilians died in the Allied bombing raids and 105,000 Iraqis died during the subsequent uprising, and from diseases that spread rapidly due to damage to the country's infrastructure. US aircraft alone dropped 88,000 tons of explosives on Iraq, the equivalent of nearly five Hiroshima nuclear blasts. Some 70% of the so-called smart bombs missed their intended targets, falling sometimes on civilian dwellings, schools, churches, mosques or empty fields. But the 30% that blasted on target wiped out Iraq's electricity generating plants and sewage treatment networks. Iraq's infrastructure – its bridges, roads, highways, canals and communication centres – was systematically destroyed.

LIFE UNDER SANCTIONS Between August 1990 and February 2003 the Iraqi people lived under one of the most stringent sanctions regimes in history. Writing in *The Guardian* in September 1999, James Buchan said:

'Humiliated in war by the West, terrorised by their own government, reduced to paupers, unwelcome anywhere in the world, the Arabs of Iraq are falling to pieces. It is not simply that with their money and savings destroyed and their goods embargoed, their living standards have fallen to the level of at least 30 years ago. In their own eyes, as Iraqis and above all as Arabs, they have been reduced to nothing. I have never seen a people so demoralised. Everybody I met, even the most repellent Baathist thug and extortionist, felt himself a victim.'

Corruption was rampant, the crime rate soared and the statistics documenting the fall in living standards and the rise in diseases and infant mortality made horrifying reading. The UN reported a shortage of medicines, vaccines and hospital equipment due to the effects of the embargo that would not have been tolerated anywhere else. However, Saddam's regime held on and would not concede any political ground internationally or domestically. Eventually this oil-rich regime had enough wriggle-room to alleviate the worst effects of the embargo. Instead the regime ignored the plight of its people, and carried on importing and developing weapons, selling smuggled oil and seeking alliances with other Arab nations. The brutality of the regime towards its own people still continued. The Iraqi opposition outside of the country estimated that the regime had killed more than three million citizens since it came to power. The imposition of these sanctions also proved to the world that in the long term sanctions do not work, except to harm the people they were supposed to protect. Slowly but surely Iraq broke out of the stranglehold of sanctions, aided by self-interested Western industrialists and so-called neutral countries. The lure of cheap, 'black gold' (oil) was overwhelming. Saddam Hussein pursued his political ambitions relentlessly and began to rebuild his military base with new weapons, increase his own wealth and loomed threateningly over the Middle East.

Only another war would topple Saddam, and the Americans and British decided to oust him by force in March 2003.

Three official reasons were given for going to war against Iraq in March 2003: to eliminate Saddam's weapons of mass destruction (WMD); to diminish the threat of international terrorism; and to promote democracy in Iraq and surrounding areas. America's negotiations at the United Nations, the drafting of resolutions and consultations with allies were nothing more than a search for justifications after the decision to attack Iraq had been taken. According to Lieutenant General Michael Moseley, Commander, 9th Air Force and US Central Command Air Forces (November 2001–August 2003), Operation Southern Forces was launched before Bush took his case to the United Nations. It involved dropping 606 precision-guided bombs on 391 targets in an effort to destroy Iraq's air defences, paving the way to use Special Forces early in the war.

THE 2003 WAR The war started with an unsuccessful strike targeting Saddam Hussein. Only 90 minutes after the American deadline for Saddam to leave, 2,000lb GPS-guided bombs struck residential quarters in Baghdad where the Pentagon believed the Iraqi leadership was meeting. If Saddam had been killed the war could have ended the day it began. Limited air strikes on Baghdad began on 20 March. US and British ground troops entered from the south and 1,000 cruise missiles were fired at targets throughout the country. An entire Iraqi division deserted, leaving the route clear for British forces to capture Iraq's second largest city, Basra. Arab volunteers, mainly Syrians and Algerians, as well as Iraqis resident in Jordan, started arriving in Iraq to fight against the Coalition. The war to topple Saddam and his regime was over when Baghdad fell on 9 April 2003.

CHRONOLOGY

2003

April	US forces captured Baghdad.
July	US appointed 25-member Governing Council of Iraqis from diverse religious and political backgrounds took office. Insurgency intensified.
December	Saddam Hussein captured at Ad-Daw near Tikrit.

2004

March	Interim constitution signed. Explosions in Kerbala and Kazimiya kill pilgrims celebrating Ashura. Moqtada Sadr's Shia militia end occupation of Najaf following mediation by Ayatollah Sistani.
April	American military occupation of Fallujah began after the murder and mutilation of four American contractors. Over 600 Iraqis died in subsequent fighting.
June	America handed power to an interim Iraqi government. The trial of Saddam Hussein commenced.
November	The Iraqi interim government declared a state of emergency for 60 days because of escalating violence.

2005

January	Increasing attacks by insurgents estimated to number 200,000 throughout the country, in an attempt to disrupt the elections. Iraq held first multi-party elections for 50 years.
August	Kurds and Shias, but not Sunnis, endorsed a draft constitution.

2006

January	The Shia United Iraqi Alliance won the elections but did not gain an absolute majority.
February	A bomb attack on the Shia shrine in Samarra unleashed a wave of sectarian violence.
December	Saddam Hussein hanged.

2007

January	President Bush announced the surge during which thousands more US troops were dispatched, mainly to Baghdad and the Sunni Triangle.
April	Province of Maysan handed over to Iraqi control.
November	Nearly 6,000 Sunnis entered into a security pact with American forces to fight al-Qaida.
December	The British officially transferred control of Basra to the Iraqis.

2008

March	Prime Minister al Maliki ordered a crackdown on militia in Basra, sparking pitched battles with Moqtada Sadr's Mehdi army. Hundreds killed.

2009

April	Britain officially ends combat operations in southern Iraq. They hand control of their Basra base over to US forces.

| June | US troops withdraw from towns and cities in Iraq. |

2010

March	Parliamentary elections.
October	Church in Baghdad seized by militants. 52 people killed in the worst single disaster to hit Iraq's Christians.
Nov/Dec	Parliament reconvened after long delay, re-appointed Jalal Talabani as president and Nuri al Maliki as prime minister.

2011

January	Radical Shia cleric Moqtada Sadr returns after four years of self-imposed exile in Iran. Al Sadr says his fighters will suspend military attacks on the US, which will resume only if the US fails to pull out.
February	Oil exports from Iraqi Kurdistan resumed, amid a lengthy dispute between the region and the central government over contracts with foreign firms.
August	Violence escalated, with more than 40 apparently co-ordinated nationwide attacks in one day.
December	US completed troop pull-out. Unity government faced disarray.

2012

	Bomb and gun attacks targeted Shia areas throughout the year, sparking fears of a new sectarian conflict.
April	Oil exports from Iraqi Kurdistan halted amid row with central government over contracts with foreign firms.
December	President Talabani suffered a stroke and was taken to Germany for treatment.
	Arab spring started in Iraq with thousands of Sunni protestors demonstrating and calling for the resignation of Prime Minister al Maliki.

2013

January	Sunni protests against al Maliki's government continued.
April	Insurgency intensifies, with levels of violence matching those of 2008
July	At least 500 prisoners, mainly senior al-Qaida members, escape from Taji and Abu Ghraib prisons in a mass break out.
September	Regional parliamentary elections in Kurdistan, won comfortably by the Kurdistan Democratic Party (KDP).
	Series of bombings hit Erbil, in the first such attack since 2007. Al-Qaida-affiliated Islamic State of Iraq claimed responsibility.
October	Parliamentary elections set for April 2014.
December	At least 35 people killed in twin-bombing of Baghdad churches on Christmas Day.

2014

| January | Pro-al-Qaida fighters infiltrate Fallujah and Ramadi after months of mounting violence in the mainly Sunni Anbar Province. Government forces recapture Ramadi, but face entrenched rebels in Fallujah. |

History   MODERN TIMES

2

April	Iraqis vote in the first parliamentary elections since the 2011 withdrawal of US troops.
	Prime Minister al Maliki's coalition wins a plurality at first parliamentary election since the 2011 withdrawal of US troops, but falls short of a majority.
June–September	Sunni rebels led by the Islamic State of Iraq and the Levant (ISIS) surge out of Anbar Province to seize Iraq's second city of Mosul and other key towns. Tens of thousands flee amid atrocities. Kurdish forces, US and Iran assist government in repelling attacks. Caliphate declared.
July	Kurdish region President Massoud Barzani announces plans for an independence referendum, given that Iraq is 'effectively partitioned'.
September	Shia politician Haider al Abad forms a broad-based government including Sunni Arabs and Kurds. Kurdish leadership agrees to put independence referendum on hold. US announces new forward strategy against Islamic State and carries out air raids in support of Iraqi army near Baghdad. International conference in Paris, including ten Sunni Arab states, but excluding Iran and Syria, agrees to support strategy.
December	The Iraqi government and the leadership of the Kurdish region sign a deal on sharing Iraq's oil wealth and military resources, amid hopes that the agreement will help to reunite the country in the face of the common threat represented by Islamic State.

2015

January	The US-led coalition against Islamic State is reported to have launched more than 900 air strikes against militant targets in Iraq since the campaign began.
April	Recapture of Tikrit by Iraqi Government forces.

OCCUPATION AND FIRST EXPERIMENTS WITH DEMOCRACY

The Office of Reconstruction and Humanitarian Assistance (ORHA), was charged with rebuilding the state. ORHA was replaced by the Coalition Provisional Authority (CPA). Ambassador L Paul Bremer III headed the CPA – the temporary governing body designated by the United Nations as the lawful government of Iraq until the country was politically and socially stable enough to assume its sovereignty. Bremer started by abolishing the Baath Party and the army – the basis of the Iraqi state. On 15 May 2003 CPA Order No 1 banned anyone serving in the four top levels in the Baath Party from serving in the post-Saddam administration. One hundred thousand people lost their jobs. Order No 2, which followed on 23 May, disbanded the army and 350,000 soldiers were left unemployed. Many joined the insurgency. In hindsight these were two very fundamental errors which showed the inexperience of those in power in the White House. The CPA started working with returning exiles from the opposition. Its approach was top-down, and failed to involve the locals in the political process. Iraq was governed by the CPA in conjunction with the Iraqi Governing Council (IGC) until the transfer of power to an Iraqi interim government on 28 June 2004.

The Americans tended to see Iraqi politics as a numbers game, which would reflect the composition of society: 13 of the 25 council members were Shia, five Kurdish, five Sunni Arabs, one Turkmen and one Assyrian Christian. Three were women and nine were returnees from exile. Like the CPA, the IGC was headquartered in the International (Green) Zone in Baghdad, which bore as much resemblance to the rest of Iraq as a safari park to a real jungle. The area outside the International Zone (called the Red Zone) was seen as hostile territory, and an unbridgeable gap was created between the rulers and ruled. The IGC's most notable achievement was the signing of a provisional constitution, also known as the Transitional Administrative Law, on 8 March 2004, which set out the framework for how Iraq would be governed after the US-led Coalition ended the occupation and before a new government was chosen.

The American military occupation of Iraq officially ended on 28 June 2004. UN Security Council Resolution 1546 endorsed the Iraqi Interim Government (IIG). But just as the downfall of Saddam was not the instant panacea that many hoped would cure the country's problems, the formal end of the occupation did not lead to a reduction of violence. 'The United States does not control the country and handing over sovereignty is like rearranging the Titanic's deckchairs,' commented Toby Dodge, author of *Inventing Iraq: The Failure of Nation Building and a History Denied*. Attacks on American forces and deaths due to sectarian strife continued to mount. Iraq's first multi-party elections in 50 years were held on 30 January 2005. The pre-election campaign was a low-key affair and many candidates kept their identity secret until the big day. Men with *keffiyah* masks handed out leaflets with horrific death threats. The United Iraqi Alliance (a Shia alliance backed by the clergy) received 48% of the votes, the Kurdistan Alliance 26%, and the Iraqi List (headed by the interim prime minister Ayad Allawi) 14%. Others (the Communist Party, the National Rafidain List (Christians), the Iraqi Islamic Party (Sunnis), The Assembly of Independent Democrats (headed by Sunni elder statesman Adnan Pachachi)) amassed 12% of the vote between them. Commenting on the elections and the political process, Gareth Stansfield, author of *Iraq: People, History, Politics* said that:

'Political life in Iraq moved from being ideologically based under Saddam to being interest and communally based following his removal. Those who voted did so as Shiis or Kurds. Those who did not vote did so as Sunnis … Iraqi society is reverting to the communal and is mobilising according to local identities of ethnicity, sect and tribe'.

As the political process continued without them, and the Shias named Ibrahim Al Jaafari Prime Minister, the Sunnis started to regret their boycott. Sunni tribal chiefs issued a list of demands, including participation in the government and drafting the new constitution. Deadlines for finalising the constitution came and went and in the end the Shias and Kurds passed the draft in the national assembly and the referendum on the constitution followed. The constitution was overwhelmingly rejected by Sunni Arabs and Turkmen, while most of the Kurds and Shias accepted it. The results of the December elections held on 15 December 2005 were much the same as those held in January, with the major two parties The United Iraqi Alliance and the Kurdish List receiving 128 seats and 53 seats respectively. However, the Sunnis and Moqtada al Sadr were now part of the government for the first time.

The third largest share was taken by the Iraqi Accord Front of Sunni Arab parties, set up in October 2005, with 44 seats. The formation of a government was problematic. The Prime Minister, Ibrahim al Jaafari, upset the Kurds by visiting

Ankara without the Kurdish Foreign Minister, Hoshyar Zebari. The Sunnis were determined to see another prime minister, as attacks by Shia gangs, associated with the Interior Ministry, increased. The political standoff was finally resolved on 22 April 2006 when the deputy leader of the Dawa Party, Nuri al Maliki, was appointed Prime Minister.

IRAQ UNDER MALIKI

Al Maliki's government suffered from the same problems as those of his predecessor: ministries were used as power bases from which patronage was exercised and paramilitary units were established in the name of security. The problems of endemic corruption, insecurity, reconstruction, insurgency, unemployment and collapsing public services were not successfully tackled. After the destruction of the Al-Askari Shia Mosque in Samarra in February 2006 (see page 190), the insurgency gathered momentum. The violent displacement of Sunnis from Shia areas and vice versa intensified in Baghdad and the insurgency continued throughout the country. The Americans, in co-operation with tribes in the Sunni Triangle, began the battle against al-Qaida, as the beleaguered central government's efforts were ineffectual. This culminated in some 100,000 Iraqis taking part in US-financed Awakening Forces. When the Moqtada al Sadr group withdrew from the governing Shia alliance in September 2007 and the main Sunni alliance withdrew from the cabinet, the survival of al Maliki's government looked doubtful. He clung to power because of American support and his opponents' inability to agree on a replacement.

Since coming to office in 2006 al Maliki consolidated the security forces. He cracked down on Shia militias in Basra in 2008 and in Baghdad's Sadr City and exerted strong control over the police and the army. He also influenced the judicial system. International human rights groups accused al Maliki of running secret jails, of widespread abuse in Iraq's detention centres and of the jailing of political opponents. After the inconclusive elections of March 2010, following which the Iraqi parliament struggled to pass any significant legislation and failed to provide a full range of basic services such as regular electricity, clean water and adequate health care, the Americans backed al Maliki. The bloc of former Prime Minister Ayad Alawi won 91 seats while al Maliki's Shia coalition won 89. Neither side was able to form a coalition until the October when al Maliki made a deal with Moqtada al Sadr's Shia which gave him a majority in the 325-member parliament. A power-sharing agreement was reached with Alawi the following month, but as it unravelled Washington focused on building a security relationship with al Malaki's government. Unemployment among young men rose to around 30% and alienation of the Sunnis grew. After nine years of occupation, Americans forces completed their withdrawal on 18 December 2011.

The most damaging legacy of al Maliki's time in office was the alienation of the Sunnis (see page 11). Despite, or perhaps because of, the ferocious onslaught by ISIS, al Maliki won the largest number of seats in the elections held at the end of April 2014 but agreed to resign after even his own party members ceased to support him. As this book went to press the prime minister, Haydar al Abbadi, formed a coalition government. This new government has to deal with the onslaught by ISIS. Abbadi has to defeat a fearsome militant foe with a rattled army and vast areas of the country outside his control.

THE ISIS ONSLAUGHT Originally ISIS was an offshoot of al-Qaida in Iraq; however, al-Qaida has distanced itself from this radical, extremist group, which is led by Abu

Bakr al Baghdadi. ISIS is thought to have between 7,000 and 12,000 fighters, 3,000 of whom are foreigners.

After achieving some military successes in Syria in 2013, the group began its expansion into the Sunni areas of north and west Iraq in 2014. In January it took control of Fallujah and then advanced into other Sunni towns including parts of Ramadi and Tikrit. In June it sent shock waves across the world when it captured Mosul. Brutality which even al-Qaida shies away from is the hallmark of ISIS. Its violence has driven thousands of Iraqis from their homes. Whole communities of Yezidis and Christians as well as Shias, who ISIS considers unbelievers, have fled to refugee camps in areas controlled by the Kurdistan Regional Government. The US intervened to save a large group of Yezidis, who were trapped on Mount Sinjar (see page 237).

Iraqi and Kurdish troops have been trying to dislodge the insurgents and since August 2014 the US has carried out hundreds of air strikes to support them. The situation on the ground is fluid; armed groups who once fought the American military have benefited from the US airstrikes in the recapture of towns such as Amerli. Iranian forces are also assisting in the battle against ISIS. But it could be a long struggle, and may only succeed if there is a popular uprising against ISIS as the Iraqi army needs the support of the local people and some of the thousands of police officers who melted away when Mosul was captured. However, after being left out in the cold following the successful campaign they waged against al-Qaida in 2006 and 2007, Sunni tribesmen may be reluctant to assist the Iraqi army and Kurdish *pershmerga* in their fight against ISIS.

Captured oil fields are providing ISIS with millions of dollars in revenue. It is alleged that they are generating income by looting banks, selling antiquities

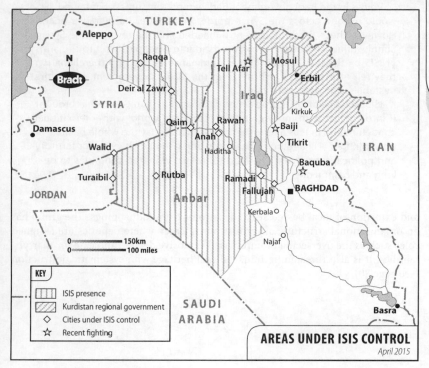

AREAS UNDER ISIS CONTROL
April 2015

The sudden and bloody emergence of the Islamic State of Iraq and al-Sham (ISIS), also known as ISIL (the Islamic State of Iraq and the Levant) and throughout the Arabic world by the acronym Daesh has caused shock waves across the Middle East and in Iraq in particular. The group was founded in 1999 by Abu Musab al Zarqawi under the name Jamat al-Tawhid wa al-Jihad (the Organisation of Monotheism and Jihad). It morphed into ISIS following its expansion in the Syrian conflict in April 2013. A mix of Salafism, Takfirism and Baathism, ISIS ideology rejects any innovation occurring after the time of Mohammed and considers anything other than a literal reading of the Koran and Hadiths as heresy. Its leadership includes disenfranchised Baathist commanders from the Saddam era who are considered responsible for its military planning and successes. Its aim is an Islamic caliphate or state under a single leader with the eradication of anything and anyone who disagrees with its interpretation of Islam.

ISIS cleverly orchestrated acts of violence culminating in the capture of Iraq's northern city of Mosul in June 2014, after just three days of fighting during which the overwhelmingly numerically superior Iraqi army offered little resistance and just melted away. Within a few short weeks it progressed through north and west Iraq until Baghdadis awoke to the shock realisation that ISIS was within an hour's drive of the capital. ISIS's encroachment into Iraq was well planned. Taking easy targets and avoiding well-defended ones it moved, to quote its leader the late Abu Bakr al Baghdadi, 'like serpents through rocks'.

Voices in the Iraqi government had warned that, unless contained, ISIS would expand across the Syrian border and shatter Iraq's fragile peace. However, these Cassandras went unheeded and the revolt of the Syrian Sunnis influenced their co-religionists in Iraq who, pushed into the arms of ISIS by the loss of their former dominance in Iraq and the alienation they felt at the lack of reforms from the Maliki Government, led to the destabilisation of Shia-led Iraq.

ISIS's expansion of its proclaimed caliphate, or Islamic State, has brought it into conflict with many countries across the world, with international condemnation of it as a terrorist organisation. Today the whole balance of power in Iraq is changing, with Sunnis, Shias and Kurds vying for territory and political supremacy. The road to normality in Iraq continues to be a long and painful one.

and extortion of local businesses and ransoms from kidnappings. The group has an organisational structure; a terrorist bureaucracy where deputies are assigned roles such as the overseeing of improvised explosive devices and care for martyrs' families. It is also threatening Iraq's cultural heritage with systematic destruction (see page 80).

3

Archaeology

INTRODUCTION

Iraq's magnificent, ancient archaeological sites have acted as a magnet for visitors to the country throughout the centuries. It is a land where clay tablets, cylinder seals, painted murals, ziggurats and ruins of temples and palaces shed light on life in ancient times. The deciphering of cuneiform script in the 19th century advanced greatly the study of these ancient sites and was paralleled with a better understanding of biblical, Old Testament texts which had motivated many archaeologists and explorers. As fresh sites were discovered, more and more cuneiform tablets were uncovered leading to yet more knowledge. In this guidebook we describe many sites in later chapters, so this chapter on archaeology discusses the subject in general terms.

It is the romance of these ancient places that has inspired travellers, archaeologists and historians for so many years. To visit that most ancient site, Tell Ubaid, most probably sited on the ancient line of the now-receded Gulf, and to see on the ground small sherds of Tell Ubaid pottery with its distinctive greenish colour and painted black stripes is to be transported back over 6,000 years to the beginnings of the long journey to our present cities and way of life. This isolated, windy, desolate place needs to be seen by all.

IRAQ'S MAJOR ARCHAEOLOGICAL SITES

Agargouf – 33km west from Baghdad (see pages 157–61)
Ashur – 112km south of Mosul (see pages 244–7)
Babylon – 90km south of Baghdad (see pages 266–72)
Borsippa – 15km south of Baghdad (see pages 276–7)
Ctesiphon – 30km south of Baghdad (see pages 163–6)
Erbil – halfway between Mosul and Kirkuk (see pages 379–90)
Eridu – 315km southeast of Baghdad (see pages 308–9)
Hatra – 100km southwest of Mosul (see pages 241–3)
Khorsabad – 20km northeast of Mosul (see pages 232–5)
Kish – 85km south of Baghdad (see pages 272–6)
Lagash – midway between the Tigris and Euphrates (see pages 344–6)
Larsa – 30km east of Samara, near Uruk (see pages 304–6)
Nimrud – 37km southeast of Mosul (see pages 239–41)
Nineveh – 400km north of Baghdad (see pages 220–4)
Nippur – 150km south of Baghdad (see pages 296–8)
Tell Harmal – in a suburb southeast of Baghdad called Baghdad Jadida (see pages 156–7)
Ukhaider – 145km southwest of Kerbala (see pages 262–5)
Ur – 15km south of Nasiriyah (see pages 309–14)
Uruk – 20km east of Samawah (see pages 302–4)

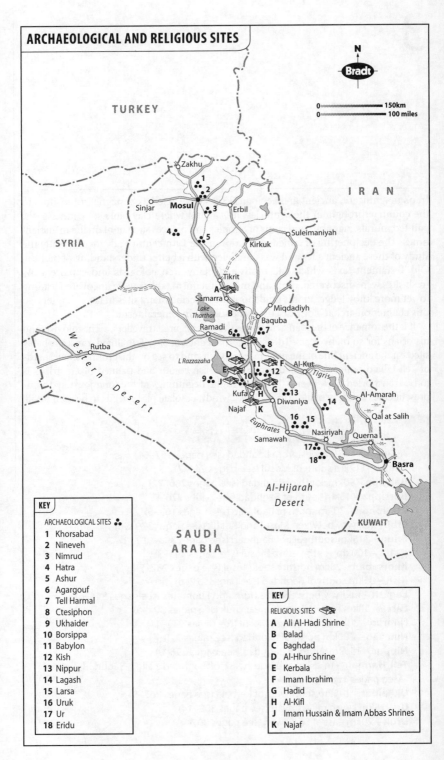

ARCHAEOLOGICAL AND RELIGIOUS SITES

N

Bradt

0 ———— 150km
0 ———— 100 miles

TURKEY

Zakhu

1
2

Sinjar   Mosul   3   Erbil

IRAN

4   5   Kirkuk   Suleimaniyah

SYRIA

Tikrit

A

Samarra

Lake Tharthar

B   Miqdadiyh

Ramadi   Baquba

6   7

Rutba   C   8

Western Desert

L Razzazaha   D   Al-Kut

E   11   F

9   J   10   12   Tigris

Kufa   H   G   13

Najaf   K   Diwaniya   14   Al-Amarah

Euphrates   16   15   Qal at Salih

Samawah   Nasiriyah   Querna

17   Basra

18

Al-Hijarah Desert   KUWAIT

SAUDI ARABIA

KEY

ARCHAEOLOGICAL SITES
1 Khorsabad
2 Nineveh
3 Nimrud
4 Hatra
5 Ashur
6 Agargouf
7 Tell Harmal
8 Ctesiphon
9 Ukhaider
10 Borsippa
11 Babylon
12 Kish
13 Nippur
14 Lagash
15 Larsa
16 Uruk
17 Ur
18 Eridu

KEY

RELIGIOUS SITES
A Ali Al-Hadi Shrine
B Balad
C Baghdad
D Al-Hhur Shrine
E Kerbala
F Imam Ibrahim
G Hadid
H Al-Kifl
J Imam Hussain & Imam Abbas Shrines
K Najaf

Fast forward to 800–600BC, and quoting from Austen Henry Layard's 1851 abridged book *Nimroud and its Ruins.*

'In the middle of April I left Mosul for Baghdad. As I descended the Tigris on a raft, I again saw the ruins of Nimroud, and had a better opportunity of examining them. It was evening as we approached the spot. The spring rains had clothed the mound with the richest verdure, and the fertile meadows which stretched around it, were covered with flowers of every hue. Amidst this luxuriant vegetation were partly concealed a few fragments of bricks, pottery and alabaster, upon which might be traced the well-defined wedges of cuneiform characters ... my curiosity, had been greatly excited, and from that time I formed the design of thoroughly examining whenever it might be within my power, these singular remains.'

Today, how many of us would love to travel down that part of the Tigris by raft and view an unexcavated mound of such proportions as we flow past?

The site of Nimrud can still inspire such romance and now the palaces and temples are revealed with the Temple of Ishtar at the foot of the great ziggurat which stands proudly over the ruins. You can imagine Agatha Christie washing excavated pots and sherds in the dig house which still stands there, while her husband, Sir Max Mallowan directed excavations. In the spring the flowers still persist making this just as Layard describes.

Authors' Note: I have my own special memory of Nimrud, despite my many visits. I recall visiting the site with my tour group and being met by Sayid Muzahim, the resident archaeologist and discoverer of the famous golden Nimrud treasure. He climbed out of a trench at the Ishtar Gate and, somewhat excitedly, showed me the two remarkably small (for Assyria) carved bulls guarding the Gate. I was not allowed to take photos, but Muzahim asked me to convey his photos and drawings to 'Dr John at the BM. Now, some years later, the two bulls are a centrepiece of the Nimrud display in the new galleries in the Iraq National Museum for all to see (see pages 142–3).

As Seton Lloyd says in his book *Twin Rivers* (1943):

'It is certain that until the beginning of the 1914 First World War, almost nothing at all was known of the history of Mesopotamia before the Babylonian kings ... by 1931, all this had changed. A conference of archaeology at Lieden in Holland were able to arrange in order and standardise the names of three main cultural periods in Iraq which preceded the beginnings of Sumerian dynasties referred to in the inscriptions. These were to be called after the names of the sites where traces of them were first discovered. The earliest Al-Ubaid, the second Uruk and the third Jemet Nasr.'

Discoveries of earliest man in the Shanidar Cave in the Kurdish mountains date from 60,000 to 100,000 years. Later sites, such as Jarmo, one of the earliest villages, date from 8000 to 6000BC. Science is continually expanding our knowledge of the early people, their environment and culture.

THE HISTORY OF ARCHAEOLOGY IN IRAQ

EARLY ARCHAEOLOGY The Western world first became interested in the antiquities of the east in the 16th century. One of the earliest visitors was a Dutch plant-collector, Dr Leonhardt Rauwolff, who combined his botanical work with a visit to the Tower of Babel in 1574. The Portuguese traveller Pedro Teixeira set sail for Basra in 1604, and visited Kerbala and Baghdad before travelling north to Aleppo in present-day Syria. The Italian Pietro della Valle wrote about his journeys in *Travels*

Pre-Ubaid 6000BC
Samarra 5500BC
Ubaid 5000–3800BC

Transit to city settlement and development of religious temple practices.

Uruk period 3800–3100BC
3500–3100BC

Late Uruk period: urbanisation and earliest writing at Uruk.

Jemdet Nasr period 3100–2900BC

Beginnings of development of writing and seals.

Early Dynastic period (Early Bronze Age) 2900–2000BC

2700–2600BC	Tell Asmar statues
2600–2100BC	Royal Tombs at Ur
2334–2193BC	Akkadian Empire
c2100BC	Second dynasty in Lagash and Gudea
2112–2004BC	Third dynasty in Ur
2112–2095BC	Construction of first ziggurat at Ur-Nammu.

Middle Bronze Age 2000–1600BC

Old Babylonian period

Late Bronze Age 1600–1200BC
1630–1170BC
1595BC

Kassite Dynasty
Sack of Babylon by the Hittites.

Iron Age 1200–550BC

Early Iron Age

1200–1175BC	Abandonment of major urban centres such as Hattusha and Ugarit.
934–611BC	Neo-Assyrian Empire
717–705BC	Foundation of Khorsabad
612BC	Sack of Nineveh by Medes and Babylonians, collapse of the Assyrian Empire.
626–539BC	Neo-Babylonian Kingdom
604–562BC	Nebuchadnezzar II building at Babylon.

Historical period 550BC **onwards**

550–330BC	Achaemenid Empire
334BC	Alexander the Great starts his conquest of Persia
331BC	Seleucid Empire
139BC	Parthian Empire.

into East India and Desert Arabia and described the cuneiform inscriptions he saw on bricks and black marble. In 1625 he brought back bricks from Ur to Europe. In 1761 the King of Denmark commissioned the first scientific mission to the area.

THE 19TH CENTURY In the early 19th century travellers crossed Iraq on the overland route from India to England and visited the ruins of Babylon and Nineveh. The great desert route between Aleppo in Syria and Basra in southern Iraq was also described in the journals of William Beawes, Gaylard Roberts, Bartholomew Plaisted and John Carmichael. Orientalists and archaeologists started arriving at the beginning of the 19th century. They included Constance M Alexander, who travelled throughout the country between 1816 and 1821 collecting Oriental manuscripts and antiquities. Between 1816 and 1821 Claudius James Rich, a resident of the East India Company at the Court of the Pasha of Baghdad, took up residence near Nineveh, and spent his time collecting manuscripts and antiquities. He published *A Memoir on the Ruins of Babylon* in 1818. Thomas Cook's first world tour of 1872 included Mesopotamia. Lady Blunt accompanied the Bedouin on their journeys towards the end of the 19th century, while Ely Bannister Soane visited both the north and south of the country in 1909. Later travellers with an intimate knowledge of the country included Gertrude Bell (see page 145) and Freya Stark, both prolific writers. Colonial officers and businessmen combined their official duties with an interest in antiquities. Henry Rawlinson, a British political agent in Baghdad, was also a philologist of unsurpassed intellect. He spoke an enormous number of Indian dialects, which he learned very quickly, and decoded the trilingual (Old Persian, Elamite and Babylonian) inscription containing a message from King Darius, immortalised on a 122m rock face at Behistun in western Iran.

Archaeological excavations began in the 1800s when Paul Emile Botta, the French consul in Mosul, unearthed Assyrian artefacts in Khorsabad. Remnants of the Sumerian civilisation were discovered near Nasiriyah by Ernest de Sarzec, the French consul in Basra. The British government subsidised the Tigris Euphrates Expedition of F R Chesney in 1835. The early archaeologists were not just interested in augmenting the display cabinets of their museums back home; with the decipherment of cuneiform came the opportunity for fame with authenticating the biblical connections of the Old Testament, and the period was characterised by a scramble for antiquities. The most important finds included Austen Henry Layard's unearthing of the Assyrian palaces of Nimrud. *The Illustrated London News* of 1840 publicised the finds, which heralded an Assyrian revival in Victorian England. Layard and his exploits inevitably evoke controversy. The Iraqis say that he plundered their country, but when the local people found ancient remains they often burned them for limestone. During most of its time under the Ottomans, Iraq was a backwater of ignorance, disinterest and corruption, and looters inspired competition between European countries to create their collections of antiquities.

Quoting Layard again with a common viewpoint of his time:

> 'almost sufficient material (in 1851) has now been obtained to enable us to restore most of the lost history of the country and to confirm the vague traditions of the learning and civilisations of its people. It had often occurred to me during my labour that the time of discovery of these remains was so opportune, that it might be looked upon as something more than accidental. Had these palaces (Nineveh and Nimrud) been by chance exposed to view some years before, no European could have protected them from complete destruction or could have preserved a record of their existence. Had they been discovered a little later, it is highly probable that there would have been insurmountable objections to the removal, even any part of their contents.'

THE 20TH CENTURY At the beginning of the 20th century, German archaeologists succeeded in introducing new discipline and meticulous recording techniques

THE RECOVERY OF THE NIMRUD GOLD

One of the greatest and most mysterious treasures to have been found in Iraq in recent times is the hoard of gold jewellery found in tombs below the floor of the Assyrian palace of Ashurnasirpal II (883–859BC) at Nimrud. The story of the 'Nimrud Gold' weaves together both the drama that is the political history of modern Iraq and the splendour and enigma of ancient Assyria. The treasure rivals Tutankhamen's in terms of splendour and similarly involves an undisturbed royal tomb.

In the 1950s, the famed British archaeologist Max Mallowan excavated at Nimrud in the North-west Palace, clearing a room in what had been the harem. He did not notice a modification of the floor-tile pattern, which was only later seen by the Iraqi archaeologist Sayid Muzahim in 1988. Subsequent excavations under the floor revealed four tombs in the south wing of the North-west Palace of King Ashurnasirpal II. More than 90kg of gold (157 items) were found, along with a stone tablet naming one of the occupants as Queen Yaba, wife of Tiglath-Pilesar III (744–727BC). The inscription on this tablet even included a 'curse of restlessness' on the spirit of those who would disturb the tomb, also translated as a warning that those 'who lay hands on my jewellery with evil intent, or whoever breaks open the seal of this tomb, let his spirit wander in thirst.' Ironically, this very jewellery was retrieved from a flooded vault.

The Central Bank vaults in Baghdad, where the precious finds were stored, were flooded during the 2003 war, some believe deliberately, in order to prevent Saddam Hussein's sons or henchmen making off with the gold. A National Geographic team organised the draining of half-a-million gallons of water, which took three weeks. Three boxes containing the treasure were then found, undisturbed since being placed there.

Abridged from an article by Diana McDonald in The Looting of the Iraq Museum, Baghdad *edited by Milbry Polk and Angela Schuster.*

into a field previously governed by luck or intuition. The *laissez-faire* attitude of the Ottoman government and then the British administration, followed by the Kingdom of Iraq, allowed foreign archaeologists – American, British, German, French, Japanese, Russians and Polish – to dig up the past. Restoration work was undertaken at Nimrud, Nineveh, Babylon, Ur and Hatra. The period between World Wars I and II, when the British archaeologist Sir Leonard Woolley unearthed the royal cemetery at Ur, turned out to be the golden age of archaeology in Iraq. It also reignited public interest in such projects and assisted funding for museums and universities worldwide. Excavations continued after World War II and young Iraqi archaeologists were keen to, and were encouraged to, train in the new discipline. The Directorate General of Antiquities assumed responsibility for research and technical activities connected with archaeology, including the administration of museums and archaeological exhibits, and the excavation and protection of sites and antiquities.

In Saddam's time the State Board of Antiquities was responsible for the restoration and preservation of antiquities and historic buildings throughout the country. The most notable restoration work took place in Babylon. Numerous buildings and main temples in the ancient city of Hatra were restored. During the 1970s the construction of dams on the Euphrates, including the Hamrin basin project, prompted salvage excavations, which led to the discovery of relics ranging from prehistoric to Islamic times. The 1991 Gulf War dampened further exploration and left a tragic legacy of looting and theft. Looting started to be a problem during the 1980–88 Iran-Iraq War when sites were not guarded as resources were diverted to the front. The sanctions period from 1990 saw a serious deterioration in maintenance of sites. Archaeology turned into 'rescue excavations' from sites which had been looted. In January 1997, *Trace*, a magazine that liaises with international police forces and the art world to find stolen art works and antiques, estimated that 4,000 items were looted during the Gulf War in 1991.

ERADICATING THE PAST: LOOTING IN POST-SADDAM IRAQ In leaflets dropped from the air on 27 March 2003, the Coalition said it did not wish to destroy Iraqi landmarks. None of Iraq's historic sites were damaged during military action. The problems started after the war: rampant looting and long-term neglect. Simon Jenkins pointed out in a *Guardian* article on 8 June 2007: 'Under Saddam you were likely to be tortured and shot if you let someone steal an antiquity: in today's Iraq you are likely to be tortured and shot if you don't.' Soon after Saddam's statue was dragged to the ground and smashed in Fardous Square the looting of the museum began. Witnesses and antiquities experts believe that the first looters were insiders who knew what they were looking for and stole the most valuable items by unlocking display cases and vaults. The staff and the caretakers at the museum did an amazing job protecting it from looters, and 1,500 paintings from the Museum of Modern Art were stored in the Iraq Museum for six months. Both the National Library and the Ministry of Religious Affairs were burned almost to the ground. Antique manuscripts and thousands of illuminated and handwritten Korans turned to ashes along with the Ottoman archive.

Iraq is a country of 10,000 archaeological sites, of which only 1,500 have been researched. Most are unprotected and as such it became open season for looters. Even when a site was guarded the guards were no match for armed gangs of looters. Sites in the remote desert of the south, such as Dahaileh, were especially vulnerable. Umma, a famous Sumerian city in the desert north of Nasiriyah, was ravaged, and what the city could have revealed about pre-Akkadian times is now in the dustbin of history; the looters having left nothing but a desert full of holes. In their contribution to *The Looting of the Iraq Museum*, Micah Caren and Marie-Helene Carleton described the farming of antiquities in southern Iraq as 'erasing the past'.

In the Kurdistan region, which has more than 3,000 archaeological sites, artefacts disappeared or disintegrated. Some sites were damaged by the expansion of agriculture and the construction of buildings, others by trenches built in preparation for war and by 'looting to order' from the sites and museums. Sites suffered from neglect due to a lack of experience, equipment and money.

Excavation and conservation work continued to suffer during the sanctions period, and few major excavations took place in the years leading up to 2003. All activities ceased in the year 2002, and most foreigners left the country.

POST 2003: SAVING THE CRADLE OF CIVILISATION Having failed to stop the looting, not only of museum artefacts but also of art works, proper border controls could have prevented them from leaving the country. Tragically Iraq's post-war porous borders were a smugglers' dream come true. To address this, Interpol set up a task force to trace Iraq's stolen treasures and in May 2003 the United Nations passed Security Resolution 1483 banning trade in Iraqi cultural property. A further resolution, 1546, was passed in June 2004 stressing the need for site protection. Thanks to these measures, looted objects began to be returned. Fencing and guardians appeared at the ancient sites, and security checks were put in place at airports and land borders, all of which gradually helped prevent further losses and stem the flow of ancient treasures out of Iraq. However, we must be realistic: Iraq was and is not unique in the illicit digging and selling of antiquities. Italy, with its Etruscan treasures, Greece with its early classical pottery sites, Turkey with its vast sites from all eras and Afghanistan with its Gandharan-Buddhist remains have all been much plagued by the illicit trade in ancient artefacts for many years, and no measures have managed to completely eradicate this.

Sadly virtually all of Iraq's archaeological sites have been damaged to some extent by wars, sanctions, the collapse of infrastructure, looting, military bases stationed within the sites themselves, accelerated decay, and questionable reconstruction methods, such as those used in Babylon in the 1980s. Most of the major sites have been looted and damaged during or since the 2003 war. The seriousness of conditions in Iraq prompted the World Monuments Fund (WMF), for the first time, to put the entire country on its biannual list of the One Hundred Most Endangered Sites. The British Museum, UNESCO, The University of Chicago and the World Monuments Fund are among the international organisations who responded with a series of major initiatives to assist with the preservation of Iraq's cultural heritage which included assessing the damage, assisting in the return of looted antiquities and helping to train a new generation of archaeologists and conservationists.

The British Museum is one of the main institutions in Britain providing information about Iraq's archaeological heritage through lectures and information programmes. John Curtis, Keeper of the Middle East Department, with special interests in Iraq and Iran, produced reports on damage to the archaeological sites in Babylon and Ur, and in 2008 site surveys were prepared of Eridu, Ur, Uruk, Ubaid, Queili, Larsa, Lagash and Kisiga. In 2009 a further investigation of Babylon was conducted on behalf of UNESCO. The British Museum launched a campaign to turn Saddam's Lakeside Palace in Basra into a museum which was due to open in 2014. They also provide training for Department of Antiquities' staff, including museum curators and conservators and staff working at the archaeological site of Babylon.

The Oriental Institute at the University of Chicago has set up a website to provide information about Iraqi antiquities looted from the Iraq Museum. The University of Michigan, the University of Southern California, Harvard University, the University of California at Berkeley, the British Museum and the British Institute for the Study of Iraq (formerly the British School of Archaeology in Iraq) are among the institutions assisting with the website and providing information, which it is hoped will deter potential buyers of looted artefacts. In December 2012 the US Embassy in Baghdad hosted a training conference on countering antiquities trafficking. In the same month police in Nasiriyah seized 131 Mesopotamian artefacts on two raids on smugglers' hideouts.

As the only UN agency with a mandate for culture, UNESCO has been keen on preserving and showcasing the rich cultural heritage of Iraq. Its culture projects concentrate on safeguarding heritage and rehabilitating institutions. UNESCO has also provided the Iraqi Government with technical expertise to fight against the looting of artefacts, protect intangible heritage and promote tourism. It is helping prepare Iraqi sites for nomination to the World Heritage List, three of which, Ashur, Hatra and Samarra, have already made it onto the list. It is active in the rehabilitation of the Erbil Citadel, the Kirkuk Museum, the Suleimaniyah Museum and the historic quarters of Basra, along with the conservation of mud-brick architecture.

ARCHAEOLOGY IN IRAQ TODAY

In 2012 the archaeologists came back. In 2012 and 2013 British archaeologists returned to southern Iraq to the site of Tell Khaiber, 20km from the ancient city of Ur, a site

THE EXCAVATIONS AT TELL KHAIBER

British archaeologists have unearthed a sprawling complex near the ancient city of Ur in southern Iraq, home of the biblical Abraham. The structure, thought to be about 4,000 years old, probably served as an administrative centre for Ur, around the time Abraham would have lived there before leaving for Canaan, according to the Bible. The compound is near the site of the partially reconstructed ziggurat, or Sumerian temple, said Stuart Campbell of Manchester University's Archaeology Department, who led the dig. 'This is a breath-taking find, because of its unusually large size (roughly the size of a football pitch, or about 80m on each side). Complexes of this size and age are rare. It appears that it is some sort of public building, possibly an administrative building, it might have had religious connections or been used to control goods to the city of Ur.'

The complex of rooms around a large courtyard was found 20km from Ur, the last capital of the Sumerian royal dynasties whose civilisation flourished 5,000 years ago. One of the artefacts unearthed was a 9cm clay plaque showing a worshipper wearing a long, fringed robe and approaching a sacred site. Beyond artefacts, the site could reveal the environmental and economic conditions of the region through analysis of plant and animal remains.

The dig began in March 2013 when the six-member British team joined four Iraqi archaeologists at the site. Decades of war and violence have kept international archaeologists away from Iraq, where significant archaeological sites as yet unexplored are located, but this dig shows that such collaborative missions are possible in parts of Iraq that are relatively stable, like its Shiite-dominated south.

Campbell's team was the first British-led archaeological dig in southern Iraq since the 1980s. It was directed by Manchester University's Dr Jane Moon and independent archaeologist Robert Killick.

chosen as the best place to start a new international collaboration in archaeological research owing to its location in an area where it was safe to work and close enough to Nasiriyah to facilitate full collaboration with the young and dedicated staff of the local Antiquities Department. It was quickly confirmed that the archaeological remains were intact and had not been disturbed by looters. Starting in 2012, the team of international and Iraqi archaeologists have been excavating annually at Tell Khaiber, supported by local labourers. The international team includes specialists in areas such as animal bone and plant remains, as well as conservators and language experts.

Tell Khaiber consists of two low mounds concealing a settlement dating to around 2000BC. On the ground, these low-lying mounds hide their secrets well, but when viewed from above by satellite, large public buildings are revealed, showing their importance in antiquity. From the pottery collected on the surface, it has been established that people first came to live there about 4000BC and the important buildings were in use around 1800BC when a western branch of the Euphrates river passed close by. Its monumental building is most likely to date to between the fall of Ur (c2000BC), and the conquest of the competing city states of southern Iraq by Hammurabi, King of Babylon, about 1763BC. Local visitors and media have already dropped in, including a great nephew of Sir Leonard Woolley. Work on analysis and publication is continuing throughout the year at the project's academic base in the University of Manchester.

After nearly a century away **Harvard** archaeology returned to Kurdistan Iraq. In 2012, Jason Ur launched a five-year archaeological project to scour a 3,200km² area around Erbil for signs of ancient cities and towns, canals and roads. Speaking to the *Harvard Gazette* he said: 'What we're finding is that this is, hands down, the richest archaeological landscape in the Middle East. Due to the history of conflict and ethnic strife in this region, there was no work done in this area at all, so it really is a tabula rasa, so it's a very exciting time but unfortunately that blank slate is quickly being erased by development.'

Boston University is partnered with educators at **Mosul University** on an innovative programme to revive higher education and cultural heritage management in Iraq. Britain is also sending archaeological teams to Iraq. A team from **Reading University** is collaborating with the Suleimaniyah Directorate of Antiquities and Heritage on excavations near Shahrizor Plain in the Zagros Mountains focusing on the Pre-Pottery Neolithic period between 9000–7000BC. **Manchester University** is involved with a re-assessment dig planned for the Shanidar Cave in Kurdistan and other sites (see page 392).

Since 1932 the **British Institute for the Study of Iraq** has been involved in archaeological work in Iraq. Since the 2003 war it has been assisting Iraqis in rebuilding their heritage and bringing Iraqi scholars and heritage staff to the UK for training and research. Educating a new generation of Iraqi archaeologists is vital. The low standard of education in the country and lack of proficiency in English is a serious problem. The top students study medicine and architecture, and archaeology is taken up by those with lower grades. Nevertheless, for many Iraqis it is still a vocation and an obsession, and in addition to Westerners eager to continue excavations in Iraq, the locals are also making a significant contribution even though finance always poses a major problem.

Teams of Iraqi archaeologists have discovered an additional 40 ancient sites in the south of the country from the Sumerian, Akkadian and Babylonian periods. They are working in the Dhi Qar Province, which has the largest number of archaeological sites totalling 1,240. Excavations have started at the 500m² Abu Rababm plateau, 150km east of the city of Nasiriyah. 'There are many archaeological sites in the region including the ancient archaeological plateau that was excavated as part of the Marshes project, the archaeological site of Abu Rabab, Abu Al-Dhahb, the Abu Massaed site and other archaeological plateaux. Now we are working in four archaeological plateaux that are located near the province and near the Marshes. This work is being done in this area because the site is located close to the province and water does not leak in the archaeological plateaux,' explained Iyad Mahmoud, the director of the archaeological team.

The plans for the development of archaeology in Iraq are ambitious, with a vision to prepare Babylon, the most famous archaeological site, and other ruins from Ur in the

A WARNING TO ALL VISITORS

The outrage at the looting in Iraq, principally that of the National Museum, has resulted in the tightening and strict implementation of rules regarding the selling, purchasing and possessing of antiques in Iraq. This has led to the strict supervision of visitors at ancient sites such as Uruk, which are strewn with pottery sherds. Any (foreign) person seen to be picking up such artefacts is in danger of being arrested. These rules have also all but ended the sale of ancient objects from antique shops.

south to Nimrud in the north, for visits by scientists, scholars and tourists. It is hoped this will contribute to the economic revival and provide a steady source of income for the local people. 'Babylon is one of Iraq's biggest and greatest projects,' Qais Hussein Rashid, Director of the State Board of Antiquities and Heritage said proudly. 'We want to have it as a model for other sites.' But Lamia Gailani, an independent Iraqi archaeologist who lives in London, said that while the project was commendable the local people want to see results yesterday, and often do not appreciate the hard work and long- term commitment required to turn dreams into reality.

THE FUTURE

On 7 August 2006 the late Donny George, President of the Board of Antiquities, resigned; ending a distinguished 30-year career. George said he resigned because the board was increasingly influenced by the militant al-Sadr Shia movement and showed scant regard for Iraq's earlier cultures. In a lecture delivered in London in 2007, Dr Abbas al Hussaini, head of the State Board of Antiquities and Heritage, said that one of the major threats to Iraq's heritage is the bombing of Islamic sites by Islamists and al-Qaeda. Sites damaged in this way include the Al-Askari (Al-Hadi) Mosque in Samarra, the Ana Minaret and Hidir Mosque in Anbar Province, the Sheikh Abdul Kader Al-Gailiani Mosque in Baghdad, the tomb of Imam Yahya bin Qasim in Mosul and ten shrines in the Diyala region.

In the last few years the predominantly Shia Government has placed much emphasis on rebuilding and restoring many of the religious buildings and sites in Iraq. (UNESCO has also been assisting with this, notably at Al Kifl) to the dismay of some people who feel that this is being done at the expense of many of Iraq's other great sites. There is a feeling that Iraq's ancient heritage, including that of its Sumerian culture, is being neglected and that not enough effort is being made to restore sites, let alone explore new ones. However, included among the State Board of Antiquities and Heritage's conservation projects are the synagogue and the Shrine of the Tomb of Prophet Nahum, situated in the Christian town of El Kosh, 40km north of Mosul. The prophet is venerated by all sects. If the board continues this all-encompassing approach then happily the future looks bright and discoveries will flow.

Another challenge for archaeologists is the attitude of many of the locals. Archaeologist Joanne Farchakh explained that what for Westerners is the 'cradle of civilisation' for the locals is often nothing more than desert land with pottery and other artefacts that they have a right to. Life in the desert is hard, and a cylinder seal, a sculpture or a cuneiform tablet which can be sold on the black market for US$50, half the monthly average salary, is always going to provide a great temptation. Iraq's ancient heritage and stone carvings will always evoke strong emotions from both the protagonists and antagonists of the conservation of the country's heritage. And the artefacts themselves still speak to us; as Elroy Flecker found out during a visit the British Museum:

There is a hall in Bloomsbury that
no more dare I tread,
For all the stone men shout at me
and swear they are not dead.
And once I touched a broken girl and
knew that marble bled.

from the poem *Oak and Pine*

Sturt W Manning, archaeologist and classicist, commented on 'the human folly and senseless violence that drives ISIS', and further said: 'The terror group is destroying the evidence of the great history of Iraq; it has to, as this history attests to a rich alternative to its barbaric nihilism'.

As ISIS swiftly and astonishingly advanced through northern Iraq, taking Mosul and forcing Yezidis and Christians to flee, the destruction began in their wake. Sinjar and Tell Afar, with its Shia Turkmen mosques and shrines were all destroyed. Mosul, with its great Muslim and Christian heritage, has seen nearly all of its churches damaged or destroyed. The mosques of Sheikh Fathi and the shrine of the prophet Sheet have also been damaged or destroyed. Most astonishing of all was the video released by ISIS of the destruction of the Mosque of Nebi Younis, which was built on the church of biblical prophet Jonah. There's also video footage of attempts to damage and loot Khorsabad, and local rumours of the destruction of exhibits that remain in the Mosul Museum. Thankfully, many of these were plaster copies.

Shockwaves have been felt throughout the world's museums in response to unproven reports of attempts to bulldoze Hatra and Ashur. These acts of violence are reminiscent of the destruction of the Bamiyan Buddhas in Afghanistan by the Taliban for similar ideological religious reasons.

But Iraq is no stranger to violence and mayhem. The taking of Mar Behnam monastery, close to ancient Nimrud, by armed ISIS terrorists and the ejection of the monks with nothing but what they stood up in, has given us a glimpse of the terror that the Mongols brought when they swept through Iraq all those centuries ago on the same hell-bent mission of conquest and destruction.

All that can be said is that ISIS will not succeed in the long term and that Mosul will be released from its hell and the damage can be assessed. Archaeology has also moved on since the early days of the last century. While we have the records and exhibits of those historic expeditions, we will make new discoveries with newly available technologies at the old sites. Nimrud will rise again and perhaps that Assyrian Palace that lies under the now-ruined Mosque of Nebi Younis (see pages 225–7) can be investigated after all. Thankfully, the great museums of the world – the British Museum, the Louvre, the Pergamon, the Metropolitan Museum and the Baghdad Museum – house an amazing range of artefacts from Iraq's damaged sites and they can be seen and shared by all.

IRAQ ONLINE

For additional online content, articles, photos and more on Iraq, why not visit www.bradtguides.com/iraq.

4

Practical Information

Travel to Iraq is not without its challenges. It is complex, sometimes maddening, often inconvenient. But the rewards are the boundless wealth of cultural richness.

WHEN TO VISIT

All visitors to Iraq must remember that nothing is certain, nothing is guaranteed. The arrangements are often chaotic. This is not a country for you if you want everything to run to plan. Most of the historical sites remain; everything else, especially the political situation, can change without warning.

The best months to visit Iraq are the cool, temperate months: April, May, September, October and November when the weather is very pleasant and warm enough to enjoy sightseeing. December, January and February tend to be cold with rain. In the mountain regions of Kurdistan heavy snow falls during the winter and the temperature can plummet with temperatures dropping below zero. The summer months (June, July and August) are very hot, often reaching temperatures as high as 50°C. For advice on what clothing to pack, see pages 101–2.

HIGHLIGHTS

BAGHDAD With a population of over seven million, Baghdad is the capital city. Located in the heart of the historic Tigris–Euphrates valley, Baghdad began life as a series of pre-Islamic settlements. In the 8th century it was transformed into the capital of the Muslim world and remained a cultural metropolis for centuries. In 1258, after its destruction by Mongol invaders, the Persians and the Turks vied for control of the city, which was finally incorporated into the Ottoman Empire in 1638 as the vilayet or province of Baghdad, an important provincial centre. In 1932 it became the capital of modern Iraq. Despite its ever-changing fortunes, the city has seldom lost its importance as a commercial, communications and cultural centre. Many years after the 2003 war, long blast barriers made of ugly concrete slabs still thread across Baghdad, defining the post-invasion city as surely as the Berlin Wall made its mark in the Cold War. As in Berlin, some have been painted with flowers and scenes from Iraq's glorious past to relieve the drabness.

BABYLON Biblical 'mother of harlots and abomination of the earth', Babylon has left its imprint on the history of the world since the time of Nebuchadnezzar II (see pages 266–72). The archaeological site is a large one, a mixture of the surviving remains of Nebuchadnezzar's Babylon and extensive modern reconstruction and restoration. Saddam Hussein reconstructed huge parts of ancient Babylon, including Nebuchadnezzar's Palace, until it became the most restored site in Iraq, and bricks inscribed with Saddam's name adorn the site. He also built his own palace on a mound by the river. Its empty shell still overlooks the site today.

BASRA AND THE MARSHES Basra, city of Sinbad the Sailor and starting point of his famous adventurous voyages is Iraq's largest and main seaport (see box, pages 318–19). Although not ancient by Iraqi standards, for centuries it has been the centre of Iraq's commercial importance, with its endless ships shuttling back and forth on the Shatt Al-Arab. Although a focal point of problems during the past 40 or so years, with its borders with Iran and Kuwait, restive tribal communities, the general hostility emanating from Baghdad's Saddam Sunni dominated regime and its repressions and killings during and following the 2003 war, happily change is now becoming apparent with new bridges across the Shatt Al-Arab and modern buildings beginning to appear. Progress is happening cautiously though, the Islamisation of Basra has altered local life; the liquor shops have gone and in the once lively streets, life is reduced and all are watchful. In contrast, the Marshes are the most beautiful part of Iraq, outshining both the Persian miniature scenery of the central Euphrates and the cool, majestic north. The area is lush, and now becoming well-watered again with small boats gliding on the calm waterways. It is an area of countless birds and at certain times of the year the shaded creeks are full of bee-eaters, kingfishers and other species flitting along the banks of the canals and waterways.

SAMARRA Inhabited as far back as the 5th millennium BC during the Chalcolithic Samaran period, Samarra was a prosperous settlement renowned for its dark-fired pottery decorated with stylised figures of animals and birds and geometric designs. Between the 3rd and 7th centuries AD it was the site of a small Sassanian Persian town and an important Nestorian bishopric with a Christian monastery. Re-founded virtually overnight, it became the capital of one of the greatest states known to history; it lost that status a mere 56 years later. Thankfully for history its quick death led to the survival of its architecture and today it is a living document and a unique witness to an empire which ruled the ancient world from Tunisia to central Asia. Modern Samarra is a town of modest distinction, but its spiral minaret, located outside the northern wall of the main enclosure, gives Samarra its high place in the list of the world's greatest architecture. Within the town, Samarra's Persian-style Shia mosque with its shining golden dome, is the final resting place of the 10th and 11th imams, Ali al Hadi al Naqi and his son Hasan al Askari. Nearby is the spot where the 12th imam, the Mahdi, vanished. The infidel treads warily hereabouts or, in other words, non-Muslims should behave respectfully in Samarra.

KURDISTAN The region of Kurdistan is a fascinating place of natural beauty, warm and friendly people, and a long, interesting and often tragic history. Although situated in the northern part of Iraq, it is in many ways a world apart. Largely unknown, or traditionally avoided by Western tourists, the region is a hidden gem. Your personal itinerary will be influenced by your own interests, transport and the time available for travel. Kurdistan is not simply about ticking off the sights; tourists are still rare here so it is not uncommon for travellers to be asked to join people for tea or a meal, or to simply talk or pose for a photo. The Kurds are a proud people eager to show Kurdistan to the world, and your encounters with these resilient individuals will undoubtedly be the most enduring memory of your visit.

SUGGESTED ITINERARIES

Iraq is a large country, and although road systems are in the main very good, there are numerous checkpoints and holdups which can result in you spending more time sitting at the side or the road than actually exploring the ancient sights! However, it is possible to visit most of the tourist attractions on a tour that adopts an intensive sightseeing schedule lasting approximately 16 days. Alternatively, you can visit just the highlights of Baghdad, Kurdistan or northern Iraq if your time is limited. A selection of possible itineraries are listed below:

WEEKEND – AROUND BAGHDAD

Day one An early start allows you to make time for the Kassite ziggurat at Agargouf, just 30km from the city centre. Dating from about 1500BC, this is probably the best ziggurat in Iraq. If you are a really early bird though, start your tour first at the Mosque at Kadhmain, situated on the banks of the Tigris to the north of the city. Opposite the mosque is a famous clothes market. Returning towards the centre, visit the railway station, which is a marble symbol of British-colonial architecture and the famous monument of Sitt Zumarrud Khatoun's tomb, dating back to the late Abbasid period (1179–1225). The Mosque and Shrine of Sheikh Omar al Sahrawardi is nearby. It is a very tranquil place and eminently photogenic. Right in the centre of Baghdad you will find the modern-day Martyr's Monument, commemorating those who died in the Iran-Iraq War (1980–88). The next stop could be the magnificent Iraq Museum which is now open. As you come into the centre of Baghdad, in Al-Rashid Street you will arrive at the Abbasid Palace, the beautiful Al-Mustansiriya School built under the Abbasids, the Murjan Mosque and Khan Murjan.

Day two Central Baghdad can be explored on foot. See pages 155–6 for a walking tour that starts at Al-Shuhada Square and takes in the Murjan Mosque, various churches, the souk and Baghdad Museum.

ONE WEEK

Kurdistan The region of Kurdistan is not large and most sites can be visited quite comfortably within a one-week period. If time is limited to less than a week, it is best to select one of the three main cities of Erbil, Dohuk and Suleimaniyah, and make this the hub for your excursions. Note, though, that local people are uncertain of many of the locations of the ancient and historical sites so you may need a guide to find some of the smaller sites.

Day one Head north to Dohuk from Erbil visiting the Yezidi village of Ain Sifni and the main Yezidi Temple at Lalish *en route* to make the most of your time. The hotels in Dohuk are fine, as are the restaurants.

Day two Travel to Zakhu and explore that city, examine the fine historic bridge and view the Turkish mountains before returning to Dohuk via the scenic Artificial Dam Road.

Day three The third day of this itinerary is possibly the best of your visit. Start your day by travelling to Amadiya, where you can explore this ancient walled town. Then to Barzan, the ancestral home of the famous Kurdish Barzani family. Then pay a visit to the Gale Ali Beg Canyon and see the impressive waterfalls, travelling *en route* along the Hamilton Road. Travel on to Shaqlawa, for an overnight stop at one of the early holiday resorts for the people of Erbil.

Day four Travel cross country via the hills and mountain roads to Koya and then Dukan, then on to Suleimaniyah. Allow up to two hours from Dukan to reach the city.

4

Days five and six Stay in one of the fine hotels at Suleimaniyah, giving you ample time to visit the attractions in the city, including the museum. The mountain views across the city from the top of Azmar Mountain are not to be missed. The second day in Suleimaniyah should include an excursion to the monument at Halabja, where the infamous poison gas atrocity was perpetrated by Saddam's forces. Finish the day off with a visit to the Red House (Amna Suraka) in Suleimaniyah.

NINE DAYS – BAGHDAD AND THE NORTH

Day one Arrive into Baghdad. Afternoon excursion to the Kadhmain Mosque.

Day two Tour Baghdad city and take in the National Museum, the Murjan Mosque, Tell Harmal, Al-Mustansiriya School and the souk.

Day three Drive first to Samarra to visit the mosque, minaret and palace and then on to Tikrit and Saddam Palace, before ending the day in Erbil, provincial capital of Kurdistan governorate, famous for its citadel.

Day four Start with a visit to Der Mar Behnam Monastery, then on to the Assyrian site of Nimrud and finally to Der Mar Matti Monastery. Return to Erbil.

Day five Make the long journey back to Baghdad via the site of Ashur and the magnificent site of Hatra, City of the Sun. Overnight in Baghdad.

Day six Stay in Baghdad for excursions to the Ctesiphon Arch and Agargouf ziggurat.

Day seven Travel to Babylon, city of Nebuchadnezzar, and Sumerian Borsippa before finishing the day in the Shrine City of Kerbala.

Day eight is your return journey to Baghdad via the Shrine Cities of Najaf and Kufa.

Day nine Depart from Baghdad.

SIXTEEN DAYS – MESOPOTAMIA

Days one–seven are the same as the nine-day itinerary above.

Day eight Drive to Ukhaider Castle via the At Tar Caves and the Christian church and monastery. Return to Kerbala for your overnight stay.

Day nine Start with a visit to Al Kifl before travelling on to Kufa. Overnight in the Shrine City of Najaf where Imam Ali is buried.

Day ten Ancient Sumer is the first stop, followed by Nippur and Uruk and possibly a visit to that most important site, Larsa. Overnight at Samawah.

Day eleven Today you visit Ur, famous for the Royal Tombs and its ziggurat, then on to Eridu and Tel Ubaid, which date back to the 6th millennium. Then finally on to Nasiriyah for your overnight stay.

Day twelve Start with a visit to the Marshes and maybe a boat ride, before travelling on to Querna where the Tigris and the Euphrates meet. End the day in Basra.

Day thirteen Tour the city of Basra with an excursion on the Shatt Al-Arab.

Day fourteen Return to Baghdad by road visiting Ezra's tomb *en route*.

Day fifteen Explore Baghdad and depart.

TOUR OPERATORS

At the time of going to press it is not possible to travel independently within Iraq. Tourist visas are issued by the Ministry of Tourism only to recognised tour operators with a minimum number of travellers. However, travelling in a small group does have advantages as this generally reduces the hassles of checkpoints, arranging internal transport and the language barrier. Although you may see many tour operators offering to take tourists to Iraq, you will generally find on closer examination that this means just the Kurdistan region. There are, however, many tour companies across the globe, especially in the Middle East, who take pilgrim groups of mainly Shia Muslims to visit the Shrine Cities in the south of Iraq. Although it is possible to travel independently within Kurdistan, many first-time visitors also choose to go with a recognised tour operator.

The companies listed below offer specialist, small-group tours, and may also be able to provide knowledgeable and sometimes specialist guides who can help you get the most out of your visit.

UK

Hinterland Travel 39 Clifton Common, Clifton, Brighouse HD6 1QW; +44 (0)1484 719549; m 07717 060415; e Hinterland@btconnect. com; www.hinterlandtravel.com. Hinterland Travel is the only UK-based tour company taking groups regularly across the whole of Iraq. It is a specialist adventure travel company, founded on over 35 years of overland adventure travel experience by Geoff Hann, co-author of this guide & Hinterland's owner & Managing Director. Hinterland offers 3 tours to Iraq – the 9-day, the 16-day & the 21/22-day combined tour which includes Turkey, Kurdistan Iraq & Mesopotamia. Ground costs start at £2,050 for the 9-day tour which includes all ground transport, group airport transfers, site entrance fees, tour guide, Hinterland Travel tour leader, some local guides, guards if necessary, hotel accommodation, b/fast & dinner. For the expected 9- and 16-day itineraries, see opposite page. See ad page 81.

IKB Travel & Tours Ltd 230 Edgware Rd, London W2 1DW; +44 (0)20 7724 8455; admin@ ikbtravel.co.uk; www.youshouldtravel.com. IKB specialises in flights to Iraq offering competitive rates for travel to Erbil, Baghdad, Suleimaniyah, Basra & Najaf. The company has been in business for more than a decade & can arrange sightseeing,

hotel accommodation, archaeological & religious tours. See ad in colour section.

Lupine Travel 12 Warnford St, Wigan, Lancs WN1 2EQ; +44 (0)1942 704525; e info@lupinetravel. co.uk; www.lupinetravel.co.uk. Founded in 2007, Lupine offers escorted tours to Kurdistan, taking in Dohuk, Erbil, Suleimaniyah & Halabja. See ad on page 82.

Robert Broad Travel 2 Boley Park Shopping Centre, Ryknild St, Lichfield, Staffordshire WS14 9XU; +44 (0)845 003 2211, (0)1543 258631; e dave@robertbroadtravel.co.uk; www. robertbroadtravel.co.uk. Established for 27 years, this is an award-winning, full-service travel consultancy offering a vast range of world-wide luxury holidays & tours with a flexible, professional & friendly service.

Undiscovered Destinations PO Box 746, North Tyneside, NE29 1EG; +44 (0)191 296 2674; e travel@undiscovered-destinations.com; www. undiscovered-destinations.com. Offering both small-group tours & tailor-made itineraries, Undiscovered Destinations focuses on countries & regions that can genuinely be described as off the beaten track.

Wild Frontiers Unit 6, Hurlingham Business Park, 55 Sulivan Rd, London SW6 3DU; +44 (0)20 7736 3968; e info@wildfrontierstravel.com;

At the time of writing Hinterland Travel has achieved six full seasons thoroughly exploring Iraq again after some long years of absence from the country. In the introduction to his tour, overland tour operator and tour leader Geoff Hann says: 'For many years in the past we regularly combined Iraq tours with other Middle Eastern countries. However, we are now concentrating on those ancient structures of Iraq that have always appealed: Babylon, Ur, Uruk, Kish and Nimrud to name but a few. Our earlier tours ceased as the disturbances, conflicts and wars between Iran and Iraq escalated to the Gulf War. Still treading warily, but with our past experience to assist us, and some new friends willing to provide us with as much help as possible, we ventured again into Iraq in October 2000. At that point we were the first British tour group to explore the country in depth for 10 years.' Several more tours followed, up to October 2003 when Hinterland ran their famous 'Post War' tour. Geoff says of this: 'The country was in shock; everything was open, the borders not manned. It was possible to travel everywhere and see everything.' This situation changed rapidly and it was not possible to visit again until 2007, when Hinterland ventured back, initially into the Kurdish region. In 2009 Hinterland again began running tours across the whole of Iraq. Geoff's knowledge and expertise in the Middle East, Mesopotamia, Iraq and Afghanistan has put the company in the forefront of Iraq tour operators and experts. For contact details, see page 87.

www.wildfrontierstravel.com. Wild Frontiers is a company that has been set up by travellers for travellers, whose ethos is to help adventurous souls get to incredible & inaccessible places in safety & as much comfort as local conditions allow.

US

The Other Iraq Tours Douglas Layton, 5072 Leucadia St, Unit I, Laguna Niguel, CA 92677; +1-619-519-2094; 964-750-301-0001; e info@theotheriraqtours.com; www. theotheriraqtours.com. Owned & operated by 2 Americans with over 25 years' experience in the region, this company specialises in luxury & custom tours to Kurdistan.

IRAQ

Babil Tours Sadoun St, Baghdad; m 0781 045 1045; www.babel-tours.com. Babil Tours offers tours accompanied by guides throughout Iraq, except in the places where, according to them, the security is not guaranteed. The agency is able to offer all types of services for tourists: hotel bookings, transport, guides for trips to a particular town & Christian & Muslim pilgrimages to holy cities & sites.

Canon Co Sadoun St, Baghdad; m 0790 114 0672; e ashur_2@hotmail.com. A full range of services for Muslim tourists of both Shia & Sunni sects, with visits to the holy Shrine Cities as well as places of interest in modern Iraq & ancient Mesopotamia.

Alhani Travel & Tourism Co Blue Sky Restaurant Building, Al-Robaiee St, Zayyona, Baghdad; m 0790 176 0000; e info@alhanitravel. net; www.alhanitravel.net. With 15 branches in Iraq, Alhani offer a range of services for visitors to the holy places & civilisation of Iraq including air tickets, hotel bookings, charter operation, airport & taxi services, shore excursions, car rental, & running organised tours of between 6 & 13 days around Iraq & Kurdistan.

Almanar Travel & Tourism Sadoun St (opposite Baghdad Hotel), Baghdad; m 0770 442 6551; e info@almanarco.com; www.almanarco. com. Established in 2004 in Iraq, Almanar is one of the largest travel & tourism companies in its field. In 2012 1,500,000 pilgrims who visited Iraq were catered for by Almanar. The company provides comprehensive cultural & religious tourism services in Iraq, the birthplace of civilisation & the prophets. The company caters for both individual customers & group bookings offering flight, hotel & restaurant bookings, visa arrangement, transportation, tour guides, hospitality packages, corporate services, car hire & cargo handling. **Kurdistan Adventures** Office 405, 3rd Floor, Talari Chwar Bakh, Saywan St, Chwar Bakh, Suleimaniyah; m 0771 152 0295; e info@kurdistan-adventures.com; www. kurdistan-adventures.com. An Australian/ Kurdish joint venture, Kurdistan Adventures combines local knowledge with Western tour operations management. They pride themselves on immersing their small groups of travellers in Iraqi Kurdish culture with safety, security & professionalism.

RED TAPE

Dealings with Iraqi bureaucracy are best left to your tour operator/travel agent. The nepotism of officialdom under the dictatorship of Saddam Hussein followed by the change from Sunni to Shia domination in ministerial posts after 2003 and the resulting inexperience and insecurity means that any dealings with Iraqi officialdom will be long-winded and often ultimately fruitless. If you have to deal with officials always be polite (but firm), try not to get angry or lose your temper and always be sure exactly what you want to achieve.

FOREIGN AND COMMONWEALTH OFFICE (FCO) ADVICE At the time of writing, the FCO was advising against travel to most parts of Iraq, check out their website for the up-to-date situation: www.gov.uk/foreign-travel-advice/iraq.

VISAS

Note In common with most Arab countries, you will probably be refused a visa if your passport contains an Israeli stamp or any crossing point with Israel including Araba border, Sheikh Hussein border, Rafah border and Taba border.

For foreign nationals there are four main types of visa:
- business/academic visas
- pilgrim visas
- tourist visas
- press and media visas.

The usual validity for a visa is three months and the maximum stay is 30 days. You will need an invitation from the commercial company, university or tour operator who will be sponsoring you. Note that individual tourist visas are not issued due to the security situation and the tour operator has to have a minimum of seven to ten persons before any tourist visa can be issued. If applying at an embassy you will need to complete the forms and supply photos, your passport and the fee (check for current cost at time of application, see page 91 for embassy contact details) plus your sponsor's invitation letter.

The alternative is to obtain the visa on arrival at the airport of your choice. This has to be arranged well in advance by your tour operator or sponsor. They will supply the documentation on your behalf and usually meet you at the airport to facilitate the process. Visa fees at the airport are currently US$82 for single entry; US$200 for multiple entry (usually for business purposes).

Important practical advice Do not attempt to travel anywhere in Iraq without your passport containing your Iraqi visa and stamp. There are an enormous number of roadblocks and checkpoints on every road in every town and city at which you and your passport will be examined.

4

DOCUMENTATION Keep spare photos, photocopies of your passport and visas, your invitation letter from your sponsor or tour operator and your tour schedule with you at all times.

HOTEL REGISTRATION You are required to register your passport at every hotel. Remember to retrieve it when you leave, or at any time when you leave the hotel.

VISITORS TO THE KURDISTAN REGIONAL GOVERNMENT (KRG) The Iraqi tourist visa granted by Iraq embassies abroad or by the Baghdad authorities covers all of Iraq, including the KRG. However, on arrival at a KRG border/airport you will be forced to obtain a KRG visa even if you have the full Iraq visa because this autonomous region insists on its own visa process. For most nationalities this is granted readily; however, some nationalities require a visa prior to arrival in Kurdistan, so it is advised that you check with your local Kurdistan Regional Office before you travel (see opposite).

If returning by road via Turkey at the end of your trip you should avoid bringing out any items which refer to the Greater Kurdistan area such as maps, magazines, flags, souvenirs bearing the word 'Kurdistan', etc. You and your vehicle will be searched on entering Turkey and if any such items are discovered these can lead to long delays and the items being confiscated and destroyed.

Please note that a Kurdish visa is valid only in Kurdistan Iraq and does not apply to the rest of Iraq. It is illegal to travel outside the KRG area without a valid Iraq visa. If you do venture outside the Kurdistan Region without the Iraqi tourist visa you can be arrested and deported out of Iraq at you own expense, usually by plane. The many road checkpoints cannot be avoided and are manned by both Kurdistan and Iraqi police and military personnel. If travelling by car, or even by taxi, make sure that you do not stray outside of the Kurdistan area. Plan your route carefully and become familiar with these joint checkpoints. They always have two flags flying, the national Iraq flag and the sunburst flag of the KRG.

Finally, realise that you need your sponsor or tour operator to be able to cut through the bureaucracy on your behalf.

POLICE AND MILITARY

It is estimated that there are probably at least 2.5 million police and military personnel on duty in Iraq. These forces make up a bewildering range of military and police units, with different uniforms and badges as each of the 18 provinces has a separate command base. These units absorb most of the young men in Iraq, paying, clothing and feeding them. These young men are invariably cheerful and accommodating, although still relatively inexperienced, and sadly often the first to become casualties when violence erupts. The older men among them though usually have experience of war and insurgency, and are much better prepared. Groups of tourists are protected by the VIP service.

PHOTOGRAPHS Do not take photos at any checkpoint or of police or army personnel. Your camera could be confiscated and hours wasted dealing with the matter.

EMBASSIES

Iraq's overseas embassies are typically small and their consular departments have very limited opening hours: in the case of London, for example, they are open to

In the current ISIS situation it is not advised that any tourists/travellers should attempt to cross the land borders between Turkey and Iraq, Syria and Iraq or Jordan and Iraq, and it is strongly advised that tourists avoid all border areas. For tourist purposes, only Baghdad and the areas to the south of Iraq should be attempted. All other areas are deemed as insecure. This situation is subject to change. At all times you should check with your tour operator and consult the current Government travel advice on their websites.

receive visa applications and return passports only 10.00–13.00 Monday–Friday. In all cases you are advised to call or check the website of the relevant embassy before visiting in person. All Iraqi embassies are closed for Iraq's national holidays, and often for the public holidays in their host countries too.

Affairs of the Kurdistan Regional Government abroad are dealt with by the Iraqi embassies and KRG offices in London and Washington, DC (see below).

IRAQI EMBASSIES ABROAD

E Australia   48 Culgoa Circuit, O'Mally ACT 2606, Canberra; +61 2 6286 7946; e cnbemb@iraqmofamail.com

E Austria   Johannesgasse 26 A_1010, Vienna; +43 713 8195; e ven1emb@iraqmofamail.com

E Azerbaijan   Baku Khakani 9, Baku; +99 412 498 1447; e bakemb@iraqmofamail.net

E Bahrain   Box 26477, Manama; +973 786 929

E Belgium   FD Roosevelt 115 1050, Brussels; +32 02 374 9711; e brxemb@iraqmofamail.net; www.iraqiembassy.us

E Canada   215 McLeod Street, Ottawa, K2P 0Z8; +613 236 9177 e Media@IraqEmbassy.ca; www.iraqembassy.ca

E France   53, Rue de La Faisanderie, 75116, Paris +33 1 45 53 33 70; e paremb@iraqmofamail.net

E Germany   Riemeisterstrasse 20, 14169, Berlin; +49 30 814 880; e beremb@iraqmofamail.net

E Jordan   Jabal Amman, PO Box 2025, Amman; +96 26 462 3176; e amaemb@iraqmfamail.com; http://iraqmissions.hostinguk.com/home.aspx

E Malaysia   No 2 Jalan Langgak Golf Off Jalan Tun Razak, 55000 Kuala Lumpur; +603 2148

0555; e quaemb@iraqmofamail.net

E Netherlands   Johan Wittlaan 16 2517 JR, The Hague; +31 70 346 6138; www.embassyofiraq.nl

E Pakistan   House No 57, Street No 48, F-8/4, Islamabad; +92 51 225 3738; e iabemb@iraqmofamail.net

E Qatar   Doha; +974 467 2263; e dohemb@iraqmofamail.net

E Romania   8 Polona Street Sector, Bucharest; +40 21 211 3179; e mosemb@iraqmofamail.net

E Sweden   Baldersgatan 6A, Stockholm; +4608 411 4443; e stkemb@iraqmofamail.net

E Switzerland   28, Ch du Petit, Saconnex 1209 Geneva; +41 22 918 0981; e jnvrep@iraqmofamail.net

E Turkey   Gaziosman Pasa Turan Emeksiz Sok no 11, Ankara; +90 312 468 4834; e ankemb@iraqmofamail.net

E United Arab Emirates   Manhal st, Haoudh 55, St 32, Abu Dhabi; +97 12 665 5152; e adbemb@iraqmofamail.net

E United Kingdom   3 Elvaston Place, London SW7 5QH; +44 (0)20 7590 9220; e lonemb@iraqmofamail.net; www.iraqembassy.org.uk

E United States   3421 Massachusetts Av, NW, 20007; +1 202 742 1600 ext 136; http://iraqiembassy.us/

KURDISTAN REGIONAL GOVERNMENT REPRESENTATIVES ABROAD

KRG Representation in the UK   Lower Ground Floor, 23 Buckingham Gate; London SW1E 6LB; 020 3301 8340.

KRG Representation in the USA   1532 16th St, NW, Washington, DC 20036, USA; 202 797 7575.

FOREIGN EMBASSIES IN IRAQ All the embassies listed here are in Baghdad unless otherwise stated. For foreign embassies in Kurdistan see page 367 or visit the website of the Kurdistan Regional Government: www.krg.org and click on the Department of Foreign Relations link.

e Afghanistan Shareh Al-Maghreb Aldifaeih, Waziria 27/1/12; ☏ 1 556 9508

e Algeria Daoudi 613/14/13; ☏ +964 154 13 824

e Armenia Hse 5, St 11, Sect 215, International Zone; ☏ 77 1321 1592; e armiraqembassy@mfa.am

e Australia International Zone; ☏ +61 2 6261 3305 (emergency 24-hours); e austemb. baghdad@dfat.gov.au; www.iraq.embassy.gov.au

e Bahrain Al-Mansour District, Locality (605) Alley (6) House (41), Al Rashid Hotel; m 0781 580 8306; e baghdad.mission@mofa.gov.bh

e Belarus Babil, Arassat Al-Hindiyah, 929/5/47; ☏ 1719 5565

e China Al-Mansour Melia Hotel Salhiyah, 8 Feb, Post Office; ☏ 1 822 7529; e chinaemb_iq@ mfa.gov.cn

e Denmark Al-Jana'a Qtr, Al-Tashree Section, B; m 0790 194 0847; www.ambbagdad.um.dk

e Finland House No 86, Zuqaq No 25, Mahallah No 925, Hai Babel, Jadriyah, PO Box 2041, Alwiyah; ☏ 1 778 6271; e in_emb@yahoo.com

e France Quartier Abu Nawas Emplacement 102, rue 55 - n'7 – Baghdad; m 1600 248 477 http://www.ambafrance-iq.org/

e Germany Mahala 609, St 3 House Nr 53, Hay Al-Mansour; ☏ 1 543 1470; e info@bagdad.diplo. de; www.bagdad.diplo.de

e Hungary Hay Al-Mutanabbi, Mansour, District 609, St 04, Bld No 43, PO B 2065; ☏ 1 543 2956

e India Hse No 6, Zokak No 25, Mohalla 306, Hay Al-Maghrib, PO Box 4114, Adhamiya; ☏ 1 422 5438; e eoibaghdad@yahoo.com

e Jordan Al-Andalus District, Mihla 617, Ziqaq 49, Hse 145, PO Box 6314; ☏ 1 542 9065; e jeiraq@ hotmail.com, jordan@uruklink.net

e Netherlands Park Al-Sadoun, Hay Al-Nidhal 103, St No 38, Hse No 10; ☏ 1 778 2571; e bad@ minbuza.nl

e Sultanate of Oman Hay Al-Andalous (Al-Dawoodi) Mahalla 613, Way No 11 Hse No 2; ☏ 1 542 1819

e Pakistan Hse No 14, St No 7, Mohallah No 609, Al-Mansoor; ☏ 1 542 5343; e pakembbag@yahoo.com

e Poland 38/75 Karadat Mariam International Zone; m 0790 234 5765; e bagdad.amb. sekretariat@msz.gov.pl

e Qatar PO Box 2445, 152 Harthiya 406, Hay Al-Kindi; ☏ 1 541 2186; e baghdad@mofa.gov.qa

e Romania Arassat Al-Hindia Street, Hay Babel Mahalla 929, Zuqaq 31, Nr 452/A; ☏ 1 778 2860; e ambrobagd@yahoo.com

e Russia Al-Moutanabbi, 05/5/4; ☏ 1 778 7887; e embscgb@warkaa.net, embscgbag@yahoo.com

e Serbia Jadriya Babil District Mahala 923, ZUKAK 35, Bld No16, PO Box 2061 Alwiyah; ☏ 1 778 7887; e embscgb@warkaa.net, embscgbag@yahoo.com

e Spain Distrito Mansur, Sector 609, Calle n 1 3, Casa n 1 1; ☏ 1 542 4838

e Turkey 2/8 Waziriyah; ☏ 1 422 0021

e Ukraine Al-Mansour, Dist 609, St 1, H 20; ☏ 1 543 9840; ukraine@uruklink.net; www.mfa. gov.ua/iraq/en

e United Kingdom International Zone opposite Al Rasheed Hotel, accessed via check point 3; m 0790 1926 280; e britishconsulbaghdad@ yahoo.co.uk; http://ukiniraq.fco.gov.uk/en

e United States APO AE 09316; m 0240 553 0589; e BaghdadPressOffice@state.gov; http:// iraq.usembassy.gov

GETTING THERE AND AWAY

BY AIR There were no international commercial flights between 1991 and 2003 when the country was under the sanctions imposed after the invasion of Kuwait. Baghdad Airport was re-opened for commercial flights in April 2004. The airport is located 16km west of the city and there is a complicated entry system for passengers due to the strict security currently in place; see pages 129 and 132 for important further information.

Kurdistan Iraq For information on flying into Kurdistan, see page 367.

BY LAND
Turkey to Kurdistan Iraq For information about overland entry through Turkey, see pages 367–8.

Iran to Iraq Northeast of Baghdad runs the route through Diyala Province to the main International Border Post of Khorasan and the Iranian border. It is approximately 90km and along the way there are some patches of good road. For further information on this border crossing, see page 173.

Jordan to Iraq The western border with Jordan is open between Karamal on the Jordanian side and Tarabil on the Iraqi side. This border is a very important one for Iraq and consequently it is closely supervised. For further information, see page 181. At the time of writing, the Iraqi side of this border is controlled by ISIS. It is not recommended that any foreigner attempts to cross here.

Syria to Iraq There are two border crossings between Iraq and Syria, one between Qusaybah on the Iraqi side and Abu Kamal on the Syrian side and the other between Al Walid on the Iraqi side and Tanf on the Syrian side. Both are currently closed (see page 181 for more details).

BY BUS There are direct bus routes into Kurdistan Iraq from Turkey. The journey between Erbil and Diyabakir takes 10–15 hours and between Erbil and Istanbul takes 36–48 hours so flying is definitely a quicker option. Cizre Nuh Buses (m *0750*

340 4773) run every day from Istanbul to Erbil via Silopi, Diyabakir and other cities in between. Can Diyabakir Buses (m *0750 895 6217/18/19*) also run daily services from Istanbul via Diyabakir. There are at least two other Turkish companies running buses from cities in Europe to Erbil via Turkey: Best Van runs a route from Istanbul to Erbil via Adana, Aksaray, Ankara and Diyabakir and the Federal Company (m *066 224 6999*; e *federal_col@yahoo.com*) who run daily services from Istanbul to Erbil. Arrival times depend on border formalities (around 2 hours from Turkey to Iraq and 5–8 hours back to Turkey). Within Iraq itself, it is possible to travel by bus, but many are old and poorly maintained and are often involved in accidents. Services are irregular and frequently change routes. Bus tickets are pre-purchased at kiosks which are not always easy to identify. Travellers are advised to exercise caution when travelling to and from Baghdad by bus as, despite the good road networks, buses and bus stations are frequent targets of suicide bombings, and suicide bombers have been known to jump on to moving vehicles and blow themselves up.

BY RAIL First mooted in 1914, the international service between Baghdad and Istanbul (and beyond) has a long, chequered history with many interruptions. The latest attempts to resume the service in 2010 were briefly successful, but it has now closed again due to the civil war and insurgency in Syria.

HEALTH *with Dr Felicity Nicholson*

BEFORE YOU GO
Travel insurance As the Foreign and Commonwealth Office currently advises against travel to much of Iraq, you are unlikely to be able to purchase comprehensive medical insurance. However, comprehensive travel insurance is generally available for travel to Kurdistan Iraq as the British Foreign and Commonwealth Office (FCO) no longer advises against travel to this region of Iraq, and it may be possible to arrange more limited cover for the rest of the country, subject to exemptions and hefty premiums. The situation is constantly changing, however, so the best advice is to make enquiries with several companies just prior to departure. Whatever cover you arrange, always leave a copy of your policy document at home with someone you trust and keep a copy of the policy number and the emergency contact number on you at all times.

Vaccinations It is advisable to be up to date with all primary immunisations including **tetanus**, **diphtheria** and **polio** – an all-in-one vaccine (revaxis) lasts for 10 years. Vaccinations against **hepatitis A** and **typhoid** are also recommended for visitors to Iraq.

Hepatitis A vaccine (eg Havrix, monodose or avaxim) comprises two injections given about a year apart. The course costs about £100, but may be available on the NHS; it protects for 25 years and can be administered even close to the time of departure. The newer, injectable typhoid vaccines (eg Typhim Vi) last for 3 years and are about 85% effective. Oral capsules (Vivotif) may also be available for those aged six and over. Three capsules over 5 days lasts for approximately 3 years but may be less effective than the injectable forms as their efficacy depends on how well they are absorbed.

Yellow fever vaccine is *required* for all travellers aged 6 months and over arriving from a yellow-fever-infected country in sub-Saharan Africa or South America but is not recommended or required otherwise. **Cholera** vaccine is not generally recommended, even though cholera occurs in Iraq, because most travellers are at low risk of infection.

Hepatitis B vaccination should be considered for longer trips (a month or more), and definitely for those working with children or in situations where contact with blood is likely. Three injections are needed for the best protection and can be given over a 3-week period if time is short for those aged 16 or over. Longer schedules give more sustained protection and are therefore preferred if time allows. Hepatitis A vaccine can also be given as a combination with hepatitis B as 'Twinrix', though two doses are needed at least 7 days apart to be effective for the hepatitis A component, and three doses are needed for the hepatitis B. Again this rapid schedule is only suitable for those aged 16 or over.

All travellers to Iraq should make sure they are fully immunised against **measles**.

Vaccinations for rabies are advised for everyone, but are especially important for travellers visiting more remote areas, especially if you will be more than 24 hours away from medical help and definitely if you will be working with animals.

Visit your doctor or a recognised travel clinic (see below) around 8 weeks before you leave.

As on any trip, a small medical kit is useful. Consider some or all of the following:

- A good drying antiseptic, eg iodine or potassium permanganate (don't take antiseptic cream)
- A few small dressings (Band-Aids)
- Sun cream
- Insect repellent; impregnated bed-net or permethirin spray
- Paracetamol or ibuprofen
- Antifungal cream (eg Canestan)
- Ciprofloxacin or norfloxacin, for severe diarrhoea
- Tinidazole for giardia or amoebic dysentery (see below for regime)
- Antibiotic eye drops, for sore, 'gritty', stuck-together eyes (conjunctivitis)
- A pair of fine-pointed tweezers (to remove thorns, splinters, etc)
- Alcohol-based hand-rub or bar of soap in plastic box
- Condoms or Femidoms

The risk of malaria is present from May to November in the northern areas of Duhok, Erbil and Suleimaniya provinces. However, for most travellers the risk is considered to be too low to need to take antimalarials. Precautions against mosquitoes are strongly advised.

There have been several outbreaks of **leishmaniasis** reported in the south of Iraq in recent years. Leishmaniasis is a chronic parasitic infection transmitted by the bites of sandflies. Insect repellents and cover-up clothing can help to prevent sandfly bites and permethrin-containing compounds should be applied to clothing, shoes and bed nets. Permethrin-treated clothing appears to have little toxicity, but for those who prefer a more natural approach then repellents containing citronella and eucalyptus oil can be used instead although they are not considered as effective. If sleeping outdoors use a bed net, which is impregnated with an insecticide such as permethrin. The edges of the net should be tucked in under the mattress. The mesh density should be at least 156 per square inch and preferably more to eliminate sand flies which are smaller than mosquitoes.

As in Western Europe, there is a danger of **rabies**. All mammals can carry rabies, though dogs are the most likely culprits. Few dogs in Iraq are kept as pets, so they are not domesticated in the same way as in Europe or North America. In particular, avoid sheepdogs as they are trained to see off unwelcome guests. Stand still and if necessary make as if you are throwing a stone in their direction, shouting angrily. Everyone should consider having a course of rabies shots before departure as treatment may not always be available in Iraq, requiring you then to evacuate. Ideally three doses of vaccine should be given over 4 weeks, so careful planning before your trip is required. Rabies is passed on to humans through a bite, scratch or a lick of an open wound. You must always assume any animal is rabid as they can look perfectly healthy, and seek medical help as soon as possible. Meanwhile scrub the wound with soap under a running tap or while pouring water from a jug for a good 15 minutes. Then pour on a strong iodine or alcohol solution of gin, whisky or rum. This helps stop the rabies virus entering the body and will guard against wound infections, including tetanus. If you think you have been exposed to rabies then seek medical help as soon as possible to obtain the relevant post-exposure prophylaxis. Those who have not been immunised will need a blood product called Rabies Immunoglobulin (RIG) injected around the wound and four to five doses of rabies vaccine given over 28–30 days. RIG is hugely expensive and is very hard to come by – another reason why pre-exposure vaccination should be encouraged as if you have had the full pre-exposure course you will not need the RIG and should need only two further doses of vaccine given 3 days apart following the exposure. And remember that, if you do contract rabies, mortality is 100% and death from rabies is probably one of the worst ways to go.

TRAVEL CLINICS AND HEALTH INFORMATION A full list of current travel clinic websites worldwide is available on www.istm.org. For other journey preparation information, consult www.nathnac.org/ds/map_world.aspx (UK) or http://wwwnc.

TREATING TRAVELLERS' DIARRHOEA   *Dr Jane Wilson-Howarth*

It is dehydration that makes you feel awful during a bout of diarrhoea and the most important part of treatment is drinking lots of clear fluids. Sachets of oral rehydration salts give the perfect biochemical mix to replace all that is pouring out of your bottom but other recipes taste nicer. Any dilute mixture of sugar and salt in water will do you good: try cola or orange squash with a three-finger pinch of salt added to each glass (if you are salt-depleted you won't taste the salt). Otherwise make a solution of a four-finger scoop of sugar with a three-finger pinch of salt in a 500ml glass. Or add eight level teaspoons of sugar (18g) and one level teaspoon of salt (3g) to 1 litre (five cups) of safe water. A squeeze of lemon or orange juice improves the taste and adds potassium, which is also lost in diarrhoea. Drink two large glasses after every bowel action and more if you are thirsty. These solutions are still absorbed well if you are vomiting, but you will need sip it rather than drink it down. If you are not eating you need to drink 3 litres a day plus whatever is pouring into the toilet. If you feel like eating, take a bland, high carbohydrate diet. Heavy greasy foods will probably give you cramps.

If the diarrhoea is bad, or you are passing blood or slime, or you have a fever, you will probably need antibiotics in addition to fluid replacement. A dose of norfloxacin or ciprofloxacin repeated twice a day until better may be appropriate (if you are planning to take an antibiotic with you, note that both norfloxacin and ciprofloxacin are available only on prescription in the UK). If the diarrhoea is greasy and bulky and is accompanied by sulphurous (eggy) burps, one likely cause is giardia. This is best treated with tinidazole (four x 500mg in one dose, repeated 7 days later if symptoms persist).

LONG-HAUL FLIGHTS, CLOTS AND DVT

Any prolonged immobility including travel by land or air can result in deep vein thrombosis (DVT) with the risk of embolus to the lungs. Certain factors can increase the risk and these include:

- Previous clot or close relative with a history
- People over 40 (increased risk over 80 years)
- Recent major operation or varicose veins surgery
- Cancer
- Heart disease
- Obesity
- Pregnancy
- Hormone therapy
- Heavy smokers
- Severe varicose veins
- People who are very tall (over 6ft/1.8m) or short (under 5ft/1.5m)

A deep vein thrombosis (DVT) causes painful swelling and redness of the calf or sometimes the thigh. It is only dangerous if a clot travels to the lungs (pulmonary embolus). Symptoms of a pulmonary embolus (PE) include chest pain, shortness of breath, and sometimes coughing up small amounts of blood and commonly start three to ten days after a long flight. Anyone who thinks that they might have a DVT needs to see a doctor immediately.

PREVENTION OF DVT
- Keep mobile before and during the flight; move around every couple of hours
- Drink plenty of fluids during the flight
- Avoid taking sleeping pills and excessive tea, coffee and alcohol
- Consider wearing flight socks or support stockings (see www.legshealth.com)

If you think you are at increased risk of a clot, ask your doctor if it is safe to travel.

cdc.gov/travel/ (US). Information about various medications may be found on www.netdoctor.co.uk/travel. All advice found online should be used in conjunction with expert advice received prior to or during travel.

TRAVELLERS' DIARRHOEA Travelling in Iraq carries a fairly high risk of getting a dose of travellers' diarrhoea; perhaps half of all visitors will suffer and the newer you are to exotic travel, the more likely you will be to suffer. By taking precautions against travellers' diarrhoea you will also avoid typhoid, paratyphoid, cholera, hepatitis, dysentery, worms, etc. Travellers' diarrhoea and the other faecal-oral diseases come from getting other peoples' faeces in your mouth. This most often happens from cooks not washing their hands after a trip to the toilet, but even if the restaurant cook does not understand basic hygiene you will be safe if your food has been properly cooked and arrives piping hot. The most important prevention strategy is to wash your hands before eating anything. The maxim to remind you what you can safely eat is:

PEEL IT, BOIL IT, COOK IT OR FORGET IT.

This means that fruit you have washed and peeled yourself, and hot foods, should be safe but raw foods, cold cooked foods, salads, fruit salads which have been prepared by others, ice cream and ice are all risky, and foods kept lukewarm in hotel buffets are often dangerous. That said plenty of travellers and expatriates enjoy fruit and vegetables, so do keep a sense of perspective: food served in a fairly decent hotel in a large town or a place regularly frequented by expatriates is likely to be safe. If you are struck, see box on page 96 for treatment.

In the major cities the water is generally safe for cleaning teeth; however, it is always safer to use bottled water both for drinking and for cleaning your teeth. Opportunities to strip off and sunbathe are obviously severely limited in an Islamic country, but the force of the Iraqi sun is powerful and there is comparatively little shade at a lot of the archaeological sites, so avoid excessive exertion during midday hours and wear a sunhat. Clothing in natural fibres is most comfortable for the hotter months but evening temperatures can drop suddenly, especially in the north, so take a light sweater too.

Take the usual precautions when walking across rough and stony ground, and through shrubbery and vegetation, against snakes, scorpions, etc. If you are entering a ruined building from broad sunlight, make a noise so that any snakes retreat.

MEDICAL FACILITIES Some of the upmarket hotels in the main cities may have doctors or paramedics on call; otherwise, the hotel reception or your embassy can recommend a doctor or dentist. In general, the private clinics in Baghdad provide better care than the public facilities, but at a higher price. Most expatriates go to either Al-Hayat Hospital (52 St, Karada), Al-Rahebat (Karada Inside St, Karada), or Karkh Hospital for Surgery. None of the private hospitals have emergency rooms. In public hospitals medical care is limited and shortages of essential supplies are common.

In Kurdistan local health care is largely funded by the KRG and while services may not quite meet the standards of some thoroughly developed and established systems, care is readily available in all major cities and towns. Private medical treatment is also widely available to foreign nationals, for example medical examinations and lab diagnostics are easily obtainable and require only a small payment of a few thousand IQDs (usually not more than US$5–10). The number for the ambulance service in Kurdistan is ＼122.

Those with serious medical problems should be evacuated to a country with state-of-the art medical facilities.

Pharmacies are numerous in Iraq and even small towns will have at least one or two which are usually well stocked. That said, take adequate supplies of any prescribed drug you need, or at least full details, so the best equivalent can be traced, because Western brands may not be available.

SAFETY

There are parts of Iraq in which it is currently not safe to travel and in all parts of Iraq caution should be exercised by foreigners at all times. At the time of writing the FCO advises against all but essential travel to Iraq (except the Kurdistan Region) and against all travel to the districts of Ramadi and Fallujah in Anbar Province due to reports of clashes between security forces and militants in parts of Anbar, including heavy fighting in Fallujah. For up-to-date security information, go to the FCO website: www.gov.uk/foreign-travel-advice/iraq.

It is necessary for any foreigner travelling in Iraq to understand and be aware of the risks and dangers. These risks and dangers vary across the country. They also depend upon whether you are residing in one place for a short time or travelling around the country. Each of these carries its own risks. Business visitors and academics will have to rely totally on their sponsoring hosts who will be responsible for providing them with their security comprising of armed personnel which accompany each group and carefully planned routes. All hotels with foreign guests will also have in-house security.

Tourist groups should always be accompanied by armed security (in civilian clothing) on provided transport. When visiting areas where there have been recent disturbances, the special police force protection squad will accompany the tourist vehicle. The somewhat complicated liaison procedures between the provinces and resulting time wasted while collecting escorts can be irritating, but at the end of the day it is for your benefit. Each province has its own procedures and ideas of how and when to protect you. Each hotel, each site and each historical and religious building will have its own guards and security. Invariably the accompanying police squads will be cheerful and good company. The downside of all this is that sometimes the perception of danger takes over and you cannot get to where you hoped to go. Also the guards and security people take their duties so seriously that sometimes you can feel unable to move freely at all. However, it is a testament to the thoroughness of the various security organisations that tourists groups have not had any real trouble in the last few years. Tourist schedules are often amended to take account of the latest incidents, and one cannot ask for more than that. Obviously at the moment in Iraq late nights out should be avoided. At certain times of year religious festivals in the Shrine Cities are attended by enormous numbers of people and care needs to be taken in these crowded places. Souk and market visits should also be carefully undertaken and only a certain time be allotted for lingering. After a few days of travelling in this manner the trust grows between everyone and everyone conforms and obeys the obvious rules of behaviour and personal discipline. Towards the end of a tour armed police are hardly noticed, but of course this can also engender complacency and one should guard against this at all times.

The traveller/tourist/business person has to also play their part. Sensible, modest clothing, no expensive jewellery and most importantly good camera discipline. Do not take photographs when asked not to and be aware that at religious sites such as Kerbala and Najaf pilgrims, especially women, do not want large cameras in their faces at times of religious privacy. Your tour guide should inform you at such places what is and is not possible. Try to avoid drawing too much attention to yourself and walk sensibly through crowds. As you will be accompanied by security personnel, crime tends not to be a problem. However, if you feel threatened or extremely uncomfortable in any situation then you must inform your guide and guards and insist on returning to your vehicle or hotel. Your survival instinct is important to you personally and not to be underestimated.

In the unlikely event of a bombing or shooting incident you will have to rely on your security personnel. Their experience and the special training they have undergone teaches them the best practices if caught in such a situation. If alone, then move away as soon as possible, avoiding the crowds in case of secondary bombs, and make your way back to your guards, group or vehicle.

KURDISTAN The security situation in Kurdistan is mostly better than the rest of Iraq. However, it is not advisable to visit areas that are out of the control of the KRG. See pages 368–9 for further information.

THE BABYLONIAN MEDICAL SYSTEM

In Napoleon Bonaparte's 'Memorial de Sainte-Helene' he humorously describes the Babylonian medical system thus: 'It was there that sick persons were exposed outside their front door. Their relatives would sit next to them and stop passers-by to enquire if they had ever had the same illness and, if so, what method they had used to cure it. At least thus, they had the possibility of avoiding those remedies which had proved fatal!'

ALCOHOL In much of Iraq alcohol is strictly forbidden and not available, certainly not in the Shrine Cities (Kerbala, Najaf and Kufa). It is sensible to avoid the few nightclubs and bars that exist for many reasons, mostly the safety factor. See pages 106–7 for further information.

WOMEN TRAVELLERS

As traditional Muslims, Iraqi society is divided along gender lines. Foreign women are often considered 'honorary men' and given the opportunity to share the company of both men and women in a way foreign men cannot. The threat of crime and physical harassment is relatively low and the locals will often go out of their way to help a woman traveller. The vast majority of female travellers to Iraq experience no adverse treatment because of their gender, as long as they dress and behave modestly and respect Islamic dress codes at Shia shrines and in the Holy Cities. It is worth emphasising though that these are highly orthodox religious places and the dress code imposed here can be a shock to Western women, even those who consider themselves regular and experienced travellers to Muslim countries. Dressing modestly here is absolutely essential which means not one strand of hair showing and dark, voluminous clothing revealing nothing more than the face and hands. Even so, do not be surprised to be refused admission to the shrines, or even their forecourts, on a whim. There are numerous airport-style checkpoints to go through even while walking in the streets, those for ladies generally placed to the right-hand side of the street and those for men to the left. You and your bag will be thoroughly searched and you will be 'advised' if your clothing does not cover you sufficiently. On my last visit, so tired did I become of this that I purchased a *niqab*, or full face veil with only a letter box style slit to see through. Even this did not meet with the approval of some of the more zealous custodians! Men, on the other hand, will be considered adequately clad in all areas by merely wearing a long sleeved shirt and full length trousers.

Women travelling alone should take the usual common sense precautions such as travelling with a companion wherever possible; making sure that they are not out alone at night and not behaving in a way likely to draw unnecessary attention to themselves. If you do feel uncomfortable in a particular situation then leave quickly and head for somewhere well populated such as a hotel, café or restaurant.

TRAVELLERS WITH DISABILITIES

Although many of the new shopping malls and some of the newer hotels, especially those being built with foreign investment, are starting to include disabled access, generally speaking Iraq is not terribly well equipped for travellers with disabilities and many of the smaller hotels don't even have European-style toilets or a lift, and you are unlikely to get any help with carrying your bags from the staff. That said, most of the pavements and roads in the major cities are well-paved. The major public transport option, taxis, are rarely able to carry wheelchairs, although as newer vehicles start appearing in the major cities this may change. The Shrine Cities are more able to cope with people with mobility problems, albeit to a low standard, as many pilgrims visit them seeking blessings and cures, and wheelbarrow-style 'carts' can be found in profusion transporting people around the shrines and their environs. If you have a disability and are considering a trip to Iraq, it is advised that you approach a tour operator (see pages 87–9), discuss your individual situation and establish what provisions can be made.

GAY AND LESBIAN TRAVELLERS

Under Saddam Hussein, Iraq did not have a law against homosexuality and that remains the case today. However, as in most Middle Eastern societies, homosexuality is generally not approved of for religious and cultural reasons, leading to it being somewhat of an 'open secret'; everyone knows it happens, but nobody talks about it. If you are travelling in Iraq with a same sex partner you are advised to refrain from public displays of affection (although two men holding hands is seen as perfectly normal and acceptable) and to be circumspect when discussing your relationship with others. Single rooms are quite an alien concept in hotels in Iraq, most rooms have two (or more) beds in them and so no-one raises an eyebrow at a request for same sex sharing of rooms – in fact there is often no alternative! The situation is a little more relaxed in Kurdistan where an acceptance of the open practice of sexual freedom is beginning, albeit in a small way in the younger generation living in the major cities such as Erbil.

TRAVELLING WITH KIDS

Iraq is a child-friendly place as Iraqis are very family oriented. Don't expect to find a lot of things specifically for children in hotels or restaurants, but they will be made welcome in these places never the less. Most restaurants have separate areas for families where the women and children always dine, so your little ones may make new friends as you eat. Protect your children from the heat and sun at exposed sites and make sure they keep drinking; children become dehydrated very quickly, especially if they have had an upset stomach. Hygiene may not be up to your usual standards so bring several packets of baby-wipes and hand sanitiser to be on the safe side. Also be aware that even very young girls may be expected to be fully covered up at the more orthodox religious sites.

WHAT TO TAKE

Iraq is hot and humid almost all year round. In the summer the temperature can reach 50°C. But between November and March it can be cooler and the nights quite cold. Take natural fibres as far as possible, synthetics create your own personal Turkish bath! Shorts for men and low-cut tops or short skirts and dresses for women are not acceptable. Though most of the country is purportedly secular, for women longish skirts and baggy trousers and a top that covers the arms to the elbows at least are appropriate. Leggings should definitely NOT be worn unless covered by a dress or baggy knee-length top. A large (shawl-sized) scarf for women is a must for visiting mosques and religious places, and a small pair of socks to pop on when leaving your shoes at the entrance to a mosque can save the discomfort of trying to walk – hop – over tiles heated by the hot Iraqi sun! Men should pack at least one long-sleeved shirt for visits to mosques, shrines and other religious places. Flip flops are useful for wearing in bathrooms.

Although toiletries are available it is prudent to take shampoo, conditioner, toothpaste, toothbrush, soap (in a container) and some intensive body and face cream or lotion as your skin can get very dry. Don't forget sunscreen and sanitary protection. As Muslim law stipulates washing under running water, bath and basin plugs are not usually provided, so a universal sink plug is also worth having with you. For the same reason, toilet paper is only usually found in the better hotels and restaurants (to be deposited in waste paper bins) so a small pack of toilet paper or wet wipes is a must. Always bring a towel (not all hotel rooms have them and some hotels can't provide them even if you ask).

The voltage in Iraq is 220V. Both UK 3-pronged and European 2-pronged plugs are in use. We advise visitors to take a universal adapter with them. English books are difficult to find in Kurdistan, so if you like reading travel prepared. Always take a compact alarm clock with you for those early morning starts and a torch in case of an unexpected power cut and to find your way after dark in places where the street lighting leaves something to be desired. Spare batteries are also worth taking; batteries are widely available in Iraq but are often of poor quality and run out quickly.

You should also bring a photocopy of your passport information pages (and keep this in a separate place to your passport) and a few spare passport photos.

MONEY

The currency used in Iraq is the Iraqi dinar (IQD). The exchange rate as of 2015 is IQD1,200 = US$1. There are few, if any, ATM machines or credit card facilities in Iraq with the exception of the large top-range international hotels. Cash is the usual method of payment, so ensure you take sufficient dollars or dinars with you for your trip. IQDs cannot be purchased outside the country, but American dollars, euros and pounds sterling can all be changed. If you are bringing currency with you, you will find the US dollar is most widely accepted and you will get a good rate of exchange. Exchange facilities are available at the airports, international hotels and exchange shops in the bazaars. All the shops are competitive and have pretty much the same exchange rates. In an emergency most shopkeepers will exchange a small US dollar note for Iraqi dinars. Most hotels will also exchange money for you, but their rates will not be as competitive.

BUDGETING

Any budget will depend so greatly on how and where you travel that it is almost impossible to give sensible advice in a general travel guide. As a rule, most travellers to Iraq will have pre-booked their trip through a tour operator, which means that they will have a good idea of what the holiday will cost them before they set foot in the country. Although pre-booked packages do vary in terms of what they include, generally they will cover everything except drinks, tips, some meals and personal purchases, gifts and souvenirs.

For the budget traveller Iraq is not one of the cheaper countries in the Middle East, and this is particularly true for Kurdistan. Genuine budget accommodation is thin on the ground. Local food is reasonably priced, and you will get a lot for your money, but hotels and restaurants catering for more international tastes charge accordingly.

BY AIR With an increasing number of **internal flights** to the airports in Kurdistan (Erbil and Suleimaniyah) it is quite possible to fly between Kurdistan and Baghdad. There are also airports at several major cities – Basra, Najaf, Nasiriyah, Kirkuk and Mosul. Internal flights are operated by Iraqi Airways (*www.iraqiairlines.com*), however, it is difficult to get details of internal flights unless you are actually in Iraq, so think of approaching a travel agent to organise flights for you. Internal flights are cheap, and tend to be frequented by locals and religious pilgrims. They are not reliable, though, and tend to be plagued by constant delays, changes and cancellations.

BY ROAD A network of well-paved and signposted highways connects Baghdad with all parts of the country. Smaller roads are not always as well maintained, however, and may only be signed in Arabic, or not at all. Road congestion in the centre of Baghdad is horrendous and you can be stuck in traffic for hours on the shortest of journeys. If you have been invited to Iraq for business or academic reasons then you will need to rely totally on the organisation who invited you for vehicles. Pilgrims will be under the supervision of a travel agent who will supply the necessary transport. Tourists can only travel around Baghdad under the control of the Ministry of Tourism or with the tour company that supplied their visa and therefore they will provide transport.

By bus Most cities in Iraq have a public bus service of one kind or another. Long-distance buses are starting to travel between the major cities, although services are not frequent. See the local city travel agents for details. A new central bus station is under construction in Baghdad, but be aware that both buses and bus stations are frequent targets for bombings, especially those running services to the Shrine Cities in the south. Local buses are predominately for the use of locals: many buses are poorly maintained and are often involved in accidents. Services are irregular; frequently change routes and all the signage on them will probably be in Arabic, causing problems unless you know the route number. Bus tickets are pre-purchased at kiosks which are not always easy to identify. In Baghdad road congestion is horrendous and you can be stuck in traffic for hours on the shortest of journeys which, in the heat of a Baghdad summer, is not a pleasant experience.

By taxi For getting around in, and between, cities, travel by one of the numerous taxis or shared taxis is the safest and most sensible option. Taxis are economical and readily available on most major roads. A ride to or from almost anywhere in the cities normally costs somewhere between IQD3,000 and IQD5,000 and you can get a seat in a shared taxi between any of the major cities for between IQD10,000 and IQD25,000 depending on the distance and petrol prices. For the departure points of these shared taxis ask your hotel or a city taxi driver 'garajee' and the name of the city where you want to go. Taxi drivers tend to have a lot of valuable information about the area and about the country so don't be shy of talking to them.

Street taxis will take you to most places in a city or between towns and rates are negotiable. Make sure your driver knows where you want to go and agree a price beforehand. It is always useful to get a business card or leaflet from your hotel and carry it with you to ensure you can get back there if you encounter language problems. In Kurdistan there are generally two types of taxis, some painted orange and white, others painted light tan. The light tan taxis are driven by government vetted drivers so are considered to be safest. They are usually newer and cleaner as well.

Practical Information GETTING AROUND

4

By car (self-hire) With the exception of Kurdistan, the advice here is simple – do not hire a car. There are some very good reasons why it is not a good idea to try to drive yourself around Iraq.

(1) As well as documents including your passport, visa and *khittab* (official permission document supplied by the Ministry to all tourists), a reasonable command of Arabic will be needed to get through the numerous checkpoints and police barriers on all the highways and roads around Iraq. Unused to seeing foreigners, security personnel are unlikely to know what to do with you, which could result in a long and dangerous (think sitting target) wait at the side of a busy highway before you are turned back.

(2) Although the highways are well signposted, local knowledge is realistically the only option when it comes to finding your way around and between smaller towns, few of which have road signs or even official or uniform names.

(3) Parking: there must be some rules attached to this, but no-one is able to tell you what these are with any certainty.

(4) Rental cars are targeted by insurgents and criminals. If you are hell bent on hiring a car then, although car hire is available in Baghdad, at least take the precaution of renting through the internet and use one of the major international car-rental companies with offices in the Middle East and hire a car which is common in the area you intend travelling in so you won't stand out.

Unlike the rest of Iraq, travel by car in the Kurdistan Region is generally safe. Private cars and drivers are available, but they can often be quite expensive. Ordinary taxi drivers may consent to being hired for a few days, otherwise approach a travel agent. Only experienced drivers should attempt to self-drive hire however, as although the roads are mostly good, Kurdish drivers are not the best. For more information on driving in Kurdistan, see page 370.

By bicycle An adventurous way to travel through Kurdistan, but only for the hardiest bicycle enthusiasts, who are not easily dismayed by local drivers and the often tough terrain, especially in the east. Be very, very aware of where you are and where you are going though and do not venture into areas near the Iranian or Turkish borders. The penalties for crossing these, even inadvertently, do not bear thinking about.

BY RAIL
By train Baghdad Central Station in Damashaq Square is the main Baghdad railway station and the largest in Iraq. For more information about the station and regular services, see pages 132–3.

By metro An overground metro line is planned for Baghdad to relieve traffic congestion and help to accommodate population growth in the capital. For more information on the proposed metro line, see page 134.

MAPS These are best purchased before travelling. Stanfords in London (*www.stanfords.co.uk*) sell maps of Iraq and the surrounding countries. Maps and city plans can be purchased in Iraq's larger cities, but few are in English, and as they are not always easy to decipher, they should be used in conjunction with local maps and your GPS.

ACCOMMODATION

There is no shortage of hotels in Baghdad ranging from 5-star establishments to modest, family-run hotels. Outside of the capital, the choice is more limited, although new hotels, including top-of-the-range ones, are starting to be built in the larger cities, and existing hotels, especially those in the medium- and lower-price bracket, are undergoing refurbishment and renovation. Ultimately this should lead to improved standards and more competitive pricing. You should note that many hotels in Iraq still don't seem to have their own websites and there is scant information generally available about prices.

In Kurdistan accommodation is generally expensive in comparison with equivalent accommodation in Europe and the US, and mid-range and even top-end prices can be paid for what would be classed as budget accommodation in other countries. Backpacker hotels can be found in all cities, but very few advertise internationally on the web or have reliable phone lines. See page 371 for more information on accommodation in Kurdistan.

Outside of cities and towns accommodation is very sparse indeed. Camping is potentially a problem due to security issues and is not recommended unless you are on an organised tour. There are no organised camp sites such as you might find in Europe at the moment, although some are planned.

EATING AND DRINKING

With Iraqi food you get a lot for your money. Roast chicken is tasty and *quzi*, a huge dish of meat (usually lamb) and rice, the exact ingredients of which vary from town to town, is not for the faint-hearted. A large selection of salads and plentiful amounts of bread accompany every meal. Arab hospitality is inseparable from sharing a meal with friends, and to share food together is one of the best and most enjoyable ways for people of two cultures to cross boundaries and to establish a friendship.

Iraqi cuisine has been influenced by the ancient spice routes, when spices were brought to the Middle East from India and Persia more than 3,500 years ago. Poets lauded the creations of Abbasid chefs that included various goat meat dishes and spitted gazelles. Iraqi dishes are extremely varied, ranging from meat and chicken kebabs to *quzi*, traditionally a whole lamb stuffed with rice, almonds, raisins and spices. The Bedouin speciality is sheep's head cooked in an enormous pot. The most famous Iraqi dish is *mazgouf*, redolent of the biblical Tigris fish: as night falls a glittering necklace of lights illuminates the water, fishermen return with their fresh catch to the open air restaurants along the river bank. Split and hung to smoke lightly over a charcoal fire, the fish is laid above the glowing ashes and filled with peppers, spices, onions and tomatoes. Every restaurant and family has its own secret recipe.

Religious festivals are times for feasts. Eid al-Fitr, at the end of Ramadan (the month when Muslims fast from dawn to dusk) is one of the most significant

4

celebrations in the religious calendar when neighbours and friends take elaborate dishes to each other's homes. A spread of food might include tabouleh, crushed bulger wheat with sweet, chopped, broad-leaf parsley. There are also imaginative salads with dressings of fresh lime or lemon, yoghurt and/or oil, again with an abundance of parsley or mint. Iraqis can create magic with aubergines. One dish, which looks misleadingly like thin, fried, crisp slices of aubergine topped with tiny dots of buffalo yoghurt, actually reveals an explosion of subtle flavours: garlic, sesame, sweetened baby peppers and other unidentified, scented excursions. Cooling wafer-sliced cucumber with dill and yoghurt, lamb, beef and chicken (always cooked with an array of vegetables mixed with sweet, thick natural fresh tomato paste) are essential to every great celebration and must be served for honoured guests.

Lavish meals are always served at births, weddings and circumcisions. On Eid al-Adha (the festival of the sacrifice which honours the willingness of Ibrahim to sacrifice his first-born son Ishmael to God whereupon God provided him with a lamb to sacrifice instead) a lamb is roasted and food is offered to the poor.

Kurdish cuisine, which has been influenced by Turkish and Iranian dishes, is rich and varied: see pages 371–2 for a detailed description.

DINING OUT Before urbanisation, a cooked breakfast and dinner were the main meals as people worked in the fields and did not return home for lunch. Today, however, lunch is the main meal, eaten after 14.00 when offices have shut for the day. Meat, lamb or chicken, in the form of kebabs, are nearly always served during the midday and evening meals. The price of a three-course meal in a local city restaurant will cost about US$15–20 per person; however, in one of the better hotels the price will probably be double that.

There are, of course, local variations. For example, the locally caught fresh fish is excellent in the mountain regions. Baghdad is famous for its mazgouf, a flat fish native to the Tigris. Half the pleasure is in watching it being prepared. It is split and roasted in the open air on stakes around a wood fire. Unfortunately, unless properly prepared, it has an overwhelming taste of mud! It is not an inexpensive meal either.

Virtually all the large hotels in Iraq, and many of the medium-sized ones, have restaurants of varying quality. The very best hotels in the major cities have excellent restaurants, with Iraqi food alongside international cuisine. In the cities and most big towns you will find a selection of foreign restaurants, usually Italian, as well as fast-food restaurants and takeaways serving wraps, burgers and pizza. Local restaurants tend to be small and scattered all over the towns and suburbs. It can be difficult to find one with a varied menu, as despite their often elaborate (and badly translated) menus, you will usually find they serve little more than chicken, rice and kebabs, with maybe soup and a side dish of beans or aubergine. Local breads, which vary slightly from town to town, are excellent if freshly baked.

The bazaars are the perfect place to find authentic, local food. Seek recommendations from the locals, taxi drivers or hotel staff.

DRINK Tea is the national Arab hot drink and there are few problems that cannot be solved over a glass of tea. Turkish coffee, which is available in hotels, is also very good. It is advisable not to drink the tap water.

Alcohol is rarely served with meals although it may be available in the bar in certain very upmarket restaurants and hotels (mostly in the cities of Kurdistan such as Erbil, Dohuk and Suleimaniyah), but you are highly unlikely to find it elsewhere and never in the Shrine Cities.

In Baghdad the liquor shops are open again after a short period of closure due to the violence directed against them. Most of these shops are located in the Karada district and along Sadoun Street. The sellers are either Yezidis or Christians. Under Saddam Hussein the rules were tightened up in an effort to prevent drinking in public, and these laws have not subsequently been rescinded. Alcohol is not served in most restaurants or clubs. Do not attempt to bring liquor to any such places however well it is wrapped up or disguised. Alcohol is not served in most hotels and many also forbid alcohol being brought onto the premises. Whenever you purchase alcohol make sure it is well wrapped in a black plastic bag and transfer it to your own bag if possible. If you do take it to your hotel room make sure you keep it out of sight and remove all empty bottles and packaging afterwards, discretely discarding these in municipal bins away from the hotel premises.

PUBLIC HOLIDAYS AND FESTIVALS

There are two main types of holidays, those in the solar calendar and those relating to the lunar calendar (10 days or so less than the solar year and linked to the sighting of the new moon)

EID AL-FITR This three-day festival not only celebrates the end of the month of Ramadan, but also allows Muslims to give thanks to God for the help and strength that he gave them to practise self-control during it. The festival begins when the first sight of the new moon is seen in the sky, and the celebratory atmosphere is increased by everyone wearing new clothes and decorating their homes. There are special religious services and processions through the streets and of course, a special celebratory meal eaten during daytime, the first daytime meal Muslims will have had in a month. Eid is also a time of forgiveness, and making amends.

RAMADAN Month-long Ramadan is not a holiday as such. During Ramadan Muslims are obliged to abstain from all eating, drinking and smoking during daylight hours and even non-Muslims must not be seen in public doing any of these. As a result it is difficult during daylight hours to find restaurants open (except in top-end hotels) and few dentists accept patients (to avoid giving mouth washes). Fasting inevitably means tempers are shorter and little work is achieved. During Ramadan many offices, especially government departments will be minimally staffed and keep erratic and shorter hours. Try to avoid such times and be patient.

EID AL-ADHA The four-day festival of sacrifice, also known as the Greater Eid, is the second most important festival in the Muslim calendar. The festival remembers the prophet Ibrahim's willingness to sacrifice his son when God ordered him to. Muslims who can afford it sacrifice a sheep or goat as a reminder of Ibrahim's obedience and the meat from the sacrificed animal is divided into three parts; the family retains one third of the share; another third is given to relatives, friends and neighbours and the remaining third is given to the poor and needy.

NOWRUZ Kurdish New Year begins on the night of 20 March, the spring equinox and runs for three days. Originally a Zoroastrian festival, it is a celebration of the first day of spring and is a time for wearing new clothes and giving gifts. Visitors to Kurdistan during Nowruz will experience the warmth and fun of a traditional Kurdish celebration. Government offices can be closed for up to a week during this period.

4

ASHURA Shia Muslims use the day to commemorate the martyrdom of Imam Hussain in 680. It is a solemn day when plays re-enacting the martyrdom are staged. Some Shia men seek to emulate the suffering of Hussain by flagellating themselves with chains or cutting their foreheads until blood streams from their bodies. Ashura has been a day of fasting for Sunni Muslims since the days of the early Muslim community. It marks two historical events: the day Noah left the Ark, and the day that Moses was saved from the Egyptians.

PUBLIC HOLIDAYS (2015)

1 January	New Year's Day
3 January*	Milad un Nabi (Birth of the Prophet Mohammad)
	(Celebrated 5 days later for Shia)
6 January	Army Day
9 April	Baghdad Liberation Day
21 March	Nowruz (regional observation Kurdistan)
1 May	Labour Day
18 June*	Ramadan starts (subject to sighting of moon)
14 July	Republic Day
18 July*	Eid al-Fitr (end of Ramadan)
8 August	Ceasefire Day (end of Iran-Iraq War)
23 September*	Eid al-Adha (Feast of Sacrifice)
3 October	National Day
13 October*	Islamic New Year
23 October*	Ashura
25 December	Christmas Day

*The lunar calendar dictates the days of these festivals which change every year

On public holidays ministries and government offices are closed. Businesses may also close. If the holiday falls at the weekend (Friday or Saturday) then the next working day is taken as the holiday.

SHOPPING

All basic requirements (toiletries, batteries, etc) are available and even away from the cities most towns of any size have a pharmacy as well as a reasonable supermarket or general store. The bazaars are the places for great bargains. Traditional metalwork, jewellery, rugs and shishas are among the best buys. Antiques cannot be bought (see box, page 78) and under no circumstances should you try to smuggle antiquities out of Iraq. Almost all traders have electronic calculators which facilitate bargaining for foreigners. Most shops are open daily 09.00–13.00 and 16.00–20.00. They are usually closed on Friday, the weekend, and on public holidays.

ARTS AND CRAFTS Textiles and loomed materials such as *shafs*, *izars*, light carpets, blankets and purses are made in most parts of the country. Baghdad is famous for silk textiles using local raw materials. Erbil, Kirkuk and Nineveh specialise in felt work. Erbil, Nineveh, Dohuk, Kirkuk and Suleimaniyah are also famous for mohair (from the Arabic word *mukhayyar*).

BOOKS Baghdad's famous Mutanabi Street Book Market was ripped apart by a car bomb in 2007. However, a plan to restore the street's historic buildings has been launched and the Shahbandar coffee house has been rebuilt. Poets and writers throughout the world have joined the 'Al-Mutanabi Street Starts Here' project to support their Iraqi counterparts.

CARPETS Compared with Iran, Turkey or Afghanistan, Iraq is disappointing for carpets and rugs. Traditional carpets are very difficult to find and there are few shops with handmade, older rugs and carpets. Attempts are being made to produce carpets in Erbil and there are some interesting local carpets sold on the street corners in Samawah. Huge and thick, with deep, untrimmed pile, they are wonderful to sleep on but impossibly impractical to carry. In every town you will find some carpet dealers, but mostly their stock is imported, Iranian-made carpets.

COPPERWORKS These handicrafts are basically Baghdadi, and Baghdad's Copper Bazaar, which runs alongside the beautiful Al-Mustansiriya College is where pots for everyday and ornamental use are beaten in the traditional manner, is justifiably famous as a popular tourist attraction. Although today the clamour of the coppersmiths is diminished as workshops close and the trade declines, it is still possible to find some wonderful examples of beaten copper antique coffee cups and pots and intricately designed trays dating back 80 to 100 years in the shops. Copperwork can also be found in Kerbala and Basra. The raw material is imported.

POTTERY The main towns known for their pottery include Kirkuk, Dohuk, Amadiya, Baghdad, Anbar, Diyala, Kerbala and Babylon.

WOODWORK A number of artisans work in wood and their pieces are mainly found in Suleimaniyah and Mosul (vases and wooden chandeliers), Dohuk (pipes and cigarette holders) and Baghdad (vases and small wooden boxes with mother-of-pearl inlay).

CERAMICS: WESTERN TECHNIQUES IN AN ARAB CONTEXT

In ancient Iraq an artist would produce a pot, a cup or the image of a god without stopping to think about the nature of creativity. He worked spontaneously. In the 6th millennium BC artists would mould clay into human forms without making a single preliminary sketch. During the Islamic period new values came into prominence. The art of ceramics was influenced by calligraphy and ornamentation.

After a break of several centuries, ceramics became an art form once again. In 1954 the first furnace for the production of ceramics was set up in the Baghdad Institute of Fine Arts. Its foundations were strengthened in 1967 when the Academy of Fine Arts was established. It was later incorporated into Baghdad University.

The country's leading ceramicists have been influenced by rich traditions and Western techniques which have been absorbed into the Arab context. Saad Shakir's work consists of fantastical shapes modelled on plants, shells, fungi and rocks. Abla al Azzawi often abandons the potter's wheel and works with her hands. The late Nuha al Radhi specialised in folkloric themes, while the work of Muqbil al Zawi has a link to the Sumerian past.

David Kanikanian produces vases and other decorative pieces from his workshop in West London's Gallery Tavid. His work is enhanced by the lustre of the glazes in which he specialises.

SOUVENIRS There is little in the way of tourist-type souvenirs on sale, though locally made soap, spices and sugar cones make acceptable and unusual gifts. You'll find shops on Karada Street, Baghdad (see page 141) selling flags, paperweights, painted plates and ornaments featuring famous Iraq monuments such as the spiral minaret at Samarra and the Lion of Babylon. There is also a souvenir shop in the airport selling Iraq T-shirts. Religious souvenirs abound around the Shrines, featuring pictures of imams Ali and Hussain. There is little left in the way of Saddam souvenirs. Postcards can be purchased in Erbil and Baghdad (in Sadoun Street).

MEDIA AND COMMUNICATIONS

Iraq has definitely emerged from the time warp of Saddam's era when mobile phones and satellite television were banned and hardly anyone used the internet. From 1969–2003, the media was severely limited and only one news network, the Iraqi News Agency, which functioned as the government TV channel was permitted. An additional five daily newspapers and four radio stations provided censored information to the Iraqi people. Any other media was barred and banned. Satellite dishes were illegal, and the breaking of any press rules meant imprisonment, torture or death. Many journalists defected as a result and went into hiding during these years. The main opponent to the Iraqi News Agency prior to 2003 was 'Aswat al-Iraq' a news outlet supported by the United States, Turkey, Germany, Russia, Great Britain, China and the UN which gave it traction and respect. After the 2003 war, the laws were revoked and journalists were allowed to report news as they saw it for the first time. Such was their enthusiasm within just a few months over 200 news publications had sprung up, including CNN, Al-Jazeera and dozens of others, and today Iraqis can choose from among hundreds of publications and scores of radio and TV stations.

TV AND RADIO Several large players dominate the market and niche broadcasters provide alternative standpoints, many of which are controlled by political or religious movements. Freedom of expression is protected by the constitution. Iraqis get much of their news from TV; radio listening has declined in tandem with the rise of TV. The Iraqi Media Network (IMN) is a government holding company for outlets including Al-Iraqiya TV and Republic of Iraq Radio. Foreign companies broadcasting in Iraq include the BBC, Paris-based Monte Carlo Doualiya radio, and US-backed Al-Hurra TV, Radio Sawa and Radio Free Iraq. Many channels are available via local relays and the BBC is relayed in Baghdad and Basra. Up to 97% of homes have a satellite dish and there are more than 30 Iraq-facing satellite networks. In the northern autonomous Kurdish enclaves, rival political factions operate their own media. CNN International and BBC World broadcasts are available in most hotels.

INTERNET Iraq's internet usage was the lowest in the region in 2012, with just 2.5 million users (around 8% of the population) according to OpenNet Initiative, with few Iraqis having internet access at home. This situation is changing rapidly however, as internet-enabled smartphones gain popularity, especially among younger Iraqis. Virtually all hotels offer internet access, usually high speed and free, and this is how the majority of visitors get on line. Most modern hotels also have conference facilities containing well-equipped business centres. Internet cafés are plentiful and can be found in the main shopping and bazaar areas of the cities as well as in some smaller towns.

TELEPHONE More than 80% of Iraqis have a mobile phone. This is hardly surprising given that the Baghdad telephone exchange was destroyed during the first few days of the First Gulf War. Rebuilt by the French in 2003, it was subsequently destroyed again and no attempt has been made at further reconstruction. The latest handsets can be bought in the numerous phone shops in every town and city in Iraq. Top up vouchers are widely available in local shops for US$10, US$20 and US$50. Iraqi mobile phone tariffs are very cheap and one of the most economical ways to keep in touch while travelling is to purchase a local SIM. The only problem with all this is that people and businesses frequently change their phone numbers.

Dialling codes When dialling a mobile number in Iraq you should remove the leading 0 of the number and prefix it with +964. Should you wish to make a telephone call to a land line number in Iraq use the international prefix 00 or 011 in place of + along with the country code for Iraq which is 964 and then the area code (see individual chapter headings for area codes) plus the local number you are calling. For calls within Iraq just use the area code and the plus the landline number.

NEWSPAPERS Most newspapers and magazines that you will see for sale in Iraq are in Arabic. Only a very limited range of international papers are available at the upmarket hotels and sometimes news magazines such as *Time* and *Newsweek* are available. There are a growing number of news sites on line however, such as *Al Mada*, an Arabic language newspaper published in Iraq; *Al Mashriq*, an Iraqi newspaper which is also distributed to other Arabic countries and *Al Sabah Al Jadid*, an Arabic-language newspaper, contains articles about politics, culture, sports, economic affairs, science and technology. Iraqi News (*www.iraqinews.com*) is the news site of an English-language newspaper covering a wide range of topics including politics, business, social issues, security, culture, entertainment and sports, human rights and more. The *Kurdish Globe* (*www.kurdishglobe.net*) is English-language newspaper published in Erbil focusing on national news, Middle East news, business, sports, world news, culture, entertainment and Iraqi culture and is distributed in Dohuk, Suleimaniyah, Kirkuk, Erbil and other Kurdish localities. *Al-Zaman* is a popular English daily newspaper based and produced in London, although it is published in Baghdad and Basra. It has an English news site (*www.azzam.co./english/*).

POST Postal services are available in the major cities and towns, although they are not well used. Most Iraqis who use the postal service do so by means of a post office box at their local post office. Iraqi postage stamps are very collectable.

4

BUSINESS

The Iraqi government is actively seeking foreign business investment, particularly in oil production. Since 2010 foreign oil companies such as BP, Exxon Mobil, Royal Dutch Shell and Eni have signed service contracts with Baghdad and are in business in the oil fields of Rumalia, West Qurna-1 and Zubair. The country needs money to develop, and there are undoubtedly large profits to be made by some, but the current combination of inefficiency, virtually impenetrable bureaucracy, nepotism and endemic corruption is a significant deterrent. In 2013 Doing Business (*www.doingbusiness.org*) ranked Iraq as 151 out of 189 economies worldwide for ease of doing business.

The security situation in Iraq is a barrier to business development at the present time. In areas such as the Kurdistan Region, where the situation is stable and which has been virtually free from terrorist attacks and bombings for a number of years, this has led to business investment in cities such as Erbil, which has rapidly become one of the fastest growing in the Middle East. It is modernising and developing as it seeks to emulate Dubai with its ability to attract wealth, patronage and more power. The argument against investment in other parts of Iraq is that the political situation may get worse before it gets better. Although foreign investors showed their optimism by spending US$56 billion in Iraq in 2011 (a 40% increase on 2010) Iraq's National Investment Commission reported that foreign investment dropped significantly after this in advance of the parliamentary elections in 2014 and the unrest ahead of it which led to the worst levels of violence the country had seen since 2008. Despite the violence and uncertainty, Iraq is slowly emerging as a country of opportunities to invest in, and fund managers and bankers are venturing back in to the country, attracted by oil wealth and a surprisingly upbeat outlook for national GDP growth.

Many Iraqi entrepreneurs are keen to develop business links overseas, especially with Europe and the US, although apart from the major international oil and chemical companies, it is a bold entrepreneur who invests in Iraq's industry and other commercial activities at this time! There are many ways of hedging the risks: learning the language, finding the right Iraqi partner and investing not just your money but your time also, making sure of course that you are fully conversant with Iraqi law and legal procedures.

BUYING A PROPERTY

Most countries in the Middle East restrict ownership of property by foreigners and up until now the government of Iraq has retained these traditional prohibitions. Although it permits long-term leases for foreigners, ownership of real property is not permitted. The Kurdistan Regional Government, through its regional investment law, does allow ownership of real property within the three northern provinces that make up the Kurdistan Region. The central government is currently considering a similar change in the law.

CULTURAL ETIQUETTE

Iraqis consider family and honour to be of paramount importance. The extended family is both a political and social force. Families hold their members responsible for their conduct, since any wrongdoing brings shame to the entire family. Loyalty to the family comes before other social relationships, even business. Nepotism is not viewed negatively; in such a culture it naturally makes more sense to offer jobs to family as they are trusted. In rural areas it is common for large extended families to live in the same house, compound or village. In urban areas, although families do not necessarily live in the same house, they generally live in the same street or district at least.

GREETINGS The most common greeting in Iraq is the handshake coupled with eye contact and a smile. The standard Arabic/Islamic greeting is '*salaam alaikum*' (peace be with you), to which the response is '*wa alaikum asalaam*' (and peace be with you). Good friends of the same sex may greet each other with a handshake and a kiss on each cheek, starting with the right. Expect to be introduced to each person individually at a small social function. At a large function, both sexes may introduce themselves.

GIFT GIVING If you are invited to someone's home you should take a small gift for your host. A souvenir item from your home country would be most acceptable, but if you have nothing suitable then a box of chocolates, pastries or biscuits would be appropriate. A basket of fruit may also be appreciated. Flowers are being given more and more these days, but only to a woman. If a man must give a gift to a woman, he should say that it is from his wife, mother, sister, or some other female relative. A small gift for children of the family would be a nice touch. You should present your gift with both hands. Gifts are generally not opened when received.

VISITING The culture of hospitality means Iraqis like to invite people to their homes. If you are invited to visit someone's home you should dress conservatively and smartly. Before entering you should check to see if you should remove shoes at the door. In many households you will find that men and women are entertained separately, with the women of the household sitting apart from the men along with the children. Foreign women however, are usually able participate in both male and female social groupings and so can get to know all members of the family. Needless to say, a Western man should always remain respectfully distant from Iraqi women and, for example, not attempt to shake hands, touch her or sit close to her.

Iraqi table manners are relatively formal. If the meal is on the floor, sit cross-legged or kneel on one knee. Never let your feet touch the food mat. It is good manners to use the right hand for eating and drinking, and certainly if taking food from a communal dish by hand, although you will find many Iraqis in these days of knives and forks now disregard this tradition. It is considered polite to leave some food on your plate when you have finished eating. Do not discuss business while eating.

BUSINESS ETIQUETTE Iraqi business people are relatively formal in their business dealings. Again the common greeting is '*salaam alaikum*' (peace be with you), to which you should respond '*wa alaikum asalaam*' (and peace be with you). The most common business greeting is the handshake with direct eye contact. Handshakes can be rather prolonged; try not to be the first person to remove your hand. Men should wait to see if a woman extends her hand. Business cards are always given out, so it would be a nice touch to have one side of your card translated into Arabic. The need to save face and protect honour means that showing emotions is seen negatively, and displays of anger are a serious no-no. If you must show disapproval it is always best to do so one-to-one, quietly and with tact. Always keep your word and do not make a promise unless you can keep it. If you want to show a commitment to something, but do not want to make a cast-iron assurance, then use vague terms such as 'I will do my best,' 'We will see,' or the local term 'Inshallah' (God willing). Iraqi business people are not afraid of asking blunt and probing questions. These may be about you, your company and its intentions.

VISITING RELIGIOUS BUILDINGS Mosques, shrines and other holy places often have their own sets of rules and you should try to observe these. If in doubt it is always better to ask rather than being disrespectful, even if unintentionally. Requirements vary, but generally will include removing your shoes, covering your head (especially women) and wearing modest clothing. Sometimes there are separate entrances for men and women, or only one gender or members of a particular religion will be allowed to enter certain places at certain times. Whatever your personal opinion you should be respectful of this.

4

DISPLAYS OF AFFECTION Public displays of affection between members of the opposite sex (even if they are married) are generally unacceptable.

TRAVELLING POSITIVELY

It's good to give something back when you travel, although the concept of charity differs in each culture and both Iraqi officials and individuals will be affronted by any actions they perceive as patronising and interventionist. One of the best ways of travelling positively is to tell your family and friends about your trip to Iraq and disseminate accurate information about the country rather than the usual negative, one-dimensional impression favoured by the press. And while you are on your travels, redistributing some of your hard-earned cash in the bazaars and tea-houses of Iraq will improve the lot of everyone. Simply by coming and spending your money here you are helping.

There are many local and international charities working in Iraq. These include:

INTERNATIONAL RESCUE COMMITTEE (www.rescue-uk.org) The IRC rebuilds schools damaged by war and trains teachers, reaching close to 50,000 students at 130 Iraqi schools. They provide free legal assistance to thousands of Iraqi returnees and displaced persons, as well as to the growing Syrian refugee population. They help displaced community leaders develop their skills in identifying and addressing essential community needs. They promote healthy families and women's well-

NATURE IRAQ (WWW.NATUREIRAQ.ORG)

The Mesopotamian Marshes are the largest wetland ecosystem in the Middle East and support a number of species of global conservation concern. The Marshes hold the only breeding population of the globally endangered Basra reed warbler and the world's highest wintering numbers of the threatened marbled duck. The Marshes are under threat from the building of huge dams in Turkey on the Tigris and Euphrates, the rivers that feed and nourish a wetland complex so important for biodiversity as well as being the homelands of the Marsh Arabs, made famous by the writings of Wilfred Thesiger.

Nature Iraq is actively campaigning to influence the building and use of these giant structures that can have such a devastating effect for the lives of people and wildlife. Another major Nature Iraq activity has been surveying more than 220 sites throughout Iraq to identify the country's key areas for biodiversity. Often in difficult and very dangerous circumstances these surveys by young Nature Iraq biologists have spanned seven years, summer and winter, and are the first step towards establishing a network of protected areas. This is wonderful conservation work from a country where the daily news is rarely uplifting. They have already produced their own bird field guide – in Arabic – the first Middle East country to do so.

But it's not just conservation in Iraq that is Nature Iraq's motivation. It may surprise many that this NGO has just made a donation of US$1,000 to the Norfolk Wildlife Trust's £1m Appeal to purchase 57ha of land next to Cley Marshes on England's north Norfolk coast. Nature Iraq has received much help from colleagues in the UK, especially through BirdLife International, and made this donation as an act of global support for the protection of marshes everywhere.

being by providing health, legal and counselling services. They help displaced young people find work and become self-sufficient through savings and credit associations and job training. The IRC ensures that displaced school children have access to clean water and proper hygiene facilities. At the Domiz camp in northern Iraq, the IRC provides camp management and a safe space for women. They are also building a secondary school so refugee children can have an education. At Al-Qaim camp, near the border with Syria, the IRC is providing free legal assistance, mobilising community groups and helping survivors of sexual violence.

AMERICARES (www.americares.org) The AmeriCares organisation remains dedicated to providing medicines and medical supplies to Iraqi civilians impacted by the war. It regularly sends medical assistance and other humanitarian aid with particular focus on internally displaced persons and those left physically impaired as a result of the wars and internal conflict.

WARCHILD (www.warchild.org.uk) Conflict and violence in Iraq has hit the education sector hard. Teachers have very little motivation as their salaries are not sufficient to provide for their families and teaching resources are not available. As a result, even those children able to attend school are not receiving a high standard of education. To help overcome this, War Child trains teachers in subject knowledge, teaching methodologies and child protection. They advocate girls' education, encouraging local adults to discuss the importance of teaching girls and work with local religious leaders enlisting their help in spreading messages about children's rights and protection. They make sure children in prisons (many locked up for petty crimes and held in squalid conditions often alongside adults) are kept as safe as possible and given the chance to get an education or vocational training. They also train social workers and lawyers to protect these children's rights and help them reintegrate with their families and communities when they are released.

THE MARSH ARABS HERITAGE PROJECT (www.amarfoundation.org) The AMAR International Charitable Foundation (AMAR ICF) is a British charity that in 2012 launched The Southern Mesopotamian Marshlands: Reclaiming the Heritage of a Civilisation, an initiative designed to help rebuild the heritage of the Marsh Arab people after decades of neglect, violent military and environmental persecution and the virtual destruction of their unique way of life. Finding that many of today's Marsh Arabs had very limited knowledge of their exceptional culture and its outstanding contribution to civilisation, the project gave more than 5,000 Marsh Arab schoolchildren and adults the opportunity to learn about and reclaim this extraordinary heritage. Simultaneously, the project aimed to build a strong new public awareness of the Marsh Arab people, increasing local, national and international recognition and respect for them by charting the development of their culture and environment over time.

NOWZAD (www.nowzad.com) A UK-based charity was set up by former Royal Marine Pen Farthing in 2007 to relieve the suffering of stray and abandoned dogs, cats and other animals in Afghanistan and Iraq. While serving in Nowzad in Helmand Province in 2006, he broke up an organised dog fight, befriending one of the dogs and naming it after the town. After the tough challenge of getting the charity started he began a second career, helping other soldiers get 'their' dogs (and later cats) home, including those from Iraq. Nowzad has re-homed over 650 dogs

Dashty arrived at the **Nowzad** shelter in 2011 with his mother and siblings. His mother, Momma Dog, and his sister Pippa went on to America and Dashty and his last brother, Jack, remained at the shelter. In mid-2012 the shelter received an email from the wife of a former soldier who had served in Iraq and who was looking to adopt a dog in honour of the dog he had to leave behind in Iraq. After several months of questions going back and forth they identified Dashty as the perfect dog for the soldier and his wife. The funds were raised quickly once a decision had been made and Dashty went to his new home in America in December 2012 where he is now living the American dream.

Winston from Iraq made the long journey home and into quarantine where he spent 6 months before being released with a full bill of health to join 'his' family. Winston is looking pretty chunky these days and he recently got to meet up with one of the soldiers who first rescued him and a fine time was had by all.

Sandbag and Dirtbag are two very famous Iraqi rescues who have settled very well into their new home. They were both enrolled in a local dog training group for the Kennel Club's Good Citizens Bronze Award, which is a 10-week course for dogs and handlers. They attended to give them the chance to associate with other dogs that weren't a threat to them, and it was very interesting to see how they interacted with other dogs including pugs, bull terriers and a huge bull mastiff. The course involved exercises such as sit and stay for 1 minute, walk to heel and recall. The boys thoroughly enjoyed the sessions and went on to achieve their Bronze awards. They have now enrolled on the Silver Award course. A few weeks after this they went to a local dog show arranged by Guide Dogs for the Blind and Sandbag was entered for the class 'Best Rescue'. The judge was wiping away tears as she announced 'there can only be one winner!' and Sandbag was awarded a rosette.

to soldiers around the world, from the US and UK to Australia, Canada and even Africa, with more going to local homes. The charity also works to promote animal welfare and responsible pet ownership and operates the only official animal shelter in Afghanistan as well as a small clinic managed by Briton Louise Hastie from Wolverhampton, who first started re-homing animals when she worked in Iraq as a contractor. As the troops started to leave Iraq, Nowzad handed over rescues from Iraq to the charity Operation Baghdad Pups, allowing them to fully concentrate on building the first ever official animal shelter in Afghanistan. But having recently joined forces with American Dog Rescue they now hope to fulfil their dream of supporting both Iraq and Afghanistan with a network of shelters whether coalition troops are in the country or not.

WORLD WIDE WELFARE (www.worldwidewelfare.org) This organisation provides humanitarian assistance such as food and non-food items, sustainable cash assistance, health care and education to orphans and their families. In Iraq the number of orphans is more than 5 million, the number of widows is more than a million and the number of people with disabilities exceeds a million.

Part Two

BETWEEN THE TWO RIVERS

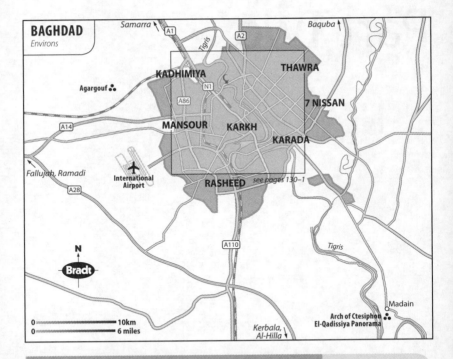

BAGHDAD SECTARIAN DIVISION AND SECURITY

Baghdad has always had ethnic communities informally grouped around religious centres: Shia and Sunni mostly, but also with a Christian presence. Before 1950 there was a large, influential Jewish population in Bataween district and near Baghdad's Great Synagogue. At the time communities were mixed and lived in relative harmony, although the Jewish population left around 1950 (see page 122). However, after the 2003 war and the invasion by the Coalition, Baghdad saw Shia and Sunni militias taking control of the political void after the fall of Saddam. Subsequently, the city has grouped itself into ethnically cleansed communities, predominantly Shia and Sunni, with the Shia being the majority. As this book goes to print, the influx of refugees fleeing from ISIS attacks, Christians and Muslims alike, has swelled the ethnic divisions. The 2014 invasion of ISIS and the Iraqi army debacle have put new life into the Shia militia, who now control some check points in the city.

SECURITY Baghdad, on the whole, has a good security system; there are police, army or militia check points on every major road and junction. Tourists should always have their documents with them and *never* take photographs at these points. The major buildings, religious places of worship and historical sites are guarded and often have blast walls around them. All the hotels are protected, mostly by their own security personnel. However, as we know only too well from our own experience, it is not possible to totally avoid the effects of urban attacks. When such an attack has taken place, the city can get locked down and travel through the streets becomes a slow process. Baghdadis have learnt to cope and are pragmatic about their situation at such times. Life goes on.

5

Baghdad and Environs

Telephone code 1

The story of the City of Peace is largely the story of continuous war. Where there is not war, there is pestilence, famine and civil disturbance. Such is the paradox which cynical history has written across the high aims implied in the name bestowed upon the city by her founder. Richard Coke writes in *Baghdad: The City of Peace* (1927) that 'In Iraq all major roads lead to the capital, Baghdad, a city that has risen like a phoenix from the ashes many times after being devastated by floods, fires and brutal conquerors. Despite its ever-changing fortunes, the city has seldom lost its importance as a commercial, communications and cultural centre.'

Located in the heart of the historic Tigris–Euphrates valley, Baghdad began life as a series of pre-Islamic settlements. In the 8th century it was transformed into the capital of the Muslim world and remained a cultural metropolis for centuries. In 1258, after its destruction by Mongol invaders, the Persians and the Turks vied for control of the city, which was finally incorporated into the Ottoman Empire in 1638 as the vilayet of Baghdad, an important provincial centre. In 1932 it became the capital of modern Iraq.

HISTORY

The banks of the Tigris, where the land was fertile and the river constituted an important trade route, were a popular site for settlements long before AD770 when the Abbasid Caliph Abu Jafar al Mansour created the round 'wagon-wheel' city, the setting of the tales of *The Thousand and One Nights*. Throughout the centuries, settlements with names similar to Baghdad were located on the site of the present-day Iraqi capital. A legal document dating back to 1800BC, the time of Hammurabi, mentions a city called Bagdadu. Archaeologists have recovered boundary stones from a city known as Pilari in the district of Bagdadi during the reign of the Assyrian king Nazimaruttas (1341–1316BC). A boundary stone from the reign of the Babylonian king Marduk-Apaliddin (1208–1195BC) mentions Baghdad, which was said to be an Armenian settlement in the 8th century BC. Baghdad has had more than 20 names, including the City of Peace (Madinat Al-Salam), the House of Peace (Dar Al-Salam), the Dome of Islam (Qubbat Al-Islam) and the Mother of Iraq (Umm Al-Iraq).

During the reign of the Abbasid caliphs (AD750–1258) Baghdad became the capital of the Muslim Empire. The Abbasids, who overthrew the Damascus-based Umayyad Dynasty, naturally wanted the centre of their empire to be close to their power base. Persian civil servants played an important part in the running of the caliphate. A permanent civil service was created, headed by a Minister of State, known as the *wazir*. Even though the Abbasids emphasised the equality of all the Muslim subjects of the empire, the caliph tended to be a remote, unapproachable figure.

Like the Mesopotamian myths, many of the stories from *The Thousand and One Nights* describe the soul's journey through life. The tales are a wonderful medley of magical stories narrated by the beautiful young Scheherazade, who is telling them to save her own life. Having suffered betrayal by a previous wife, brutal King Shahryar partly through vengeance and partly to prevent the same thing happening again, slew all his subsequent wives shortly after marrying them. But Scheherazade stayed alive by keeping him occupied for a thousand and one nights with a series of fascinating and amusing tales of magical transformations, genies and wishes, terror and passion. These enchanting tales, which include *The Seven Voyages of Sinbad the Sailor, Ali Baba and the Forty Thieves* and *Aladdin and the Magic Lamp*, as well as less well-known tales such as *Prince Behram and the Princess al Datma*, an early version of Shakespeare's *The Taming of the Shrew*, became popular in 9th-century Baghdad, the capital of the Abbasid Empire, when they were translated from Indian languages and Persian into Arabic. Their subsequent translation into French and other European languages guaranteed their universal popularity. During the 19th century, Sir Richard Burton's unexpurgated translation of *The Thousand and One Nights* containing all the sensuality and lushness of the original was printed as private editions for subscribers only, as in Britain the exotic, erotic and bawdy content of many of the stories offended prudish Victorian society.

THE FOUNDER OF BAGHDAD In *The Monument*, Samir al Khalil describes the building of Baghdad thus: the city's founder, the Abbasid caliph Abu Ja'far al Mansour, fancied himself an architect. He imagined the new seat of government as an elaborately walled fortress perfectly circular in shape. A splendiferous royal palace, to which was attached a great mosque, was placed in the exact geometrical centre. The rest of the city radiated outwards like the segments of an orange. Given the singular geometry of this vision, the only critical decision concerned the dimensions of the circumference. It seems the caliph did not trust drawings. Nonetheless, he had to judge the rightness of his decision correctly before construction could begin. So he had his labourers dig a shallow trench into the soil following the outline of the intended circle. Into this a mixture of oil and cotton seeds was placed and set ablaze. The caliph watched the magnificent spectacle from a spot overlooking the great River Tigris, which had seen so many civilisations born of its fertility come and go, pronounced himself satisfied, and ordered construction of the massive outer ring's walls to begin.

The *Encyclopaedia of Islam* points out that the site was chosen for military, economic and climatic reasons. The plain was fertile and could be cultivated. It was a meeting place of caravan routes, and monthly fairs were held there, ensuring provisions would be plentiful for the army and the residents. It was in the middle of Mesopotamia and enjoyed a temperate and healthy climate, without malarial mosquitoes.

Caliph Mansour referred to his settlement on the west bank of the Tigris as 'City of Peace' (Madinat Al-Salam), despite its fortress-like appearance, which gave it the air of a city ready for war. The design was in fact based on a circular Roman military camp with four gates equidistant from each other: Al-Basra (south), Al-Kufa (north), Damascus (west) and Khorasan (east) led to four main roads that linked the city centre with the regions outside. It was surrounded by a deep ditch followed by the first wall. A space of 57m was left empty for defence purposes.

Then came another brick wall with 28 great towers and a space of 170m where the caliph's loyal subjects built their houses. Another wall separated the caliph's palace, with its famous green dome, and the mosque. The mosque's area was a quarter of that of the palace, but it was gradually expanded because of the increasing number of worshippers. The ceiling of the mosque was decorated with golden crescents and its walls were inlaid with green mosaics surrounded by teak wood. It is said that Caliph Mansour employed 100,000 workers and craftsmen to turn his dream city into reality. Materials were brought from neighbouring towns. Wasit lost its five famous wrought-iron gates and both Damascus and Kufa had to supply a gate. The bricks from the ruins of Babylon and Ctesiphon were also used.

The 85ha city was finally completed in 766. Mansour was obsessed with security and the city had its own prison: Matbak prison. He ordered 100 graves to be dug for him to escape desecration at the hands of his enemies. The real place of his burial was such a well-kept secret that today no-one is sure where he is buried. Mansour's city was a city for the government and the court and not for the people, and commercial activities were severely restricted, prompting a merchants' town called Karkh to grow up outside Kufa Gate. The canals were the focal point for trade, where coppersmiths, reed-weavers and sellers of cooked meats congregated. New suburbs were built and Mansour's round city soon became the nucleus of a larger town. Mansour also built an army camp on the east side of the Tigris named Rusafa. In 768 a new mosque and palace were constructed in Rusafa, near a great cemetery where many of the caliphs were buried. Today part of central Baghdad has retained this name. Mansour was an exemplary individual in his private life and nothing of an unseemly nature was ever permitted at his court, despite his reign being continually interrupted by rebellions, religious disturbances and wars. As well as founding a new capital city he placed the imperial administration on a firmer footing than it had been for a generation and created a stability which permitted material, intellectual and literary growth. The founder of Baghdad may justly claim a place as one of the great organising monarchs of the world, and his descendants continued to occupy the throne in the capital city for 500 years.

GROWTH AND PROSPERITY The 8th and 9th centuries were Baghdad's golden years. Gavin Young, author of *Iraq: Land of Two Rivers*, described how 'Baghdad became the richest city of the world. Its wharves were lined with ships from China bringing porcelain; from Malaya and India with spices and dyes; from Turkestan with lapis lazuli (used as a gem) and slaves; from East Africa with ivory and gold dust; and from Arabia with pearls and weapons.'

A fledgling banking system fostered the growth of trade. There was self-regulation of fraud by merchants and traders who formed a specific guild to root out corrupt practices. As well as a focal point of trade, Abbasid Baghdad was a preserver and translator of past knowledge. The foundation of the city corresponded with the introduction of paper from China, which encouraged literary endeavours – especially as paper was manufactured in Baghdad. The city became a leading centre of learning from which Greco-Roman wisdom was passed on. The writings of Aristotle and Plato were translated in the House of Wisdom and advances in medicine, astronomy and other disciplines laid the foundations for modern Western sciences. In 1235 Caliph Mustansir built Mustansiriya University on the banks of the Tigris. It was also the time of the poet Abu Nuwas, a famous literary figure whose works are often quoted today. Educational institutions similar to the ones developed in Baghdad were also introduced in the other cities of the Abbasid Caliphate, which extended from the Mediterranean to India.

The Jews were an ancient, respected community in Mesopotamia. Even when Cyrus allowed them to return to Palestine in the 6th century BC, many chose to remain in Babylon where the famous Talmud of Babylonia was subsequently produced. Also known as the Bavli or Babylonian Talmud, this extensive commentary on the written and oral law of Israel was compiled between AD500 and 600 and is a comprehensive record of how Jewish scholars preserved a humane and enduring civilisation. Representing the primary document of rabbinic Judaism, it throws considerable light on the New Testament as well.

During the time of the Abbasid Caliphate (AD750–1258) and the subsequent years of Ottoman rule (from 1534), Jews played an important economic role in Iraqi society. Among the Ottomans, they lived as protected minorities (*dhimmis*) who were given freedom to worship, conduct business and own property. Towards the end of the 19th century many Baghdadi Jews moved to other towns, especially Basra, a thriving port after the Suez Canal was opened.

During the 1930s relations between Jews and Muslims began to deteriorate due to Jewish agitation for a Zionist state in the Middle East. Iraq, as the first Arab state to gain independence and be admitted to the League of Nations, saw itself as the centre of pan-Arabism and Arab resistance to Zionism. The Germans established an influential embassy in Baghdad and began disseminating anti-Semitic ideas. In 1934 the Arabisation programme led to the dismissal of Jews from administrative positions under the pretext of reorganisation, so their places could be filled by a rising generation of educated Arabs. The year of 1941 was the year of the Farhud, a word denoting the breakdown of law and order. Jewish properties were looted and burned and Jews were beaten up and killed in Baghdad, Mosul, Kirkuk, Erbil, Basra, Amarah and Fallujah. Official figures put the dead at 187, but Jewish sources claim at least 400 people lost their lives. Not all Iraqis condoned the indiscriminate violence and rape: many Jews were sheltered by Muslim families and Salih Bashayan, a prominent Muslim figure, assigned his men to guard Jewish properties. But despite these humanitarian gestures the tradition of hundreds of years of co-existence between the Jews and Muslims had come to an end, prompting a mass migration of Iraqi Jews to Palestine or the USA in the 1950s after the Suez War.

The Arabs' disastrous defeat during the 1967 war with Israel led to the public hangings in Baghdad of Jews as spies. According to the Jewish Agency's emissary to Iraq, Jeff Kaye, the last Jewish wedding was held in 1978, and by 2003 there were only 34 Jews remaining in Baghdad, half of whom were over 70. In July of that year the Jewish Agency flew six elderly Iraqi Jews to Israel. The 2,600-year-old community's last remaining synagogue is in the city centre neighbourhood of Batawneen. '*It is surrounded by a high wall – you wouldn't know there's a synagogue there until you entered the forecourt,*' Kaye told the *Jewish Chronicle* in June 2003. '*The building is well preserved, contains some beautiful ancient artefacts and is large enough for 300 worshippers.*' Present estimates of the Jewish population in Baghdad range from seven or eight to none.

Respect for their Iraqi heritage and a historical connection to Baghdad and other places in Iraq is still alive among the Jewish communities who fled to Europe or settled in Israel. The Sassoon and the Saatchi families in the UK are prime examples.

During Abbasid times social and welfare services, financed by the paying of *zakat* (an offering for the poor and needy similar to the Christian tithe), were developed, along with free hospitals where only doctors with a diploma could practise. *Zakat* is one of the five duties (pillars) of Islam and the welfare system was centred on the mosques that financed the services through the social funds (*waqf*) to which believers contributed a percentage of their income. The care of the sick was also financed by the caliphs. Most of the leading physicians were Christians and relations between the Christian and Muslim communities were extremely cordial. Order was maintained by the police force, the legal system, and an army made up of 125,000 regular troops in addition to irregulars known as *harbiyah*. Spies were sent to all major foreign capitals, especially Constantinople. The Board for the Inspection of Grievances eased the caliphs' judicial responsibilities. Judges (*qadis*) presided over both civil disputes and matters pertaining to religious law. The Islamic ideal that every Muslim should be able to complain about injustice brought the Office of the Censor of Morals (*muhtasib*) into being. He dealt with matters ranging from the provision of water supply and the control of weights and measures, to inspection of dolls to make sure they did not contravene the religious ban on idols. He even found husbands for widows.

THE DECLINE OF BAGHDAD Caliph Mansour was succeeded by his son Mahdi. Aware of the harshness of his father's reign, Mahdi's generosity seemed boundless, especially on pilgrimages to Mecca and Jerusalem, during which he distributed millions of dirhams. The next caliph was Harun al Rashid (the orthodox). As the caliph of *The Thousand and One Nights*, he entered almost every home and his name is as familiar to the world at large as that of Baghdad itself. Harun left many of the administrative duties to Jaffar the Barmecide, who built a new palace on the east bank of the river that was the scene of wild drinking parties. Some of the more important government offices were moved across the river to East Baghdad, close to Barmecide's residence. East Baghdad became an administrative centre, a role that it maintained until the beginning of the 20th century. But Jaffar's luck ran out when, in a fit of anger, Harun threw him into prison and had him executed. This left the caliph with immense administrative responsibilities, which he found difficult to bear in his old age. Another serious political mistake was the division of the empire between his three sons: Mamum, Amin and Mutasim. The conflict between the brothers played itself out in the struggle between the Arabs and the Persians in the empire who supported one brother against another.

When Harun died in 809, Amin was firmly ensconced in Baghdad with his father's treasure. He took up residence in Mansour's old Golden Gate Palace. This prompted Mamum, supported by the Persians, to launch an attack on the city. The tide had turned and the slow decline of Baghdad began with an attack on its western suburbs. The siege lasted for almost a year. In the end Amin tried to escape in a small boat, which overturned when it was pelted with stones. He was taken prisoner after he managed to swim ashore, and was promptly put to death.

RE-BIRTH AND CONFLICT The life of the city was now focused on three districts on the east bank of the river. During the reign of Mamum, who was also a religious scholar and the second of the only two caliphs in Islamic history who knew the entire Koran by heart, Baghdad was a city of intellectual brilliance and under his regime one day a week was always set aside at court for literary, scientific or philosophical discussion. In the House of Wisdom an army of translators worked around the clock to make sure all significant foreign works were available in Arabic. Poets shed

Harun became the fifth caliph of the Abbasid Dynasty in 786. During his rule the Abbasid Caliphate reached the height of its power and his court was famous for its splendour. Harun's empire extended from the Mediterranean to India. He was a great patron of the arts and a single sonnet could earn a poet 5,000 gold pieces, a robe of honour, ten Greek slave girls and a horse from the royal stables. Harun was responsible for the rebuilding of the mosque of Mansour.

However, over time Harun al Rashid began to develop jealousy against the imams due to the great influence and popularity which they enjoyed among the people. Eventually he had Musa al Kadhim, the 7th of the 12 Imams and regarded by Sunnis as a renowned scholar, arrested while he was praying at the tomb of the Holy Prophet. He incarcerated him in Al-Sindi ibn Shahek prison for four years before having him poisoned in 802 and his corpse buried in a cemetery outside the Straw Gate to the west of Baghdad. Thirty years later his grandson, the 9th Imam, was buried in the same place. A town grew around the tombs of the Imams called Kadhmain (meaning the two Kadhims) and the site of their burials is now said to rest within the Kadhimiya Mosque. The Festival of Imam Musa al Kadhim which takes place on the 7th day of the month of Rajab is a celebration of his life and death.

the restrictions of rigid classical forms and prose writing in Arabic began. There are many records of court debates on religious subjects between Muslims and men of other faiths, centred on the mustazilates, who advocated free will and reason and the Sufis, oriented towards pure mysticism. Both schools of thought had a profound influence on the Islamic faith.

During the reign of Mamun's successor Mutasim, the capital city of the Abbasid Empire was transferred from Baghdad to Samarra between 836 and 892. However, Baghdad maintained its importance as a leading trading and cultural centre. Within the city, the Turks were now the masters, with their allegiance to Samarra amounting to little more than the payment of taxes. Mustain, a grandson of Mutasim, could not tolerate this situation any longer and decided to enlist the support of the Arabs to rid Baghdad and the Abbasid Empire of the troublesome Turks. The confrontation took place in Baghdad, which suffered its second siege. Mustain and his men were defeated but the people of Baghdad became increasingly rebellious and unwilling to submit to Turkish domination. During the reign of Mutadid (892–902) the capital moved back to Baghdad, and he succeeded in restoring to the Abbasid state some of the power and provinces it had lost during the turmoil of the previous decades, a process continued under his less able son and successor, al Muktafi. Despite this, the last 350 years of Abbasid rule were characterised by internal strife and struggles between various religious sects.

MONGOL RULE In 1256 much of the city was destroyed by floods and two years later the Mongols invaded, leaving between 800,000 and 2 million people dead. Genghis Khan, the famous Mongol leader, united a number of ferocious tribes and turned them into a formidable war machine that devastated western Asia and threatened Europe. The caliphs underestimated the strength of the barbarians and at first successfully repulsed their raids and drove them out of Iraq. Hulagu, Genghis Khan's grandson, followed his grandfather's edict 'to treat those who submitted to his arms

THE ILKHANID DYNASTY

- Meaning 'subordinate khan' in Farsi, the Ilkhanid Dynasty can be dated back to 1253, when Hulagu, grandson of great Mongul leader Genghis Khan was tasked with conquering Persia. The Ilkhanid Dynasty ruled paramount in that country from AD1256 to 1335.
- By 1258 the Ilkhanids had also captured Baghdad, and after consolidating their position in Persia they united the fragmented region into a cohesive political and territorial entity. By the end of the 13th century, they had lost all contact with their Mongul roots and had embraced Sunni Islam. This was followed by a golden period in which Persian arts and culture flourished, giving birth to such writers and scholars such as Rashid al Din.
- In 1310 the reigning Ilkhanid Khan Oljeitu converted to Shia Islam. This conversion gave rise to great unrest and only his death in 1316 prevented civil war breaking out. His successor, his son Abu Said, reconverted to Sunni Islam in an attempt to keep the peace. However, unrest continued to grow and when he died in 1335 without leaving an heir, the unity of the Ilkhanid Dynasty was finally destroyed, although various minor rulers continued to govern parts of the former Ilkhanid Dynasty for a further 20 years.

kindly, but to exterminate those who resisted; to conquer the lands from the banks of the Oxus river to the borders of Egypt and to compel the caliph of Baghdad to be submissive.' He began by sending the caliph a letter complaining that he had not received assistance in his campaign against the Assassins (an esoteric Muslim sect), and reminded him of the Mongol's previous conquests. The caliph was not intimidated and replied:

> 'O young man, just commencing your life, who, drunk with the prosperity and good fortune of ten days, deem yourself superior to the whole world, and think your orders equivalent to those of destiny: why do you address me with a demand which you cannot secure.'

War was inevitable. The people, sensing the imminent disaster, paid boatmen exorbitant prices to transport them to what they saw as the safety of the city walls. But only the Christians were spared at the request of Hulagu's Christian wife. After a week of merciless slaughter the people of Baghdad sent a delegation to Hulagu begging him to stop the bloodshed. He agreed, but by this time all the city's major buildings had been either damaged or destroyed and the city's treasures were looted. Famine and disease followed the Mongol onslaught and Cairo replaced Baghdad as the cultural centre of the Muslim world.

One of the most successful Mongol rulers was Orud Kia. In 1284 under the influence of the Jewish doctor Said ud-Dawlah, the taxation system was reformed and the power of the military curbed. In 1302 Ghazan was the greatest Mongol ruler: he introduced a new standard of weights and measures, redeveloped lands devastated during earlier invasions, set up an efficient postal service, and mosques and public baths in poor areas and ensured their upkeep. After a revolution in central Asia in 1400 Timur (Tamerlane) emerged as the head of the Mongol Empire. He was a master opportunist who used Islam to justify whatever act of megalomania he wished to pursue. In 1401 he unleashed his wrath on Baghdad, where the Jalayrids had created a new kingdom, ordering only the preservation of mosques and hospitals. The destruction of all other buildings and the killing of citizens 'from eight to eighty' was decreed. His 90,000 men were instructed to bring at least one human skull each to camp. Those who failed would pay with their lives.

The first Mongol capture of the city had left it with a ruling foreign dynasty. The second capture was more like a raid and the invaders did not establish themselves as a ruling power. Turkish tribes then displaced the Mongols as rulers of Baghdad: the Black Sheep (1419) and White Sheep (1473) Turkmen took turns at misruling, rather than ruling, the city and the country. The nomadic Arab tribes turned large areas into pasture lands for their flocks and were more occupied with their internal disputes than the establishment of a centralised administration. The destruction of the irrigation system led to the further marginalisation of the city, which was no more than a bargaining chip between rival Turkmen tribesmen, a town of half-ruined bazaars through which foreign travellers passed unimpressed.

THE OTTOMAN ERA During the 15th and 16th centuries the Ottomans and the Safavid Persians competed for control of Baghdad. In 1508, Shah Ismail of Persia occupied the city, destroyed the tombs of Sunni saints, constructed a large hostel for Persian pilgrims at Kadhmain and appointed Ibrahim Khan as the first Persian governor of Baghdad. The city was once again developed as a commercial centre. But the Turks could not accept Persian domination. Thirty years later the Ottoman Sultan Suleiman the Magnificent took Baghdad from Persia, but his rule was detested by the Shias and the non-Muslim population. In 1621 the Persians again took Baghdad but lost it 17 years later to the Ottoman Turks. When they retook the city the Turks were eager to ensure the loyalty of the citizens, so local dignitaries were encouraged to visit the Turkish court, Sunni mosques were

AL-RASHID STREET

Iraqis have a lot of affection for Al-Rashid Street, which has been witness to some of the most important events in Iraqi history. It was once the centre of Baghdad's political and cultural life as well as a great place to go for a bargain. Throughout most of the 20th century, it was home to some of the city's most popular cafés, restaurants, markets and entertainment venues. In its heyday Al-Rashid Street with its old style architecture was beautiful.

Named after Harun al Rashid of *Arabian Nights* fame, the street runs along the east bank of the Tigris river in the heart of Baghdad, following the original route between the north and south gates of the old walled city. The Ottoman Turks planned and built the street in 1910, demolishing any houses in the way. Supposedly, it gets its winding shape from all the families who paid bribes to save their homes from destruction! In 1925, Al-Rashid Street was the first in Baghdad to be paved for vehicles. In the wake of this businesses sprang up alongside, and by the 1940s, it was the place to go for late-night entertainment with 30 nightclubs, 20 cinemas and 9 theatres along its 2km length. Baghdad's best-known cafés: the *Umm Kulthum*, named after the Egyptian diva whose music they played and the *al Zahawi*, named after the poet and philosopher were in the street. The haunt of artists, students and the intelligentsia, Al-Rashid Street became the Mesopotamian equivalent of the Parisian Left Bank in the 1950s.

Al-Rashid Street has a dark side too. It has been a popular place for political demonstration dating back to 1919 when Iraqis gathered there to protest against the British occupation. In an era when few newspapers were available it became a rebuilt and agriculture was encouraged. Baghdad became the regional capital of a Turkish province. Some of the Turkish governors were resourceful and forward-looking, while others were weak and incompetent. Yusef Pasha was in the latter category and the city fell into the hands of Bakr, an officer who asked the sultan to legalise his rule. The request was refused and Bakr enlisted the aid of the Shah of Persia, Abbas, to defeat the Turkish troops sent to oust him. But he did not allow the Persians to take over the city on behalf of the Shah. During the siege that followed famine set in and many of the city's hapless citizens deserted at night to the Persians. In the end Bakr's son Muahhad smuggled Persian troops into the city, the gates were opened and the keys handed to the Shah. Bakr was executed, many Sunnis were sold into slavery and the city was left in a state of disrepair. The Turks, led by Sultan Murad, made several attempts to re-take the city and finally succeeded in 1638 with the assistance of the Abu Rishah tribes on the Euphrates, who sent 10,000 camel loads of provisions. The sultan left the city at the head of his victorious army by the Talisman Gate, which was bricked up, and so from 1638 until World War I, Baghdad was part of the Ottoman Empire and was governed from Istanbul.

The Persian threat never completely subsided and they invaded Iraq in 1818, but troops were held in check by the outbreak of a cholera epidemic.

Bubonic plague and devastating floods of 1831, which washed away two-thirds of East Baghdad and much of West Baghdad, followed. The population of the city dropped from 150,000 to 50,000. The city recovered slowly from disease, natural disasters and horrendous internal disputes and as Turkish influence declined, European influence increased. See pages 50–2 for further information on Ottoman rule.

meeting place for those seeking the knowledge of the printed word and political propaganda. A hothouse for the recruitment of political activists, in 1959, a young Saddam Hussein fled Iraq from the street after taking part in an attempt to assassinate the then Iraqi Prime Minister Abdul-Karim Kassim.

Many of Al-Rashid Street's theatres, shops and cinemas closed when that self-same Saddam Hussein came to power, although a few of the most famous cafés and markets lingered on. But the 2003 war took a heavy toll on Al-Rashid, leaving few businesses still operating in its wake. The street was hit hard by bombings and kidnappings, and the Central Bank was looted so badly at the beginning of the war that the street was closed to all but pedestrians for many years afterwards.

Today Al-Rashid Street is no longer beautiful. The traffic has returned, although the blast walls remain. When you enter the street now, you see a tangle of electric wires over your head and hear the noisy sound of the generators. After years of violence and neglect, the old shops and houses badly need renovation. When you walk down the street you feel the buildings are going to come down on you. Al-Rashid Street has lost most of its old charm.

Although no longer rich with heritage, there may still be a future for Al-Rashid Street. One of its side-streets, Al-Mutanabbi, which was torn apart by car bombs for years, is now beginning to see the restoration of some of its famous bookstalls and shoppers are starting to come back. In May 2010, the mayor of Baghdad announced the signing of a US$7 million contract to revitalise the street, which was completed in 2015.

THE 20TH CENTURY World War I brought increased activity as Baghdad became the base of operations against the British. The Turks finally left the city in 1917, but not before the military commandant destroyed as many official records as he could. The Talisman Gate was blown up as a parting gesture. General Maude entered the city and delivered a famous speech in which he urged the people:

> 'Through your nobles and elders and representatives, to participate in the management of your own civil affairs in collaboration with the political representatives of Great Britain, who accompany the British Army.'

The army did not leave immediately, even though the threatened Turkish return never took place. A new city administration took over the running of Baghdad, electricity was introduced and improvements were made to the streets and water supply. When the plague broke out again in 1919, a large-scale inoculation programme was organised by British doctors and nurses. The country's first constitutional assembly met in 1924 after the women's hospital in Karkh was renovated and turned into the Parliament House of Iraq. Until the 1920s the city maintained its largely medieval appearance. But after independence in 1932 it started to expand. Attention was paid to the construction of schools and hospitals, the infrastructure, and a system of bunds (embankments) to protect the city from floods. According to John Warren and Ihsan Fethi, authors of *Traditional Houses in Baghdad*:

> 'Flood, decay and the city planners together destroyed almost all parts of the city which were over 50 years old. With the exception of a scattering of old mosques and of two much-restored 13th century structures (the Abbasid Palace and Mustansiriya School), the city of Baghdad dates from the end of the First World War (1918).'

After World War II, Baghdad slowly became an industrial centre. The first large-scale factory was a woollen textile factory, followed by a number of cigarette factories and a brewery. Plants for making bricks and other construction materials also sprang up, along with factories for cement, soap making, tanning and leather goods, soft drinks and confectionery. Other early industries included flour mills, print shops and car repair shops. The construction sector in the city, small machine shops and the service industries provided employment for peasants who converged on Baghdad from the rural areas. Squatters lived in hastily erected reed and mud huts on the outskirts of the city, where one of the squatter settlements was turned into Ath Thawra Township (renamed Saddam City in 1980 and later Sadr City). In 1955 Iraq was a founding member of the Baghdad Pact, a mutual defence treaty with Iran, Pakistan and Turkey. The fact that it was signed in Baghdad was an indication of the city's growing importance in world affairs. Between 1963 and 1980 Iraq was gradually nationalised, and the new wealth of the 1970s, generated by the nationalisation of the oil industry and a four-fold increase in oil prices, led to a growth spurt that saw the construction of motorways, bridges, new residential areas and an upgrading of the sewage and water supply systems. Several bridges connected the two sides of Baghdad along the east and west banks of the Tigris. The main streets were Al-Rashid Street (the financial district, the copper, textile and gold bazaars, cheap hotels and restaurants), Al-Jammouri Street (historical mosques, government offices), Sadoun Street (a commercial area with expensive hotels and cinemas) and Abu Nawas Street (with many outdoor cafés). The rich lived near the race-track in magnificent villas. Baghdad became a city of contrasts, where minarets and skyscrapers competed for attention and traditional craftspeople co-existed with business people in Western suits. Once the capital of the Muslim world, Baghdad became a modern metropolis: a city of the future that would never forget its past.

Saddam Hussein, determined to make his mark in Iraqi and Arab history by securing his place on the international stage, was responsible for Baghdad's decline in the last decades of the 20th century. For further information on Saddam Hussein, and the period since the Americans and British ousted him by force, see pages 57–61.

BAGHDAD TODAY In 2015, 12 years on from the 2003 war, long concrete blast barriers made of ugly slabs still thread across Baghdad, protecting public buildings and lining arterial roads and defining the post-invasion city. In 2014 the city was designated the Capital of Arab Culture. Ali al Shallah, Chairman of the Iraq Parliament's Committee of Arab Culture, emphasised that 'celebrating Baghdad as a Capital of Arab Culture was an important event, particularly as it happened in tandem with positive changes sweeping the capital'. For the Arab Summit held in Baghdad in the same year, many parks were renovated and the approaches to the airport transformed. The once-scarred face of Iraq's capital city is beginning to regain some of its magnificence.

Despite the bombs and the grenade-taking of innocent lives there is an opinion, albeit balanced by depression and despair at the difficulties for ordinary people, that life is returning to parks, restaurants and markets. The Government has been forced to produce a better way of life if it wishes to stay in power. This is happening slowly, salaries have increased but so has the cost of living. Public highways are being improved, and even Al-Rashid and Sadoun Streets are being repaired. Iraqi expats are bringing money and influence into the city. Time will tell if, when the blast walls obscuring Baghdad disappear, it becomes the City of Peace once more.

GETTING THERE AND AWAY

BY AIR Baghdad's airport reopened for commercial flights in April 2004, following the severe damage it sustained during the 2003 war and the subsequent extensive renovations. The airport is located 16km west of the city and there is a complicated entry system for passengers due to the strict security currently in place. With regard to passenger facilities the airport has a few souvenir shops, money exchangers and cafés, toilet facilities and duty-free shopping, taxi services plus visa services.

Arrival from abroad Once through immigration and baggage collection, authorised taxis and buses are available to take you through to the taxi/bus park some distance from the airport building. Here you change to regular taxis, buses or private vehicles which will take you through to Baghdad city (allow 30–40 minutes and more on a bad traffic day for this journey). Taxi fares range from US$25–50 depending upon where you want to go.

Getting to the airport Logistically, your journey to Baghdad Airport is a complicated matter. You should allow for heavy traffic in the early morning and give yourself plenty of time to pass through the initial city checkpoints. Unless you are travelling with the Government or diplomatic services you have to leave your regular taxi, bus or private vehicle at the taxi/bus park located some distance from the airport and complete your journey to the airport building by a special authorised taxi or bus, as no unauthorised vehicles may go beyond the taxi/bus park to the airport. Owing to the necessary heavy security you must always have to hand your air ticket/printout and passport. The procedure now requires your authorised taxi to stop at two checkpoints

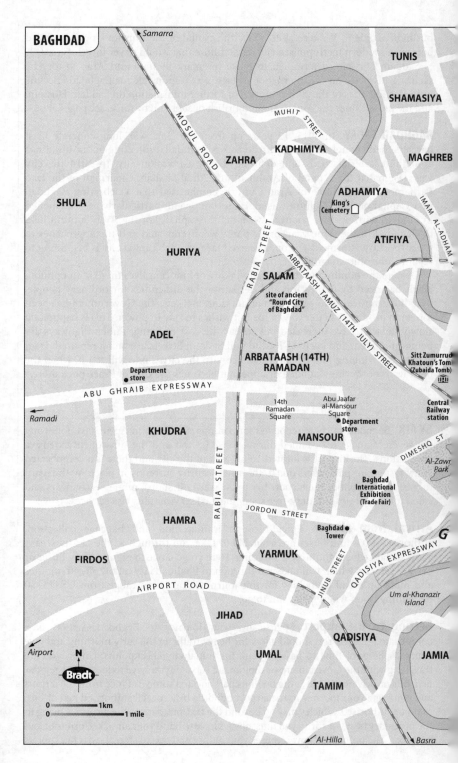

BAGHDAD

↗ Samarra

TUNIS

SHAMASIYA

MUHIT STREET

KADHIMIYA

ZAHRA

MAGHREB

MOSUL ROAD

ADHAMIYA

King's Cemetery

SHULA

IMAM AL-ADHAM

ATIFIYA

HURIYA

RABIA STREET

SALAM

ARBATAASH TAMUZ (14TH JULY) STREET

site of ancient "Round City of Baghdad"

ADEL

ARBATAASH (14TH) RAMADAN

Sitt Zumurrud Khatoun's Tomb (Zubaida Tomb)

Department store

ABU GHRAIB EXPRESSWAY

14th Ramadan Square

Abu Jaafar al-Mansour Square

Central Railway station

← Ramadi

KHUDRA

Department store

MANSOUR

DIMESHQ ST

Al-Zawr Park

RABIA STREET

Baghdad International Exhibition (Trade Fair)

JORDON STREET

HAMRA

Baghdad Tower

G

FIRDOS

YARMUK

JINUB STREET

QADISIYA EXPRESSWAY

AIRPORT ROAD

Um al-Khanazir Island

JIHAD

QADISIYA

↗ Airport

N

JAMIA

Bradt

UMAL

0 ____ 1km
0 ____ 1 mile

TAMIM

↙ Al-Hilla

↘ Basra

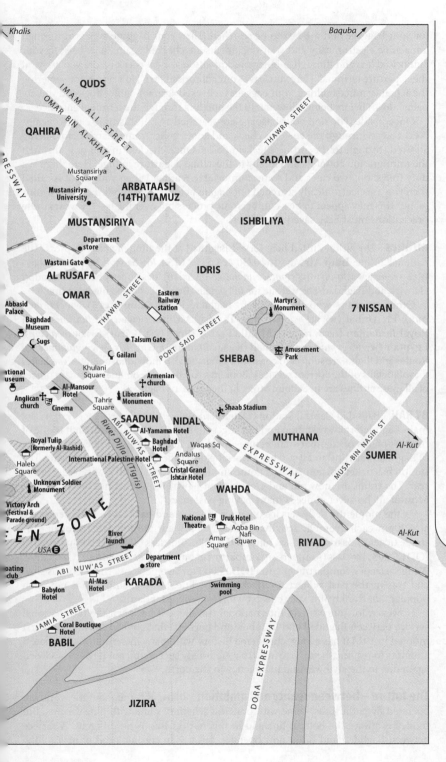

Khalis

Baquba ↗

QUDS

IMAM ALI STREET

OMAR BIN AL-KHATAB ST

QAHIRA

ESSWAY

THAWRA STREET

SADAM CITY

Mustansiriya Square

Mustansiriya University

ARBATAASH (14TH) TAMUZ

ISHBILIYA

MUSTANSIRIYA

Department store

Wastani Gate

AL RUSAFA

IDRIS

OMAR

THAWRA STREET

Eastern Railway station

Martyr's Monument

7 NISSAN

Abbasid Palace

Baghdad Museum

Sugs

Talsum Gate

Gailani

PORT SAID STREET

SHEBAB

Amusement Park

Khulani Square

Armenian church

ational useum

Al-Mansour Hotel

Anglican church

Cinema

Tahrir Square

Liberation Monument

Shaab Stadium

Royal Tulip (formerly Al-Rashid)

SAADUN

River Dijla (Tigris)

NIDAL

Al-Yamama Hotel

Baghdad Hotel

Waqas Sq

MUTHANA

Al-Kut

Haleb Square

International Palestine Hotel

ABI NUW'AS STREET

Andalus Square

Cristal Grand Ishtar Hotel

SUMER

MUSA BIN NASIR ST

EXPRESSWAY

Unknown Soldier Monument

WAHDA

Victory Arch (Festival & Parade ground)

EN ZONE

National Theatre

Uruk Hotel

Aqba Bin Nafi Square

RIYAD

Al-Kut

USA

River launch

Amar Square

ABI NUW'AS STREET

oating club

Department store

KARADA

Babylon Hotel

Al-Mas Hotel

Swimming pool

JAMIA STREET

Coral Boutique Hotel

BABIL

DORA EXPRESSWAY

JIZIRA

131

for your baggage and the taxi to be searched. Then your baggage is passed through a machine electronically and your documents are checked again. Now back to your authorised taxi and through another checkpoint/document check before you arrive at the departure terminal. Here you leave your authorised taxi. However before entering the actual terminal building your baggage is checked again by sniffer dogs and you are patted down before being allowed into the building through the terminal entrance.

Once inside, you and your baggage are searched again, this time electronically. Next you go through the customs check and another electronic search before being allowed through to the airline check-in desks. Once checked in you pass through the immigration counters and finally to the actual departure lounge. Here there is a duty free shop, two cafés and some comfortable seating. When your flight is called then you are electronically searched once again before being allowed on board your plane. This may appear to be a cumbersome process but over the last few years these precautions must have saved many lives.

Airlines The airlines listed here served Baghdad at the time of going to press. The national airline, **Iraqi Airways** (m *0750 423 5555, 0750 466 6444;* e *Iraqairwayssul@ yahoo.com; www.iq-airways.com; see ad in colour section*) flies directly between London Gatwick and Baghdad. See website for full details. Bookings can be made on line.

Other operators who fly directly to Baghdad include **Emirates** (*www.emirates. com*); **Fly Dubai** (*www.Flydubai.com*); **Turkish Airlines** (*www.turkishairlines.com*); **Royal Jordanian** (*www.rj.com*); **Middle East Airlines (via Beirut)** (*www.mea.com*); **Egyptair** (*www.egyptair.com*); **Etihad** (*www.etihad.com*); **Gulf Air** (*www.gulfair.com*). Routes and flights are subject to constant change, so visit individual operator's websites for full details of the current services. Bookings can be made on line. The main offices of all these airlines are in Sadoun Street in the centre of Baghdad.

BY RAIL Baghdad Central Station (*Damashaq Sq; www.transport@scr.gov.iq*) is the main Baghdad railway station and the largest in Iraq. Built by the British it is one of the best pieces of colonial architecture anywhere. Its clocks and dome are a feature of Baghdad's skyline and it still has a working post office on one of its platforms. The station has ticket offices inside its dome and four platforms with ready access to the rear. The trains are now old and creaking but new rolling stock has been ordered. Most of all, however, it needs many paying passengers.

At the moment a daily service operates to Basra and back again with departure at 6.20pm each evening, arriving in Basra at 5.30am the following morning. A single ticket to Basra costs (seat only) IQD7,500; 2nd class (4 person compartment) IQD17, 200; 1st class (four person compartment but with better seating) IQD20,000. A night sleeper compartment costs IQD25,000 for two persons. The service is slow and was in the past subject to attacks on the line. Subsequently it has not been popular, but frankly it is very cheap by international standards.

However, for tourists and international travellers, it has been the international service between Baghdad and Istanbul (and beyond) that commands interest. First mooted in 1914 it has a long, chequered history with many interruptions. The latest attempts to resume the service in 2010 were briefly successful, but it has now closed again due to the civil war and insurgency in the north.

The future – between reality and ambition Railways throughout the world are operated by enthusiasts; some with practical schemes, some with pipe dreams. But money is always the bottom line and in this respect Iraq is no different. A service between Baghdad and Basra now operates, but it is in chronic need of new rolling stock and better facilities at each station *en route*. If it were possible to cut down the length of the journey with improved tracks many people would prefer to travel by rail than by road to Basra. It is proposed that the old Baghdad to Samarra line will soon operate once more, although again improvements to the track and facilities will be needed. Between Baghdad and Mosul a new track is slowly being laid alongside the old one (see page 94) and when this route is open again it potentially has an exciting future. Internationally, the romance and dream of the old railway connecting Basra and Baghdad to Aleppo and Istanbul and connecting them to the Orient Express will always be there, but international politics and security are so important that finance pales in comparison. But this line will live again in the future. It is with great pleasure that we can announce some progress with this. Two superb Chinese-built modern, fully equipped trains complete with engines and sleeper carriages were delivered in July 2014 and stand proudly in the station. Designed to operate at a programmed 160km per hour, they have already increased traffic from the station on the Basra line. However, the track is in need of an upgrade and that (along with the ongoing security situation) means that the old timetables still have to be adhered to, resulting in a more comfortable journey, albeit at the old speed.

BY ROAD A network of well-paved roads connects Baghdad with all parts of the country. Travellers are advised to exercise caution when travelling to and from Baghdad by bus, as despite the good road networks buses and bus stations are frequent targets of suicide bombings. The Nahda bus station in Baghdad from which buses depart to the mainly Shia cities of the south has been the target of car bombings and suicide bombers have been known to jump onto buses and blow themselves up.

GETTING AROUND

The concrete blast wall placed around all major buildings and along many streets makes finding your way around the city, even with the benefit of a map, very difficult, with many side streets suddenly coming to a halt behind one of these. The innumerable checkpoints manned by the police and army and often protected by armoured vehicles cause massive traffic jams at rush hour and slow all progress through the city at the best of times. A sudden security crisis will bring the traffic to a complete standstill, sometimes for days. Any vehicle containing a foreigner will immediately be pulled over at a checkpoint and the documentation of all the people, including Iraqi drivers and security personnel, will be closely scrutinised, along with passports, visas and especially your *khittab* (official permission document supplied by the Ministry to all tourists). In combating your frustrations at these delays, spare a thought for the Baghdadis who have to experience these frustrations on their journey to and from their workplace each day.

BY PUBLIC TRANSPORT Baghdad is currently reliant on buses and taxis for public transport. For the tourist, travel by one of the numerous taxis or shared taxis is the safest and most sensible option. Road congestion in the centre of Baghdad is horrendous and you can be stuck in traffic for hours on the shortest of journeys, which in the heat of a Baghdad summer is not a pleasant experience in an un air-conditioned and crowded bus. For more information about travelling by bus, see page 103.

BY CAR If you have been invited to Baghdad for business or academic reasons then you will need to rely totally on the organisation who invited you for vehicles.

5

Pilgrims are under the supervision of a travel agent who will supply the necessary transport for them. Tourists can only travel around Baghdad under the control of the Ministry Tourism or with the Tour Company who supplied their visa and will provide transport. For the rare person not fitting any of the above categories the advice is simply do not hire a car. For further information, see page 104.

BY RAIL An overground metro line is planned for Baghdad to relieve traffic congestion and help to accommodate population growth in the capital. Starting from Al-Mustansiriya University, the 25km first phase will cross the River Tigris on a new bridge near the existing Sarafiya Bridge to reach the Kadhimiya district. It will then follow Muthanna Airport Road to terminate near Baghdad Central railway station at Alawi, where the depot will be located. Fourteen stations are planned. Further stages will run from Alawi, through the Karkh and Bayaa areas to Saidiya and on to Jadiriyah and Karada, looping back to Alawi. This project is separate from long-standing proposals for an underground metro, which were revived in 2011.

TOURIST INFORMATION

There is no official tourist information office in Baghdad at the time of going to press. Enquiries can be made to the Board of Tourism (\+964 (1) 537 2870/69), the National Bureau of Tourism (\+964 (1) 537 0454) or the Common Bureau of Tourism (\+964 (1) 537 2522).

TOUR OPERATORS

At the time of going to press it is not possible to travel independently within Iraq but the Ministry of Tourism will issue tourist visas to recognised tour operators with a minimum number of travellers. See pages 87–9 for a list of international and Baghdad-based tour operators currently taking clients into Iraq. These tour operators are able to provide knowledgeable and sometimes specialist guides who can help you get the most out of your visit.

WHERE TO STAY *See map, pages 130–1.*

Baghdad has a wide range of accommodation from 5-star establishments to modest family-run hotels. One of the best hotels, Golden Tulip (formerly the Al-Rashid) Hotel in the international zone, has recently been refurbished to very high standards and caters mainly for international business people. You should note that many Baghdad hotels still don't seem to have their own websites and there is no information generally available about prices. However, many of those in the medium- and lower-price brackets are undergoing renovation in the hope that the security situation improves. The the hotels listed below are just a sample of those available and are the ones we have been able to visit. In the future there will be many more and standards will improve and prices reduce as competition increases. Virtually all of the hotels in the luxury and upmarket range can arrange airport pickups – just ask (and ask the price, if any) at the time of booking.

LUXURY

Royal Tulip (formerly the Al-Rashid Hotel) (449 rooms) International (Green) Zone; m 0771 809 4859; e info@royaltulipalrasheed.com; www.goldentulip.com. The most luxurious hotel in Baghdad & possibly the whole of Iraq,

AL-RASHID HOTEL

Baghdad's most famous hotel, originally built for the Oberoi chain in the early 1970s, has an interesting history. In its early days it hosted all the major conferences and Saddam Hussein would often visit as president of Iraq. Opulently furnished, it had private dining rooms: the Gold Room with all furnishings in gold, the Silver Room and the Bronze Room, along with its many conference rooms and restaurants. The gardens were attractive and the swimming pool was a particular attraction in the early days when such facilities were scarce.

Located close to central government under Saddam and then on the boundaries of the Green Zone it was subjected to attacks. In 1982 it was attacked by the Iranian air force and badly damaged. During the First Gulf War it became the centre for world media reporting.

A famous mosaic depicting US president George Bush senior was cemented into the floor of the front entrance, positioned so that visitors were forced to walk over his face. It was removed in 2003 following the American occupation of Baghdad.

The hotel was hit by US rockets several times in the initial period before the 2003 invasion. After the invasion the hotel was used as a base for the Coalition and military forces. This led to a rocket attack by insurgents which damaged the hotel and caused several deaths and injuries. In later years it was subjected to periodic rocket attacks without much success.

Renovation has taken place frequently at the hotel over the years. It is now in the hands of a private company, the Tulip Group, and is a luxurious, comfortable hotel which feels very secure. It has some interesting shops in its arcade and is very expensive.

the Royal Tulip has tastefully decorated rooms & suites, & has been designed for both traveller & business people. The spacious lobby & well-landscaped garden & terrace are welcoming & friendly, & the hotel has all the facilities you could require with little extras to give you that added touch of home. The hotel has high-speed Wi-Fi access throughout; AC; a cash machine; coffee shop; gym; gift/newsstand; sauna/spa/health club; swimming pool; business centre & 24-hour security. Rooms have tea-making facilities, satellite TV, hair dryer, safety deposit box & room service – & bullet-proof glass in all the windows! The hotel has a restaurant (Al-Rayhanaa) with a daily international buffet, a cigar lobby lounge, a terrace café (Al-Rayhanaa Terrace) with nargiles, snacks & drinks), a banqueting restaurant (Al-Zahir), the National Restaurant for à la carte lunch & dinner, a BBQ Restaurant & Terrace, swimming pool bar & nightclub. $$$$

🏠 **Cristal Grand Ishtar Hotel** (307 rooms) Fardous Sq, off Sadoun St; m 0770 677 0701;

www.cristalhospitality.com. The tallest building in Baghdad & the tallest structure in Iraq after the Baghdad Tower, the Cristal Grand Ishtar was renovated in 2011 for the Arab summit. It has a business centre, a fully equipped gym, an outdoor swimming pool, spa, steam room & sauna. The hotel has the impersonal air of many international hotels, but all the rooms are spacious & recently modernised with complementary high-speed Wi-Fi, tea-making facilities, safe, satellite TV & minibar. The hotel even offers an evening turn-down service. As well as 24-hour room service, guests have the choice of 3 restaurants, the Al-Warkaa with à la carte international cuisine; the Al-Dananeer serving fusion cuisine & the Blendz Café serving snacks, pastries, coffees & cocktails throughout the day. The rear of the hotel backs on to the River Tigris, but sadly access is blocked by concrete blast walls due to the security situation. $$$$

🏠 **International Palestine Hotel** (406 rooms) Fardous Sq, off Sadoun St (across from the Cristal Grand Ishtar); m 0790 144 3571. This hotel draws attention because of its oddly shaped balconies which look like Empire fighter ships from *Star Wars*. It gained international fame when it housed foreign journalists during the US-led invasion of Iraq. It re-opened in 2012 after a 2-year facelift. Despite this, the hotel is quite average, dark & dingy, with facilities & service not up to the high standard you would expect for the amount you pay. The rooms are spartan with laminated wood, dark curtains & low levels of lighting. Some were not so clean & required repairs. The restaurant menu is limited for international travellers. There is an 18th-floor bar with a panoramic view, which is one of the few places in Baghdad you can get an alcoholic drink. Friendly service. **$$$$**

UPMARKET

🏠 **Al-Mansour Hotel** (306 rooms) Al-Salhiya St; ☏ 537 3227; m 0790 426 6851/0740 157 5938; e mansourhotel@yahoo.com; www.almansourhotel.com. Charmingly situated overlooking the Tigris with 10ha of gardens; the Al-Mansour has slightly smaller rooms than the Cristal Grand Ishtar. It has 4 restaurants, including French & Chinese (situated in the gardens), a health centre & an outdoor swimming pool & business centre. The rooms have Wi-Fi, AC, TV with in-house films & minibar. Staff are very helpful & friendly. An all-round good hotel, it feels very secure with many checkpoints in the area & the hotel is surrounded by concrete blast walls. **$$$**

🏠 **Baghdad Hotel** (175 rooms) Sadoun St; ☏ 717 1882; e hotel.baghdad@yahoo.com; www.baghdadhoteliraq.com. Built in 1956, this is one of the oldest hotels in Baghdad. Centrally situated overlooking the River Tigris, it has a health club, sauna, steam bath & swimming pool, & a business centre. The hotel has a restaurant serving international cuisine, a café serving teas & snacks & a nightclub. All rooms are spacious with AC & private balconies, minibar & satellite TV. **$$$**

🏠 **Coral Boutique Hotel** (80 rooms) Baghdad University Rd, Jadiriyah; ☏ 781 4400; e info@coral-hotelbaghdad.com; www.coral-international.com. Located in Jadiriyah, one of the nicest & safest areas in Baghdad, this hotel is run to international standards & is quite competitive compared to other hotels in the area. Rooms are clean & new with modern furniture, Wi-Fi,

minibar & comfy beds. Bathrooms are a decent size with hot water. The hotel has a good restaurant offering international food with large portions & reasonable prices, although choice at the b/fast buffet is limited. Room service is good & fast, & the employees are friendly. **$$$**

MID-RANGE

🏠 **Babylon Hotel** (310 rooms) Zuweia; ☏ 776 1964. A 16-floor hotel situated on the banks of the Tigris, 20-mins' walk from the centre of Baghdad. It has a health club, games room, indoor & outdoor swimming pools & a business centre. Rooms have AC, fridge, TV & some have a minibar. This hotel is popular with Iraqi businessmen. **$$**

🏠 **Al-Mas Hotel** (50 rooms) Kahrmana Sq, Karada; m 0782 128 2495; e almas.hotel@ymail.com. A nice, clean, functional hotel, the Al-Mas has a 24-hour front desk & a garden, a ticket service, luggage storage & free parking. Within easy walk of Sadoun St, it has 2 restaurants, one of which is buffet-style. Rooms are clean & comfortable with a balcony, and all have Wi-Fi, a flat-screen TV, AC, an electric kettle, a hair dryer & free toiletries. **$$**

🏠 **Uruk Hotel** (40 rooms) End of Al-Nedhal St (near the National Theatre); ☏ 718 9776; e info@urukhotel.com; www.urukhotel.com. Behind a rather kitschy façade, a very good hotel with friendly employees, traditional Iraqi hospitality & more atmosphere than most Baghdad hotels. Despite a noisy neighbourhood (the shops across the road sell alcohol) the hotel is quiet with modern, clean rooms. The b/fast buffet has a wide choice & the waiters are attentive. The reasonably sized rooms have comfortable beds, Wi-Fi, flat screen TV, a safety deposit box in the wardrobe, AC & tea-making facilities. Bathrooms are clean with a shower over the bath with constant hot water, toilet & bidet, rails over the bath to hang laundry, a shaving mirror, space around the wash basin for toiletries, a hair dryer & clean towels. The hotel has a tiny, underused swimming pool outside the b/fast room with clean water. **$$**

🏠 **Al-Yamama Hotel** off Sadoun St; m 079 013 5823; e al_yemama2010@yahoo.com. Specialises in looking after pilgrim groups. The hotel has restaurant facilities for groups & has 3 floors of rooms for groups. It has been refurbished over the last 2 years & is a basic, comfortable hotel with good security. **$$**

BUDGET/SHOESTRING

⌂ **Palm Beach Hotel & Restaurant**
(40 rooms) Abu Nawas St; m 0740 010 6827;
e Emil-palmbech@outlook.com. Comfortable,
en-suite rooms. The hotel has Wi-Fi and a nice
reception area. It overlooks the River Tigris facing
the International Zone and is ideally suited for
visits to the centre of Baghdad. **$**

✗ WHERE TO EAT AND DRINK *See map, pages 130–1.*

Baghdad is famous for its mazgouf fish restaurants. Mazgouf is a flat fish native to
the Tigris. Half the pleasure is in watching it being prepared. It is split and roasted in
the open air on stakes around a wood fire. Unfortunately, unless properly prepared,
it has an overwhelming taste of mud! It is not an inexpensive meal either. At present
there is only really one main restaurant open for mazgouf, which is in the Abu
Nuwas Park and is said to be one of the best. The other restaurants are shut due to
security problems, but as they are clustered in a popular spot by the river and open-
air park, they will no doubt pick up again.

RESTAURANTS SERVING IRAQI FOOD

✗ **Saj Al-Reef** Karada 62 St, near the University of
Technology; m 0750 313 0008; ⏰ lunch & dinner.
The speciality is *raj saj,* a roasted bread stuffed with
meat, chicken, etc. It also serves oriental & western
meals like pizza, rice & meat, kebab & Mexican food.
The take-away section serves snack food.

✗ **Crispy** Al-Wathiq Sq, Karada; m 0790 271
0770; ⏰ 09.00 –23.00 daily. Popular family-style
restaurant serving traditional Iraqi food.

INTERNATIONAL CUISINE

✗ **Italian Reef Restaurant** Arasat Alhindia St;
☎ 717 4582; ⏰ 10.00–midnight daily. This family-
owned restaurant opened in 1995 & serves Italian,
Mediterranean & Middle Eastern food, hamburgers
& desserts.

✗ **Aroma Restaurant,** Babylon Hotel St,
Jadiriyah; m 0780 999 2999. Stylish restaurant
which looks like a hotel. Good atmosphere, music,
décor & service. Great range of reasonably priced
food, inc Italian food & grills, & a buffet on Fridays.
It also serves perfect coffee & cakes.

✗ **Mazaya Restaurant** Al-Mansour St; m 7801
522 2006; ⏰ lunch & dinner. Great food ranging
from Italian to Iraqi, Chinese to Middle Eastern.
A clean, friendly restaurant with good, though
sometimes a little slow, service. Conveniently
located in Al-Mansour St close to the Mall.

✗ **Bosphorus Restaurant** Al-Mansour St.
Stylish family restaurant serving Turkish food.
Comfortable & spacious, food is well presented &
service is good.

✗ **Al-Areesha Restaurant** Imam Al-Adham
St, Al-Adhamiya; m 0770 064 4996. Located in
a very beautiful old area near the river, this is a
lovely place to visit in the evening to soak up the
atmosphere. International food of a high standard,
the service is great & the staff are friendly. Large
portions & prices are reasonable.

✗ **Burger Joint Restaurant** 14th Ramadan
St, Al-Mansour district. Clean & modern interior:
iPads are used to take orders, which must be a first
in Baghdad. Ex-pat opinion is that this restaurant
serves the best burgers in Baghdad. Frequented
by local youngsters, it has a friendly atmosphere.
Serving a variety of burgers & fries (inc veggie-
burgers), this is the place to come if you fancy a
taste of home.

✗ **Ice Pack Restaurant** International Zone,
Karada and Al-Mansour district. Serving pizza,
milkshakes & ice cream, these branches of Ice Pack
have recently opened. They have a huge range of
ice-cream flavours. Modern setting, clean, bright
with friendly staff, standards are consistent across
all of their locations. Free Wi-Fi & great prices.

ENTERTAINMENT

Baghdad's social life is conducted in safe places, in people's homes and
neighbourhoods where they are known or in public spaces where they feel
comfortable. Although Baghdad has been edging towards a cautious normality,
albeit under a very heavy security presence at almost every junction, the security

situation means that most Baghdadis are still heavily restricted in what they can do. Subsequently they are reluctant to venture out of their local area after dark due to fear of kidnapping and the difficulties of passing through innumerable roadblocks and checkpoints. Hence social life generally revolves around family and dining out at small, local restaurants and mainly takes place during daylight hours. Although there are no bars, alcohol is tolerated in the central neighbourhoods of the capital with Christian populations. At the height of the city's sectarian tensions it was available in only the most secretive of back-door transactions. In hard-line neighbourhoods such as Sadr City, selling alcohol will still get you killed.

There is a little disco boat that coasts on the Tigris at weekends, although this is largely for groups of young men. New private parks have sprung up in the city's green spaces to rival the long-established Zawara Amusement Park, with its rides and gardens, popular with both families and groups of young men and women. One of the recent additions to the Baghdad social scene is the Olive Leaves, formerly a farm near Jadiriyah, where you can find several restaurants and a playground set among palm trees beside the river. A popular spot in summer, when it catches the breeze from the river, it is a safe place for children to play. Baghdad has a National Theatre, a National Ballet, a few cinemas and a number of art galleries. Any visitor to Baghdad expecting nightlife, however, will be sorely disappointed.

LIFE MUST GO ON

Until recently going to a restaurant, one of the few evening diversions available in Baghdad, would have been considered dangerous and areas such as Karada and Mansour would have been empty by 6pm. Now things are starting to change.

'People used to be scared to go out at night. I feel happy this has changed. Baghdad is a big city and we need to enjoy culture. We used to go to the theatre and cinemas all the time before the war', says Elaf Mohammed, a 29-year-old civil engineer accompanied by her husband Osama and 3-year-old daughter. 'It is so good that we can do so again.'

While the Baghdad cinemas that once showed international and Arabic films remain closed, bar a few matinee screenings, it is a sign of progress perhaps, that families now have the option of going to the Baghdad National Theatre in the evening. The fact that the city is hosting evening shows at all is progress, according to director Ghanim Hamid. 'Things are undoubtedly better security-wise,' he says. 'People can finally come out and enjoy themselves in the evening. The main problem, for us, is that there is not much money around to stage productions that we can be proud of.'

For Khalid Ahmed, a bus driver from Adhamiya, an evening at the theatre is a welcome boost for his wife and three children. 'I passed the theatre in my car the other day and I saw a poster advertising the play, so I thought I'd take the family,' he said. Other people share his positive outlook. 'We are able to organise different activities,' said Mufidh al Jaziri, a former culture minister who now heads an association which supports the arts. He helped organise a human rights film festival in 2012 and hopes to recreate a time in the 1950s when, he says, 'Iraq was in the lead in modern poetry, novels and short stories'. And yet, he adds sadly, art and music will not truly grow until the country's politics and security settle into real peace.

PRACTICAL RULES FOR THE CONSUMPTION OF ALCOHOL In Baghdad the liquor shops are open again but keep a low profile due to the violence directed against them. Most of these shops are located in the Karada district and along Sadoun Street. Alcohol is not served in most hotels and many hotels forbid alcohol being brought onto the premises. For further advice on the availability of and penalties for consuming alcohol, see page 107.

THEATRE The National Theatre in Fatah Square, Karada, was built during the Iran-Iraq war and in its heyday hosted sell-out foreign productions of Shakespeare and Chekhov. Closed during the 2003 war, it re-opened in 2009. Today it is protected by police who are deployed in large numbers in surrounding streets during and after performances, and theatre goers are subjected to thorough vehicle searches and security checks. The theatre holds an audience of 1,000 and seats cost approximately IQD10,000.

CINEMA At one time Baghdad had numerous cinemas showing a variety of films, local and international. However, recent years have seen the closing down of most cinemas which have been turned into commercial outlets. As in other countries across the Arab world, shopping malls are being built with integral multiplex cinemas and this will be the way forward for cinema in Iraq in the coming years.

MUSIC Music plays an important part in daily Iraqi life, although recently music was declared *haram* (sinful) for Muslims by the Islamic fundamentalists and has begun to disappear from the streets. Many music shops are closed under threat of violence. What is left on the shelves are Arabic artists and very few Iraqi musicians. Those who still want to record travel abroad to find a production company. The Opera and Concert Halls have been closed, with the exception of the National Theatre.

Most orchestras and companies have disbanded because so many artists have left the country. The **Iraqi National Symphony Orchestra** continues to rehearse and perform more or less regularly, even abroad. The orchestra began life as the Baghdad Symphony Orchestra in 1944 and is still going strong. It has 90 members and in 2010 it put on 23 full orchestral concerts around Iraq, including *Rhapsody in Blue*, Grieg's *Piano Concerto*, Wagner and Brahms as well as specially commissioned works by Iraqi composers. In November 2011 it played Rimsky-Korsakov's *Scheherazade*, a grand, challenging piece that took two months of rehearsal. In 2012 the orchestra appeared at the National Theatre as part of a ceremony to celebrate Baghdad Day. The orchestra's home is the Institute of Fine Arts in the Al-Mansour district of Baghdad, not a concert hall, but a theatre with a smallish orchestra pit. The auditorium capacity is 900 and all concerts are free, thanks to government support. Karim Wasfi, the chief conductor, believes that in a sense they represent a collective achievement for the country. His mission is to make the orchestra open to every part of Iraqi society, and indeed every sect is represented in it – Christians, Shias, Sunnis and Kurds – men and women. Karim has launched a youth orchestra and even pays disadvantaged children to come to concerts. When attending the National Theatre, audiences have to contend with security checks, personal searches and police surrounding the building, as well as a long walk to get to the building from the car parks which are miles away.

CULTURE

ART GALLERIES During the Saddam era there were six art galleries in Abu Nuwas Street alone. Today there are fewer than six in the whole of Baghdad. The arts have suffered greatly, artists have been threatened and many of the best have left the country along with musicians, poets, writers and much of the intelligentsia. A three-storey art gallery has opened on Abu Nuwas Street and there is also a statue of Scheherazade telling the stories of the Arabian nights to King Shahryar. Opening times vary and change, so you should check ahead by phone, email or website.

Dijla Art Gallery Abu Nuwas St, opposite the Scheherazade statue; m 0790 133 0880; www.dijlaart.com. A prominent gallery specialising in contemporary Iraqi art. Established in 1997 by Zainab Mahdi, it is dedicated to encouraging & promoting the art of Iraqi art pioneers as well as emerging & established artists working primarily in painting, sculpture, graphic & ceramic art. It has 12 viewing rooms & is also a venue for cultural activities such as lectures, open debates & musical performances.

Hewar Art Gallery Al-Wazerya, near the Turkish embassy; ✆ 425 0086; www.qasimsabti.com. In 1992, Qasim Sabti founded the Hewar Art Gallery in Baghdad, which has since become an important & active oasis for Iraqi artists (*hewar* means

dialogue). The gallery has a garden in the back, where there is a charming café, surrounded by lush plants & sheltered from the sun by a corrugated tin roof supported by antique columns.

Orfali Gallery m 0790 609 0669; www.orfaligallery.com. Established by Wadad Orfali who has participated in numerous exhibitions in & out of Iraq, inc in Moscow, Paris, Warsaw, Spain, USA & the UK.

Madarat Gallery Al-Wazerya; m 0790 178 9622; www.artiniraq.net. Madarat Gallery is a cultural centre in Baghdad. Opened in January 2006 by Attitudes SAC (an NGO which promotes culture in Iraq) it hosts cultural events such as exhibitions, music concerts & cultural sessions.

LIBRARY Despite death threats and the murder of some of its staff, librarians at Iraq's **National Library and Archive** (*Inia; Al-Adham St, nr Al-Maidan Sq*) are doing their best to rebuild it: 60% of the archive materials and 95% of the rare book collection were either destroyed or went missing during the looting that followed the capture of Baghdad in 2003. Before the destruction, the library and archives held 417,000 books, 2,618 periodicals dating from the late-Ottoman era to modern times, and a collection of 4,412 rare books and manuscripts. Saddam loyalists burnt the entire Republican Archive, which contained the records of the Baathist regime between the years 1958 and 1979. Also completely destroyed were the Baathist court proceedings detailing the charges against and trials of party opponents. The library was set up in 1920 with the help of Gertrude Bell, Oriental Secretary to the British High Commissioner.

SHOPPING

Al Mansour Mall, Hay Al-Mansour, opened in 2013. Built over four floors, this air-conditioned mall contains a 3-D cinema, an indoor amusement area with a carousel, bumper cars, a roller coaster and a giant bouncy slide, women's, men's and children's fashions, sportswear, jewellery, foreign exchange, restaurants and cafeterias. It has an electronic protection system, including surveillance cameras and is heavily patrolled by security personnel. **Maximall** in Al-Mansour Street is more akin to a department store that a traditional mall. The first floor is a supermarket, the second floor sells clothing, the third features furniture and home goods, while the top floor has a food court and a play area for children. Here you can find cheese from Denmark, huge frozen prawns from the Persian Gulf, or enjoy a nargile pipe on the outdoor balcony overlooking the domes of Saddam Hussein's vast unfinished mosque, planned to be the biggest in the world. The fifth-floor gym and beauty salon are off-limits to men. The mall has strict security checks in place and people and bags are searched on entry.

The **Copper Bazaar**, alongside Al-Mustansiriya College, off Al-Rashid St, where pots for everyday and ornamental use are beaten in the traditional way, is justifiably famous as a popular tourist attraction. Today the clamour of the coppersmiths has diminished as workshops have closed and the trade declines. But it is still possible to find some wonderful examples of beaten copper antique coffee cups and pots and intricately designed trays in the shops dating back 80 to 100 years, although the crowds are long gone. Around this end of Al-Rashid Street are modern textile bazaars where traditional Arab clothing and modern designer clothes jostle for pride of place. And all are sold at bargain prices. Some of the nearby streets are narrow with interesting buildings, nearly all decaying and crying out for restoration. There are old Jewish Buildings, several ruined synagogues and old caravanserai buildings running from here down to the river. When the author trod these now near silent streets in the 1970s he was often lost among the teeming throngs. The once-famous **Mutanabi Street book market** was ripped apart by a car bomb on 5 March 2007. A plan to restore the street's historic buildings has been launched and the Shahbandar coffee house has been rebuilt. Poets and writers throughout the world have joined the 'Al-Mutanabi Street starts here' project to support their Iraqi counterparts. **Karada Street** is full of trendy shops and markets selling clothes, shoes, jewellery and more. It is busy with families in the late afternoon and evenings, especially at weekends.

SPORTS/FITNESS

Baghdad's top-end hotels typically have their own pools and fitness facilities and these are probably the most modern and high-quality sports venues in the city. Some may be open to non-residents for a daily fee, it is always worth enquiring. Please be aware though that outside of hotels, it is usual in Muslim countries to have separate public bathing facilities for men and women/children, or for the facilities to be open at different times to each of these groups. Times can change regularly, so it is always worth enquiring ahead.

OTHER PRACTICALITIES

COMMUNICATIONS Baghdad has definitely emerged from the time warp of Saddam's era when mobile phones and satellite television were banned and hardly anyone used the internet. There are hundreds of satellite channels now and most people have a mobile phone. Virtually all hotels offer internet access, usually high speed and free, and this is how the majority of visitors get on line. Baghdad's telephone exchange was destroyed during the first few days of the First Gulf War. Rebuilt by the French in 2003, it was subsequently destroyed again. Not surprisingly no attempt has been made at further reconstruction, and telecommunications in Iraq are now exclusively of the mobile variety. The latest handsets can be bought in the numerous phone shops and sim cards and top ups are readily available all over Baghdad. The only problem is that people and businesses frequently change their phone numbers.

MONEY There are exchange facilities in the arrivals hall at Baghdad airport. In central Baghdad there are numerous money exchanges which are quick and easy to use. In particular you will find a number of these in Sadoun Street and the Karada district (among the gold shops). All the shops are competitive and have pretty much the same exchange rates.

Bathed in the rainbow-coloured light of an old Baghdadi window, Ali al Makhzomy explains his plan to get technology-obsessed young Iraqis to read books; old-fashioned books with pages. Eleven years after the toppling of Saddam Hussein, young people who despair of a future in Iraq are still trying to emigrate. Many of those who remain hope that their country will someday emerge as a new version of ultra-modern, oil-rich Dubai. Makhzomy, 26, and his friends would prefer to take Baghdad back to a more elegant past. 'We really want the Baghdad of the 1930s or 40s or 50s to return. It was more civilised,' he says. 'How do we know? We read about it.'

In a room on the second floor of the wood-panelled Al-Atrakchi House café, Makhzomy is starting an informal public library with about 800 books to encourage the clientele to take time to read – and to escape the world outside. Bombings have been common in Baghdad for so long that violence is almost less of a concern to many Iraqis than the sheer difficulty of daily life. Traffic jams due to road closures and checkpoints have turned his bus ride to work into an ordeal. When Makhzomy reads books on his iPad, people ask what he is doing. 'I tell them, I'm reading. You should try it,' he says.

It has not always been this way. Iraq is the land where writing was invented and Baghdad was famous for its book market. But basic literacy has plummeted and strict security measures mean few people can just walk off the street into a library. Baghdad's famous Mutanabi Street, where merchants set out piles of used books on Fridays, has been mostly rebuilt after a devastating bombing seven years ago. Crowds show up for poetry readings and cultural events on weekends. But on a recent day, there were more young men crowded around a stall selling fake designer sunglasses than there were buying books. On a nearby street an elderly bookseller in a suit and tie is surrounded by shelves of books but no buyers. 'Young people don't read any more,' he laments.

Makhzomy is not among them. He inherited his love of books from his mother and his father, a lab technician who died in 2001 and from whom he inherited

WHAT TO SEE AND DO

MUSEUMS
Iraq National Museum (*Nasir St, Karkh; www.iraqmuseum.org*) The looting of the Iraq Museum was the story of a cultural genocide. 'If a country's civilisation is looted its history ends,' commented Riad Mohammed, an Iraqi archaeologist. The museum, which first opened in 1923, occupies an area of 4,700m². It was expanded continually until 1983, culminating in 28 large exhibition halls, with displays pre-dating 9000BC and reaching right up to the Islamic era. The museum's collections included some of the earliest tools ever made, gold from the famous Royal Cemetery at Ur, and Assyrian bull figures and reliefs from the ancient Assyrian capitals of Nimrud, Nineveh and Khorsabad. The former president of Iraq's State Board of Antiquities, the late Donny George, recalled in the introduction to *The Looting of the Iraq Museum Baghdad: The Lost Legacy of Ancient Mesopotamia*, 'As I walked through the museum, I passed gigantic Assyrian wall carvings, some 15m long and about 5m tall, showing ceremonies in ancient Nimrud and Khorsabad. Giant human-headed winged bulls that had once guarded the gates of the Assyrian capitals loomed overhead. Buried for thousands of years they blazoned forth as

many of the books that now make up his collection. Makhzomy, who works at the Ministry of Culture, is funding the project on his own. He first tried it in a modern café in the glitzy new Mansour Mall, Baghdad's first large shopping centre, but he found patrons there more interested in shopping than in culture. He has since relocated most of his books to Al-Atrakchi House, where the owner has re-created the atmosphere of historical Baghdad cafés. 'In Baghdad, we have maybe 1,600 houses from the 18th century, but there is no preservation,' says Abdul Razak al Atrakchi, whose family has sold antiques and carpets in Iraq for more than a century. 'Nobody cares about heritage.'

Atrakchi opened the café six months ago in the upmarket neighbourhood of Mansour, adorning it with antique windows, doors and tiles he had collected from the market. Wooden benches covered with cushions are arranged around traditional Baghdadi tables inlaid with flowered ceramic tiles. Upstairs in a room lined with bevelled mirrors, elegantly dressed men and women who remember the old Baghdad (and whose average age appears to be about 70) listen to a lecture on poetry. Makhzomy and Atrakchi say they believe that if literary culture again became part of everyday life, Iraq's younger generation could rebuild the country. The library that Makhzomy is starting includes books from his own collection on history and politics, poetry and novels. He was given books at the Baghdad International Book Fair but rejected many of them because they were religious texts emphasising adherence to Islamic law. 'The society we want to support is liberal, where democracy rules and you can say whatever you want,' Makhzomy says. 'We are trying to get all kinds of books, but we want to encourage youth to be open-minded.'

In addition to the library he has formed a group of volunteers to clean up historic places and introduce young Iraqis to museums. 'You find many young people who say, "I just want to leave Iraq," Makhzomy says. 'They see violence everywhere, no respect for the law, traffic jams... but with these cultural activities, we link Iraq's heritage to their hearts.' That will, he believes, 'give them a reason to stay.'

though carved only yesterday, to proclaim the majesty of the greatest empire in the ancient world. In other cases were some of the earliest known pieces of elaborate pottery, jewellery and statues from Ur, Babylon, Nineveh, Nimrud, Ashur and the score of cities scattered along the Tigris and Euphrates rivers. All in all, the Iraq Museum was one of the greatest collections of cultural treasures in our world. And today it is no more.'

After the capture of Baghdad by American troops in April 2003 the museum was looted, and an estimated 15,000 items were stolen, including Abbasid wooden doors and Sumerian, Akkadian and Hatraean statues, gold and silver materials, necklaces, pendants and pottery. Several famous pieces, such as the Warka vase, were returned, but the collection of 4,800 cylinder seals is still missing and half of the objects looted from the museum are still unaccounted for. Refurbishments are continuing: the Islamic Halls are basically ready and the Assyrian Halls are complete. Building work on an annex at the entrance is now complete. Up until the beginning of 2015 the museum was open by invitation only, but it re-opened to the public in February and took the next step in its rehabilitation to being one of the world's great museums. Given what has happened in the last few years this is a momentous act of faith and, actually, courage. Everyone is confident, the new staff are young and eager and the professionals are realising that they are not alone with this work. The British Museum has assisted the Iraq Museum with conservation, archaeological and curatorial assistance, as have other museums across the world. This inspires self-confidence and provides a fresh impetus to the study of ancient Mesopotamia.

Natural History Museum (*www.en.uobaghdad.edu.iq*) Established in 1943, this museum is part of Baghdad University. During the looting after the 2003 war rare fish fossils and insect, mammal, reptile and amphibian collections were destroyed, and now there is no exhibition hall, although there is an e-museum which can be accessed via their website.

National Museum of Modern Art (*Haifa St; m 0771 106 7936*) Contained in two big halls used as galleries, storage rooms and an office, the National Museum of Modern Art is home to a collection of more than 19,000 art works of pioneer artists in Iraq. Officially under the administration of the Ministry of Culture, it is housed in the same main building as the Ministry. The collection represents the art history of the Iraqi people, their traditions and heritage. As well as making these works accessible to visitors, the museum also runs educational workshops about Iraqi arts and promotes cultural ties within Iraq and with other countries and cultures.

Baghdad Museum (*Mamoun St, Rusafa District, near Shuhada Bridge on the east bank of the Tigris'* ⊕ *Sat–Thu*) Traditional professions and popular customs of old Baghdad are represented at this museum in colourful life-size models. Many of those professions and customs are fast disappearing so are very interesting to see, even as tableaux. For instance, you will see an old water seller, the harem and wedding preparations. Paintings, photographs, maps and other illustrative material depicting Baghdad's history and rulers are also on display.

HISTORICAL BUILDINGS
The Abbasid Palace This remarkable building on the corner of 17 July Bridge and Al-Rashid St/Ahmedi Square with its beautiful arch is a fine example of Islamic architecture, reminiscent of that found in Samarkand. It was constructed during the reign of Caliph al Nasser Lidnillah (1179–1225). The only Abbasid palace left in Baghdad, it has a central courtyard and two stories of rooms, with beautiful arches and *muqarnases* (ornately decorated cornice supports) in brickwork, and a remarkable *iwan* (a rectangular vaulted hall, walled on three sides with the fourth side open) with brickwork ceiling and façade. When it was partly reconstructed in recent times another *iwan* was built to face it. Because of the palace's resemblance in plan and structure to Al-Mustansiriya school some scholars believe it is actually the Sharabiya School, a school for Islamic theology built in the 12th century, mentioned by the old Arab historians. Parts of the building were reconstructed by the State Establishment of Antiquities and Heritage during the Saddam era and a collection of historical remains are exhibited, representing certain stages of the country's Arab Islamic history.

Al-Mustansiriya School The Al-Mustansiriya School, on the left bank of the Tigris, near Martyrs Bridge, is one of the most impressive reminders of the Abbasid age. Built on the orders of the Caliph al Mustansir Billah, it was completed in 1234, an architectural feat of its time. The college marked a new stage in the development of learning in the Islamic world. Religious colleges had formerly been concerned with only one of the four Islamic schools of law; here for the first time was a college

GERTRUDE BELL

Born in 1868 into a wealthy industrialist family, Gertrude Bell is often described as the first woman to get a first in modern history from Oxford. As with many things in her life though, things weren't always as they seemed with Miss Bell. In actual fact she was the first woman to pass the *requirements* for a first in history at Oxford in 1888 when she was 20, although since women were not allowed to get degrees at Oxford until the early 20th century, she never actually got the degree.

In the years that followed, she came out at Court, learned Persian, Arabic and Turkish, wrote books, climbed the Matterhorn, joined the Anti-Suffrage League, translated Sufi poetry, suffered a broken engagement, studied cartography and archaeology and travelled the world. Becoming a skilled photographer in a day where photography really required skill, she took thousands of photographs of ancient sites and ruins, photographs which to this day are the best record of the buildings and structures, many of which have fallen further into decay or disappeared altogether. By her thirties, she was an expert on Arabian desert travel and politics. Much of her success was due to her understanding the importance of following the proper local customs and the advantage she had of being able to speak with the women as much as with the men. Never condescending, she had charm and tact and generally made a good impression on everyone.

Miss Bell became increasingly involved in the archaeological and political affairs of the Middle East from the early 20th century onwards. In 1911 at Carchemish she met a young, blond-haired, blue-eyed Oxford graduate, the archaeologist T E Lawrence whom she later would join in the military. Her frustrated love affair with married soldier and administrator Dick Doughty-Wylie ended when he was killed in the Dardanelles campaign in 1915. Recruited by British intelligence during World War I, she attained the rank of major, later serving as a Political Officer and then Oriental Secretary to the High Commissioner in Baghdad. But it is Bell's exploits in Iraq that deserve attention. Still working for the Foreign Office, in 1916 she moved to Baghdad as an advisor to Sir Percy Cox, the Consul General. The only woman invited by Winston Churchill to the Cairo conference of 1921, she was instrumental in drawing the borders and defining the administration of modern Iraq and installing Faisal I as a Western-style constitutional monarch friendly to England.

One area where Miss Bell was ahead of her time was when she helped write the antiquities laws for Iraq. She passionately believed that the antiquities excavated in the country should stay there, a revolutionary attitude in 1920 when the usual arrangement was that the archaeologists took the choice spoils, leaving little for the country of origin. She also established the Iraq Museum in Baghdad, which under her direction became the home of some of the world's most priceless antiquities.

By 1926 Miss Bell had been friend and advisor to soldiers and sheiks, presidents and prime ministers, and even the occasional king. But her busy (and at times hard) life took its toll. Although devoted to her father, she never considered retiring to England. Living alone in Baghdad and in failing health, on the night of 11 July, she took an overdose of sleeping pills. Whether it was accidental or intentional isn't known, but the consensus is generally the latter. She was found dead the next morning.

intended to teach the doctrines of all four schools: Hanafi, Maliki, Shafei and Hanabli. In addition to teaching Islamic theological sciences and the Koran, applied sciences such as medicine, pharmacy and mathematics were taught. The library, which contained about 80,000 books, was one of the most important centres of learning in the Muslim world.

Sitt Zumurrud Khatoun's Tomb
Situated within Sheikh Marouf al Karkhi's mausoleum in the middle of the cemetery on the west bank of the Tigris in Al-Karkh district, behind the railway station, this peculiarly shaped building dates back to the late Abbasid period (1179–1225) and was constructed by Zumurrud Khatoun, wife of Caliph al Mustadhi Bi-Amrillah, as her own mausoleum. A prominent figure of the Abbasid period, she was also the mother of Caliph al Nasir din Illah. She built the Al-Shafiya School which was inaugurated in 1192, the Al-Khaffafeen mosque on the banks of the Tigris, a Ribat (an Islamic religious and military construction) as well as her own tomb before she died in 1303. The building's most important feature is the dome transforming itself from an octagon into a 16-sided figure and back again. It is one of the most important pieces of architecture in Baghdad, and its Iraqi builder has excelled in designing and building the dome using bricks. The building has witnessed various architectural phases, the last of which was carried out by Nadhim Pasha in 1910. The Department of Antiquity and Heritage renovated the Mausoleum in 1972. Today, the tomb is entered from a square-planned, domed structure that was built to replace an earlier one. From this area, a staircase rises up to the base of the *muqarnas* dome while a tight corridor just over 1m high leads to the octagonal burial chamber. The light inside the vault emanates from small holes cut in the *muqarna's* dome producing a glowing effect. Some people mistakenly believe the mausoleum belongs to Zubaida, the wife of the Abbasid Caliph Harun al Rashid, but she is buried in the Quraish cemetery in Kadhmain (see opposite).

Khan Murjan
(*Al-Rashid St, opp Murjan Mosque & next to the Central Bank*) Khan Murjan is the only completely roofed caravanserai in Iraq. Its brick-built ceiling is enormous and stunning, and it is one of the finest caravanserai in the Middle East. It provided lodgings for the merchants travelling along the caravan routes as they passed through Baghdad in the 13th century and later. Over the centuries it has been much restored and even in the time the author has been visiting, it has gone through many changes. In the 1970s it served as a restaurant and nightclub for the elite with belly-dancing, music and good food. Later it became a souvenir shop and tea shop. Today, with a rising water table causing flooding, it is sadly empty and neglected and in need of restoration again.

Al-Wastani Gate
This gate can be seen from the Al-Sahrawardi Shrine (see pages 148–9) but on the other side of the Khalid bin al-Walid Expressway. The only surviving one of four medieval gates of Baghdad, its date of construction is approximately 1120. It has a tower and a dome. The gate is being restored again, but you can walk around it.

Baghdad Railway Station
(*Damashaq Sq*). The main Baghdad railway station and largest in Iraq, it was built by the British between 1948 and 1953 to designs by J M Wilson who had worked under Lutyens in New Delhi before he came to Baghdad. It is without a doubt one of the best pieces of colonial architecture anywhere. Its clocks and dome are a feature of Baghdad's skyline and it is well worth a visit. The railway station once offered telegraph services and had a bank, a saloon,

a shopping area and a restaurant, as well as an office with printing presses which printed train tickets. Renovation of the station was started in June 2006 and is still ongoing. It still has a working post office on one of its platforms, as well as ticket offices in the dome.

MOSQUES AND SHRINES
Kadhmain Mosque In the northern neighbourhood of Kadhmain about 5km from the centre of Baghdad on the banks of the Tigris, Al-Kadhimiya is one of the oldest districts in Baghdad. Before the construction of the city, Al-Kadhimiya was one of the oldest towns in Iraq and was known as Shoneezi, an Arab name meaning black grain. When the Abbasid Caliph Abu Jafar al Mansour started the construction of the circular city of Baghdad in AD762 he put aside an area on the west bank of the Tigris for a cemetery for his family interments which became known as the Quraish Cemetery. Among those believed to be buried there were Caliph al Ameen, Zubaida (Harun al Rashid's wife) and Jafar al Mansour himself. Also buried there were of two of Prophet Mohammed's descendants, Imam Musa al Kadhim who died in 799 and his grandson Imam Mohammed al Jawad (see box, page 124). A township sprang up around their tombs which became known as Al-Kadhmain. The mosque was reconstructed in 1515 and later many additional rooms and galleries were added. Today, Kadhmain is the largest Shia mosque in Baghdad. The monumental entrance to the sanctuary is dominated by two gilded and glowing domes and four impressive minarets all coated with gold. A further four smaller minarets are also gold coloured. Entering the holy shrines one is overwhelmed by a feeling of majesty and amazement. The galleries and cloisters are decorated by ceramic tiles with geometric and foliage engravings and Koranic verses. In addition there are magnificent decorations made from mirrors and precious metals such and gold and silver. There are two famous clocks outside the shrine, one overlooking the Qibla Gate and the other the Al-Murid Gate on the eastern side. The clocks, facsimiles of London's Big Ben clock, were erected in 1883. Although their towers have subsequently been rebuilt they still enjoy great historical and aesthetic value. Kadhmain Mosque and Shrine has today become one of Islam's architectural wonders, and the mosque is always very crowded, thronged with Shia pilgrims from all over the Islamic world. In recent years the mosque's forecourts have been greatly enlarged. Opposite the mosque is a bustling market selling all sorts of religious souvenirs.

The Murjan Mosque In the centre of the city on Al-Rashid Street, opposite Khan Murjan and next to the Central Bank is the Murjan Mosque. Dating from the Jalayirid period which lasted until 1410, it was built as part of the Mirjaniya School by Amin-ef-din Murjan. From its inscriptions we know that Murjan, a commander of Uways, started building the madrassa with its mosque under Hasan Buzurg and finished the building under Uways in 1357. This madrassa was for the Shafis and Hanafis. Only the gate of the *madrassa*, or later mosque, now remains. It is famous for its ornamental brickwork and wonderful Kufic inscriptions in the prayer hall. Its location (next to the Central Bank) has made it a target for attacks in the past, but thankfully it has only suffered from minor damage, which has been repaired. The forecourts are currently being reconstructed.

Sheikh Abdul Kader Al-Gailiani Mosque This mosque on Kifah Street, Rusafa district, is the burial place of Sheikh Abdul Qadir al Gailiani, a 10th-century Muslim saint. The district around the mosque (Bad Al-Sheikh) also bears reference to him. The shrine was originally a religious school built by the Hanbali scholar Sheikh al Mubarak bin Ali al Mukharrami (d1119), later improved and enlarged by his pupil Sheikh Abdul Qadir al Gailiani a great scholar who was born in Gailan district to the south of the Caspian Sea in 1077. A descendant of Imam Ali, he came to Baghdad when he was young and became a teacher at the school. Practising self-denial and good deeds, he soon surpassed his masters. As his reputation spread he became a sheikh of the highest order, respected throughout the Islamic world and many miracles were attributed to him. Disciples and students gathered around him and he established the Al-Qadiriya order, one of the most widely spread Sufi orders in the world. Following his death in 1166, he was buried in the school's cloister, which later was used as a mosque. In 1534 Sultan Suleiman the Magnificent built an enormous dome of brick and gypsum over the tomb and prayer section of the mosque. The clock of the shrine was erected in 1898. Its tower was built by Abdul Rahman al Naqeeb, the first Prime Minister of Iraq in modern times who died in 1927. It was made at the famous Pona workshops in Bombay, India. It is 30m high. In 1970 the shrine was renovated, the two blue and white domes were restored and new ones were built. Further restoration in 2007 was halted when the shrine was the target of a car bomb which caused damage to it and to the new minaret that was under construction. Work remained suspended for many years until the complex could be surrounded by high concrete blast walls. This has now been done and the renovation work is nearly completed.

Al-Imam Al-Adham Mosque (*Adhamiya District*)

All visitors to Baghdad should see the mosque and mausoleum of al Imam al Adham, a famous and holy place to Muslims and one of the finest pieces of architecture of its type in Iraq. The district in which it is situated was a famous part of Baghdad during the Abbasid period when it contained a cemetery known as Al-Khaizaran Cemetery. Imam al Adham was born in Kufa in AD701. He met some of the aged Companions of the Prophet. A teacher who undertook the task of *Fatwa*, instead of codifying established practices, he applied logic and consistency in legal doctrines, thus establishing a method for tackling future problems and expanding the jurisdiction of law in Muslim society. He became a great scholar and introduced the Al-Hanafi doctrine into Islam. When he died in 767 he was buried in an existing mausoleum here and the district became known as the district of Abu Hanifa and Al-Adhamiya. His mausoleum has undergone various structural and architectural developments over the years. In the time of the Seljuk Sultan Alb Arsalan (1029–72), the building was renovated and a great dome was built on it. The present dome of the mosque was built in 1638. The mosque itself was built in 1871. It underwent renovation in 1903 and the exterior cloisters were added in 1948. One of the landmarks of the Imam Al-Adham Mosque is its big clock which was built by local craftsmen in the workshop of Abdul Razzaq Mahsoub al Adhami during the period 1921–29 and erected into its present position in 1958. Today with its huge prayer halls, the proportions of the monument and the distribution of the sources of light make this mosque one of Iraq's major shrines and prestigious places of worship for thousands of pilgrims each year.

Al-Sahrawardi Mosque and Shrine

Located on Sheikh Omar Street, and now surrounded by the car workshop district, is the mosque and shrine of the Sufi saint Sheikh Omar al Sahrawardi. A Sufi of the Al-Shafi school, he was known throughout the Islamic world for his teachings. He was born in Persia in 1144 and died in Baghdad in 1234. The shrine was built about 1225; its cylindrical dome has similarities to that of the dome of Sitt Zumurrud Khatoun's Tomb (see page 146) and is one of the oldest in Baghdad. It is also known for its slight tilt. Underneath the dome is the tomb of the saint and close by in a small alcove room is a simple slab under which purportedly lie the remains of Mustasim-billah, the last Caliph of Baghdad. In the author's experience this shrine has always exuded a feeling of peace and an odour of sanctity. There is a Kufic-style inscription above the entrance to the Sheikh's tomb. Today, like most of the historical and religious places in Iraq, the shrine has been renovated with new brick walls laid against the old; even the important outside front entrance façade has been renovated and new brick work added. Will its centuries' old peace ever return, or is that just a Western-European feeling for the old?

Suq Al-Ghazil Minaret Halfway up Caliph Street, near Shorja is a new mosque with an ancient minaret, all that remains of the Caliph's Palace Mosque which was built in the 10th century. The latter mosque was built by al Muktafi (902–908) but the existing minaret was actually built much later, in 1289 on certain parts which pre-date it considerably. It rises 33m above ground level with a base that has 12 sides measuring 21m in total and an ornate balcony. It takes its name today from the nearby spice market, Souk Al-Ghazil.

Umm Al-Qura Mosque (Mother of all Cities) In the Al-Adel area of Baghdad is the city's largest Sunni mosque. Originally called the Umm Al-Maarik (Mother of all Battles) it was designed to commemorate Iraq's 'victory' in the First Gulf War. However, not one of its monuments is dedicated to the soldiers who were killed in the war. Rather it serves as a personal tribute to Saddam Hussein himself, and it has been speculated that it was intended to have been his final resting place. Costing US$7.5 million to build, the mosque's foundation stone was laid on 28 April 1998, Saddam's 61st birthday. It was completed three years later in time for the tenth anniversary of the Gulf War. The building is constructed from white limestone with blue mosaic decorations. Red, white and black Iraqi flags are painted on the peaks of the inner minarets. Many of the architectural features of the mosque and the surrounding complex allude to either Saddam or the war (or both). It has four 43m-high minarets on its perimeter, each resembling the barrel of a Kalashnikov rifle and signifying the 43 days that the war lasted. Around the dome are another four 37m-high minarets, each in the shape of a Scud missile on its launchpad. A reflecting pool rings the dome in the shape of the Arab world. In the middle there is a monument of Saddam's thumbprint with his initials set in gold. The 28 fountains of the lake, the four inner minarets and the 37m height of each minaret together represent the date of Saddam's date of birth 28 April 1937. Behind an ornate door in an inner sanctum there used to be 650 pages of the Holy Koran rumoured to be penned in Saddam's own blood mixed with ink and preservatives, producing a red and brown colour with a tinge of blue. The calligraphy was the work of an Iraqi artist, Abas al Baghadi. On 28 August 2011, the mosque was attacked by a suicide bomber during prayers, killing at least 28 people.

Saddam Mosque The skeleton of the Saddam Mosque towers eerily above the centre of Baghdad. Built to be a replica of the Mother of All Battles Mosque, although five times bigger, it would have been the third biggest in the world after Mecca and Medina had it been completed. The cranes are still on site. There is a dilemma about its future. It cannot be demolished because it is a mosque; and it cannot be completed because of its association with Saddam.

CHURCHES There are a number of churches in Baghdad but after the violence against the Christian community in recent years (see page 22) many are locked up and difficult to visit.

Roman Catholic Church (*Al-Khulafaa St*) Also known as the Latin Church, the Roman Catholic Church is a massive architectural masterpiece built in 1866 on the site of a smaller church known as the Temple or Monastery of St Thomas the Apostle. The 10m structure resembles a cross with a towering dome. It has many impressive statues and is used by the Orthodox Copts of Iraq.

The Armenian Orthodox Church Located on Maidan Square off Al-Rashid Street, the Armenian Orthodox Church is also known as the Meskenta Church (from a woman who was martyred in the 5th century) or the Church of the Virgin Mary. One of the oldest churches in Baghdad, it was built in 1640 by Armenians on land they were given by the Ottoman Sultan Murad IV. Subsequently used by Nestorian Christians who played a significant role in the construction of the church, it later reverted back to the Armenians who completed the construction. It was further reconstructed in 1967. On 15 August each year a special ritual is held at the church to celebrate the Assumption of the Virgin Mary to heaven and Christians from across Baghdad and Iraq visit the church to witness the ritual and to participate in it. Certain local traditions and customs which pay tribute to St Meskenta's sacrifice are also held at the church, for example worshippers put an iron chain around their necks. If it unlocks automatically then their prayers will be answered.

The Chaldean Church (*Ras Al-Grayyel, near Wathba Sq*) Built in 1889 and called the Church of Mary Mother of Sorrows, it was later enlarged and a cloister was added making it one of the largest churches in Baghdad.

The Anglican Church of St George (*opp Mansour Hotel, Haifi St*) Built in the 1930s for a small Anglican community, including British subjects who resided in Iraq and who worked for British institutions. Today the Church runs a multi-faith medical clinic from its premises which specialises in the treatment of rare diseases.

MONUMENTS
Jawad Salim's Nasb Al-Hurriyah (Freedom Monument) On the central roundabout of Al-Tahrir Square, this is Baghdad's most famous monument. It consists of 14 separate 8m bronze castings providing a visual narrative of the 1958 revolution and reflecting on Iraqi history through Assyrian and Babylonian bas-reliefs.

The Martyrs Monument Located on the east side of the River Tigris near the Army Canal 4km from Fardous Square, this extraordinary monument of blue hearts was designed by Ismail Fattah al Turki and built by Mitsubishi in 1983 as a shrine to the million or so Iraqis killed during the eight-year war with Iran. Set by two lakes, the shrine is imposingly huge. The interior foundation is supposed to represent the tears of the relatives. In Saddam's time there were glass cases full of belongings of the dead including pens, nail clippers, letters home, glasses and dog tags. Today it has become a monument to Shia and Kurdish victims of Saddam's regime. Gruesome mannequins display firing-squad executions and the unearthing of mass graves. Although the setting is superb and there is no doubt that there cannot be many modern monuments to equal it in the Middle East, there are few visitors. I believe Iraqis do not wish to be reminded of these terrible

The International Zone, originally the home of the presidential palace of Saddam Hussein and the administrative centre of his regime, is now the centre of Iraq's parliament and government and home to the present president. The Zone also houses the largest American embassy in the world and several other smaller embassies such as the British and other Commonwealth consulates. It also contains the Victory Arch and the Unknown Soldier Monument.

However, to visit you must have an invitation from someone or an organisation currently in the Zone. You need two forms of photographic ID. Ideally you need your invitee to meet you at one of the crossing points to facilitate everything (there are a number of entrances).

years of aggression against Iran. The monument is not an easy place to enter as special police permission is required and the last group of tourists to visit found the interior completely locked.

The Victory Arch Located in the International Zone, which stops most would-be tourists from visiting is the Victory Arch. Also known as The Monument, this is Iraq's Arc de Triomphe, proclaiming victory in the eight-year Iran-Iraq war, according to the official Iraqi version of history. Situated next to the Monument of the Unknown Soldier, near the former Republican Palace and festival and parade ground, it is a gigantic structure with Saddam's hands holding two swords. The Monument provided the inspiration for Sami al Khalil's book. Khalil tells us that because no Iraqi foundry was big enough, the arms were cast in sections at the Morris Singer foundry in Basingstoke, England – the largest professional art foundry in the world. The swords, on the other hand, were cast in Iraq, and the official invitation card informs us that the raw steel was obtained by melting down the weapons of Iraqi martyrs who died in the fighting. The arches were built in duplicate, marking the two entrances of a vast parade ground.

The Unknown Soldier Monument Designed by Iraqi architects Abdulla Ihsan Kamel, Rifat Chadirji and Ihsan Shirzad, the Unknown Soldier Monument in Sadoun St was built in 1950. While resembling a flying saucer, it is actually supposed to represent a helmet and traditional shield dropping from a warrior's dying grasp. Situated on an artificial hill it is shaped like a low, truncated cone. Stepped platforms lead to the dome and the cubic sculpture on top. It is believed that the repeated circular and elliptical motifs echo the ancient circular city walls of Baghdad. The cube is made of seven layers of metal and said to represent the seven levels of heaven in the Islamic faith. The steel structure to the left of the dome which is meant to resemble the minaret of the Great Mosque in Samarra, used to light up in the Iraqi national colours of red, white, green and black Three ramps lead directly from the bottom to the top of the tomb signifying the Euphrates and Tigris rivers coming together and merging into the Shatt Al-Arab. After the fall of Saddam Hussein, the tomb was looted and damaged and is now closed and inaccessible to visitors.

Al-Amariya Shelter This air-raid shelter, located in the suburb also called Al-Amariya, was used by civilians during the First Gulf War. On 13 February 1991 it was hit by two bombs. At the time of the bombing, there were hundreds of Iraqi

Baghdad and Environs **WHAT TO SEE AND DO**

5

civilians in the shelter. More than 400 people were killed. The blast sent shrapnel into surrounding buildings, shattering glass windows and splintering their foundations. The shelter has been maintained as a memorial to those who died within it. In the eerie interior the hole left by the two bombs is intact, the craze of bombed metal and wrapped girders strangely beautiful. There are photographs of the victims and shadows, purportedly of those who died, have been burnt into the walls. Umm Ghadia, who lost eight of her nine children in the bombing, moved into the shelter to help create the memorial and serve as its guide

STATUES
The Statue of Sadoun (*Nasr Sq, Sadoun St*) Abdul Muhsin al Sadoun was born in Nasiriya in 1889 and died in Baghdad in 1929. After World War I he became Minister of Justice and in1922 Minister of Interior following which he became Prime Minister four times. In his fourth term of office there were serious difficulties with the colonialists in Baghdad and shot himself. The statue was created in 1933 by an Italian sculptor.

The Mother (*Al-Umma Park*) Created by the Iraqi sculptor Khalid Rahal in 1961 it represents the mother who is confident of her son's future now that the revolution has given hope and confidence to the next generation.

Kahrmana Square This is one of Baghdad's famous squares, located at a crossroads between the two areas of Karada. In the centre is a sculpture which was erected in the 1960s. There are two theories as to what this sculpture depicts. Known locally as **Ali Baba Square**, some assert that it is a representation from the story of Ali Baba and the 40 thieves, immortalising Ali Baba's housekeeper pouring boiling oil on the heads of the 40 thieves hiding in big jars. The other theory is the story as told in old tales dating back to the pre-Islamic era, featuring a bright, courageous girl called Qahramama, whose father sold oil out of huge jugs in the market. One night, Qahramama heard noises and getting up, saw a fugitives hiding in the empty jugs while the police searched for them. Qahramama poured oil in to the jugs, one by one and when they were almost full, the fugitives stood up and started screaming, revealing their hiding places to the police who were able to catch them. This monument has always been a great favourite with Japanese visitors who loved to have their pictures taken next to it. After the last war, the people of Japan assisted with the rehabilitation of the monument, which included planting the surrounding square with colourful flowers and painting the jugs green, which does not really complement the artistic shape of the monument.

Abbas bin Firnas The road to Baghdad International Airport has a monument to the poet and inventor **Abbas bin Firnas** (AD810–887). He developed his own theories about the possibility of human flight and his experiences earned him the name of the first Arab aviator in history, although as his only recorded attempt consisted of him covering his body with feathers and appending wings to himself, it was somewhat unsuccessful, leading only to a broken rib. Still Muslims duly establish him as the first human to have attempted flight, 1,028 years before the Wright brothers did so with a little more success. Although sources say that Bin Firnas later devised a flying machine (after having studied and mechanically dissected flight processes used by birds) and attempts are thought to have been successful, he was afterwards tried as having wanted to change man's god-given nature and sentenced to seclusion in his home. Bin Firnas was known for the wealth of his inventions, including the water clock which he named *al meeqat*, a technique for cutting crystals and producing medical lenses, the production of transparent colourless glass and several kinds of planispheres (a map of half or more of the sky with a window showing only the part of the sky that is visible at any one point in time). Among his strangest inventions was his 'celestial dome' where people would gather to gaze at stars, clouds and lightning. He also invented a metronome which he used to determine the times of prayers and sunrise and sunset, and a machine resembling an astrolabe in its ability to monitor the sun, moon, stars and planets and their circuits and orbits. Described by his peers as the sage of Andalusia who imparted their community with a wealth of tools and arts, he was also a proficient philosopher and a tormented poet. The Bin Firnas moon crater was named after him as a tribute to his scientific achievements.

PARKS
Al-Zawra Park A family-friendly place, Al-Zawra Park feels very secure. The park has two entrances, one from Al-Zaytoon Street (which is less crowded), the other at the side of Al-Rashid Hotel. The park is home to the Middle East's second-largest Ferris wheel, which is 60m high and has 40 cabins with an overall capacity for 240 people. The total cost of the Ferris wheel was said to be US$6 million. The amusement park is currently being upgraded and 16 new rides opened in 2013–2014, including the Happy Swing, Gravity, Pirates, Family Ship and Aerial Slides, and other roller coasters and water rides. If you visit in March you will be able to enjoy the annual flower festival where you'll see (and smell) some of the best roses in the world. There is also a small zoo where a rare white Bengal tiger cub was born in 2013 and a lake with boat rides.

The Baghdad Amusement Park On the Al-Rusafa side of Baghdad is a new park which opened in 2013. It has a large number of modern rides, an electronic games hall and a bowling alley, as well as restaurants, a display of tropical fish, large green areas and water fountains. The place is secure, comfortable and ideal for families. The park is currently charging a nominal entrance fee, just IQD500 per person (US$0.43) and the price of each ride ranges from IQD1,000 to 2,000 (US$0.86 to US$1.72). The park also has restaurants and stalls selling ice creams and fruit juices.

Abu Nuwas Park Abu Nuwas Park runs for 2km along the east bank of the Tigris in central Baghdad. Abu Nawas was an early medieval poet, half Arab and half Persian, who wrote poems celebrating wine and romance, which ensured trouble during his lifetime and fame after his death. In keeping with his liberal tradition, the park that bears his name is relaxed, although getting in requires going through a checkpoint or two. Once inside, though, it doesn't feel like Baghdad at all. Families have picnics on blankets spread under trees and children play on the grass. A fountain at the edge of the Tigris shoots up water as coloured lamps make the jets pulse red and purple. Music mixes with the shouts of vendors selling nuts, sweets and balloons. At its centre is an amusement park with bumper cars, a giant inflatable slide, video games and an amusement arcade.

OTHER PLACES TO SEE
Sadr City Once called Saddam City, Sadr City lies east of Army Canal and Jamila Square. In dramatic contrast to the ostentatious displays of wealth springing up elsewhere in Baghdad these days, Sadr City, home to two million Shias, is one of

5

the poorest neighbourhoods in the city with crushing unemployment and 20-to-a-house poverty. It is certainly not a tourist attraction and it is not advisable to try to visit Sadr City at the moment. However, in the future when it is possible to visit the places where American forces frequently clashed with the Mehdi army and car bombs killed hundreds of people, this will provide a penetrating flash of insight into the hardships of daily life in Iraq, which is still a struggle for survival for many people.

Maamoon Telecommunication Centre Tower Not far from the Qadisaya Expressway, the Maamoon Telecommunication Centre Tower, previously known as the Baghdad or Saddam Tower, was badly damaged during the First Gulf War and had a broken rocket at its base for many years (now removed). Damaged again during the Second Gulf War, it was renovated and re-opened. At the top of the tower was a revolving restaurant, with panoramic views across the whole city, which were especially stunning at night when the whole of Baghdad could be viewed in its illuminated splendour below (although the distance between the restaurant and its basement kitchen meant that food was often cold by the time it arrived at the table). Sadly, it is currently closed but no doubt as security improves it will open again.

The Royal Cemetery is in Adhamiya by Shabab Square and contains the graves of the kings of Iraq: King Faisal I; King Ghazi and King Faisal II, along with Queen Hazeema, wife of King Faisal I, and Queen Aallya, wife of King Ghazi. Also in the cemetery are the graves Jaafer al Askrai, the Iraqi Minister of Defence who was one of the most prominent Iraqi leaders during the period of Arab Great Revolution, Rustim Haider, King Ali, the father of Prince Abd Illah and his sister the Princess Jalella along with those of other members of the royal family killed during the military coup on 14 July 1958.

The British Military Cemetery in Wazeriya District, close by the old Turkish Embassy building has suffered a great deal over the last 40 years from neglect and lack of care. However, it now appears to be being cared for again. British and Commonwealth graves are in the majority here, most dating from World War I. Many graves have been relocated here from other cemeteries elsewhere in Iraq. The largest mausoleum is that of General Sir Stanley Maude, who in 1917 took Baghdad from the Ottomans, dying later the same year from cholera. There are some other interesting monuments, including one to the British troops who died on the march to Turkey following the fall of Kut and another to the Turks who died opposing the British Forces taking Baghdad.

The Christian Cemetery This cemetery in Nidhal Street contains may diplomatic graves, notably that of Gertrude Bell (see box, page 145), who has a simple grave, which is still well cared for and tended today by the custodians of the area who speak in respectful tones when referring to 'Miss Bell'. At both cemeteries you will have to ask for the key.

CITY TOUR SUGGESTIONS A suggested day out around Baghdad requires an early start and a good day with no traffic jams and quick movement through checkpoints. The security personnel accompanying you will ultimately decide if you can venture as far as Agargouf. Alternatively, you could take a half-day walking tour around the old part of the city.

City tour with vehicle An early start to your tour allows you to make time for the Kassite ziggurat at **Agargouf** (see pages 157–61). The site is 30km from the city centre. Dating from the 15th century BC, this is probably the best ziggurat in Iraq. If you are a really early bird though, start your tour first at the **Mosque at Kadhmain** (see page 147). Built in the 16th century on the site of the shrines of two of the Prophet Mohammed's descendants, Musa al Kadhim and Mohammed al Jawad, it is situated on the banks of the Tigris to the north of the city. The shrine has a magnificent golden dome and impressive minarets. Opposite the mosque is a famous clothes market. Returning towards the centre, next take the road past the **railway station**, which is a marble symbol of British, colonial architecture (see page 132). If you have time, visit the booking hall. Just before the station is the famous monument of **Sitt Zumarrud Khatoun's tomb**, dating back to the late Abbasid period (1179–1225) (see page 146). It is remarkable for its octagonal shape. The **Mosque and Shrine of Sheikh Omar al Sahrawardi** is on Sheikh Omar Street. This famous mystic and theologian was born in Iran and died in Baghdad in 1225. The shrine has an extraordinary conical dome, in Seljuk style. It is a very tranquil place and eminently photogenic. Close to the hub of the city is the modern-day **Martyrs Monument** which cost US$40 million to build. It commemorates the deaths in the Iran-Iraq War (1980–88) (see pages 58–9). In the hall underneath the huge double-hearted egg-shaped structure are the inscribed names of the dead. The next stop could be the magnificent **Iraq National Museum** which opened its doors again to the public in 2015 (see pages 142–4). As you come into the centre of Baghdad, in Al-Rashid Street you will come to the **Abbasid Palace** (see page 144), the beautiful **Al-Mustansiriya School** built under the Abbasids (see pages 144–6), the **Murjan Mosque** (see page 147) and **Khan Murjan** (see page 146).

Walking tour Your starting point should be the Al-Shuhada Square (also known as the fish market, just by the bridge of the same name). In the square is a very old, traditional tea house, with Turkish-style benches and tables. The locals still congregate at the tea house to drink tea and play backgammon. From this side of the river, there are fine views of the Ottoman palace and clock tower. Walking across the Al-Shuhada Bridge (without taking photographs of the military checkpoints) you come, on your right-hand side, to the **Al-Mustansiriya School** with its inscriptions (see pages 144–6). Facing the school to your right are some interesting antique, jewellery and carpet shops. If you climb up to the roof of the school you will find many good places from which to take panoramic photos across the city and the river.

Past the school and at the end of this small street, a little to the right, is a small, covered souk containing an old, traditional tea house in front of the mosque. Returning to Souk Street and taking a left, you will plunge into the souk itself. Pass through the cloth section to the copper section. This part of the souk is very famous, but is diminishing in size every year. There are some extremely interesting examples of beaten copper and brass still to be found here. At the end of this street you enter into Al-Rashid Street where fresh food, fish and fruit are sold. This end of Al-Rashid Street is blocked off by military personnel guarding the red-painted National Bank of Iraq. Do not take photos here either!

Fork slightly left in front of the bank and you will come to the **Murjan Mosque** (see page 147). The gate to the mosque, despite the rubble and water around it, is quite amazing with its highly decorated brickwork. After passing the mosque, proceed through more cloth stalls and at the next street on your left you will find three churches. These are the **Chaldean Church** (see page 150), the **Syriac Catholic Church** and the **Assyrian Catholic Church** which may all be well locked up. This short street brings you to Jumhurrye Street. Almost opposite you will see the **Suq Al-Ghazil Minaret** (see page 149). The minaret was the only part of the mosque left by the Mongols of the original mosque which was here. Also close by is the Bird Market, which has not really returned to its former size following a bombing some years ago.

Retracing your steps to Al-Rashid Street, just past the National Bank is a left turning which will take you past the **Khan Murjan** caravanserai (see page 146) to the river. On reaching the riverbank turn right and trying to ignore the piles of rubbish and general decrepitude, note that there is a toilet on the right by the mosque should you need to avail yourself of this. Turning into the souk again, walk past the Al-Mustansiriya School onto Armin Street by the bridge you crossed at the beginning of your tour. Facing you is the Stationery Souk leading into the **Book Market** (see box, pages 142–3). Also to your right is the **Baghdad Museum** (see page 144), now refurbished and an interesting place with its wax tableaux.

Walk along the Stationery Souk and proceed to the Ottoman Palace, past the burnt out National Library and the old British Post Office on your right. There are some fine, old buildings in this area, all in need of restoration. Now you come to the old Ministry of Defence building and finally the **Abbasid Palace** (see page 144) with its wonderful inscriptions and arches. From the Abbasid Palace, make your way to the 17 July Bridge, where your transport back to your hotel should be waiting for you.

AROUND BAGHDAD

TELL HARMAL Once the ancient town of Shaduppum, Tell Harmal was a small heavily walled town of no special importance. Its main period of occupation falls abou 1800BC, when it formed part of the Kingdom of Eshnunna (some 30km away in the Diyala plain, east of Baghdad). Its ancient name signifies the place of writing, and it appears to have been specifically a centre for priests and scribes. Excavations have yielded tablets revealing unique evidence of Babylonian administration. These include literary, legal and economic documents as well as one of the most famous of Babylonian texts which anticipates the theorem of Pythagoras. Tell Harmal gives a good idea of what an ancient Babylonian town would have been like. The priest's house has been restored and the whole site can be viewed from the roof of this two-storey building. It has a parapet and ventilation shafts that are still found in many of Baghdad's old houses. The main temple foundations have been restored, with copies of the guardian lions at the entrance. The remains of dwelling houses, characterised by an internal courtyard, have been preserved.

Getting there Tell Harmal is in the environs of Baghdad in the southern suburbs of Jadida.

What to see and do The town was surrounded by a massive brick wall with buttressing towers, of which only the foundations now remain. The outline of the walls has been restored. The ancient gateway, preserved as the modern entrance, leads to a street with a temple of typical Old Babylonian plan on its north side; the lower parts of its walls having been preserved in cement. The temple doorway is flanked by the projecting towers, and gives access through a gate chamber into a courtyard. Facing the entrance at the west end is the façade of the principal shrine, with the doors protected by two seated lions, copies of terracotta originals now in the Iraq Museum. Steps lead into a broad ante-cella, from which a second doorway

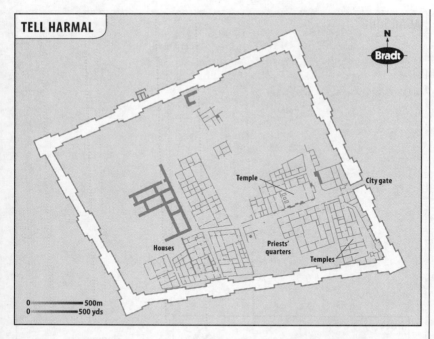

TELL HARMAL

N

Bradt

Temple

City gate

Houses

Priests' quarters

Temples

0 ——— 500m
0 ——— 500 yds

opens into the cella. A niche in the rear wall marks the position of a dais for the cult statue which would have faced worshippers as they entered the courtyard. Another similar, but smaller, sanctuary opens off the northwest corner of the courtyard, and other rooms on this side were probably priest's lodgings and domestic quarters.

The remains of dwelling houses can be found elsewhere on the site, and a characteristic example of one with an internal courtyard is preserved on the south side of the street opposite the temple. In the southeast corner a pair of shrines of a different type have been completely reconstructed. Their façade, again decorated with pilasters, is pieced by two doorways each leading into a long nave containing the entrance to a broad cella at the far end. The divine statue would have again stood on a dais inset into the rear wall, facing the length of the shrine. Each unit includes a small vestry or store, and from the nave of the southern temple a stair leads to the roof with its characteristic parapet and ventilation shafts.

Today, the site is situated in the middle of a rubbish-littered suburb and is somewhat disappointing. It has been much neglected but is now being restored. A fence has at last been put around the site. It is interesting to walk up onto the roof of the reproduction priests' house and see the traditional method of air-conditioning vents on the roof, and to look out over the whole site.

AGARGOUF Also known as Aqar Quf and in ancient times as Dur Kurigalzu, this Kassite capital city dating from c1500–1150BC is one in a long series of capital cities, from 3rd millennium BC Kish to Abbasid Baghdad, that all lay in northern Babylonia, the narrow waist of Mesopotamia where its great highways meet. This site may have been a border fortress of Babylonia in the 3rd millennium BC, but the visible remains date from the late 2nd millennium. It was re-founded by the Kassite king Kurigalzu in the 15th century BC and remained the administrative capital of southern Mesopotamia until the fall of the dynasty about 1170BC. The Kassites, like the Babylonians and the Sumerians, built large ziggurats and groups of sacred

5

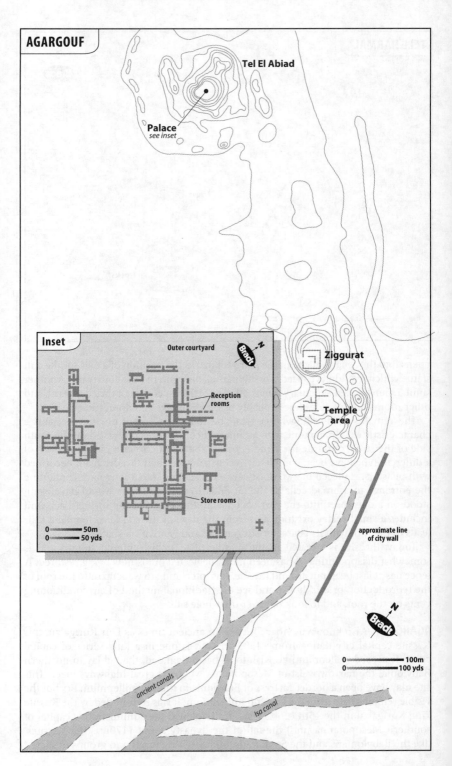

AGARGOUF

Tel El Abiad

Palace
see inset

Inset

Outer courtyard

Reception
rooms

Store rooms

0 ——— 50m
0 ——— 50 yds

Ziggurat

Temple
area

approximate line
of city wall

0 ————— 100m
0 ————— 100 yds

ancient canals

Isa canal

buildings, among which were several temples. The temples and palaces at Agargouf were used until the end of the 2nd millennium BC, when the Kassites ceased to be a dominant power in the region. Political control then reverted to Babylon, but occupation of the site continued through much of the 1st millennium BC. Around 1150BC the Elamites raided Babylon and in the course of this raid they also set fire to the Kassite capital. After this destruction, the site was occupied intermittently over the centuries and as late as the Muslim conquests.

Getting there Agargouf is approximately 33km from Baghdad city centre on the Damascus road, located on the right bank of the 15th-century AD Saklawiyeh Canal and just north of the old Ramadi–Amman road.

What to see and do The most stunning feature, visible for miles around, is the core of the ancient ziggurat which has been restored up to its platform, the remainder giving a very good idea of what the original site was like. Built of sun-dried bricks interspersed with layers of reed matting, it still stands to a height of 57m above the plain. The platform of this storied tower consists of a coffering of baked bricks measuring 81m by 67m. Its corners correspond to the four points of the compass. The baked-brick face of the lower stage and its upper pavement have been restored, together with the axial stairway: two other flights of stairs once rose to meet it from the corners of the façade, as at Ur. To the southeast you can still see traces of the central flight of steps, built of baked bricks. Two more flights of steps, one to each side of the central flight and perpendicular to it, also lead to the upper parts of the edifice. Layers of reeds are placed every eight or nine courses in the body of the ziggurat and sometimes these are bound and serve to join the different parts of the structure. These plaited ropes can be as much as 15cm thick. The remains of a religious building are found 100m west of the ziggurat. This temple was built in three different stages during the Kassite period. Close by you can also see the remains of the paving of the esplanade. Originally this structure, which formed a huge terrace 650m by 28m, was built of unbaked bricks, but it was later covered by a coffering of baked bricks. A temple dedicated to the god Enlil took up most of the terrace. The remains of the paving of the esplanade are visible.

The palaces of the Kassite kings were built about 1km southwest of the ziggurat in artificial hillocks grouped together under the name of Tell El Abiad. Rising 24m above ground level, this mound has only been partly excavated. Four levels that correspond to four different or re-worked structures have been discovered in this hill. The oldest level probably corresponds to the founding of the town at the beginning of the 15th century BC. The last construction, the one that the Elamites burnt down around the year 1250BC, can be attributed for the greater part to Marduk Apal Iddin (1168–1155BC).

The north corner of the outermost courtyard served as the administrative and reception area. Opening off it were two long chambers, originally decorated with painted friezes of courtiers entering through their doorways. To the south a depression marks the site of a second courtyard, one of many in the whole building which was surrounded by triple rows of rooms, in some of which, at the southern corner, can still be seen low vaulted chambers opening off of a central passage. This was the royal storehouse and treasury, in which were found many examples of Kassite art, now in the Iraq Museum, including a decorated ceremonial mace head, a gold bracelet with paste inlay, fragments of inlaid glass vessels and a graceful and lifelike terracotta figurine of a lioness, which is justly famous.

The Kassites were a highland, tribal people from the east, possibly the Zagros Mountains. A people at least partly Indo-European and expert horsemen; they were the longest-ruling dynasty in Babylonian history. They were first mentioned in 18th century BC texts, particularly from Sippar, as individuals or tribal groups, hiring themselves out for agricultural or military work. Relations with the sedentary Babylonians were not always peaceful. Within 200 years they had spread over a wide area of the Near East, and, when the Hittite king Mursilis I raided Babylon in c1595BC bringing to an end the dynasty of Hammurabi, the Kassites were able to assume power.

The Babylonian King List records 36 kings of the Kassite Dynasty, but of the first 200 years the sources reveal very little. In c1475BC King Ulam-Buriash defeated the Sealand Dynasty in the south and unified Babylonia, initiating more than 300 years of stability and prosperity. Babylonia became a major power, both in diplomacy and trade contact with other powers, as revealed in the Amarna letters. The Kassite kings Kadashman-Enlil I and Burnaburiash II exchanged ambassadors and gifts and arranged diplomatic marriages with Egypt, Hatti and Assyria. Major buildings and restoration works were undertaken in the principal cities and Kurigalzu I founded a new capital named after himself at Dur-Kurigalzu (Aqar Quf)

The most characteristic aspect of Kassite material culture are *kudurrus* or boundary stones. Kassite kings rewarded favoured subjects with grants of royal land and *kudurrus* commemorated these gifts and designated their boundaries. Other innovations were the systematic breeding of horses and new developments in chariot technology. Kassite kings promoted the collection and composition of literature and many of the standard literary works found in later Neo-Assyrian libraries are copies of Kassite originals and compilations. Under the Kassites, Akkadian became the common diplomatic language of the near east, as used in the Amarna letters. Of the original Kassite language we know very little and it cannot be related to any other known language. No Kassite text has survived and its main sources are two Kassite-Akkadian dictionaries which list divine and personal names and some basic vocabulary. Our word 'Kassite' comes from the Akkadian 'Kassu', but in fact they called themselves 'Galzu'. In religion they worshipped Babylonian gods, although coronations took place in a special shrine in the palace at Babylon consecrated to two Kassite mountain gods – Shuqamuna and Shimaliya.

The Kassite Dynasty was ended by an Elamite invasion in c1155BC, but Kassites continued to live in Mesopotamia, and even hold important official posts, until at least the 9th century BC. Thereafter, they are attested as a war-like tribal people in the hills of eastern Iraq and Iran, and perhaps supplied troops for the Achaemenid army against Alexander the Great, who had to campaign against Kassite groups in the mountains. One classical account states that the Kassites were expert bow men who lived in caves and ate acorns, mushrooms and the smoked flesh of wild animals.

The site today Despite the ongoing and intermittent terrorist activity around the area (the Abu Ghraib Prison is fairly close and Fallujah is not far away) work refurbishing the site is being carried out at intervals after years of neglect. The site is now well protected, a new front gate is in place and picnic tables and chairs, benches and lighted paths are being constructed. The pathway steps to the ziggurat have been renewed and the temple reconstructions of the 1980s also refurbished. This site has always been a favourite picnic spot for Baghdadis and it also affords the best site in Iraq to view and understand how a ziggurat is constructed.

AL-MAIDAN (THE CITIES) Now we come to the more complex historical sites that strew this area. As with so much of Mesopotamia it is the rivers Tigris and Euphrates that dictate the course of history causing cities and their trade to fall by the wayside as the rivers change their courses. Al-Maidan or The Cities is the Arabic name for the area around Salman Pak and Ctesiphon. The village of Salman Pak, which overlies a small part of Ctesiphon, contains the mosque tomb of the Barber of the Prophet.

Salman Pak Most visitors to the area are likely to start at the village of Salman Pak. The road to Salman Pak has been widened in recent years and as you approach the village you will see that the road surface is being repaired and buildings on either side of it are being fitted with sewerage and drainage pipes. This possibly has more to do with increased visits by pilgrims to the shrine than with improving the lives of the inhabitants, who do not look at all happy at the transformation of their town. Everywhere there are soldiers, police and barriers. However, it has to be said that this village (and indeed the whole area) has had a very unhappy dissident recent past. Close by was a base for Saddam Hussein's Revolutionary Guards and later a base for Moqtada Sadr's Shia militia, as well as a base for the American Forces supervising the area. Because the American base was frequently attacked, they had to make twice-daily patrols with mine detectors and troops. Today the guardians of the shrine have formed a local committee, and, led by the chief guardian, are working to wholly promote harmony and solve local disputes between the evenly matched (in size) Sunni and Shia communities. Hopefully the sectarian killing and troubles will eventually become a feature of the past; certainly the committee hopes and thinks so. The people here are impressive and it is one of the few places where foreigners and non-Muslims can feel more at ease.

The shrine for which the village is famous is, or rather was, a nice, quiet and cool place with a simple dome and minaret. However, it has now been doubled in size by the addition of a new courtyard (Iranian-style) and reception centre. This is rather to the dismay of many traditionalists who remember it as it was from their childhood. 'It was where you were traditionally taken for your first haircut', a Sunni Arab told me rather plaintively, as he had hoped to have his own child's first haircut here. Inside the shrine are the tombs of the Companions of the Prophet, namely Salman al Farisi (the Persian); Jabir ibn Abdullah al Ansari and Hud Haysan ibn al Yamani: all three of whom are much venerated and respected.

Getting there Salman Pak is 24km south of Baghdad city, past the ongoing cleaning of one of the city's worst slums, past the old Saddam base and down a turning after the old American military base. The road is strewn with checkpoints as not long ago it was controlled by the Mather Sabra Shia militia, whose forces manned the checkpoints.

 Where to stay and eat The town has a vegetable market and shops, but little else. There are no eating places and no hotels.

What to see and do
The Mosque of the Prophet's Barber After the conquest of Iraq, during the reign of Caliph Omar, this area was chosen by some of the Prophet's companions as a

THE PERSIAN-ZOROASTRIAN CONNECTION Salman the Persian or Farisi is revered by Muslims and considered a traitor by Zoroastrians and nationalist Iranians. One way or another, he is an important part of history and has gained much notoriety. The Prophet Mohammed (570–632AD) declared Salman was of his House, the **Ahl Al-Bayt**. This designation placed him at the Prophet's right hand. Salman was also a member of the **Sahaba**, Mohammed's inner council and therefore one of the few, if any, non Arabs in Mohammed's inner circle. As Salman was intimately involved with the Zoroastrian and Christian religions, he would have brought that knowledge and experience to these groups. Both Muslims and Zoroastrians have practices in common, for example both pray five times a day. It was said that he was 'stuffed with knowledge and wisdom – an ocean that does not dry up'. Salman was perhaps the most literate within the inner circle and stands in juxtaposition to the Prophet's own illiteracy.

Shia, Alawi and Sufi Muslims hold Salman al Farsi in high regard. The Alawi consider him to be the 'Bab' (door) within an esoteric trinity which includes Ali and Mohammed. There is some speculation that the name Mus-salman contains Salman's name. This could be coincidence. Salman, born as Rouzbeh in Persia in AD568 was reputed to have been a Magian, ie a Zoroastrian charged with maintaining an ever-burning fire. Apparently Salman became enamoured by Christianity, converted and travelled to Mosul and Rome. He then became the servant of a Jewish merchant, in the company of whom he travelled to Arabia where he met Mohammed. This event was preordained by one of Salman's Christian mentors, even down to Salman finding a mark on Mohammed's back. By the time he met Mohammed, Salman had experience with the Zoroastrian, Christian and Jewish religions and peoples. It was common for Arabs to declare their tribal affiliation to others. When asked about his tribe, Salman declared, 'I am the son of Islam. I was lost, so Allah guided me to Mohammad; I was poor, so Allah made me rich with Mohammad; I was a slave, so Allah released me with Mohammad: this is my tribe!' He is also reputed to have declared 'I am Salman, the son of Islam from the children of Adam.' Later Salman participated in the battles against his countrymen, the Persians, following which he was instrumental in the establishment of a Muslim administration in Kufa.

After Mohammed's death in AD632 Salman was appointed governor of Al-Maidan by the Arabs. He died around 655 at the age of 76 during the reign of the 3rd caliph Othman. The place where he died and which now contains his shrine is named after him – Salman Pak.

place to live, among them Salman al Farisi, who was designated governor of Iraq by Omar. He was originally called Rozaba, but after he embraced Islam, the Prophet gave him the name Salman. The people of Iraq called him Salman Bek, meaning Salman the pure one. He died in AD655.

Mausoleum of Salman al Farisi The mausoleum is composed of an esplanade, with two gates and several halls, some of which hold religious classes. At the top of the mausoleum are two minarets and four domes: one above the tomb of Salman al Farisi, two at the top of the mausoleum of Jabir ibn al Ansari and Assayed Taher and the last on top of the mosque itself. On the right-hand side of the mausoleum there is the Friday mosque. An awning to stop the rain and provide shade from the sun is erected for outdoor praying. At the far side of the esplanade is a small door inscribed with the Prophet's saying: 'Salman belongs to Ahl Al-Bayt' which leads directly to the tomb. The tomb is located in the middle of a small, nicely decorated mausoleum, with a grid overlooking the adjacent hall and a metal door leading to the tombs of the companions Hud Haysan ibn al Yamani, Jabir al Ansari and Assayed Taher. At the top of the mausoleum is a wooden case decorated with silver and a bronze lamp on each corner.

At the exit there is a hall which has a small library of Korans. The building was recently restored and its ceiling decorated with beautiful Islamic inscriptions.

The Tomb of Hud Haysan ibn al Yamani To the left of the tomb of Salman al Farisi is the tomb of another of the companions, Hud Haysan ibn al Yamani, who was an expert in the Koran and Sunnah (the way of life for Muslims based on the life and teachings of Mohammed). His tomb and that of the companion Jabir al Ansari were originally on the bank of the Tigris but flooding in 1931 prompted their transfer to the current location. This mausoleum has the same dimensions as that of Salman al Farisi. At the top of the tomb there is a wooden case nicely decorated with an aluminium framework on top.

Ctesiphon At the point where the land of the twin rivers narrows north of Babylon is one of the iconic architectural monuments of Iraq, the **Arch of Ctesiphon**. Although the Arch seems to have stood proudly aloof and majestic in its isolation for centuries, it actually is the remaining symbol of thousands of years of this region's history. Here once stood the Arsacid capital of Ctesiphon, one of many ancient cities clinging to the Tigris river for their survival. Capricious, the river changed its course and so humans followed, leaving behind their palaces and their graves. Today, all that remains of this splendour are the ruins of the White Palace or Taq-i-Kisr, spanned by the Arch, proudly soaring 29m in height in a single span. Towering over the entrance of a throne room which measured 25m by 43m, the whole of this vast chamber was once covered by a single flower embroidered carpet known as 'the Spring of Chosroes'. Built in the 3rd–4th century AD, it is the largest single-span brick arch in the world and one of the most beautiful and iconic ruins in the east. At the time of going to print, it had recently undergone another significant restoration.

History Each phase of the history, as far as can be traced, has left some mark; either through discarded texts or simply archaeological attempts to interpret the texts and discover more. We start with Opis, an early 2nd millennium BC Sumerian city on the eastern bank of the Tigris, which later became a prominent capital of Babylonia. Little is known about Opis, another lost city of the Babylonian era. It was the site of the defeat of Nabonidus, last king of Babylon, by the Persian King Cyrus in 539BC. Was Ctesiphon built on its foundations? Next in time comes Seleucia on the Tigris, founded by Seleucus I on the western bank of the Tigris river between 306–281BC. Seleucus was a successor to Alexander the Great, and under him the city became one of the greatest of its time. Seleucus' kingdom stretched from Asia Minor to the Hindu Kush, and at its inception, Seleucia was the kingdom's metropolis. Before long, however, the capital moved to Antioch in Syria, better placed for contact with the Mediterranean world with its major markets and rival powers, and Seleucia remained what geography had destined it to be; a centre of east–west trade, supplied by arterial traffic routes from the Persian Gulf and inner Asia. Next came

5

the Parthians, led with determination by their Arsacid dynasty, who swept across Seleucid Persia and Media and in 144BC confronted Seleucia itself on the Tigris. After conquering the city they then moved across the Tigris to the eastern bank where, for reasons which can only be guessed, they halted and camped, perhaps on the site of ancient Opis. The camp eventually became the palace and garrison town of Parthian Ctesiphon.

In ancient times a ship canal, the Nahr Al-Malik, linked the Tigris with the Euphrates and at this strategic point the two great cities now confronted each other across the Tigris. The advancing Parthians may for this reason have abstained from the destruction of so much accumulated commercial wisdom, without any compensating political advantage. The two cities, one Greek and the other Oriental, tolerated each other's presence. Rivalry showed its teeth in the earlier part of the 1st century AD, when Seleucia seems to have come somewhat the worse out of the conflict. This may have been little more than a momentary setback; but in the following century three Roman emperors: Trajan, Lucius Verus and Septimus Severus, led hungry and destructive armies against Ctesiphon, with momentary success. Neither city could have benefited from these excursions. Finally in AD165 Legate Avidius Cassius, commander of the troops of Verus, razed Seleucia. Ctesiphon suffered similarly, but survived. Some centuries later Ctesiphon was taken by the Persian Sassanians, their capital and Seleucia was renamed as Veh-Ardasir (the good city of Ardasir). At this time Seleucia was an insignificant remnant of a city, while Ctesiphon was once more a prosperous capital. The latter's last major conflict with the Roman power came in AD363, when it was vigorously attacked by Julian the Apostate and was saved from capture only by a timely javelin in the ribs of that redoubtable Emperor. Henceforth Ctesiphon spread far beyond its original boundaries and turned into a cluster of small towns rather than a single city, hence the name Al-Maidan (the Cities), which was adopted by the Arab conquerors in AD636. After the Arab conquest Ctesiphon declined in importance until the vast site became the untidy miscellany of mounds and cultivation which we see today. Its importance was taken first by Basra and Wasit and, after AD762, by Baghdad.

Getting there   Ctesiphon is 31km southeast of Baghdad, on the east bank of the Tigris, partly overlaid by the village of Salman Pak.

What to see and do   The topography of Seleucia and Ctesiphon is complicated by the fact that the Tigris, which formally divided them, has changed its course so that it now cuts through the site of Ctesiphon, leaving the greater part of this city on the 'wrong' or Seleucid bank. Neither city has been adequately explored but it would appear that Seleucia (see pages 166–7) was laid out on a rectangular plan while Ctesiphon was roughly a circle, as was the later Baghdad. Both cities had extensive suburbs which have only in part been identified. Of the vast potential of this immense dual site, let it be said at once that whatever future excavations may reveal, the outstanding feature will remain the massive brick *iwan*, the Arch of Ctesiphon which looms over the plain long before the visitor arrives. It is a truly astonishing spectacle. It consists of a mighty elliptical vault rising to a height of 29m, and 25m wide at its base. This vaulted salon is, or was, flanked by two wings enriched by six or more arcades, of which only the lowest was in part functional. (The north wing collapsed in 1909 as a result of flooding.)

The Arch   Described as the widest single-span vault of unreinforced brickwork in the world, the overwhelming magnitude of the Arch is not its only quality. The subtlety with which its curve changes centre and ultimately produces what is inadequately called an oval shape, gives the whole structure a lightness and intelligence, which lift it out of the rut of purely mechanical engineering.

If the vault may properly be described as a masterpiece, **the wings,** which flank and 'support' it, are more controversial. They have been criticised for the lack of consistent axes in their arcaded decoration and for the unstructured fashion in which the panels are superimposed one upon another, with no great regard for the verticality which we expect and find, for example, on the exterior of the Coliseum at Rome. Is this to say that the Ctesiphon building was not designed by a classical architect? Medieval buildings of repute are not always pedantic in this matter. At Ctesiphon it has been counter-claimed that the extreme shallowness of columns and arcading (their projection is 0.3–0.6m only) reduces the whole design to free pattern, rather than a scholastic structure; the intention being to emphasise horizontal lines to carry the eye up into the air. It is a characteristic example of the oriental disregard of mathematical law in favour of impressionistic design, and may be held to give the Ctesiphon façade the quality of an oriental rug.

We have to remember, too, that the brickwork was originally plastered and coloured, no doubt with a vividness and gaiety that would itself distract the mind of the viewer from architectural deviation. The Ctesiphon façade, with its towering central feature, is neither copy-book Roman architecture nor any other kind of copy.

Arab tradition has it that the vast vaulted hall was the Iwan-i-Khosrau, the throne room where the royal Sassanid conducted business and ceremony in the Persian fashion, which demanded regular contact between monarch and people. The hall or *iwan*, with its adjoining rooms, was a central feature of a large palatial complex, preceded by a considerable space for assembly and parade. Many, perhaps all, of the apartments behind the main vault and its lateral wings were vaulted. To the south and the east, separated from the main block, incomplete excavation has revealed extensive buildings, of which, facing the main hall at a distance of 100m, was apparently a second *iwan* of comparable width, but unascertained depth. To the south of the principal block, traces were found of a large rectangular building or enclosure, some 100m from north to south and 69m from east to west, built of mud brick with a baked-brick skin and with internal pedestals or buttresses. The building is known locally as ad Dhabi (Hyena Hill), or as the Karim Al-Kisra.

Of the stucco and other veneers which formerly graced these buildings, nothing can now be said save that they once existed. Fragments show that there were coloured marble wall-facings and glass-mosaics on some of the ceilings. Floors were of marble or of brick coated with gypsum. Excavations at other Sassanid buildings in the neighbourhood have been a little more productive; enough to indicate a great variety and some considerable liveliness of design, including medallions and friezes enclosing animals and birds and a conventionalised flora, together with occasional human figures of a crude but not inexpressive kind. Unhappily these fragments have mostly perished beyond recall in the saline sand and cannot be reassembled in any sort of over-all picture. In particular they have lost practically all the polychromy which was of their essence: yellow, red, brown ochre, ultramarine, black. In some instances there appears to have been an inlay of precious or semi-precious stones. The result must have been one of splendour, if of a somewhat ostentatious kind.

Ctesiphon today After years of neglect and fighting, during which trenches were constructed around the Arch along with their accompaniment of razor wire, the museum was completely looted and the gardens, once lovingly tended by the Department of Antiquities, were turned into a soccer field by local children, the site is being cleaned up and the fences are being restored. Over the last few years the site has had to be guarded due to threats from insurgency organisations, but now the resultant gun pits are being removed. The decision has been made to again preserve the Arch, and renovation is taking place of some loose slabs which fell due to adverse weather conditions, the site having always been prone to flooding. Archaeologists are also beginning to explore the site again.

The area in the front of the Arch was formerly a large park. The buildings approximately 1,000m away facing the Arch were built under the Saddam regime in the early 1980s and consisted of a hotel, a restaurant, a reception area and tall building called the **El-Qadissiya Panorama**. Only the shell of the Panorama building survives today. Constructed in the shape of a terraced Mesopotamian ziggurat, it was built to house a panoramic dramatisation depicting the 7th-century AD Battle of Qadissiya, at which the Arab Muslim army under the command of Saad Ben Abi El-Waqasse defeated the Persian army. Dozens of North Korean artists painted battle scenes on a 1,500m² screen, the viewing of which was accompanied by audio effects recreating the clatter of armour, shouting of warriors and neighing of war horses. Unfortunately locals looted the building, the shell of which now awaits a new future. Residents of Baghdad once came to picnic at Ctesiphon, but its green lawns and palm trees are withered now.

Seleucia on the Tigris In its time Seleucia on the Tigris was the greatest and most populous city in the Middle East, founded by Seleucus I (Nikator) the successful general who took the eastern part of Alexander's empire in about 304BC. For most of the 3rd and 2nd centuries BC Seleucia on the Tigris was the Hellenistic city of the world, comparable in size and population (some ancient texts claim a population of 600,000) to Alexandria in Egypt, and greater than Antioch in Syria. Its central position allowed it to control much of the east–west trade and the administration of the Seleucid Empire. The Parthians under Mithridates I conquered the city in 141BC and it then became their western capital. Tacitus, the Roman historian, described the city walls, mentioning that even under Parthian rule it was a fully Hellenistic city. Burnt down by the Roman Emperor Trajan in AD117, ceded back to the Parthians, and then completely destroyed by the Roman general Avidius Cassius in AD165. Following the Parthians, came the Sassanians who, 60 years later, founded a new city under Ardushir I, called Veh-Ardasir. The Italian excavators of the site found it to be a fresh construction, although it eventually encroached onto the suburbs of Seleucia. Under the Sassanians the Christian Nestorian Church was based in nearby Sela and other towns in Al-Maidan. Seleucia in the 3rd and 4th centuries became an important centre of Christianity, establishing its pre-eminence with several synods, notably that of 424, and became very active in the spread of Christianity in the East. Today archaeologists are finding churches and monasteries as far afield as central Asia and China, all founded under the banner of the Church of the East. Interestingly, Mandaeism, Manichaeism and Judaism were also developed in this section of Babylonia in and near Seleucia in these centuries.

Excavations of the site along with that of Opis were undertaken by Professor Leroy Beraj Waterman of the University of Michigan between 1927 and 1932 and again between 1936 and 1937 under Clark Hopkins and Robert H McDowell. From 1964 to 1968 and then from 1985 to 1989 the University of Turin, directed by Antonio Invernizzi and Giorgio Gallein, excavated at the site.

Getting there Seleucia on the Tigris is on the other side of the river to Salman Pak and needs to be approached via the Southern Highway (which runs from

Baghdad to Basra). To explore properly you will need a local guide as the small roads are so obscure and can often end up in a local date-palm plantation!

What to see and do The Arabic name for the site is Tell Umar. There are a series of mounds, the largest of which is also called Tell Umar. The excavations reveal a partially excavated theatre, temples and many houses. The excavations uncovered four levels of occupation and many artefacts were discovered illustrating a little-known period of history. The blending of Greek and Eastern elements can be almost described as a missing link between Hellenistic and Sassanian styles according to the excavator, Dr Waterman.

Some years ago I eventually got to Seleucia on the Tigris, only to be confronted by a meadow on which stood a giant missile protected by ground to air missiles! Needless to say I was not supposed to see this. Nevertheless, it was a thrill to be able to stand in a Greek temple where perhaps Seleucus I (Nikator) had once stood. His coins, the first coins of the town, often depicted some of the elephants that were his symbols. He had granted the Indian king Chandra Gupta his daughter and part of Alexander's conquered territory east of Iraq in exchange for 500 war elephants. This formidable force gave Seleucus a great deal of power in his acquisition of Alexander's Middle East conquests. For the armchair historian and traveller the area promises years of study and fascination.

Sippar (modern Tell Abu Habbah) The name Sippar in ancient texts sometimes refers to Abu Habbah, together with its neighbouring twin city, modern Tell ed-Der. The city was occupied from the Uruk period (3900–2900bc) through to Neo-Babylonian times. There's later evidence of Parthian times, but then occupation seems to cease. Sippar appears in the Sumerian King List as one of the cities divinely chosen to rule over Sumer before the flood. Its temple to the sun god Shamash was an important religious institution that was known all over Mesopotamia throughout the ages. There were, or so it seems, two cities named Sippar, one on either side of the Euphrates. This one (Tell Abu Habbah) was a dual city, half of which was under the protection of the sun god Utu of Sippar (Shahmash in Akkadian language) and the other half under the goddess Anunit. Sippar is also known as Sepharvain in the Old Testament, which alludes to this city. The other Sippar on the west bank of the river was known as Sippar-Amnanum.

Sippar is mentioned in a few ancient texts, which give information about it as follows:

1792bc	the city was conquered by the early Babylonian kings
1174bc	Kutia-Nalhenta III, King of Elam sacked the city after he had conquered Babylon
481bc	the Sippar Temple activities cease around the time that Xerxes the Persian king put down a Mesopotamian revolt

The site was first described by A W Selby and J B Bewsher (1860) and was excavated by Rassam (c1880), Vincent Scheil (1894), a Belgian team (1972/3) and the University of Baghdad (from 1978 onwards).

Getting there Sippar is almost 60km directly south of Baghdad. Leaving the city out onto the Hilla Road, Highway 18, it takes approximately 40 minutes to reach Al-Mahmudiyah. Just before this town is a turning to the right which will take you past the Sippar site. However, you will most probably need a local guide to find the site itself, which is behind a ditch and a small bridge near some farms. Its most notable landmark is the massive ruins of the ancient mud-brick walled embankment,

What to see and do The site covers approximately 100ha, with two tells surrounded by the ruins of the city's ancient mud-brick wall, and covered by a dike which protected the city against flooding. The southwestern mound was the religious quarter, with a ziggurat and temples, with the city proper on the northeast mound. Sippar was famous for its cloister where 'special or sacred' women dedicated to Shahmash (Naditu women) were housed. These prestigious women included the daughters of kings. Excavations have uncovered streets of two-roomed houses, which were possibly the Naditu cloister. Also, in the religious quarter, a Neo-Babylonian library was discovered containing thousands of cuneiform tablets. More than 27,000 tablets were excavated by Rassam from both cities of Sippar and these are still being studied today at the British Museum. A most prized exhibit in the British Museum is the tablet of Shahmash from Sippar (see box, below).

Today the site has a neglected air, having had so few visitors over the last few years and more than its share of looters. However, as it is such a notable early Mesopotamian site and because it is located so close to Baghdad, it is well worth the effort to get there.

THE TABLET OF SHAHMASH

The tablet of Shahmash is a small stone tablet dating back to the early 9th century BC on which the God Shahmash is shown seated on a stool under a canopy. In his hands are a rod and a ring, which are the symbols of his divine authority. Facing him is the figure of the Babylonian king Nabu-apla-iddina standing between two interceding deities. Below the figures, inscribed in cuneiform text, is the story of how at a time in the past the temple of Shahmash at Sippar became neglected and fell into disuse and how the image of Shamash had been destroyed. It goes on to relate how, during the reign of King Nabu-apla-iddina, a terracotta image of Shahmash was discovered on the banks the Euphrates which led to the King having a fabulous golden model of Shahmash made, embellished with lapis lazuli. He also restored the Shahmash Temple to its former status and glory.

In due course, however, the temple again declined. The tablet next appears in the pages of history some 750 years later, following its discovery by King Nabopolasser (625–605BC). By this time the tablet had been broken into two large pieces along with some smaller fragments, so King Nabopolasser had a copy of it made and placed the original, broken pieces in a clay box which was then buried under the temple floor for safekeeping.

The Babylonian tablet again saw the light of day in the 19th century when it was recovered from Sippar by Hormuzd Rassam. It can now be seen in all its glory in the British Museum.

6

East and West of Baghdad

To the east of Baghdad is Diyala Governorate, an agricultural area famous for its palm groves and orchards. It has numerous archaeological tells dating back to the Ubaid period, 6000BC, and thousands of clay tablets from the Babylonian period. In 2007–08, the governorate was under Sunni insurgent control and al-Qaida in Iraq moved its base of operations from Anbar to Diyala. In December 2011, the governing council declared itself a semi-autonomous region due to differences with the Shia dominated government. In April 2015, 100,000 people were displaced by fighting as ISIS regained ground from the Iraqi army.

BAQUBA *Telephone code 25*

Baquba is the capital of Diyala Governorate. In medieval times it was a halting point and caravanserai on the Silk Road between Baghdad and Khorasan in Iran. Owing to its proximity to two major sources of water, Baquba began life as an agricultural town. Today it is known as the capital of Iraq's commercial orange production.

SECURITY WARNING At the time of going to print there is a significant problem with security in both Diyala and Anbar provinces. Foreigners are advised against all but essential travel to the areas and will be turned back at the checkpoints if not in possession of the correct accreditation. Should you consider trying to visit if/when the situation changes in the future you should monitor the situation closely. Take extra care if you do decide to travel there and consult your embassy for the latest advice.

HISTORY The capital of the ancient Upper Nahrawan district, Baquba was originally irrigated by water from the Diyala river via the Nahrawan Canal, early work on which can be dated back to the Parthian period. In the reign of the Sassanid king Khosrau I (AD531–579) a network of canals was developed in the vicinity of Baquba, which the Abbasids repaired and expanded into a large-scale canal system that reached its peak in the 9th and early 10th centuries. The canal system was divided into three parts or sections. The initial feeder canal was called Al-Katul Al-Kisrawi (the cut of Khosrau). This canal took water from the Tigris river at Dur Al-Arabaya to Baquba, where it joined the Diyala river. During its course three smaller canals, also taking water from the Tigris, flowed into Al-Katul Al-Kisrawi: the Yahudi (the Jewish); the Al-Mamuni (named after Caliph al Mamun (AD813–833) and the Abu l-Jund (the father of the army) which was built by Harun al Rashid (AD786–809). After this point the canal turned south and became known as the Tamarra.

In AD937–938, Ibn Raiq breached the Nahrawan Canal in an unsuccessful attempt to impede Bajkam's advance to Baghdad by flooding the region with its

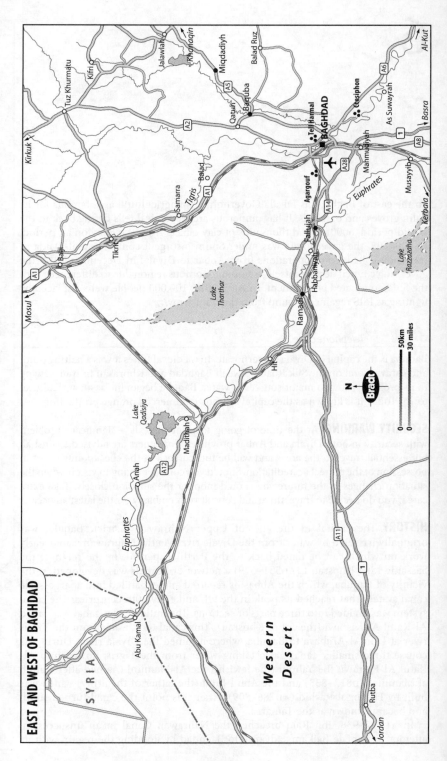

SYRIA

Western Desert

Jordan → Rutba

Abu Kamal

Euphrates

Lake Qadisiya

Anah — Madithah

Hit

Ramadi

Lake Tharthar

Habbaniyah

Fallujah

Lake Razzazah

Agargouf

Euphrates

Tell Harmal — **BAGHDAD**

Ctesiphon — As Suwayrah — *Basra* →

Mahmudiyah

Musayyib

Kerbala →

Qatun — Baquba

Balad

Tigris

Samarra

Tikrit

Baiji

Mosul →

Kirkuk →

Tuz Khurmatu

Kifri

Jalawlah — Khanaqin

Miqdadiyh

Balad Ruz

→ Al-Kut

N

Bradt

50km

30 miles

0

0

waters, a move described as 'simply the most dramatic example of a widespread phenomenon of the time; and ... symbolic of the end of Abbasid power'. His actions destroyed the agriculture of Baquba and the surrounding towns and villages, which had up to that point been known as the bread-basket of the Abbasid capital. Following this the lower and middle parts of the Nahrawan Canal were abandoned for nearly 14 years, until the Buyids under Muizz al Dawla carried out repairs. Despite this, and further restoration by the Seljuk governor Bihruz in 1140, the canal network never achieved its former importance and gradually declined through neglect until it was largely silted up. Matters were not helped by it being used as a road by Seljuk troops and by the 13th century the canal network was finally destroyed and the countryside alongside it was abandoned. Baquba briefly grew in importance in the 14th century when the road between Baghdad and Khorasan was diverted north to pass through it.

In the late 19th and early 20th centuries, Baquba became a centre for Assyrians fleeing the Assyrian genocide taking place in the Ottoman Empire. In 1918 the British army convinced the Ottomans to let them have access to about 30,000 Assyrians from various parts of Persia, who they relocated to refugee camps in Baquba. Although it took just 25 days to move them to Baquba, at least 7,000 died of exposure, hunger or disease and others were killed in attacks by Kurds and Arabs. Once at Baquba the dangers were not over, and they had to defend themselves from further attacks. In 1920 the Baquba refugee camps were closed and the majority of the inhabitants decided to go back to the Hakkari Mountains in Turkey, while the remainder dispersed throughout Iraq into the existing Assyrian community.

During the 2003 US-led occupation of Iraq, Baquba was the scene of some of the heaviest militant activity, along with the Sunni strongholds of Fallujah, Ramadi and Samarra. In 2006 al-Qaida in Iraq named Baquba as the capital of their Islamic State of Iraq, following which, in early 2007, they withdrew large numbers of their forces from Baghdad to Diyala Province. Around 3,000 of these were located in Baquba, where they fortified observation posts and fighting positions, planted mines, booby-trapped houses and established supply bases and training camps. This insurgent control continued through 2007 and into early 2008. However, by mid 2008 an increased effort by US forces and Sunni tribesmen, coupled with a substantial Iraqi army presence in the Baquba region, dramatically hampered al-Qaida in Iraq's activities. In December 2011 the governing council in Diyala Province, suspicious of the Shia dominated government of Prime Minister al Maliki, declared itself a semi-autonomous region, an announcement which led to the outbreak of protests in the ethnically and religiously mixed province. Insurgent attacks and sectarian bloodletting have been rampant in Baquba in the decade since 2003, with violence surging in 2013 in the run up to Iraq's provincial elections and again in 2014 as ISIS (Islamic State of Iraq and al-Sham) sought to disrupt the elections and create an Islamic caliphate in Northern Iraq and Syria.

GETTING THERE
By road The city is located 50km to the northeast of Baghdad on the Diyala river. The alternative route from Baghdad to Kirkuk is via Tuz Khurmatu along Highway 2 and Highway 3, which skirts Baquba.

WHAT TO SEE AND DO At the time of going to press it had not been possible for the authors to travel into Baquba for many years. Baquba is a religiously mixed city which makes it especially vulnerable to the sectarian violence that has surged

across Iraq following the withdrawal of US troops. Deadly attacks are an almost daily occurrence, with bomb attacks on mosques and other public buildings commonplace. There have been numerous large-scale bombings targeting civilians, security forces personnel and government facilities as well as violent demonstrations. The city was home to an important museum which contained finds from some of the earliest archaeological work carried out in Diyala Province, but it is not known what condition it is in or what remains of the contents following the widespread looting which was carried out after the Second Gulf War.

Authors' Note: For the reasons above the following information regarding sites around Baquba, while being as accurate as possible in the circumstances, is inevitably somewhat outdated and incomplete.

AROUND BAQUBA

Located 30km southeast of Baquba, **Eshnunna** (Tell Asmar) was an ancient Sumerian-Akkadian city dating back to 3000BC. It was one of a number of independent, self-governing city-states contemporaneous with Lagash, Umma, Kish and Uruk. The remains of the ancient city of Eshnunna are now preserved in the mound of **Tell Asmar**, which was excavated between 1930 and 1936 by a team from the University of Chicago. These excavations revealed that in common with its contemporaries, Eshnunna had at its centre a walled enclosure built of mud brick and dominated by the huge Abu Temple. This temple went through a number of phases of construction including the Early Dynastic Archaic Shrine, Square Temple and Single-Shrine. The remains of these, along with artefacts found by

ESHNUNNA'S SUMERIAN CULTURE

Picture Eshnunna at its peak. The year is 2700BC. As you approach the town you will pass through small, flat fields, criss-crossed by irrigation channels, before coming to a high wall pierced by numerous gateways. Passing through one of these, you then find yourself walking through streets flanked by low, mainly flat roofed, mud-brick houses. In front of you, rising higher still, is another great wall, roughly oval in shape, which encloses the outer precincts of the temple. If you manage to gain entrance to this hallowed place you will find yourself in the central courtyard of the temple itself. Looking around you, you might see a procession of priests heading towards a square building raised up on a high platform at the far side of the courtyard. Like a medieval keep, the sanctuary of the temple god Anu looms over mere mortals below. By Akkadian times, the renowned tutelary deity of the city was Tishpak, but in Sumerian Eshnunna many gods are worshipped, with a few taking precedence over the rest. The most important Sumerian gods are Anu the god of the sky; Enlil (Ki) god of the earth and Ea, god of the deep.

Worshipped along with these nature gods in Eshnunna were others, who all had their own festival and rites. Each year Dumuzi, the god of vegetation, died and descended to the underworld till spring came when he was resurrected by the goddess Inanna whom he then ritually married. The obvious symbolic cycle of life and death in nature contained in this rite has parallels among the other ancient religions; with the story of Osiris and Isis in Egypt; with Persephone of the Greeks; and with the Syrian, Thammuz.

archaeologists, has helped form the basis of the classification of the Early Dynastic period into three parts ED I, ED II, and ED III. Twelve geometric gypsum sculptures were found in the Square Temple, and are some of the best known examples of ancient Near East sculpture. However, the most famous find was that of a Sumerian statuette found in 1933–34, one of a group of sculptures buried in a pit next to the altar of the Abu Temple. Dating back to the Early Dynastic period (c2900–2600BC), it is the figure of a Sumerian man, thought to be a priest because it lacks the full beard and long hair of other male statues of its type, standing reverently before his god. Just 40cm in height, it is made of gypsum inlaid with shell and black limestone. During this period statuettes were often placed in sanctuaries as votive offerings and were later buried when the temple was remodelled or rebuilt. More than 1,500 cuneiform tablets, which were also discovered by archaeologists, are still being examined by experts more than 80 years later. Although following the excavations several volumes detailing the findings were prepared for publication, World War II intervened and dispersed the group of scholars that had worked in the field, leaving more than 12,000 objects awaiting publication for the general public. Only a few monographs on the architecture and some of the major finds (statuary, cylinder seals, pottery) have been published spasmodically over the years by a few of the remaining collaborators.

THE INTERNATIONAL BORDER CROSSING IN DIYALA PROVINCE TO IRAN

Northeast of Baghdad runs the route through Diyala Province to the main International Border Post of Khorasan and the Iranian border. To reach the border first take Highway 4 via Baquba to Al-Miqdadiyah and then Highway 5 via Khanaqin until you reach Khorasan at the border. It is approximately 90km and along the way there are some patches of good road. The border post and road in the vicinity of it have been refurbished in recent years, but the border formalities have not! Allow at least 2 hours, depending on the security situation that day to clear the border crossing. It helps if you have assistance waiting for you on the Iranian side and obviously you will need to make sure that all your documentation is absolutely correct and up to date.

KHANAQIN Although a mainly agricultural town Khanaqin also has a fairly extensive oilfield, mirrored on the other side of the border in Iran. The town's population of approximately 70,000 is predominantly Kurdish, with some small groups of Shia Arabs and Turkmen. Although not actually in the Kurdistan Regional Government area, Khanaqin is still controlled by Kurdish forces. The town is divided by the Alwand river which is spanned by a rather magnificent, many-arched bridge, probably built in the early part of the 18th century under the Zands, an Iranian dynasty. Khanaqin has the usual local cafés, restaurants and basic hotels. It is not a place for foreigners to linger during these times, although the Kurdish population are warm and welcoming.

Other Iraqi/Iranian borders are principally for the use of the local population.

FALLUJAH

Further west and located in the Anbar Province on the Euphrates river, Fallujah was once a city of 200 mosques. In recent times it has been the scene of some of the bloodiest battles in the hostilities between US and Iraqi forces and the insurgents.

SECURITY WARNING Fallujah is currently one of the most dangerous places in Iraq and it is not possible, or advisable, for foreigners to go there. Heavy fighting has taken place on the highway that links the city to Baghdad and the Iraqi military regularly shell the city and carry out air strikes targeting suspected al-Qaida fighters. With an increasingly sectarian war in Syria rippling throughout the region and Iraqi political alliances unravelling, the battle for Fallujah at the time of going to press was even more complex than it was 10 years earlier, when US troops devastated the city to wrest it from al-Qaida.

HISTORY Fallujah dates back to Babylonian times. Its name is thought to be derived from the Syriac word *pallgutha* meaning 'division' or 'canal regulator' as Fallujah is located where the waters of the Euphrates river divide into a canal. During the Sassanid era AD227–636, the region served as a warehouse or barracks for Persian troops (the word *anbar* meaning 'storehouse' in Farsi) and it was one of the main commercial centres of the Lakhmid Kingdom. When Rauwolf of Germany visited Fallujah in the 16th century, while searching for the site of ancient Babylon, he noted that it contained 'several ancient and delicate antiquities, still standing but in great desolation'. Under the Ottoman Empire, Fallujah was a popular resting place on one of the main desert roads west from Baghdad. In the spring of 1920 the British, who gained control of Iraq after the collapse of the Ottoman Empire, sent Lieutenant Colonel Gerard Leachman, a renowned explorer and a senior intelligence officer, to meet with a local leader, Sheikh Dhari, to renegotiate repayment of advances made to him by the government and to persuade him to remain loyal to the current administration. Exactly what happened depends on the source; officially he was shot in the back by Dhari's son, but according to the Arab version, the sheikh had his sons shoot Leachman in the legs. The sheikh then beheaded him with his sword. Leachman's death sparked an immediate outbreak of tribal uprisings between Fallujah and Hit and was responsible for General Haldene's advance on the area in September 1920. During the brief Anglo-Iraqi War of 1941, the Iraqi army was defeated by the British in a battle near Fallujah.

The discovery of oil changed the fortunes of the city and due to its location on one of the major highways out of Baghdad, it increased from a small, anonymous town in 1947 to one with a population of about 473,000 inhabitants before the 2003 war. Saddam Hussein's era was a time of heavy industrialisation for the city which saw the construction of several large factories, including one later closed down at the time of the searches by the weapons inspectors as it was suspected of manufacturing chemical weapons. Many of Fallujah's residents were thought to be Saddam's intelligence officers and many held high ranks in the army. During the 1991 Gulf War the city suffered one of the highest numbers of civilian casualties when, during the bombing of its bridges, a stray bomb hit a crowded market and killed 200 people. At the beginning of the 2003 war the city was not damaged, although when the Iraqi army stationed in the area abandoned its positions, looters quickly targeted government sites, including the Dreamland compound, a Baathist resort. In 2004 Fallujah became notorious when insurgents killed four American security contractors, whose mutilated bodies were subsequently filmed and displayed on TV footage around the globe. Fallujah, Ramadi and other nearby cities became battlegrounds over the following years as sectarian bloodshed mounted. In 2007, Prime Minister Nuri al Maliki sent reinforcements to dislodge militants from Fallujah and nearby Ramadi, which had become a focus for the 'surge' of US forces. In 2013 sectarian violence between Sunni and Shiite Muslims, as well as the overspill of the conflict that has engulfed nearby Syria, resulted in the largest civilian casualties in Fallujah for five years, and by 2014, al-Qaida-linked militants held control of much of the city and nearby towns, fighting off efforts by Iraqi forces to regain control and using military equipment belonging to the Fallujah police, whose headquarters they seized. At the time of going to print, the fighting in Fallujah continues with the Shiite-dominated Iraqi security forces striving to expel the Islamic State of Iraq and Syria (ISIS) faction from the surrounding Anbar Province and to win the loyalty of the region's Sunni tribes. 'The tribes are really torn between different groups,' said Iraq's deputy national security adviser, Safa Rasul Hussein. 'We've seen in some tribes the father has a position and his son has a different position ... Some from the tribes are fighting with ISIS, but some are also fighting against them.'

GETTING THERE   Fallujah is located 70km west of Baghdad.

AROUND FALLUJAH

About 1.5km north of Fallujah lie extensive ruins which are identified with the town of **Anbar**, an ancient Sassanid town, located at the confluence of the Euphrates river and the King's Canal (today the Saqlawiyah Canal) known in early Islamic times as the Nahr Isa and in ancient times as Nahr Malka. Known as Firuz Shapur or Perisapora to the Greeks and Romans, Anbar was founded around AD350 by the Persian king Shapur II. It was sacked and burnt by the Roman Emperor Julian in AD363 during the Roman invasion of the Sassanid Empire, after which most of its inhabitants migrated north and founded the city of Hdatta. The name of the town was then changed to Anbar.

Abu al Abbas as-Saffah, the founder of the Abbasid Caliphate, made Anbar his capital, and it remained so until the founding of Baghdad in 762, after which it still remained a place of much importance throughout the Abbasid period. The fortunes of Anbar then declined and today it is entirely deserted apart from a profusion of ruin mounds, most of which are an indication of the former importance of Anbar. Nearby are the remains of the former Babylonian Jewish city of **Pumbeditha,** famed for its Talmudic academy which was moved there from Nehardia in Babylonia in AD259 by Judah ben Ezekiel and which, together with the city of Sura, was one of the two most important centres of Jewish learning in the world, whose scholarship gave rise to the Babylonian Talmud. The medieval Jewish traveller Benjamin of Tudela visited 'el-Anbar which is Pumbeditha in Nehardea' in 1164 and said it had 3,000 Jews living there.

HABBANIYAH   Located between Ramadi and Fallujah, **Habbaniyah Tourist Village** was once one of the biggest tourist resorts in Iraq. Built by the French in the late 1970s, a tourist guide published by the Iraqi government in 1982 described a 'six-floor four-star hotel, three restaurants, bars, a night club, 50 plus chalets, two large swimming pools, a sailing club, a horse-riding arena, four tennis courts, a supermarket, an open-air theatre and an Arab tent casino'. During the Second Gulf War it was transformed from Iraq's top luxury resort into a shelter for around 15,000 refugees, mostly Sunnis driven from the capital due to death threats from Shia militias and refugees from the offensive against Fallujah. The lakeside beach was used as a laundry and refugees caught fish from the lake to eat. All that remained of the village's once lush gardens was dirt and scrub. Rusted carousel horses suspended in the air, and eerie, headless elephants were all that was left of the fairground ride. By 2008 the future of Habbaniyah Tourist Village looked bleak. However, in 2009

Coalition forces provided financial aid to the resort in an attempt to get it back in business. A five-floor, 200-room hotel was rebuilt in the centre of the Village by the beachfront, as well as a boardwalk, food kiosks, a playground and amusement rides. Business picked up and the resort began to get busier with sometimes as many as 3,000 local visitors a day during festivals and religious holidays. Business owners at the Tourist Village attribute the increase in visitors to better security and accessibility to the area.

Initially a joint effort led by the Iraqi army, Iraqi police and Coalition forces helped increase security in the area, Iraqi police then took sole responsibility for providing security. Today Habbaniyah Tourist Village is again closed to tourists, although it is still used for government purposes (see box, below). There are plans to reopen the Village once the situation in Fallujah stabilises and the security situation improves.

In 1921 the British forces took over the Turkish base at Habbaniyah and eventually built it up to become the largest Middle Eastern British military base during World War II. **The Royal Air Force Station Habbaniyah**, more commonly known as **RAF Habbaniyah**, (originally **RAF Dhibban**) is about 65km west of Baghdad. It was

ANBAR FESTIVAL OF ARTS

Some of Iraq's foremost painters took part in an art festival in Anbar Province on 21 January 2013 as part of the preparations to celebrate Baghdad as 2013 Capital of Arab Culture. The festival, sponsored by the Iraqi Ministry of Culture and hosted at the Habbaniyah Tourist Village, aimed to select artists to participate in the celebration honouring Baghdad later in the year. Said Ministry spokesman, Abdul Qader al Jumaily said: 'All the works done at the festival will be entered into a competition to select the best art piece, best painting and best imagery and idea and the winning pieces will be highlighted at the Baghdad celebration'.

The Anbar festival was a major event featuring works depicting provocative scenes and vignettes through fantastic paintings that invoked the history, present and future of Iraq as well as the unity of its people. Submissions included sketches, watercolours, oils and charcoal paintings on canvases. The committee furnished the necessary materials and selected scenic locations for the artists to paint in. Festival director Mutih al Jumaily said the event was the first of its kind at the Habbaniyah Tourist Village. In addition to the participation of some well-known artists, a group of young people worked on their paintings together in art galleries and on the shores of the Habbaniyah Lake. 'Youth participation in various festivals and artistic and literary events is very important because this segment of the population represents the next generation that will build up the country', Anbar Cultural House director Fawzi Mutlaq said. He went on to describe the festival as one of the most successful arts events ever held in Anbar. 'Participation on the part of Iraqi painters showed the country's unity and its rejection of the ideology of terror', Mutlaq said, adding that 'this solidarity was reflected in their artwork, which depicted the indivisibility of the people in all their segments, setting forth a model for brotherhood and endurance in the face of terror. This unity was further manifested through artwork that showed an ordinary citizen, a policeman and a soldier guarding their nation and striving to protect its security and stability'.

operational from October 1936 as a peace-time RAF station, maintained under the Anglo-Iraqi treaty of 1930, which permitted a British base west of the Euphrates. In the late 1930s Imperial Airways established a staging post on Lake Habbaniyah for the Flying Boat Service between the UK and British India (and later Singapore and Australia) using Short Empire flying boats. The lake provided the necessary landing area for these aircraft, which carried mail and passengers. This service was operational from October 1936 until the 31 May 1959 when the British were finally withdrawn following the July 1958 Revolution.

Habbaniyah was the permanent headquarters of the RAF in Iraq during World War II, although its location in the middle of the desert, 300 miles by air from the nearest bases on the Persian Gulf and 500 miles from the bases in Palestine, made it particularly vulnerable. In April 1941 it was threatened with attack by Iraqi forces. There were no operational units on the station, but there was a Flying Training School and a number of trainer aircraft. Work immediately commenced on fitting guns and bomb racks to these aircraft and by the end of the month some 70 were serviceable for operations. At the same time intensive training courses were instituted in bomb aiming and air gunnery. When the Iraqi forces besieged Habbaniyah this improvised striking force was the backbone of constant air raids on enemy positions and, together with the nightly raids on their gun emplacements by the RAF Levies defending the station, was mainly responsible for the withdrawal of the Iraqi forces from the plateau adjoining the airfield during the night of 5–6 May.

On 31 May 1959 the British finally withdrew and the base was handed over to the Iraqi air force. Renamed Rashid Airfield, it remained a major Iraqi military airbase over the following years and is now in an enclosed military area.

Habbaniyah War Cemetery is enclosed by a high brick wall within the former RAF cantonment. Originally the pre-war RAF cemetery, it was used during the war not only for RAF casualties but also for the burial of soldiers killed during the 1941 operations and for all servicemen who died through illness or accident while serving in PAIFORCE. The war graves are mainly in special plots, alongside pre-war RAF and civilian graves (RAF dependants and civilians employed by the RAF) and the graves of servicemen who died after the war. They include 14 men of the King's Own Royal Regiment killed at Fallujah on 23 May 1941 and buried where they fell, whose graves were moved afterwards from Fallujah into the cemetery by the Army Graves Service. Altogether 60 casualties of the fighting in Iraq during May 1941 are buried here. The post-war army burials include 24 men who were killed in April 1957 when a Jordanian RAF plane crashed in the vicinity. There are 162 Commonwealth burials of the 1939–45 war commemorated here including 10 Polish and 1 Norwegian foreign national burial and a further 117 non-World War burials. Built into the wall at the extreme end of the main avenue of the cemetery is the Habbaniyah Memorial to those whose graves in Iraq are so situated that they cannot be permanently maintained.

RAMADI *Telephone code 24*

Ramadi is the capital of Anbar Province. It is the largest city in the province having grown considerably during the past 20 years, and it now extends more than 60km along the Euphrates river just northwest of Lake Habbaniyah. Its indigenous inhabitants are Sunni Muslims from the Dulaim tribe, whose numbers have swelled in recent years as Ramadi has become a dormitory town for those working in Baghdad.

6

SECURITY WARNING Since 2003 heavy fighting has taken place sporadically in and around Ramadi between the Iraqi army and the tribal forces on one hand and armed insurgents on the other, meaning that it has not generally been possible or desirable for foreign travellers to visit. Since the beginning of January 2014 the Baghdad–Ramadi highway has been closed and other roads outside the city have witnessed fierce fighting. All the entrances and exits to Ramadi as well as the main roads and some of the bridges in the city have been closed by the government due to the high number of casualties sustained in these clashes.

HISTORY Although now a large city, Ramadi is also a very new one. Ancient settlements have existed in the vicinity for millennia, but the modern city of Ramadi was only founded in 1869 by the Ottomans as a base for communications with, and control of, the Dulaim tribe living in the region. It later became the chief customs port for entry into Iraq from Northern Syria along the Euphrates Road. In 1917 Ramadi was the site of clashes between the British army and what was left of the Ottoman forces (see box, below). A dam was built across the Euphrates near Ramadi during the 1950s. The city once had a large Jewish community, but the Jews left for Israel in the same decade. Between 2003 and 2006 Ramadi was a base of resistance to US occupation forces. After the fall of Fallujah in 2004, the Islamic State of Iraq, a group which was part of al-Qaida, declared the city to be its capital and the city came under the control of the insurgents. Law and order broke down and street battles became common. In August 2006 the insurgents killed Abu Ali Jassim, a moderate Sunni sheikh who was encouraging his tribal kin to join the Iraqi police. They

THE BATTLE OF RAMADI

The Battle of Ramadi was fought in September 1917 between the British and the Ottomans during the Mesopotamian Campaign of World War I. An important Ottoman garrison was quartered in Ramadi, and their presence was preventing the British from advancing further along the Euphrates river. The British had already attacked the garrison earlier in the year, but had been repulsed and had been forced to retreat to the town of Dhibban with heavy casualties.

In preparation for the assault the 15th Indian Division constructed a bridge and roadway on the north bank of the Euphrates so that the Ottomans would expect the attack on Ramadi to come from that direction. Meanwhile, the 6th Cavalry Brigade was quietly taking up positions to the west in readiness for the Ottoman retreat.

On 28 September two brigades of the Indian Division attacked and fought their way into Ramadi. Having observed the preparations being made across the river, the Ottomans were ready for this, but were taken by surprise by the use of armoured cars by the British Forces. Unprepared and unable to defend themselves against these, the Ottomans swiftly capitulated. Their attempts to escape from Ramadi by fleeing west across the desert to the town of Hit were prevented by the cavalry and the following day the Ottomans surrendered the town to General Maude.

The British use of armoured cars in the battle was one of the first in World War I and was a decisive factor in their swift and comparatively bloodless victory. Unfortunately, a subsequent attempt to capture the town of Hit, also using the armoured cars, failed on account of poor road surfaces and it was called off before the town could be reached.

refused to return his body to his family for burial in accordance with Islamic law. Angered by this, 40 sheikhs from tribes across Anbar Province set up the Sahwa Al-Anbar better known in the West as the Anbar Awakening. Led by Sheikh Sattar the tribes mobilised against the Islamic State of Iraq insurgents. In less than a year the Anbar Awakening spread across the whole of Iraq, reducing the levels of insurgency and violence everywhere they operated. In the final days of 2013, however, Ramadi was again subjected to violent clashes following which the provincial government and Iraqi army closed all the entrances to the city.

GETTING THERE Ramadi is approximately 141km west of Baghdad by road.

AROUND RAMADI

The **Ramadi Barrage** lies west of Ramadi on the Euphrates river. It has two sections, the northern barrage which slows or stops water as required and the southern barrage through which the water is then diverted into a canal feeding water into Lake Habbaniyah. When the barrage was built it was intended to use water for irrigation during the summer months. However, it was discovered that the very large evaporation losses, together with the dissolution of salts from the soil leading to high levels of salinity, seriously diminished water quality and rendered it unsuitable for irrigation purposes.

THE INTERNATIONAL BORDER CROSSINGS IN ANBAR PROVINCE TO SYRIA AND JORDAN

Located west of Baghdad in Anbar Province, the route from Baghdad to Amman in Jordan and Syria travels west for just short of 900km. The major road is the Saddam Highway which runs roughly parallel to the old roads and highways. The Saddam Highway was built to accommodate and facilitate the truck traffic which brought goods into Iraq from Jordan and the port of Aqaba. Since the inception of the highway, the volume of traffic making this journey has increased immensely. However, its western situation is strategic; and with a profusion of airfields and other military posts surrounding it, it has been much bombed and has been a target in all conflicts since the Iran-Iraq War in the 1980s. Consequently, at times the highway has been badly damaged and its bridges broken. Set in unremitting desert landscape, the road lends itself to high-speed driving in places and its reputation as a dangerous road is still prevalent, though today as much for hijackers and insurgents as for high-speed crashes. Although flying between Baghdad and Amman is the preferred option for travellers, many cannot afford to do so and have to travel by road. There are still some cafés and restaurants alongside the highway.

The old road begins as Highway 10 out of Baghdad and tracks the Saddam Highway passing through Fallujah, Habbaniyah and Ramadi. All these towns are currently hotbeds of tribal division and al-Qaida-led insurgency, so best avoided. However, it is easy to travel on Highway 10 and then divert onto the Saddam Highway to avoid these towns before returning to Highway 10.

Described below are the three main routes to international borders in Anbar Province.

ROUTE 1 The first of the routes runs directly towards Syria. Travelling west of Ramadi, you change to Route 4 at Han Abu r-Rayat which follows the route of the Euphrates for 162km to the Syrian border at **Qusaybah/Abu Kamal** (Syrian border town). This road is the ancient path of war, trod since the earliest periods by invaders from and to the west. The Euphrates river is navigable in parts and of course provided the source of water for marching troops in desert lands. In recent times it has become a more dangerous smugglers' route, for antiques, guns, explosives and insurgents. The US forces tried very hard to plug this gap in Iraq's defences but have never managed to do so completely. Tribal Arab loyalties have always come first.

At the time of going to print, this border crossing was shut due to the Syrian Crisis, but it is an interesting route to travel when it is possible to do so as it transverses Iraq through to northern Syria following the Euphrates along which are clustered many small tribal towns and villages. It makes for much more interesting viewing than the direct, but boring, road to Amman. There are a number of small towns on this route between Baghdad and the Syrian border.

Located on the Euphrates, **Hit** was always an important river port. A small, walled agricultural town with a population of around 100,000, it has been famous for its bitumen wells and springs since Babylonian times. Herodotus mentions Hit as the source of the bitumen used by Nebuchadnezzar II to seal and waterproof the

THE NAIRN BROTHERS

Of New Zealand origin, with possibly Scottish ancestry, Gerald and Norman Nairn served in the British Army during World War I. They ran a motorcycle dealership in New Zealand before the war and so were experienced and knowledgeable mechanics. The brothers recognised a business opportunity in the Middle East selling cars. With backing from a Beirut Arab family they set up business.

After a shaky start they opened a taxi business between Beirut and Haifa. This cut the travel time for the 112km journey to less than a day, compared with the three days it usually took for horse-drawn conveyances. From then on their business grew from strength to strength with the emphasis on tour and bus services. It took time for the brothers to experience and discount different types of vehicles that could operate efficiently in the hot and dusty desert conditions and later the attempts of Syria's bandits to try to disrupt their services. The British Consul in Damascus in 1923 asked them to explore the feasibility of crossing the Syrian Desert by car. On 2 April 1923 the Nairn brothers set off on the first of their exploratory trips from Damascus to Baghdad. Three days later the convoy – a Buick, an Oldsmobile and a Lancia – arrived in front of the Maude Hotel in Baghdad. From then on the brothers offered a mail, diplomatic bag and bullion transporting service to the various embassies and consulates in Damascus and Baghdad. Soon the desert crossing became the route of choice for celebrities, including Gertrude Bell, Freya Stark and Agatha Christie. By 1936 the company was dealing with the Iraq Petroleum Company and carrying workers, technicians and food to the pump station sites.

After World War II the use of air transport grew and this coupled with increasing political difficulties in the area led to the decline of the service. In 1950 the brothers, tired by all the modern difficulties, handed the company shares to their employees and ceased to be involved in the business. Without them, the desert service continued a short while longer before folding in 1956. Norman Nairn died in 1968 and Gerald in 1980.

grand Processional Way in Babylon. The modern oil pipeline to the Mediterranean crosses the Euphrates here at Hit. The next important town is **Al-Hadithah,** another agricultural market town on the river and important as the largest hydro-electric facility in Iraq, the **Hadithah Dam.** There was a continual source of conflict here between the mainly Sunni affiliated tribes and the occupying American forces. The Iraqi Government continues to face the same conflict. **Anah** is also on the riverside and has a population of more than 20,000. The market town for a large, fertile, agricultural area is 260km from Baghdad and 90km from the Syrian border. Anah has a very ancient part to it, possibly the remains of a settlement dating back to 2000BC and variously described as Hanat by Babylonians, as An-at by the Assyrians and Ana by Christian Arab writers. The town has always been on the path of invaders: the Roman Emperor Julian mentions taking the place in AD363. The Persians, Parthians and Sassanians all travelled this way and passed through this town. A famous octagonal minaret was built in the 11th century AD. Restored several times it was allegedly destroyed in 2006 by insurgents, but this isn't confirmed.

The Syrian border is at Abu Kamal and if you continue to follow the Euphrates for 136km, you will reach the city of Deir-e-Zor.

ROUTE 2 The second of our Syrian border routes takes us to the border called **Al-Walid** on the Iraq side and **Tanf** on the Syrian side. It is approximately 126km west of Rutba. At the divergence of the road into two, the major branch carries on to Jordan. The lesser road is Highway 13 to Syria. To the side of Highway 13 you will see what was once a hydraulic pumping station, known as H3. It is now the site of the largest military airfield in Iraq, much attacked during the last war. This road, after the border, travels through the desert to Palmyra. Once again at the time of going to print this border post was closed.

ROUTE 3 Finally the last western border, is with Jordan. Take the Saddam Highway or Route 10 which leads to **Tarabil** on the Iraqi side and **Karamal** on the Jordanian side. This border is a very important one for Iraq and consequently it is closely supervised. Documentation is all important and it can take anything from 2 to 7 hours to cross here. The post gets closed occasionally when insurgency levels rise, but such is its importance to the economies of both Jordan and Iraq that they strive to keep it open at all costs. Sadly it has also become an important crossing point for refugees and there is now a refugee camp here. Allow 10–15 hours of flat, monotonous driving from Baghdad to Amman.

RUTBA

Rutba is a Sunni city and the first major populated area as you enter Iraq from either Jordan or Syria by road. Standing at a crossroads of desert tracks surrounded by hills that border a dry wadi, it occupies a strategic location on the Amman–Baghdad road and the Mosul–Haifa oil pipeline. During the British mandate Rutbah Wells, as it was then known, was a stopover for Imperial Airways flights to India and Rutba Fort (see box, pages 182–3) and was a rest house on the overland route from Baghdad to Damascus.

HISTORY Rutba grew up around the ancient drinking-water wells which were frequented by desert nomads before most opted for a sedentary existence. Once the town was known as the 'Rutba Rest House' as it was the first major staging

Standing outside the hotel in the early morning was a long, experienced-looking motor coach. It was touched everywhere with brown dust. The words 'Nairn Transport Co,' were written on its side. It was a heavier, longer version of those coaches which roll so swiftly through the English countryside. Its normal route was Damascus to Baghdad. Its driver was known to everyone as Long Jack.

A broad-shouldered man over 6ft in height, he wore a pair of old flannel trousers and a leather golf jacket. He was one of those men who seem to have a schoolboy hiding somewhere inside them. He asked for my passport and told me he had been born in Wellington, New Zealand and had come to Syria as a boy of 11. The Nairn brothers, Gerry and Norman, were also New Zealanders. They had served in Palestine during the War and then started their desert transport company. They had given him a job as a driver – and how many times he'd driven the coach to Baghdad and back he really couldn't say! 'We have two drivers in each desert car,' he explained, 'one sleeps while the other drives and so we keep it up all night'

The distance between Damascus and Baghdad is 843km and the Nairn coaches accomplish the journey in 24 hours with only two official stops: one, at Rutba Fort, halfway and the other at Ramadi, the Iraqi passport station. Before cars crossed the desert, the journey was possible only by camel caravan, and sometimes took two months.

A heat haze trembled over the plain. Our eyes, seeking for variety, seized eagerly on any rock or low hill or even the ragged line of a wadi, just as at sea one looks with pleasure at a passing ship. At some point, where I believe there was a post or some barbed wire we passed into Iraq. There was no customs house or passport office – that happens near Baghdad - nothing but the plain rising and falling, scattered with stones and gravel like the dry bed of an enormous lake.

The afternoon wore on. The sun was behind us to the west. The shadows lengthened. We saw the swift twilight go and darkness come to the desert. It grew colder and the stars shone. With only a pale finger of light left in the sky, we came to a gaunt square building standing in the treeless desolation: a walled fort with stone towers at the four corners. The flag of Iraq flew over the gate; a wireless mast rose from one of the towers; and two or three cars and some lorries stood on the sand, while an armed sentry in a blue uniform marched up and down. This was Rutba Fort – the halfway house to Baghdad.

I went through the postern gate into a dark courtyard. Soldiers were lounging round the guardhouse, gazing curiously, for the arrival of a desert coach is probably a great event in their lonely day. In contrast to the desert outside, this courtyard, with its bustle of life, was exciting. It also had the urgency and the drama of events that happened behind four closed walls: it was almost as if men were preparing for a siege. I could hear a dynamo throbbing, and when doors opened in the low building that ran round the four sides of the fort, I could see a yellow oblong of light, dark men at desks, soldiers delivering a message, a wireless operator with earphones on his head.

post *en route* to Baghdad for caravans (and later in the 1930s for the Nairn desert coach service) from Damascus. In colonial times Rutba was a British airbase and public radio station. In the Saddam era it remained a military customs and communication centre and was notable as the site of a large part of the old Iraqi air-defence warning system. A large number of military personnel were housed there

While I was blundering around in the dark, wondering where I should find something to eat, for although Rutba has plenty of light for its offices it spares none for its courtyard, a door opened and out came a little man. He wore a white mess jacket and looked like a Goanese steward from some P and O ship. 'A wash and brush up sir?' he asked in English. 'There is hot water'. I followed him into a room where about 20 camp wash stands were ready for travellers. Besides each was a white enamelled jug of hot water with a spotless towel neatly folded and placed over the top. There was soap everywhere – English soap – and several clean hair brushes. I felt pride and happiness rising in me, for this was undoubtedly English; but when I turned to ask the little man to explain it, he had gone.

On the veranda outside I saw a sign 'To the lounge'. I followed it, pushed open a door and saw a truly amazing sight. In a room dotted with little wickerwork tables a number of men and women were sitting in basketwork chairs round a stove. Most of them were English. Some were smoking cigarettes and others drinking tea. I ventured in and sat next to a woman in a tweed costume who was reading an old copy of the *Bystander*. This was the rest house which the Nairn Company keeps at Rutba, and the people were passengers on their way east or west. Leading from this room was a little dining room with tables set for dinner, all neat and clean and – English. There is a wonderful English way of setting a table which we don't notice at home because we see it so often. The cloth droops almost to the ground, decently covering the table's legs and it generally has ironed creases in it. The knives and forks are set with precision. Not with Gallic insouciance or Latin fire, the cruet is given a place of honour besides a bottle of sauce. Tumblers, the right size for half a pint of ale, stand to the right-hand and inside each one is popped a little bishop's mitre – a folded table napkin. No other nation sets a table like that, and I determined to pour Lea and Perrin's sauce over everything that night, out of sheer love for England.

Pinned to an announcement board next to an apology for the high price of bottled beer, was a notice that brought me back to reality:

NOTICE

Passengers are warned when leaving the fort always to keep the fort in sight. Cases have occurred of passengers becoming lost (through losing their bearings) when out for a stroll, owing to darkness falling suddenly and the fort not being in sight. The result of this causes danger to passengers and trouble to the police

BY ORDER, THE ADMINISTRATIVE COMMANDANT

My eyes lingered lovingly over 'when out for a stroll' which brought memories of Eastbourne into Mesopotamia. No-one but an Englishman could have talked about having 'a stroll' at Rutba.

Taken from *Middle East* by H V Morton (Methuen, London, 1941)

before the warning station was destroyed in the 1990–91 Gulf War. After 2003 the base was occupied by the Allies. It reverted to Iraqi army control in 2010.

GETTING THERE Rutba is located in Anbar Province on the Baghdad–Amman Road.

SECURITY WARNING In the past Rutba had fuel stations, restaurants, small hotels and rest houses. At the time of going to print, Rutba was a hotbed of insurgent activity and one of the many towns in the province harbouring insurgents. Therefore, it is another place to which foreigners are advised not to travel at this time.

BALAD

Moving back towards Baghdad and then directly north we next come to Balad in Salah ad Din Province within the borders of the so-called 'Sunni Triangle'. It is a major place of pilgrimage for Shia Muslims particularly from Iran, as it is the site of the mausoleum of Syed Mohammad ibn Imam Ali al Naqi who died in AD866. As Balad lies between Samarra and Kadhiman (now part of Baghdad) pilgrims will often visit all three holy places in one trip.

GETTING THERE Balad is 80km north of Baghdad on Highway 1, the Baghdad–Mosul road, approximately 30km south of Samarra.

OTHER PRACTICALITIES Today the small town of Balad has no hotels or facilities for tourists.

WHAT TO SEE AND DO The **Mausoleum of Syed Mohammad ibn Imam Ali al Naqi** is a typical large Shia shrine with a magnificent dome and minarets. The entrance way is covered with flower-pattern tile work and the archway has gold Kufic script

AN INTRIGUING HISTORICAL LEGACY

While they're a sad sight to the aviation enthusiast, there's something eerily fascinating about abandoned aircraft and plane graveyards. Whether it's the sight of yesterday's cutting-edge technology rusting away in the timeless dust of the desert, or the rich history surrounding military forces and hardware in general, plane graveyards make for great exploring. Balad Air Base contains a graveyard of armoured vehicles and tanks, and row upon row of abandoned Russian MiG-23s, some of which had been partly dismantled and others which have been buried in the desert sands. This ruinous plane graveyard reflects the fate of Iraq's air force both before and after the 2003 US-led invasion.

It is thought that the rot set in prior to the 2003 invasion. It is known that two squadrons of MiG-23 Floggers were based at Balad during the 1980s, so the planes may well have been quietly decaying in the desert sands since the end of the Gulf War in 1991. Representing an air force that barely got off the ground in the wake of invasion; these dilapidated MiG-23s were abandoned by the Iraqis, looted and left neglected amid other junk and detritus. However, after quietly rotting away for years, they were discovered by American troops and after being dragged out from their various hiding places around the former air base their stripped-out carcasses were liberally daubed in graffiti. Today these MiGs now look more like pieces of urban art than once-operational aircraft. One of the previously buried MiG-25 Foxbats was even recently excavated and transported to the US.

For both the military historian and avid modern art collector, this place is a mouth-watering prospect for future investigations.

adorning it. Inside the large rectangular tomb is encased in a silver cage topped by a gold roof. The gateway suffered minor damage when attacked by insurgents over the last few years, so the shrine is now surrounded by railings and there are the usual checkpoints to go through before you can get into the outer courtyard. The shrine attracts Shia couples who come here to seek blessings (*nadr*) for the birth of a child. The place where the shrine is built used to be the cemetery of Shias. During the time of Caliph Hujjaj bin Yusuf thousands of Shias were imprisoned and not allowed to leave Balad. Many died and were buried here, and the cemetery has now also become a place of worship.

Balad's other claim to fame is its air base and army camp. Known as **Al-Bakr Air Force Base** in honour of Hassan al Bakr, the President of Iraq from 1968 to 1979, it is the major air base of the Iraqi air force. Operating out of the base were two squadrons of MiG-23 fighters which saw action particularly during the Iran-Iraq War. Soon after the US invasion and the capitulation of Iraq, the US forces took over and occupied Balad air base. Because of its strategic position and facilities, including runways and hangers, it soon became the most important such base in Iraq. At its peak it housed over 36,000 personnel. It also became the headquarters of the US Special Forces in their two-year hunt for Saddam Hussein and subsequent battles against al-Qaida insurgents. British air force and SAS personnel were also based here. The base passed back into Iraqi forces' hands on 8 November 2011.

SAMARRA

Samarra, on the left bank of the Tigris, has a strange and glorious past. Thought to have been first settled 7,000 years ago, during the 9th century AD it was transformed virtually overnight from a piece of desolate ground with no buildings and no inhabitants save a Christian monastery, into the capital of one of the greatest states known to history, but it lost its status a mere 56 years later. At its peak it was known as Surra Man Ra'a (he who sees it is delighted) but following its sudden desertion the people began to call it Saa Man Raa (he who sees it is displeased). Thankfully for history, its quick death led to the survival of its architecture and layout with little change or destruction, and today it is a living document and a unique witness to an empire that ruled the ancient world from Tunisia to central Asia. Modern Samarra is a town of modest distinction. It possesses a circuit of mid-19th-century fortifications dominated by a Persian-style Shia mosque (the Al-Aksari Mosque) with a once-shining golden dome. Within the mosque are the resting places of two holy men of Islam, the 10th and 11th imams Ali al Hadi al Naqi and his son Hasan al Askari and nearby is the spot where the 12th imam, the Mahdi, who was reportedly born in Samarra, vanished. Non-Muslims should take particular care around Samarra.

Samarra was known to the Greeks as 'Souma' and to the Romans as 'Sumere' a fort mentioned during the retreat of the army of the Emperor Julian in AD364. In Syriac it is 'Sumra' and is described as a village. The metaphor of 'Having an appointment in Samarra' signifying death is a literary reference to an ancient Babylonian myth: Death is both the narrator and a central character.

SECURITY WARNING Samarra is a place where religious tensions can run high. There are strict security checks to go through in the vicinity of the Al-Askari Mosque (including checks carried out by the now infamous 'golf ball' explosive detectors). Taking photographs of the mosque is strictly forbidden and cameras

WHO IS IMAM MAHDI?

According to the Shia version of Islam the 10th imam, al Hadi al Naqi, was forced from his home in Medina by the powerful Sunni caliphate in Baghdad and was sent to live in Samarra where he could be kept under closer supervision. It is believed that he was then poisoned on the orders of the caliphate, as subsequently was his son Hasan al Askari, the 11th imam. Fearing a similar fate, Muhammad al Mahdi, the 12th imam (known as the Mahdi or Hidden Imam), went into hiding or occultation, a kind of suspended state. Legend has it that shortly before he disappeared; the Mahdi visited the shrine of al Naqi and al Askari in Samarra. According to Richard Hooker on *The Hidden Imam* (*www.wsu.edu*) website:

'The core of the Shi'ite religious world view is the legend of the Hidden Imam, Muhammad al Mahdi (the Guided One). While the stories of the first eleven Imams are historical in nature, the history of the 12th Imam is mystical and miraculous. Born Abu'l-Kasim Muhammad in AD868, when al Askari, the 11th Imam died in 874 he declared himself to be the 12th Imam and went into hiding. The Shias believe that he hid himself in a cave below a mosque in Samarra; this cave is blocked by a gate which the Shias call *Bab-Al-Ghayba*, or the 'Gate of Occultation'. This is one of the most sacred sites in Shia Islam, and the faithful gather here to pray for the return of the 12th Imam.

'The central Shia doctrines revolving around the Hidden Imam are the doctrines of occultation (*Ghayba*) and return (*Raja*). The doctrine of occultation is simply the belief that God hid the Mahdi away from the eyes of men in order to preserve his life and has miraculously kept him alive ever since. Eventually God will reveal the Mahdi to the world and he will return to guide humanity. His return is the most significant future event for the Shia faithful and will occur shortly before the Final Judgement and the end of history. The Mahdi will return at the head of the forces of righteousness and do battle with the forces of evil in one, final, apocalyptic battle. When evil has been defeated once and for all, the Mahdi will rule the world for several years under a perfect government and bring about a perfect spirituality among the peoples of the world. After the Mahdi has reigned for several years, Jesus Christ will return (*raja*) as will Hussain and others.'

must be handed in at the gate before entering the outer courtyard. Access to the mosque is not always permitted, depending on the situation in Samarra at the time of visiting, and at the time of going to press it was closed to even the locals. It is not advised that visitors linger here any longer than they need to.

HISTORY Samarra was inhabited as far back as the 5th millennium BC during the Chalcolithic Samarran period, the precursor of the Ubaid period. Known as Tell Sawwan, it was a prosperous settlement renowned for its dark-fired pottery decorated with stylised figures of animals and birds, and geometric designs. Between the 3rd and 7th century AD it was the site of a small Sassanian Persian town with a Christian monastery. Re-founded in 690 BC by the Assyrian king Sennacherib as Sur-marrati, the city expanded after the Qatal Al-Kisrawi canal was built to bring water from the Tigris river to the region by King Khosrau I Annushirvan (AD531–578). King Khosrau also built a commemorative tower (modern Burj Al-Qaim) to the south of Samarra and a palace with a walled hunting park at the northern inlet (modern Nahr Al-Rasasi) near to Al-Daur. A supplementary canal, the Qatul Abi Al-Jund, was opened by the Abbasid caliph Harun al Rashid and a planned city was laid out in the form of a regular octagon, but he abandoned it unfinished in 796.

The city further blossomed in the 9th century when it became the capital of the Abbasid Empire, although the circumstances of its selection as the capital city are shrouded in mystery. What is known is that in 836 Caliph al Mutasim and his court left Baghdad and established a new capital at Samarra. Yaqubi, the contemporary Arab historian, relates that before he came to power, al Mutasim purchased young Turkish slaves in Samarkand each year as reinforcements in the Caliph's campaigns against the Byzantine Empire. Eventually he had at his command thousands of these young Turks who, when they went out riding, 'would gallop and collide with people right and left'. After the death of Harun al Rashid in 809, the designated heir to the caliphate was murdered by an older half-brother, who had been overlooked in the line of succession as his mother had been only a Persian slave girl. The ensuing battle for the caliphate resulted in the besieging of Baghdad, which left it much destroyed and its occupants bitter, due in part to al Mutasim's Turks getting out of hand and murdering and pillaging. When al Mutasim assumed the caliphate his subjects became further alienated as the Turks abused their increasing power. Perceiving that the Turks now posed a threat to his position, al Mutasim may well have gambled on a complete change of environment, with the attendant universal employment bringing renewed loyalty from his subjects and control over the wayward Turks. A move to Samarra would give his dynasty a fresh start by making a visible break with the previous regime.

The move took place and once there al Mutasim set to work on a large and imaginative scale to create a new environment of which he could become the master. He spared no efforts to build his new metropolis as Yaqubi relates; al Mutasim assembled 'workmen, masons, and artificers, such as smiths, carpenters and all other craftsmen, including marble-workers'. He collected 'teak and other kinds of wood and brought palm-trunks from Basra'. Elsewhere it is recorded that he sent to Egypt with orders that 'the columns and the marble should be taken from the churches. Those of Alexandria were pillaged, and from the pilgrim-church of St Menas in the desert behind Alexandria were removed its coloured marbles and its famous polychrome pavements. From all directions caravans laden with the loot of late antiquity converged upon Samarra'.

Al Mutasim was a benign ruler. He paid the Christian monks in Samarra a substantial indemnity in a period when less civilised methods of sequestration would have passed without comment. He built the Friday Mosque and three palaces, one of which, on the right bank of the river, was linked with the main body of the town by a bridge of boats. Parallel with the Tigris river, he built the Al-Shari Al-Azam or Grand Avenue, which formed the axis of the city plan. This was subsequently extended as the city spread with the addition of new palaces, mosques and residential suburbs. The Turks were quietly quartered away from the city in the hope they would not unduly harass the citizens of Samarra.

Between 859 and 860 Caliph al Mutawakkil, a son of al Mutasim, instigated further building work, designed to match the glory of his father. 'Now I know that I am indeed king!' he is recorded to have exclaimed, 'for I have built myself a city and live in it'. The new city was separately identified as Al-Jafariya. In Samarra itself he continued work on the Al-Jami Mosque and minaret, a synthesis of Babylonian ziggurat and Islamic architecture. Built of baked brick disguised by a rendering of stucco, the walls were buttressed by round-fronted towers on square pedestals pierced by 16 doorways. Within were quadruple colonnades round three sides and a large sanctuary nine columns in depth and 24 in width. The *mihrab* or prayer niche was square in plan, as was the early custom in Iraq and Persia, and was flanked by two columns of rose-coloured marble. The spandrels of its high arch also bore traces of gold. It is recorded that the mosque rivalled that of Damascus with its unsurpassed mosaics. At first Samarra flourished as vigorously as her ambitious founder; however, in 892 after a short but eventful time as the Abbasid capital, a successor to al Mutasim led his patient subjects back to the ruins of old Baghdad and the reign of Samarra was over.

Samarra played a very important role during the Mesopotamian campaign of World War I and the old barrage, which was built by the British army there to control the headwaters, can still be seen close to the town. Baghdad was flooded on more than one occasion by forces controlling this barrage, and it is still possible to see some of the original old gun emplacements on it. Samarra flourished again as a result of the building of the Al-Tharthar Dam in 1956. This modern replacement for the barrage built by the British is more efficient at preventing flooding in Baghdad as it diverts the flow of Tigris river during its rise into the Al-Tharthar Valley and the newly created Lake Tharthar. Many people living in the valley were displaced when this happened and moved to the city of Samarra, leading to a big increase in its population.

GETTING THERE Samarra is accessible by road on the left bank of the Tigris, 130km north of Baghdad.

WHAT TO SEE AND DO As you approach the city from the main road it appears to be perched on a platform of earth and stones by the river. This platform is made up of the ancient and historical remains of Samarra. From here you can also see the great Malwiyya or spiral minaret, and close by the golden dome of the Al-Askari Mosque containing the Shrine of al Naqi and al Askari in the centre of Samarra. Crossing the bridges by the water barrages brings you to the centre of the city and what seems to be a plethora of concrete-slab blast walls. Everywhere there are police and barriers across the roads. Following the massive destruction of the shrine in 2006–07, it is being painstakingly rebuilt and already the half rebuilt dome is beginning to shine again; however, even the Iranian pilgrims have been denied access to it so far. Entering the shrine needs permission from the Ministry of Religious Affairs, so all visitors have to wait a while longer before it is possible to visit the mosque and shrine again.

Driving slightly to the left of the town brings you to the Malwiyya Minaret and Al-Jami Mosque built by Caliph al Mutasim. Restored under the Saddam regime in the 1980s the mosque is again being renovated and the foundation stones around the minaret are being exposed. A viewing garden is being laid out with skill around the mosque containing seats and flower gardens, and the foundations of a reception house and a small museum are now in place. Progress is rapid, and maybe in 2015 all will be in place. Some slight excavations are being made close to the minaret, so it will be interesting to see what is revealed. Just outside the mosque enclosure are the foundations of two small Christian churches. You will need to ask the guardians of the site if you wish to view them.

The best advice is to climb the minaret. From the very top you can see the progress of the shrine's restoration in the centre of the city. To the north are the mounds that cover the foundations of the cities of al Mutasim and his son al Mutawakkil, stretching 20km into the distance. Note: Just to the north of the

'After a long day of work, the king was exhausted, and he knew exactly what he needed to refresh. He entered his private chambers and called for his hookah to be brought. His wife walked in and looked at him. "There is no more tobacco," she said. The king shot a look of anger at her. "Who is it that made the tobacco haram for me?" he demanded. She looked back at him with a defiant smile and said, "The same one who has made me halal for you!"'

Born Sayyid Muhammad Hasan ibn Sayyid Mahmud al Hussaini al Shirazi in 1814 in Shiraz, Iran, Mirza Shirazi was an exceptionally intelligent child blessed with an extraordinary memory, who started his religious studies at the tender age of four years. By the time he was eight, he had already completed preliminary level studies, and at the age of 12 he began attending advanced lessons in jurisprudence and methodology in the seminary of Shiraz. Eventually he travelled to Isfahan and then to Kerbala and Najaf in order to study under the most prominent scholars of the time, including Jawahari and Ansari. Upon the death of Jawahari, Mirza Shirazi became one of the most prominent Shia scholars in the world.

Although Samarra contains the burial sites of Imam al Naqi and Imam al Askari, it had always been a predominantly Sunni area and pilgrims often faced difficulties when visiting the holy shrines. In 1874 Mirza Shirazi decided to migrate to Samarra and establish its first Shia seminary. The school trained many prominent scholars and jurists until it was closed by Saddam Hussein. Mirza Shirazi also initiated a project to renovate the mosque containing the graves of the 10th and 11th imams which had fallen into disrepair.

In 1888 the Shah of Iran granted the British Imperial Tobacco Company exclusive rights to produce, sell and export all of Iran's tobacco in return for annual royalties to him to give the Shah much-needed financial help. However, the tobacco crop was widely considered a valuable national asset by the Iranian people who were proud of the rich variety and quality of their tobacco as well as depending on its revenues. Therefore, selling the rights to it to a foreign company caused widespread outrage. Despite protests taking place across all of Iran, the Shah refused to back down so leading Shia and Sunni scholars in Iran to write to Mirza Shirazi asking him to intervene and save the Iranian economy from the Shah's destructive policy.

In response to this cry for help, Mirza Shirazi issued his famous Tobacco Edict, declaring that using tobacco was akin to waging war against the 12th imam. All across Iran, farmers refused to grow tobacco, merchants refused to sell tobacco and servants refused to serve tobacco. Even the Shah's wives stopped smoking in an act of solidarity with the Iranian people and the Shah's own servants refused to prepare his hookah. Eventually the Shah was forced to cancel the agreement. Since it was a temporal edict, Mirza Shirazi was then able to withdraw it so that production and usage of tobacco could continue as usual.

Mirza Shirazi passed away in Samarra in 1894. His body was taken to Najaf, and he was laid to rest near his mentor Ansari in the courtyard of Imam Ali's shrine.

minaret you can see the chemical plant that attracted so much attention from the UN inspectors led by Hans Blix in their hunt for chemical and nuclear weapons, of mass destruction in 2002. All in all Samarra should be on everyone's list to visit, even those who are in Bagdad for the briefest time.

Al-Askari (Al-Hadi) Mosque Situated in the centre of the modern city, the mosque with its great shining golden dome contains the tombs of the 10th imam al Hadi al Naqi and his son the 11th imam Hassan al Askari. Their shrine is particularly important to Shia Muslims and has been visited by thousands of pilgrims over the years. It also contains the shrine of Muhammad al Mahdi, known as the Hidden Imam (see box, page 186). Also buried in the mosque are Hakimah Khatun and Narjis Khatun (the mother of the Mahdi) both of whom are female relatives of the Prophet and highly regarded by both Shia and Sunni Muslims. Traditionally, although these shrines are predominantly Shia ones, they have been cared for by the Sunnis, as Samarra's native population are largely Sunnis who, it is believed, are descended from these saints. Until recently the mosque had two minarets, delightful tile work and was crowned by a huge dome 22m in diameter constructed from 7,200 golden covered bricks. Disaster struck on 22 February 2006 when armed groups bombed the mosque. There were no casualties, but the structure of the mosque and its golden dome were badly damaged. Then on 13 June 2007, two near simultaneous blasts destroyed the mosque's two minarets. In July of the same year UNESCO announced that the 'Shrine city of Samarra' had been declared a World Heritage Site. Since then both Sunnis and Shias have been working on the reconstruction of the mosque, which it is hoped will soon be once again open to worshippers.

Al-Jami Mosque Built by al Mutasim and extended by his son al Mutawakkil, the mosque was one of the largest Islamic mosques ever built, with 17 aisles and walls panelled with mosaics of dark blue glass. It was destroyed in 1278 after Hulagu Khan laid waste to Iraq. However, it is the **Malwiyya** or spiral minaret located outside the northern wall of the main enclosure which gives Samarra its high place in the list of the world's greatest architecture. In the words of British archaeologist Sir Mortimer Wheeler:

'What matters most about the Samarra minaret is not its formal origin but its startling originality. Strikingly bold and simple in design, functional, elemental, finely proportioned, comfortable to the eye. Here we have in the 9th century many qualities which bridge the centuries. The malwiyya is truly a great and rather lonely masterpiece.'

The minaret, or tower from which the muezzin called the times of prayer, stands on a square foundation which is connected by a ramp and small bridge with the adjacent entrance to the mosque, and there may once have been an outer wall enclosing both mosque and minaret. The minaret is encompassed by a spiral ramp 2.25m wide at the base. Above each circuit the width of the tower is diminished by the width of the ramp, which makes five complete turns in an anti-clockwise direction. The ramp becomes steeper as it rises in order to keep a constant height for the successive stages. At the top were the remains of a little pavilion which rested on eight columns; however, in 2005 the minaret was targeted by insurgents (reportedly because they thought US troops had been using it as a sniper position) and the remains of this little building were destroyed.

Apart from tubular towers, Muslim minarets are of two main kinds. Those with simple diminishing square or round stages (as in the Ibn Tulun Mosque in Cairo and the Great Mosque of Kairouan in Tunisia) are commonly derived historically from the telescopic form of the famous lighthouse on the Isle of Pharos at Alexandria. The spiral or helicoidal type of Samarra and Abu Dalaf can be traced back to an ancient Babylonian ziggurat or temple-tower of which the most notorious was the Tower of Babel at Babylon itself. Herodotus has been quoted in this connection. He says that the Tower of Babel consisted of eight receding rectangular stages, reached by a path which wound 'round all the towers'. This feature was still visible in the 12th century, so the Arab architects may quite possibly have borrowed the idea, transferring it from a square to a circular shape.

Borrowing of this kind would be completely in accordance with Arab procedure. The Islamic Arabs started upon their conquering mission with no established architectural tradition of their own. They improvised as they went along, adapting their minarets from Alexandria or Babylon, and their multi-aisled sanctuaries from the multi-aisled Christian churches which littered their path. With these general borrowings they took much detailed artistry, so that, for example, the sanctuary of the Holy Mosque of Kairouan is a veritable forest of Roman and Byzantine columns collected from around the region.

The *malwiyyas* of Samarra and Abu Dalaf are truly great masterpieces.

Bayt Al-Zakharif Located to the west of the Al-Jami Mosque and minaret this house was an important private residence. It was excavated by the Iraqis in 1965 who discovered in it carved stucco panels forming revetments approximately 1m high. Fifty other houses from the same period have also been excavated and many more remain to be explored.

Bayt Al-Khalifa Al Mutasim built his major palace complex on the east bank of the Tigris around an existing pre-Islamic settlement and the site of a Christian monastery. It is not easy to picture how Samarra would have looked at this time as there has been extensive overbuilding of the site since then. It is possible to ascertain that a roadway, the Grand Avenue (Al-Shari Al-Azam) ran 3km south from the palace complex to the markets and the mosque of Al-Mutasim (both of which are now buried under the modern town of Samarra) and extended on through the whole length of the city. To the east of the Grand Avenue are the remains of the barracks where the Turkish troops were quartered by al Mutasim and to the west the barracks of the Maghariba soldiers of Egyptian origin. To the north of the Al-Jawsaq Al-Khaqani palace are the remains of another military cantonment called Khaqan Urtuj. Two further cantonments can also be found near the site: Ushrusaniyya in the village of the same name 4km south of modern Samarra and Karkh Faryruz at the village of Shaykh Wali, which also housed the rebellious Turkish mercenaries. The area east of the city encompassed the walled hunting park called Al-Hayr.

The palace complex **Al-Khalifa** was built by Khaqan Urtuj Abu al Fath Ibn Khaqan, who was a Turkish military commander. It is situated on the Grand Avenue overlooking the Tigris river. At 125ha it is one of the largest Arab Islamic palaces discovered, exceeded only by the Al-Jafari Palace to the north of Samarra (see page 194). Comprising two parts, the **Dar Al-Amma** or public palace where al-Mutasim held court and the **Al-Jawsaq Al-Khaqani**, his private quarters, Bayt Al-Khalifa was excavated by Viollet and Herzfeld before the World War I and more recently by the Iraq Directorate of Antiquities. The site is dominated by the square Dar Al-Amma, which leads to a garden on the bank of the river. Behind this can be seen a court, two basins, a polo ground and the private, enclosed palace, Al-Jawsaq al-Khaqani. The palace complex includes living quarters, halls, administration rooms, *diwans* and guards' barracks in addition to leisure facilities.

Among the remains you can see the Bab al-Amma, the formal ceremonial entrance to the public palace overlooking the river, the palace of al Hayr and the circular basin, each containing pools, rooms and *iwans* used by al Mutasim and his family for rest and recreation. This palace complex still preserves its complete original layout and is the only case of an imperial palace from later antiquity whose plan is so completely preserved. However, even though excavations have been conducted in the palace complex on and off for over a century, about three-quarters of the area still remains unexplored and the western garden has been flooded following the construction of the Al-Tharthar Dam in the 1950s. In the 1980s the palace was renovated and the original walls were plastered and made good. Spaced among these walls were placed bricks commemorating Saddam Hussein's reconstruction. Today the site, following its use as a police barracks, is beginning to crumble again and requires further refurbishment.

Al-Huwaysilat Palace Situated on the west bank of the river to the north, Al-Huwaysilat Palace is identified with the Qasr al Juss in the medieval Arabic chronicles.

Built as a leisure palace for al Mutasim, it consists of two buildings, the Lower and the Upper. The Lower Palace consists of a square building whose sides are 140m. It is located within a square-shaped outer enclosure surrounded by a wall which is 370m on each side and reinforced by a series of towers, four of which are main round towers, 3m in diameter. In the middle of each of the four sides of the enclosure there is a main entrance. The palace also has a number of halls, rooms and courtyards.

Al-Mashooq Palace (the Palace of the Beloved)
Built by al Motamid in AD876 on the bank of the Al-Ishaqi river, looking out over the west bank of the Tigris some 10km northwest of Samarra, the palace is monumental in scale. It is the best preserved of the Abbasid palaces at Samarra. Its plan is rectangular, with dimensions of 136m by 90m. It consists of a large brick construction mounted on a high artificial platform of barrel vaults, with many courtyards and a number of rooms and halls opening onto the central spaces or connected to them by entrances. The internal division in the palace is tripartite. The walls of the palace are 3.6m wide, reinforced by round towers with rectangular bases. Between each pair of towers are three large niches with polylobed arches. The outer walls and gateways were fully restored in the 1980s.

Qubbat Al-Sulaybiyya
South of Al-Mashooq Palace is Qubbat Al-Sulaybiyya. This domed building was probably a mausoleum for three of the caliphs who ruled in Samarra: al Muntasir, al Mutazz and al Muhtadi. It is an octagonal-shaped building in the middle of which there is a square hall surrounded by an octagonal ambulatory surmounted by a hemispherical dome. The palace was heavily restored in the 1970s.

Balkuwara (Al-Manqur) Palace
Built by Caliph Al-Mutawakkil ala Allah for his son Abdullah al Mutazz in about AD854, the palace is situated to the south of modern Samarra on the bank of the river. Despite the effects of time and nature, archaeological explorations have revealed the plan of the building. It is rectangular in shape, 575m by 460m, with its corners oriented to the cardinal points. Comprising three parallel internal rectangles, the middle one contains the important parts of the palace. The site was excavated in 1911 by Ernest Herzfeld for the German Archaeological Expedition. Today all you can see of the building are mounds of earth with some fired brick.

Al-Istablat
Approximately 111ha in size, this palace complex, surrounded by an ancient military camp, is located on the west bank of the Tigris about 15km south of Samarra. It was built by Caliph al Mutawakkil in AD851 and consists of a small rectangle containing the palace Al-Arus which is connected to a large rectangle with blocks of houses. The length of the small rectangle is about 500m and the width is 215m. The length of the large rectangle is 1700m and its width is 550m. These rectangles are surrounded by a massive enclosure wall.

Husn Al-Qadisiyya
Abandoned unfinished in AD796, Husn al Qadisiyya is an octagonal-shaped mud-brick city. The plan was based on a circle of 1.5km in diameter. The length of each side is between 620m and 627m and its perimeter is 4.5km. According to the texts it was built by Caliph Harun al Rashid on the model of the Round City of Baghdad.

Al-Musharrahat Palace
Located about 6km east of Samarra, it is built on the site of one of the palaces which Caliph Harun al Rashid built when he excavated the

Nahr Abu Al-Jund Canal. The debris from the canal excavation was laid under the area of the palace to form a high mound. In front of the palace is the basin known as Birkat Al-Buhturi after the famous poem by the Abbasid poet al Buhturi.

Tell Al-Alij This is an artificial mound for the caliph to view horse-races. Probably built by al Mutawakkil, it is 21m high and is positioned at the start of a 10.5km racecourse. Originally it would have contained a pavilion for the caliph to watch the horse-racing. There were three other racecourses at Samarra.

Al-Jafari Palace Dating from AD857–861, this was the new caliph's palace built by al Mutawakkil. It is located north of Samarra and is the largest palace ever constructed in the Islamic world at 211ha. It has never been excavated, but the site is well-preserved.

Abu Dalaf Mosque The ruins of Abu Dalaf Mosque are situated about 20km to the north of Samarra at neighbouring Jafariya. This mosque also has a spiral minaret, built on a smaller scale and slightly later than the minaret at Samarra by Abu Dalaf, a commander of al Mutawakkil in AD860–861. Like the mosque and minaret in Samarra upon which it is modelled, Abu Dalaf Mosque is also built of fired brick. Although its minaret has the same form as the Malwiyya, it is only 20m tall and therefore much steeper with a much narrower ramp. Only some remnants of the inner arcade still stand, along with the minaret, alone in the middle of the desert. Owing to security concerns it is currently very difficult to get permission to visit this site.

TIKRIT (SALAH AD DIN) *Telephone code 21*

The city of Tikrit will always be associated with Saddam Hussein who was born in the nearby village of Al-Awja. During the Saddam era, Tikrit was the important home of the tribal Tikritis.

SECURITY WARNING At the time of going to print it was not possible for tourists to stay in Tikrit due to the security situation.

HISTORY Tikrit dates back to Babylonian times. The Babylonian king Naboholasar camped there when he was attacking the city of Ashur in 615BC. Interestingly, in view of its later history, Tikrit was home to the early Christian church, and Christians were living there from the 1st century AD. It flourished as a Christian centre during the first three centuries of Arab rule. Recent studies and excavations show evidence of at least seven, some say nine, churches in Tikrit and many monasteries in and around it. In 1036 it was the stronghold of the Uqaylid Dynasty, descended from the Bedouin. The great Syrian Orthodox cathedral was destroyed in 1089 by the Muslim governor of the province. Salah al Din al Ayubbi, founder of the Ayyubid Dynasty and known as Saladin in the west, was born in Tikrit in 1138. Saladin, a Kurdish warrior, became the Sultan of Egypt and was known as a champion of Islam for his role in capturing Jerusalem during the Crusades. Sultan bin Malik Shah besieged Tikrit in 1156 and by then most Christians had fled to Mosul. Like much of Iraq, Tikrit was devastated during the Mongol invasion of the 14th century.

In the 1990s Saddam built a huge palace complex in the town overlooking the Tigris. It was not a place for happy families as his wife and mistress resented each other. Extravagance was the name of the game: the hillside had nine palaces, the one with the best view reserved for Saddam. Maybe he wished he had paid the contractors what they were owed – they exacted their revenge by linking the sewage system to the air conditioning...

'It was a different town from the one I passed through in 1991', John Simpson recalls in *The Wars Against Saddam*. 'Then it had seemed like just another untidy, backward little place; now real money had been spent on it. Several of the buildings were faced with marble. A statue of Saddam on horseback stood at the junction where the road from the bridge met the main street which ran through the town.'

Saddam's anticipated 'last stand' in Tikrit never transpired. When several thousand marines with 300 armoured vehicles converged on the town on 13 April 2003, they met little resistance. Before his capture on 13 December 2003, Saddam sheltered in and around Tikrit for six months. The 'spider hole' from which he was ingloriously extracted was just outside ad-Dawr, a small town 15km south of Tikrit. The town was not a victim of the post-war orgy of looting, however, as Saddam's government looked after its people. He may be hated in most of Iraq, but nostalgia for Saddam lives on in Tikrit. Fighting to retake Tikrit from ISIS prompted 28,000 people to flee. Mass graves containing hundreds of bodies of soldiers killed by ISIS were found in April 2015.

GETTING THERE The main Highway 1 from Baghdad to Mosul bypasses Tikrit. This was arranged during Saddam's time as a security measure.

WHERE TO EAT AND DRINK There are two restaurants in Tikrit on the main road through the town, on opposite sides of the road and facing each other. One is called The Baghdad Restaurant and the other is called Al-Dhyafa Restaurant. Both serve typical Iraqi cuisine – kebabs, rice, salad, chicken and pilau rice. In both restaurants the food is plentiful and well cooked, but both are expensive by Iraqi standards.

WHAT TO SEE AND DO The **Saddam Mosque** in the centre of the city is one of the cleanest, best lit and best air-conditioned in the country. In the centre of the town to the east, and on the road to Kirkuk, bridging the Tigris and looming over the town in a baleful presence, is the huge, empty, monumental palace of Saddam Hussein. At present it is a fenced off, forbidden place. **The Palace Complex** was the scene of the famous film clip of Saddam firing a rifle into the air from a balcony overlooking his troops. In tribal fashion members of Saddam's family lived close by the president in sumptuous large palaces and houses all built in the distinctive Saddam style. It was also good politics to live close to the influential members of Saddam's council, such as Tariq Aziz who eventually became Vice President. In due course, this Government-clique town became a hived-off area with no entry allowed for ordinary people and barriers at every entrance. The Palace Complex was occupied by American troops until 22 November 2005, when it was handed over to the governor of the province. Up until the ISIS invasion in July 2014, it was used by the Iraqi police and army for its headquarters.

In layout the town is open and a straight road runs directly through it. There is a much used side road which goes northeast to Kirkuk. The distinctive Saddam architecture can be seen in the mosque in the centre of the town as well as featuring in many other minor buildings. As you drive north through Tikrit on your right-hand side there is a walled-off enclosure which housed the visitors' palaces and the entrance gate to the ministers' houses. Some of these continue to be occupied by the present government ministers. Ten years after the fighting in Tikrit ended, the buildings still showed damage. The houses stretch down to the river, which is fairly fast flowing with a pumping station and weir built for the residents' needs. Located by the river are the ancient walls of Tikrit. The old city mosque is on the nearby hill along with the remains of the Cathedral Church of the Middle East. In the 6th century Tikrit was the principal Archbishopric of the Middle East and hugely influential in Christian Iraq. Today, however, little remains of this glory.

In 2014 the town was taken by ISIS but in 2015 it was retaken by Iraqi forces. The town was reported to have been severely damaged but we cannot ascertain to what extent.

AROUND TIKRIT

AL-AWJA Saddam's birthplace is an ugly, dusty little village. Most of it was flattened in 1987 after a shot was fired at Saddam's motorcade as he travelled through it. **The Shrine and Mausoleum of Saddam Hussein and his Family** is in Al-Awja, which is home to the Saddam branch of the Tikrit tribe. The shrine has a smallish dome and an open courtyard in front of it. In this courtyard are 12 graves of the Hussein family, including sons and Saddam's cousin, the reviled Chemical Ali. The graves here are concrete, with longish slabs inscribed with the occupant's name. Under the round dome of the shrine itself lies the grave of Saddam, ornamented with wreaths of flowers. Around the room on all the walls are pictures and photos of Saddam and his life. Outside, the shrine gardens are laid out at the rear of the dome. It seems astonishing that this building exists, given the hate that has been generated in Iraq towards him. In some ways though, the very fact that it exists shows the pragmatic view of death in Islamic culture.

In September 2014 sources in Baghdad stated that Saddam's body had been moved from this grave by his family and taken to an unknown destination. The other graves, it was reported are intact, but the extent of damage to the mausoleum is unknown.

BARJI (BAYJI)

Barji is probably the major industrial centre in Iraq. Situated at the crossing point of a new road system and at a junction on the Mosul–Baghdad railway, Barji has more than 200,000 inhabitants. It is the home of one of the largest oil refineries in Iraq, Al-Bayji Refinery, and the Bayji Thermal Powerplant, which is reputedly the largest in the country and a major contributor to Baghdad's electricity supply.

HISTORY Barji has a recent, but chequered history. Prior to the First Gulf War it was thought that a chemical weapons manufacturing facility was located in its environs. The refinery and petroleum facility were bombed at the beginning of 1991, towards the end of the air campaign. In 2003 UN inspectors investigated both the State Company for Fertilizers and the Arab Company for Chemical Detergents in Barji, but no trace of chemical or other weaponry was found. The Bayji Water Treatment Facility re-opened in 2003 after a major refurbishment funded by the Coalition Provisional Authority.

In recent years, although the refinery has recovered from the damage caused by the war and the deterioration it suffered due to a lack of vital parts needed for its maintenance when the sanctions were in place, it has become a target for insurgents keen to disrupt the flow of oil. Output at Barji was disrupted for several days after an attack in February 2011 and in February 2013 Iraq's Oil Ministry reported that insurgents had blown up the fuel pipeline, which carries seven million litres per day, for the third time that month, halting fuel supplies and forcing the Ministry to use tankers. However, the outlook remains positive with new oil containers constructed and a new hospital being built for its workers. In February 2014 Siemens Energy announced that they had been awarded an agreement to perform service and maintenance at the 600 megawatt Barji Gas Power Plant. In July 2014 Iraqi security forces reported that ISIS militants had taken control of a portion of the Barji oil refinery. Security forces drove the militants off, but over the following months Barji became a flash point for multiple clashes between security forces and ISIS fighters and this situation continues in 2015.

GETTING THERE Barji is on the main Highway 1, 180km north of Baghdad and 43km north of Tikrit.

WHAT TO SEE AND DO Although a growing town, Barji is essentially a local place and dormitory for the industrial workers and their families. For the traveller there is one main street, which has the usual modest wayside restaurants and tea houses.

East and West of Baghdad   BARJI (BAYJI)

6

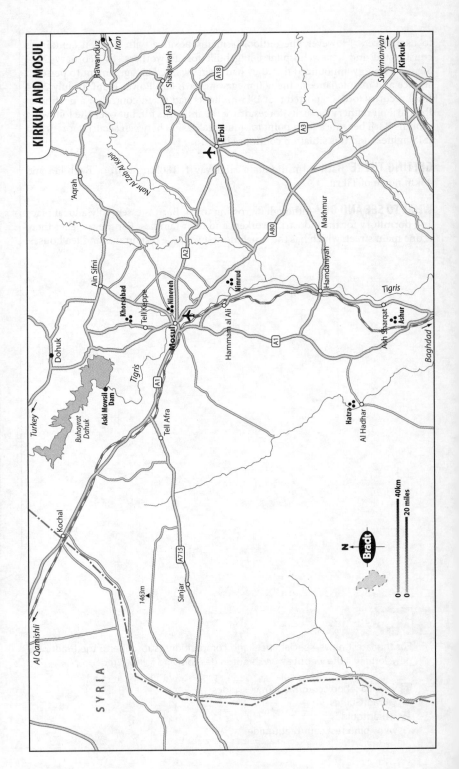

KIRKUK AND MOSUL

7

Kirkuk and Mosul

KIRKUK *Telephone code 050*

Kirkuk Governorate lies between the Zagros Mountains in the northeast, the Lower Zab and Tigris rivers in the west, the Himrin mountain range in the south and the Sirwan (Diyala) river in the southwest. The governorate straddles the strategic trade routes between Turkey, Iran and Iraq.

The area was referred to in Syriac chronicles as Beth-Garmai – the land of warmth. Before gas deposits were identified the area was regarded as having supernatural powers. Women used to move the earth with a stick and if flames appeared they believed they would give birth to a boy. Natural gas was used for centuries by shepherds and local people for heating and for cooking.

SECURITY WARNING At the time of going to print there is a significant problem with security in Kirkuk and Mosul. Kirkuk is under the control of Kurdis Peshmerga forces and Mosul is under the control of ISIS. The situation is in a state of flux. Foreigners are advised against all but essential travel to the areas and are turned back at the checkpoints on the approaches to these cities. Should you consider trying to visit if or when the situation changes in the future you should monitor the situation closely. Take extra care if you do decide to travel there and consult your embassy for the latest advice.

HISTORY Known to the Assyrians as 'Arrabkha Arfa', Kirkuk dates back to Sumerian times. It stands on the site of the ancient Assyrian capital of Arrapha, a settlement dating back 5,000 years. Because of the strategic geographical location of the city, Kirkuk was the battle ground for three empires, the Neo-Assyrian Empire, the Babylonian Empire (cuneiform writings found at the foot of the citadel indicate that it was known as Erebga) and the Median. All controlled the city at various times, although Arrapha reached its zenith under the Assyrians in the 10th and 11th centuries BC. The Assyrian king Nasirbal II built a citadel between 884BC and 858BC as part of his military defence. During the Roman era, the city was known as Kergi Sluks and later as Kergini. King Sluks was responsible for the construction of a strong rampart with 72 towers surrounding the citadel.

In AD1294 Marco Polo referred to the town as Circura. The name Kirkuk first emerged during the time of the Turkmen state of Kara Koyunlu (1375–1468). During Ottoman times Kirkuk was part of the province (vilayet) of Mosul. The Kurdish claims to the city date back to the late 19th century when they made up three-quarters of the population of Al-Tamim Province around Kirkuk. Following the end of World War l, the British occupied Kirkuk, under the Armistice of Mudros. At this time the population of the vilayet of Mosul was 61% Kurd, 28% Turkmen and 8% Arab. Both the Ottomans and Great Britain desperately wanted control of the vilayet, of which Kirkuk was then a part, and as the 1923 Treaty of

IRAQI TURKMEN

There are estimated to be some three million Turkmen in Iraq, but despite being the third largest ethnic and cultural group (after the Arabs and the Kurds) they make up less than 2% of the overall population. They are found mainly in the northeast of Iraq along the border between the Kurdish and Arab regions in an arc of towns and villages stretching from Tell Afar, west of Mosul, through Mosul, Erbil, Altun Kopru, Kirkuk, Tuz Khurmatu, Kifri and Khaniqin.

Descendants of the Turkish-speaking Oguz tribes from Central Asia, Turkmen migrated to Mesopotamia over several hundred years starting in the 7th century AD. Following the collapse of the Abbasid state in 1258, a number of Turkmen states were founded in Iraq, including Akkoyunlus, Karakoyun-lus, Ilhanis and Celayirlis. The Ottomans encouraged the Turkmen to settle at the entrances of valleys that provided access to Kurdish areas and to repel raids, leading to Turkmen being viewed historically as protectors of the Ottoman Empire from tribal raids. This historic pacification role has subsequently led to strained relations with the Kurds.

The majority of Turkmen are Muslims but they are not divided along sectarian lines. Approximately 60% of Turkmen are Sunnis, while the balance are Ithnaashari or other Shia. Shia Turkmen tend to live in the more southerly and rural areas. Tiny extreme Shia communities (for example, Sarliyya and Ibrahimiya) exist in Tuz Khurmatu, Tauq, Qara Tapa, Taza Khurmatu, Bashir and Tisin, and Tell Afar. There are also about 30,000 Christian 'Catholic' Turks and some Jews living in Iraq. One of the most important historical places to visit in the city of Tuz Hurmatu (Turkmeneli) is the Gawer Kalasi, which means 'Christian castle' in the Turkmen language.

The Turkmen speak a Turkish dialect and although some have been able to preserve their language (despite a strong linguistic Arabisation policy by Saddam Hussein), the Iraqi Turkmen today are being rapidly assimilated into the general population and are no longer tribally organised.

Lausanne failed to resolve the issue, the matter was sent to the League of Nations. A committee travelled to the area before coming to a final decision: the territory south of the 'Brussels line' belonged to Iraq. By the Treaty of Angora of 1926, Kirkuk became a part of the Kingdom of Iraq.

The discovery of oil during the 1920s turned Kirkuk into Iraq's fourth-largest city, and with the development of the petro-chemical industry, the city gained even greater prominence. Drilling first began at Bawa Gurgur in Kirkuk in 1927 and drilling rigs soon became a constant landmark. Refineries, which provided a good source of employment, were developed in the area and the population increased dramatically. Before the discovery of oil Kirkuk was a largely a Turkmen city. From the 1940s the ethnic balance began to change as Kurds migrated from the villages to work in the city, and soldiers stationed in the Iraqi garrison remained in the area. Gradually the demographic balance in the city changed in favour of the Kurds, who had large families of between 10 and 20 children. According to the 1957 census, 48.3% of the city's residents were Kurds, 28.2% Arab and 21.4% Turkmen. Arab control of Kirkuk's oil fields had always been a priority for the central government. From the 1970s Saddam Hussein's Baath Party embarked on a major relocation programme, transferring tens of thousands of families from

Kirkuk, Sinjar, Khaniqin and other areas to purpose-built resettlement camps. But the Kurdish migration into Kirkuk continued during the Anfal campaign, when hundreds of villages in Kurdistan were destroyed. The relocations intensified after the failed 1991 uprising.

Today the city, no stranger to suicide car bombings and political assassinations, is one of the most dangerous in Iraq. It is a tinderbox of conflict, mainly fuelled by the continuing internecine ethnic and sectarian violence between the Turkmen, Kurds and Shias; Christians, Yezidis and Muslims. The cosmopolitan nature of Kirkuk has been destroyed. Turkish and Kurdish sectarian tensions, fuelled by uncertainty and fear of the future, have polarised the communities. Despite this continuing instability, efforts have been made to restore the citadel, and one of the city's governors made the decision to paint the buildings dating from the 1930s and 1940s white. A number of old houses (such as the one belonging to a merchant named Ali Agha) and the bazaar, which has more than 300 stalls, have also undergone some restoration. Kirkuk is a market for the region's produce, including cereals, olives, fruits and cotton. It also has a small textiles industry. As Kirkuk has not benefited from the oil reserves in its vicinity, it is aiming to expand its agricultural sector to boost the local economy and reduce reliance on food imports.

GETTING THERE Kirkuk is located in the governorate of Kirkuk, 236km north of Baghdad.

AUTHORS' NOTE At the time of going to press travel into and around Kirkuk was not easily possible and had not been so for several years, although after ousting ISIS, the Kurds are now in control of the city. Therefore the information below, while being as accurate as possible in the circumstances, is bound to be somewhat outdated and incomplete.

GETTING AROUND It is possible to get around Kirkuk on foot, by taxi or bus.

WHERE TO STAY AND EAT The centre of the city is the place for hotels. We've not been able to visit the hotels to check them out for this edition, but in the past the following hotels have been used by visitors to Kirkuk: the **Kirkuk Hotel,** located on the corner of Majida and Al-Aqwaf Street; the **Sunoba Hotel**, located at the beginning of the Baghdad–Kirkuk Road; the **Bawa Gurgur Hotel** in the city centre, located in an old Turkmen khan, similar to a medieval inn, and **Takia**, an old-style Kurdish guest house located near the railway station. There were also plenty of second-rate, no-star hotels in the centre of Kirkuk, but these were definitely not recommended for tourists.

SHOPPING The main shopping market in the centre of Kirkuk is known as the **Bazari Pirehmerd.** The more modern **Hewraman Shopping Centre** can be found 2.7km from Kirkuk University on the outskirts of the city. Kirkuk also has a number of modern shopping malls located in its vicinity, including the **Kirkuk Mall** and the **Maxi Mall.** In December 2013 Iraqi security forces stormed the **Jawahir Mall** in an armed operation aimed at wresting control of it back from armed insurgents. Iraqi forces were able to take control of the situation and rescued 11 people, but not before a number of casualties were sustained.

ENTERTAINMENT Kirkuk has an **Olympic Stadium and Swimming Pool**. There are several parks in the environs of the city, including **Kirkuk Park**, **Imam Qasim Park** and **Efendiler Park**, near to Baghdad Street in the centre of the city.

OTHER PRACTICALITIES Kirkuk has two major hospitals **Kirkuk General Hospital** and **Dar Al-Salam Hospital**, both of which are located in the city centre. Kirkuk General Hospital, which has a new dialysis unit, is one of the main hospitals in northern Iraq, where the most severe and complicated cases are referred and treated.

WHAT TO SEE AND DO Kirkuk is a city of stone and alabaster buildings. The River Al-Khasa or Khas Jai passes through the city and divides it into two parts. The city was not bombed during the two gulf wars and its ancient shrines are intact, if in various stages of neglect and dilapidation. **Kirkuk Citadel** or castle can be found standing in what is considered to be the oldest part of the city on an artificial mound 40m high, in the area between the two bridges over the river. The citadel has an elevation of 18m from the surrounding street. At its highest point it reaches 368m, including the height of buildings located on its surface. The mound is believed to have been built by King Ashurnasirpal II between 884 and 858BC as a military defence line for the city.

The citadel is divided into three main sections: Al-Meidan District which is located in the north; Al-Qalaah District which is located in the centre, and Al-Hamam District which lies in the south. The citadel is home to the **Tombs of the Prophets Daniel, Haneen and Uzair**, as well as the **Red Church**, so called because in AD409 a pagan king ordered hundreds of Christians to be beheaded there. Since that time it has been known throughout Iraq as 'the graveyard of the Chaldeans' on account of the massacre. However, Chaldeans today prefer instead to recount the epilogue to the story in which a general named Tahmazgerd, under orders to carry out the murders, watched one young mother killed with her two children. Seeing their 'faith, serenity, and the trust of the widow', the story goes, Tahmazgerd converted to Christianity, and later was beheaded himself. Today the Red Church has some interesting mosaic engravings still remaining on its old walls.

According to the Koran, King Nebuchadnezzar ransacked the dwellings of the Israelites and slaughtered them, leaving their bodies decaying in the sun. When he saw this, Uzair was devastated and despaired of the glory of the cities ever being revived again. As he grieved, sleep overcame him and he fell asleep for 100 years.

Then Allah awoke him. He got up and went to look for his donkey, but he found only the bones of its decaying skeleton, although his food was as fresh as it had been when he had fallen asleep. As he wondered about this, Allah asked him if he knew how long he had been asleep. He said, 'for a day, or less'. Allah then told him that he had been asleep for a hundred years! His perishables had remained fresh by the grace of Allah, but his donkey as a living creature had undergone the natural process of death and dissolution. Then Allah brought his donkey back to life in front of his eyes and Uzair acknowledged Allah's supreme power.

Uzair is known as Ezra in the Torah, the Hebrew Bible. In the Book of Ezra he returned from exile in Babylon and re-introduced the Torah in Jerusalem (see also page 340).

The citadel is also home to numerous mosques, including the **Great Mosque, Mosque Fuduli, Mosque Arian** and **Hassan Backees Mosque,** and a number of traditional houses named 'Tifour'; 'Abdul Ghani'; 'Siddeeq Allaf'; 'Sayid Fatih'; 'Michael' and 'Toma' for their owners. Most of the structures within the citadel are characteristically built with white stone and plaster, and the roads are paved with a kind of brickwork called 'Farshi'. The market shops in the citadel have been built since ancient times in a unique architectural style known as 'Al-Qeisaria' with four doors, each being a metaphor for one of the four seasons. In 1997 a geographical survey and excavation carried out on the citadel led to the discovery of a large gate or door leading to what was thought to be a further city underneath it, however since then there have been no further reports of work in this area by specialists in the field of archaeological excavations, and the secrets of what may lie behind it remain unexplored.

The **Tomb of Daniel** is a shrine to the prophet Daniel who was Governor of Babylon when the area was ruled by Nebuchadnezzar. Originally the site was a Jewish synagogue, then later it was turned into a Christian church and finally into a mosque. The mosque is about 400m square with an arch and two domes on a decorated base, beside which there are three minarets dating back to the end of the Mongol period. It houses four tombs believed to belong to Daniel, Shadrach, Meshach and Abednego. So great is the reverence and respect that the people of Kirkuk feel towards the prophet Daniel, that they aspire to be buried near to his tomb, and the nearby graveyard is considered to be the first cemetery in Kirkuk.

The **Qishla of Kirkuk,** located off Madjidiya Street, behind the General Police Directorate, was built in 1863 to be the headquarters of the Ottoman army in Kirkuk (in Turkish Qishla means a place for the army to stay in winter). The site is large, occupying about 2ha. There is a small museum in the Qishla, and the Institution of Cultural Heritage has plans to renovate the southern part of the Qishla and turn it into a bespoke museum and cultural centre.

Grand Kirkuk, which is located in the centre of city, was built in 1963. Kirkuk's largest mosque, covers more than a 1,000m^2 and is big enough for 1,500 people to

The story of the prophet Daniel comes from the book of the same name in the Bible. He was a noble of the tribe of Juda. While still a youth, Daniel was taken captive to Babylon by Nebuchadnezzar in 605bc. There, with three other youths, Shadrach, Meshach and Abednego, he was educated by Asphenez, the master of the eunuchs, in the Chaldean language and the arts of divination, magic and astrology. After three years Daniel and his companions appeared before the king who promoted them to a place in his court as they proved superior to all the other 'diviners and wise men'.

Soon afterwards Daniel demonstrated his powers by being the only one who could interpret the meaning of the king's terrible dream. Daniel rose into high favour with Nebuchadnezzar, and was promoted to ruler of 'the whole province of Babylon' and chief of all the wise men.

As was common in those days King Nebuchadnezzar had built a huge golden image in the city, which all the people had to fall down and worship. Anyone who failed to do so was thrown into an immense, blazing furnace. Shadrach, Meshach and Abednego refused to worship this pagan idol and so were brought before the king to explain: *'O Nebuchadnezzar, we have no need to answer you in this matter. If this be so, our God whom we serve is able to deliver us from the burning fiery furnace, and he will deliver us out of your hand, O king. But if not, be it known to you, O king, that we will not serve your gods or worship the golden image that you have set up'.* Furious at this, the king had the furnace heated seven times hotter than normal. Shadrach, Meshach and Abednego were bound and cast into the flames which were so hot they killed the soldiers who had escorted them to their fiery fate. But as Nebuchadnezzar peered into the furnace, he marvelled at what he saw: 'four men unbound, walking in the midst of the fire, and they are not hurt; and the appearance of the fourth is like a son of the gods'. Shadrach, Meshach and Abednego then emerged unharmed, not even singed or smelling of smoke. Awestruck, the king pardoned them and granted them freedom to worship, along with the rest of the Israelites in captivity.

pray in it. One of the major mosques in the region, it has a decorated dome and golden minarets. It is decorated in the Islamic architectural style, with a white-painted interior decorated with Islamic verse.

Recently renovated, **St George Church** is also in the city centre and is still in daily use. It belongs to the Holy Apostolic Catholic Assyrian Church of the East which was founded in AD33.

AROUND KIRKUK

BABA GURGUR Famous for its eternal flames that have been burning for more than 4,000 years, Baba Gurgur (father of fire) is a large oilfield on the outskirts of the city. Described as far back as Herodotus c484–425BC (and believed by some to be the fiery furnace into which King Nebuchadnezzar threw Shadrach, Meshach and Abednego for refusing to worship his golden idol, see box, above) the flames have a significant symbolic value for residents of Kirkuk. It is believed that the heat of the eternal flames was used by shepherds to warm their flocks during winter, and women would visit Baba Gurgur asking to have a baby boy, an ancient practice which probably goes back to the time of fire worship. The burning flames are the result of natural gas and naphtha seeping through the cracks in the area's rocks.

We lose biblical track of Daniel following the death of Nebuchadnezzar in 561BC, the intimation being that he lost his high office and retired. He next appears during scenes of revelry in Baltasar's palace on the eve of Cyrus's conquest of Babylon in 538BC. While Baltasar and his court feasted, drinking their wine from precious vessels taken from the Temple in Jerusalem, there appeared a hand which proceeded to write on the wall: *'Mane, Thecel, Phares'*. These mysterious words meaning 'numbered, weighed, divided' were interpreted by Daniel, to mean that the king was about to lose his kingdom to the Medes and the Persians, a prophesy which came true that very night when Baltasar was slain and succeeded by King Darius who was a Mede (Darius Hystaspes 485BC). Daniel, now at least 80 years of age, remained in favour under Darius, who considered making him ruler over all of his kingdom. However, the other chief ministers jealously sought to ruin Daniel by convicting him of treason. To this end, they persuaded the king to pass a decree forbidding anyone, under penalty of being cast into the lions' den, to petition either god or man for 30 days. Daniel, however, continued to pray three times a day at his open window facing Jerusalem, as they knew he would. This was reported to the king who was forced, unwillingly, to cast Daniel into the lions' den. God sent an angel to shut the mouths of the lions so they would not hurt Daniel, as he was blameless before his God and his king. Upon hearing what had happened Darius freed him, punished his accusers and decreed that all his subjects should now honour and revere the God of Daniel.

The prophet Daniel is not specifically mentioned in the Koran; however, the Koran generally confirms that the books of the Torah, and the prophets, were revealed by Allah and so Islam accepts the prophethood of those mentioned in the Old Testament. Daniel is thus considered a prophet by Muslims, based upon the information contained in the Old Testament, which is not expressly refuted by the Koran.

A description of the area can be found in a 1939 issue of *The American Journal of Science*:

'Near to the wells is a pool of muddy stagnant water, covered with a thick scum deeply tinged with sulphur. A few hundred yards to the east of the top of the same hill is a flat circular spot, 50 feet in diameter, perforated by 100 or more small holes, whence issue clear smokeless flames, smelling strongly of sulphur. In fact, the whole surface of this perforated spot of ground appeared as a crust of sulphur over a body of fire within; the surface being perforated by a dagger, a flame instantly issued, rising, sometimes even higher than the others.'

Baba Gurgur became the first modern oil well in Iraq when the Turkish Petroleum Company struck oil there in 1927. The discovery soon turned into a major environmental crisis as thousands of barrels of oil gushed out, inundating a depression known as Wadi Naft that carried water off the low foothills. Crude oil escaping down to the open desert threatened the local inhabitants and their properties and risked polluting their water supply. It took ten days from the first eruption to close the control valve and shut off the supply of oil. By the time the well was capped, over 95,000 barrels of oil a day had spewed into the desert. The approaching rainy season raised the spectre of another disaster; if the rains came and the wadi flooded, the oil would be carried down to the river and would pollute water supplies across the whole of Iraq. Pumps were urgently installed in an attempt to pump the oil back into the wells, but they made little impression. In desperation, large quantities were finally set alight. Eventually when the rains came the area was clear of oil. Baba Gurgur was considered the largest oilfield in the world until the discovery of the Ghawar Field in Saudi Arabia in 1948.

QALAT JARMO Lying east of Kirkuk, 11km from the village of Chemchemal on the road between Suleimaniyah and Kirkuk, Qalat Jarmo is one of the oldest Neolithic archaeological sites in the Middle East. Its original occupation is estimated to date back to c7000BC. The site is important for revealing traces of one of the world's first village-farming communities and, at the time it was discovered, Jarmo was the earliest archaeological site with evidence of this. Excavations here have yielded information on human society's transition to sedentary agricultural practices. Robert Braidwood from the University of Chicago spent several seasons excavating the site between 1948 and 1955, revealing a village of 20–25 houses situated in an oak and pistachio woodland belt dating back to between 7250 and 5750BC. The inhabitants, of Jarmo, estimated to have numbered at most 100–150 people, lived in square, mud-brick, multi-roomed houses built of pressed mud with a complex division of residential space and courtyards, including mud ovens, hearths with chimneys, and baked-in clay basins sunk in the ground. They lived on emmer, einkorn wheat, barley and lentils; ate with bone spoons, sewed with bone needles, and the stone spindle-whorls discovered by the archaeologists show that they could weave or plait flax and perhaps even wool. This, along with their domestication of dogs and goats, suggested that they lived a settled agricultural way of life. The approximately dozen layers of architectural building and renovation yielded evidence (in the later levels) of the introduction of ceramic vessel technology suggesting that the site spanned two time periods which are known as the Pre-Pottery and Pottery Neolithic. Other artefacts found at Jarmo, such as milling stones, flint sickle blades and (again in the later layers) painted pottery sherds and figurines of animals and humans, hint at the technological innovations made in response to the new agricultural practices. In addition, obsidian tools at the site indicate the practice of long-distance trade, as the closest source of obsidian at the time was located in Anatolia. Pre-ceramic Jarmo was first dated by radiocarbon tests on snail shells at about 4750BC but further tests on charcoal gave a higher figure and a date of c6750BC, which is now thought more realistic.

Please note: There are no signs to this site and taxi drivers and locals are unaware of its whereabouts. On a visit in 2009 the author, his local drivers and a group of tourists were arrested by the police when driving to this site as it is on the border between the Arab region and Iraqi Kurdistan and were held for several hours in the police station. Therefore, the current advice is not to attempt to visit Jarmo at this time unless you have a police escort.

YORGAN TEPE An important Hurrian city, part of the empire of Mitanni and source of a large cuneiform archive, **Yorgan Tepe** (also known as Nuzi) is a mound 13km southwest of Kirkuk containing the remains of an ancient settlement. The Hurrians came from the Caucasus into northeastern Mesopotamia and Anatolia in the late 3rd millennium BC. They spoke a language not related to any known linguistic group, which is still poorly understood because there are few cuneiform texts. The Hurrians achieved their greatest prominence between 1500 and 1200BC as part of the empire of Mitanni, which was controlled by an Indo European elite of chariot warriors. Mitanni was one of the great international powers, which competed for power and influence through diplomacy and arms. In the 2nd millennium BC the Hurrians absorbed the town and renamed it Nuzi. At this time Nuzi was a provincial town in the kingdom of Arrapha which was administered by a governor. The history of the site during the intervening period is unclear, although the presence of a few cuneiform tables from Old Assyria indicates that there were trade links with nearby Ashur. After the fall of the Hurrian Empire of Mitanni to the Hittites, the city was destroyed by the Assyrians in the middle of the 2nd millennium BC.

The site, which consists of one medium sized multi-period tell and two small single-period mounds was first occupied during the Akkadian period in the late 3rd millennium BC when it was known as Gasur. The site has 15 occupation levels, including:

- the neolithic period dating from the second half of the 4th millennium BC;
- the remains of a Sumero-Akkadian settlement (the original city of Gasur) dating from the second half of the 3rd millennium BC;
- the Human city of Nuzi dating from the first half of the 2nd millennium BC.

Although tablets from Yorgan Tepe began appearing back as far as 1896, the first serious archaeological efforts only began in 1925 after the orientalist Gertrude Bell noticed tablets appearing in the markets of Baghdad. Excavations were carried out under the auspices of the Iraq Museum by Edward Chiera, Robert Pfeiffer and Richard Starr in 1931 which revealed the acropolis and temple of Nuzi. The city was surrounded by a wall, beyond which were situated the houses of the suburbs. The inhabitants engaged in farming and animal husbandry. Copper implements and several thousand tablets were discovered. The palace, situated in the centre of the mound, contained more than 100 rooms, many of which were arranged around a central courtyard. The functions of some of those rooms have been identified as reception areas, apartments, offices, kitchens and stores. The walls were decorated with impressive mural paintings, fragments of which were unearthed in the ruins of the building, and had unusual provisions for drainage and sanitation, including an example of a toilet flushed by water piped from above. An archive of thousands of cuneiform tablets in Akkadian discovered at the site tell us about the royal family, as well as the organisation of the internal administration of the palace and its occupants and give details of personal and public life in terms of mercantile activity and social customs. The two shrines of Nuzi Temple had elaborate decoration, including wood panelling in the form of clapper boards pegged to the brickwork, while other wall faces were decorated with nail-shaped bosses of glazed terracotta. The levels of Hurrian occupation have been fully excavated, and the findings published in a series of volumes. The vast majority of finds are from the Hurrian period during the 2nd millennium BC with the remainder dating back to the town's founding during the Akkadian Empire. Around 5,000 tablets are held at the Oriental Institute, the Harvard Semitic Museum and the Iraq Museum in Baghdad. Perhaps the most famous item found is a map of the local region dating from the Akkadian period. An archive contemporary to the Hurrian archive at Nuzi has been excavated from the Green Palace at the site of **Tell Al-Fakhar**, 35km southwest of Nuzi, and the history of Nuzi is closely interrelated with that of the nearby towns of Eshnunna and Khafajah.

Mosul is known as the 'City of Prophets' because of the number of shrines in the city built within it for both biblical and Islamic prophets and saints. Iraq's second-largest city, Mosul, was originally built as a citadel or outpost for the Assyrian Empire on a hill called Qleat, on the right bank of the River Tigris, opposite the site of ancient Nineveh. The area was inhabited as early as 6000BC. Mosul has had many names, including Al-Mosul, meaning 'the link' as it is at the centre of a hub of different destinations east and west, north and south, or a place of reunion. It was also known as the city with two spring seasons; God's city; the city of the prophets and the green city. The famous cotton fabric 'muslin' derives its name from Mosul, where it was first made. Mosul is also famous for its rich culinary tradition including Kebbet Mosul, a healthy high-fibre food made from the shell of crushed wheat (*burgul*) and stuffed with meat.

History is alive in Mosul, which has plenty of archaeological ruins dating back to Assyrian times. Old Mosul has 38 living quarters called *mahala*, each self-contained with its own market, bath (hamam), church, mosque and cemetery. Some quarters even have their own traditions and dialects related to the tribal origins of their inhabitants. Originally all the living quarters were on the west bank of the Tigris, within the parameter wall of old Mosul with its nine gates. In 1630 the Ottoman Wali, Bakr Pasha, added four more gates. Visitors and caravans could only enter and leave the city during daylight hours as all 13 gates were shut at sunset. A deep trench was filled with water for defence and this saved the city during the great siege by Nadir Shah. The remnants of the city wall and some of the gates can still be seen today. Mosul was one of the most ethnically mixed cities in Iraq: Arabs, Syriacs, Armenians, Kurds, Turkmen, Jews, Christians, Muslims and Yezidis all called Mosul home. It is the ancient centre of the Christian community, who have a special attachment to it because they believe St Thomas the Apostle lived in Mosul on his way to India. Before the coming of Islam, most of the Arab tribes who lived in the area were Christian.

SECURITY WARNING At the time of going to print it is impossible for visitors to travel to the area and should they be foolish enough to try to approach the city they would quickly be turned back at the numerous checkpoints located on its approaches. Should you consider trying to visit if/when ISIS is ousted from the city after a major military offensive you should monitor the situation closely and check government advice and warnings prior to travelling.

HISTORY The site became an important commercial centre from the 6th century BC when on the site of present Mosul the little town of Now Ardashir, named after the first Sassanid king was founded. It became a Byzantine city after the defeat of the Persians in a battle near Mosul in AD627. But just ten years later it fell to Muslim rule during the time of the second caliph Umar (634–644) after one of his commanders, Rabaibn Akfal al Anzi, took control of it without a fight. The Umayyads took a special interest in the development of Mosul, and during the reign of the last Umayyad caliph, Marwan II (744–750) it became the capital of the province of Jezireh. In the Abbasid period it was the chief town of the district of Diyar Rabiah. Following the decline of the Abbasid Caliphate, Mosul became a principality; first under the Hamdanids (929–991) and then under the Oqaylids (996–1096). The town was then seized by the Seljuk Turks who appointed a governor or *atabek* to administer it. In 1104 at Harran the ancient Carrhae, the *atabek* of Mosul repulsed a Crusader expedition against the province

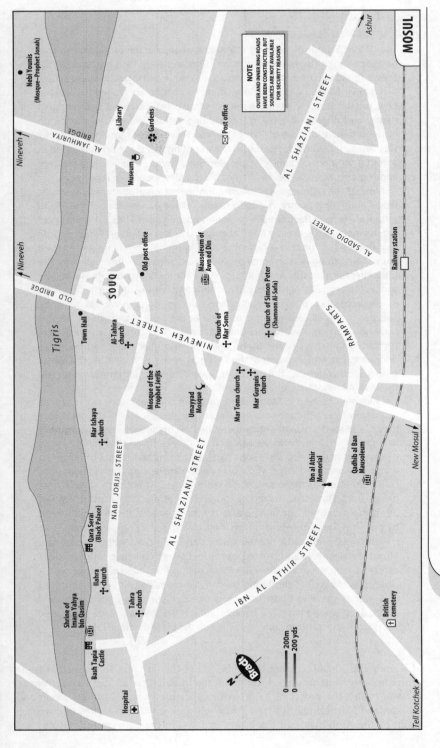

MOSUL ARTS AND CRAFTS

The 'Mosul School of Painting' refers to a style of miniature painting that developed in northern Iraq in the late 12th and early 13th centuries under the patronage of the Zangid dynasty. In technique and style the Mosul school was similar to the painting of the Seljuk Turks, who controlled Iraq at that time, but the Mosul artists had a sharper sense of realism based on the subject matter and degree of detail in the painting, rather than on representation in three dimensions, which did not occur. Most of the Mosul iconography was Seljuk, including, for example, the use of figures seated cross-legged in a frontal position. Certain symbolic elements, however, such as the crescent and serpents, were derived from the classical Mesopotamian repertory.

Most of the paintings were illustrations of manuscripts, mainly scientific works and lyrical poetry. A good example of the earlier work of the Mosul school is a copy of the frontispiece painting dating from a late 12th century of Galen's medical treatise the *Kitab Al-diriyak* (*Book of Antidotes*) which depicts four figures surrounding a central seated figure holding a crescent-shaped halo. The painting is in a variety of whole hues with blue Kufic lettering. The total effect is majestic. Another mid 13th-century copy from the same text suggests the quality of later Mosul painting, with vital realism in its depiction of the preparation of a meal and of horsemen engaged in various activities. This painting is as awe-inspiring as those of the early Mosul school; yet it is somehow less spirited. By this time, however, the Baghdad school which, combined the styles of the Syrian and early Mosul schools, had begun to dominate. With the invasion of the Mongols in the 13th century, the Mosul school came to an end, but its influence continued in both the Mamluk and the Mongol schools of miniature painting.

Craftsmen centred in Mosul also influenced the metalwork of the Islamic world from North Africa to eastern Iran. Under the auspices of the Mosul School they developed an extraordinarily refined technique of inlay, particularly using silver on bronze and brass. After delicately engraving the surface of the piece, strips of gold and silver were carefully worked so that not the slightest irregularity appeared in the whole of the elaborate design. The technique was carried by Mosul metalworkers around the Middle East, and similar metalwork pieces from Damascus, Baghdad and elsewhere are still known as Mosul Bronzes. Among the surviving pieces is a brass ewer in the British Museum by the artist Shuja ibn Mana, which is inlaid with silver and dates from 1232. It is inscribed with battle scenes, animals and musicians within medallions. Mosul metalworkers also created pieces for Eastern churches, for example, a candlestick by the artist Shuja ibn Mana dating from 1238 in bronze with a silver inlay. As well as displaying the familiar medallions it is also engraved with scenes showing Christ as a child. Rows of standing figures, probably saints, decorate the base. The background is decorated with typically Islamic vine scrolls and intricate arabesques, giving the piece a unique look.

of Jezireh and Mosul. During the Abbasid era the city was an important trade centre because of its strategic location on the Indian, Persian and Mediterranean caravan route. The power of its governors increased with Nuriddin Zangi and his son, and Nuriddin built a new Friday Mosque which was visited and written about by the Arab historian Ibn Jabayr in 1184. In the 12th century, Mosul was subjugated and sacked by Saladin, who served under Nuriddin in Egypt, and it declined in importance.

In the 13th century Badruddin Lulu, the former regent, declared himself independent and took the title of sovereign, which he held from 1222–59. The city was then plundered and destroyed by the Mongol invasion in 1261. It was rebuilt by Osman I (1280–1324), the first Ottoman sultan, who divided Iraq into the three provinces (vilayets) of Mosul, Baghdad and Basra. The city remained under Ottoman rule for six centuries, when it was able to resist many attacks, until 1918, when, following the victory of the Allies and the collapse of the Ottoman Empire, Mosul was detached from the Turkish Empire and became a provincial capital in the new State of Iraq.

The 20th century Under the British Mandate, the future of Mosul was a key issue in the negotiations which took place to determine the boundary line between Iraq and Turkey. The inhabitants of Mosul took part in a referendum, conducted by a special committee, the outcome of which was that they chose to remain as part of Iraq. Following this, although Mosul settled down under the Iraqi monarchy until the Revolution of 1958 it was still witness to turbulence and upheaval. The inhabitants of Mosul also participated in the revolution of May 1941 against the British occupation and took part in political activities against the monarchy and the government in 1952, 1956 and 1957.

In those days Mosul itself was a city with a fascinating maze of narrow and wide alleyways (*awjat*) and interesting streets and roads along both banks of the river, which served as a flood barrier. Gavin Young, author of *Iraq: Land of Two Rivers*, writing in 1980 tells us that:

'Mosul improves the closer you get – your first sight of Mosul from the south is a bit disappointing: the buildings are modern and have a utilitarian look. Yet, nearer, you can cheer up. You begin to see better things: the river and the corniche and the old houses that still stand on the water's edge and the parks. Also you see minarets and church spires and domes above the rooftops.'

The minarets, spires and domes, while being the places for a panoramic view of the old city, also watched over an unfurling ecological and environmental disaster. Dams upstream in Turkey had turned parts of the mighty Tigris Basin into a giant car park. The urban sprawl of modern Mosul had expanded to both banks of the Tigris and engulfed Old Mosul, Nineveh and surrounding areas. There were 67 new residential zones and the city had been overtaken by a great burst of modernity. What used to be a discernibly Middle-Ages-type city with many tenements and alleyways had been divided into parts by major roads circling and cutting through it. In 2001 much building development took place and some suburbs had an air of prosperity, with occasional streets of exceptional wealth in evidence.

Because of the current occupation of Mosul by ISIS, the city, no stranger to suicide bombings and terrorist attacks, is one of the most dangerous in Iraq, and probably the world, especially for foreigners and particularly Westerners. There is talk of a proposal to oust ISIS to enable the city to regain its historical and cultural role as one of the three major cities in Iraq and one of the first historic metropolitan areas in the world, but there doesn't appear to be a definite plan or date. At the time of going to press travel into and around Mosul was not safe and had not been so for several years.

GETTING THERE

By air The airfield base now known as Mosul International Airport is located close to the city and was first established by the British Royal Air Force in the 1930s. After the British left in 1969 it became an important base for the Iraqi air force. After the war in 2003 it became an American air force base. Then it was considerably updated with a brand new air traffic control tower and a restored passenger terminal in 2006. In 2011 the airfield was returned to the Iraqi Government and international flights began soon afterwards as good facilities were readily available and the security situation was stable. Iraqi Airways began running regular services to Dubai, Istanbul and Baghdad; Jupiter Airlines to Dubai; Royal Falcon to Amman; Royal Jordanian to Amman and Turkish Airlines to Istanbul.

However, the airport was suddenly closed down in September 2013 without warning and has been closed ever since.

By road Mosul stands on the right bank of the Tigris opposite the site of ancient Nineveh, 400km northwest of Baghdad. Highway 1 connects the city with Baghdad and there are good road connections from the Kurdistan Regional Government areas such as Dohuk and Erbil, which is less than 30km away by taxi or bus.

By rail There used to be a rail connection from Baghdad to Mosul; however, at the time of going to press this is suspended, although a new track is being constructed alongside this line. A date for completion of this is not yet known. The Mosul railway station was originally built by the British Army and opened in 1938. Its adjoining hotel, now an empty building, is somewhat famous. It features in several books by Agatha Christie as she passed through it on her way to visit Nimrud to be with her husband Max Mallowan on his digs. See page 132 for information and origins of the rail system in Iraq.

AUTHORS' NOTE At the time of going to press travel into and around Mosul was not possible and had not been so for several years. Therefore the information below, while being as accurate as possible in the circumstances, is bound to be somewhat outdated and incomplete.

WHERE TO STAY AND EAT Mosul was renowned for its ancient cafés which served as gentlemen's clubs, each frequented on a daily basis by professionals or traders. They were popular meeting places where information was exchanged and contracts sealed. Bab Al-Tub Square (Cannongate Square) in the centre of the city was the place for popular cafés, cheap hotels and restaurants, and opposite the university there was a string of reasonable restaurants offering a range of Iraqi food. In the past, tourists visiting Mosul have stayed at the **Nineveh International Hotel**, (m *0771 073 3330; info@ninevehhotel.com*), overlooking the Tigris river or the **Youth Hostel** on Rifat Haj Sirri Street on the Kikuk–Baghdad–Mansour road. Along the corniche there were many reasonably priced, comfortable hotels of mid-range standard.

SHOPPING Nineveh Street, which runs from east to west through the city, is the main, longest shopping street in Mosul. Side streets lead to the jewellery market and other shops. The marketplace near the old bridge that connects the two sides of the city used to be an important exchange centre for the agricultural products of the mountains, including watermelons.

WHAT TO SEE AND DO Mosul has a profusion of early Christian churches reflecting the schisms and splits which took place as Christianity developed its formal structures and unity. Almost every branch of Christianity is, or has been, represented by a church in Mosul. It was visited often in the 19th century by various clerics of protestant persuasion who were fascinated by the Christian heritage in this region.

In modern times, it is the fractures among the ethnic factions which have come to the fore that take our notice. The residents of Mosul include Turkmen, Arabs and Kurds, all backed by vested interests abroad, and, as a result, possession of power in the city is highly sought-after. In Mosul, the sons of Saddam Hussein, Uday and Qusay and their young cousin took refuge in the city and were killed by the Coalition forces in 2003. All traces of the building where they met their deaths has been erased. The legacy of Saddam is still feared in many quarters. Once, as travellers, we are free to visit the city again in the future, Mosul will be on every travellers 'must see' list.

Then the visitor to Mosul will find many ancient archaeological sites to view, especially on the western edge of the Tigris river. Mosul contains the remains of castles and palaces built for bygone rulers as well as fortresses built to defend the city and to store ammunition and supplies. The remains of an **Assyrian Fortress** can be found on Kulaiat Hill. Demolished in 612BC, it was later rebuilt around AD1261 in the centre of Mosul between the Saraya bath house (*haddabaa*) and the Mosque Zainab Khatoon, extending up to the Bab Al-Nabi quarter and the Bab Al-Jabalain quarter. It contained various buildings, hamams, mosques, and army facilities. Today its remains extend under Nineveh Street to the Al-Nouri Mosque. The military and civilian court house, built in 1842 for administration and military purposes is now home to the military hospital and the civil courts. The square in front of it is the **Garden of the Martyrs.**

The Mosul House Museum
This museum is located near the Hurriya Bridge and the Numaniya Mosque in the centre of the city. Housed in one of the beautiful old residences in Mosul with an impressive marble façade, it was badly looted during the 2003 war. It contained many interesting finds from the ancient sites of the old Assyrian capital cities Nineveh and Nimrud, as well as life-size models depicting traditional life in Mosul in tableau form.

Bash Tapia Castle (Big Castle)
Called Castle Pashtabi by the Turks due to its imposing and impregnable location on a high promontory to the north of old Mosul overlooking the Tigris river, this huge building was built with stucco and stone to accommodate thousands of soldiers and their ammunition. At its zenith it extended to the Qara Serai in the south and the place of the Imam Mohsen in the west. It had an underground tunnel network with two well-known doors: one leading to the army field in the west, and a secret, emergency door leading to the River Tigris, which was only opened in times of great need. The tunnel network also extended to the house of the Queen in the Qara Serai. The castle played an important role in the blockade of Mosul in AD1156 before being demolished during the siege by Timurlaine in 1393. It was later rebuilt by the Ottomans (who called it Eaj Galae) on the banks of the Tigris in front of A-Maidan market. It was surrounded by walls and a moat, which separated it from the facing army barracks and training ground. After the end of the British Mandate, it was taken over by the Department of Water and Electricity and in its grounds a municipal building was constructed along with a garden café. Nowadays, all that remains are neglected and dilapidated ruins.

Qara Serai (the Black Palace) To the south of Castle Pashtabi is the Qara Serai or Black Palace, so called by the Ottomans as its walls were blackened as the result of smoke from the fires of the inhabitants. It was built in the 13th century by Sultan Badruddin Lulu (1213–59) as a royal palace. Badruddin Lulu was an Armenian by birth who, unrestrained by the Muslim prohibition of portraying the human form, adorned his palaces with magnificent figures in decorative panels. The grounds of the palace contained gardens with fountains and beautiful statues. In there was a parade ground for the training and reviewing of troops. Later the palace grounds became a park for the people of Mosul. Sadly, the building has been neglected and allowed to virtually disintegrate.

The Umayyad (Great Nuriddine) Mosque Known also as Al-Jami Al-Kabir, this mosque near the corner of Al-Shaziani and Nineveh streets, was originally named after Nuriddin Zangi who built it in 1174. It is famous for its crooked 52m minaret known as the humped one (Al-Hadba) and its elaborate brickwork. It is said to be the oldest mosque in Mosul and is located in the vicinity of an ancient church once dedicated to St Paul and 40 martyrs. It was renovated by Marwan ibn Muhammad (AD744–50) but then destroyed at the time of the Mongol invasions and rebuilt again in 1150 when Mosul was hit by a plague which killed a large number of people. Ibn Battutah, the 14th-century Tunisian adventurer, wrote that it contained a marble fountain and a *mihrab* with a Kufic inscription. According to local tradition the minaret gained its tilt after bowing to the Prophet Mohammed who passed overhead while ascending

THE GATES OF MOSUL

Many of Mosul's citizens are unaware of the reasons behind naming a number of their shops 'Al-Bab' or 'the door', despite the absence of any door!

The reason is that these names date back to the period in which the wall around Mosul was built. It was constructed firstly of milk and mud and then rebuilt with stone and stucco at the time of Said bin Abd al Malik. Harun al Rashid (AD786–809) later demolished the wall; however, in the era of Sharaf al Daula Alukaili (around 1081) it was partly reconstructed. Later it was reinforced by the Seljuks. In the time of Nurridin Zangi, Atabek of Mosul (c1127–46) the wall was fortified and surrounded by a deep trench. At this point in its history it had nine gates – Al-Bab Al-Emadi; Bab Al-Jasaseen; Bab Al-Medan; Bab Kinda; Al-Bab Al-Gharbi; Bab Iraq; Bab Al-Qasabeen; Bab Al-Mashraa and Bab Al-Jisr.

During the Mongol siege of the city, several parts of the wall were destroyed, opening up a number of gaps in it. Over the centuries the wall was been rebuilt and maintained. Extensive renovations were made in 1630 by the governor Bakr bin Ismail Pasha Ben Younes al Mosuli resulting in the number of gates being increased to thirteen as follows:

1. Bab Al-Jisr – the Gate of the Bridge, as this gate was near the Ottoman Bridge
2. Bab Al-Toop – the Brick Door Gate, also known as Bab Al-Qasabeen, Gate of Butchers
3. Bab Liksh – the Straw Gate, the door of straw or grass, which was sold beside it each day
4. Bab Al-Sarai – the Palace Gate, located near the Government House
5. Bab Al-Hurria – the Gate of Freedom, also known as Bab Al-Jasaseen (Gate of Plasterers) and later as Bab Al-Wabaa, Gate of the Epidemic, as it was

to heaven. However, Christian tradition is that the tilt is due to the minaret bowing towards the tomb of the Virgin Mary, is believed to be located near Erbil. The minaret was restored and stabilised by UNESCO engineers before the First Gulf War.

Al-Imam Muhsin Mosque
This modern mosque is situated in the Al-Maidan district of Old Mosul, about 1km north of the corner of Al-Shaziani and Nineveh streets. It was constructed on the ruins of the Nour-ul-Din Arsalan School, which was built in 1210. The only remaining part of the original building is a rectangular room with two flat pulpits made of limestone bricks.

Mujahidi Mosque
Standing at the entrance of the corniche, the Mujahidi Mosque is also known as the Al-Khuther or Red Mosque. Dating back to the 12th century, it has a beautiful dome and elaborately wrought *mihrab*.

Mosque of the Prophet Jerjis
This ancient mosque in Al-Shaarien market area is located at what is believed to be the burial place and shrine of the prophet Jerjis, although there is no definite information on the existence of the prophet or his grave. Built originally as small mosque it was later expanded. Although it is difficult to date the mosque exactly, the motifs and Kufic inscriptions in it indicate that is from the 12th century with the explorer Ibn Jubair writing about it at that time, and it is known that it was renovated and expanded by Timurlaine in 1392–93. It is believed by some to contain the tomb of al Hur bin Yousif.

closed when an epidemic appeared and opened as a door of freedom in the Ottoman Era.

6   Bab Shatt Al-Qalaa – the Gate of Castle Beach, named after a castle in old Mosul named Eajqalaa
7   Bab Al-Emadi – the Gate of Emadi, who was a relative of Imadel-Din Zengi
8   Bab Al-Sir – the Secret Gate, this was the gate leading from the Eaj Castle to the river
9   Bab Eyen Kbreat Sulfur – the Spring Gate, the gate leading from the castle Pashtabia to the river which were once upon a time linked by a secret door
10 Bab Al-Baidh – the Gate of Eggs (previously the Kinda Gate) as eggs were sold beside the gate every day.
11 Bab Shatt Al-Makawi and Shatt Al-Hasa – gates that were named after a legislator in Mosul Al-Mashraa.
12 Bab Sinjar (previously known as the Gate of the Field or Bab Al-Meedan)
13 Bab Al-Jaded – the New Gate, which was built to replace the Gate of Iraq after the expansion of the city to the south

These gates which connected the city with surrounding villages and the Tigris, enabled the residents of Mosul to easily access water for drinking, laundry and to wash wool in the river water. Over the years further gaps appeared in the walls caused by war, neglect and vandalism; however, the wall remained intact in the main until World War I, when the Turks demolished a large portion of it. Just a few remaining parts of the wall, now in ruins, stand in Qara Serai, Pashtabia and Barood Khana. In the Al-Badan district a few fragments of Bab Al-Baidh and Bab Al-Toop can be found.

Mosque and Shrine of the Prophet Sheet The mosque was built by the governor Mustapha Pasha al Nishangi in 1647 after he saw in a dream the tomb of Nabi Sheet in this location which was outside the city wall. He asked one of Mosul's traders named Haj Ali al Nomah to dig in the place he saw in his dream to reveal the grave and then to build a dome over it. He did what the governor commanded and this became known as the Shrine of the Prophet Sheet. In the year 1791 a mosque was built beside the shrine known as the Mosque of Nabi Sheet, about 1km southeast of the corner of Al-Shaziani and Nineveh streets.

Mashad of Yahya ibn Al-Kassen The tomb of Yahya ibn al Kassan is surmounted by an octagonal pyramid, thought to date back to the 13th century. Located on the right bank of the Tigris river, 1.5km north of the corner of Al-Shaziani and Nineveh streets, it is famed for its conical beehive dome, decorative brickwork, sculptured and inlaid wall panels containing calligraphy inscribed onto Mosul blue marble and the carved wood sarcophagus. It has also been used as a school, the Al-Badriyah School. This monument is one of the principal objects of interest in Mosul.

Shrine of Imam Yahya bin Qasim This shrine is located in the north of Mosul, near Bash Tapia Castle. It was built by Badr al Din Lolo in AD637.

Churches The churches of Mosul are fascinating buildings containing much of the early heritage of 'Eastern Christianity'. A few of its principal churches are listed below, although Mosul has other churches in the winding streets in its centre. Sadly, many of the churches, and some of the city's mosques, have been badly damaged or destroyed by ISIS and looters.

Mar Toma (St Thomas) is one of the oldest historical churches in Mosul and thought to be the oldest still in use today. The church is named after St Thomas the Apostle who preached the gospel in the East. It is believed to be built over the site of the house occupied by the Apostle during his visit to Mosul, about 100m to the west of the corner of Al-Shaziani and Nineveh streets. The three altars are its most interesting feature. The exact time of its foundation is unknown, but it can be assumed that it pre-dates 770, since al Mahdi, the Abbasid caliph, is mentioned as listening to a grievance concerning this church on his trip to Mosul in that year. Its present structure suggests a 13th-century style.

The **Church of the Immaculate (Al-Tahira),** near Bash Tapia, started life as the Church of the Upper Monastery in c300 and became a Chaldean Catholic Church in 1600. It was reconstructed in 1743, and is considered one of the most ancient churches in Mosul.

The oldest Chaldean church in Mosul is the **Church of Simon Peter (Shamoon Al-Safa),** and is located about 300m south of Mar Toma church. It was built in the 13th century and named after Shamoon al Safa or St Peter (Mar Petros in Assyrian Aramaic). It began life as the Church of St Peter and St Paul and was home to the nuns of the Order of the Sacred Hearts. Under the vault there is a beautiful inscription in Syriac. Built in a combination of brick and marble, its architecture is typically massive and the church remains cool inside even on the hottest day.

Mar Petion Church was the first Chaldean Catholic Church in Mosul, after the union of many Assyrians with Rome in the 17th century, although it actually dates back to the 10th century. Currently lying 3m below street level, the church has been destroyed and rebuilt many times. A hall was built on one of its three parts in 1942. As a result, most of its remaining architectural features are somewhat confused.

The **Mar Hudeni Church** was named after Mar Ahudemmeh (Hudeni) Maphrian of Tikrit who was martyred in 575 and is the oldest church of the Tikritis in Mosul. It dates back to the 10th century and was restored in 1970. There is a well in its yard which contains mineral water and a chain fixed in the wall, which was thought to cure epileptics.

Not far from Mar Toma, **Mar Gurguis (St George's Monastery)** dates back to the late 17th century, and is probably one of the oldest churches in Mosul. Pilgrims from different parts of Iraq still visit the church yearly in the spring holiday. A modern church was constructed over the old church in 1931, destroying much of its remaining architectural and archaeological history. The only original parts which remained from the old church were a marble door-frame decorated with a carved Syriac inscription and two niches dating back to the 13th or 14th century.

The **Church of Mar Soma** is thought to be the oldest Protestant church in the Middle East; it was established in 1840.

Located at the corner of of Al-Shaziani and Nineveh streets, the **Clock Church (Al-Saa)** is a Latin church that was built in 1862. It is named after the clock it contains, which was donated to the church by the wife of Napoleon III. It is also known for its fine marble and stained glass.

AROUND MOSUL

MAR BEHNAM MONASTERY Also called Deir Al-Jubb, or the Cistern Monastery, Mar Behnam is believed to have been built in the 4th century. The monastery consists of a mausoleum, a convent and a church. Its outer walls and façade have been restored, as have the walls of most of the monastery and church. The relief and paintings by the altar date back to 1143. The Jubb, or cistern, contains the tombs of the martyrs who were killed with Mar Behnam and his sister Sarah by the troops of their father, King Sennacherib, after their conversion to Christianity at the hand of Mar Matti. The monastery also has a most interesting collection of sculptures. Today it is administered by the Syrian Orthodox Church and at the moment has a rotation of priests in charge of it. It also serves as a retreat for visiting Christian families.

History A famous place of Christian pilgrimage, the convent was founded, as legend has it, at the site of the martyrdom of St Behnam (see box, pages 218–19) by a Persian Christian called Isaac. When passing the spot on the way to Jerusalem to seek a cure for an ailing servant who was like a son to him, Isaac had a visitation from St Behnam. The servant was cured and in gratitude Isaac had a convent built next to the saint's mausoleum. The titular saint was assimilated by the monks with al Khidhr who was respected by the Muslims with the particular aim of safe guarding the monastery against the Mongols. The sculptures also reveal some assimilation to St George.

Getting there Mar Behnam Monastery is located 35km southeast of Mosul and one hour's drive from Erbil. The nearest large town to Mar Behnam is **Al-Hamadaniyah**, a mostly Christian town of Arabs and Kurds with some modern Orthodox Syrian churches and mosques. Being on the front line of Arab Iraq and the Kurdistan region, Al-Hamadaniyah has its own mainly Christian armed militia who guard all the religious buildings. Some further 15–20km west of Al-Hamadaniyah you come to the small, ethnically mixed village of Khalid, where the monastery can be found.

Mar Matti was born in the village of Apgarshat, north of Amed City in the province of Diyarbakir in Turkey at the beginning of the 4th century. He came from a pious and religious family and had two sisters and a brother named Zacharias. When his parents died while he was still a youth, Mar Matti entered the Monastery of St Serges and St Bacchus next to his village and spent the next seven years learning Psalms and the Syriac language. Following this he joined another monastery in Zouknin in Diyarbakir and studied theology and ecclesiastical spirituality. Mar Matti was increasingly drawn to asceticism, isolation and seclusion, so he left the monastery at Zouknin in search of hermits with whom he could live. Finally, he found four monks living simply near a small spring, spending their days in prayer and worship of God. He built a hut there and joined their way of life.

The Roman Emperor at that time was Julian, a pagan, who returned the Roman Empire from Christianity to paganism. Julian persecuted Christians and this persecution finally reached Mar Matti and the monks. To escape this, Mar Matti and 25 monks (including St Zakai, St Abrouhoum and St Daniel) moved to live in a small hermitage on Mount Magloub on the banks of the Khabour River where they continued to worship and maintain their ascetic lifestyle. Mar Matti then visited the Sassanian province of Nineveh, the city of Nimrud, and one of the states of the Persian Empire, where he became known for his holiness and his gift of healing the sick. All these events took place between the years 361–363.

THE LEGEND OF PRINCE BEHNAM AND PRINCESS SARAH The story goes that one day Prince Behnam, son of King Sennacherib, went hunting with 40 horsemen. They pursued a large deer until, tired from the chase, they rested by a spring, near the mountain of residence of Mar Matti. They fell asleep, and as they slept an angel appeared to Behnam and told him that the Lord of Heaven had chosen him

What to see and do The Convent Church has been restored several times. It was built to a rectangular design with the appearance of a fortress. It is entered through a portico by two doors with straight lintels; they are adorned with a cross and two small figures and have relieving arches. The sculptured and decorated framework of the doors carries a long Syriac inscription and two figures of saints. On the two pillars to the left of the altar there are handsome bas-reliefs with many traces of paintings, unfortunately mutilated. The pillar nearest the altar represents St Behnam, armed and on horseback, felling his enemies; above him two little angels support a large crown. The rectangular frame is decorated with a Syriac inscription dated in the year 1861 of the Seleucid era (1550). The sculpture probably masks one of the old doors of the sanctuary. There is another sculpture opposite this bas-relief. The choir stall was reconstructed in 1164. The sculptures of the façade and the interior date from the middle of the 13th century and count as being among the finest examples of Atabek art. This style can also be seen in certain mausoleums in Mosul. The church occupies the southeastern corner of a modern monastery. Fifty metres away is the saint's tomb, which consists, on the outside, of a massive square chapel with a small cupola. From this you descend into a kind of underground chamber and come to a large room, the ancient baptistery, where fine Syriac inscriptions are engraved in marble. The inscription on the altar gives the date 1617 of the Seleucid era, corresponding to the year 1306.

and instructed him to climb the mountain to see a saint from God who could perform miracles. In the morning Prince Behnam told his companions about this revelation and guided them to the cave of Mar Matti, who welcomed them with pleasure. Mar Matti then accompanied the Prince to the city in order to heal his sister, Sarah, who was suffering from leprosy. On entering the palace Behnam told his mother, the Queen, what had happened and she allowed him to take his sister to see the saint. When they reached Mar Matti he prayed for Sarah and hitting the ground with his stick a spring of water miraculously appeared. (This spring still flows today and can be found near the city of Qaraqosh). Mar Matti baptised Sarah, along with Prince Behnam and his companions and she was healed. Mar Matti then returned to his cave on the mountain.

Behnam and his companions returned to the city and spread the news of Sarah's healing. But this did not please King Sennacherib, who was angry that his children had embraced Christianity. Fearful of his threats, Behnam gathered together his companions and his sister and they fled to Mar Matti for sanctuary. Enraged by this Sennacherib ordered his soldiers to pursue them and kill them all. This they did; and at the moment of their deaths the ground shook beneath the soldiers' feet and the King lost his mind. Despite the efforts of the best doctors in the land he could not be cured.

When it seemed that there was no hope left, Behnam appeared to his mother in a dream and told her that the King could only be cured by Mar Matti. She immediately sent to the hermitage for the saint who healed the King in the name of Jesus Christ. After his recovery the King, remorseful for what he had done, embraced Christianity and proclaimed his faith across his kingdom. He helped Mar Matti and his monks to build the first monastery, and the monastery became a holy and blessed place for all believers and seekers of healing.

Mar Behnam August 2014 Once again religious prejudice and brutal force showed its ugly face when the forces of ISIS took the monastery, forcing the priests to leave at a moment's notice with just the clothes they stood up in and refusing to let them take the monastery's holy relics. The fate of them and the village, the church and the ancient monastery building are unknown at this time.

MAR MATTI MONASTERY The monastery of Mar Matti is considered to be one of the most significant Christian sites in Iraq. This holy mausoleum is under the patronage of the Syrian Orthodox Church. It is also renowned for its beauty and dramatic location as well as its cool climate. The views from the monastery, which dates from the 4th century, are magnificent. In the words of Oswald Parry, author of *Six Months in a Syrian Monastery*, 'it clings like a swallow's nest against a wall'.

History Mar Matti was founded in the 4th century by a Syriac Christian called Matti (Syriac for Matthew) who had fled from persecution in Diyarbakir in modern-day Turkey to make his home on the mountain among the mostly Nestorian population who lived there. Under Mar Matti's leadership, the community developed a true monastic ethos, and according to legend, the monastery was built by the king to show his gratitude after being cured by Mar Matti (see box, above). Mar Matti was appointed the first abbot and thousands of monks from Nineveh and Persia have subsequently taken part in its monastic life. No-one knows the monastery's original design, because the conquests and catastrophes that have occurred during its history have caused many of its decorations and sculptures to be destroyed or ruined. In the year 480, nearly a century after its founding, the monastery was engulfed by a tremendous fire. The flames destroyed the entire building, leaving nothing but empty ground. At the end of the 5th century it was rebuilt and monastic life continued there. It was renovated around the year 544. After several centuries of peace, it was again abandoned after being overrun and looted by first the Mongols and then Timur when he invaded Iraq. For a long time it remained a ruin, until around the end of the 16th century under the Ottomans when it flourished again. Between 1970 and 1973 it was wholly renovated, many parts were being rebuilt and connected to mains electricity for the first time. Some of its original structures can still be viewed today, including the altar, the saint's tomb, the cell of Mar Matti, the water cistern and some caves, caverns and cottages.

Getting there Mar Matti is on top of Mount Magloub; by road it is about 35km northeast of Mosul. A good road built under the Saddam regime takes you to the monastery itself.

What to see and do Today Mar Matti is recognised as one of the oldest Christian monasteries in existence. The Monastery is currently maintained by the Syrian Orthodox Church. Five monks live in the building which is also used as a religious retreat. Several small villages and a new church have recently been built on the slopes leading to the monastery for Christians fleeing persecution in Baghdad and Mosul. The monastery is also noted for a considerable collection of Syrian Christian manuscripts. When we last visited in 2014 the monastery was being greatly extended with a new wing being built. This new wing is designed to provide permanent accommodation for the increasing number of Christian refugees seeking sanctuary from the current persecutions as well as allowing the monastery to serve as a summer retreat and relief for families from Mosul and Baghdad.

NINEVEH (MODERN KUYUNJIK) Known from the Bible, Nineveh was the capital of the Neo-Assyrian Empire. Lying close by the Tigris, its great mounds comprise the mound surmounted by Nebi Younis, the neighbouring palace mound and the ancient centre mound all surrounded by the city walls. These ruined mounds lie directly across the Tigris from the city of Mosul, whose modern suburbs of Kuyunjik threaten to engulf them. First, tentatively recognised in the 12th century by Benjamin of Tudela as Jonah's city, it remained for Pietro della Valle at the end of the 17th century to describe the ruins of the city, whose ancient walls enclosed an area of approximately 750ha. He also described the network of canals and aqueducts which, along with the River Khosr, provided the water for Nineveh and its famous gardens and parklands.

In 1820 Claudius Rich, the British Consul, again proposed that the site was that of Nineveh, though this was only confirmed when the cuneiform tablets discovered there were translated. It should be noted that the Nineveh of Layard's books is not this site but Nimrud. Excavations from those by Botta in 1842 up until recent times have revealed a great deal of information about the site. The most important finds made there were probably the two libraries of clay tablets found in the palaces of Sennacherib and Ashurbanipal by Layard and Rassam in the 1850s.

History The name Nineveh is of Sumerian origin. The origins of the town itself are very ancient; the site appears to have been occupied since the 5th millennium BC.

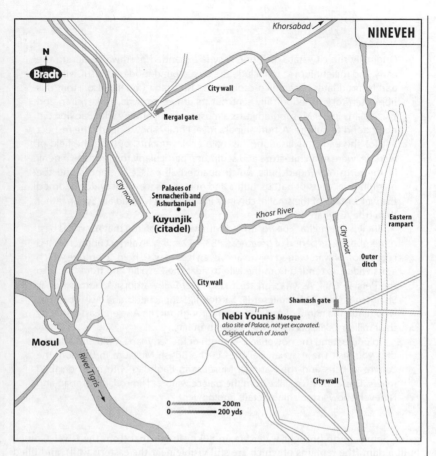

The lower levels of the tell of Kuyunjik have revealed the presence of pottery of the Tell Halaf type. It was a cultural settlement during the Sumerian and Babylonian periods, though the remains of a Sumerian occupation of Nineveh are of little importance, and we have to wait until the end of the 3rd millennium BC to find the name of Nineveh mentioned in the famous Cappadocian Tablets (c2200BC). But by that time Manishtu (c2335–2321BC), the son of Sargon, founder of the powerful Akkadian dynasty, had already built a temple here, the E-Me-Nu-E. The construction of this edifice is attested by inscriptions on archaic cylinders attributed to Shamishad I. In the 16th century BC, Nineveh probably fell into the hands of the Kassites with the rest of Assyria. Nor was Hurrian influence negligible, for the goddess Ishtar of Nineveh was transported into Egypt by a Mitannian king named Dushratta. During the 14th century BC the Assyrian kings succeeded in lifting the Kassite yoke from their country and asserting their independence.

About 1280BC an earthquake ravaged the city's temples and palaces and Shalmaneser I had to undertake their reconstruction. Nineveh appears to have been promoted to the rank of capital in the reign of Tiglath-Pilesar I, about the end of the 11th century BC. It was ruled by a number of great Assyrian kings, such as Sargon II who neglected the city. However his successor, Sennacherib (705–681BC), undertook a big construction programme and endowed the city with powerful ramparts. They occupied a perimeter of more than 11km and had 15 monumental

Originally the city-state of Ashur, Assyria expanded northwards during the early 2nd millennium BC to include the area around modern Mosul. Nineveh and Nimrud later became co-capitals and Khorsabad briefly also. From this home territory it periodically sent out its armies to Syria, Turkey, Iran and particularly lower Mesopotamia. Its almost constant enmity with Babylon did not extend to culture. Ashurbanipal's royal library shows clearly the respect felt for the earlier civilisation. The main achievements, outside the field of warfare, were in architecture and sculpture, particularly the protective genii in the form of winged bulls which guarded all palace entrances and the magnificent reliefs of battles, hunts and military processions which adorned the walls. Many of the smaller carvings in ivory from Nimrud are Syrian rather than true Assyrian work.

But it is as a military power armed with weapons of iron that Assyria is best remembered. Its period of greatness, 883–612BC was an almost uninterrupted succession of wars waged to win and, even less easy, to hold an empire which at its widest extended from the Nile to near the Caspian and from Cilicia to the Persian Gulf. Assyria's greatest kings were all warriors: Ashurnasirpal II; Shalmanesar III; Tiglathpileser III, Sargon II, Sennacherib and Ashurbanipal, who made the name of Assyria feared throughout the Ancient East partly by their military skill, partly by their sheer brutality.

To understand the power and strength of the Assyrian Empire it is advised that you visit the Assyrian galleries in the British Museum in London, the Louvre in Paris and the National Museum in Baghdad with its Khorsabad reliefs. These massive slabs from the palace walls of Nimrud, Khorsabad and Nineveh show astonishing details and power.

gates. Sennacherib brought water via an 80km-long canal from the River Gomel, built a dam (the remains of which are still visible near the eastern wall), and filled the city and the surrounding countryside with gardens and orchards to which he brought some rare trees. His successors Esarhaddon and Ashurbanipal continued this work by constructing sumptuous palaces for themselves. Ashurbanipal's principal palace, built on the present site of Kuyunjik, contained a magnificent library of 25,000 cuneiform texts.

The city became a joint capital of Assyria with Ashur and Nimrud early in the 1st millennium BC, and its location in the centre of the Assyrian lands between the Tigris and Zab gave it an added administrative and religious importance. Successive rulers built up the city and made it the centre of the civilised world from 705BC onwards until it was destroyed by the Medes in 612BC. The walls of the last Assyrian capital were strong enough to resist a first attack by the Medes with their Babylonian allies, but the city was at last taken by assault in 612BC. This date marked the end of the Assyrian empire. The Medes took advantage of a great flood to bring up their battering-rams against the walls by rafts. The city was plundered and razed to the ground so completely that Xenophon, passing near the site during his famous retreat in 401BC did not notice it. In the Roman period even the memory of its position had been forgotten. Lucian of Samosata in Syria, less than 250 miles from Nineveh, writes in AD151: 'Nineveh has perished; no trace of it remains; no-one could say where it had existed.' It was only identified again when Claudius Rich investigated in the 19th century, followed by a raft of famous explorers and archaeologists, including Emil Botta in 1842; Austen Layard from 1845; Rassam from 1851; Henry Rawlinson in 1854; Budge and Smith for the British Museum, between 1876 and 1903 and Campbell Thomson from 1904 to 1927. In the 1960s the Iraqi Directorate of Antiquities resumed work at Nineveh in order to make the antiquity of the site a visible reminder of the past and to turn it into a museum. To preserve the perimeter of the inner city, the team restored parts of the old wall and some of the gates. Between 1987 and 1990 American archaeologists from Berkley University joined them working on some of the city's residential quarters and the Halzi Gate.

Clearly, little of the long history of Nineveh has come to light so far. Nineveh was found far too early, before archaeological techniques had been developed.

Getting there
By road Nineveh is now a suburb of Mosul and is located on the northern outskirts of the modern town, 400km north of Baghdad. It occupies a vast, irregular rectangle of mounds lying against Mosul on the left bank of the Tigris.

What to see and do In 2001 Gwendolyn Leick in her book *Mesopotamia – The Invention of the City* described Nineveh:

'The ancient mound of Nineveh is nowadays almost engulfed by the urban sprawl of the city of Mosul. Dual carriageways pass just outside the old ramparts and modern houses cover a large area of the old city. But Nineveh's proximity to a living city means that it is implicated in the political affairs of our time. The looting of antiquities has become more common as clandestine markets have generated some form of undeclared income in an economy crippled by the UN sanctions against Iraq. A lack of finance and materials for the maintenance of the ruin sites has accelerated the deterioration of the monuments, creating a "world-heritage disaster" according to one American archaeologist ... In the mid-nineteenth century the dimensions of Nineveh could still be clearly seen: a not quite rectangular site enclosed by a massive wall some 12km in length. The largest mound lay along the west side of the city walls and was known by its Turkish name of Kuyunjik. A smaller mound was occupied by a mosque built within the remains of an earlier Christian monastery, which was known as Tell Nebi Younis, the mound of the Prophet Jonah, who was believed to have been buried there. This smaller mound was also inhabited by some villagers and is still occupied to this day. Only a few soundings have, therefore, ever been possible on this mound.'

One of the most astonishing features of this site is its size: the city wall has a circumference of over 12km. There are 11 gates in all, and five have been excavated. The original statues of giant bulls still flank the entrance to Nergal Gate, but the towers are a modern reconstruction. Inside Nergal Gate is a small museum where models of leading Assyrian towns are on display. The east wall on either side of Shamash Gate by the Erbil road has also been rebuilt. On Kuyunjik Hill are the remains of two magnificent Assyrian palaces: Sennacherib's palace and Ashurbanipal's palace built between 690 and 650BC. Ashurbanipal's palace had a library of 25,000 texts in cuneiform, which preserved much of the lore and knowledge of ancient Mesopotamia.

The throne room of **Sennacherib's palace** has been re-excavated and roofed. Some of the relief slabs depicting the king's victories have been left at the site. Some were looted in the 1990s and later appeared on the antiquities market in

Europe. Most of the sculptures are now in the British Museum and the Louvre. Impressive collections of Assyrian sculptures from the sites of Nineveh, Khorsabad and Nimrud are found in all the major museums of the world. Some were bought, some were given away by the Ottoman rulers, and excavators received permission to remove others. Post 2003, a number were looted.

Sadly in 2014 the palace, although now fenced and re-roofed, has greatly deteriorated due to the previous neglect, especially during the sanctions of the 1980s. This is one of the most depressing sites in Iraq. The protective overhead coverings of tin have been stolen and the remnants of panels have been destroyed by the sun and robbers. Luckily, would-be looters have not managed to get through the locked doors at the **Nergal Gate Museum** in Nineveh and the storage facility and excavation house have not been damaged. While the danger from looters has been eliminated, Nineveh is still threatened by the expansion of new suburbs, and the reliefs are decaying due to a shortage of conservation materials.

It is difficult to explore Mosul and its major ancient sites of Nineveh and Khorsabad because of the sectarian and ethnic tensions of this divided city.

JONAH – BUT NO WHALE!

Jonah is one of the later prophets in the Hebrew scriptures and a minor prophet in the Bible. The book of Jonah differs from the other prophetic works in being in prose and consists almost entirely of a straightforward tale describing an event in Jonah's life. It is not a historical narrative but a work of fiction, a parable. And, in spite of popular belief, there is no whale in it! The story of Jonah in the Koran is remarkably similar to the biblical version.

The unknown writer tells us that Jonah was sent by God to prophesy against the wickedness and sin of the city of Nineveh, which was one of Israel's bitterest enemies. Jonah, however, ran off in the opposite direction and took a ship westwards from Joppa, a Mediterranean seaport on the coast of Palestine. In response God caused a violent storm to arise, which was only abated when the sailors threw Jonah overboard. However, instead of drowning he was swallowed by a great fish. Three days later the fish vomited Jonah onto dry land and he finally followed God's command and went, rather reluctantly, to Nineveh. There, to his surprise the people listened to him and repented, putting on sackcloth and covering themselves in ashes. God was compassionate and did not destroy them.

This made Jonah angry and he accused God of being gracious and merciful to Israel's enemies. As he sat sulking in the hot sunshine, God caused a plant to grow up to shade him from the heat. However, the following day God caused the plant to be attacked by a worm and wither away. Jonah pitied the plant and cried out that he too may be allowed to die. God remonstrated with Jonah for being concerned about a plant, but not about Nineveh. Then comes the moral of the story: Jonah was full of pity for the plant which lasted but a day, yet he had no mercy in his heart for the thousands of inhabitants of Nineveh and their cattle, unlike God whose boundless love includes his enemies, the men of Nineveh, as well as his chosen people.

The writer's aim in this pithy, good-humoured tale is to protest against narrow-mindedness and intolerance towards other races. It contains many Aramaic words and expressions, indicating that it is one of the later books of the Bible.

AROUND NINEVEH

Nebi Younis The town of Nebi Younis is on the slopes of the mount of ancient Nineveh, surrounded by an impoverished village. The Mosque of Nebi Younis is said to be the burial place of the biblical prophet Jonah (see box, opposite). Today there is an old Nestorian church converted into a mosque at the site where the local Muslims venerate the memory of the prophet Jonah. A village of tortuous alleyways is built behind the mosque. There is no other church in Mosul dedicated to Jonah, and Muslim and Christian pilgrims visit the shrine together to honour the memory of the prophet. Over the years, archaeological excavations here have mainly centred on the larger mound of **Kuyunjik**. This is because Nebi Younis is sacred to Muslims and a mosque has been built near his tomb, which makes excavations in the area impossible. Archaeologists attempting to excavate the Assyrian palace underlying the mosque foundations ran into serious trouble with the clerics and effectively abandoned this work. The smaller palace mound, Nebi Younis, has defeated all serious attempts at excavation, although certain work has been carried out, on account of the sanctity of the mosque and shrine that surmounts it.

Excavations at Kuyunjik were begun by Paul-Emile Botta, the French Consul at Mosul in 1842. Botta's excavations were continued by Sir Henry Layard, Rassam, Loftus and Smith during the last half of the 19th century and by L W King in 1904.

In 1847 Henry Layard excavated at Kuyunjik as part of his major excavation at Nineveh and discovered the Palace of King Sennacherib (704–681BC) in the northern part of the mound and that of Ashurbanipal in the south. This palace contained more than 70 rooms, and 3km of walls decorated with reliefs showing hunting scenes and commemorating battles and religious ceremonies. Since these sculptures were all several metres beneath the surface, Layard's method of excavating was to tunnel along the base of the walls and through the doors. Occasionally he dug a vertical shaft to bring light into the tunnel. Both tunnels and shafts have now fallen in, and all one can see of the excavations are irregular depressions in the centre of the mound. These finds, together with others from Khorsabad and Nimrud, have supplied all the principal museums of the world with their collections of Assyrian sculpture, in spite, for instance, of a loss of 120 cases of artefacts when a group of rafts carrying them to Basra foundered in the Tigris.

From 1931 Reginald Campbell Thompson dug down over 27m into the mound and established that three-quarters of it was prehistoric. This deep dig helped to establish pre-historic Assyrian chronology covering 3,500 years from 6000BC to 3000BC. Five levels were identified which were named Ninevite 1 to 5 by the archaeologist Max Mallowan who also worked on the site. Much Halaf pottery was found (named after Tell Halaf in Syria where similar finds had already been made) and the depth of the excavations meant that this could now be reliably dated to between c5300 and 4500BC.

Beyond the mound of Nebi Younis lies **Yarimjah,** a mound which gave its name to the archaeological site in Agatha Christie's *Murder in Mesopotamia.*

In part due to the quantities of Halaf pottery which covered it, the mound of Tepe Reshwa better known as **Tell Arpachiyah,** a *tell* dating back to Halaf and Ubaid periods situated on the Tigris east of the centre of Nineveh, was chosen as one of the first sites to be excavated in an attempt to find out more about the prehistory of northern Mesopotamia. Originally a small village, it is now contained in the urban sprawl of Nineveh itself. Excavations show the remains of a 4th-century BC settlement on the top of the small mound with evidence of later occupation: the site was most notably occupied during the Halaf and Ubaid periods (5800–4900BC). Excavated in 1932 by Max Mallowan and John Rose, this site has a very long history.

Little is known of its earliest occupation, although pottery has been found dating from this period, especially deep straight-sided bowls usually decorated with cross-hatching or lozenge patterns in rows.

Excavating through the centre of the tell, ten levels of architecture were discovered. The Halaf settlements yielded a long pottery sequence and a series of ten circular buildings, 3.6m to 9.5m in diameter, some having rectangular anti-chambers. These structures have been likened to the much later Mycenaean *tholos* tombs but their function is unknown. In the lowest levels stone foundations of circular buildings with straight walls and either flat or domed roofs were

SIR MAX MALLOWAN 1904-78

'An archaeologist is the best husband
any woman can have:
the older she gets,
the more interested he is in her'

Agatha Christie, 1954

Max Edgar Lucien Mallowan was an English archaeologist and student of Leonard Woolley's who excavated at Ur, Nimrud and Nineveh from the 1920s to the 1950s. Long associated with the British School of Archaeology in Baghdad, he is probably best known as the husband of the novelist Agatha Christie.

Born in London in 1904, he studied classics at New College, Oxford. After gaining his degree, he began his long career as an archaeologist, specialising in ancient Middle Eastern history. His first appointment was as an assistant to Sir Leonard Woolley at Ur where he met and married Agatha Christie in 1930. He then worked for a short time with R Campbell Thompson at Nineveh, before becoming a field director for a series of expeditions jointly run by the British Museum and the British School of Archaeology in Iraq. In 1932 he conducted his first independent dig at the Halaf period site of Tell Arpachiyah in Iraq, as well as at Chagar Bazar and Tell Brak in Syria. He was also the first to excavate archaeological sites in the Balikh Valley in 1938.

During World War II he worked in air force intelligence in the RAF Volunteer Reserve in North Africa, being based for part of 1943 at the ancient city of Sabratha in Libya.

After the war he held various posts at the British School of Archaeology in Baghdad. He was also appointed Professor of Western Asiatic Archaeology at the University of London in 1947, and there he again excavated in Iraq, this time principally at Nimrud following in the trowel prints of Layard and making several important archaeological discoveries. In later years he took up a research fellowship at Oxford and held various academic posts including Vice President of the British Academy; President of the British Institute of Persian Studies and a trustee of the British Museum. He was knighted for his achievements in 1968. His works include *25 Years of Mesopotamian Discovery* (1956); *Early Mesopotamia and Iran* (1965); *Nimrud and Its Remains* (1966) and *Elamite Problems* (1969). His autobiography was published as *Mallowan's Memoirs* in 1977.

In 1976 Agatha Christie died. One year after her death Mallowan married the archaeologist Barbara Hastings Parker, who had been his epigraphist at Nimrud. He died on 19 August 1978, aged 74.

discovered, which were named 'tholoi' and which have been found at other Halaf-period sites in Mesopotamia. In later levels theses tholoi increased in size and had rectangular rooms attached to them. The last level of occupation during the Halaf-period is the most interesting and the one for which Arpachiyah is noted. The circular style of architecture is replaced completely by rectangular buildings and cobbled walkways radiate out from the centre of the site. In one building, which became known as the 'Burnt House' named for the cause of its collapse, numerous artefacts were found including delicate tricoloured pottery plates decorated with elaborate geometric designs, seals and sealings, stone vessels and items made of obsidian (volcanic glass), including plaques and beads, votive figures and carved and real knuckle bones. The archaeologists surmised that the 'Burnt House' had once belonged to either a potter or to an important official. Tell Arpachiyah was abandoned at this point. The most recent occupation of the site dates from the Ubaid period (c5200BC). Several buildings and a graveyard have been discovered from this period. Graves excavated from here show links with earlier burials from the Halaf period. In both Halaf and Ubaid burials at Tell Arpachiyah there was evidence of cranial modification or artificially deformed skulls of both males and females caused during infancy through the shaping of a baby's head while it is still malleable.

The most recent excavations at Tell Arpachiyah were carried out in 1976 by Ismail Hijara on the outermost edge of the mound. Hijara discovered numerous structures and some quite remarkable pottery. He also uncovered further burials in the area south of Mallowan's discoveries. These consisted of a pit into which a large globular and tall-collared jar containing a skull had been placed. Next to the jar two painted pottery bowls and one of stone were found. A collective grave of four skulls, three of which had been interred in pottery bowls and the fourth in a squat jar was also uncovered. Hijara interpreted the skull burials as the ritual interments of people of high social rank within a religious centre.

Tepe Gawra About 25km north of Nineveh is the site of a settlement concurrent with Tell Arpachiyah. Finds here support the theory that Tell Arpachiyah may have been a thriving pottery making and export centre.

TO THE NORTH OF MOSUL

TELL KEPPE Tell Keppe, or TalKayf as it is known by the Arab Muslims, was once one of the largest Chaldean towns in Iraq. However, it is now considered an extension of the city of Mosul, with a population close to 25,000 people. It is estimated that only a few hundred of its native inhabitants continue to live in Tell Keppe, the rest, forced by anti-Christian discriminatory practices and violent terrorist acts have left their Mesopotamian homeland for the US and Tell Keppe is now a majority Arab Muslim town.

History The name Tell Keppe, meaning hill of stones, is Aramaic. It is so named from its location over a ruined suburb of Nineveh, capital of old Assyria. The name first appears at the end of the 5th century BC, after the fall of Nineveh to the Chaldean-Medes alliance by Xenophon, the Commander of the Greek army's campaign in northern Mesopotamia in 401BC. In common with most Chaldean towns around Nineveh, Tell Keppe suffered savage attacks at the hands of the Mongols, the Persians and the Kurds. In AD1436 and again in 1508, Tell Keppe, along with the other Chaldean towns of Tell Esqof and El Kosh and the Rabban Hormizd

Monastery, was attacked by the Mongols, resulting in the death of hundreds of its inhabitants and the destruction of its churches and buildings. In 1743 under King Nadir Shah the Persians attacked Tell Keppe along with Karamles, Bakhdida, Bartilla and other towns, slaughtering thousands of inhabitants and destroying their churches and crops. In 1833 the Kurdish governor of Rawanduz attacked Tell Keppe and El Kosh and unleashed a savage wave of killing, kidnapping and destruction. Families originating in Tell Keppe have played an impressive role in Iraq, those who migrated to Baghdad from the mid-19th century onwards were the first to use steam ships on the Tigris river, introduce the concept of modern hotels and publish the first Iraqi newspaper dealing with women's issues, *Fatat Al-Arab*, in 1937.

Getting there Tell Keppe is less than 13km northeast of Mosul by road.

What to see and do Unfortunately, due to the presence of Tell Keppe's modern cemetery, it has been difficult to excavate the ancient *tell*. However, the water irrigation canals that were built by the Assyrian king Sennacherib (705–681BC) to irrigate the land around Tell Keppe have been unearthed, and excavation by the Iraqi Directorate of Antiquities succeeded in finding vases dating from 2000BC, as well as other, much older items, from prehistoric times. Several old ruins of churches and monasteries dating from early Christianity were also found in Tell Keppe, which currently has five old churches along with a large new one. Today the town is home to hundreds of Assyrian refugees from Syria.

AROUND TELL KEPPE
Rabban Hormizd Monastery For a spectacular view of the region visit the ancient Chaldean monastery of Rabban Hormizd, an important monastery of the Chaldean Church carved out in the mountains on the escarpment over the village of El Kosh, 48km north of Mosul. Named after Rabban Hormizd (*rabban* is Syriac for monk) who founded it in about AD640 as an Assyrian monastery, it has been the official residence of the patriarchs of the Eliya line of the Church of the East site, which is the oldest and largest patriarchal line from 1551 to the 18th century. After the union with Rome in the early 19th century it became a prominent monastery of the Chaldean Church.

The monastery flourished until the 10th century and by the end of the 15th century served as the patriarchal burial site. Nine patriarchal graves, from 1497 to 1804, are still located in the corridor that leads to the cell of Rabban Hormizd. In about 1743, due to pestilence and the attacks of the Kurds, the monastery was abandoned but in 1808, the Chaldean Catholic Gabriel Dambo (1775–1832) revived it and installed a seminary.

E A Wallis Budge, who visited Rabban Hormizd Monastery in 1890, described the monastery with these words:

'Rabban Hormizd Monastery is built about half way up the range of mountains which encloses the plain of Mosul on the north, and stands in a sort of amphitheatre, which is approached by a rocky path that leads through a narrow defile; this path has been paved by generations of monks. The church is of stone and is of a dusky red colour; it is built upon an enormous rock. In the hills round about the church and buildings of the monastery are rows of caves hewn out of the solid rock, in which the stern ascetics of former generations lived and died. They have neither doors nor any protection from the inclemency of the weather, and the chill which they strike into the visitor gives

Nahum was a minor Old Testament prophet venerated as a saint in Eastern Christianity whose name means comforter. He wrote about the end of the Assyrian Empire and its capital city Nineveh, in a vivid, poetic style. His writings can be taken as either a prophecy, written about 615BC just before the downfall of Nineveh, or as a history, written just after its downfall in 612BC.

Nahum declared that Nineveh was to be destroyed; the heart of the mighty Assyrian Empire, which had crushed Judah and brought terror into the heart of all the nations, was to be judged by God for her cruelty and wiped from the face of the earth. A great contrast indeed to the message of Jonah (see box, page 224)!

Nahum describes Nineveh's attackers, who we know were an alliance of Medes, Scythians and Chaldeans, in vivid detail: the red shields and cloaks of the Medes, the flashing armour and the forest of spears. Although Nineveh's commander tries to deploy his defenders, the invaders open up the sluices controlling the river and flood the city. Great buildings have their foundations swept away. The palace collapses. Nahum likens Nineveh to a pool being drained: her pride, strength and wealth ebbing away in the slaughter of her people and the plunder of her treasure. Nineveh, which previously had been like a lion's den – secure in her strength and a breeding place of violence – now lies destroyed. Nahum chants a battle-song against Nineveh: She is a 'city of blood', built on slaughter and maintained by her stolen wealth. Now she will get the treatment she has handed out to others. The prophet describes her as a prostitute, devoted to paganism and witchcraft, now exposed, stripped and humiliated before the eyes of the world. The damage is final and irreversible: Nineveh has finally suffered the fate she so richly deserved.

No other of the minor prophets equals the sublimity, the vehemence and the boldness of Nahum: Nineveh's ruin is vividly expressed.

The feast of St Nahum is celebrated on 1 December in the Eastern Church (which follows the traditional Julian calendar), 14 December in the Gregorian calendar. He is commemorated with other minor prophets in the Calendar of Saints of the Armenian Apostolic Church on 31 July.

an idea of what those who lived in them must have suffered from the frosts of winter and the drifting rain. Some of them have niches hewn in their sides or backs in which the monks probably slept, but many lack even these means of comfort. The cells are separate one from the other, and are approached by narrow terraces, but some of them are perched in almost inaccessible places, and, unless other means of entrance existed in former days, could only have been approached by the monks crawling down from the crest of the mountain and swinging themselves into them. I saw no marks of fire in any of the cells. Some cells have a second small cave hewn out behind the larger one which is entered through an opening just large enough for a man of average size to crawl through. The monks eat meat on Easter Day and Christmas Day only, and their usual food consists of boiled wheat and lentils, and dark coloured, heavy bread cakes. They drink neither wine nor spirits, and they have neither light nor fire. They drink rain water which they preserve in rock cisterns. They are called to prayer by the ringing of a bell at sunset, midnight, day-break, and at certain times of the day. The number of the monks in 1820 was about fifty; in 1843 it was thirty-nine; in 1879—80 it was sixteen, and in 1890 it was about ten'.

El Kosh (Alqosh) The village of El Kosh is known as the birthplace and final resting place of the Old Testament prophet Nahum who was known as 'the Elkoshite'.

History The history of El Kosh probably pre-dates the Assyrian Empire. The earliest known mention of it appears in the phrase 'this rock was brought from Alqosh's Mountain' carved behind a mural inside King Sennacherib's palace that was discovered in Tell Kuyunjik and which is believed to date back to c705BC. A number of places within El Kosh have ancient Assyrian names, including Sainna which utilises forms of the Assyrian for 'moon' and Bee Sinnat pertaining to the Sumerian moon god Sin, who was worshipped by the local inhabitants along with a local god El-Qustu. According to tradition, those living in Nineveh would visit El Kosh every Akitu (the Assyrian and Babylonian New Year) to re-enact the Enuma Elish (the Sumerian Epic of Creation) and to take part in a religious ceremony honouring Sin, during which an image of the god would be carried in a procession back to Nineveh. Forty days later the inhabitants of Nineveh would return the statue of the god to its original place in El Kosh.

Since its establishment, El Kosh has been a religious centre, whether for Sumerian and Assyrian gods or for Judaism. Hebrews brought by the Assyrian army during the 8th and 9th century BC also made their home in El Kosh. Al Qoun, who was believed

THE ALQOSH

The Alqosh, or Alqoshniye, speak Syriac, a dialect of Aramaic, the ancient language spoken by Jesus of Nazareth. Historically, the men wore long trousers and *zaboon*. Instead of a turban, they wore their hair in plaits. Women wore colourful *posheya* or Assyrian head-scarves decorated with beads with gold and silver ornaments around their neck and ears. Around their forehead they placed a golden belt that skirted the *posheya* at the front and from which black strings dangled down both sides of the head. They wore skirts of various colours and a decorated top extending from the shoulder to the knees. They also wore their hair in plaits, adding to these with long strands of wool extending to the ankle.

The Alqosh mainly practised dry agriculture and relied on the fertile plains to the south for agricultural products like grain, wheat, beans, melons, grapes and cucumbers. Farmers followed the old-fashioned ways of farming, handed down through the centuries, which made them vulnerable to the forces of nature such as drought, epidemic and pests.

Towards the beginning of the 1960s agricultural machinery such as tractors and harvesters began to be used, along with fertilisers and insecticides. However, as Alqosh has no river it relies on springs and ancient wells for irrigation, supplemented by rainfall. Farms belong to the government and are rented by tenant farmers who also raise cattle, sheep and bees.

Until recently El Kosh was an important marketplace for the surrounding Kurdish, Yezidi and Arabic villages. A number of trades are practised by its residents, including: shoe making; carpentry; saddlery; knitting and needle work; dyeing; tailoring and jewellery making.

Many Alqosh have left Iraq since the 1970s and it is estimated that at least 40,000 Alqosh and their descendants now live in the US. Conversely, many Assyrians from Mosul and Baghdad fled to El Kosh for safety after 2003. Although there is no official census for the village, the population is estimated as somewhere between 2,500 and 20,180.

to be the father of the prophet Nahum (see box, page 229), was the son of a Hebrew family brought to El Kosh by King Shalmaneser V, who reigned 727–722BC. Later, inhabitants of El Kosh became some of the earliest Christian converts. According to the memoirs of Mar Mikha of Dohuk, when he visited the town in 441AD he was welcomed by priests of a church built on the ruins of the temple of El Kosh's ancient god Sin. El Kosh's stature grew when Hormizd built the Eastern Christian monastery named after him in the nearby mountains of Alqosh in 640AD. It was the seat for many patriarchs of the Assyrian Church of the East, and from it came Yohannan Sulaqa who united the Assyrian Church with the Catholic Church in 1553 to establish the Chaldean Church. Before that, the inhabitants of El Kosh followed the Nestorian faith of the Assyrian Church of the East. From 1610 to 1617, the Patriarchate of El Kosh, under Mar Eliyya VIII, entered into full communion with Rome, following which from about 1700, El Kosh also had a Catholic minority. The patriarch Eliya Denkha signed a Catholic confession of faith in 1771, but no formal union resulted till the reign of Patriarch Yohannan VIII (Eliya) Hormizd, and by 1780, most of the inhabitants of El Kosh accepted the union with the Catholic Church. El Kosh became a victim of its own success, however, and in 1743 was attacked by the Persian king Nadir Shah.

In 1828, El Kosh was again attacked, this time by the army of Mosa Pasha, Governor of Amadeya, who arrested and imprisoned several monks and priests and caused substantial damage to Rabban Hormizd Monastery. This was followed in 1832 and 1833 by attacks by the Kurdish governor of Rawanduz whose hatred of Assyrians was well known, killing over 600 of its inhabitants. In 1840, his brother, Rasoul Beg, surrounded El Kosh for several months, after which he set the monastery on fire and stole over 500 of its valuable books.

Getting there El Kosh is located on the east bank of the Tigris, about 3km north of Mosul, in the Bayhidhra Mountains overlooking Nineveh's northern plateau alongside other Assyrian towns such as Telassqopa (Tell Skuf), Baqofah, Sharafiya, Batnaya and Tell Keppe.

What to see and do El Kosh's stone dwellings are spread along its mountainous slopes up to the tip of its plateau. They share similar decorations with the other villages on the Nineveh plains. The more modern parts of the town, with their cement and brick buildings are to the south. El Kosh is divided into four quarters: Sainna quarter to the west, Qasha quarter to the east, Odo quarter to the north, and Khatetha quarter to the south. In the centre of El Kosh you will find the shrine of the prophet Nahum (see box, page 229) who predicted the end of the mighty Assyrian empire:

'Thou hast multiplied the merchants above the stars of heaven ... they are crowned as the locusts, and the captains as the great grasshoppers, which camp in the hedges in the cold day. But when the sun arises they flee away and their place is not known where they are. Thy shepherds slumber, O King of Assyria: thy nobles shall dwell in the dust. Nineveh laid waste – who is going to pity her?'

El Kosh was abandoned by its Jewish population in 1948, when they were expelled from Iraq and the synagogue that purportedly houses the tomb is now in a poor structural state, to the extent that the tomb itself is in danger of collapse. When the Jews left, the iron keys to the tomb were handed to a Chaldean man by the name of Sami Jajouhana. Few Jews are able to visit the historic site, yet Jajouhana continues to keep the promise he made to his Jewish friends, and looks after the tomb. A team of US and UK construction engineers, led by Huw Thomas, were looking at ways to save the building and the tomb, and money was been allocated for proposed renovation in 2008. However, due to the current prohibition on travel to the area, it is not possible to say if this has taken place.

AROUND EL KOSH Just 3km to the west of El Kosh lies the ruin of **Shayro Meliktha**, a temple containing a carving of Sennacherib aiming an arrow from his bow. Also in the vicinity are various caves, including: **Guppa D Mmaya** (cave of water), **Guppa Ssmoqa** (the red cave) and **Guppetha D Toomin** (small cave of Toomin) located to the north, and **Guppa D Magoar Gama** (the thunderous cave) and **Guppa D Hattarein** (the cave of the cotton carders) located to the northeast. **Shweetha D Gannaweh** (the sleeping bed of the robbers) is a hill located to the north of El Kosh which some experts believe was a sacred site of the god Sin. **Kerrma D Raysha** (the peak's vineyard) is the site of an ancient vineyard at the peak of the mountain. **Besqeen**, an old orchard is located behind El Kosh Mountain in a rough trail valley. Three families own this orchard which is part of the remains of a monastery built here some ten centuries ago. **Galeeya D Dayra** or **Galeeya D Qadeesha** (valley of the saints or valley of the monastery) is a valley in the northeast corner of El Kosh leading to Rabban Hormizd Monastery (see pages 228–9). Until recently the monastery was occupied by monks who worshipped within its walls and tended its orchards and farms. Opposite the monastery and towards the plain of Nineveh is the **Virgin Mary's Monastery** (Guardian of the Plants). Built in 1856, it is a huge monastery still inhabited by monks.

KHORSABAD Also known as Dur Sharrukin, the 'Fortress of Sargon' is located in a region of tells, monasteries and churches. Unlike other ancient cities, it was not an important centre of communications and was constructed solely for Sargon's benefit. The city was nearly 2km from side to side and was surrounded by a wall containing seven gates. Little remains of the magnificent royal palace, temples and ziggurat. During the 19th century many of the stone reliefs were removed. The Sibitti Temple near the Palace of Sargon has been excavated and its foundations restored. ISIS has attempted to destroy the site with bulldozers but as it is a very large site, this has not proved easy, thank goodness.

History Khorsabad was founded by Sargon ll, King of Assyria 721–705BC as a new capital city to replace Nimrud (Caleh) where his predecessors had resided since the early 9th century BC. No traces of earlier occupation have been found on the site, and it is presumed that there was, at most, a village there beforehand. Thanks to extensive archaeological work we know a great deal about Khorsabad during this period, as there is an abundance of written texts between Sargon and architects associated with its building, which show the depth of the king's involvement in its planning and execution. They also indicate that the construction of the city wall and its gates was divided up among craftsmen and builders from different provinces right across the empire, who were responsible for procuring their own building materials. Soon after the city was finished, however, Sargon was killed in battle, and his son Sennacherib removed his administration to Nineveh. Little is known of the history of Khorsabad in the 7th century BC. The site was occupied until 612BC when it presumably shared the fate of other Assyrian royal cities and was sacked during the Median invasions of 614 and 612BC. Following this there was only a brief and impoverished reoccupation and, as at Nimrud, a village stood on the ruined citadel in the Hellenistic period. Unlike Nineveh, Khorsabad was never an important centre of communications and its sudden rise and decline less

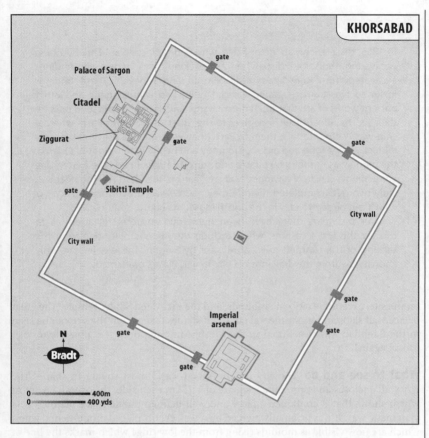

than a century later apparently reflect only the whim of a single monarch. Owing to its relatively short lifespan the stratigraphy of Khorsabad is straightforward, and its architecture well preserved. It was rediscovered in 1843 by Paul-Emile Botta, the French Consul at Mosul, who while excavating unsuccessfully at Kuyunjik was informed that the locals regularly dug up sculptured stones at Khorsabad. He hurried there and after a week's work, came to the erroneous conclusion that he had discovered the last capital of Assyria and telegraphed 'Nineveh has been discovered'. This was a hasty judgement, later to be repeated by Layard who made a similar mistake when excavating at Nimrud, and thought it to be Nineveh itself, before he again was proved wrong. Further work was carried out by Victor Place in 1852–54. Excavations of Khorsabad between 1929 and 1935 by the Oriental Institute of the University of Chicago concentrated on Sargon's palace complex and the main citadel as well as the city's defensive walls.

Getting there
By road Khorsabad is 20km northeast of Mosul and 20km northeast of Nineveh on a minor tributary of the Tigris river.

Other practicalities Due to the difficulties in Mosul, few visitors have reached Khorsabad in recent years. The site is by the side of a major road and opposite a teeming, populous village (the children here can be difficult). There is little to see

7

KHORSABAD'S LOST TREASURES

In 1855, the Frenchman Victor Place, who had replaced Paul-Emile Botta in excavating Khorsabad, dispatched 235 packing cases loaded with findings excavated from Khorsabad, Kish, Nimrud and Nineveh. These findings included two human-headed winged bulls, two winged genii and other ancient works of art. Crammed onto a barge and several overloaded rafts for their journey down the Tigris river to the Shatt Al-Arab and Basra where a ship was waiting to take them to Paris, they were attacked several times by raiders. After a long and arduous journey and nearly within sight of Querna, the barge was rammed by pirates and sunk. The rafts fared little better; one containing a statue of a winged bull later sank in the Shatt Al-Arab near Kut. Only two rafts completed their journey and delivered their precious cargo, which can be seen today in the British Museum and the Louvre.

Over the years there have been numerous unsuccessful attempts to recover the lost treasures, which include the famous relief depicting the sacking of the Urartian town of Musasir by Sargon. These reliefs are only known now from the drawings of Félix Tomas, Place's draftsman.

on the site, except the city gate mounds, and the excavated Sibitti Temple. The great palace wall slabs and monumental guardian statues taken from the site can be seen in the Baghdad Museums (and in the Mosul Museum, once it is possible to visit Mosul again).

What to see and do The city of Khorsabad was almost square in shape. The city wall encloses an approximate square of 1.75km each side, the overall layout of which shows that it contained a large and well-defined public space planned in a systematic way. It was originally pierced by seven, evenly placed monumental gates, which are now visible as mounds rising from the low ridge which marks the line of the fortifications. A vast complex including the royal palace, a number of temples and a ziggurat stood on a terrace straddling the northwest wall and immediately overlooking the modern highway from Mosul to Ain Sifni. Little of the palace plan can be now traced, but the ruins of the modern excavation house overlie its small internal courtyard, with the throne room immediately to the northeast. South of the terrace and linked to it by a stone bridge, of which the abutments are still visible, was the great citadel, separated by massive walls from the outer city. The citadel housed Sargon's palace complex, named é-gal-gaba-ri-nu-tuku-a or 'palace without rival' and the Nabu Temple, which were built on a higher level on artificial terraces of rough limestone and mud-brick and were connected to each other by a corbelled stone bridge. It was usual for Assyrian palace compounds to be built at the edge of a citadel overlooking a river or landscape. This area also housed four large residences occupied by the vizier and other ministers. The temple of Nabu, the god of writing and wisdom, was an outstanding complex with nearly 50 rooms arranged around five courtyards. The temple's façade was decorated with brightly coloured glazed bricks depicting lions, eagles, bulls and trees. The palace itself was a giant complex consisting of ceremonial, residential and administrative quarters in over 200 rooms arranged around three large courtyards.

Just outside the citadel to the southwest, and close to the modern road, the temple dedicated to the Sibitti (the seven planets), was recently excavated and restored. A second large mound on the southwest city wall marks the headquarters of the arsenal, the outer bailey of which occupied all this corner of the city. Like the arsenal of Nimrud, it contained a secondary royal palace, only a small part of which has been excavated.

TO THE EAST OF MOSUL

Bahizani and **Bahshiqa**, 23km east of Mosul, both sit among acres and acres of evergreen olive groves, at the foot of Mount Maqloub on the way to Mar Behnam monastery. These villages are home to Syrian Orthodox Christian and Yezidi communities (see pages 22 and 25), who live in harmony together. Although the main Yezidi shrine of Sheikh Adi is in Lalish (see page 401), Bahizani and Bahshiqa are also home to many Yezidi leaders and the towns have numerous Yezidi shrines and religious festivals, including a colourful festival held every spring.

TO THE WEST OF MOSUL

Directly west as far as the Syrian border on Highway 1 and its southern off-shoot, the country becomes dry and desert-like. This route, through Jebel Sinjar, is little known to modern travellers. It is the old caravan route to Raqqah in Syria. It passed through many interesting places, such as Sinjar with its Roman remains and a Yezidi temple and Eski Mosul, a very historical city of the Abbasids. It was also one of the routes taken by the Roman invaders in their incursions into Mesopotamia. Historically, it is a forgotten corner of Iraq which awaits the discerning traveller.

SECURITY WARNING Unfortunately at the time this book goes to print, travel in the area is extremely unsafe due to the current insurgency in Syria and is the path for weapon smuggling and terrorist activities.

TELL HASSUNA Perhaps the most fascinating prehistoric site excavated in Mesopotamia, Hassuna is both a Neolithic site and typical of the major prehistoric cultures of northern Mesopotamia. It has given its name to the pottery ware present in its lowest levels dated to the 6th millennium BC. This pottery may be related to that of the upper levels at Jarmo and is widely distributed from Susiana to southern Turkey (Sakce-Gozu and the Amuq). It was usually a buff ware in simple shapes, sometimes burnished, sometimes painted or incised with a simple geometric pattern. In higher levels it was replaced by Samarra ware.

History An important prehistoric site, dating back to the 6th millennium BC, Hassuna was an early agricultural village and is the type site for the cultural assemblage defining this period characterised by the proliferation of sites on the open steppe of north Mesopotamia, where few preceding Aceramic-Neolithic sites are known. Its height reaches 7m above the valley and occupational debris show a 200m by 150m rectangle. Excavated in 1943–44 it was found to represent an advanced village culture that was widespread throughout northern Mesopotamia at that time. Although no architectural remains were found in the oldest levels, it was assumed that a semi-nomadic society occupied the site and, according to the ashes of camp-fires found, lived in a kind of tent. People had moved to the foothills of northern Mesopotamia where there was enough rainfall to allow for dry agriculture, making them the first farmers in the region later known as Assyria, combining sheep and goat herding, hunting, and wheat and barley cultivation. Along with farming, these early inhabitants made Hassuna style pottery (cream

Hassuna was re-discovered in the 1940s by Seton Lloyd who excavated the site with the Iraqi Department of Antiquities. In his book, *Foundations in the Dust*, he describes the primitive beginnings from which the great city state of Sumer evolved over a period of some 2,000 years. He recounts that during the months that the mound was under excavation, the horizon of prehistory receded several centuries. Revealed in the simplest terms of archaeological evidence was a new and earlier chapter in the history of civilised man. As a nomad he first ventured out of the mountains onto the grassy uplands above the Tigris, and at the junction of two rivers he first camped, remaining long enough to reap a store of wild barley. In the lower stratum of the mound were found the ashes of his camp fire. Grouped around them were the simple paraphernalia of his household – flint weapons, bone implements and crude pottery vessels. At the next stage he had learnt to sow as well as to reap, and his nomad habits were forgotten. Higher in the mound, primitive adobe houses began to appear along with improved pottery ornamented with painted designs. Near the surface was a well-built village with the practical economy of an agricultural community almost completely developed.

Seventy centuries later the modern village of Hassuna is run on much the same lines.

slip with reddish paint in linear designs). They lived in small villages or hamlets which rarely exceeded 500 people. The houses were adobe built around open, central courtyards. The inhabitants used fine-painted pottery rather than the crude pottery of earlier times. Hand axes, sickles, grinding stones, bins, baking ovens and numerous bones of domesticated animals indicate that they lived a settled, agricultural life. Obsidian and flint were also used to make tools. Beads, pendants and some small ornaments have been found, some set with turquoise which was perhaps imported from Persia. Figurines of the mother goddess type made of baked clay and jar burials containing food are indicative of the inhabitants' religious beliefs. Fine stone vessels were manufactured and could be exchanged. Overall, the Hassuna finds demonstrate that even as early as the 6th millennium BC extensive trade was carried out throughout a large part of the ancient Middle East.

Getting there The site is located just west of the Tigris river, about 35km southwest of Nineveh.

SINJAR Directly west of Mosul situated on the desert road at the foot of the Sinjar Mountains lies Sinjar (ancient Sinjara). The town is mainly inhabited by Yezidis, who venerate the mountain ridge, considering it the place where Noah's Ark came to rest after the biblical flood. Sinjar was also the site of the filming of the 1973 film *The Exorcist*.

History Ancient Sinjar was declared a colony by Marcus Aurelius around AD170 and was populated by a Roman garrison. It was captured in 260 by Shapur I, after which control of it bounced back and forth between the Persians and the Romans several times. It was finally handed back to Shapur II in 363, and effectively formed the frontier between the Roman and Persian empires for centuries. It was famed for its prosperity in Abbasid times. In 1170 Nuriddin conquered it *en route* to Mosul.

When ISIS seized large swathes of territory in central and northern Iraq unprecedented terror was unleashed on the Yezidi minority who were regarded as devil worshippers. For ISIS the Sinjar area near the border with Syria, home of the Yezidis, is strategically important and the Sunni fanatics prompted a mass exodus from the town of Sinjar on 7 August 2014 when its Yezidi residents were given an ultimatum: convert or lose your heads.

According to UN statistics at least 130,000 people fled from Sinjar to Dohuk, or Erbil where the Kurdistan Regional Government is doing its best to cope with an influx of refugees. At least 40,000 Yezidis, many of them women and children, sought refuge in nine locations on Mount Sinjar, a craggy, mile-high ridge identified in local legends as the final resting place of Noah's Ark. Food and water was dropped by American planes and the refugees were escorted to safety by the *peshmerga*.

August is the month when Yezidis traditionally gather at the holy shrine of Lalish: in 2014, 2,500 people flocked to the temple seeking sanctuary from ISIS.

Some members of the Yezidi community are calling on the Kurdistan Regional Government to set up Yezidi militias to protect areas inhabited by the Yezidis similar to the Sunni Awakening Forces set up in 2005 as a defence from al-Qaida.

Originally from Sinjar, Hamat Khalaf who has lived in Germany for the past 15 years but returned to help his family, said that the Yezidi people want to leave Iraq to go anywhere, to Germany, the Netherlands, America. 'They just want to get out. There's no safety here: they've seen too much and they don't want to go through it again.'

Reflecting on the latest outrage against his community, a Yezidi politician said: 'In our history we have suffered 72 massacres. We are worried Sinjar could be the 73rd.'

Getting there Sinjar is located on the desert road approximately 129km west of Mosul on the slopes of Jebel Sinjar.

What to see and do The modern town of Sinjar is located to the east of ancient Sinjar and contains a Yezidi cemetery and several remains of very old mosques and minarets. On the old desert road running through Sinjar, there are many important tells, or ancient mounds covering villages, settlements and towns going back to the 3rd and 4th millennium BC. This old desert road is approximately 185km long and runs to the Syrian border, a route once taken by camel trains to the important water and market towns of El Haseka and Raqqa in Syria. The Iraqi–Syrian border is only 57km from the town. **Tell Maghzaliyah**, which is situated on the southern slopes of Jebel Sinjar, contains the remains of an agrarian pre-ceramic fortified settlement dating back to the 7th or 8th millennium BC. Culturally and chronologically this settlement can be compared to Jarmo and Cayonu Tepisi.

TELL AFAR Considered by some to be the biblical Assyrian city of Telassar or Thelasar inhabited by the children of Eden at the time of Sennacherib, Tell Afar is located in an open desert plain at the southern base of the Aedea Mountains. Tell Afar has a large Turkmen population, unlike its neighbouring towns and villages which are made up largely of Yezidis and Arabs.

History According to Austen Layard, who visited the area in the 1840s, Tell Afar was once a town of some importance. It was mentioned in the writings of the early Arab geographers and it has been linked to the Telassar of Isaiah in the Bible. In 1837 Tell Afar was occupied by Turkish troops who used it as a base to control the movements of the Yezidi tribes in neighbouring Sinjar. Remains of the fortress they built can still be seen today in the centre of the town on the top of the hill. Garrisoned at the fortress were Turkmen members of the Daloodi tribe who, following the withdrawal of the Ottoman army, became the first civilian occupants of the modern town of Tell Afar, built around the fortress. In the 1880s Tell Afar became an administrative area in the newly formed Sinjar District. In 1920 it briefly gained notoriety as a base of operations for a planned revolt against the then ruling British.

Getting there

By road Tell Afar is located approximately 50km west of Mosul and 60km east of the Iraqi–Syrian border on the major east–west highway which spans the Nineveh Governorate and intersects Iraq's main central north–south highway near Mosul.

What to see and do Tell Afar is divided into 18 districts – Saad; Qadisiyah; Todd A-O; Sarai; Mohalemeen; Madlomin; Uruba; Wahada; Nida; A'a lot; Hassan Qoi; Mothana; Khadra; Jazeera; Taliha; Kifah; Malain and Qalah, each maintaining their identity owing to the tribal nature of the city. Several extended families in an area will identify with a local sheik who represents them in dealings with the local administration. The town is comprised of closely packed, interlinked buildings. Many residents of Tell Afar have strong family links to, and relatives in, Turkey and so share many similarities with Anatolian Turkish culture. Arab culture is also apparent and you will see men wearing traditional Arab *dishdashas* and checked headdresses, alongside Western-style clothing. The cuisine found in the town is representative of this cultural mix, and includes unseasoned grilled lamb and beef, unleavened bread, rice, vegetable-based soups and local produces such as potatoes, tomatoes, raisins, cucumbers, etc. The streets themselves define the individual districts, separating one from another as they haphazardly cut through the town. Located in the centre of the town in the Qalah (castle) District are the remains of the Ottoman fortress which was renovated by the British after the World War I. During the 2003 Gulf War, the fortress was further augmented and used as the mayoral, municipal and police headquarters.

AROUND TELL AFAR About 10km southwest of Tell Afar are the six mounds of **Yarim Tepe**, an early farming village dating back to the Neolithic Hassuna era (c6000–5500BC). A Russian team excavated the mounds, known as Yarim Tepe I and Yarim Tepe II, in the late 1960s and 1970s and found remains from the Halafian culture dating back to the Hassuna era. Yarim Tepe I contains the remains of an early Hassunian farming settlement consisting of courtyards and small streets with rectangular mud-brick buildings and public granaries. Among the artefacts found were saddle querns, stone pestles and sickles, various vessels and female statuettes. The discovery of copper ore, copper beads and a lead bracelet are evidence of the oldest metallurgy in Mesopotamia, while the finds of cattle bones attest to the beginning of cattle raising. Burials of children in vessels were also discovered. Yarim Tepe I belongs entirely to the Hassuna Period. No later phase of occupation has been found here, and it has been suggested that this site served as a burial ground for the nearby Halaf settlement at Yarim Tepe II.

Yarim Tepe II was a settlement of the Halafian culture (5th millennium BC) containing round mud-brick dwellings, cultic buildings, granaries and potters' kilns. Stone farming implements and the bones of both domestic and wild animals were found. The pottery included figured vessels in the shape of elephants and women. Pendant seals, including a very old copper seal, were also found, as well as cremations and burials of skulls. Later excavations in the upper strata of one further small tell (Yarim Tepe III) were dated back to the Halaf and Ubaid periods. This site contained over 100 mostly single-roomed houses of differing sizes. Artefacts discovered in the remains included copper and lead ornaments, small seated clay figures and small stone or clay disks, which may have been early versions of later stamp and cylinder seals.

Approximately 20km further south is **Tell Irmah**. Tell Irmah has a large artificial hill enclosing the remains of a ziggurat and its surrounding village. The site was occupied until the Assyrian period. By road, approximately 65km from Mosul on Highway 1, is **Eski Mosul**. An important town of the Abbasids, it was probably built on the site of the Persian town of Sharabad. The ruins of its historical castle were submerged when the **Mosul** (Chambarakat) **Dam**, formerly known as the Saddam Dam, was constructed in the early 1980s. The reservoir of the dam, which is the largest in Iraq, submerged many archæological sites in the region when it was inundated by the Tigris river in 1985. Continuing west, approximately 120km from Mosul and some 9km north of the road is the village of **Qairyet el Khan** with the remains of a caravanserai dating to 1240. The Arab historian Yaqut described this area as a Christian one. The remains of a Roman camp or fort built to guard the ancient roadway lie just off the modern road.

TO THE SOUTH OF MOSUL

NIMRUD (ANCIENT CALEH) Although mentioned in the Old Testament by the name of Caleh, Nimrud is mostly known as the royal capital of the Assyrian Empire in the 9th and 8th centuries BC. Rediscovered by Layard in 1845, the statues and inscriptions he sent back, together with his book on his discoveries *Nineveh and its Remains* (only later was the site correctly identified as Caleh) first stirred the public imagination in the way that the archaeological discoveries of Troy, Tutankhamen or Ur did later. The queen of crime writing, Agatha Christie, spent some time in Nimrud during the early 1950s with her husband, the archaeologist Max Mallowan (see box, page 226). Her stay in Iraq provided the inspiration for *Murder in Mesopotamia* and *They Came to Baghdad*. Her murder-mystery writing in Iraq is documented in the book *The 8.55 to Baghdad* by Andrew Eames.

History The city was probably founded in c1280BC by Shalmaneser I on a site which had been occupied from prehistoric times, as 13th century texts suggest that it was already a place of importance. After falling into decay, it was re-founded on a larger scale by Ashurnasirpal II (883–859BC), when he made Nimrud the royal capital, initiating the large-scale building programme that was to continue sporadically under his successors. He constructed a new city wall some 8km in circuit and made from mud brick, which enclosed a roughly square area of 360ha. Surrounded by its own fortification wall a citadel mound occupied some 20ha at one corner of the city, containing a royal palace and nine temples. In these palaces were found enormous stone-winged bulls, carved reliefs and, on a quite different scale, exquisitely carved ivories which once adorned the royal furniture. His successor, Shalmaneser III (858–824BC) added a ziggurat and a temple in the citadel area, and another collection of ivories was found by archaeologists in Shalmaneser's arsenal in the outer town. Nimrud was the capital until it was succeeded by Khorsabad in 707BC. Thereafter, it remained an important city. Extensive renovation was undertaken by Esarhaddon (680–699BC). The Medes and Babylonians sacked the city in 614–612BC, and some of the ivories excavated from Ashurnasirpal's palaces show traces of the fire which accompanied the destruction they wrought. Some occupation may have continued, although it is uncertain whether Nimrud is the ruined Median city Larissa mentioned by Xenophon. There was a village settlement here in Hellenistic times.

Getting there

By road Nimrud is approximately 35km southeast of Mosul and 1 hour's drive from Erbil. The nearest large town is Al-Hamadaniyah.

What to see and do Several palaces and temples have been incompletely excavated in the citadel. Most imposing is the 'North-west Palace'. More than 200m by 120m, it was built by Ashurnasirpal II and renovated by Shalmaneser III (and probably later kings until the reign of Sargon II). Four vaulted tombs beneath the palace were excavated by the Iraq museum in 1989 and 1990. Inscriptions found in one of the tombs suggest that they are the graves of several Assyrian queens. These graves contained large quantities of gold jewellery and precious vessels and together constitute one of the greatest treasure troves ever found in modern times.

The restored south façade of the Palace of Ashurnasirpal II is decorated with reliefs, and the two doorways flanked by winged lions and bulls lead into the throne room. A few slabs were stolen from the wall of the palace during the post-2003 war looting, after which the site has been the scene of exchanges of gunfire between looters and guards.

Owing to its precarious position on the borders of Arab Iraq and Kurdistan, little further excavation work has been done at Nimrud since the retirement of Muzaham, the last director of archaeology here. He carried out the last major dig at the site; the excavation of the Ishtar Temple and Gate at the foot of the ziggurat. Here he unearthed the most remarkable small guardian bulls, sculptured in the Assyrian tradition but only just over 1m in height. Unknown anywhere else, they are now displayed in the Iraq National Museum in Baghdad. Since those days the site gets a periodical cleaning, and in 2013 the north side of the ziggurat foundations were cleared and exposed. Much to the horror of the civilised world, ISIS attempted to blow up the excavated walls but the extent of the damage is not known.

HATRA City of the Sun, Hatra was the first, and for a very long time, the only UNESCO listed site in Iraq. It is the only large ancient city in the 'round' in Iraq. The massive, circular city walls and towers and its inner masonry buildings are a great contrast to the mud-brick sites in the rest of Iraq. Although Hatra can be likened in situation, aspect and to some extent culture, with Palmyra and Dura Europos in Syria, it was an enigmatic city which probably originated from a combination of strategic and religious factors. The city gives a different impression from Palmyra at first glance with the circular plan of its city walls and the enormous vaulted structures in its central temple complex. The written language was a local dialect of Aramaic, with no Greek inscriptions being found and only three Latin ones from the brief period of Roman occupation. But the religious life of the city appears to have been almost completely Semitic. However, from our view point, as travellers to the city, its layout appears to be more familiar than the early Mesopotamian city sites and we can more easily recognise the architectural features from a Western past.

Security warning Although the site was well guarded by site police, the army and government authorities are not able to protect visitors, therefore the site is impossible to visit at the moment. Rumours are circulating that the site was bulldozed by ISIS in early 2015.

History Although the date of the foundation of Hatra cannot yet be determined with any accuracy, it was the capital of a client kingdom under an Arab ruler in the 1st century AD, when it was in the possession of an Arab dynasty probably founded by a prince called Sanatruq, who was obliged to recognise the suzerainty of Parthia. Serving as a religious centre for the Bedouin and a bulwark against the aggressive Roman armies, the majority of the buildings now visible probably date from this time. During the Parthian period Hatra withstood two memorable sieges. In AD116 that of Trajan failed before the formidable walls, containing seven gates and reinforced by round towers which guarded the town. In 198–199 Septimius Severus attempted to seize the place, with no greater success. Subsequently, after the eviction of the Parthian power by the Sassanids, Hatra became the ally of Rome. It was the Sassanid king Shapur I who put an end to Hatra's prosperity when he stormed the city around 258 and destroyed it. Hatra was subsequently abandoned.

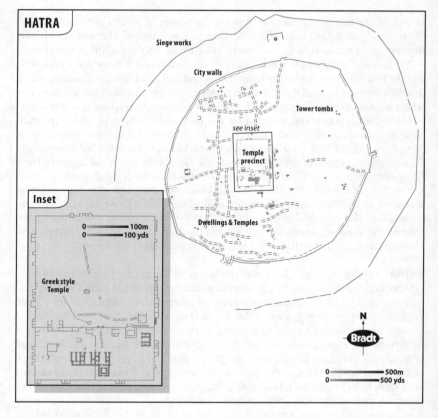

HATRA

Siege works

City walls

Tower tombs

see inset

Temple precinct

Inset

0 ——— 100m
0 ——— 100 yds

Greek style Temple

Dwellings & Temples

N

Bradt

0 ——— 500m
0 ——— 500 yds

Getting there

By road Some 25km out in the desert west of Highway 1 and 100km south of Mosul, the site is in desert terrain at an important junction of tracks and roads.

What to see and do The approach to Hatra from Highway 1 takes you past a few small settlements of local Bedouin. In the early days the local people, for a few dinars, would entertain you for tea. However, on the horizon are large military buildings which tell a different story; the area was a military site under Saddam and the Iraqi military continues to use it today. Sadly mass graves containing executed Kurdish women and children, victims of Saddam's Anfal Campaign, have been found here buried in a trench south of Hatra.

As you approach the site and are stopped at the army checkpoint, you are close by the original guest house hotel. This hotel was once administered by the Nineveh Hotel of Mosul and had two floors of bedrooms and a ground floor restaurant. In the 1980s obtaining a booking here was somewhat of a hit or miss arrangement. Since those days the building has been used by the Iraqi military and the US army and is now back with the Iraqi army. Hopefully in the future it can be restored to an ideal site hotel.

From a distance you will have seen the great construction crane, which has loomed over the site for at least 15 years. Hopefully one day it will be removed. A thousand metres in is the city entrance, through the outer walls and then through the inner city wall. It thrills the eyes to see such masonry in Iraq, and it

The Nimrud ivories, a cache of Iraq's greatest and most valuable antiquities are currently in storage in the vaults of Baghdad's National Central Bank and the Iraq Museum's storerooms. Some fragmentation has been caused by mould, as the ivories were submerged when the vaults of the bank were flooded. A throne base from Fort Shalmaneser, Nimrud and the banquet scene stele from the North-west Palace are in the Mosul Museum. It is hoped that it will be possible to put them back on display to the public one day. In the meantime we recommend that where possible a visit to the British Museum to view the Assyrian sculptures and bas reliefs on display there should be undertaken before visiting Nimrud and Nineveh.

is no wonder that the city defied its besiegers in the past. Once through the inner gate is the Greek-style temple, almost unique in Iraq, with the high Persian-style *iwans* behind it. Then you take in the brick reliefs of camels on the buildings close to the temple, proclaiming the main purpose of Hatra, that of a caravan city. The outline of the walls that protected the town can be easily traced by following the embankment around a circumference of more than 3km in diameter. They were built of ashlars and were reinforced by powerful bastions or round towers. A deep, wide ditch completely encircled the walls on the outside. The town's administrative sector, situated at its centre, was isolated from the rest of the town by a rectangular courtyard; seven gates gave access to it, the principal gate being on the east. Entering the enclosure by this gate you cross a great rectangular courtyard, then pass another wall isolating the courtyard from a group of religious buildings. On this side the precinct wall is pierced by two gates flanked by imposing towers. Each of the two gates gives access to a great *iwan* built on the axis of the entrance. On the left you will see the ruins of the temple of the Sun, which contains two small *iwans* and a larger one leading to the sanctuary proper, which contains a central chamber, formerly vaulted, surrounded by vaulted galleries.

To the right of the southern entrance to the precinct are the remains of a temple dedicated to the goddess Shahiro; it consisted of an *iwan* flanked by chambers to the east and by a gallery to the west. In 1961 several statues of princes, high priests and other notables of the town were brought to light here. In the southern sector of the precinct are the remains of two other temples; the one on the south was probably dedicated to the goddess Allath. In the northern sector of the precinct, opposite the northern entrance, are the ruins of a great *iwan* flanked by two smaller ones; this formed the main section of a temple not yet identified. The sanctuary, which lies next to it to the north, was probably consecrated to Mithras, whose cult spread throughout the whole Roman world from the 2nd century AD onwards. Between 1951 and 1955 the remains of 12 small temples were also unearthed; they were probably erected in the 1st or 2nd century. Near the double gate giving access to the central precinct were discovered the important remains of a Hellenistic temple and several statues of Apollo, Poseidon, Eros and Hermes. Within the city ramparts, you can see the remains of several funeral towers and stone wells. Statues of princes, high priests and important figures in the history of Hatra were discovered on the site in 1961 and transferred to the museums of Baghdad and Mosul.

The site has a history of looting, and although many attempts were made to loot its statues during the period of sanctions (1980–89), these statues can now be seen in the National Museum in Baghdad.

THE GOLDEN TREASURES OF NIMRUD

In 1989 and 1990 one of the world's great treasure troves was discovered at Nimrud. To find royal tombs with their contents still untouched is something virtually unknown in the Assyrian Empire. Many Assyrian kings were buried at Ashur, but their tombs have all been found empty of contents. Amazingly, after a hundred years of digging and after the final departure of the British Museum team, for whom the city had almost become their preserve, treasure was finally found. The story is a fascinating one.

Sayid Muzahim, the Iraqi director of the site, was supervising the clearance of the fallen walls and rubbish from the domestic quarter of the North-west Palace. Muzahim described to me how this thankless task suddenly became alive, as he noticed bricks indicating a vaulted roof, possibly that of a tomb. He kept very quiet about this until he had cleared more ground personally as the Nimrud site had proved vulnerable to looters. He then excitedly called Dr Donny George, Head of the Department of Antiquities and Heritage who immediately drove the 400km from Baghdad to Nimrud. Over three nights he and Muzahim entered the first tomb and photographed its contents. Then three more tombs, their contents intact, were discovered. Altogether almost 90kg of gold ornaments, crowns, cylinder seals along with many bronze objects were discovered and cleared. Several of the skeletons discovered in the tombs have been identified. One is that of Mulissu, wife and queen of King Ashurnasirpal II (883–859BC) discovered in Tomb 3. Another skeleton has been identified by inscriptions as that of Queen Yaba, wife of Tiglathpileser III (744–727BC).

Then in 1991 the First Gulf War began and this treasure disappeared from public sight. Its whereabouts was really not known for sure, although it was thought to be somewhere in Baghdad, probably in the National Museum, for safekeeping. As the wars progressed these treasures were feared lost, stolen or melted down. But no, the gods were kind and when the flooded Central National Baghdad Bank vaults were finally drained and forced open under supervision in 2003, three treasure boxes were found undisturbed. Now the treasure is safely stored and has been provisionally examined and enumerated, but it still awaits the time required to study the workmanship and provenance of individual pieces and finally to display it when safe to do so.

ASHUR (QALA'AT SHARQAT) Situated in low hills by the banks of the Tigris and opposite the growing village of Sharqat, Ashur is an enormously important site for the understanding of the Assyrian Empire. The city has had an unusually long history of occupation in contrast to other Assyrian capitals. It was a sacred site; the seat of the God Assur or Ashur, who was originally a local deity, but ultimately became the chief god of the city of Ashur and Assyria, and, with the latter's conquests, became supreme over all the other gods of Mesopotamia.

Security warning At the time of writing it is impossible to visit the area and there have been reports of damage to the site by ISIS.

History Ashur was founded at the beginning of the 3rd millennium BC, but it wasn't until later that it came to play an important role in the political life of Mesopotamia. According to tradition, an enclosure wall was built c2300BC by King Kikkia. The

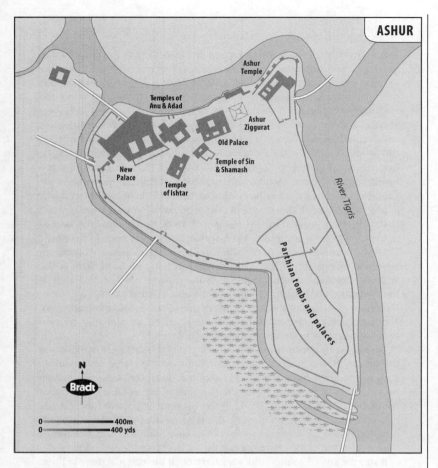

ramparts were restored on several occasions afterwards, in particular by an Assyrian king, Shamishad I. Ashur was the first capital of the first kingdom of Assyria. In the 13th century BC Tukulti-Ninurta I carried on his ancestor's work and enlarged it. He dug a deep, wide ditch in front of the walls. To commemorate his victory over Babylon, he dedicated a temple and ziggurat to the god Ashur. From this time the empire of Assyria grew and eventually came to encompass most of the Middle East and parts of Asia.

Sometime towards the end of the 11th century BC, Ashur became too exposed to invaders from the west and so the capital was moved to Nineveh. Thanks to its temples (which were restored by Sargon II (721–705BC) and Sennacherib (705–681BC) in particular) Ashur did not, however, decline in importance until the fall of the Assyrian Empire in 614BC. Its ruins were left to the elements for nearly 500 years until in the 2nd century BC the Parthians established themselves in the area and built a new city with a Hellenistic layout over the levelled remains of the old Assyrian capital. The largest building at that time was the huge Parthian Palace. Several temples and palaces, discovered among the Assyrian ruins, demonstrate the recovery in Ashur's fortunes. The Parthians stayed at Assor, as it was then called, for 300 years. It was probably sacked by Trajan in AD116, at the time he was besieging Hatra. Septimius Severus followed suit in 198, leaving the city almost totally destroyed. The population gradually declined, and the invasion of Shapur I, who

The destruction of the Assyrian Empire in 614–612BC left the city of Ashur destroyed and desolate for some centuries. The city was revived in the Parthian period and so was the cult of Ashur. Little is known about this god's personality. There are no myths or stories about Ashur that we can know and even his symbol has not been clearly identified. On some Assyrian reliefs there appears a winged sun disc with a bearded male holding a bow and arrows which could be identified as a representation of Ashur, but no confirmation can be found for this at the moment. Ashur's origins are obscure; possibly he originated as a west Semitic god or a Hurrian god. Most probably he was a manifestation of a weather god, with links to Mount Ebih (the mountain range southwest of the city), since he is listed as 'Lord of Ebih' in texts from the Ur III period (c2500BC). In the course of time, many other powers were ascribed to him. Perhaps inspired by the example of the Sumerian god Enlil, famous at Uruk, he became a supreme ruler of the pantheon of gods in the north. However, in contrast with the Babylonian deities whose family relationships stemmed from a complex pantheon, Ashur is left undefined. Only in the aftermath of Sennacherib's anti-Babylonian policy, which culminated in the destruction of Babylon (689BC) and the abduction of Marduk and other Mesopotamian deities, did Ashur's divine persona become more complex, although clearly patterned on that of Marduk. Indeed, the Sumerian creation epic was rewritten to feature Ashur instead of Marduk.

Sennacherib's efforts to make Marduk a god of the past were not followed through by his successors. Esarhaddon returned the statue of Marduk to Babylon, and rebuilt the temple his father had destroyed. Ashur once again became what he had always been, the local deity, but not just of the city of Ashur, but of the whole Assyrian Empire. His most important function was to be the focus of Assyrian identity. This is borne out by official inscriptions which stress the close connection between King, State and God, but also by the frequent use of Ashur in personal names. The epicentre and origin of this cult was the city of Ashur. Ashur may have been the national deity in times of great empires, when his name struck great fear into the populations of the Empire as inscriptions tell us, but ultimately Ashur is the God of the city of Ashur. He was there at the beginning of Assyrian history and was still there after the demise of the Mesopotamian states. Even today Nestorian Christians who live in northern Syria and northern Iraq call themselves 'Assyrians' and their official symbol is the god within the sun disc whom they believe to be Ashur, not only God, but a guardian of their identity.

captured Ashur in 257, delivered the coup de grace. It was completely forgotten during the Sassanid and Arab periods and only after the excavations carried out from 1903 to 1914 by a German expedition under Walter Andrae, was it possible to place the site of ancient Ashur with any certainty. The archaeologists discovered the remains of palaces, temples, walls and a town. They also cut a sondage (test) pit beneath the Temple of Ishtar which revealed levels dating back to the 3rd and early 2nd millennium BC, the first use of this technique in Mesopotamian excavations.

Getting there

By road Ashur is located 112km south of Mosul, in a magnificent setting on a stony promontory overlooking the Tigris on the east, near the Himrin Mountains. It is also easily reached from Hassuna and Hatra when exploring the area.

What to see and do The most striking feature of the site today is the ziggurat and temple devoted to the god Ashur, called the Temple of the Universe. The ziggurat dominates the ruin, and you should climb to the top in order to obtain a general view of the site and its position if you can. This main ziggurat (the city had three) was built on a square of 65m and like the majority of Mesopotamian ziggurats comprised of a central massif in unbaked brick with a coffering of baked bricks. Originally it belonged to the Temple of Enlil, the principal deity of Ashur; then it was dedicated to Ashur when the latter became chief deity in the reign of Tukulti-Ninurta I (1260–1232BC). In the 9th century BC Shalmaneser III restored it. Today it is considerably dilapidated. A gallery cut in the central massif of unbaked bricks allows a view of the structure's gigantic proportions. In 2013 the facing stones and ground levels of the ziggurat were exposed, and further work is being done as and when possible to prepare the site for visitors in the future.

Not far from the ziggurat, at a point of the salient on which the town is built, you will find the site of the temple of Ashur, one of the most ancient of temples. Founded in the 3rd millennium BC, it was restored or rebuilt several times, notably by Sargon II and Sennacherib. A temple with three *iwans* was built on this site by the Parthians in the 1st century AD. Further to the west stood the Temple of Anu-Adad, which contained two ziggurats measuring 36m by 35m. This building seems to have been begun in the 12th century BC in the reign of Assurreshishi and completed under Tiglath-Pilesar I (1115–1093). Its plan was appreciably modified in the time of Shalmaneser III (859–824BC), when the ziggurats had a side of not more than 26m. In the Assyrian period several palaces were built. The oldest stood between the great ziggurat and the temple of Anu-Adad; it was built about the beginning of the 2nd millennium BC and was occupied as a residence until at least the reigns of Adad-Nirari I (1310–1281BC) and Tiglath-Pilesar I, who carried out several restorations. The basements of the palace were later converted into a royal necropolis.

A little to the southeast of the Temple of Anu-Adad stood another double temple dedicated to the divinities of Sin and Shamash. It was built in the 16th century BC in the reign of Assurnirari I and was continually modified until the time of Sennacherib (705–681BC). The Andrae excavations revealed the existence of several temples dedicated to Ishtar, the oldest dating back to the 3rd millennium BC. Because of the city's great religious significance a succession of Assyrian kings were buried here, although their tombs were robbed in ancient times. Erosion by the waters of the Tigris is also damaging the site. Excavations which were carried out in early 2002 revealed some small houses and religious buildings, a very sophisticated drainage system and new tombs. The inner part of the city, which is home to the Parthian graves and palaces is fenced off.

IRAQ ONLINE

For additional online content, articles, photos and more on Iraq, why not visit www.bradtguides.com/iraq.

8

The Road South

We now travel along the road south to Basra, mythical home to Sinbad. The south is a land of contrasts; it is the most fertile land in Iraq located between the two rivers and steeped in ancient history – not only of Iraq but also that of much of our own civilisation. Encircling this fertile region is a rim of desert lands that border Syria, Jordan and Saudi Arabia. Added to this, the south is also the Shia Islamic heartland with the shrine cities of Kerbala and Najaf. We are embarking on a voyage of discovery into the past and present, with magnificent archaeological sites such as Babylon, Ukhaider, Nippur, Uruk and Ur.

HISTORY

RELIGIOUS HISTORY The Sunni-Shia (orthodox–heterodox) schism in the first half of the 7th century AD occurred due to differences over the leadership of the Islamic community after the Prophet Mohammed's death in Medina in AD632. The Prophet died without leaving any instructions regarding his successor. Just as the Prophet was basically a religious and spiritual teacher, but at the same time, due to circumstances, a temporal ruler and statesman, Islam has been since its very birth both a religious discipline and, so to speak, a socio-political movement. It is basically religious because the status Mohammed attained as the Apostle of God appointed and sent by Him to deliver His message to mankind, and political because of the environment and circumstances in which it arose and grew. Like Shiism, Islam's inherent nature has always been both religious and political, and these co-existing aspects are found side by side throughout its history. (See pages 19–20 for a full explanation.)

THE 20TH CENTURY The beginning of the 20th century was a time of increased Shia political activism when the *mujtahids* cultivated the image of the leaders

---

AUTHORS' NOTE

GETTING AROUND The reader has to be aware that travel in the south of Iraq is mostly fine on the major highways and towns, but travel to some of the more obscure ancient sites located in the countryside is fraught with difficulties such as very poor or non-existent roads and the presence of many checkpoints to pass through.

ACCOMMODATION Although we have provided details of the main (and sometimes only) hotels that we feel able to recommend, there are often many more very basic hotels in most of the towns and cities covered below, which would only be acceptable if there was absolutely no alternative.

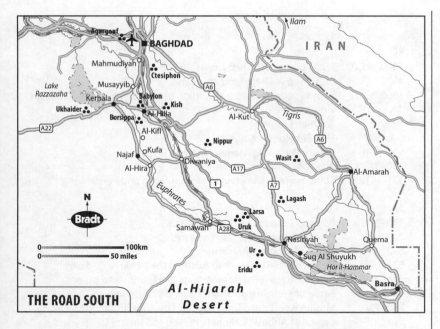

THE ROAD SOUTH

Al-Hijarah Desert

of the Muslim opposition. It was also the time of the introduction of a Shia secular education, a major departure from the curricula of the religious schools (madrassas) of the holy cities. In World War I a *jihad* was declared against the British by Turkey. It failed, and Iraq was fully occupied in 1918, but the *mujtahids* filled the power vacuum created by the departure of the Ottomans. By the 20th century some 5,000 Indians had settled in the holy cities. The first migrants were well-to-do members of the royal Nawabs family who arrived with their subjects. When their munificence decreased, the number of poor Indians in southern Iraq increased to the point where a 1929 report by the Protector of British Indian Pilgrims described Kerbala as 'a sink of Indian pauperism'. The 1920 revolt against British rule was supported by both the *mujtahids* and the *sayyids* (descendants of Prophet Mohammed) who perceived their positions to be threatened by them. The revolt was crushed.

Successive Sunni governments would seek to eradicate the power of Shia *mujtahids* and institutions in the country and to reduce the links between Najaf and Kerbala and Iran. While the Sunni ex-Ottoman officers and the royal family installed by the British had their differences, they were united in their desire to keep the Shias firmly under their thumb. The religious establishment struck back, and a *Fatwa* was issued stating that any Muslim who took part in the elections to the constituent assembly in 1924 would be shunned by his fellow Muslims and forbidden from going to the public bath. But the influence of the *mujtahids* and the *sayyids* started to decline. The Shias did not have a strong leadership, the Persian language presented a communication barrier between the *mujtahids* and the Arab masses, and the spread of secular education undermined the role of the madrassas. A modern legal system was established and the *sayyids* lost their traditional role as mediators. The government put an end to preaching about the Shia faith and arrested Shia emissaries who tried to convert the Turkmen in northern Iraq. The leadership of the Shias shifted from Najaf to the Iranian city of Qom following the death of Abu al Hassan Ishahani in 1946.

BC

6000–4000	Eridu, perhaps the first city as we know it.
4000	Kish, Nippur, Ur forming city states.
1900	Babylon emerged from the union of the Sumerian and Akkadian kingdoms.
1400	Assyrian Empire.
606–539	Neo-Babylonian Kingdom.
539–330	Rule of Persian Achaemenid Dynasty.
330–323	Alexander the Great.
331–AD129	Kingdom of Seleucid ruled Mesopotamia and Persia.

AD

130–226	Parthian Persians ruled ancient Iraq.
227–636	Rule of Sassanian Persian Dynasty.
632	Death of Prophet Mohammed.
637	Defeat of Persians by Arab forces at the battle of Qadasiyah.
661–750	Muslim world ruled from Damascus by Ummayad caliphs.
680	Battle of Kerbala led to Sunni-Shia divide in Islam.
750–1280	Muslim world ruled from Baghdad by Abbasid caliphs.
836	Capital of Abbasid Caliphate moved to Samarra for 56 years.
1258	The sacking of Baghdad by the Mongul Hulagu Khan and the founding of the Ilkhanid Dynasty.
1261	Caliphate moved from Baghdad to Cairo.
1408	The sacking of Baghdad by Timurlaine.
1509–33	Ismail Shah, founder of Persian Safavid Dynasty, conquered Iraq. The Persians favoured the Shia religious establishment.
1534–1918	Iraq ruled by the Ottoman Turks, who favoured the Sunni religious establishment.
16th century	Iranians converted to Shiism in large numbers.
18th century	Southern Iraq became a magnet for Persian religious scholars and their students after the Sunni Afghans captured Isfahan in Persia.
1737	Kerbala replaced Isfahan as the main centre of Shia scholarship.
1801	Kerbala sacked by Wahhabis.
1803	Construction of Hindiyya canal alleviated Najaf's water problems.
1805	Wahhabis laid siege to Najaf.
1843	Najib Pasha occupied Kerbala and returned it to Ottoman control.
1860s	Indians from Awadh migrated to Najaf and Kerbala in large numbers.
1875	Iranians exempted them from paying taxes.
20th century	Large-scale conversion of Iraqi tribes to Shiism, most of whom settled down and started farming.
1918	Religious scholars filled power vacuum created by the departure of the Ottomans and the end of World War I. The British Mandate began which led to the modern state of Iraq.
1920	Revolt against British rule.
1924	*Fatwa* issued against any Muslims who took part in the elections to the constituent assembly.
1930	Pilgrims began arriving by train, rather than camel train. Their stay in the holy cities was limited to 3 months.
1935	Shia lawyers in Baghdad and *mujtahids* presented a manifesto to

	the government calling for greater participation in parliament, government and the civil service and greater investment in Shia areas.
1938	Holy cities (Najaf and Kerbala) failed to develop alternative sources of income. Declining revenues from pilgrims and fees for the transportation of bodies to be buried in the holy cemeteries caused economic problems. Around half of Najaf's population unemployed.
1940s & 50s	Shias increased demands to secure government civil service posts.
1946	Leadership of the Shias shifted from the southern Iraqi city of Najaf to the Iranian city of Qom after the death of Abu al Hassan Ishahani.
1970s	Thousands of Shias expelled to Iran under the pretext of their Iranian origin.
1980	Execution of renowned Shia scholar Muhammad al Baqir Sadr and his sister Bint al Huda.
1980–88	Iranian pilgrims banned from Iraq during the Iran-Iraq war, economy of the holy cities suffered.
1991	Protests in the city of Diwaniyah against Saddam's refusal to leave Kuwait, followed by popular uprising throughout southern Iraq, crushed by Saddam's regime.
1998	Assassination of Ayatollah Ali al Gharavi.
1999	Assassination of Mohammed Sadiq Sadr.
2001	Tribal leaders and mayors in the south undertake to ensure Saddam's pictures and statues cleaned after acts of vandalism. Death in suspicious circumstances of Shia scholar Hussain Bahr al Uloom.
2003	Thousands of Shia pilgrims celebrated Ashura in Kerbala, the performance of rituals previously banned by Saddam's regime.
2004	Explosions in Kerbala and Kazimiya kill pilgrims celebrating Ashura. Moqtada Sadr's Shia militia end occupation of Najaf following mediation by Ayatollah Sistan.
2006	Two aides to Iraq's most senior Shia cleric, Grand Ayatollah Ali al Sistani, assassinated.
2007	Maysan handed over to Iraqi control. Moqtada Sadr returned after 4 months in Iran and called for Sunni–Shia co-operation to end the occupation. The British officially transferred control of Basra to the Iraqis.
2008	Prime Minister al Maliki orders crackdown on militia in Basra, sparking pitched battles with Moqtada Sadr's Mahdi Army. Hundreds are killed.
2009	Britain officially ends combat operations in southern Iraq. They hand control of their Basra base over to US forces.
2011	Radical Shia cleric Moqtada Sadr returns after 4 years of self-imposed exile in Iran. Al Sadr says his fighters will suspend military attacks on the US, to be resumed if the US fails to pull out in time.
2012	Bomb and gun attacks target Shia areas, sparking fears of a new sectarian conflict. Nearly 200 people are killed in bombings targeting Shia Muslims in the wake of the US withdrawal.
2013	Renewal of sectarian targeting of Iraqi Sunnis in southern Iraq.
2014	ISIS invasion of Iraq.

While the *mujtahids* were crushed, the Shia sheikhs were assimilated into the ruling establishment. They were rewarded for keeping order in the countryside and ensuring the steady flow of tax revenues to the government. They formed a strong alliance, which lasted until the revolution of Abdul Karim Qasim which overthrew the monarchy in 1958. As the holy cities declined in importance, the sheikhs failed to develop alternative sources of income and continued to rely on the dwindling money brought in by pilgrims and the corpse traffic. Government investment was negligible and by 1938 around half of Najaf's population was unemployed. The government also made life difficult by placing restrictions on the amount of rice that could be sold to Saudi tribes. In 1951 the quota was set at 3,000 tons for Najaf and 500 tons for Kerbala. There was also competition with Samawah and Zubair, two other granary centres. Baghdad, the city of bright lights and economic opportunities, became the focus of Shia migration. Despite the *Fatwa* on participating in elections which alarmed many Shias, they were eager to secure employment in government service. In 1935 Shia lawyers in Baghdad and the Arab *mujtahids* drafted a manifesto in an attempt to unite rival Shia sheikhs and force the government to accept their demands. These included Shia participation in parliament, government and the civil service in accordance with their numbers, government investment in health and education in Shia areas, inclusion of Shia teachings in the law school and the distribution of religious endowments to all Muslim institutions. The government did not respond to calls for negotiations over these demands, and the conflict between the government and the tribes of the middle Euphrates intensified: railway lines were torn up, martial law was declared, the villages of rebellious tribes were bombed. In the end the representation of Shia tribal sheikhs in parliament was increased.

During the 1940s and 1950s the power struggle between the Shias and Sunnis intensified as young, educated Shias were eager to secure government and civil service posts. They also resented their under-representation in the army and police force. State education in rural areas and Shia access to state education was largely the achievement of two main figures in the Ministry of Education: Abd al Karim al Uzri and Muhammad Fadil al Jamali. The government bureaucracy expanded, the number of Shia employees increased, but the Sunnis remained dominant in the state's institutions, pushing the Shias either towards the Iraqi Communist Party or the Islamic opposition. The Shias' support for the communists declined during the 1960s when they saw little change in the power structures. The Baathists failed to attract the Shias in large numbers as they advocated pan-Arabism, which the Shias equated with Sunnism. When it became clear that the Baath Party was controlled by the Sunni Tikritis (Saddam Hussein's tribe) many Shias shifted their allegiance to the Islamic Dawa Party under the leadership of Muhammad Baqir al Sadr. His books – *Our Philosophy* (published in 1959) and *Our Economic System* (1960) – presented an alternative political and economic ideology. The Baathists executed Baqir al Sadr and his sister Bint al Huda, a renowned female Islamic scholar, and expelled thousands of Shias to Iran under the pretext of their 'Persian connection'.

After the invasion of Kuwait and Iraq's defeat, the Shias (encouraged by outside influences), and the Kurds in the north, revolted against Saddam's regime. On 10 February 1991, Iraqis in the southern city of Diwaniyah encouraged by southern and outside political forces and the seeming weakness of Saddam after the invasion of Kuwait rose up and protested, resulting in much bloodshed. But no strong Islamic figure emerged to lead the resistance, which was mercilessly crushed by the regime's troops. The regime did not hesitate to shell the shrines and mosques in Najaf and Kerbala where the rebels hid. Tanks were painted with the slogan 'no more Shias after today'. By the end of March 1991 resistance was confined to guerrilla attacks, mainly in the marshlands. In an attempt to secure the loyalty of the Shia inhabitants of the south, Saddam found it necessary to appoint a Shia from Kerbala, Sadun Hamadi, as Prime Minister, and to hold meetings with important religious and tribal leaders from the south. In a gesture of reconciliation the damage to the shrines was repaired. But despite these gestures aimed at appeasing the Shias, the regime was determined to eliminate the influence of the religious establishment. A number of religious scholars, including Hussain Bahr al Uloom, died in suspicious circumstances. The Third River Project which reduced the water supply to some of Iraq's finest rice fields also undermined the south. Unable to make a living, many of the farmers moved to other areas. The south did not recover economically after the war as damage to the infrastructure, especially sewage and desalination plants, resulted in further impoverishment, and the small towns and villages had an air of decrepitude.

AFTER THE 2003 WAR The bitter memories of the allies' perceived betrayal of the 1991 uprising dampened the welcome extended to the Coalition forces throughout much of southern Iraq. Many people feared that Saddam would be allowed to return and the cycle of fear was not broken until his capture on 13 December 2003. Many of the Shias who received the worst treatment from Saddam's regime also suffered disproportionately during the 13 years of sanctions when the south was left to decay and disintegrate and, partially due to Iranian influence, adopted a viciously anti-Western stance. The Coalition forces encountered some of the heaviest resistance in Nasiriyah and Najaf. The south was guarded by troops loyal to Saddam who fought fiercely while the ordinary people, fearful of a re-run of the slaughter that followed the 1991 uprising, watched. The inhabitants of the heartland of Shia Islam welcomed the ousting of Saddam's regime as a signal for the end of oppression and a chance to gain political power from which they had been excluded since the days of the Ottoman Empire. But this new-found freedom is viewed with concern by moderate Shias and intellectuals. In the words of Iraqi writer Nabil Yunis Damman:

'We do not wish to emerge from the cloak of fanatical nationalism only to enter into the cloak of religious extremism. Just accept that there will be an Islamist government that will fall short of Iranian theocracy, but that will be nothing like Western-style democracy'.

In the holy cities a strict code of Islamic law is already being imposed. The women are clad in black, none venturing outside without a headscarf, posters of Islamic clerics decorate the streets, Iranian goods are in the shops, Iranian currency can be used and Farsi is spoken as well as Arabic.

KERBALA (SHRINE CITY) *Telephone code 32*

The first major Shrine City on the route south towards Basra is Kerbala. The name Kerbala is derived from the Babylonian word *kerb* (a prayer room) and *El*, Aramaic for God – hence God's temple. Kerbala's Shia sanctuaries are objects of great veneration and the city contains the shrines of Hussain ibn Ali, son of Imam Ali, and Abbas, Hussain's half-brother. Hussain is known among Shia believers as the Prince of Martyrs (*sayyid al shuhada*) because he was killed in his challenge

Daniel Bates and Amal Rassam, authors of *Peoples and Cultures of the Middle East*, described how 'Shahs, sultans, emperors and other rulers have all made gifts in demonstration of piety and perhaps in pursuit of legitimacy' to the holy shrines. Even quite recently the former Empress of Iran, Farah Pahlavi, donated two massive gold and jewel-encrusted doors to the sanctuary of Kerbala. The cupolas of leading shrines are leafed in gold and coloured mosaics, mirrors and gold and silver calligraphy embellish the walls. Every year thousands of pilgrims flock to Najaf and Kerbala, some with donations of gold and expensive jewellery. The cities are among the richest in Iraq, with pilgrims and agriculture contributing to the economic boom. Iranians are flocking to the holy cities in large numbers and buying property. Iranian currency is accepted and the cities are full of Iranian imports especially religious icons. Business has never been better for souvenir merchants and those involved in the religious tourism industry which caters for millions of pilgrims every year

Throughout the 19th century the Iraqi Shias were united during the procession in Kerbala. Sometimes it was difficult to distinguish where religion ended and politics began, as the processions in Kerbala and other cities often turned into anti-government protests. From 1930 onwards successive Iraqi regimes struck back by banning the processions. The people protested and the cycle of resistance and oppression continued until the overthrow of Saddam Hussein. Even today the celebrations are still filled with tension, as Shia pilgrims are now being targeted by sectarian suicide bombers.

Both Najaf and Kerbala made their money from the steady flow of pilgrims, mainly from Iran and India. The pilgrims had to be housed, fed, taken to the shrines and even provided with a 'temporary wife' (*mutah*). Things started to change during the 1920s and 1930s. The pilgrims began arriving by train, rather than on camels and mules, they needed passports and visas and could only stay in the holy cities for three months. The Iranian government made life difficult for its citizens (and for the Iraqis) by stopping the pilgrimage under the pretext that it was an obsolete Shia tradition that wasted money outside the country. Inside Iraq itself, the wealthy Shias did not support religious activity to any great extent and were not noted for their generosity in caring for the poor and needy. Religious schools were on a downward spiral; Kerbala was no longer the Shia seat of learning; Iranian students who did not receive allowances from home left Iraq; the secular education system competed with the religious establishment; the *mujtahids* did not always use the funds they received for the benefit of their students and the previously independent religious establishment began to rely on the state for funds. Gradually, the Iranian city of Qom took over as the centre of Shia learning. During the Iran-Iraq War (1980–88) Iranian pilgrims were not allowed to visit the holy cities, whose economy duly suffered.

Today Iranian and Shia pilgrims from all over the world are once again making their way to Kerbala. Following the imposition of sanctions against Iraq by the West in the 1990s, the majority of tourists who visited Iraq were pilgrims and this is still the case today. As many as 10,000 religious tourists a day have been seen in the holy cities, bringing in revenue of around US$2 billion a year.

to the accession of Muawiya's son Yazid to the caliphate. The tragic Battle of Tuff, in which Hussain and Abbas were martyred together with many others, became the most important event in Shia history and mythology. Kerbala emerged as a focus of devotion, particularly for Persian Shia believers. The city has been strongly influenced by the Persians, who were the dominant community, making up 75% of the population at the turn of the 20th century, when there were around 50,000 people in the city.

HISTORY In 1737 Kerbala replaced Isfahan as the main centre of Shia scholarship. The Ottoman governor Hassan Pasha (1704–23) had made life easier for pilgrims by building and renovating khans *en route* from Baghdad. In 1801, following the sacking of Kerbala by the Wahhabis, many students and *mujtahids* moved to Najaf, which in turn became the main Shia religious centre. Kerbala continued to maintain strong links with Iran though, and the Kammuna family, related to the Shahs, were custodians of the shrines and practically ran the city until the time of the British mandate. The most influential figures were two brothers, Fakhr al Din and Muhammad Ali Kammuna, who were both deported, the former for organising supplies to the Turkish forces and the latter for spreading anti-British propaganda. The control of the city then passed to seven *mukhtars* (tribal leaders), who started receiving a salary from the municipality. They were succeeded by Iraqi government employees. The influence of the Persians was curbed both by British attempts to establish an Arab character for the city and by a series of nationality laws, including a law that made it illegal for foreigners to occupy government posts. Arabic also became the language of administration. By 1957, Persians accounted for only 12% of the city's population, and most of these accepted Iraqi nationality. After the popular uprising in 1991 the Persian-looking bazaars of Kerbala were not rebuilt, but the pilgrimages continued. In March 2004, at the Festival of Ashura, thousands of pilgrims converged on Kerbala, beating their breasts with their fists and symbolically whipping their backs with chains, a ritual which had been banned for 30 years under Saddam. The excessive blood-letting of 2004 has subsequently been quietly discouraged.

The piety and unshakeable belief of the Muslims who visit the sanctuaries is illustrated by heart-rending acts of devotion, such as kissing the railings that surround the shrines. The atmosphere in this oasis of spirituality, in a country often characterised by violence, disaster and suffering, can be overwhelming. In 2013 some 15 million pilgrims took part in mourning rituals in the city.

GETTING THERE
By air In May 2007 final approvals were granted for the building of an international airport at Kerbala on the site of a former Iraqi air force base which was abandoned after the 1991 Gulf War. Although the foundation stone was laid in 2009, work is yet to begin on Al-Furat Al-Awsat or Kerbala Northeast, or Middle Euphrates or Imam Hossein Airport (the proposed name changes depending on which publication you read) and at the time of writing the government is in dispute with many farmers claiming legal tenure of the land needed for its construction. Don't expect to be able to fly into Kerbala any time soon.

By road Located 105km south from Baghdad, on Highway 8, the city is easy to get to as it is signposted from every direction. Note all the approach roads have outer and inner checkpoints. Security measures are fully implemented 24 hours a day.

Ashura, the tenth day of the Islamic month of Muharram (the Islamic calendar is based on the lunar cycle), when the massacre at Kerbala occurred in AD680, is one of the most popular times of pilgrimage. Events surrounding the death of Hussain are recounted in Shia mosques throughout the world and acted out as a *shabih* (passion play), accompanied by frenzied grief and self-flagellation. At the beginning of the 20th century, the *shabih* was so popular that in some villages in southern Iraq as many as 60 'actors' took part. As in the battle of Kerbala, they were divided into two rival camps. During the play actors on horseback were cheered by the audience who handed them rifles. The play ended when bullets were shot over the heads of the actors.

GETTING AROUND The only way to get around Kerbala and the bazaar areas is on foot as the roads are inaccessible to traffic, with concrete road blocks and checkpoints preventing vehicles entering for security reasons. However, these areas are compact enough to cover on foot. Outside the cordon of barriers and checkpoints, street taxis are widely available. Often you will see older and frailer pilgrims being transported from the roadblocks to the shrines in wooden carts and barrows, which are available for hire for a small fee.

Every year during the Festival of **Ashura**, it is traditional for pilgrims to walk between Baghdad and Kerbala and on to Najaf. Thousands join in with the trek, each with their colourful banners. They are provided with food by the local people along the way, who regard it as a religious duty to do so. They use local mosques to rest and to sleep in at night.

 WHERE TO STAY Despite there being around 300 hotels in the city, Kerbala is still underdeveloped in terms of accommodation for the millions of Shia pilgrims who make the pilgrimage to the religious sites there each year. It has no luxury hotels that meet international standards, despite the huge demand, and although hotel prices can be high, the level of quality of the accommodation can be very poor. You will find numerous small, local hotels on every street in Kerbala. Although they are classified 3-stars, 2-stars or 1-star, these ratings do not correspond in any way to European equivalents. Their clientel is almost exclusively pilgrims or local Iraqis, travelling in family or larger groups. The hotels are more often than not basic, with mainly family rooms, and lacking Western-style toilets. The dining rooms often bear more than a passing resemblance to school dining halls from the 1960s and 1970s.

Construction of more upmarket accommodation is under way, with the **Shaza Karbala Hotel** being built as part of the 620-roomed Al-Rawdatain Residences. It will be a 5-star hotel spread across the first three floors of the complex. Very few non-Muslims visit Kerbala as, with its strict adherence to Sharia principles (including no alcohol, a strict dress code for women in public and constant checkpoints to go through even when walking along the streets), it is not conducive to relaxation. Furthermore, apart from the shrines, there is nothing in the way of sightseeing. The few Western non-religious visitors tend to stay in the hotels listed below.

Upmarket

Karbala Rayhaan by Rotana (185 rooms) Bab Baghdad Main St; 332993; www.rotana. com/rayhaanhotelandresorts/iraq/karbala/ karbalarayhaanbyrotana. This hotel has a spa, fitness centre & 3 restaurants. The rooms have AC, complementary tea- & coffee-making facilities & high-speed Wi-Fi. There is a shuttle bus to the airport at an additional cost. *Rooms start from US$145 pp per night.* **$$$**

Mid range

Safir Hoda Wali Hotel (349 rooms) In the centre of Kerbala (less than 1km from Hussain's shrine); m 0770 941 3011; e info@safirkabala.com. An award-winning hotel, which was completed in 2008 & is part of the Safir Resorts & Hotel chain, though oddly enough it does not feature on their website (even though 2 hotels in Damascus do!). Nice hotel with good restaurants, catering mainly for Iraqi workers & local tourists. **$$$**

Naher Al-Jannah Hotel Bab Baghdad (in front of Alhusaenea's River); ⍾ 333847; e alnahher@yahoo.com. Rooms start from US$75 per night. **$$**

Alnoor Alsatte Hotel (70 rooms) Maitham Tamar St; m 0780 032 9004. All rooms have satellite TV, a minibar, an electric kettle & shower. The restaurant serves a buffet-style b/fast. Free Wi-Fi is available in all areas. Al-Imam Al-Abbas Shrine is 2 mins' walk from the hotel & Najaf Airport is 60 mins by car. *Rooms start from US$70 per night.* **$$**

Jarash Hotel m 0790 262 3728; e garashhoteel@yahoo.com. A good, comfortable hotel, with constant levels of service & a reasonable restaurant. Free Wi-Fi. From the hotel it is just a short walk to the shrines. **$$**

✕ WHERE TO EAT There are many dining-hall-style local restaurants which cater for pilgrims who can arrive in groups of hundreds at a time from a particular country or city, or as part of an extended family group. There are also small kiosks selling tea and street food along the main streets to the shrines and within the bazaar. The more upmarket hotels (such as the Karbala Rayhaan by Rotana, see above) have Western-style restaurants, but the cheaper hotels catering for tourists often have restaurants with long tables, where the same pre-packaged meal is endlessly placed in front of diners as they sit down. Needless to say in these establishments men and women are expected to sit at the appropriate male- or female-only table which are on opposite sides of the dining room from each other.

✕ Karbala Rayhaan by Rotana Hotel Bab Baghdad Main St; ⍾ 32 33. This hotel has three restaurants, Al-Fardous, offering buffet and à la carte meals all day; Al-Nakheel, an Oriental restaurant open in the evenings, and Al-Noor Café and Lounge, which is situated in the hotel's reception and is open all day.

SHOPPING The old city bazaars which are clustered around the shrines are a veritable treasure trove of tacky religious souvenirs, cheap clothing and footwear, endless jewellery shops and secondhand knick-knacks. Sugary sweets, so loved by the Iranian pilgrims are in abundance. For female visitors (particularly Western ones who may feel that they are not suitably clad), there is no problem in obtaining the correct attire to fit in with the pilgrims.

OTHER PRACTICALITIES It cannot be emphasised too strongly that Kerbala is a highly orthodox, religious place. Alcohol is strictly forbidden. For women, dressing modestly here is absolutely essential (see page 100 for important advice on what is expected in Kerbala).

Shoes, cameras and mobile telephones need to be left outside when you visit a shrine. These can safely be deposited at the stands outside the shrines designated for this purpose. You will usually be given a token to retrieve them on your return and a few IQDs will be expected in payment. Women visitors, especially Western, non-Muslim ones, will generally be expected to wear the *abayah* provided by the shrine, irrespective of how well covered up they may be by their own clothing. As these are not washed very frequently, this can be a somewhat unpleasant experience, particularly as the local way of securing these is by gripping the material firmly with the teeth. Bring safety pins and hair-grips with you, especially if you are not very tall, as the *abayahs* are all one size and length and can be a positive trip hazard for the unwary.

CORPSE TRAFFIC

For Shias it has always been desirable to be buried close to either Imam Ali in Najaf or Hussain in Kerbala. The mass Shia conversions in Iran and Iraq in the 16th century started the 'industry' that has come to be known as 'Corpse Traffic'.

In the early days corpses were transferred principally from Iran by caravan contractors who worked for the Shrine Cities. As the cities developed into major pilgrim centres, this traffic increased and became an important source of income. The conversion of the Iraqi Bedouin to Shia Islam also enhanced the trade as the Bedouin saw this as a way to reap heavenly rewards. The image of Imam Ali as the protector of the dead still holds strong even today among the rural tribes of Iraq.

'The livelihood of shroud makers, grave diggers, tomb builders, servants in the shrines as well as the *ulema* and students was always closely connected to the corpse traffic. The newly arrived corpse was washed, wrapped in a shroud and taken for burial, accompanied by hired mourners and *ulema* who chanted Koranic verses. The servants of the shrines used to circulate the corpses within the shrines before burial, an act of which was considered meritorious for the dead and for which the servants were well paid. Students were paid for trimming the lights and for reciting prayers over the graves of the dead where families had sent money for that purpose.' (from *The Shias of Iraq* – Yitzhak Nakash)

The trade has fluctuated along with the fortunes of the cities and indeed those of Iraq itself. Under British rule attempts were made to try to regulate the traffic and these days, with modern health regulations, the trade has become more formal and organised. It is still possible when visiting the Shrine of Ali to sometimes see a cortege carried by chanting men circulating around the shrine for the blessing prior to burial.

The presence of Moqtada al Sadr and his Mahdi Army was felt in Iraq following the overthrow of Saddam. Moqtada al Sadr is extremely popular among the Shia masses, and many Iraqis saw him as a heroic symbol of resistance to the occupation by the Western forces. He identified Iraq's main enemies as the occupation forces, the Saddamists (Baathists) and the Nawasib (radical Sunni Muslims who see the Shias as heretics who have to be exterminated). He is also opposed to al-Qaida. Despite his anti-American stance he subsequently participated in the political process and his followers gained seats in the Iraqi Parliament and even reached ministerial positions, running the health and transport departments.

Al-Sadr's appeal comes from the mixture of religion (he called for an Islamic democracy) and nationalism, which he espoused. His background also proved invaluable. He was the youngest son of Muhammad Sadiq Baqr al Sadr, a senior cleric assassinated in 1999 by Saddam's agents after trying to counter secularism in Iraqi society, opposing the Iraqi Communist Party and the Baath Party, and helping set up the religious Dawa Party. In his thirties, al Sadr's followers elevated him to the rank of hujjat al-Islam (sign of Islam, the third highest rank in the Shia clerical hierarchy).

When Saddam's regime was ousted, al Sadr, from his power base of a network of charitable institutions, instructed his followers to distribute food and patrol the streets in the poor Shia suburbs of Baghdad. His ability to mobilise the Shia masses was clearly illustrated in April 2007 when an estimated 1.5 million people turned up for a massive rally in Najaf demanding that the government agree to a timetable for the withdrawal of foreign troops. The Mahdi Army took control of Sadr City, the Baghdad shanty town with a population of two million, much of Baghdad and some areas in southern Iraq. The Shias relied increasingly on the Mahdi Army to protect them from sectarian violence and suicide bombers, but al Sadr denied that death squads killing Sunnis were really members of the Mahdi Army. His followers clashed regularly with American troops, the Iraqi army and police and members of rival Shia militias.

An attempt to assassinate al Sadr was revealed in the book *The Occupation of Iraq: Winning the War, Losing the Peace* by Ali Allawi, the former Finance Minister. The Iraqi National Security Adviser, Dr Mowaffaq I Ruabie, negotiated an end to fighting with al Sadr in Najaf in August 2004. Al Sadr wanted the old city of Najaf to have special status like the Vatican. Al Ruabie was due to meet al Sadr in a house in Najaf to finalise the agreement, but as he headed for the house marines bombarded it. Al Sadr had not arrived yet and so escaped. Fearing for his life, he left Iraq in January 2007. He returned later that year and in a characteristically fiery sermon in Kufa to 6,000 worshippers called for Sunni-Shia co-operation to end the occupation. Moqtada Al Sadr and his Mahdi Army officially stood down in May 2007. In February 2014 he announced his withdrawal from politics but in June his supporters held several marches declaring: 'We can deal with ISIS ourselves.'

Note Tourist groups will need to be accompanied by an Arabic-speaking Iraqi Muslim guide to obtain the best out of your visit. They can negotiate for any camera use (sometimes allowed, sometimes not) hopefully for the entire group, but more usually just one camera per group is allowed, and just in the outer courtyards and

The Road South   KERBALA (SHRINE CITY)

8

prayer halls. Entry for non-Muslims into the actual shrine rooms is forbidden. Otherwise you will be welcomed by the guardians who are responsible for the shrines and who are only too pleased to show you around.

WHAT TO SEE AND DO The town is split into two: Old Kerbala, famous for its shrines, and New Kerbala, the residential district containing Islamic schools and government buildings. There are more than 100 mosques and 23 religious schools in the city, the sole reason for travellers to visit.

The mosques of Hussain and Abbas stand out on their own as islands in the middle of a city whose activities are centred around the wants and needs of the pilgrims. **Hussain's Mosque and Shrine** is surrounded by a wall with eight gates. The main gateway is surmounted by a clock tower decorated with glazed blue and gold earthenware. The three small bulbs on the dome, which is covered in gilded copper, indicate the importance of the mosque. It is said to have been built on the site of the Battle of Kerbala, fought in AD680 between Ummayyad partisans and the supporters of Ali, who were led by Hussain. It has a gilded dome surrounded by two golden minarets. The date of the construction of the first sanctuary is unknown, but it is known that in 850, Mutawakkil ordered its destruction and forbade pilgrimages to this holy place. In 979 Azud el Dowleh, a Persian governor, built a mosque on the site. This burned down in 1016 but was subsequently rebuilt. The shrine consists of the mausoleum, galleries, hall and courtyard measuring 95m by 75m. There are ten gates, each with an archway and decorated with tiles and Arabesque. The Mecca gate is also known as 'The Golden Gate' as it is covered in gold and silver. The shrine has 65 galleries, many with rooms especially reserved for religious students, which later became graves for the *ulama* (scholars).

The second major shrine in Kerbala is that of Abbas, Hussain's half-brother, who died with him at the battle of Kerbala. The Abbas Shrine has nine gates decorated with glazed tiling leading into the mosque. The outer gateway is adorned with earthenware stalactites and surmounted by two small amortisements in the shape of minarets. The third gateway is flanked by two minarets, the lower parts of which are decorated with glazed bricks. A balcony supported by corbelled stalactites is surmounted by ribbed amortisement covered with gilded copper sheeting above each minaret. The shrine is 4,370m². On the sides of the courtyard are several galleries and rooms in which *ulama*, sultans, emirs and ministers have been buried. In the middle of the shrine is the tomb of Abbas, over which there is a huge dome with Koranic verses and the Prophet's sayings inscribed in gold. The dome is flanked by two tall minarets. The sanctuary proper is surmounted with a cupola in glazed earthenware. The mausoleum is made of pure gold and silver, with inlays of mina (blue stones) and precious stones. The vault of Abbas contains treasures and antiques that cannot be valued. It has more than 16 Korans, one of which is written in Kufic style, plus gold, golden lamps, Persian carpets, gold crowns and chains inlayed with precious stones.

There is now a fenced walkway between the two shrines and sleeping areas alongside for the many pilgrim families. The shrines themselves are being enlarged again, with newly tiled walls around each building, to the point of being almost unrecognisable to even a most recent visitor of a year ago.

AROUND KERBALA

The city is a continually expanding sprawl, with new suburbs and housing in various stages of construction. For the Western visitor the mass of electrical wires across the streets in the suburbs has to be seen to be believed. A newly built road now takes visitors through the suburbs to join up with the old Haj road to Saudi Arabia by way of **Lake Razzazaha (Bahr Al-Milh),** Iraq's second largest lake, which is located northwest of Kerbala city. Created in 1969 thanks to a drainage canal built to subvert the Euphrates' flood waters, it is approximately 76km long (from the beginning of the Al-Majarah channel to the White Valley near Kerbala city) and 40km wide, with a maximum depth of 17m. Once it was the centre of the local fishing industry, a lake teeming with commercial activity, fish and avian life. Today Lake Razzazaha is littered with abandoned fishing nets and the debris of the small wooden boots that used to ply their trade here. Two decades ago, the lake spanned an area of 1,800km² It was fed by the Euphrates river and nearby Lake Habbaniyah as well as rainfall, groundwater sources and the occasional flooding. Various fish species thrived in the lake, as did migrating birds, and the fishermen earned a good living. But the last floods occurred in the late 1990s, following which Saddam Hussein ordered the closure of waterways that fed the lake after the southern Iraqi Marshes became a refuge for Iraqis involved in anti-government, Shiite Muslim-dominated rebellions. Since then it has been dying a slow, dry death, and it is feared that it may dry out completely in the next few years. Saline levels in the remaining water have risen dramatically and some species of fish have disappeared, along with some of the birds that used to inhabit the area. The fishermen have also started to move on.

AT-TAR CAVES The At-Tar caves are a complex of some 400 caves carved out of the flanks of a series of marly (fine-grained sedimentary rock) escarpments alongside Lake Razzazaha. From March 1971 to December 1977, the At-Tar caves were excavated by the Japanese Archaeological Expedition in Iraq.

History According to carbon-14 dating, it appears most probable that the primary carving of these caves dates from the middle of the 2nd millennium BC. Although very few archaeological findings datable to the primary carving have been found, a number of burials have been unearthed in the crushed stone, which are datable by carbon-14 dating to between the 3rd century BC and the 3rd century AD. These burials contained human skeletons and in the region of 4,000 fragments of textile, leather goods and rush mats. Three distinct methods of burials were found as follows:

1) Bones wrapped with textile and placed on rush mats laid upon crushed rocks;

2) Bones wrapped with textile and placed on a pile of textiles which was laid on crushed rocks;

3) Bones wrapped with textile and placed on a pile of textiles on rush mats which were then laid on crushed rocks.

Sometimes leather was used to cover the bones, textiles and rush mats.

Getting there The At-Tar caves are situated 110km southwest of Baghdad and about 80km west of Babylon. The site of the caves occupies the easternmost border of the Iraqi southwestern desert (Syrian Desert), standing just off the main Haj desert road. The caves are not signposted, but are easily seen from the road. Vehicles can drive so far towards them, after that it is a case of getting out and walking. As explained above, Lake Razzazaha is shrinking, so the caves are no longer on the lakeside, but are surrounded by desert sands.

Other practicalities There is no infrastructure in place for tourists at the caves, no admission fee, guides or guide book. You are free to wander around and explore, climbing up the dunes and rocks to enter the caves where this is possible and within your physical capabilities. The wind and the constantly shifting sands mean different parts are visible and accessible at different times. They can also often make visibility and photography very difficult.

What to see and do The caves have horizontal ceilings and extremely uneven floors, caused by extensive digging as well as by the prevailing weather conditions. Some caves even have sudden descents as deep as 4m. Some of the caves were carved in such a way that they connected up with each other like a maze. Some of the caves are now totally filled from floor to ceiling with crushed stones, but others are still open, including the caves dug at the central portion of the hill. Sand, blown in from the desert by wind, has accumulated on the crushed stones especially near the cave entrances, which can make access difficult.

UKHAIDER

Dating back at least to AD600, this palace-fortress, whose name means a little green place, is located in the desert far from civilisation. The majestic structure is nearly 21m high with vaulted rooms surrounded by fortified walls. Partly because of its remote location in the desert and partly owing to the stout combination of stone

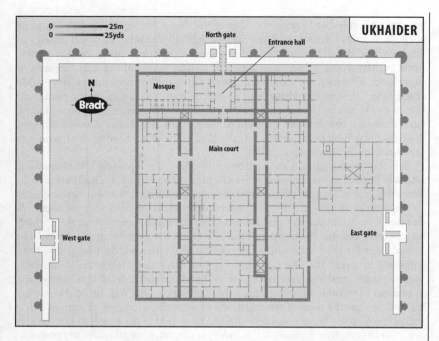

0 ————— 25m
0 ————— 25yds

North gate

Entrance hall

N

Bradt

Mosque

Main court

West gate

East gate

and wooden ties in its construction, Ukhaider is one of the best preserved and most impressive antiquities of Iraq. Coming into view from a considerable distance, the first sight of this colossal façade as one approaches from the desert, whether by camel or car, is a thrill even for the most unimaginative traveller.

HISTORY By all accounts it seems probable that Ukhaider dates from a period when the Arab principalities along both fringes of the Arabian desert had become aware, by their contacts with Persians on the one side and Romans on the other, of the merits of buildings more solid than goat-hair tents, as well as the possibilities of a more sedentary and luxurious life than that familiar to their hardy Bedouin ancestors. Scholars argue as to whether Ukhaider was built a little before the time of Mohammed and the Arab wars of conquest (so should be considered as a blending of Persian and Byzantine art), or whether it dates from the early years of the Islamic era (and can therefore legitimately be claimed as one of the archaic jewels of Arab architecture). Further investigations and some excavating have now satisfactorily demonstrated that both these theories are in some measure correct. One of the courts in the palace itself was found to contain a *mihrab* (a prayer niche indicating the direction of Mecca), along with other evidence showing that it had served as a mosque. Therefore it is correct to say that it was built (at least partly) in the early Islamic period. However, several unfinished (and therefore locally carved) Byzantine capitals, some even with the familiar 'wind-blown acanthus' ornament, used in conjunction with Persian vaulting and other Sassanian architectural features, indicate that the builders of Ukhaider ignored Arab styles of architecture which already existed in Yemen and the Hejaz, preferring to draw their inspiration from non-Islamic countries instead.

As well as disagreement among archaeologists as to when Ukhaider was actually built, there is also disagreement as to its purpose. Before the discovery of the *mihrab*, Ukhaider was attributed to the time of the Lakhmid dynasty of Arab princes, who ruled at Hira on the edge of the desert in the 6th century. As to its purpose, it is known that the Lakhmids established a number of desert palaces in this area, one of which was intended as a sanatorium for an ailing Persian prince, while the remaining palaces also appeared to have been built as health resorts of some kind. Alternatively, the contemporary Ghassanid princes on the Syrian side of the desert are known to have built a series of 'hunting palaces' on the road from Mecca to Damascus. However, Ukhaider does not give the impression of falling into either category. Another suggestion, made by the late Shukry Aloussy, was that the palace was built by a Christian Arab called Ukhaider, a Kindite chief, who was expelled from Arabia in about 635.

A further theory is that it was built by Isa ibn Musa, the nephew of Caliph Mansur, who was famous in his declining years as a millionaire recluse. Isa had been heir to the caliphate, but Mansur, having other ideas for the succession, spent a great deal of his reign trying to get rid of him. He used every trick in the book to bring about his demise, but without success. Following a failed attempt to poison him, from which he recovered but lost his beard and the hair of his head, Isa became a permanent invalid. Mansur then enlisted the help of Khalid the Barmecide, who got 30 false witnesses to swear that Isa had consented to surrender his rights. Meanwhile, Mansur summoned him to bring his son to the palace and ordered his chamberlain to pretend to strangle the boy in his father's presence. This was the final straw for Isa, and he signed a deed of renunciation in exchange for an honorarium of half a million gold coins. Then, disgusted with life, he retired to his estates to live the rest of his life in complete isolation. If this theory is correct, it seems extremely probable that the half million was partly spent on building Ukhaider.

One of the first European travellers to stumble upon the ruins of Ukhaider was an unknown Englishman, who in the middle of the 18th century gave a brief but astonishing report of his discovery to Niebuhr, the German geographer. Then in 1909 Gertrude Bell included it in one of her desert pilgrimages and conscientiously made plans of the walls, not realising that a Frenchman called Massignon had already done so two years previously. For Gertrude Bell, it was 'of all the wonderful experiences that have fallen my way the most memorable'. She said: 'I have sometimes found myself longing for an hour out of a remote century, wherein I might look my fill on the walls that have fallen, and stamp the image of a dead world indelibly upon my mind. The dream seemed to have reached fulfilment at Ukhaider. There the architecture of a bygone age presented itself in an unexampled perfection to the eye. It was not necessary to guess at the structure of vaults or the decorative scheme of niched façades – the camera and measuring tape could register the method of the builder and the results which he had achieved.'

Ukhaider was indeed her dream come true. The cool interior of the castle gives a vivid impression of what living in the early Islamic period was like to even the most unimaginative visitor.

GETTING THERE Ukhaider is located 45km southwest of Kerbala, 200km from Baghdad.

WHAT TO SEE AND DO The site consists of a fortified enclosure approximately 160m by 160m, about a third of whose area is occupied by a rectangular palace building. The main gate, which is heavily protected with masonry, leads straight into the palace. On the right, on the outside of the walls, there is a long annexe building. Inside the main gate is a wide entrance hall which leads into the central Court of Honour. This part of the building was originally three stories high, and stairs lead upwards on the right-hand side of the hall.

On the opposite side of the Court of Honour, facing the entrance, is what Gertrude Bell called a 'Liwan Group' of reception rooms. The great arch of the central *iwan* was originally framed in a *pishtaq* or frontispiece, a most characteristic feature of Persian architecture. The cloistered court, now identified as a mosque, is on the right of the entrance. Small and partly reconstructed with fragmented marble columns of different origins (taken from Byzantine churches) the mosque's *mihrab*, which faces in the direction of Jerusalem rather than Mecca, has generated considerable controversy. The remainder of the ground floor is mainly taken up by five bays or detached groups of living quarters, each with its own courtyard. A passage runs all around the top of the outer fortification wall, giving access to the vertical slots in the machicolations, meant for dropping uninviting substances on anyone attempting to attack the base of the wall.

During the past 20 years the castle has been heavily restored to over-perfection from the crumbling deserted desert ruin seen by Bell. The building is ideal for exploration.

AROUND UKHAIDER

Approximately 10km from Ukhaider are the ancient Christian settlement sites of **Al-Qusair**. Al-Qusair was an important centre of Christianity before the coming of Islam to Iraq in the 7th century. In 2009 a team of Iraqi archaeologists excavating at Al-Qusair unearthed what is believed to be the oldest church in Iraq. Built in the 2nd century, it is part of an extensive monastery containing several churches. It is believed that the excavated parts contained three halls as well as the altar. Although the archaeologists' aim was to fully unearth the church and display the remains to the public, all digging is currently in abeyance and it is not known when it will start again. Items which were found at the site have been handed over to the Iraq National Museum in Baghdad. This site is an extraordinary place situated out in the desert and totally obscured when the wind blows. Left just as you find it by the archaeologists who had to abandon it when threatened by insurgents, it fires the imagination with its small heaps of pot sherds and the plastered walls of the monastery. Not to be missed; one day excavations will begin again and the Christian past of this whole area will be much enlightened.

Ukhaider also sits close to where the road splits and the Haj road travels on to the Saudi Arabian border via **Nukhaib** and the border town of **Judaidat Arar**. The road these days is used mainly by heavy trucks carrying goods between the two countries. With the many road checkpoints and no Saudi Arabia visa to legitimise our presence, we have not explored this road much beyond Ukhaider and Ain Al-Tamr.

Approximately 15km past the Al-Qusair track turning and close to the lake is the historical city and once important town of **Ain Al-Tamr** (ancient Shuthatha). Ain Al-Tamr was built in the pre-Christian era and flourished in the early Christian era, but did not acquire any particular importance until the Arab conquest, when it became a thriving military and trade centre and an important military base for the Arab invasion of Persia and Central Asia. It was also the birthplace of Musa Ibn Nusair, the Arab general who conquered Spain in the 8th century AD. Historically, there is little to be seen there today. It was once a very large oasis, famous for its dates and camels, but a little fly blown from the visitor's viewpoint and hardly worth the extra mileage unless totally dedicated.

AL-HILLA Telephone code 30

Moving slightly inland brings you to Al-Hilla, the capital of Babylon Province; its name means beauty in Arabic. The main claim to fame of Al-Hilla is that it is close to ancient Babylon, some 25km to the east, which is one of the pearls of Iraq and a place which many people have been enthralled to read about for centuries.

HISTORY A town known as Al-Jamiayn was founded in the 10th century AD on the banks of the Euphrates river. Then in 1101 on the opposite bank of the river Sayfu-i-Dawla Saddiqa built a village called Al-Hilla. Slowly Al-Hilla grew up from these foundations, with many of the houses being built with bricks taken from the site of ancient Babylon. It has been said that some of the largest and finest houses in the town 'borrowed' some of the famous coloured tiles from ancient Babylon. Al-Hilla also became a Shia centre of learning and religious education. Later, under the Ottomans, it became an important administrative centre and this continued under the British Mandate. In the 19th century, the Hilla branch of the Euphrates started to silt up and much of the agricultural land was lost to drought. However, this loss was reversed by the construction of the Hindiyya Barrage by the British between 1911 and 1913, which diverted water from the deeper Hindiyya branch of the Euphrates into the Hilla canal. The latest history does not read well; unhappily, after the demise of Saddam Hussein, mass graves containing over 3,000 bodies were discovered in the city area, victims of his regime and the persecution of the Shia. Some 60,000 such victims have so far been discovered in pits across the south of Iraq. Today the city is a sprawling industrial conurbation with a river port and large grain market.

GETTING THERE Al-Hilla is 100km south of Baghdad on the Hilla branch of the Euphrates close to the sites of ancient Babylon, Borsippa and Kish.

WHAT TO SEE AND DO The Euphrates runs through the middle of Al-Hilla. It is surrounded by date palm trees and other forms of vegetation, providing a cool, green oasis in the middle of the otherwise arid landscape. It is extensively irrigated with water provided by the Hilla canal, which enables it to produce a wide range of crops, fruit and textiles. There is a large central mosque and several shopping streets. It is also a focal point for sectarian violence and normally visitors are advised to travel through Al-Hilla quickly and straight on to Babylon.

BABYLON

'Babylon the great, Mother of Harlots and the abominations of the earth', so it sayeth in the book of Revelation in the Bible. The Babylon that has left its imprint on the history of the world is the Babylon from the time of Nebuchadnezzar II onwards – two centuries of glory and decadence when the arts and sciences flourished and when there was an unprecedented boom of prosperity.

HISTORY Although the high water table has made investigations deep into Babylon's early history almost impossible, excavations show that in Akkadian times (around 2350BC), Babylon was a small village. During the next six centuries it grew in size and importance until it became the capital of the famous law-giver and social reformer King Hammarupi (1792–1750BC). After his reign and for the next thousand years or so it was surpassed by other Mesopotamian cities in power and influence. After being partly rebuilt following its sack by the Assyrian king Sennacherib in 689BC, it was set out in new lines by Nabopolassar, founder of the Neo-Babylonian Empire, and this work was continued by his celebrated son, Nebuchadnezzar II, who succeeded him in 604BC. Having first driven out the Egyptian forces occupying Syria, he set about

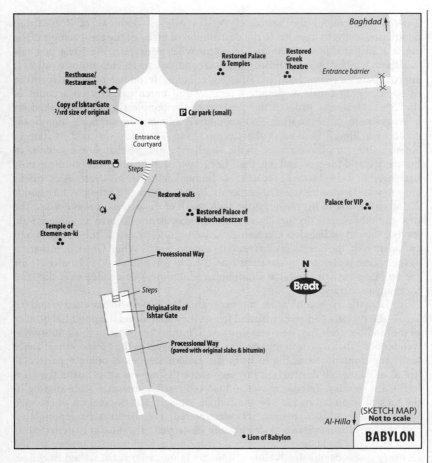

BABYLON

(SKETCH MAP)
Not to scale

Key items on map:
- Baghdad
- Restored Palace & Temples
- Restored Greek Theatre
- Entrance barrier
- Resthouse/Restaurant
- Copy of Ishtar Gate ²/₃rd size of original
- Car park (small)
- Entrance Courtyard
- Museum
- Steps
- Restored walls
- Restored Palace of Nebuchadnezzar II
- Palace for VIP
- Temple of Etemen-an-ki
- Processional Way
- N / Bradt
- Steps
- Original site of Ishtar Gate
- Processional Way (paved with original slabs & bitumin)
- Al-Hilla
- Lion of Babylon

completing his father's vision of making Babylon the most magnificent city in the world. He laid out broad streets and squares on a grid pattern, paved with bricks and lined with imposing buildings. One of the most impressive structures was the great **Processional Way,** which passed through the Ishtar Gate, resplendent with its two pairs of towers embellished with alternate rows of bulls and dragons in relief against a background of blue glazed bricks. He also rebuilt and restored the massive city walls and the Temple of Marduk (often associated with the biblical Tower of Babel) as well as creating for himself a magnificent palace (the Southern Palace) which was most likely linked to the Hanging Gardens themselves. Finally, he strengthened with new walls the banks of the River Euphrates. Although it ran through the centre of the city at that time, it subsequently moved steadily westwards and now just skirts the ruins.

This extraordinary period of construction was, however, short lived. The fortunes of the city declined sharply after the death of Nebuchadnezzar in 562BC and it fell without a struggle to Cyrus, the Persian king, in 539BC, and became somewhat of a backwater. The seat of Persian power moved to Persepolis, far to the east, and Babylon was relegated to a satrapy (Persian province) called Ebirnari, meaning 'Beyond the River'. However, Persian domination was resented; and a subsequent rebellion was put down by Darius, who reconquered the province.

Towards the end of the period of Persian rule an outbreak of Zoroastrian fanaticism seems to have led to the destruction of many of the great temples. The ziggurat in Babylon was a mound of rubble when Alexander the Great first saw it, although it had apparently been in good condition when Herodotus wrote of it approximately a century earlier. (Strangely enough, Herodotus makes no mention of the Hanging Gardens, despite a lengthy and much exaggerated account of the city.) Alexander ordered the clearing of the temple site and embarked on a programme of restoration and rebuilding, but before anything significant could be achieved he died in the city in 323BC. His body was laid in state in Nebuchadnezzar's throne room in the Southern Palace so that all the soldiers in his army could file past and pay their last respects, indicating this building must have been in a good state of repair then. Immediately after his death, Alexander's empire was divided between his generals, Babylon falling to Seleucus I. In about 275BC the centre of his power, along with much of the population, moved to the new capital Seleucia on the Tigris, close by what is now known as Salman Pak, leaving the city of Babylon increasingly decaying and deserted. This led Strabo to comment that 'the Great City has become a great desert'. When Greek domination of the region was ended by the Parthians, the city was plundered for materials for the building of their capital at Ctesiphon and darkness descended over the land for many centuries.

Initially, the irrigation system was maintained by those who marched to and fro across the region as empires rose and fell, as they all realised the potential bounty of the land between the two rivers and saw to it that the source of this bounty was well tended. That was until the coming of the Mongols in the 13th century. These terrifying nomads, sweeping in from the eastern steppes, brought a particular brand of wholesale destruction not seen since the incursions of Attila the Hun in the 5th century. Terrible massacre followed terrible massacre, culminating in the sack of Baghdad in 1258 by the Ilkhan, Hulagu. The population of the city, approximately 800,000 people, was slaughtered; the countryside depopulated and the irrigation systems systematically destroyed. The Mongols departed as quickly as they had come, but just as the region was beginning to make a partial recovery it was dealt a death blow in 1401 by Timur, who again sacked Baghdad. The countryside was reduced to a dismal tract of miasmic marsh alternating with arid desert, a situation that has only been reversed in the 20th century.

ROBERT KOLDEWEY 1855–1925

Born in Blankenberg, Germany, Robert Koldewey studied archaeology, architecture and the history of art. He acquired his experience and great expertise excavating not only in Mesopotamia, but also in Syria, Greece, Italy and Sicily.

During his time at Babylon (1899–1917) he unearthed many cuneiform tablets and excavated the foundations of the Tower of Babel, the Processional Way and the Ishtar Gate. In addition, he identified what he thought was the substructure of the famous Hanging Gardens of Babylon

His greatest claim to fame in archaeological circles, however, is due to the methods he developed of tracing mud walls and distinguishing these from fills and foundation trenches – techniques which are still being used today.

Although a patient and methodical man in his work, Robert Koldewey could be amusing company and was much admired by his peers.

In the 19th century the city was visited and excavated on a small scale many times by Layard, Rawlinson and Rassam among others. The centre of the city was extensively excavated between the years 1889 and 1917 by a German expedition from the Deutsche Orient–Gesellschaft led by the architect Robert Koldewey. Various areas were cleared, including the Ishtar Gate. The tiled remains on top were dismantled and re-erected in Berlin, a project which took over 20 years to complete. Amazingly, the remains survived the World War II and can be viewed in all their glory in the Pergamon Museum.

GETTING THERE Babylon is 85km south of Baghdad, just off Highway 8 on the road to Al-Hilla (25km).

OTHER PRACTICALITIES The site is totally fenced off with guards at the gates. In order to gain access you need written permission from the Ministry of Tourism in Baghdad or Al-Hilla. There is an admission fee for foreigners (currently US$20). There is a souvenir shop which is currently closed, as is the museum. Both of these were looted by local people after the fall of the Saddam regime in 2003.

WHAT TO SEE AND DO The site is a large one. It is a mixture of the surviving remains of Nebuchadnezzar's Babylon and extensive modern reconstruction and restoration. Saddam Hussein reconstructed huge parts of Babylon, including Nebuchadnezzar's Palace, until it became the most restored site in Iraq. Bricks inscribed with Saddam's name adorn the site. He also built his own palace on a mound overlooking the site and the river.

The centre of the ancient city is an appropriate place to begin a tour of the site, behind the two-thirds sized copy of the Ishtar Gate. Behind this gate is a walled quadrangle, adorned with freshly restored murals depicting ancient Sumer. Here also is the now closed **museum** and disused **visitors' centre.** (Although somewhat tacky, in the 1980s and 1990s, it was one of the few places in Iraq where you could buy interesting cards, stamps and copies of brick tiles, glazed and unglazed. Little did we know then the fate that awaited the site in the future.) Leaving the quadrangle through the facing gate, you come to the steps and path leading to the famous **Processional Way**. Positioned alongside the rebuilt palace (which is to your left) and high off the excavated ground, it is fenced off by metal railings which have been in place undisturbed for many years (despite what has been said in the press about damage sustained during the recent conflicts, it does not seem to me to have been disturbed over the last 30 years). The original roadway, made of stone slabs coated with bitumen, does not seen to have changed and a few slabs have visible inscriptions on them. The Processional Way continues until it reaches the original Ishtar Gate. To the left of the Processional Way is the vast and amazingly rebuilt **Palace of Nebuchadnezzar II**, King of Babylon. Some of the remaining original palace wall foundations still contain inscribed bricks carrying his name. There is an entrance here into the palace. On the right-hand side of the Processional Way is a temple building dedicated to the **mother goddess Ninmahi**. Once restored, this building is now in great need of repair again, although even in its current state, it gives a good impression of what a Neo-Babylonian temple would have looked like in this city.

From here steps descend to the **Ishtar Gate**, the foundations of which are still covered with the original decorations of bulls and dragon-like chimeras (composite animals with the physical attributes of a snake, lion and eagle). These brick are unadorned reliefs, not glazed or painted. The second gate or upper part on these foundations was originally finished with beautiful glazed-brick panels depicting bulls, dragons and lions (the symbol of Ishtar). However, these were dismantled and taken in thousands of pieces to Germany after World War I, by the German archeological team that excavated Babylon, and painstakingly reconstructed in the Pergamon Museum in Berlin. Notwithstanding, the foundations are still an amazing sight and, in the right light, the terracotta bas-reliefs situated on the walls make for magnificent pictures. As mentioned elsewhere, the high water table has always caused problems here and in 2013 urgent work was carried out on the site to prevent this rising further and damaging the remains. During this work, and some 6m down from what appeared to be the original ground level, archaeologists uncovered yet another bas-relief chimera in line with the others. Could this newly revealed level mean that there is a much older and more extensive gate still waiting to be uncovered?

Returning to the Processional Way, this would once have been bordered by great walls. The walls you can see today are significant reconstructions; the originals would have been lined with the glazed-lion frieze which can now be seen in the Pergamon Museum, containing an estimated 60 glazed lions in all.

Turning from the Processional Way brings you face to face with the **Summer Palace**, a great jumbled mass of brickwork; paved floors at various heights reflecting continuous building and rebuilding through the centuries. This is the site of the last organised dig undertaken on the site of Babylon in the 1980s by the Iraqi archaeologist Hai Katth Moussa. A great library of baked documents along with numerous other artefacts was discovered. There is speculation that this Summer Palace was the site of the fabled **Hanging Gardens**. The site aches for more excavation to be undertaken.

Returning to the ancient past, sitting isolated on flat ground is one of the most iconic symbols of Iraq: the **Lion of Babylon**. Sculptured from basalt, the lion is depicted astride a captive. Marks on the lion's back indicate that originally it was fitted with a saddle. This massive, almost modernist-appearing piece of art has many theories about it. Certainly there is no basalt stone for many hundreds of miles. Could it be a trophy of war taken from the Hittites of central Anatolia? Another theory is that a figure of the goddess Ishtar may have stood on a saddle on the lion's back. In any event it is now a symbol of Babylon and certainly worthy of a photograph or two.

Turning back, past the remains of the last dig you come to the original surrounding inner palace and temple wall before returning to the great **Palace of Nebuchadnezzar II**. Extensively reconstructed by Saddam Hussein in 1983, its massive walls reach a great height. Still in situ at the base of some of the original walls you may see a few Nebuchadnezzar bricks, stamped with the king's name. The Throne Room of the palace is vast with a central platform which was originally the site of the king's throne. The superb tiled murals with which these walls were decorated are also exhibited in the Pergamon Museum. Saddam Hussein intended to make Babylon the symbol of Iraq's glorious past and the showpiece of Iraq. In some ways he succeeded; without this restoration it would be difficult to imagine the sheer immensity of such a building, but by walking through it, perhaps with a glance or two at the bier where Alexander the Great was laid in death, the palace comes to life. Perhaps Nebuchadnezzar and Saddam were not that far apart in their ambitions. Saddam also copied his predecessor by stamping the bricks used in the restoration work with his own name, stating on them that he had rebuilt this palace. It has been estimated that the reconstruction cost in the region of US$40 million and that approximately 60 million bricks were required.

Just past the entrance into Babylon, the site of the **ziggurat** and **Temple of Marduk** is marked by the mounds to the right of the road. The ziggurat, or stepped tower,

Joan Oates writing in *Babylon* (Revised Edition, Thames and Hudson) tells us where the Hanging Gardens may be:

'At the very northeast corner of the Palace the excavators found an underground "crypt" consisting of a series of 14 vaulted rooms surrounded by an unexpectedly thick wall, the vaults clearly having been constructed to support some enormous weight. This massive and unusual building, together with the presence of a type of well unknown elsewhere in ancient Babylonia, with three shafts laced together in a manner suggesting a hydraulic lifting system with an endless chain of buckets drawn up in a continuous rotation, led the excavators to conclude that they had found here the remains of the renowned Hanging Gardens, considered by classical writers as one of the seven wonders of the ancient world. It must be noted, however, that it was here that the lists of rations for the Jewish exiles were found, and the plan itself suggests that this odd structure might have served as a warehouse and administrative unit. Classical tradition attributes the famous gardens to Semiramis, but Berssus credits them to Nebuchadnezzar, who is said to have built them for his Median wife, Amyitis, to remind her of her mountain homeland'.

known as **Etemen-an-ki** or the 'House of the Foundation of Heaven and Earth' was originally 30 cubits (15m) high. Over time it eventually developed five more levels, each smaller than the preceding one, giving it the appearance of a stepped pyramid. On the topmost level stood the high temple of Marduk. When Alexander the Great arrived in Babylon the ziggurat was in ruins, so he had some of the rubble cleared in preparation to restore it. However, his early demise meant that nothing further was done. Over the following centuries many bricks and tiles were carried away by the local people for building material. Today all that can be seen are the mounds and a large hole where the ziggurat once was. Close by is a rather interesting small mosque and shrine containing the tomb of a Companion of the Prophet. Further along are **Ninmakh's Temple** and **Alexander's Amphitheatre and Storerooms** which have been restored. This amphitheatre was first built in the time of Alexander the Great and then rebuilt again under the Seleucids. The Greeks reconstructed it based on the original model. It was again restored in the 1980s to today's version.

Looming, almost brooding, over the remains of ancient Babylon is the enormous megalomaniac **Palace of Saddam Hussein**. It is not known if he ever stayed here, but in the 1980s it was forbidden to take photos of the place and sometimes you could see the sun glinting off binoculars held by the guards as they watched the visitors to the site. The site is ideally situated as a military defensive position, as it is close by a major road and not far from Al-Hilla, (a large town suitable for supplies), it is close to water and its ancient walls and mounds are ideal for military defences. During the 2003 war, it was first used by the Iraqi army as a fuel and ammunition dump and base, then the American troops took up residence after a quick tank fight in the environs, its large, cool rooms and great views over the surrounding country making it an ideal vantage point. Once the US and Polish troops left, local people moved in. Fittings were broken, wooden panels stripped, toilets and shower units ripped out, and almost anything that could usefully be used by the locals was removed. Local youths played basketball in one of the main rooms, causing further damage. Today the building lies empty; semi derelict, chandeliers hanging broken, its walls still bearing the graffiti of the troops once housed there. A few plaques remain on the outside and in the reception hall, featuring Saddam Hussein in a

The Road South   BABYLON   8

variety of poses, reminiscent of the old Soviet murals of communist times. It is still possible to go inside, and the views across the river and the site are worth the somewhat precarious climb to the higher floors and the roof. However, parts of the building are unsafe and the guards actively discourage visitors. The future of this somewhat amazing building is in the hands of local policy makers, as many ideas as to its future use are floated – art gallery, museum, hotel: only time will tell.

The Babylon site has always suffered a lack of maintenance, with insufficient time and money being spent on it. Now, this is being recognised. Having visited the site of Babylon in my capacity as a tour operator on and off since 1979, it is not easy to identify any actual war damage caused by the American forces. The looting of the museum and the removal of ancient inscribed bricks from the walls of the palace was carried out by gangs of locals. However, ground disturbance and ground compacting for helicopters, motor vehicles and gun pits did take place on unexcavated ground, leading archaeologists to fear for the future when archaeological excavations are carried out again. Certainly on several occasions when visiting the site while the US troops were still there, I observed that soldiers were only allowed to visit the main ruins in groups and that they had to be accompanied by an official site guide.

In conclusion, to obtain the best from the site, read, read and read. There are so many books and so much internet material available about the past and present history of Babylon. They will enrich your visit.

AROUND BABYLON

Babylon, Kish and Borsippa can all be visited in one day and make a fine excursion either from Kerbala or Najaf. Before the Second Gulf War the Hotel Babylon, close by Al-Hilla, was the ideal base for exploring the ancient world of the Sumerian Era. Hopefully this may become possible again in the future.

KISH Kish is the name applied to a series of tells or mounds covering an area stretching 8km east to west and 2.5km north to south. Today the area is a confused landscape of modern irrigation canals and mounds, some of which cover ruins, while others are the remains of dumps from earlier excavations. The various mounds represent a series of settlements which, though closely related, were not always part of the same town and were not all inhabited simultaneously. However, through common usage, the entire area is now referred to as Kish. Kish was the capital of King Sargon, founder of the Akkad Empire and the city of Akkade (and possibly the first empire known to the world) and famed for his 'King's List' (see box, page 274).

History The name of Kish appears at the beginnings of Mesopotamian civilisation and only disappears with the decline of the great eastern empires. The Sumerian city

KING SARGON OF AKKADE

Initially a governor of Kish or cup bearer of the then king (c2340–2284BC), Sargon later became king and founded the dynasty of Akkade. Much of the information about his reign comes from inscriptions on monuments that he erected in the Temple of Enlil at Nippur. He gained control of southern Mesopotamia and then went on to subdue Elam and later Mari, then Ebla and Central Anatolia. Sargon laid the basis of the post-Mesopotamian kingdom and his sons, and notably his grandson, Narah Sin, carried on this achievement.

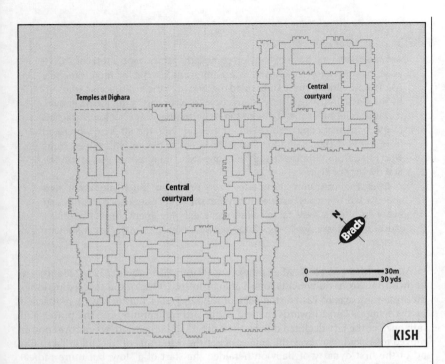

Temples at Dighara

Central courtyard

Central courtyard

N

Bradt

0 ———————— 30m
0 ———————— 30 yds

KISH

of Kish was founded at the beginning of Mesopotamian history, and was occupied from the Ubaid period (c5000BC) until it's abandonment in the 6th century AD. Four dynasties established their capital successively at Kish, the first was in the time of El Obeid (4000–3400BC). Between the early 3rd millennium BC and the late first millennium AD, there was continuous occupation on at least one of the tells at Kish, and excavations have uncovered numerous examples of the waxing and waning of Kish's fortunes during this period. Kish was one of the foremost cities in Mesopotamia in the 3rd millennium BC, and it was shown in the King's List as being the capital of the first Babylonian dynasty after the flood. The prestige and derived authority that the title 'King of Kish' bestowed on its holder was such that it was still claimed by kings in the 1st millennium BC. Much of the wealth and power in ancient Babylonia was concentrated in the king, and the prestige and prosperity of a town waxed and waned in direct relation to the presence or absence there of a royal dynasty. The benefit of this patronage to a town may be gauged by the extent of the royally sponsored building work undertaken there, evidenced by structural remains, inscriptions on stamped bricks, year names and other texts.

The era of the great Kings of Kish begins around 2900BC in the Mesilim Period (named after one of its most famous kings). An inscribed mace found at Lagash mentions Mesilim, a prince of Lagash and vassal of the King of Kish. Kish's most famous king was Sargon, founder of the great Akkadian Dynasty (c2400– 2220BC) who may originally have been a cup bearer at the court of Ur for Zababa, King of Kish. After Zababa's death, Sargon seized his throne and fought an epic battle in which he captured Lugalzaggisi and conquered all of Mesopotamia as far as the Persian Gulf. To the west he invaded Mari (Syria), and pushed as far as the Taurus (Turkey). He may also have captured Cyprus and its precious copper mines. Following this Kish was abandoned in favour of Akkad near Sippar, however Sargon did not neglect the city completely and carried out many restorations within it.

THE KING'S LIST

Around 1800BC a scholar of Babylon compiled a list showing a total of 24,510 years of power for 23 kings whose names are Semitic, or more precisely Akkadian, in origin. These kings ruled the land from the institution of kingship by the 'Gods until his own day'. Many copies of all or part of this list are known. It was also found in the library of the Assyrian king Ashurbanipal. Attached to this particular copy of the main list it begins with the 8th king who ruled from 5 towns 'then came the flood'. The main list begins with the 23 kings who ruled from Kish. The length of reigns are in hundreds of years from the first dynasty of Kish.

Over the centuries these lists have provoked much argument and speculation: not really resolved today. But they offer a sequence of kings and every so often a 'new' tablet offers some enlightenment. Note: the British Museum possesses well over 40,000 known tablets plus many yet unknown.

Among his successors, Manishtuso and Naram-Sin (about 2320–2284BC) are known to us from documents found at Susa in Iran. One of the succeeding kings built the ramparts of Kish at the edge of the Euphrates, but he was then attacked by the King of Larsa towards the end of the 3rd millennium BC. The power and influence of the city declined during the brief Akkadian period, when royal power moved to Akkad. However, the emergence at the beginning of the 2nd millennium BC of the first dynasty of Babylon heralded the start of a slow, but more radical decline in the prosperity of Kish. Shifting water courses, increased salinisation and marginal climatic changes may have exacerbated the situation. Fundamentally, though, the city was a victim of the change in the way power was distributed in Babylonia, a change which took place in the first half of the 2nd millennium BC. In about 1860BC the city walls were razed by a king of the 1st Babylonian Dynasty.

Throughout the 3rd and early 2nd millennium BC, Babylonia was a collection of squabbling kingdoms each centred on a major city. Hammurabi's conquests (1848–1806BC) changed all this, replacing small fiefdoms with a kingdom covering most of Babylonia with its capital at Babylon. This led to the ending of the royal patronage of these cities, which was so vital to the upkeep of city walls, temples and canals. Many of them also suffered at the hands of conquering armies, which also hastened their decline. During the reigns of the first two kings of the first dynasty of Babylon, Sumu-abum and Sumu-la-El, Kish became a pawn in the power struggle between Babylon, Larsa and Isin, and control of the city frequently changed hands. As Babylon rose in importance during the 2nd millennium BC, the power of Kish declined and the temples and city walls suffered from destruction and neglect. Although restoration and rebuilding was occasionally carried out and the occupation of the town continued, the city of Kish went into a decline.

With the fall of the first dynasty of Babylon in 1651BC, and the movement of power north to Dur-Kurigalzu during the Kassite period, Kish's position as a small provincial town rather than a major city was emphasised. There is little archaeological evidence of occupation at Kish during the Kassite period, none of which suggests that the town ever approached its former glory. Kish's resurgence took place almost a thousand years later, during the Neo-Babylon period (8th–7th century BC), when Marduk Apal Idin II broke free from Assyrian control. However, he was defeated in 710BC by Sargon II and Kish became part of the Assyrian Kingdom again. During the Babylonian period Nebuchadnezzar II restored some of the temples at Kish.

In AD1818 excavation was undertaken at the site by Ker Porter. This work was continued by Fresnel and Oppert in 1852. Following this and for a long time thereafter the locals dug into the tells to extract antiques to sell. When these started to arrive in Europe, they drew scholarly attention to the site. Methodical excavations were undertaken in 1912 by H de Genouillac, which led to the discovery of a temple and other monuments. This work also enabled archaeologists to fix the city's history to an extent on certain points. Excavations were also carried out by Oxford University in 1925, by the Field Museum of Chicago in 1933 and by Professor Fujji in 1992.

Getting there Kish is located 85km south of Baghdad and 15km east of Babylon in the northern alluvial plain of Mesopotamia.

Other practicalities Kish has no guards or guides, but the site is fenced. A local guardian keeps an eye on the place and will turn up when you arrive.

What to see and do The portions of the site of particular interest and where much of the excavation work has been conducted, are **Tell Uhaimir** (site of the ziggurat and the principal shrines of the city), **Tell Ingharra** (ancient Hursagkalamma and the site of two ziggurats forming part of a large religious complex) and **Mound W** (site of extensive Neo-Babylonian remains).

To the left of the track the first tell is just a confused mass of mounds, which, to judge by the great number of tablets found here, might well be the scribes' quarter. To the right, and separated from the scribes' quarter by a wide depression which was probably an old canal, stands **Tell Ingharra**, the most important of the mounds, not only in its extent but also for the remains of a Sumerian palace archaeologists unearth in it. Only the façade and a courtyard with brick columns now survive.

A little to the north of this palace, two temples of the Babylonian period (6th century BC) have been discovered. The larger of the two, on the west, the **E-Hursag-Kalamma**, is thought to be dedicated to the goddess Ninlil. It measured 92m by 83m. The smaller temple which is situated on the east, was attached to it on the corner. This temple was called **E-Tur-Kalamma** and was probably dedicated to the deity Nin-e-Anna. Both temples were built on the same lines as those generally found in Babylon. They contain an inner courtyard with four great gates, one at the centre of each side. The E-Hursag-Kalamma also has subsidiary gates. Each temple has a cella or small inner chamber situated along its southwest face. Both were precisely arranged so that their four corners corresponded to the four points of the compass. They were built from unbaked bricks without inscriptions, with the exception of the pavement of the cellae, which was built of plano-convex baked bricks probably manufactured in the Babylonian period. Both are very ancient and probably rebuilt by Nebuchadnezzar and Nabonidus.

To the south of these temples are the remains of two ziggurats which were originally joined to them. At the time of Genouillac's excavations they rose to 17.2m and 17.7m respectively. Excavations carried out to the east of Tell Ingharra in 1931 uncovered the remains of several Sassanid villas decorated with rich ornamentation, the largest of which attributed to Bahram Gor (AD420–438), is opposite the temples. Another of the villas contained a pool with a mechanism for raising and pumping water.

To the northeast of Tell Ingharra is the El Bender tell where the remains of a Parthian fortress can be seen. The massive remains of the ziggurat of the **Temple of Zababa**, within a group of ruins, are to the northwest. This ziggurat measures

55m by 63m and stands 19.5m high. Its faces are decorated with projections and are shielded by an enclosure wall of baked bricks stamped with the name of Sargon II. The ziggurat is constructed of unbaked bricks, although the remains of the original covering of baked bricks can still be seen at the top. On all five tiers the beds of palms which are part of its construction can still be seen. The upper platform of large baked bricks formed the base of the upper building, the **House of the Numbers, or El-Kisibba**. To the west of this structure there are a series of heavily excavated shallow mounds, remains of the old city which is contemporary with Hammurabi. Archaeologists have discovered many in Sumerian texts from this period in this area.

AROUND KISH There are numerous tells covering the remains of ancient towns in the area around Kish. Among these is **Tell Barghuthiat**, located 27km away. About 800m to the north of Tell Barghuthiat, is the **Jamdat Nasr** mound. Texts excavated here have been instrumental in establishing Mesopotamian chronology. Picture writing was used during the Jamdat Nasr period (3100–2500BC), although the earliest examples go back to the preceding Uruk period (c3200BC). Pottery from this period has also been discovered, polychrome with geometrical decoration in black, red or brown which was thrown on a wheel and finished with a polished slip.

ANCIENT BORSIPPA (BIRS NIMRUD)

These ruins were long considered to contain the ruins of the Tower of Babel, as Birs Nimrud is dominated by the mass of its ziggurat, a striking landmark which can be seen from miles afar.

HISTORY In Babylonian times the Ezida was a temple as big as that of Marduk. It was built to the same design. The original date of the ziggurat is unclear but it underwent some restoration by Nebuchadnezzar II as cylinders bearing his name were discovered in the foundations. The ruins were often described in the writings of 19th-century travellers, including Rich and others. In 1852 Oppert carried out excavations here, and in 1902 Robert Koldewey unearthed, on the nearside of the ziggurat, the remains of the Ezida, the Temple of Nabu. Nabu was the god of the scribes, whose emblem was a stylet or a bird, and who was held in great veneration among the Babylonians and Assyrians. His cult was linked with that of Marduk, the god of Borsippa, who it was believed personally visited the festivals of the New Year at Babylon.

GETTING THERE Birs Nimrud is on the road from Al-Hilla to Kufa.

✕ WHERE TO EAT At the edge of the site, at the point where vehicles park, there are a few stalls selling soft drinks, nuts and crisps.

OTHER PRACTICALITIES There are police guards on the site and based next to the Mosque of Abraham.

WHAT TO SEE AND DO As you reach the site, the first great mound is that of a Sumerian palace or temple. We shall never really know because built on top is the mosque associated with the prophet Abraham and much visited by local people. The pictures taken at sunset looking across to the other great mound surmounted by the ziggurat and the temple area are spectacular.

There are extensive ruins to the northeast of the tower, near a small Muslim mausoleum. The E-Ezida temple, originally as big as that of Marduk, is constructed from unbaked bricks and occupies a rectangle 92m by 100m, its four corners corresponding to the four points of the compass. On the northeast side of the main entrance there is a great rectangular courtyard, 28m by 41m, leading on the southwest side to the sanctuary. A whole collection of rooms and courtyards, approximately 80 in number, form the subsidiary offices of the temple. Its outer northwestern enclosure wall, about 100m long, has been partly excavated.

The ziggurat, about 46m high, stood some 50m to the southwest of the temple. It measured around the base 45m by 61m. Its present appearance is that of a steep hill crowned by a great section of wall forming a tower built of baked bricks. To the southwest of the platform are great dark blocks of partially vitrified bricks, the result of some violent conflagration in the past. Viewed from the ziggurat, the walls surrounding the site are clearly easy to discern.

AROUND BORSIPPA When you return to the main road the way that you came, just before the main road is a local shrine and mosque dedicated to Abu Bakr, a member of the family of the more famous Abu Bakr, who was the second caliph and a companion of the Prophet. This is another important place of Iranian Shia pilgrimage.

AL-KIFL OR CHIFAL

'Chifil itself is small, lies along the Euphrates River and has an old covered suq at the back of which stands the shrine. Dr Abdul Sittar al Azawi, a jolly, French-speaking Islamist from the Directorate General of Antiquities in Baghdad, was busily at work restoring the shrine and digging about it to discover just what this quite large site actually contains. There is for example, a leaning brick minaret, Abbasid apparently, without a mosque, and this poses an archaeologist's problem: a minaret without a mosque is like a head without a body. But Ezekiel's shrine is sturdily visible under its honeycomb minaret, Seljuk, like that of Sitta Zubeida in Baghdad. The synagogue part has great thick square flanks and arched ceilings, beautifully hand-painted walls and Hebrew texts carved in wood. All of which are being preserved with great care; five shrines in one vaulted hall are covered in reverential green cloths. The Arab workman and guardians who entered with me removed their shoes before doing so; and politely but firmly recommended me to do the same. Some old men of Chifl told me that the Jewish population here numbered about four hundred until the 1950s when they moved to Palestine.'

Taken from Iraq: Land of the Two Rivers *by Gavin Young, 1980*

HISTORY The earliest building which is believed to have been erected on this site was a tomb over the reputed grave of the prophet Ezekiel, who lived among the Jews exiled to Babylon in the 6th century BC. Ezekiel warned of the destruction of Jerusalem and foretold the restoration of Israel. Among the Jews of ancient times this was a highly revered place of pilgrimage. Two medieval Jewish travellers who visited the place wrote accounts of it; however, their descriptions do not tally with the existing tomb which is most probably attributable to the Ilkhanid period. Islam identifies Ezekiel (Hizkil) with the Koranic prophet Ohu-I-kifl. It is not known how the tomb came to be known as Dhul-Kifl; the identity of Dhu l-Kifl; his relationship to Ezekiel; the date the tomb was converted to a Muslim tomb; the reason for this or the date of the most recent alterations to the building. The answers to these questions would no doubt help to explain the religious and historical context of this building.

The Muslim reverence of Dhul-Kifl apparently stems from the fact that this personage is mentioned twice in the Koran in connection with a series of prophets, firstly in Sura XX1, v, 85 as follows: '*And (mention) Ishmael, Idris and Dhul-Kifl. All were of the steadfast*', and secondly in Sura XXV111, v, 48, which runs as follows: '*And make mention of Ishmael and Elisha and Dhul-Kifl. All are of the chosen*.' Religious scholars are not agreed on the antecedence of Dhul-Kifl; whether he was a prophet or just a pious servant of God. According to Goldziher, Dhul-Kifl is the second name of Ezekiel. Other researchers suggest Dhul-Kifl is the Arabic and Islamic form of Ezekiel. If correct, this would explain the relationship between the two names and make clear the change from the original name of the tomb, which took place during the Ilkhanid period. The authorities, who are all agreed that the conversion took place during the reign of Sultan Uljaitu, do not give any reason for it. Hamid Allah Mustaufi al Qazwini states that the Sultan Uljaitu took from the Jews the privilege of the guardianship of the tomb of Dhul-Kifl and handed it over to the Muslims. He also built a *masjid* with a minaret in the place. According to Herzfeld the *turba* (tomb) should also be attributable to Uljaitu, mainly because its present appearance is quite different from that described by the above mentioned medieval Jewish travellers.

After the addition of the *masjid* and the minaret in 1316 the place became purely Islamic and remained thus until the beginning of the 20th century. According to Massignon, the building, which includes the *turba* and the *masjid*, was reconverted to a Jewish sacred place through the influence of the Jewish multi-millionaire Menahim ibn Danyal, who was also responsible for the restoration of the building. Apart from the minaret, no element of Islamic religious architecture can be traced at present on the site.

GETTING THERE
By road The shrine is situated in a village known as Al-Kifl, midway between Al-Hilla and Najaf, about 130km to the south of Baghdad.

By air Some visitors fly to Al-Najaf International Airport and then continue on by road.

SHOPPING With an old tea house and traditional bread makers, close by the walls of the mosque is an early and atmospheric covered souk street. There are few such village or small town souks as this remaining in Iraq. The shopkeepers are very friendly and welcoming.

OTHER PRACTICALITIES The site has been taken over by the Religious Affairs Department and is being extensively restored prior to being re-opened later. When it opens again to the public, female visitors will have to be completely covered and cameras and mobiles will no doubt continue to be discouraged. The site has zealous guards who keep a close watch over all visitors.

WHAT TO SEE AND DO The Ilkhanid shrine complex is composed of a **minaret**, a *masjid* and a *turba*, topped with a *muqarnas* dome. Despite the considerable architectural and decorative importance of the building, very little information regarding these aspects has been published. The historical inscriptions on the minaret, translations of which were published by Herzfeld, makes it clear that it was commissioned by the Mongol ruler Uljaitu Khudabanda who died in 1316; the building was completed by his son and successor Abu Sa'id soon afterwards. Although the minaret has suffered damage in the past, it still retains most of its original structure and brick ornament. Early photographs of the minaret show a staircase attached to the northwest corner of the base over a pointed arched recess which led to the roof of a room with an arched entrance linked with the base. This room and staircase no longer exist.

The **minaret** exhibits some of the most elaborate extant ornamentation of medieval Iraqi minarets, and some say that it is the last and unsurpassed example of this elaborate traditional technique. The cylindrical shaft of the minaret is 10.27m in circumference and 20m in height. It has several ornamented zones. The lowest part of the shaft containing the entrance is composed of courses of cut brick in common bond. This zone is bordered on its lower and upper parts by a row of bricks set vertically. This zone is followed by a decorative band composed of pieces of rectangular plain brick combined with square brick plugs carved in low relief with a four-pointed rosette. The pattern of this band is purely geometrical. The plain brick pieces are set so as to build up cross shapes with the square plugs set on a slight level in between them. The cross pattern is one of the most popular motifs on the brick minarets of both Iraq and Iran. The next section is 2.27m in width and has an elaborate Kufic inscription, which is built up of small pieces of terracotta tessellation. It is striking not only for the small pieces comprising the words, but also for the stylish pattern of alternate upright and inverted triangles in which the words are arranged. The letters of the inscription are set in angular Kufic. The unique style of the writing and the way each individual word is built up is undoubtedly the most impressive artistic feature of this minaret. The inscription is very difficult to read, both because over half of the inscription is missing and also due to the highly stylised way in which it was executed, but it is thought to say 'For the love of Mohammad and Ali.' Another inscription, which was already badly damaged when Herzfeld visited it at the beginning of the 19th century, is carved in relief on terracotta slabs, each of which contain several letters on a dense arabesque background. The translation runs as follows:

> ... the august Sultan Ghiyath al Dunya wal-Din [Khudab] anda Mohammad, may his grave be pleasant, and it was finished under the reign of his son, the Sultan ...

> ... Allah, be He exalted, and demanding His most generous reward, the exalted Amir, the Just, King of the Umara, the promoter and establisher of justice, the protector ...

The present **mosque** has been subjected to a great deal of alteration, most of which took place during the late Ottoman period when the building was reconverted for use as a Jewish sacred place. Until recently there was no *mihrab* in the *qibla* wall, and the exterior and interior façades of the walls were plain plaster. The interior façades were decorated with polychrome painted motifs composed of naturalistic leaf and flower scrolls of quite recent date. This was combined with Hebrew texts painted on the upper walls or in frames hung on the walls. Scholars speculated that these Hebrew decorations replaced those of the Ilkhanid period, which formerly decorated the mosque. The altered and restored state of the mosque, coupled with the lack of earlier descriptions or photographs, means that the only way to identify original elements would be by rigorous examination of the present structure, something which has not taken place. It is thought though that it still retains some features of its original structure, which could date from 1316, including the vaulting, the arches and the exterior façade of the *musalla*.

Today This most ancient religious place has undergone further reconstruction. For many centuries the site had as its focal point the ancient tomb of Ezekiel, surmounted by its wonderful architectural spire, which it is now possible to visit. The building is Ilkhanid in style, with adaptations of Judaism such as synagogue furnishing including Torah cupboards and a ladies' balcony. Behind the actual tomb are the tombs of several Companions of the Prophet. Deep excavation trenches close by these tombs show layers of archaeological evidence indicating an extensive history of this site stretching back well before Islam and possibly even pre-dating Ezekiel. Outside of the tomb buildings are the ruins of the Ilkhanid mosque and minaret as described above. With the clearing of the ground around the minaret, the full extent of the mosque has been revealed, and its old walls and gateways are full of interest.

Currently, a new minaret and buildings are being constructed on top of some of the old mosque and therefore when you visit the site full Islamic strictures apply – no cameras, no phones and full Islamic clothing for women. To me, a Westerner, this most ancient place had a special appeal with its mix of cultural influences and that slight crumbling of the past that motivates you to go away and read again about it, and perhaps look for references to it in the Old Testament. I am saddened at what is being done here. But perhaps we in the West have to recognise that Islam is not particularly interested in the old, but only in the opportunity to worship. Paradoxically, the town has a modern mixed history. The Jewish inhabitants left in the exodus of the 1950s. Many Palestinian refugees lived here for some years afterwards, and in the most recent years al-Qaida and sectarian elements have given the town a reputation for insurgency. Several years ago many Asian Muslims visited the site; now none are allowed (although we hope this will change).

KUFA

Formally a small town on a branch of the River Euphrates, Kufa was the first capital of the Abbasid Empire. Before Baghdad became established as the capital, Kufa, Basra and Wasit were the most important towns in Iraq. In the early days of Islam, Kufa was the bastion of support for Ali in his struggle against Muawiya. From an important political-military centre, its role changed to that of a cultural centre where one of Islam's main codes of law (the Hanifa code) was developed. Today, it is home to the second-oldest mosque in Iraq, containing the tombs of many pious men of religion, including Aqeel bin Talib and Hani bin Erwa, as well as the pulpit of Ali. The mosque area has been heavily restored with new walls around the mosque. The shrines have also been rebuilt and embellished.

HISTORY Kufa was founded by Saad Ibn Abi Waqqas, Commander-in-Chief of the Arab forces, soon after the Arab conquest of Mesopotamia AD638 by the Lakhmids, vassals of the Sassanid Persians. When Ali moved to live in Kufa in 657 it became the capital of those who recognised him as the fourth caliph. Ali was assassinated here, while praying in the mosque in 661. Today the main mosque of Kufa, with its golden dome and tombs of Muslim bin Aqeel and Hani bin Erwa, stands on the site of that original first mosque, which excavations have shown was square in dimensions in accordance with all the very early mosque buildings. To the south of the mosque is the site of the ancient Dar el Imareh, a palace built by Saad Ibn Abi

Waqqas. Kufa's prosperity did not last long following Ali's death, however, and when Ibn Jubair visited it in 1184 he described it as a town fallen into ruins: 'It is a big city with old building ... it was built with brick and it has no walls ... the old mosque is at the end of the city in the east side and there is no building behind this mosque from the east side'. Ibn Battutah also visited it and commented that although it was 'distinguish because of the cemetery of the prophet companion and the settlement of the scientists and Al-Imam Ali Holy Shrine ... ruination covered it'.

GETTING THERE Kufa lies 10km north of Najaf, along the road to Al-Hilla.

GETTING AROUND All of Kufa that pilgrims and visitors come to see is contained in a very concentrated spot around the main mosque. Nearby there are huge parking areas for pilgrim coaches. Taxis are available in the town centre to travel to Najaf; however, most pilgrims travel around in their own vehicles. The majority of the pilgrims to this mosque come from Iran.

WHERE TO STAY AND EAT Most visitors, apart from some of the religious pilgrims, base themselves in hotels in Najaf, which is only 10km away (see pages 285–6). They also return there to eat. There are many local snack-style eating places in Kufa selling soft drinks, fruit, nuts, biscuits and sweetmeats.

SHOPPING There are numerous small stalls and street vendors selling the usual little religious souvenirs such as bracelets, necklaces and pictures commemorating Imam Ali.

OTHER PRACTICALITIES Kufa has always adhered to very strict Shia Islamic law. Today the town is under the control of the Madhi militia, who have their headquarters there. Non-Muslims are not allowed into the mosque. Again, it is very important that women are well covered in all areas as is customary in such places. The guardians of the mosque are very pleasant people, but can be fairly described as inflexible on such matters. On a recent visit I was severely admonished by a small boy of about 8 years old when a strand of hair blew from underneath my headscarf!

WHAT TO SEE AND DO
House of the Caliphate (Dar Al-Imara) This is believed to be one of the world's oldest Islamic monuments. Built in 16AH (AD637), it was formerly the secular administrative headquarters and palace for the whole of Iraq. It consisted of an outer square wall, each side of which was 170m long and 4m thick. Six semi-circular towers punctuated each side (with the exception of the northern side, which had only two towers). It has now been restored and the walls and the bases of the six towers which once supported the walls can be seen.

Behind the House of the Caliphate lies the House of Imam Ali which contains a well, a library and items relating to the story of Imam Ali's life and death including the stone on which his body was laid out and washed prior to his funeral. Non-Muslims are sometimes allowed to visit this place at the whim of the guardians.

Al-Kufa Mosque and the Holy Shrines
Kufa Great Mosque is revered for many reasons, most notably as it was the place where Imam Ali was fatally injured while praying. The first mosque at Kufa was marked out by Saad Ibn Abi Waqqas in 638. Its boundaries were fixed by a man who shot an arrow towards the south, then another towards the north, another to the west and a fourth to the east. It was almost square

in plan and enclosed by a ditch only. Its sole architectural feature was a covered colonnade which ran the whole length of the south side. Little changed until 670, when it was enlarged and rebuilt. The mosque underwent some restoration in the Umayyad period, and an account, written in 1187, notes that it had high marble columns supporting a flat roof, although almost nothing remains now from this time. The present mosque, which is of quite recent construction, retains several ancient features along with an additional monument built during the 14th century. The mosque's important features are the *iwans* and the *mihrab* which believers must face when praying. The mosque contains nine sanctuaries:

1. The sanctuary of the prophet Abraham. Some believe that Abraham's house was here and it is from this location that he departed to fight giants (Al-Amaliqa) in the Yemen.
2. The sanctuary of Al-Khudir.
3. The sanctuary of Prophet Mohammed. So named, even though the Prophet never visited Iraq, because it is believed that after he ascended to heaven he visited a mosque and performed a double-kneeling prayer in front of the Mosque of Al-Kufa, the House of Adam and the Sanctuary of the Prophets.
4. The sanctuary of Amir al Mu'minin (Ali bin Abi Talib).
5. The sanctuary of Adam.
6. The sanctuary of Gabriel.
7   The sanctuary of Imam Zainual Abideen bin al Hussein.
8. The sanctuary of the prophet Noah.
9. The sanctuary of Imam al Sadiq. Historical references say that Imam Jaafar Bin Mohammad Asadiq prayed frequently here, now the site for congregational prayer.

In addition to the above the mosque also contains four ancient Islamic sites:

10. Bait Al-Tusht (the Tub of Washing). According to legend a young unmarried maiden was swimming in a pond when a leech entered her body and grew within her, causing her belly to distend. Her brothers, believing she was pregnant, decided to kill her and sought guidance from Imam Ali. Imam Ali ordered that a washing tub be brought to this place, filled with water and the young maiden should sit in it. After a while the leech slipped out of her body and her life was saved.
11. Dakatu Al-Qadha (the Judgement Seat). So known because in this place Imam Ali gave religious decisions and guidance to Muslims based on the Koran and the rubric of the Prophet Mohammed.
12. Mihrab Al-Nafelah (prayer niche).
13. Safinat Noah (Noah's Ark). This brick-built monument, also known as Safina or ship, as it is shaped like a boat, is situated partly below ground level. Local tradition identifies this as the place from which Noah's Ark, made on the order of God shortly before the flood, departed.

There are five gates into the Mosque: Al-Hujah Gate, which is the main entrance, Al-Thuban (the serpent), Al-Rahma (mercy), Bab Aqeel and Al-Murad (Erwa) Gate. The Gate of Mercy is the ladies entrance. In the centre of the courtyard there is a sundial (Al-Mizuala)

Al-Kufa Mosque contains four minarets. Located alongside its northwestern side and accessible by the **Gate of Mukhtar** (Bab Al-Mukhtar) is the **Holy Shrine of Al-Mukhtar bin Abi Obeid bin Masood Al-Thaqafi** (also known as Abu Ishaq), a magnificent shrine with nave colonnades, surmounted by a large, structured dome covered with the blue tiles of Kerbala. Contained within this complex are also the shrines of **Muslim ibn Aqeel** and **Hani ibn Erwa**. These shrines contain the remains of the revolutionary Mukhtar al Thaqafi, Muslim ibn Aqeel, who was a first cousin of Hussain ibn Ali and his companion Hani ibn Erwa.

Nearby lies the mosque of the prophet's companion **Zaid Bin Sihan** built in the 19th century. Zaid was one of the leaders of Ali's army who was martyred with him at the battle of Al-Jamal. In front of the main gate to this mosque lies the mosque of his brother **Saasaa Bin Sihan**, who was also a companion of Ali.

NAJAF *Telephone code 33*

According to tradition Ali, feeling his death approaching after he had been stabbed in the great mosque at Kufa, ordered his people to place his mortal remains on a camel and allow it to wander at random; where the camel stopped, there he was to be buried. The burial place was kept secret, and no funeral monument was raised.

Home to the Holy Shrine of Imam Ali, the fourth caliph and son-in-law of the Prophet, resplendent with its golden dome and minarets, Najaf is a major city of mosques and shrines. There is no quarter or street without a mosque, either small for the locals or large and attended by visitors to the city. The city's large cemetery (Wadi Al-Salam) is considered the holiest and most sought after place for burial among Shia believers. Najaf is also one of Islam's most important seminary centres for the training of Shiite clergymen (al Hawzah al Ilmiyyah), and has many religious schools. Every year millions of pilgrims visit the Holy Shrine of Imam Ali, whose shining golden dome is visible from a distance of 75km away.

HISTORY Considered one of the holy cities, or 'Atabat', along with Kerbala, the fortunes of Najaf have changed greatly over the years. The history of Najaf begins with the murder of Imam Ali at Kufa some 14 centuries ago which led to the Sunni-Shia divide in Islam, a divide that still evokes strong emotions today (see pages 19–20). This tragic event led to the construction of magnificent shrines in the desert and the blossoming of the city of Najaf. According to the Shiite tradition, the first mosque in Najaf was built in 791 by Caliph Harun al Rashid; however, historians say that the tomb of Imam Ali was first discovered around 750 by Dawood Bin Ali al Abbas, then rebuilt by Azod Eddowleh in 977; that it was burnt later and then restored by the Seljuk Malek Shah in 1086, and finally rebuilt yet again by Ismail Shah, the Safawid, in about 1500. During Ottoman times, the city of Najaf was plagued by two main problems: raids by Arab tribes and the lack of a reliable water supply. Both of these affected the pilgrim trade and the economy of Najaf to such an extent that by the beginning of the 17th century the number of inhabited houses in the city had dropped from 3,000 to 30. In the 18th century, Najaf was attacked and besieged by the Wahhabis; however, by the beginning of the 19th century, the conversion of many of the Arab tribes in the surrounding area to Shia Islam had all but ended the raiding. The water problems were addressed in 1803, when the cleansing of existing waterways was instigated and the Hindiyya canal was built. These changes rejuvenated the city's fortunes, the pilgrims returned and the city's population doubled. By the early 20th century Najaf exercised an enormous religious and political influence, far beyond the borders of Iraq, having escaped effective government control throughout much of the Ottoman period. The city had at least 19 functioning religious schools and was often the seat of the leading Shia *mujtahid* of the day, who would receive large donations from Shia followers around the world.

Following World War I and the fall of the Ottoman Empire, Najaf came under the control of the sheikhs of the Zuqurt and the Shumurt tribes, who received an allowance from the British. In 1918 the British tried to increase their control of the city and Captain Marshall was put in charge of Najaf. Yitzak Nakash, author of *The Shi'is of Iraq*, described how Marshall took up residence in a house just outside the city walls: he attempted to organise a police force in the city which was not subject to the authority of the sheikhs and sought to regulate the payment of municipal taxes. At his suggestion the allowance that had been paid to the sheikhs was discontinued. Faced with a serious threat to their authority the sheikhs rebelled and had Marshall murdered. But the city's problems were not over. Its inability to supply the Anaza (a tribe allied to the British) with grain ignited a rebellion supported by the junior *ulema* (scholars) and *mujtahids* (scholars who can make legal decisions based on their interpretation of legal sources and the Koran). It ended with a siege of the city, the cutting off of its water supply and the end of the rule of the sheikhs.

Over the last few years, the steady flow of pilgrims into Najaf has resulted in a commercial boom and rapid construction in the area around and leading to Imam Ali's shrine. Business is brisk, especially in shops selling religious souvenirs. Work is underway to expand the shrine. Started in 2004 at an estimated cost of US$50m, it will be on-going for many years to come. Large-scale development projects have been undertaken: three new electrical substations were completed in 2006 at a cost of US$4.8 million each. A new road has been built from the old city to Kerbala. Ambitious plans are underway for the construction of parks, gardens, rest houses, libraries and housing. The Al-Najaf International Airport opened in July 2008. 'Most people now have a good job and lots of opportunities,' Governor Adnan Zurfi said as he described the increasing attention being paid to health care, housing for the poor and education in the city.

GETTING THERE

By air Located on the eastern side of the city, Al-Najaf International Airport (📞 *334 935*; 📱 *0770 802 4606*; 📧 *info@alnajafairport.com; www.alnafafairport.com*) opened in 2008. It is not possible to fly directly into Al-Najaf International Airport from the UK; however, the following airlines have direct flights into the airport from their home countries – Turkish, Qatar, Kuwait Airways, Air Arabia, Iran Air, Middle East Airlines, Gulf and Fly Dubai. Iraqi Airways have domestic flights to Najaf from Baghdad, Erbil, Suleimaniyah, Mosul and Basra. Around 1,000 people use the airport each day, most of them pilgrims from Shiite-majority Iran and Bahrain, but numbers increase tenfold or more during major festivals such as Ashura, when Shiites flock to Imam Ali's shrine. The airport is open sunrise to sunset at the time of writing, but it had very little in the way of facilities for passengers.

By road Najaf is located about 190km south of Baghdad and 80km from Kerbala on Highway 8.

GETTING AROUND The only way to get around in the centre of Najaf and the bazaar areas is to walk, as the roads are inaccessible to traffic with concrete road blocks and checkpoints preventing vehicles entering for security reasons. However, these areas are compact enough to get around on foot without too much difficulty. Outside the cordon of barriers and checkpoints, street taxis are widely available.

WHERE TO STAY Although hotel accommodation is not limited, given the huge numbers of pilgrims visiting Najaf every day, bookings should be made in advance wherever possible. Many new hotels are being constructed to accommodate the influx of pilgrims, but despite this Najaf is still underdeveloped in terms of accommodation, restaurants and other tourist facilities. You will find numerous smaller, local hotels on every street in Najaf. Classified as 'second rank' hotels, their clientele is almost exclusively pilgrims or local Iraqis, travelling in family or larger groups. These hotels are basic, often with mainly family rooms and lacking Western-style toilets. Dining rooms are frequently communal-style and often segregated into male and family areas.

Very few non-Muslims visit Najaf, as with its strict adherence to Sharia principles (including no alcohol, a strict dress code for women in public, frequent segregation of the sexes and constant security checks even when walking along the streets) it is not the most comfortable or relaxing place to visit. Apart from the shrines, there is nothing in the way of sight-seeing, and it can be difficult for non-Muslims to gain admission into these at times. The few Western, secular visitors tend to stay in the hotels listed below. Bear in mind it is not appropriate to expect completely Western standards in hotels in Iraq.

Luxury/upmarket

🏠 **Hotel Asr Aldur** (5 floors) Zainul Abdeen Rd; m 0780 101 9019; www.qasraldur.com. Located in the heart of the old city, very close to the shrine & Wadi-Al-Salam cemetery, this is one of the best & newest hotels in the area, catering mainly for large groups (the majority of their customers are on organised tours). Clean & well run, in marked contrast to many of the run-down hotels in the vicinity, with a big marble lobby, free b/fast, lunch & dinner & free Wi-Fi. The staff are helpful & speak good English. The bedrooms are large with separate, though slightly down-at-heel wet-room-style bathrooms with both Western (seated) & Arabic (squat) toilet. The hotel has a large restaurant which serves a wide variety of Middle-Eastern cuisine & kebabs. Free soda & water is always available. The hotel also has a coffee shop. The bazaar is directly opposite the hotel, down a narrow side street. **$$$$**

Be aware this hotel is inaccessible to vehicle traffic as there is a large checkpoint & concrete vehicle barriers at the top of the road. Therefore you have to wheel your luggage to the hotel yourself, or use one of the many local barrow-boys.

Mid-range

🏠 **Al-Ghaleb Hotel** (75 rooms) Imam Ali St; www.alghalebhotel.com. A 4-star hotel located 10-mins' walk from Imam Ali's shrine. The hotel has a bar/lounge & restaurant serving Western and local cuisine, Wi-Fi & free shuttle bus service to Najaf Airport. Rooms are somewhat small & crowded, though clean & newly furnished, with refrigerators, AC & TV. **$$$**

🏠 **ZamZam Hotel** (83 rooms) Revolution Sq; m 0780 880 3407, 0780 122 8828; e reception@ zamzam-group.com. The hotel has en-suite rooms with a refrigerator & satellite TV. It has a coffee shop on the top floor with views all across the city & a restaurant overlooking the sea of Najaf. $$$

🏠 **ZamZam Tourist Complex** Safi Safa St; m 0780 121 0237. This is the sister hotel to the ZamZam Hotel (above). It has a similar range of facilities. $$$

Budget/shoestring

🏠 **Al-Nabaa Hotel** near Al-Maidan Sq; ☎336 0236,337 3088

🏠 **Qasr Al-Badr Hotel** near Al-Maidan Sq; ☎336 4057

🏠 **Al-Qibab Al-Thahabiya Hotel** Al-Muheet St; ☎337 2711

🏠 **Sal-Ameen Hotel** Zain Al-Aabedeen St; ☎337 1601

🏠 **Al-Qasim Hotel & Restaurant** Al-Rasool St; ☎337 0409

🏠 **Al-Jawad Hotel** Al-Rabita St; ☎337 3361

🏠 **Shubar Hotel & Restaurant** Al-Tossi St; ☎336 2357

🏠 **Yathrib Hotel & Restaurant** Zain Al-Aabedeen St; ☎334 2959

🏠 **Al-Rusul Hotel & Restaurant** Madinat Al-Zaerin 964; ☎337 0361

🏠 **Barakat Al-Abbas Hotel & Restaurant** Madinat Al-Za'eriny; m 0780 100 2149

🏠 **Misbah Al-Huda Hotel** Madinat Al-Za'erin; ☎337 3396

🏠 **Al-Wadi Al-Jameel Hotel & Restaurant** Al-Sour St; ☎337 2177

🏠 **Tabook Hotel & Restaurant** near Al-Maidan Sq; ☎336 6918

🏠 **Al-Daoha Hotel & Restaurant** near commercial centre; ☎336 0470

🏠 **Shaheed Al-Mihrab Hotel & Restaurant** behind Nadi-A-Mowadafeen (the civil officers club); ☎336 5332

🏠 **Al-Muna Hotel & Restaurant** Kerbala St; ☎336 0797

✗ **WHERE TO EAT** There are many 'dining hall' style local restaurants which cater for pilgrims who can arrive in groups of hundreds at a time from a particular country or city or as an extended family group. There are also small kiosks selling tea and street food along the main streets to the shrines and within the bazaar. All the larger hotels have restaurants which are open to non-residents.

✗**Sobat Restaurant** Sobat St, Ghadeer District; m 0780 800 6700; e sobatrestaurant@ outlook.com. European, Middle Eastern & vegetarian cuisine. This restaurant comes highly recommended for good food in elegant surroundings.

SHOPPING Najaf is a city of alleyways, markets and squares. The most famous of these, with over 200 shops, is **Al-Suq Al-Kabeer** (the Big Market), located in the centre of the old city starting at Al-Maidan Square and running to the gate of the Imam Ali Shrine. It is well known for its jewellery, pottery, spices, prayer beads, perfumes in small ornate bottles, carpet shops, goldsmiths, cloth and sweets. Everything is available here from satellite phones to religious texts and souvenirs, including brightly coloured paintings of imams and mosques. There are many small markets branching off it, including: **Al-Shebibi Street** to the left-hand side of the entrance to Al-Suq Al-Kabeer. This is a small market specialising in shoes. **Al-Safareen Suq** is in the first branch of the main entrance of Al-Suq Al-Kabeer and traditionally contained blacksmiths' shops. **Suq Al-Qasabeen** (the butchers) is in the second branch after Al-Safareen Suq and contains the shops of butchers and other foodstuff. **Al-Sagha Suq** (goldsmiths' market) is on the left-hand side when coming from Imam Ali's shrine. The shops sell gold. Najaf is famous for precious stones, especially its beautifully shaped, transparent pearls and rings made from these pearls are believed to bestow many benefits on the wearer. Further along you come to the **Al-Tejar Suq** (merchants' market) which specialises in selling cloth. **Al-Abaycheya Suq** (the cloak market) it is one of the oldest markets in the city. Originally the place where the traditional, heavy Iraqi cloaks worn by the merchants were made, nowadays it sells mainly men's clothing. Finally, **Al-Masabech Suq** contains shops selling of all types of spices and foodstuff. In addition to these, there are numerous small branches in the market containing a myriad of shops such as **Al-Mishraq Market,** where you will find vegetables and foodstuff and **Al-Huwaish Market,** the book market.

Despite the security concerns, the city's ancient bazaar stays open until approximately 11pm.

OTHER PRACTICALITIES It cannot be emphasised too strongly that Najaf is a highly orthodox religious place. Alcohol is strictly forbidden. Dressing modestly here is absolutely essential and for women that means not one strand of hair showing and dark, voluminous clothing revealing nothing more than the face and hands. Even so it is sometimes not possible for non-Muslims to enter Imam Ali's Shrine. There are numerous airport-style security checks to go through while walking in the streets, those for women generally placed to the right-hand side of the street and those for men to the left. You and your bags will be thoroughly searched and you will be 'advised' if your clothing does not cover you sufficiently. While these checkpoints are not manned 24 hours, they are open until at least 11pm or until the bazaars and shrines close to visitors.

Shoes and often cameras need to be left outside when you visit a shrine. These can safely be deposited at the stands outside designated for this purpose. You will usually get a token to retrieve them on your return and a few IQDs will be expected in payment. Visiting women, especially Western, non-Muslim ones will generally be expected to wear the *abayahs* provided by the shrine, irrespective of how well covered they may be by their own clothing. See page 258 for further information on *abayahs* provided at religious sites.

The climate of the city is a typical desert climate. In summer, especially in July when the hot wind (Al-Semom) is blowing, the temperature may reach 45°C. During the winter months, however, between December and February, the weather is very cold, but dry. The rainy season is in spring and autumn.

WHAT TO SEE AND DO
Shrine of Imam Ali Enclosed in a mosque named Al-Haidariya Shrine, is the spectacular Shrine of Imam Ali. Built in the same style as those of Kerbala, Samarra and Kadhimain, it comprises a rectangular enclosure surrounding a two-storied sanctuary, containing the tomb, with a great dome over it. The area of the shrine is 13,240m² and it is bordered by a 12.5m fence. There are five main gates for visitors to enter the shrine. These are the Clock Gate (also called the Great Market Gate) which is

NAJAF: A FESTIVAL OF SKILL AND COLOUR

The shining golden dome of Imam Ali's shrine in Najaf is visible from a distance of 75km. In *Iraq: Land of Two Rivers*, Gavin Young recalls 'The façade of Ali's tomb, seen from the northern gateway, is richly beautiful – the gold tiles have darkened handsomely with age. And through the doorway to the tomb itself you can see the glistening stalactite effect of mirrors and the harsh neon lights that are features of all major shrines of Iraq. Pink, blue and yellow patterns of birds and flowers bedeck the archways into the courtyard. Heavy wooden doors lead in from the street opposite the covered *suq* (market) where you can buy worry-beads (*sibhas*), finely worked gold ornaments or ankle-length cloaks for winter or summer, some hemmed with gold braid'.

located in the centre of the east wall of the shrine; the Qibla Gate which is located in the centre of the southern wall of the shrine and so named because it is located towards the Muslim *qibla*; Gate Al-Tusi, located in the northern wall of the shrine and so named because it faces the tomb of Al-Shaykh Al-Tusi; the Gate of Muslim bin Aqeel, located next to the Clock Gate on the right-hand side as you enter the shrine and the Gate of Easement Al-Faraj, which is located in the centre of the southern wall of the shrine.

The most prominent and visible part of the shrine is its resplendent golden dome. Approximately 25m from the roof of the shrine, its diameter is about 16.6m. Wrapped in tiles of gold foil, the dome is surrounded by a belt of gold Koranic verse against a background of startling blue enamel. The whole edifice stands on a square-shaped ornate structure. At the eastern side of the shrine are two golden minarets (that to the north is 29m high, the one to the south is 29.5m) each made of 40,000 gold tiles, inlaid in some places with blue enamel. The predominant colour of the exterior is bright shining gold and the entire exterior of the mausoleum is inlaid with a mosaic pattern of light powder blue, white marble, gold again with an occasional splash of Middle East rust. Within the shrine the surrounding walls have many open rooms or *iwans* that are laminated with Kerbala mosaic which in turn is decorated with a number of Koranic verses, pictures of plants and beautiful inscriptions. Some of these inscriptions contain valuable historical information which is considered to be a record of rich Islamic heritage.

In the centre of the shrine is located the **Honourable Courtyard**, and located on its east façade is the **Golden *Iwan***, which is wrapped in gold foil and inlaid with blue enamel. Opening on to the Honourable Courtyard are six gates leading to the principal corridors of the mosques where visitors can pray. This is linked to the main hallway by five doors leading to the courtyard of the Holy Shrine, in the middle of which is **Imam Ali's tomb** – or the Honourable Grave, the most important part of the shrine. It consists of a rectangular-shaped structure 6.35m by 5.15m by 2.2m high. Inside this and located directly on the Holy Shrine itself is a sealed box made from the most precious types of wood. The tomb of Imam Ali is surrounded by a cubical windows made of gold and silver, decorated with Islamic inscriptions and magnificent engravings of plants in pure gold. The façade of the tomb, seen from the gateways, is richly beautiful, the gold tiles having darkened handsomely with age. Through the doorway to the tomb itself you can see the glistening stalactite effect of mirrors and the harsh neon lights that are features of all the major shrines of Iraq.

Today, despite the huge developments around the shrine, there is still an atmosphere of peace, respect and devotion in the shrine itself. The atmosphere is not so emotionally charged as in Kerbala. It feels more mature, more respectful to Allah (God) and Imam Ali as his servant. You have to go through the usual routines of checking in cameras, mobile phones, etc, and the checking of women's clothing, but the welcome is genuine. Although the shrine is subject to much upheaval at the moment, the glittering 17th-century tiles, the gold coverings and the Holy Shrine itself, surrounded by the faithful, are sights not to be forgotten.

Other mosques in Najaf

Family mosques The most prominent scholars and well-known families in Najaf have their own mosques, the most famous of these being: **Al-Tusi Mosque** to the north of the Shrine of Imam Ali in the Al-Amarah quarter, **Al-Hindi Mosque** in Al-Rasoul Street to the south of the shrine, **Al-Hannanah Mosque** on the left side of the road between Najaf and Kufa, **Al-Shakiry Mosque** in Imam Ali Street at the entrance to Najaf and **Kashif Al-Ghita Mosque** also in the Al-Amarah quarter.

The Visitation to the Shrines of the Imams is a doctrinal recommendation for Shia believers only. Unlike the pilgrimage to Mecca (the Hajj) the visitation is not confined to any specific time of the year. There are, however, a number of special dates, when it is particularly auspicious. Among the various shrines those of Najaf and Kerbala carry the highest importance.

The Visitation of the Shrines of the Imams is intended to acknowledge their authority as the leaders of the Muslim community following the death of Mohammed, and to maintain the contact and understanding between the Shia believer and his imam, who is capable of interceding with God on his behalf on the day of resurrection. Besides serving as an act of constant renewal between the believer and his imam, the visitation is also aimed at preserving the collective Shia memory and group identity as distinguished from that of the Sunnis.

Religious seminaries, libraries and cultural centres Najaf was the home of Ayatollah Al-Sistani, a revered cleric with thousands of followers. The religious university, known as **Hawza Ailmiah**, is the focal point of religious movements and has produced many well-known poets and religious intellectuals. There are a number of private libraries belonging to religious families, such as the library of Ali Kashif Al-Ghita, Hadi Kashif Al-Ghita, Bahr Al-Ulum and Al-Qazwini. The famous public libraries are: **Imam Al-Hakim Library** in Al-Rasoul Street, **Al-Alameen Library** in Al-Tusi mosque and **Al-Haidary Library** and **Ameer Al-Muminin Library** in the Al-Huwaish quarter. Ameer Al-Muminin library contains more than half a million books and manuscripts in all fields of knowledge, including a rare Koran, which it is believed was written by Imam Ali himself in Kufic style with no dots on the letters. This Koran, written on deer skin, has the stamp of his son, Imam Hassan as proof of its authenticity. Shia cultural establishments in Najaf are restoring and preserving ancient manuscripts. Over the past few years the Kashif Al-Ghita religious school has saved more than 1,800 religious manuscripts onto 74 CDs.

Wadi Al-Salaam Cemetery The Peace Valley Cemetery, known as Wadi Al-Salaam Cemetery is to the north of the Shrine of Imam Ali, beginning at the end of Al-Tossi Street. It is on UNESCO's tentative list of World Heritage Sites, highlighting its significance as one of the largest cemeteries in the world. It includes the remains of millions of Muslims and dozens of scientists, guardians and people of faith as well as the graves of prophets Salih and Hud. The cemetery extends from the centre of the city to the far northwest and forms 13% of the area of the city measuring 917ha. Wadi Al-Salaam cemetery has lower graves (burials) and high graves (towers). There are also special family burial chambers. As well as burial inside vaults there are rooms carved underground, accessible by a ladder. Because of the merit accorded to being buried in this cemetery and the honour of being interred near the remains of Ali, Muslims come from all over the world to conduct the funerals of departed family members in Najaf in order for them to be entombed in this cemetery. This 'tomb traffic' generates a huge income, which has and continues to be a very important source of revenue for Najaf. A worldwide industry has grown up around this, specialising in transporting bodies to Najaf by air, land and sea and preparing and interring them upon arrival.

The Road South   NAJAF

8

It is related that the commander of the faithful, Ali, once sought solitude and went to a place on the edge of the city of Najaf for seclusion. One day, while Ali was glancing at Najaf, he suddenly saw a man approaching from the desert, riding a camel and transporting a corpse. When the man saw Ali, he walked up to him and greeted him. Ali returned the greeting and asked the man 'Where are you from?' The man answered 'From Yemen.' 'And what is this corpse?' 'It is my father's corpse: I came to bury it in this land.' 'Why do you not bury him in your own land?' 'It is my father who ordered me to do so, and he said one day there will be buried a man in Najaf whose intercession with God was far reaching.' 'Do you know who this man is?' asked Ali. 'No' said the man. Ali then said 'By God, I am that man. Go and bury your father'.

Ibrahim al Musawi al Zanjani – quoted in *The Shiis of Iraq* by Yitzhak Nakash.

Other shrines in Najaf

Minor shrines To the west of the Shrine of Imam Ali, about 500m from the shrine, lies the **shrine of Imam Ali Bin Al-Hussein Zain Al-Abedeen**, grandson of Ali, who made frequent visits to his grave. The shrine was originally outside the old city wall, which fell into ruin many years ago. The shrine itself was destroyed during the 1991 uprising. Other historical references mention another shrine of Imam Ali Bin Al-Hussein Zain Al-Abedeen lying beside the shrine of Ali, near Bab Al-Faraj on the western side of the shrine. Nearby lies the **Safi Safa Shrine** or shrine of Atheeb Al-Yamani, the Yemeni who was known as Safi Saf, and who ordered his son to take his body to Najaf for burial after his death (see box, above). This shrine is also currently ruined and awaiting renovation. There are also some very ancient gravestones in this area, dating back to the 8th century, and there is a stone near the entrance dating back to 759.

The **Shrine of Kumail Bin Ziad Bin Al-Haitham** is in the Al-Thewaya in Al-Hanana Quarter, about 100m from the main street between Najaf and Kufa. The total area of the shrine is about 5,400m². Circular in shape, the tomb is in the middle on a small hill. Above the shrine there is high dome. The inner tomb is covered with silver box engraved with Islamic arts and many corridors surround the tomb for visitor access. The shrine was opened in 2008 after much restoration and rebuilding. Kumail Bin Ziad Bin al Haitham was one of the Prophet Mohammed's companions. He was also a scientist and ruler of the area around Najaf during the time of Imam Ali. He was killed by al Hajaj, the King of Iraq, around 82AH (AD701) when he was 70 years old.

Al-Hannanah Mosque Close to the Shrine of Kumail Bin Ziad Bin al Haitham (see above) in Al-Thewaya in Al-Hanana Quarter is Al-Hanana Mosque. It is one of the most revered mosques in Najaf which covers about 7,400m². In the middle of the mosque is the place where it is believed that the head of Imam Hussain was put after his martyrdom in 61AH (AD680). Historical references also indicate that the body of Imam Ali passed through this location on its way to Najaf. The shrine had been renovated and extensively reconstructed.

Shrine of the Prophets Hud and Salih This important shrine is located at the entrance to Wali Al-Salam cemetery near Al-Tosi Street. Both prophets are in one

A US tank veered hard right, smashing a tombstone; a mortar slammed into a catacomb with an ear-shattering roar and Iraqi snipers dodged among the graves; it was hard to imagine that the hallowed cemetery at Najaf is also known as 'The Valley of Peace'. But this was August 2004 and the sacred burial site – the biggest in the world – became a battleground after followers of the radical Shia cleric Moqtada al Sadr occupied the nearby Imam Ali Mosque, a site so holy Imam Ali himself declared it: 'the gates to paradise.' I was working for the US television network Fox News and we were the first Western crew to set up a live link from the graveyard, to cover the unfolding Najaf conflict. It was mid-summer and the 45°C temperature was overwhelming; so hot the heat from the blistered earth burned my soles through my shoes.

As far as the eye could see: thousands of graves, mausoleums and catacombs; quite literally a city of the dead. More than five million people have been buried in this hallowed graveyard since the 7th century AD, and, covering five square miles, it's the biggest on the planet. Some family vaults were topped with adobe-style homes, made from a mixture of what appeared to be ochre-coloured mud and rocks. Entering the ground floor, here was where the body was prepared for interment, and set in the floor a kind of trap-door through which you could see the coffins on shelves.

We interviewed one of al Sadr's supporters, Abdul Zahra Hadi, who had been sniping at US soldiers. 'We ambush their patrols and the Americans cannot get into the area, because it's full of winding lanes and underground mausoleums', he said. 'We can hit and run and hide inside the many tombs.'

Incredibly, despite heavy fighting the graveyard was still functioning, and we met the Ansari family from Tehran, Iran who had brought a grandfather for burial. The head of the family, Ali, 52, told me his father's dearest wish was to be buried there. So, despite the dangers from flying bullets and mortar rounds in the graveyard, they had come. The stand-off at Najaf by Moqtada al Sadr and his followers had ended by September 2004 and once again the graveyard returned to tranquillity.

But the damage to hundreds of graves and mausoleums was immense; human remains, buried for centuries, had been disturbed. Even the dead did not sleep in the so-called Valley of Peace.

John Cookson, former Baghdad correspondent for Fox News

---

tomb, above which there is a small dome covered with blue mosaic. The present mosque over the shrine was constructed in 1918. According to legend the prophet Hood was sent to bring Islam to the Nation of Ad, but they did not believe him. So they were punished with a strong wind. The prophet Salih was sent to Thamood where he performed a miracle by producing a pregnant camel from the rocks in the mountains. However, they killed the camel and were punished.

Najaf Sea To the south of the old city near the Safi Safa Shrine in an expansive area with very beautiful scenery, you can see the natural depression which once contained the **Najaf Sea**. Nothing remains now of the sea itself except its name; historians think that it was probably a land-locked lake whose waters finally disappeared in the 19th century. It is said that in its heyday the Najaf Sea was used by ships carrying goods and people and that the remains of many shipwrecks were found on its shores as the waters receded and evaporated. Today the Najaf Sea is considered to be one of the most fertile agricultural areas in Najaf, with fields of vegetables and glades of palm trees.

Religious schools in Najaf The scholastic movement in Najaf has a long history dating back to the 10th century AD when students and theologians started to come to Najaf to teach or learn from the famous religious scholars. Sheikh Abu Jaafar bin Mohammad bin Hassan Tusi, a highly renowned scholar from Baghdad who moved to Najaf in 448AH (AD1056), had a prominent role in developing and extending the religious schools in Najaf among the cities of the Arabic and Islamic worlds. Since that time Najaf has maintained its place as a leading centre for religious study, with many religious scholars from across the Islamic world coming to study in its religious schools and to learn from its masters. **The School of Imam Ali's Shrine** is one of the oldest schools in Najaf and until quite recently students still lived in rooms on the upper floor of the shrine. Most of the religious schools in Najaf today are located in the centre of the old city, including **Najaf Religious University** located on the road from Najaf to Kufa, just after Thawrat Al-Eshreen Square. Established in the 1950s by Mohammad Klantr, the university consists of three floors, containing classrooms, libraries and dormitories for the students. To the left of the main entrance is the mosque, where the daily group prayer is held. **Great Al-Akhuand School**, located at the end of Al-Hoiesh market, was established in 1902 by Sheikh Mohammad Kazem. **Yazdi Great School** also located in Al-Hoiesh, on Al-Rasoul Street, it is known for its impressive construction and ornate style. It was established in 1906 by Muhammad Kazim Tabatabai Yazdi

Al-Shaylan Khan In the centre of the old city, at the beginning of Al-Khawarnaq Street beside Al-Khawarnaq high school, lies Al-Shaylan Khan, which is considered one of the biggest and most stately historical buildings in Najaf. Built in the Ottoman era as a hall to receive visitors, it subsequently became the centre of the Ottoman ruler in Najaf. The Khan consists of two floors and covers an area of 1,500m² to a height of 12m. It has three cellars as well as rooms arrayed around its courtyard. Its walls and entrance are decorated with Islamic designs. It was considered one of the national symbols for the citizen of Najaf in the struggle against the Ottoman and British colonialism. During the revolution against the Ottomans it was the headquarters of the Civil Najaf Government. Finally, it became a prison for British prisoners after their defeat at the battle of Al-Raranjiya in the Revolution of 1920. Records show it held 148 prisoners at this time – 80 British soldiers, 2 officers and 66 Indian prisoners of different religions. The walls of Khan still contain the writings and drawings of the British prisoners.

City walls According to historical records, up to six city walls have been built around Najaf in the past to protect it in the face of repeated attacks and invasions. The construction of the last wall by adr-Azam Mohammad Hassan Khan Nidham al Dawlais is believed to date back to 1802. It took eight years to build and comprised of towers and observatories for spotting invaders, as well as niches for firing at the enemy through. There was also a defensive ditch situated just outside the wall. The wall defended Najaf in 1915 against the Ottoman Turks, in 1918 against the British colonial power and again during the Great Revolution of Iraq in 1920.The last remaining part of the wall can be seen at the end of Al-Sadeer Cross Street near the Sadeer Street Literary Association.

QASR AL-KHAWARNAQ (AL-KHAWARNAQ MANSION) Situated near Al-Manathera and towering over the Najaf Sea, this mansion is surrounded by palm trees, green areas and villages. Built by al Numan Bin Emre al Qais, it is unique in its architecture. Only the ruins remain today.

The Chari Sada (River Sada) marks the boundary between Najaf and Kufa. It was dug in 1132AH (1719) to bring water to Najaf. A stone arch **Al-Gantara Hajariya** was constructed across it, the remains of which can still be seen at Alwat Al-Fahal. There are four brick minarets on the arch. Locally it is referred to as Om Qoron (with horns).

On the Pilgrims Road, near Al-Ruhba village and about 30km from Najaf can be found the ruins of **Al-Ruhba Khan**. The Khan, which measured about 100m by 80m, was constructed from stone with a domed roof and half-square towers in

GRAND AYATOLLAH ALI AL SISTANI

Once referred to in the media as the most influential man in the country, Grand Ayatollah al Sistani is the most senior Shia cleric in Iraq and the prime marja' or spiritual reference for Shia Muslims everywhere. He is thought of as a peaceful and wise religious leader.

In 2004 he, and only he, was able to derail American plans for the drafting of a constitution before elections and he brought a halt to three weeks of fighting in Najaf between Moqtada al Sadr's Mahdi Army and American forces.

The Grand Ayatollah is totally opposed to violence; when terrorists have set off suicide car bombs killing hundreds of Shia pilgrims he has ordered that there be no retribution.

Now a frail man with a black turban and a snow white beard, al Sistani was born in Mashhad, Iran on 4 August 1930. He began his religious education in the holy city of Qom. In 1951 he travelled to Iraq to study in Najaf under the late Grand Ayatollah Abdul-Qassim Khoei. When Khoei died in 1992 Sistani ascended to the rank of Grand Ayatollah and made Najaf his permanent home.

Keeping a low profile and living in virtual seclusion in a decrepit alley in Najaf enabled al Sistani to survive the persecution that killed many other Shia clerics in Saddam's Iraq. His influence was exerted through a network of junior clerics who conveyed his teachings to every Shia neighbourhood in Iraq and through an internet company in the Holy City of Qom. He regularly answered questions by email.

In his *Fatwas* al Sistani urged Shia clerics to get involved in politics. He supported the elections in 2005 but when the United Iraqi Alliance, a mixture of Shia religious parties, Sunnis, Kurds, secular groups and independents won he said: 'You were elected so it is up to you now. Don't drag me into it.' When ISIS began massacring Shias he urged Iraqis to join the army.

Austerity is a hallmark of his lifestyle. When his air-conditioning unit broke down he had it repaired and gave the new one purchased for him by his staff to a poor family. Yet he oversees a multi-million dollar network of charities and religious foundations throughout the world.

To date al Sistani has not appointed a successor. Moderate Shias fear that the vacuum he leaves will be filled by radicals eager to see the Shia south split from the rest of Iraq.

the corners of the main entrance. **Khan Al-Mosala Al-Ruboa** (Quarter Khan) lies about 20km from Najaf, and is so named because it is a quarter of the distance from Najaf and Kerbala. Pilgrims used to stay at this khan for the night on their way to visit the holy shrines. It was constructed in the Ottoman era towards the end of the 19th century. It comprises two halls separated by a wide door and containing many rooms, stables and a well. The external walls are supported by half-square towers. **Khan Al-Hamad** (Desert Khan) or **Khan Al-Nos** (Half Khan) lies about 40km from Najaf in the Al-Haydaria District. **Khan Al-Nekhaila** is in Kerbala Province, half way between Najaf and Kerbala. Some 16km to the south of Najaf on the Pilgrims Road and west of Al-Fuhba village are the remains of the **Om Qoron Minaret**. Such minarets or towers were built along the desert roads as signposts to guide travellers.

AL-HIRA

Just 20km from Najaf and 10km south of the Euphrates is the site of the famous city of Al-Hira. Today it is part of Al-Manathera Qada in Najaf Province, but in the 4th–6th centuries it was the capital of the caliphate of the Lakhmids, the kings of Al-Manathera. Its name is derived from either the Aramaic word meaning 'the city' or from the Serianic word 'herta' meaning 'camp and sit'. The kingdom was a vassal of the Sassanids and helped control the borders of Persia and the Byzantine Empire. Al-Hira has 14 major mosques including those in the villages of Al-Rumaytha, Albo Khareef, Al-Siniya, Al-Desm and Al-Radawiya.

HISTORY The kingdom of Hira has been ruled by approximately 33 kings of the Al-Manathera Dynasty. The first was Malik bin Fahim and the last was al Nuaman bin al Monther (AD580–603) the last king of the Lakhmid Kingdom. The collapse of the dynasty was brought about by the Persians and then during the Battle of Hira in 633, the town was taken by the Muslims and declined in importance. It is also claimed that the first Arabic script was developed here, and certainly Arabic literature was developed by al Akhtel, a Christian, in c640 and the script was used by poets Jasir and al Farazdaq as Al-Hira became an important centre of Arab culture. Between the 5th and 11th centuries Al-Hira was a diocese of the Syriac Church of the East, and its inhabitants were Arab Christians whose language was Aramaic. It also had a substantial Jewish community and was famous for its Jewish religious schools.

GETTING THERE Al-Hira is approximately 20km southeast of Najaf on the road to Diwaniyah.

WHAT TO SEE AND DO There are no visible remains of the city of Al-Hira to be seen today. In the past, however, Al-Hira was famous for its monasteries such as Deer Al-Athara, Hanna Al-Sagheer, Hanna Al-Kabeer and Hind Al-Kubra. Although Yaqoot al Hamawi mentioned these monasteries in his book *Moajam Al-Buldan*, little if anything remains of these, and even locals are not sure where they can be found. The great Euphrates changed its course frequently and subsequently settlements rose and fell as did the sustenance provided by the river to these communities.

HEADING FURTHER SOUTH

Leaving behind the Shrine Cities, the beating heartland of the Shia faith and beliefs and the vanished city of Al-Hira, we advance south with Diwaniyah, Samawah and

Nasiriyah as our major reference city points, all on Highway 8 and south of the Saddam Highway. Along the highway and within easy reach are the most famous Sumerian sites – Uruk, Larsa, Eridu and Ur. The Saddam Highway northeast of Diwaniyah connects with Highway 8 at Nasiriyah. North of the highway is the famous site of Nippur (Warka) but so also are the more difficult sites to reach – **Adab, Kissur, Shurrupak, Tell Ukra, Umma** and **Tell Farah**. Heavily looted and difficult to get to, visitors to these insecure sites are viewed with suspicion by the local people for obvious reasons. So we give below a brief description of these sites for the dedicated travellers and historians among us.

Adab (Bismaya) located 35km south of Nippur in Wasit Province is the ancient Sumerian city of **Adab**. Adab was an important early Sumerian city from the time following the Great Flood, according to the Sumerian King's List. First excavated by Edgar J Banks of the University of Chicago between 1903 and 1905, unfortunately Banks' results were never properly published, and only today is the material that was recovered from the site being examined. The city of Adab was first mentioned in the very early texts discovered in other cities in Mesopotamia and appears to have been in 'city leagues' at various periods with Ur, Lagash and Nippur. The excavations have revealed many buildings, some dating from the time of Shulgi and Ur-Nammu, kings of the 3rd Ur Dynasty in the latter part of the 3rd millennium BC. The city was divided by a canal which flowed around a ziggurat creating an island of it. All that remains of the city today is a series of *tells*. Distressingly, the site has been much looted. Adab awaits the spade of a new generation of archaeologists.

Travelling further south after Adab, and lying in between the Saddam Highway and Highway 7 are a series of tells marking the location of **Kissura**, another ancient site of interest. Much looted, we are unable to visit the site today due to its location in semi-wet lands. Close to the Saddam Highway there is another series of ancient sites, including **Shuruppak** (close by **Tell Farah**). Shuruppak is another ancient Sumerian city approximately 50km south of Nippur which can be reached either from Diwaniyah or Nasiriyah, travelling to the north of the Saddam Highway near Tell Farah. The city at its peak extended to almost 200ha (2600–2350BC), but the earliest settlement on the site can be dated from the Jemdat Nasr period (c3000BC). The city appears to have been finally abandoned at the end of the Ur III Period. Excavations at Shuruppak were conducted by Ernest Heinrich (1902) and Erich Schmidt (1931). The city had a number of fine buildings and many cuneiform tablets have been discovered at this site. It was celebrated in Sumerian legend as the scene of the deluge which destroyed all humanity except one lone Sumerian, the son of the last king Ziusudra, the Sumerian 'Noah'. Shuruppak is not an easy place to visit; it has been looted heavily and local people are understandably suspicious of strangers for that very reason.

Next on our list is **Umma (Tell Jokba)**. Situated south of Tell Farah, Umma is another famous and extensive Sumerian site. Easily reached from either Samawah or Nasiriyah distance-wise, you should allow a day to get there and explore it properly. Umma was an ancient city state known from Sumerian legends and from the huge number of cuneiform tablets discovered here. The 21st-century BC calendar of Shulgi found here is the immediate predecessor of the later Babylonian Calendar. In ancient cuneiform texts Umma is mentioned in connection with its epic border dispute with the neighbouring city state of Lagash. Umma reached its peak as a city c2275BC–2165BC. It later became an important provincial city during the Ur Dynasty. It was visited by the early travellers and archaeologists such as William Loftus and John Punnett Peters in 1854 and 1885 respectively. The site has been looted over a long period of time, probably since the turn of the 20th century, and today it is a mass of illegal holes mostly dating from 2003 and onwards.

There are other sites that I have not mentioned; current maps show some of them. The history of these ancient places can be found in many books and it is a delightful journey of discovery as you move from one book to another and then progress to visiting the sites on the ground for yourself. Unfortunately, it is too soon to expect to cover these sites on the ground in Iraq at the moment, but hopefully it will be possible for the ordinary traveller or tourist to do so in the near future.

DIWANIYAH *Telephone code 36*

The capital of Al-Qudisiyah Province and strategically located on the Baghdad to Basra railway line, Diwaniyah in Arabic means 'guest house'. The locality of Diwaniyah is irrigated by the Euphrates, making it highly fertile and highly cultivated with rice fields, vineyards, orchards and palm trees. The city has grain and date markets. Today it is a sprawling provincial sort of town, without a seeming heart. The housing is generally of poor quality, but it has a fine university which serves the province, and much research is being done here concerning agriculture and entomology. The combination of wet lands and semi-arid desert regions make for interesting contrasts.

In the last two years the Baghdad Government has funded a new generation power station and made large housing commitments for the city. For the traveller, however, there are few facilities on offer here, and no real reason to linger.

HISTORY Although situated in an ancient Sumerian hinterland, Diwaniyah is a relatively modern city with no real history. As with Samawah and Amarah on the Tigris, it began life as a market and tribal meeting place by the river. Its traceable history is mostly one of tension between tribes and religious sects and resistance to whoever attempted to rule Iraq. The population is mainly Shia Arab and the Al-Sadr Shia Party has been the resonant political voice of influence. Major battles have occurred here in the years since 2003 between the militia, the US forces and the old government under President al Maliki, however, in the past few years these tensions seem to have diminished.

GETTING THERE Diwaniyah is on the left bank of the River Euphrates about 180km southeast of Baghdad.

Travellers from Baghdad and Najaf visiting Larsa and Uruk need to travel through Diwaniyah on their way south to visit these sites. But there is no good reason to delay your journey by halting here.

NIPPUR (NAIFAR)

In Mesopotamian times Nippur lay on the banks of the River Euphrates. It was linked by this river to Sippar in the north, Kish downstream and Shuruppak and Uruk further south. Nippur's position in the geographical centre of Babylonia was an important factor in its development and growth.

HISTORY The ancient Sumerian city of Nippur was an important religious capital from the end of the 4th millennium BC, but was most probably founded in the 6th millennium BC. It possessed a famous sanctuary consecrated to the god Enlil, who was considered the chief deity of the Sumerian pantheon. The prosperity of Nippur declined with the coming of the 1st Babylonian Dynasty at the beginning of the 2nd millennium BC. The

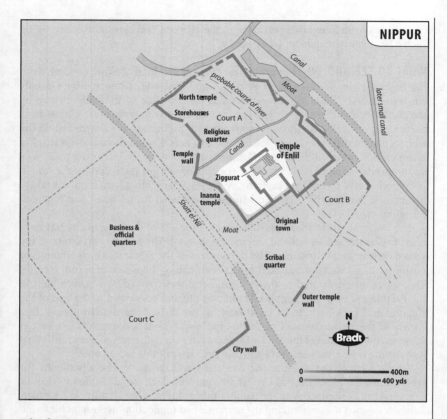

NIPPUR

North temple
Storehouses
Court A
Religious quarter
Canal
Temple of Enlil
Temple wall
probable course of river
Moat
Canal
later small canal
Ziggurat
Inanna temple
Shatt el-Nil
Court B
Business & official quarters
Moat
Original town
Scribal quarter
Outer temple wall
Court C
City wall
N
Bradt
0   400m
0   400 yds

cult of its patron deity no longer received the same enthusiasm from the pilgrims, who transferred their devotion to the Babylonian gods, of whom Marduk was the chief. For all that, the temple of Enlil was no less supported even up to the time of the later Babylonian period (7th to 6th century BC). The city then passed into the power of the Achaemenians, then the Seleucids. The Parthians occupied it from the 2nd century BC to the middle of the 3rd century AD and built a palace here. It was probably only in the 10th century in the Muslim period that Nippur was finally abandoned. The site was first excavated by Layard in 1851, then by the University of Pennsylvania in the 1890s and then intermittently between 1948 and 1990 by the Oriental Institute of Chicago. During these excavations numerous clay tablets with cuneiform inscriptions were discovered.

GETTING THERE The site is 36km from the city of Diwaniyah. You have to return to the Highway from Diwaniyah, cross it and go to the village of Afak. Cross the village canal and head north. The mounds of Nippur soon appear along the old Shatt el-Nil river bed in the middle of the Babylonian plain.

WHERE TO STAY AND EAT In Afak, the small village you pass through on the way to Nippur, falafel sandwiches and tea can be bought. The nearest accommodation should be in Diwaniyah, but as there are no reasonable hotels there it is preferable to travel on to Samawah (see pages 300–1).

OTHER PRACTICALITIES The old dig house is situated just off the road at the edge of the site. Here you have to show your *khittab* and check in with the guards. A track for vehicles from here takes you close to the ziggurat and close to the city. Being such a large site, a map helps (see page 297).

WHAT TO SEE AND DO Nippur's ruins cover more than 2.6km² of land, with the highest point reaching 25m above ground. The site is bisected by a deeply cut watercourse. There are several mounds on each side of the gully formed by the old Shatt el-Nil river bed. The site in itself is a joy to walk over: it must have been a magnificent city. Today it is strewn with millions of pot sherds left by the archaeologists and excavators. You are walking across some thousands of years of history in a way very difficult to find outside of Iraq. Around the city are many tells and mounds, some of which conceal remains of villages inhabited by the Jewish people who were forced into captivity by the Assyrians when Jerusalem was taken. Incantation bowls with Aramaic lettering have been found here (see Baghdad Museum, page 144).

The western part of the Great Tell marking the site of the ancient city has been identified as the residential and commercial quarter. The eastern part contains the sacred quarter and is dominated by the remains of the ziggurat, which amounts to no more than a mass of unbaked bricks dominating the whole area of the ruins. This tower was dedicated to the god Enlil and was covered by a palace built in the Parthian period. The temple of Enlil was situated below and to the east of the ziggurat and goes back, in its latest state, to the second Babylonian period. In a corner of the perimeter wall of this temple two foundation deposits left by Ur-Nammu, the first king of the 3rd Ur Dynasty, have been discovered; they testify that he built the E-Kur, meaning probably the perimeter of this sacred area.

To the west of the ziggurat the American archaeologists also discovered the remains of a temple of the 3rd Ur Dynasty, part of which was dedicated to Inanna, as several bricks stamped with the name of this goddess by Shulgi, King of Ur, prove. Beneath the two towers flanking the entrance two foundation deposits were found containing a bronze figurine of Shulgi. In another part of the tell, beneath an Arab cemetery dating from the 10th century AD, several superimposed buildings have been found, the latest level having been occupied during the Achaemenian and Seleucid periods. In the deeper levels the Americans found tablets from the ruins of a building which has been identified as a school of scribes.

ISIN

Located on the eponymously named Isinnitum Canal, Isin was inhabited from at least the 3rd millennium BC and possibly even earlier. Experts consider it may have been first occupied as early as the Ubaid period in the 5th millennium BC through to the 1st millennium BC. An ancient Semitic capital city, in the 17th century BC King Enlil-bani built a temple to Nintinuga, the goddess of healing, here and she became the patron deity of the city. An ancient fertility cult was also practised in ancient Isin, in which the king annually acted out a sacred marriage, by having sex with a priestess representing Inanna, the goddess of love and war.

HISTORY Isin's history can be split into two main periods. The first of these, the Isin-Larsa period, began when the Isin Dynasty was established by the Amorite king, Ishbi-Erra, around 2000BC. Ishbi-Erra was a courtier of the last king of Ur, Ibbi-Sin, who left Ur following its conquest by the Elamites and installed himself as ruler at Isin. From there he expelled the Elamites from the area and expanded his empire to include Ur, Uruk and Nippur. Ibbi-Sin expanded Isin, building palaces and temples and administrative centres. He installed his ministers as governors in the provinces and developed trade links via the Persian Gulf. Subsequent kings of the Isin dynasty continued its expansion. One of these, Lipit-Ishtar was responsible for promulgating a set of laws, the Lipit-Ishtar Code which is believed to be one of the earliest known codified laws. Inscribed onto tablets of stone in the Sumerian language, they start by fulsomely praising the deeds and reign of Lipit-Ishtar and end with a curse on all those who disregard the laws, and listing the gods, including Enlil and Anu, who will be evoked to carry this out. Although the first half of the tablet containing the laws has never been found, the remainder gives a fascinating glimpse of everyday life in Isin, covering the governance of land, orchards, slavery, inheritance, marriage, boats and oxen, including:

- If a man cut down a tree in the garden of another man, he shall pay one-half mina of silver.
- If a man's wife has not borne him children but a harlot from the public square has borne him children, he shall provide grain, oil and clothing for that harlot. The children which the harlot has borne him shall be his heirs, and as long as his wife lives the harlot shall not live in the house with the wife.
- If a man rented an ox and damaged its eye, he shall pay one-half its price.

Although the exact reasons for Isin's decline are not known, it is thought that a lack of water played a part in its downfall. Furthermore, the capture of Ur by the governor of Larsa and Lagash, Gungunum, disrupted Isin's trade links with the Persian Gulf and caused great economic hardship. Gungunum's successors then re-routed the Isinnitum and other canals, exacerbating water and trade difficulties. The *coupe de grâce* came when around 1860bc Enlil-bani took advantage of Isin's political and economic weakness to seize power and thus bring to an end the dynasty of Ishbi-Erra. Subsequently Isin was conquered by the king of Larsa, Rim-Sin, and again at the beginning of the 18th century bc by the Babylonian king Hammurabi.

The second rise of Isin occurred at the end of the 2nd millennium bc under the rulers of the 2nd Dynasty of Isin (1146–1010bc) following the Elamites' overthrow of the Kassites. Under Nebuchadnezzar I they attacked Elam in the heat of summer, when the temperatures generally made fighting impossible. This victorious campaign heralded a flourishing of the Isin Dynasty, which lasted for over a century and gave Isin control over the cities of Ur, Uruk, and Nippur. Unfortunately, the later fate of Isin has not been established, as the city has not been fully excavated.

GETTING THERE Isin is near the site of modern Ishan Al-Bahriyat in Qadisiya Governorate, 20km south of Nippur and about 75km southeast of Baghdad.

WHAT TO SEE AND DO Rediscovered and briefly excavated in 1924 by Stephen Langdon in tandem with his excavations at nearby Kish, the majority of the excavations at Isin were carried out in the 1970s and 1980s by a team from Munich's Ludwig Maximillian University led by Professor Barthel Hrouda. Since then the site has been neglected and repeatedly looted, leaving little of value remaining. The remains of Isin lie on a flat plain in an uninhabited region. The site itself comprises a low, but sizable mound, about 1.5km across and with a maximum height of 8m. Remains of many large structures have been identified, the largest being temples. However, despite its major Sumerian past, Isin would not feature on any usual tourist itinerary. It is a site for the dedicated historian or archaeology enthusiast.

On 21 May 2003, Col John Kessel and Professor Macguire Gibson of the Oriental Institute at the University of Chicago toured various sites in southern Iraq by helicopter. After visiting Uruk, Professor Gibson 'flew north to Isin where I had already heard from a German visitor that it was being badly destroyed. Her report was correct. At least 200 to 300 men were at work on all parts of the site, and the damage was clearly of long duration. We landed and the men came up waving. They were surprised that the US troops would think that it was wrong for them to be doing the looting. They lied by saying that they had been working only a few days, only since the German woman has been there and told them to do so. We told them that it was forbidden, and the army men fired over their heads to speed up their exit. A boy with a tractor and cart, the only vehicle on this site, wanted us to pay him his taxi fee, since we had chased off his fares. The next day, the German woman returned to Isin with a German camera crew, to find hundreds of men at work again. Clearly, an occasional visit by a helicopter is not going to save the sites. Only the imposition of authority in the entire country, as well as the reconstitution of the State Board of Antiquities with its full complement of guards, backed by Coalition power, can preserve what is left of these major Sumerian sites.'

Scholar Simon Jenkins, in a subsequent report, noted 'the remains of the 2000BC cities of Isin and Shurnpak appear to have vanished: pictures show them replaced by a desert of badger holes created by an army of some 300 looters.'

According the researchers at the Oriental Institute, tens of thousands of artefacts, including cuneiform tablets and cylinder seals, have been illegally excavated, smuggled out and sold to dealers and collectors.

SAMAWAH

Capital of the Al-Muthanna Governorate, Samawah lies midway between Baghdad and Basra, on both sides of the Euphrates river. Samawah is home to the small and rare trade in wild truffles, which grow in the desert regions of the province.

HISTORY In the 3rd century AD Samawah was founded by the Himyarite Tribe of Banu Qudaa. The tribe were exiled from the Yemen following the trials of the Lakhmids and they settled in the southern part of the Lakhmid Kingdom in the area around Samawah. The historical route between Mesopotamia and Saudi Arabia ran through Samawah, and it has been a main trading thoroughfare for Iraqi produce to Saudi Arabia throughout its otherwise unremarkable history. Today Samawah is primarily Shia, the town having been practically cut off by Saddam after the Gulf War. Historically though, Samawah was a mixed Jewish and Shia city, the remaining Jewish community emigrating to Israel in the 1940s and 1950s. Today, however, there is still a small population of Assyrian Christians in the city.

GETTING THERE Samawah is 280km south of Baghdad on Highway 8.

WHERE TO STAY AND EAT There are two recommended hotels in Samawah, but don't expect completely Western standards in hotels in Iraq. There are also a number of very basic, local hotels which may be just acceptable if there is no alternative.

The best advice if you need to stay in one of these is to visit personally, inspect the rooms and check what is included in the price first.

If you're looking for a restaurant, take a short walk from the Al-Khalij Hotel towards the river and bridges where there is a very pleasant riverside restaurant with a varied menu including chicken, kebabs and pizza.

Upmarket

⌂ **Qasr Aldur Hotel** (30 rooms) Off the main roundabout as you enter Samawah from Diwaniyah; m 0771 311 3111, 0781 200 4040; e qsghdeer@yahoo.com. This is comfortable with a pleasant foyer & a reasonably priced restaurant serving local food. Rooms are clean & well furnished with good en-suite bathrooms & hot water. Wi-Fi is available. *Double rooms start from US$100 per room per night.* **$$$**

Mid range

⌂ **Al-Khalij Hotel** (15 rooms) Main Street, Samawah; m 0780 818 0243; e alkhalij_hotel@yahoo.com. A basic hotel with limited facilities, but it is a very pleasant place with a genial proprietor. Although it does not have a restaurant, a cold b/fast of bread, yoghurt, juice, etc, is brought in for guests. *Rooms cost US$50 per person per night.* **$$**

WHAT TO SEE AND DO There are four bridges in the city centre crossing between the two sides. On the west bank you will find the commercial part of the city, the **Old Town** with its Byzantine maze of crowded markets and streets, the **Jewish Quarter** (Agd Al-Yahood) and the covered market (Suq Al-Masgoof) dating back to the Ottoman Period. A Jewish Synagogue (the Torat), which is no longer in use following the emigration of the Jews in the 1950s, can also be found in the Qushla quarter of the city which is located on the east bank of the river. There is an interesting cottage industry of carpet makers in Samawah, primarily employing women. Although the quality of the carpets is a little coarse, the designs are most distinctive. Samawah has the advantage for the local carpet makers of the ready availability of cheap wool from the desert Bedu (who use Samawah as their main trading post) combined with cheap labour, which is abundant in this poor city. The residents of Samawah have enlivened the drab grey concrete walls surrounding government buildings and schools by covering them in paintings depicting scenes of everyday life in Samawah. This tradition, which began in the early 1970s, was forbidden under the Saddam regime, however it has flourished again since 2003 with many new paintings depicting the changes that have taken place in Samawah since its liberation.

AROUND SAMAWAH

When travelling around the villages in the vicinity of Samawah you will see the tall chimneys of kilns built by the locals for baking bricks. Sun-baked bricks are still made by hand and dried using traditional methods dating back to Sumerian times. **Lake Sawa** is a large salt lake located 25km north of Samawah. The lake has no obvious source, no rivers flow into it and there is no evidence of any ancient link to a sea. The water is extremely salty due to heavy evaporation and the lake supports no marine life, although the high salt levels make it so buoyant that birds can often be seen walking on its surface. The lake is surrounded by embankments, raising the water in it to above ground level, and the high level of salt in the water means that if these dykes are breached, they are able to repair themselves spontaneously and so prevent the water from escaping. The Salt Sea (**Bahr Al-Milh**) located 20km southwest of Samawah is the main source of salt production in Iraq and large refineries have been built there to process it.

Known today as Warka and in the Bible as Erech, Uruk was one of the greatest city-states of Sumer. Occupied from the late 5th millennium BC until around the Arab invasion in the 7th century AD, it is famous for its mythical dynasty of 12 kings reigning for 2,310 years, one of which was the hero Gilgamesh.

HISTORY The site seems to have been first settled in the late Ubaid period, towards the end of the 5th millennium BC. However, Uruk's real predominance started with the Uruk period, named after the site. During this thousand-year time span, in the 4th millennium BC, Uruk developed into the most important city-state, colonial power and sophisticated centre of cultic and administrative capability in the whole of Mesopotamia. In its dynastic time Uruk was both a political power and a religious centre (thanks to the religious supremacy of its goddess Anul. The city declined in importance after the rise of the third dynasty of Ur in c2100BC, but remained occupied until the Parthian period, a span of some 4,000 years.

Architecturally, the Uruk period is best known from the series of immense religious buildings excavated in two cultic centres of the city, the Inanna precinct and the Anu Ziggurat. These include the Limestone Temple, the Stone Building and the Stone Cone Temple, all of which probably date back to c3600BC. Many new monumental buildings were also constructed during the Late Uruk period, in the late 4th millennium BC. During this time Uruk was the central power in an economic and political empire which reached up to the Euphrates into northern Syria and Anatolia as well as into Iran to the east. It is thought that within this area the world's earliest form of writing, proto-cuneiform, was first developed and

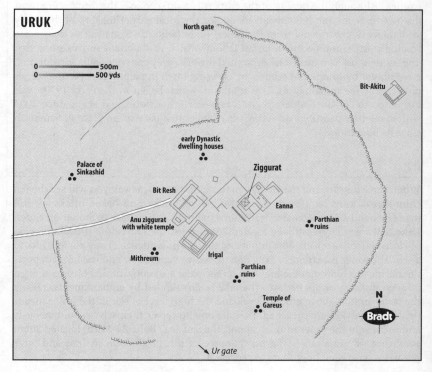

used in Uruk before spreading across much of Mesopotamia. Simplified pictures representing objects, such as a foot, associated ideas (walking) or other words pronounced the same way were drawn onto clay tablets and baked. These later evolved into impressed cuneiform signs and true cuneiform writing.

Through the Early Dynastic period c3000–2350BC, Uruk maintained its importance, with the construction of a new city wall, some 10km in length, which is attributed to Gilgamesh. By the middle of the 3rd millennium BC the ruler of Uruk, Lugal-Zaggesi, had conquered all of southern Mesopotamia, before being defeated by Sargon, founder of the Akkadian Empire. Further building activity continued during the Akkadian and Ur III periods, up to 2000BC when Uruk went into a decline for several centuries.

Later in the 2nd millennium Uruk to some extent regained its role as a major city with the launch of a massive programme of building in the cultural areas of the city. In the centuries after the death of Alexander the Great, Uruk was ruled by three important rulers who it is thought are buried in three large tumuli north of the city ruins. Uruk later came under the control of the Parthian and Sassanian empires. The city gradually declined until its final abandonment around the time of the Arab invasion in 634AD.

GETTING THERE Just outside the environs of Samawah, out on the main highway to Nasiriyah is the marked left turning road following an old course of the Euphrates to what is probably the most important site in Mesopotamia – Uruk.

WHERE TO STAY There is no accommodation or facilities for tourists at Uruk, so for your bed at night return to Samawah (see pages 300–1). Allow at least one hour for the drive.

OTHER PRACTICALITIES Situated along an old course of the Euphrates, and with a circumference of at least 14km, the ruins stretch across a vast area of the plain and this truly astonishing site takes time to view and to walk over. Improvements have been made with the new (2013) all-encompassing site fence, with a gated entrance and guard house. Here you will need your *khittab* (permission document) plus the receipt for the ticket purchased by your guide at the office of the Director of Archaeology in Samawah (US$20 per person for foreigners). This office is in an obscure location in a building with no number in a street with no name. So you will need the services of an Iraqi speaking guide to arrange this for you. From the guard house it is a short drive to the German dig house and storage buildings and the house of the Arab guardian of the site and his family. On this site all visitors are accompanied by site police.

Note: At Uruk you must remember to bring a hat and carry water, for in certain months you may be walking in 40+°C degree heat under a fierce sun with no shade.

WHAT TO SEE AND DO The first excavations at Uruk were conducted by William Loftus in the mid 19th century. A long series of German excavations at the site commenced in 1912 and continued until the 1970s. Despite this, the earliest levels of the site have not been extensively explored, largely because of difficulty of access through the accumulation of later deposits and buildings, but also because of modern groundwater levels. The prehistoric culture discovered in the lowest levels excavated represents the appearance of the civilisation of Sumer, and shows several innovations as compared with the Ubaid period. Pottery is unpainted and for the first time made on the wheel, with better defined shapes often mimicking those of metal vessels, and fitted with spouts or handles. Buildings are larger, more elaborate and decorated with the famous 'cone mosaics', in which terracotta cones with painted heads are pressed into wet mud plaster forming a decorative pattern. Examples of these can be found all across the site.

It is thought that the site may originally have consisted of two settlements or cultic centres, the Inanna precinct and the Anu Ziggurat, which surrounded shrines to the male and female deities Anu and Inanna. The archaeological remains of the Temple of Inanna, its archives and ziggurat are of prime importance. Remains of mud-brick structures, some perhaps temples in the Inanna precinct have been excavated and typical Ubaid painted pottery and baked-clay implements were discovered in them. In both areas religious buildings have been excavated including the Limestone Temple, the Stone Building and the Stone Cone Temple, all of which probably date back to c3600BC as well as more recent structures. The Greek influence on the art of Uruk can be seen in the many baked-clay figures which have been excavated dating from this period.

Uruk is also famous for finely carved seals implying personal ownership. Initially made in the 'stamp' form, these later gave way to the more common cylinder seal, many of which have been found by archaeologists on this site. At the dig house area there are now new blue placards describing the history of the site. There are also placards implanted in front of every major excavated building on the site, which can be somewhat intrusive to the keen photographer!

From the dig house you will see the rail tracks and wagons left behind by the German archaeologists and excavators, and which were used to move the immense amounts of spoil dug out of the site. For the lay visitor to absorb the atmosphere and gain the overall impression of the site, first walk past the great temple excavation to the foot of the Anu Ziggurat, noting the mosaic cones and sherds under your feet. As you climb the ziggurat you will see that the staircase is made of sun-dried bricks. Observe the details of its construction, made from layers of palm fronds and lime. From the top of the ziggurat you will have magnificent views across the whole of the site. Around the ziggurat you will see the ruins of the temples and the temple precinct walls. In the distance is an intriguing mound, the so called Tombs of the Greek Kings. Descend the ziggurat and cross north over the huge piles of excavation spoil and pot sherds to the Seleucid Temple and Parthian temples and palaces. Dwarfed by these mounds, your eyes and feet are immersed in mosaic cones and pottery fragments dating back many millennia. You are in the centre of thousands of years of history of which the wind and rain bring up further evidence daily. If you are lucky you may see a desert fox or hare scampering away from you.

After reaching the temples, walk along past the Parthian mounds, palaces and tombs and struggle up to the other ziggurats and temple buildings. Here you can see the most amazing palace complex, with walls covered in lapis lazuli. This beautiful stone, imported at vast cost from Afghanistan, once covered all the walls of rooms in this palace. Here also you will see every so often brick columns revealed under piles of rubble, their remains illustrating the grandeur of the palace of which they were once part and the skill of the craftsmen, long gone, who fashioned them. As you finish your walk and return to the site house, note the remains of the mosaic walls contained in the other palaces.

LARSA (MODERN TELL SENKEREH)

Larsa is a tell near Ur representing one of the ancient city states of Sumer, where King Ur-Gur is said to have built the E-Babbar ziggurat and the temple dedicated to the sun god, Shamash. Larsa is also the site of the biblical Chaldean town of Ellasar of which Arioch was the King (Genesis: Chapter14). Larsa has never been properly explored archaeologically, and most of its history has been established by way of documents from other sites.

HISTORY Larsa was founded around 2750BC by a Semite conqueror from Amurru, in modern day Syria, who overthrew Ibi-Sin, king of Ur. The city prospered under King Naplanum (c2025–2005BC), a contemporary of King Ishbi-Erra of Isin. Naplanum was succeeded by 13 more kings, many of whom became dominant in Babylonia and were instrumental in the emergence of the Semitic Akkadian Empire which replaced the Sumerian era. Larsa flourished in this period of Sumerian decline, when following the overthrow of the King of Ur in c1950BC by the Elamites and Amorites, Larsa and Isin became rivals for the supremacy of Mesopotamia. To start with Isin predominated; however, by the reign of kings Gungunum and Abisare (c1932–1895BC) in Ur, records show that Larsa was in its ascendancy. During the sovereignty of King Warad-Sin (1834–1823BC) Larsa prospered, improved irrigation helped farming and husbandry and long-distance trade in crops and animal products such as fleeces stretched from the Euphrates to the Indus. Schools were founded and, as the numerous business records inscribed on clay tablets found dating from this period attest, the arts flourished. Larsa's greatest ruler was King Rim-Sin, who destroyed Isin in c1794BC, before being attacked by Hammurabi of Babylon in c1763BC. Rim-Sin appealed to his allies, the Elamites, who came to his assistance; however, they were defeated by the armies of Hammurabi, leaving Larsa in the hands of the Babylonian conqueror, who assumed primacy of the whole area.

GETTING THERE AND AWAY The site of Tell Senkereh, as the remains of ancient Larsa is known locally today, can be found approximately 20km to the east of Uruk, part way between Ur and Erech on the left bank of the Euphrates.

OTHER PRACTICALITIES Although guards have been designated for the site, you are highly unlikely to see one during your visit. Large areas of the site are covered with wind-blown sand or eroded brick. The site is unfenced.

WHAT TO SEE AND DO The remains of Larsa, which comprises the mound with its ziggurat rising above them, cover an oval about 6km in circumference. Although some evidence suggests the site was occupied during the Ubaid period, the earliest excavated phases are Early Dynastic in date (c2900–2350BC). Excavations have concentrated on the Temple of Shamash and the ziggurat. Several large houses of the Old Babylonian period have also been uncovered.

Known in earlier days as Sinkara rather than Tell Senkereh, the site was first excavated briefly by William Loftus in the 1850s. Loftus centred his efforts on the Temple of Shamash, where he discovered inscriptions of Burna-Buriash II of the Kassite Dynasty of Babylon and Hammurabi of the 1st Babylonian Dynasty. Loftus described the mound of the ziggurat and the temple as a 'low, circular platform, about 6km in circumference, rising gradually from the level of the plain to a central mound 22m in height. Judging from the inscriptions, the kings Hammurabi, Burna-Buriash and Nebuchadnezzar II of Babylon restored or rebuilt the Temple of Shamash'. Bricks excavated from the reign of Nebuchadnezzar II identified the site as ancient Larsa, and Loftus speculated that Larsa and its suburb, Senkereh, ceased to be inhabited around the time of the Persian conquest in the 1st millennium BC.

Further excavations were briefly carried out by Walter Andrae in 1903. Edgar James Banks who visited the site in 1905 found widespread looting by the local population taking place there. A more scientific examination of the site had to wait until 1933, when Andre Parrot conducted brief excavations. Parrot uncovered the ziggurat, the Temple of Shamash, and a palace believed to be that of Nur-Adad (1865–1850BC), as well as many tombs and other Neo-Babylonian and Seleucid remains. Parrot again excavated the site in 1967, followed by Jean-Claude Margueron, who worked on the site intermittently until 1970. For 13 seasons between 1976 and 1991, an expedition of the Délégation Archéologique Française en Iraque, led by J-L Huot, excavated at Larsa.

A century after Banks, looting was again discovered to have taken place at the site. In June 2008 a team from the British Museum visited Larsa and reported that following extensive looting in 2003 a guard tower had been erected and the presence of guards seemed to have been effective in deterring further looting. However, when they visited the guard tower had not been used for some time (as demonstrated by a nest with a young hawk within the observation platform). From the top of the E-Babbar and neighbouring smaller mounds they observed little evidence of looting holes, and saw no clear evidence of recent disturbances at the site.

Continuing south to Nasiriyah and Basra, we can first view the sites that resonate down through history back to the dawn of transition from hunter gatherer to the settled to the village and town and city.

TELL UBAID

The small tell of Ubaid is the site of an ancient Sumerian city which provided the important pottery sequence that defines the Ubaid period. Today (2015), this site seems a desolate, lonely little mound of a place. But it is a remarkable signpost to our civilisation, and just to be here is enough.

GETTING THERE Tell Ubaid is 6km west of Ur in Dhi Qar Governorate, a few kilometres from Nasiriyah where the Saddam Highway and Highway 8 cross. Close by here and just within sight of the road there is a turn off to the left onto a small desert road which leads to Tell Ubaid. It is the only turning and once you have made it you will know you are on the right track as you will find a view of Tell Ubaid in the distance below you.

OTHER PRACTICALITIES The site is incompletely fenced, not gated and crossed by vehicle tracks. There are no designated guards for Ubaid, but guards from Ur have responsibility for protecting the site.

WHAT TO SEE AND DO The majority of the remains are, not surprisingly, from the Ubaid period. To the southwest of the site is an extensive cemetery, with graves dating back to the Ubaid and Early Dynastic periods (c3000–2350BC). The remains of a mud-brick temple platform and staircase dating from Early Dynastic III (c2500BC) to the 3rd Ur Dynasty (c2000BC) have been excavated. The temple has not survived, but decorative elements of the building can be found at the base of the platform. These originally included copper lions with bitumen cores and a copper panel showing the lion-headed eagle, Imdugud. Simple houses from the late Ubaid period (c4000BC) have been uncovered containing typical Ubaidian painted pottery.

Ubaid was probably abandoned at the beginning of the Early Dynastic period. The first large excavation of Tell Ubaid was conducted in 1919, initially by Henry

The Ubaid period is a prehistoric era which represents the earliest settlement in southern Mesopotamia. It was first identified by Jacques de Morgan at the beginning of the 19th century and dates back to between 5500BC and the beginning of the Uruk period, around 4000BC.

Ubaid culture began to spread into Mesopotamia around the 5th millennium BC, replacing the Halaf Culture. In southern Mesopotamia the Ubaid period dates from around 5200–3500BC, but in the north it developed later, around 4300BC. Some experts think that the characteristics of the northern Ubaid period may have been developments from the preceding Halaf period, rather than being directly influenced by the south. Overall, though, Ubaid culture is one of great homogeneity throughout Mesopotamia and the whole area from the Persian Gulf to the Mediterranean.

The Ubaidians themselves were a pre-urban people who lived in large agricultural village settlements growing wheat, barley and lentils and tending livestock such as sheep, goats and cattle. It is believed that they built the first temples in Mesopotamia. Ubaidian sites included Lagash, Eridu and Ur, all of which later became important centres of the Uruk civilisation which followed.

Excavations have uncovered Ubaidian remains throughout the whole of southern Mesopotamia. Ubaid pottery was painted in geometric designs and often fired at very high temperatures, resulting in a greenish colour. It was decorated with geometric and sometimes floral and animal designs. Many vessels appear to have been made on a slow wheel and had the first-known loop handles and spouts.

Other artefacts typical of the Ubaid period include distinctive baked-clay figurines, both male and female, with conical headdresses, coffee-bean shaped eyes, and with a slightly lizard-like appearance.

Tools such as sickles, bent clay nails (thought to be for attaching reed matting to clay walls), net-weights and socked axes, were often made of hard-fired clay in the south. In the north stone, and sometimes metal, were also used for tools, and copper artefacts appear occasionally.

Hall and later by Leonard Woolley (in 1923–24). Woolley's excavations uncovered parts of a platform of a temple 4,500 years old. The temple had decayed, but Woolley found objects which may have decorated it. Thought to be dedicated to Ninhursag, Sumerian mother goddess, it was surrounded by an oval-shaped enclosure wall. While much of the temple has now been dismantled, the platform, with façades faced with baked brick is almost intact, although much of the temple decoration has been removed. The wall-faces nearby were decorated with three-dimensional friezes of animals, including lions, moulded in high relief and sheathed in copper. These temple decorations can now be seen in the British Museum. Further fieldwork was subsequently carried out by the British and Americans in the 1920s and 1930s, including those of P Delougaz and S Lloyd in 1937.

In June 2008 the site was visited by a team from the British Museum who reported that the tell had been extensively damaged by military installations when it was established by the Iraqis as a command post in early 2003. They observed a 4m-square hollow about 1.5m deep on the summit of the mound which was probably the position of a radar station, along with numerous other hollows and pits around the mound, which may have been dug by the military.

According to Mesopotamian tradition, the Sumerian city of Eridu ranks as 'the oldest city in the world'. Interestingly Eridu is explicitly described by ancient writers as 'standing upon the shores of the sea' and Ur, situated only a few miles away, 'had quays at which ocean-going vessels discharged their cargoes'. Both of these cities today are almost 160km from the shoreline.

HISTORY The city's origin is lost in the mists of antiquity. It may have been founded before the great deluge echoed in Sumerian literature. It was certainly occupied in the El Ubaid period, during the first half of the 4th millennium BC, and possibly earlier.

The founder of the 3rd Ur Dynasty, Ur-Nammu (2123–2106BC), restored its temples and built a ziggurat which today still rises above the rest of the ruins. Its destruction by the Elamites at the end of the 3rd millennium BC and the diversion of the course of the River Euphrates in the time of the Larsa Dynasty (beginning of the 2nd millennium BC) brought about its gradual abandonment. In the Neo-Babylonian period, the last period of architectural grandeur for the ancient land of Sumer, its temples are no longer mentioned. Excavations at this site began in AD1850 and have continued intermittently over the years.

GETTING THERE Eridu is further along the road from Tell Ubaid. It is possible to lose one's way, but continue past a firing range and a pumping station and eventually you will come to the site.

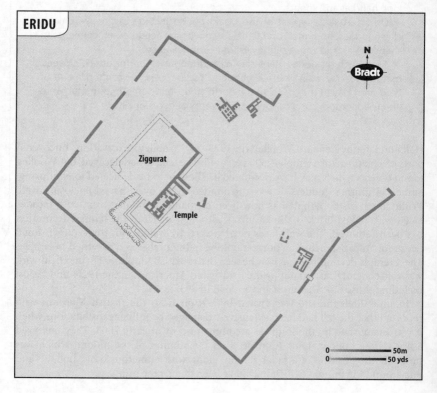

OTHER PRACTICALITIES The site is not easy to access, as often you have to drive down very muddy tracks and it also near modern sites of some sensitivity. Visitors rarely manage to visit.

WHAT TO SEE AND DO The ziggurat stands on a great rectangular terrace 200m by 120m, covering older remains. It consists of a core of unbaked bricks covered in baked bricks stamped with the name of Ur-Nammu. The ziggurat stands on a platform of 15m². A triple staircase, the centre stairs of which were covered in stone slabs, led to the upper level. A total of 16 temples have been discovered to the south of the tower in different levels of excavation. An extensive cemetery dating back to the Ubaid period has been excavated. There is also evidence of later occupation of the site, up until the 4th century BC.

When you reach this desolate, windy city mound, which is strewn with Ubaid and later-period pottery and even early sickles, you will feel amazed as to how anyone could have lived and settled here. Today even the local tribes-people have moved away. But in the past the sea, rivers and marshes abounded here as you can see from the masses of sea shells on the site. Here is silence with only the wind for company; you can feel it is not only the end of a world but it could also be the beginning of our civilisation, the oldest city in the world. Sadly the site was the scene of fighting after 2005 and although just 22km from Ur and its military base, troops only came here in armed, track vehicles. It is not safe to pick up anything metal as bullet rounds and detonators can be found on the ground around the site.

UR (TELL MUQEIHAR)

Ur, together with Babylon, is probably the best known city of Mesopotamia. The wealth of modern literature and the glittering objects in museums worldwide has made this so. Ur is known locally as Tell Muqeihar or 'mound of bitumen', a name taken from the 18m-high ruins of the ziggurat, which dominated the otherwise desolate site. During the 3rd Ur Dynasty (c2124–2015BC) Ur was probably isolated from the plain by the Euphrates, which is thought to have flowed to the west of the ziggurat at a distance of perhaps 200m and by a system of canals which acted as a protection for the city. At this time the city had two harbours, one to the north and the other to the southwest. The rest of the city was entirely taken up by the official and residential quarters.

HISTORY Although it had been inhabited since the end of the Neolithic age, 'Ur of the Chaldees', Abraham's native city, first comes on the historical scene in the El Ubaid period (about 4000–3400BC). At the time of the 1st Ur Dynasty, the beginnings of which can be placed in about the 27th century BC, Ur succeeded the older dynasties of Kish and Uruk and became the great Sumerian metropolis. Five kings succeeded one another over a period of 171 years and the destruction of this dynasty seems to have been achieved in the latter part of the 26th century BC by Eannatum, the vassal prince of Lagash. After a period of disturbances in which the kings of Elam, Kish, Uruk, Adab, Mari and Lagash fought fiercely for the hegemony of Sumer, the Akkadians, under the leadership of Sargon of Agade (2400–2344BC), brought about the unification of these territories.

About 2255BC the Guti hordes from the Zagros Mountains invaded Mesopotamia and finally put an end to this dynasty about 2220BC. After a time, the old Sumerian principalities seemed to recover a measure of independence under the leadership of these barbarians. Around 2131BC Utu-Hegal overthrew the Guti power and became King of the Four Regions. After reigning for seven years he in turn was overthrown by his own vassal Ur-Nammu, first governor and then King of Ur, who defeated

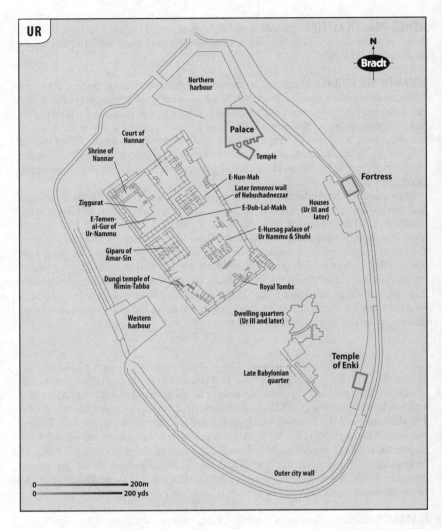

UR

N

Bradt

Northern
harbour

Palace

Temple

Court of
Nannar

Shrine of
Nannar

E-Nun-Mah

Fortress

Later *temenos* wall
of Nebuchadnezzar

Ziggurat

E-Dub-Lal-Makh

Houses
(Ur III and
later)

E-Temen-
al-Gur of
Ur-Nammu

E-Hursag palace of
Ur Nammu & Shuhi

Giparu of
Amar-Sin

Dungi temple of
Nimin-Tabba

Royal Tombs

Western
harbour

Dwelling quarters
(Ur III and later)

Temple
of Enki

Late Babylonian
quarter

Outer city wall

0 ⎯⎯⎯ 200m
0 ⎯⎯⎯ 200 yds

the King of Uruk and took the title King of Sumer and Akkad. This reversal of the situation after the long Akkadian supremacy and the sombre Guti interlude ratified the ephemeral renaissance of the Sumerian civilisation. Five kings succeeded one another and constituted the 3rd Ur Dynasty for 108 years (2123–2015BC). The Sumerian kings continued the policy of expansion of the kings of Akkad and made war against Elam; Shulgi, King of Ur from 2105 to 2058BC, penetrated as far as Urbillum (now Erbil) and Shimurra the present Altun Kopru. In about the 25th year of his reign he married one of his daughters to the King of Anshan (Elam) and became its suzerain. Bur-Sin (2057–2049BC) succeeded him and undertook a campaign against Assyria where he appointed an Akkadian governor, Zarikum (he who squints); Urbillum was sacked in 2055BC. Gimil-Sin made a reconnaissance into Elam and attacked Anshan, but was unable to subjugate Simash. Ibi-Sin (2039–2015BC), the last king of the dynasty of Ur, engaged in an unfortunate war against Simash, who got possession of Susa. On another front the Amorites led by Ishbi-Irra from Mari attacked Nippur and Kazallu. Ibi-Sin finally succumbed in 2015BC.

Ur, his capital, was taken and destroyed by the Elamites and the last Sumerian kingdom broke up into small rival principalities which were to be united under the leadership of the 1st Babylonian Dynasty.

In the Kassite period a king of Babylon, Kurigalzu, set about the restoration of the city's sanctuaries, which had been more or less abandoned, but Ur gradually declined. In the 6th century BC, Nebuchadnezzar II restored the *temenos* (sacred area) with its six gates and rebuilt the great ziggurat. The city was captured by the Persians at the same time as Babylonia (539BC) and standing as it did at a distance from the Euphrates, which had moved away to the east, its prosperity slowly diminished until Ur practically ceased to exist around the year 400BC.

GETTING THERE There is a 22km local road which runs via Tell Ubaid and Eridu to Ur. By road from Nasiriyah it is 12km south to the site of Ur.

WHAT TO SEE AND DO Before undertaking the tour of Ur you are recommended to climb the ziggurat if you are allowed to. By doing so, you will clearly see the whole area of the ruins spread out panoramically below you. From the top of the steps and to your right if you look down on the major building you will see the Haram or sacred enclosure, which is surrounded by a trapezium-shaped wall dating from the Neo-Babylonian period, the outline of which can still be seen. Inside the Haram you will see several ruins, including the E-Dub-Lal-Makh to the southeast and, beyond it, the hypogea of the 3rd Dynasty. The last of these summit shrines was built by Nabonidus, a Chaldean king of Babylon, and replaced by a 3rd-Dynasty sanctuary which must have survived all through the 2nd millennium BC.

The visible remains of the ziggurat itself are of two widely different periods, an early structure built by Ur-Nammu about 2300BC having been enlarged and rebuilt by Nabonidus. The 6th-century BC ziggurat was a very different structure from that of the 23rd century BC. It was much higher, much more bulky, and above the first terrace, which remained unchanged; it bore no relation to its predecessor.

The 3rd-Dynasty mausoleum contains the Royal Tombs which form the eastern limit of the great cemetery. The graves vary in date from the beginning of the Early Dynastic to the end of the Akkadian Period, and were consequently superimposed and often inter-penetrating. The majority have disappeared in the process of excavating, but some of the vaulted tombs in which important people were buried still remain. The actual structures of these are interesting. They are built of stone rubble or baked brick. Some have several compartments, covered by barrel-vaults or occasionally true domes. Those which Sir Leonard Woolley was fortunate enough to discover unrifled produced a great wealth of jewellery and precious objects, much of which may now be found in the Iraq Museum in Baghdad and the British Museum in London. There are many beautifully designed vessels of gold and silver with jewellery and personal ornaments; toilet sets, musical instruments, gem-encrusted daggers and many art treasures. Woolley identified a few graves as the tombs of royal personages, and these, in addition to the personal adornments and furniture buried with the deceased in the actual tomb chamber, included the bodies and paraphernalia of a considerable retinue of attendants sacrificed so that they might accompany their lord on his journey to another world. One individual called Abargi, who is believed to be the husband of Shubad (see box, pages 312–13), had been attended to the grave by a company of soldiers, courtiers and women, whose bodies could be seen laid out in rows in the open shaft in which the tomb-chamber was built. Even wagons with their

In 1854 J E Taylor, who was British Consul at Basra, excavated the base of the ziggurat and from inscriptions he found there he identified the site with 'Ur of the Chaldees', biblical home of Abraham. Further excavations were carried out by the University of Pennsylvania and the British Museum (1918–19), but the best-known work was carried out by the archaeologist Sir Leonard Woolley during the period 1922–34.

Work at the site established that Ur's earliest inhabitants lived in huts with mud-coated reed walls, not dissimilar to those later built by the Marsh Arabs. They used flints as tools and made figures and decorated pottery from clay, known as Ubaid pottery from the eponymous Ubaid period. They were also traders, trading their wares with distant cities. This level of occupation ceased abruptly, following a severe flood which left a layer of silt between 1m and 4m deep covering most of the lower site. Woolley believed that this flood covered not just Ur, but the whole of low-lying Iraq and was the Great Flood of Noah referred to in the Bible and mentioned in the Sumerian *Epic of Gilgamesh*. Following the level of the flood, the site was re-occupied and similar types of artefacts were unearthed as found in the layers beneath the silt – inscribed tablets, jar sealings and seals.

In 1922, while clearing a cemetery area close to the ziggurat platform, Woolley came across the so-called Royal Cemetery. The upper graves had been buried under the middens of subsequent inhabitants, but their inscriptions dated them back to the Akkadian Dynasty. Below them tombs from the Early Dynasty III (c2500BC) were found. Ancient tomb robbers had been at work in these, and many were despoiled; however, some were found intact and in the most sumptuous, that of Meskalamshar, a spear with a golden shaft was found, alongside gold-mounted daggers, an axe head and other items of jewellery. His engraved helmet of beaten gold, one of the finest examples of Sumerian workmanship ever found, was still in place on his head.

Sixteen of the brick-lined tombs were found to contain not only the bodies of the deceased royalty, but also numerous of their servants. The grave of Queen Shubad was found to contain the bodies of 64 maid servants and 4 harpists, all wearing ceremonial dress and jewellery. Even the donkeys that had pulled the wooden sled used to carry the Queen's body into the tomb were also slain, along with their drivers. As in burials from the 1st Egyptian Dynasty (where humans were later replaced by statues), the attendants (numbering between 6 and 80) who accompanied the royal corpses to their graves were part of the burial ritual. It is thought they entered the tombs voluntarily, and took poison in the hope of continuing in service to their masters in the next life. The contents of this tomb, although flattened by the weight of the overlying debris, were intact and the queen's headdress, jewellery, inlaid lyres and a pair of statues of standing goats made of gold, lapis lazuli and white shell, along with many gold and silver objects are among the most magnificent antiquities discovered in Iraq.

draught animals were included. Many more graves were discovered. The site of this city is huge and remarkable remains can be seen of the harbour temples and the great city wall which is an astonishing piece of work and almost oval in shape.

The site today This site has been connected to the air-force base and its perimeters for a long time. The air base was built and occupied by the British air force during the 1930s, then the Iraqi air force, followed by the US air force and is

The vaulted mausoleum of Ur-Nammu and those of his successors Shulgi and Amar-Suen were also excavated by Woolley. King of the 3rd Dynasty (c2110–2015BC) Ur-Nammu rebuilt the walled city, the ziggurat, the royal palace and many other religious and public buildings. Woolley discovered more than 2,000 inscribed tablets which painted a vivid picture of the economic life of Ur and its trading links, which stretched as far away as India. The texts also described the offerings and taxes paid to Nannar, the moon god who was the chief deity of the city, as well as literary works and even school reports. A victory stele was also discovered which detailed some of Ur-Nammu's military activity across his dominions in Iraq.

In 1930 Woolley started to dig in the residential suburb southeast of the sacred enclosure. This area dated to the Isin-Larsa period (c2000BC) when Ur was conquered by the semi-nomadic Semites and Isin became the capital in its place. Its ruler, Ishme-Dagan rebuilt a palace at Ur for his daughter Enannatum whom he dedicated as high priestess to Nannar. He also reconstructed the ziggurat and its terraces, work which was continued by his successor, Warad-Sin of Larsa. Woolley's excavations showed that the buildings here were linked by narrow streets and entered through a gateway into a courtyard, from which led off reception rooms, guest rooms, servants quarters, the kitchen, bathroom and store rooms. The main living quarters were on the upper storey, the rooms having balconies which overlooked the courtyard. Some of the houses had private chapels and some belonged to merchants, who expanded or downsized their property as their fortunes waxed and waned. Elsewhere a public place of worship and a school house were discovered and Woolley estimated that at its peak the city may have had more than 250,000 inhabitants. Ur suffered a further blow in 1737BC when it was again destroyed and it lay fallow for many centuries until in c1400BC King Kurigalzu rebuilt the Ningal Temple, the Egishshirgal (great gateway) into the sacred enclosure and the House of Tablets.

Under the Chaldean Kings Ur once again entered into a period of greatness. In the 6th century BC, King Nebuchadnezzar II started rebuilding Ur, work which was continued after his death by Nabonidus, his successor. The main temples were remodelled, and a further four levels were added to the ziggurat, increasing it to seven in total. The Harbour Temple and the Palace of Belshalti-Nannar were built, within the ruins of which Woolley found an ancient 'museum' containing a carefully preserved Kassite boundary stone, part of a statue of Shulgi, King of Ur (2029–1982BC), as well as objects from the Larsa period and copies of inscriptions from the 3rd Dynasty (of which the originals also survive). A small drum-shaped clay object was inscribed with an inventory of some of the items.

Ur continued to be occupied until the late-Persian period when the River Euphrates changed its course leaving the city buried beneath sand and rubble. The most recent document that has been excavated from the site was dated 316BC.

now back in Iraqi hands. In the early days, certainly in the 1970s, access to the site was limited due to the security measures put in place by Saddam's regime. After 2003 these measures were re-introduced under the Americans. Now we are able to access this site again. In 2014 it had been partially re-fenced and gated. A reception centre was added and golf buggies are available for people to travel in around the site. Walkways have been constructed between the ziggurat, the Royal Tombs and the re-constructed Abraham's House. From the top of the ziggurat you can clearly see the harbour depressions, the various temples and the palace foundations. The Royal Tombs are fenced off, partly to protect them, but also because their roofs are damaged and potentially dangerous to tourists. Close by the tombs you can see the 'Pit' or 'Woolley's Pit'. This 35m-deep excavation was an attempt by Woolley to plumb to the ground levels of the site, and Woolley subsequently cabled a telegram to London newspapers to say that he had found evidence of the biblical flood in the pit. Behind the Royal Tombs are some large spoil heaps and the foundations of many ancient houses, a few of which have been reconstructed. It is claimed that this is the place where Abraham lived with his family. Plans are still current for some minor archaeological work, but mostly the site is being planned as an important tourist and visitor centre.

NASIRIYAH *Telephone code 42*

Nasiriyah was once the most important point of entry to the Marshes. The marshlands around Nasiriyah once provided up to 70% of the country's fish and dairy products. Today, however, there is only enough for local consumption. The population of Nasiriyah is nearly exclusively Shia Muslim with small Mandean and Sunni Muslim communities. Until 1951 the town was home to a sizable Jewish community.

HISTORY The city, which dates back to 1870, was originally a meeting place and market for the local tribes. It was named after its founder Sheikh Nasir Sadun. During World War I in July 1915 around 400 British and Indian soldiers were killed in the battle for Nasiriyah, fought against the Turks who controlled the city. During the 1991 Gulf War the Coalition forces decided not to proceed any further into Iraq than Nasiriyah, following the liberation of Kuwait in accordance with UN resolutions. During this period all the bridges in the Nasiriyah area were bombed by the British air force, and only in 2014 were the temporary pontoon bridges constructed after the bombings replaced with permanent structures. The Shia population took part in the uprising against Saddam Hussein, which he subdued with heavy loss of life and destruction.

During the 2003 Gulf War the tranquillity of life in Nasiriyah was severely disrupted once again when the Americans tried to capture a nearby bridge over the Euphrates. They fought one of the longest battles of the war and reacted to snipers with house searches and arrests. 'Sniper Alley' was almost completely demolished as the Coalition advanced towards Baghdad. Even today Nasiriyah maintains its dissident reputation for unrest, and the security situation is still in flux.

GETTING THERE Located on the Euphrates, Nasiriyah is 208km north of Basra and 375km southeast of Baghdad, near the ruins of the ancient cities of Ur and Larsa.

GETTING AROUND The centre of Nasiriyah is quite small and it is easy to travel around on foot.

WHERE TO STAY AND EAT As in all these cities there are small hotels of the basic variety and also many small eating places and cafés. Opposite Al-Janoob Hotel are several tea houses and a local restaurant.

Al-Janoob Tourist Hotel (100 rooms) Theqar-Nasreya-Al-Naher St; m 0770 738 8398, 0780 669 1108. Situated along the corniche by the riverside, this hotel was established many years ago & has recently undergone major refurbishment. The hotel has a restaurant which serves reasonably priced food. *A single room costs US$90 & a double room US$160 per night.* **$$$**

SHOPPING In the main street and around the principal city roundabout are all the bazaar streets.

WHAT TO SEE AND DO All the bridges across the river adjacent to the central bazaar street were bombed during the two Gulf wars and have now been replaced. Unlike many Iraqi cities there are still a few bronze statues commemorating various political and religious leaders still standing. One along the river front, which commemorates the Ottoman battle against the British forces in 1915, is interesting as there are so few left in Iraq. In the past, before the Marshes were partly drained under Saddam, it was possible to begin your exploration of the Marshes from Nasiriyah by boat down the river. This will again become possible in the future.

AROUND NASIRIYAH There are two routes to Basra from this city. The minor route (Road 16) travels through the fringes of the Marshes via Al-Kabash to Querna (see page 317) and on to Basra. This route enables you to see the condition of the Marshes today and what is being done to revive them, and the attempts to reduce poverty among the tribes. For the keen photographer this is the best route to Basra.

TELL KHAIBER

Consisting of two mounds, Tell Khaiber, a mere 20km from Ur, has much to teach us about the ancient Ur city state. The tell appears to consist of large buildings, surrounded by a great deal of surface pottery dating from between 4000 and 2000BC. It was first documented by Henry T Wright in 1965 and mapped by the Iraqi State Organisation for Antiquities in 1972.

But its real significance is that it is the first dig (2013–14) by co-operating archaeologists (Iraqi, British and Italian) since the 1980s. Long may this continue. As professor Stuart Campbell and Dr Jane Moon from Manchester University have stated: 'the project is also building partnerships with local practitioners and local institutions'. The story of Tell Khaiber is begging to be told.

The second route, on Saddam Highway and Highway 8, skirts the Marshes and traverses the dry (previously wetlands) desert-like lands to Basra more directly. South of these roads are the provinces of Muthanna and Al-Basra. These desert lands, criss-crossed by desert tracks and very minor roads, border the Kingdom of Saudi Arabia. There are one or two known historic sites in the area, namely Kalat Abu Ghar and Qasr Shagrah, that are not currently possible to visit.

Note: The Saddam Highway continues south of Basra city to Safwan and Abdali, which are the border towns and crossing points between Iraq and Kuwait.

FOLLOW BRADT

For the latest news, special offers and competitions, subscribe to the Bradt newsletter via the website www.bradtguides.com and follow Bradt on:

- www.facebook.com/BradtTravelGuides
- @BradtGuides
- @bradtguides
- www.pinterest.com/bradtguides

9

Return from Basra

The region of Basra, the city of Sinbad the Sailor and the starting point of his famous adventurous voyages, is the most beautiful part of Iraq, outshining both the Persian miniature scenery of the central Euphrates and the cool, majestic north. The whole area of the south is lush and watered, full of trees and gardens, small boats gliding on the calm waterways. It is an area of countless birds and a variety of animals and, at certain times of the year, the shaded creek just below Ashar is full of bee-eaters, kingfishers and other birds flitting through the date gardens, the slanting sun through the trees producing a magical effect. Basra is Iraq's largest and main seaport. Although not ancient by Iraqi standards, for centuries it has been the centre of Iraq's commercial importance, with its endless ships shuttling back and forth on the Shatt Al-Arab.

When it comes time to leave, you can, of course, travel back to Baghdad the way that you came (on Highway 8) but to see more of the country we suggest two alternative routes, dependent on the time that you have available and where your interests lie. Whichever route you choose, it is advisable to leave Basra early, by 6am at the latest, which will clear you through the Basra traffic at a cool time of day with good light.

The first option, Highway 6, will take you northwest to Baghdad on a clear road, well served by restaurants and tea stops, although it is prone to flooding in certain sections around Amarah. It follows the route of the Tigris river and runs close to the Iranian border and the Marshes. This has been a source of problems at times when international politics has shown its face as it does from time to time here. This route also travels through the area which is supposed to have been the Garden of Eden. It is true that this is, and has been in the past, an extremely fertile region owing to an abundance of water, sun and irrigation canals. It is approximately 74km to Querna, which is the first town of interest on your route (see pages 328–9). From Querna your next stop will be Al-Uzair (see pages 340–1), a village on the banks of the Tigris. Quite close to the Iranian border and Marshes, is the putative 4th-century BC tomb of Ezra, the Old Testament prophet, priest and scribe who led the party of Jews returning from their Babylon exile and who came to be known as the father of Judaism. Ezra's work involved the reconstitution of the Jewish community based on the Torah and his influence on Jewish law, tradition and family life cannot be underestimated.

BASRA Telephone code 40

'Basra retains a romantic aura. So does the whole area of the south from the Shatt Al-Arab up to Al-Amarah on the Tigris and Suq-esh-shiukh on the Euphrates: it is lush, watered, full of trees and gardens and canoes gliding on the mirror-surfaces of calm lagoons. It is an area of countless birds and a variety of animals. You feel that lions, possibly dragons or the Great Roc of *A Thousand and One Nights* may appear. Its people, I judge, are the most beguiling of all Iraqis.'

from Iraq: Land of Two Rivers – *Gavin Young*

Gavin Young lived in Basra for two years during the 1950s. Today the visitor can capture *some* of that romantic aura, but the last 30 years of war, invasion and insurrection have left their mark on the city. Much needs to be done to renew, cleanse, construct and revitalise this port.

Basra vies with Mosul as Iraq's second city. It is the principal port of Iraq and is situated on the banks of the Shatt Al-Arab (the waters formed by the union of the Tigris and Euphrates). The adjacent terrain is low lying and deeply intersected by creeks and small watercourses peopled by date palms which do much to enhance the region. The city is penetrated by a complex network of canals and streams, vital for irrigation and general agricultural use. These canals were once used to transport goods and people throughout the city, hence the misnomer 'Venice of the East' ascribed to Basra. Today the drop in the levels of water and the extreme pollution of the waterways has made such use impossible. The budding port of yesterday has diminished and moved south of the city centre, and the Shatt Al-Arab is no longer so crowded with large shipping and boats scampering in all directions. The port area is surrounded by devastation and derelict land. The actual docks cannot be visited without special permission. These docks are capable of handling large ships and container freight traffic which the Shatt Al-Arab cannot.

The weather is the major drawback to Basra. The summer humidity is intense and temperatures often soar to above 50°C.

HISTORY The early history of Basra and its immediate environs is somewhat obscure and waiting for modern archaeological techniques to explore it. But its position at the head of the Gulf and the outlet of the twin rivers and its proximity to the ancient Sumerian cities means that it must always have been an area of strategic

SINBAD THE SAILOR

The legend of Sinbad the Sailor and his voyages around the world has been recounted for more than 1,000 years. A merchant from the city of Basra, Sinbad made seven voyages to the lands and islands around the Indian Ocean to restore his lost fortune. On each voyage Sinbad came across foreign lands and strange creatures, allowing him to use his intelligence and courage to overcome a dangerous creature or an evil tyrant, always finding a solution by using his ingenuity, diplomacy and strength. As one story ends, so another begins forming a dramatic and exciting cycle of heroic acts. Overcoming numerous dangers, Sinbad manages to acquire great wealth during his travels.

The stories of Sinbad the Sailor appear in the classic book the *'Thousand and One Nights'*, (or the *Arabian Nights*, as it later came to be known), a collection of Persian, Arab and Indian tales interweaving Eastern social history and myth. Their origin is a mystery: no-one knows who first told them or where. Some believe the tales first appeared in *Hazarafsaneh* (*Thousand Stories*), a collection of Persian folktales, though opinion is divided. The original tales were often dark and adult, with wisdom seen as a powerful if not invincible tool in many of the stories.

On Sinbad's first voyage, he and his crew visit an island that turns out to be a huge sleeping whale. When they light a fire, the whale wakes up and dives underwater, taking Sinbad with it; however, he is rescued by another ship and taken home. In the second voyage Sinbad visits a desert island where he discovers an enormous egg, measuring up to 50 paces in circumference, belonging to a bird called a roc. (In Arabian legends roc are gigantic birds, often referred to as importance to be controlled by people with power, locally or internationally. One of the earliest records is that of Nearchus of Crete, the admiral appointed by Alexander the Great to build and sail his fleet along the coast from the mouth of the Indus river (now Karachi) to the head of the Gulf, the Shatt Al-Arab. Alexander himself returned with the bulk of his army through the Baluchistan Desert, losing many thousands of men and camp followers *en route* to Susa and Babylon. Nearchus had many adventures exploring the coast, and made his way eventually up part of the Tigris to meet Alexander. He mentions a small port and ship building facility – perhaps this was a precursor to Basra? Who knows? There are other mentions in history. The first Arab encampment (AD638) was built on the site of an older Persian settlement. Also, the Basra city area was known by the local Arab tribes as Al-Khaiba due to the existence of an ancient city called Al-Kharba. Following the Arab/Muslim invasion of Iraq and Iran (from 637 onwards), Basra was founded by Utba bin Ghazwan on order from the second caliph Umar ibn al Khattab, originally as a military base (as was Kufa) with a mosque built of mud and reeds. Of that and of the original palace nothing can be seen today. Basra was strategically placed for the subjugation of Iraq and Iran and this led to its growth. In 639 Umar established the city of Basra, with five districts and appointed the first governor, Abu Musa al Ashami. He was also to carry further the subjection of Persia.

The third caliph, Othman ibn Affan, was murdered in 656 and Ali ibn abi Talib was appointed fourth caliph. In the years during and after this caliphate, Basra was at the forefront of the political strife which arose between the competing religious factions of Islam, based in Damascus, Medina and Basra. The volatile social situation between the Arab army, who were the aristocracy, and others provoked unrest and insurrection, and Basra loomed into history once again in 656 with the

the 'Great', and capable of carrying off elephants for food. They appear in various tales in the Arabian Nights and are also mentioned by Marco Polo on his travels.) When the bird appears, Sinbad grabs its claws and is carried away to the Valley of Diamonds. Eventually rescued by merchants, he returns home laden with the precious stones.

During Sinbad's third voyage, he is captured by dwarves and taken to the home of a one-eyed giant who starts eating members of his crew. Sinbad manages to escape but is then lured to another island by a serpent that tries to eat him. Again, Sinbad escapes and is rescued by a passing ship. Shipwrecked on his fourth voyage, Sinbad and his crew are taken prisoner by cannibals who plan to eat them. Sinbad escapes to a strange kingdom where he marries the daughter of the king. When she dies, however, Sinbad is buried alive with her. He succeeds in escaping yet again.

On the fifth voyage Sinbad's ship is destroyed by an angry roc, which drops huge stones on it from the air. Washed ashore on an island, he meets and kills the Old Man of the Sea. On his sixth voyage Sinbad is again shipwrecked on an island where he finds precious stones and visits the city of Serendib, whose king returns him home with even more wealth.

On his seventh and final voyage, Sinbad returns to Serendib. However, on the way home he is attacked by pirates and sold into slavery. Sinbad discovers an elephant burial ground containing a huge store of ivory tusks, so his owner grants him his freedom and enough ivory for him to return home a rich man.

raising there by Zubeir ibn al Awwam and Talha bin Ubaidullah of a force to resist the claim of Ali, the Prophet Mohammed's cousin, to the caliphate after the murders of caliphs Umar and Othman. The famous Battle of the Camel (656) between Aisha, the Prophet Mohammed's widow and Ali, the Prophet's son-in-law and the fourth caliph took place outside Basra to the west and it merely emphasised the disorder and vested interests. The battle resulted in the deaths of both Zubeir and Talha. Zubeir was buried on the battle site and that is why the small town that has grown up there is called Az Zubayr to this day. Ali was murdered in Kufa in 661 and various governors were appointed to Basra by succeeding caliphs. These governors not only had the responsibilities of governorship, but also those of the on-going campaigns that spread Islam through Persia and on to central Asia.

The foundation of the schism between Sunni and Shia Muslims took place against the backdrop of political and religious unrest in Basra and Kufa. Hussain ibn Ali, a pious man, the grandson of the Prophet Mohammed and son of the fourth caliph, set out from Medina with his family and tribal followers to Basra to reclaim his heritage. But the Governor in Damascus under the new caliph crushed Hussain's supporters in Basra, and Hussain and his entire family and followers met death at their hands near Kerbala. So began the path of blood and martyrdom that is still with us today. (See pages 19–20 for more on the schism.)

Now began 200 years of unrest, revolts and invasions. Remarkably in the 8th and 9th centuries, under the Abbasids, a great flowering of intellect took place in the city. Poetry and science and religious intellectuals, as exemplified by the Sufi mystic Rabie Basra, flourished. The city has carried this reputation to the present day. The great Friday Mosque was constructed in more peaceful times as the city grew. Then came the Mongols. In 1258 the Mongols under Hulagu Khan sacked Baghdad, and Basra capitulated to avoid a massacre and came under their control. A further decline and Basra re-located a few miles upstream.

The 16th century saw the explosion of European sea powers. First came the Portuguese who used the city to replenish their ships supplies and to trade, followed by the Dutch and the British. The Turks were also using the port by 1624 and the Portuguese assisted the Basra pasha (governor appointed by the Ottoman caliph in Istanbul) to repel a Persian invasion, following which they were granted a share of the customs and freedom from tolls. From the period 1625–68 Basra and its surrounding area was in the hands of local chieftains. However, from 1668 the Ottoman Turks extended their rule and took Basra to formally include it as part of their empire. A brief period of occupation in 1779 took place under the Zand Dynasty and Karim Khan Zand introduced Shia religious practices to the city. After much agitation, similar to elsewhere in their empire, in 1884 the Ottomans detached a southern part of the Baghdad vilayet and created a new vilayet of Basra in recognition of the growing importance of the city. The European traders, now well established, exerted considerable influence on the provincial government in this matter.

World War I At the turn of the 20th century, with the turmoil and clamour of nationality and political reform taking place throughout the Ottoman Empire, war came to Basra. With the influence of Germany now prominent, Turkey joined the war on their side. Soon after, at the outbreak of war in October 1914 between the Ottoman Empire and Great Britain, the British landed a Mesopotamian expeditionary force near Basra and the city was in British hands at the end of November.

Initially planned by the British Government of India as a pre-emptive move to protect British oil interests in the Persian Gulf, the capture of Basra began a process which ended in the British occupation of the three vilayets of Basra, Baghdad and Mosul by the end of 1918. These actions laid the foundations for the establishment of the state of Iraq and it is from this period that the history of that state begins.'

from A History of Iraq – *Charles Tripp.*

Under this occupation the British modernised the port by building wharfs, access roads and warehouses. All shipping had previously had to moor out in the Shatt Al-Arab, and goods and people were transferred to the shore by small boats. In 1930 these port installations were transferred to Iraqi ownership. Eventually Basra became the most important port in the Gulf for international shipping. During World War II it was very important for receiving equipment and supplies to be sent to Russia. The British Mandate of the vilayets was followed by the Kingdom of Iraq. Iraq was formally admitted to the League of Nations as an independent state governed by a constitutional monarch, King Faisal, installed by the British. This monarchical government was overthrown in July 1958 and a new republic formed, led by General Abd al Karim Qasim as Prime Minister. This was the end of direct British involvement with Iraqi governments. Basra as a city of trade, oil and agriculture continued as before. But just as the Iraqi state has had so many changes of political power, so has Basra been at the heart of many of these, albeit in the south, due to its predominantly Shia community and its strategic position at the head of the Gulf. From 1958–79, when Saddam Hussein was sworn in as President, many changes in power took place. Then in 1980 the Iraqi forces invaded Iran. This Iran-Iraq war ended in 1988 when a UN ceasefire resolution was accepted by Iran.

Iran-Iraq War The war lasted for eight years and had a devastating effect on Basra. The economy of the city had been constantly growing as the city became more prosperous although the poor, predominantly Shia, working in the date groves and rice fields could see little benefit. Basra became a front line and was constantly shelled in the latter part of the war. Many of the date palms were cut down and irrigation projects ceased. The port facilities came under attack in the fighting (the Iranian frontier was only 50km away) and the city never really recovered from the disaster of these days.

The First Gulf War After the end of the Iran-Iraq War came another conflict that involved Basra: the invasion of Kuwait in 1990. The author visited Basra briefly in 1989 and at that time the centre of the city had many shelled buildings and the canals through the centre were being cleared by foreign labour of the mess of cement and rubbish.) Saddam Hussein was fully aware of the fact that the ending of the war with Iran, the crushing of the Kurdish rebellion and the continued suffering of the Shias did not remove political pressure on his own position. The country was in debt, the Iraqi population had suffered immensely with more than 900,000 dead. The colossal amount required to refurbish the economy and keep the oil fields in production meant that Saddam had to produce some results or lose power and his life. He was unsuccessful in persuading OPEC to raise the price of oil and persuading Saudi Arabia and Kuwait to transfer the US$40 billion debt from loans to grants. So in August 1990 to keep his home critics assuaged, his forces invaded Kuwait by land, air and sea using Basra as their base. The occupation of Kuwait was accomplished within 24 hours. This annexation was presented as Saddam Hussein's cumulating achievement of Iraq's national goals, rectifying the injustice committed by British imperialism in separating Kuwait from Iraq when the boundaries of the state were drawn. The rest of the Arab world did not agree and joined the UN forces led principally by the US and Britain. The First Gulf War began and ended in February 1991 with huge damage to the oilfields of Kuwait and parts of Basra. The aftermath was dire: in March 1991 uprisings broke out across the south in the Shia cities of Basra, Al-Amarah, Nasiriyah, Najaf and Kerbala. They were said to be spontaneous against a hostile regime, but the rebel forces proved helpless against the Iraqi forces and these cities were recaptured with much destruction and loss of life. Thousands fled to Saudi Arabia and thousands more sought refuge in the southern marshes. Saddam had broken the southern Shia commanders and had retained power. He now deliberately neglected Basra city and the port suffered with decreased shipping in the Shatt Al-Arab and Basra shipping lanes, due to the bombing by the allied forces. A terribly difficult time ensued for Iraq, with the period of sanctions and the 'No Fly Zones' (both north and south). The greed, ruthlessness and desperation of the regime of Saddam Hussein who refused to abide by UN Resolutions led eventually to the Second Gulf War.

The Second Gulf War Basra was in a parlous position still recovering from the First Gulf War with so much destroyed. It was a focal point of problems: difficulty with its border with Iran and now Kuwait; restive tribal communities throughout the region of the south; and the general hostility emanating from Baghdad's Sunni-dominated regime with all its repressions and killings. Then began the Second Gulf War as the mainly US and British forces issued ultimatums following the UN Resolutions which were ignored. Hostilities began on 20 March 2003 with airstrikes throughout Iraq from Basra to Baghdad. This time, though, there was little support from the Arab world. The British and US forces captured the port of Umm Qasr on 25 March 2003 after some strong resistance, and Basra city fell soon afterwards and finally came under the control of the British in April 2003. Over a million people had to suffer without fresh water and electricity while this conflict had been taking place. The city and its environs had been heavily bombed and its citizens terrified. Many tried to flee. As with many Iraqi cities extensive looting by the people took place in Basra. Government buildings were destroyed; banks and hotels attacked and burnt out until British forces gained some semblance of control. The British now began a torrid period until the city was passed out of their control on 17 December 2007. With good intentions the US cleared the harbour and approaches at great financial cost and modernised it. The city institutions and services were overhauled and training programmes, which included the police force, were provided. Since 2007 the British have been training local customs, and navy forces, and attempting to promote internal and national border security. Despite the efforts of the British, the pervasive influence of Shia militia influenced local people and attacks by international and internal insurgents targeted foreign troops. Many worthwhile projects for the welfare of Basra citizens were deliberately sabotaged by vested interests.

In the meantime the battle for hearts and minds of local people was being fought by al Sadr's Mahdi Army (which controlled the police, the ports and customs), the armed wing of the Supreme Islamic Council, the Badr Brigade (which controls the intelligence commander), the Fadhile Party, a branch of the Sadrist Movement (which controls the tactical support unit) and about 20 tribes, which have their own smuggling business. Loyalties were a moveable feast with the militiamen switching sides depending on who paid the most.

The British forces, too few and underfunded due to lack of goodwill in Basra and the reluctance of the Government in the UK to fully support its own troops against a swell of negative British public support, lost the battle. Eventually, enough was enough; the Maliki Government, army and a combined Iraq and US force descended on the city and the Mahdi militia were forced to leave. Today the city, with the departure of the Coalition forces and the Mahdi militia, has gained some control although it is still struggling to renew itself.

Happily, change is now becoming apparent, with new bridges across the Shatt Al-Arab and new buildings beginning to emerge. A sports complex, constructed some distance from the city centre is looking superb. Progress is being made but optimism must be cautious; it is too early to expect a change. The Islamicisation of Basra has altered local life and conflict still simmers under the surface. The alcohol shops have gone, some of the owners were murdered and the purchasing of alcohol has now been forced underground. In the once lively streets, life is reduced and all are cautious and watchful.

THE ECONOMY The largest oil fields in Iraq are based in Basra Province and most of the oil exports leave from the Basra Oil Terminal. Contracts have been signed for the refurbishment of the facilities and the outlook is bright for the future. Inevitably, the growing petrochemical industry plays a large part in this area, with many factories enlarging. Agriculturally, this whole region is very fertile. Rice, maize, barley and wheat are major products. The once-famous Basra date industry is slowly recovering, but it will be years before the newly planted palms are productive and meanwhile Basra's reputation for the finest dates faces fierce worldwide competition. The port facilities for shipping and transport are a large part of the city's economy and indeed of the whole of Iraq. Umm Qasr is its main deep-water port, with dedicated areas for specific goods. The one good thing that has possibly emerged from all these latest wars is the widening and deepening of the port facilities.

GETTING THERE
By air Basra International Airport (886 3999) is located 20km northwest of Basra city. No airlines fly direct from the UK, but the following foreign airlines all fly from their home countries into Basra International Airport – Turkish (from Istanbul); Emirates and FlyDubai (from Dubai); Qatar (from Doha); Eithad (from Abu Dhabi) and Royal Jordanian (from Amman). Iraqi Airways fly into Basra locally from Baghdad, Erbil and Suleimaniyah, as well operating international flights from Amman, Beirut, Damascus, Dubai, Istanbul and Delhi.

Note: As in Baghdad, the road to the airport has many checkpoints and you will need to change from your taxi to another special authorised car when you approach the airport. Therefore, try to leave your hotel at least 3 hours before you need to arrive at the airport. Check-in is also a long process so expect waits and delays. There is a little coffee shop that is open most of the day and night, and a small gift and refreshments shop similarly open. The airport is fairly clean, if a little dusty; a wide-screen TV shows BBC News 24 or football and there are a few rows of plastic chairs for seating. Although the terminal is air-conditioned it's still quite hot. Expect to be shunted from departure lounge to departure lounge on the way to your flight.

You may need someone to pick you up from the airport as there have been instances of travellers being refused permission to leave without a local 'escort'. However, this could be a driver from the hotel you have booked into or a local company. Make sure that you agree a price for the transfer before starting the journey.

By train An overnight train service from Baghdad departs daily at 18.30 and is scheduled to arrive at 06.10 the next morning; however, delays are common. The train usually carries a restaurant car and sometimes 'tourist class' carriages. The railway station is a somewhat bare, basic building with minimum facilities.

By road Basra is situated 67km to the north of the Arabian Gulf and 549km southeast of Baghdad.

GETTING AROUND The city sprawls greatly. For the local, working population there is an extensive system of minibus transport, mostly with their set routes. But local knowledge is required to use this facility. **Taxis,** as in most of Iraq are the preferred mode of transport for visitors. Your hotel is the best and really the only way to organise your travel around the city. It will be safe and sensible to use their services. Taxis hailed from the street are not recommended for security reasons.

It is not advised to **hire a car** and drive yourself. The security procedures in place at this time (2015) make this method of travel virtually impossible. However, once security improves and it is possible to negotiate the numerous checkpoints without a local escort then car rental can be arranged via various international car rental companies who advertise a worldwide service.

WHERE TO STAY Basra lacks good, European-style, reasonably priced hotels, and some of the top-range hotels will use this fact to try to rip off customers. You will find that in some hotels room rates fluctuate dramatically, and you can be quoted from US$200 to US$800 for the same room depending on the season or if they are hosting a conference in the hotel or not.

Around and behind the Basra International Hotel are many mid-range and budget hotels and restaurants. These mainly attract local Iraqi and foreign workers so don't tend to advertise internationally or have websites. Many are heavily, or even fully, booked for months in advance, being the only places to stay for the influx of business people and workers in Basra. Standards in these hotels vary enormously. The best advice is to visit the area, check availability and price in person, and view the room and facilities before making a booking.

The streets in this hotel area are indescribably filthy and polluted and full of potholes. Building work is going on all around. A torch is highly recommended if you are visiting shops or restaurants after dark, although walking anywhere after dark currently in Iraq is not recommended.

Luxury

Basra International Hotel (205 rooms) m 0781 555 5472; e info@ basrahinternationalhotel.com. Previously the Sheraton, the Basra International Hotel opened in 2012. Located by the Shatt Al-Arab Corniche, many rooms have a magnificent sunset view. The hotel has a swimming pool, a tennis court, fitness centre & 5 restaurants. It's not cheap & definitely not 5-star by European standards, but for what you get it's still probably the best choice in Basra & the security getting in & out is quite tight. The rooms are comfortable & spacious with AC, although you may feel you are in a 1980s time warp with the velour bed covers & wooden decoration. The bathrooms are big, but despite the refurbishment broken fittings & fixtures are not unusual & in common with many hotels in Iraq you have to ask for towels, etc. Check-in is slow & service is quite inconsistent. The hotel has Wi-Fi but you have to pay extra & there doesn't seem to be a uniform charge so it is worth negotiating if you can. Check beforehand what is & is not included in the price you are quoted (for example b/fast, service charge, etc) to avoid any nasty shocks when you come to pay the bill.

The restaurant offers a daily open buffet with a variety of dishes including fish, chicken & meat. Cost of the open buffet is around US$45, exc drinks. Adjacent to the lobby is a small coffee & narghile shop that has a lovely view of Shatt Al-Arab. There is also a small shop. *Rooms cost US$240–730 pp per night.* **$$$$**

Mnawi Basha Hotel Cairo District. The Mnawi Basha Hotel is located on a quiet side street in an area where many international companies have their offices. Although away from the rush & bustle of central Basra, it is not that distant from the city centre as well as being handy for the airport. The hotel is probably one of the best 3- or 4-star hotels in Basra & the most expensive after the Basra International. Security is very good, with 3 checkpoints before entering the hotel. The hotel has a swimming pool, steam room & sauna. Overall it is very clean, the rooms are large, modern & well maintained, with comfy beds & nice furnishings, inc those in the bathroom. There is AC in all areas and complimentary Wi-Fi. The staff are friendly & glad to assist. The buffet b/fast is varied & good quality. *Rooms start from around US$130 pp per night.* **$$$$**

Upmarket

Shams Al-Basra Hotel (81 rooms) Watan St; m 0780 000 3654; e info@shamsalbasrahotel.com; www.shamsalbasrahotel.com. Shams Al-Basra is an upmarket hotel in the middle of Basra's commercial & leisure district near to Shatt Al-Arab, & a 30-min drive from the airport. An airport shuttle is available on request. The hotel has a modern feel to it: rooms are carpeted, furnished with wooden furniture & equipped with a minibar,

LED TV, desk & AC. There is free Wi-Fi in all areas. The modern restaurant is open to non residents. **$$$**

Kasr Al-Sultan Philistine St; m 0780 100 521; e qser_alsitan@yahoo.co.uk. Middle-range, clean, comfortable hotel with a good restaurant & friendly, obliging staff. Mainly frequented by visiting Iraqi businessmen, this is a popular hotel & is often fully booked. *Single rooms start at US$70 pp per night and doubles from US$100 pp per night.* **$$$**

Mid-range

Jundian 3 Hotel Al-stklal St; \ 064 1254; m 0780 021 1110; e jundian.3hotel@yahoo.com. A basic hotel with all facilities, frequented mainly by foreign construction workers from many small companies, inc Turks, Iranian & Chinese. The hotel also has a restaurant serving basic local food at reasonable cost. *Single rooms from US$50 pp per night & double rooms from US$60 pp per night.* **$$**

Budget/Shoestring

Jundian 2 Hotel Al-Watan St; \ 061 8006; m 0781 221 2428. This is the slightly downmarket sister hotel to the Jundian 3 Hotel (see above). **$**

✗ WHERE TO EAT Apart from the restaurants in the hotels listed above, there are some eating options in the front of the Central Bazaar and facing it across the canal are many fast food places and booths. Chips, salads and falafel sandwiches are the favourites and very tasty for a quick midday snack. Close to the Mnawi Basha Hotel (see above) are a selection of local restaurants, including the **Rose Garden**, which serves good quality food and narghile pipes.

✗ Hamdan Restaurant Al-Saady St, Al-Ashshar; ☺ All day & evenings. Local food at reasonable prices.

✗ VIP Basra Café Al-Jazaar St; ☺ All day, shows European football matches on large screen

TV. Serves narghile pipes & fresh fruit juices.

✗ Restaurant Janat m 0780 817 0606; ☺ All day. Wide selection of food including pizza, gateaux, fruit juices, burgers, kebabs & grills.

SECURITY SITUATION As in all the cities in Iraq, in Basra the security situation dominates. To visit most places, and all still have guards, a *khittab* or permission document is required. Even a couple of years ago it was not safe to be on the streets as a foreigner on your own. Today, the threat is diminishing, although as in many cities worldwide it is still not safe in certain areas after dark.

WHAT TO SEE AND DO The place to wander, if so inclined, is the **Corniche** where you can contemplate the flowing Shatt Al-Arab. But to catch a glimpse of old Basra visit **Ashar**. Ashar is the heart of the city, the old commercial centre, home to the merchants of the 18th and 19th centuries. Situated one street north of the bazaar area, its covered bazaar and mosque mark the end of the narrow creek that links it and the river to Old Basra. Today the older parts of Ashar are still attractive. A few of the beautiful old-style houses with walled gardens and balconies leaning over into the narrow streets remain with beautiful wooden façades in the style of old Arab architecture (called Shanasheel). They have character and are worth wandering through – a delight to see, giving you an idea of what old Basra must have looked like. They are quite extensive: explore some of the alleyways behind the houses and note the old shutters and doorways and interestingly shaped windows; the shops smelling of spice, herbs and coffee, and the old-world atmosphere that pervades there. Scattered in this area are also mosques and churches. The churches are very difficult to gain admission to, not surprising considering the persecution Christians in this area have been, and are still being, subjected to.

Head towards the bazaar area in the direction of the Shatt Al-Arab where you will find the many streets of the **Central Bazaar**. Although crowded, the myriad of streets are full of almost everything that a port city would import from around the world. Upstream is Margil, the garden suburb fanning out from the forest of cranes at the wharves of the Old Basra port and the railway station; and a little further you cross to the island where Basra's airport was sited until the 1960s when it was moved to Shuaiba.

A little further on is **Babylon Square** and facing this is **Fun City**, an area at the start of the Corniche with a Ferris wheel, lit at night, and other outdoor entertainment with tea and naghile stalls. Close by on the waterfront is the last remaining bronze statue, that of the poet and journalist **Badr Shakir al Sayyeb** (1926–64) by the artist and sculptor Nadakadhum. Originally there were statues all along the Corniche, life-sized Iraqi soldiers facing and pointing to Iran, along with a much larger statue of Saddam Hussein. Following his demise, all these were looted and melted down. Located by the one remaining statue are jetties for the motor launches which can be hired for a trip along the Shatt Al-Arab. Allow IQD20,000–25,000 per launch for a group, for a simple ride which will take you past Saddam Hussein's yacht, moored by the bank and as far down as his palace complex – more if you want a longer trip or across to the other bank.

There are many creeks on the far side, with palms reaching down to the water and water birds. In the evenings the people of Basra stroll down the Corniche with their families, buying nuts or tea from the stalls lining it. Along the way there are moored boats converted into restaurants and the rebuilt Sheraton Hotel. Heavily damaged and looted in 2003, the hotel was totally refurbished and is now the Basra International (see page 324). The views from the upper stories of the sun setting over the waters of the Shatt Al-Arab and the bridges are quite spectacular. Further along towards the end of the Corniche is the large old city hospital. Just past this building is the gateway to **Saddam Hussein's Palace Area**.

At this gateway foreign visitors need to show their permission document to enter. It may be possible to obtain permission from the military by telephone, but be prepared for a long wait. If you can gain admission the palace area is well worth a visit. There are four major buildings, with many smaller outbuildings. One palace has been taken over by a major TV centre, so is not open to the public. But the other palaces, in various states of dereliction, are viewable. Occupied by British troops when they seized the city, they initially suffered little damage, but were looted and vandalised after the British left. The modern interior woodwork, ornate plaster ceilings, fine glass and general design, albeit larger than life, is completed with superb workmanship. The design of the exterior doors and lanterns are in harmony and the fine bas-reliefs in stone are reminiscent of Mussolini's 1930s' architecture. What to do with such vast-roomed buildings? Apart from the aforementioned TV studios, another is earmarked for the new **Museum of Basra**. Assisted by experts from the British Museum and others, work is now on-going to create this, and there are plans in place to turn the whole area into a cultural centre. 'It will be the principal museum in southern Iraq and we hope people will look to it as a model museum in the region,' said John Curtis, keeper at the British Museum.

Christian churches exist in Basra: the Latin Church on The 14th of July Street, an Armenian Church and a Syrian Orthodox Church. There is also an interesting church belonging to the Mandeans. Once a large community in the south of Iraq, only a few Mandeans remain, maybe a thousand or so in Basra and a few hundred in Nasiriyah and the Marshes. They are a very ancient community, probably influenced by the even older Essenes, a monastic community in 1st-century Palestine, who had many similar religious practices.

The major place of worship is on the outskirts of Basra, the **Imam Ali Mosque**, 10km west of the centre and close to the airport. The Al-Imam Ali ibn Talib Mosque was the first mosque to be built in Iraq at the beginning of the Arab Conquests, and the first mosque outside the Arabian Peninsula. It is an important place for pilgrimage as Imam Ali prayed here. The mosque has been rebuilt many times, the latest reincarnation being completed by Saddam Hussein. All that is left of the first mosque is a remnant of the minaret and the columns and slabs of the original courtyard which faithfully reflect the very first mosque of Mohammed in Medina. The mosque is controlled by the Mahdi Militia and it is absolutely forbidden for women to enter unless clad in the *abayah* provided.

The city has a variety of mosques with varying degrees of antiquity.

Basra Sports City is a newly built multi-use sports complex that was completed in 2013 as the main venue for the 2013 Gulf Cup of Nations. However, owing to concerns over preparations and security the tournament was moved to Bahrain instead.

The **English Cemetery** suffered heavily during the recent wars and the memorial formerly situated there is now located in the airport area. Sadly, **Sinbad Island** (an island in the Shatt Al-Arab by the Khaled Bridge, which before the war was a casino and night club area with restaurants, is now almost flattened and the remaining buildings are occupied by squatters.

AROUND BASRA

AZ ZUBAYR Just south of Basra is a traditional picnic spot. Formerly the name of the whole area, the old Emirate of Zubair, it is named after Zubair bin Auiwa, one of the earliest converts to Islam, who embraced the religion when he was just 15 years old. He fought for the cause of Islam and was martyred at the Battle of the Camel in 656. The surrounding terrain is dry, dusty and treeless. Hardy Shia farmers scratch a living from postage-stamp farms dotting the sides of the road from Khawr Az Zubayr Port to Az Zubayr town. Nearby is a sprawling munitions storage facility which once housed the Iraqi navy's mine-warfare school. The modern, well-built but now crumbling guard towers standing sentinel at each corner of the base confirm it was once a tightly guarded military secret. The high security fence that rings the facility has long since been stripped of wire and any other useful items by looters. Now scores of locals wander unimpeded between the bunkers seeking anything of value, providing an added complication for divers attempting ordnance clearance. Camp Chindit, originally run by the British, was also located in Az Zubayr. There were approximately a hundred British troops stationed at the camp, until control was handed over to the Iraqi army in September 2005.

ABUL KHASIB This town, 26km south of Basra, has a strange claim to fame: the highest density of palm trees in the world! It is also the birthplace the famous Iraqi poet and journalist Badr Shakir al Sayyeb, whose statue can be seen on Basra's Corniche.

UMM QASR Iraq's largest deep-water port close to the Kuwait border was once a small fishing village and smugglers' haven. By 1961 it had been developed in a small way and has continued to grow ever since. It was the first population centre to be taken by the invasion forces in both World War I and the subsequent Gulf wars. USAID upgraded the port and dredged a deep-water channel, giving access to large vessels.

SAFWAN About 54km from Basra, this town near the Iraq–Kuwait border, is where the ceasefire agreement was signed at the end of the 1991 Gulf War. The town itself is relatively nondescript. It is possible to cross the border here into Kuwait if you have the correct documentation. Relations between Iraq and Kuwait have improved remarkably following the overthrow of Saddam Hussein's regime: on 30 August 2004 Iraq and Kuwait agreed to restore full diplomatic relations and have subsequently signed economic co-operation protocols. Kuwait has made donations in support of Iraqi refugees and in return Iraq has co-operated with the return of the antiquities taken from the Kuwait Museum by its forces during the invasion of Kuwait by Iraq.

QUERNA

About 75km northwest of Basra city, Querna is famous for being the possible site of the biblical Garden of Eden. Today, there is little there to remind one of paradise, and its recent history has been less than peaceful.

HISTORY Legend has it that Querna was once a city built by Seleucus I, the general who succeeded Alexander the Great on the latter's death in Babylon, in honour of his wife Apamea. But no traces of that city have been found.

Owing to its geographical location there has probably always been a settlement and market here for the use of the marshland tribes people. The Ottoman Turks had a garrison stationed at Querna and a customs tobacco tax collection point.

During the Mesopotamia Campaign of World War I, Querna was the site of a battle between British and Ottoman troops. In December 1914 British forces captured Basra, forcing the Ottoman troops to retreat to Querna. Situated at the conflux of the Tigris and Euphrates rivers, Querna was a strategic point for the British who were keen to consolidate their position in Basra and to protect the Abadan oilfields of Iran.

The British force, accompanied by several gunboats, attacked the Ottomans who were dug in at Querna. While the gunboats kept the Ottomans under fire, British troops managed to cross the Tigris. The troops then advanced across open ground but, unable to cross into Querna itself, were forced to retire. Following the arrival of reinforcements, they tried again several days later. By then, however, the Ottomans had moved back into the positions they had lost in the previous engagement so the British had to re-take those positions. As before, however, although they drove the

Ottoman troops back, they again could not cross the river. In view of this setback, troops were then sent along the banks of the river Tigris to find a place to cross. This they did successfully, cutting off the Ottoman retreat to the north in the process. The following day the Ottoman commander, Colonel Subhi Bey, the Wali of Basra, surrendered his forces to the British.

GETTING THERE About 75km northwest of Basra, Querna is near to the town of Nahairat, at the point where the rivers Tigris and Euphrates merge to become the Shatt Al-Arab.

WHERE TO STAY AND EAT A small tourist hotel was built in Querna by Saddam Hussein to encourage tourism to the area. Following its destruction in the Iran-Iraq War, the Querna Tourist Hotel has been rebuilt and it is the only hotel in Querna. Located next to Adam's Tree, it has a rather dismal and gloomy air about it. The restaurant serves teas, beverages, sandwiches and snacks. On a lighter note, in the gardens there are some large and friendly goats. It is very good to see them so well looked after and still with us.

WHAT TO SEE AND DO The hotel site has been improved in recent years, and tourists are starting to visit again. Adam's Tree stands in the grounds. Although legend has it that this is the biblical tree of life, it is actually a somewhat sickly looking fig tree, more dead than alive. However, from the paved area around it there is a nice view of the coalescence of the Tigris and Euphrates, one clear and blue, the other sludgy and brown.

THE MARSHES

> 'Reed-house, reed-house! Wall, O Wall, harken reed-house. O man of Shuruppak, son of Ubaru-Tutu: tear down your house and build a boat – abandon possessions and look for life ... and take up into the boat the seed of all living creatures.'
>
> *The Epic of Gilgamesh,* The story of the flood

The Marshes (Al-Ahwar in Arabic) are unique to Iraq where nature seems to preserve its virgin aspect. They cover a large area surrounding the Tigris and some of the Euphrates and the union of the Tigris and Euphrates rivers, the Shatt Al-Arab just below Querna. Stretching from Kut in the north to Basra in the south this vast expanse of marshland dotted with shallow lagoons occupies a total area of about 10,000km² and is the home of an endless variety of birds, fish, plants, reeds, and bulrushes. A trip to the marshlands of southern Iraq was once a journey in time to the era of the Sumerians who lived in the area 6,000 years ago. In 1991 there were 250,000 Marsh Arabs in their ancestral homelands. In 2003 the number was 40,000 but with the return of displaced persons, the total population has now regained the 1991 numbers.

Until the intensification of drainage through the Third River Project during the late 1980s and throughout the 1990s, the Marsh Arabs (**Madan**) built cathedral-shaped reed houses known as Sarifas. Made from a mixture of earth and papyrus, pressed hard to form a base called *chebasheh*, the reed houses have elaborate latticework entrances and attractive designs that go back to ancient times. Viewed from a distance, their communities looked like hundreds of islands, clustered together into small townships. The main mode of transport through the reedy waterways is a long, slim canoe, made from reeds and bitumen, known as a *mashuf,*

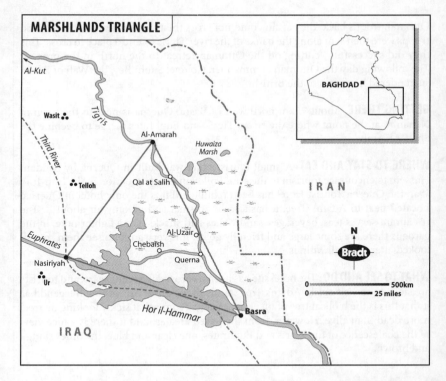

MARSHLANDS TRIANGLE

Al-Kut

Wasit

Tigris

Third River

Telloh

Al-Amarah

Qal at Salih

Huwaiza Marsh

IRAN

Euphrates

Chebaish

Al-Uzair

Nasiriyah

Ur

Querna

Hor il-Hammar

Basra

IRAQ

BAGHDAD

N

Bradt

0 ———————— 500km
0 ———————— 25 miles

from which they caught fish using spears. A delightful scene is a Marsh wedding, when the bride is carried in a lovely 'regatta' made up of her own *mashuf* and those of her party, all loud with men's lilting songs and women's joyous cries.

During the Iran-Iraq War (1980–88) the watery haven of the Marsh Arabs became a launch pad for attacks by Iranian armed forces. Iraqi army deserters and the regime's opponents also hid in the area, prompting the central government to accelerate a land reclamation project started decades earlier to drain saline water from waterlogged farmland north and west of the marshes. This idea was later modified to drain the marshes themselves. Massive engineering works, consisting of a series of dams hundreds of kilometres in length, were constructed to drain the waters of the Euphrates away from the area. This threatened a unique culture. The poetic words of a refugee who fled from the region tell us that: 'The birds died, the animals died, the people died, the world died. There is no water, there is no life, and we are naked in our misery.'

But the tragic story, summarised in this poignant poem, has a happy ending. As the Saddam regime ended, people began to open floodgates and break down embankments that had been built to drain the marshlands. In 2003 Basra Marsh was linked with the central marsh when the Iraqi army blew up a road leading to Basra to stop the advance of the British army, and by mid-2004, the marsh dwellers had re-flooded many of the areas that had been drained. The Huwaiza Marsh on the Iran–Iraq border was re-flooded with the assistance of Iranian engineers. Writing in *The Independent* on 5 January 2004 from the Sahel River, southern Iraq, Robert Fisk pointed out that many Marsh Arabs had long ago exchanged the water buffalo for the Mercedes and become traders: 'Other tribes moved in and planted crops in newly irrigated land. But the people that the explorer Wilfred Thesiger and

Gavin Maxwell so charmingly introduced us to in their books have survived and Saddam's regime has not. A small tide of dark-blue water was seeping back into the desert, creeping around Mahamar, Manzan, Meshal and all the lost villages of the marshes. It is a beautiful, enchanting, peaceful sight, a place where, centuries ago, the legendary Sumerian hero Gilgamesh fell asleep and let the plant of life slip from his grasp.'

Since that time hundreds of Iraqis have been trained in marshland management techniques and policies. A series of community-led environmental awareness campaigns has been organised by local leaders and residents, and an internet-based Marshland Information Network (MIN) has been set up. Water-distribution pipes and common distribution taps have been installed and sanitation systems have been implemented. The region's thin-grained rice, introduced in around 1000BC, considered one of the finest and most nutritious in the world, is again being grown.

HISTORY According to legend, the Babylonian God Marduk, who lived in a primordial universe where 'all the lands were sea', built the first reed platform, similar to the floating reed platforms once found in Hor il-Hammar and Hor il–Hawazia. Old Arabic books suggest that the Marshes were the aftermath of a devastating flood which took place around AD620. Archaeological indications, however, suggest that they were formed long before even Sumerian times, when the Arabian Gulf waters began to recede southwards, leaving behind marshlands alongside the rivers Tigris and Euphrates as river sediment built up the land.

Over the centuries, the Marshes have been fed by the spring floods of the Tigris and Euphrates. The Sumerians introduced the ancestors of the water buffalo from India and domesticated them in around 4000BC. The reeds, up to 6m in height, provided house-building material, the birds and fish a ready supply of food, and the self-sufficient, simple life of the marshland's inhabitants remained unchanged for centuries. Birds like duck and heron bred in the reeds and there was also a plentiful supply of carp and eel. Fishing had its own ethics. Nets were taboo and were only used by a low caste known as the berbera. The Marsh Arabs, excellent swimmers, displayed remarkable skill with a spear and could kill a fish from a moving canoe. They also laid poison bait as an aid to catching fish. Gavin Young, author of *Return to the Marshes*, points out that life was good in those remote times: 'The green, well-watered gardens, orchards and seemingly endless date forests of Sumer; the gloriously intricate cobweb of canals and dykes that made Mesopotamia the granary of the Near East; prosperous farmers with their thousands upon thousands of sheep and cattle; singing boatmen in the giant reeds fishing and hunting undisturbed: such was the golden prospect when southern Iraq was young. A paradise – to be lost later through conflict and neglect.'

The buffalo and fisher-people of the Marshes could not lead their idyllic life without becoming involved in the battles of Mesopotamian history and the tooth and claw struggles between its rulers. During the reign of the Assyrian king Sennacherib, the tribes of the marshlands rebelled and the king sent his troops into the area in canoes. His victory in the 6th century BC has been immortalised in a bas-relief that is now in the British Museum.

With the coming of Islam the pure Arab camel-breeders from the Arabian Peninsula met the marsh men, learned their ways, intermarried and introduced the Islamic faith. After defeating the Persians in AD635, Caliph Umar decreed the founding of two cities in the south of Iraq: Basra and Kufa. Both were military bases. The houses in the two cities were at first made of reeds: the first mosques were built of reeds and clay, and then clay and brick. The two cities became major Islamic centres

CHRONOLOGY

4500–1900BC	Sumerians pioneered the building of reed houses and the domestication of water buffalo.
6th century BC	The Assyrian king Sennacherib conquered the rebellious tribes in the marshlands and absorbed them into his empire.
AD635	Caliph Omar decreed the founding of two cities, Basra and Kufa, in the south of Iraq.
8th century	The Abbasid caliph Harun al Rashid succeeded in re-opening the water courses of the Babylonians.
883	Ali the Abominable, leader of a slave rebellion, who captured Basra and threatened Baghdad, was executed.
1533	The tribes of the Gharraf and the central Hawazia marshes of Basra made obeisance to the Turkish sultan, Suleiman the Magnificent, who captured Baghdad.
1865	The Ottomans who ruled Iraq paid increasing attention to the marshlands and tried to persuade the tribes to settle and cultivate land and their sheikhs to become Turkish officials.
1914–18	Struggle between the British and Ottomans for control of Iraq. The tribes in the marshlands often changed allegiances as they wanted to back the winner.
1920–30	Thousands of marshlands inhabitants left to join the newly formed Iraqi army and police force, and to work in the towns as porters, night-watchmen, building workers and servants.

and Basra soon emerged as an important port due to its strategic location between East and West. These momentous political developments proved almost fatal to the agricultural economy on which Iraq depended. The dikes, which the Sumerians had kept in immaculate condition, were left to decay until a conservation-oriented Sassanid king tried to rebuild them. Even the public execution of 40 dike-builders who were not up to the job failed to halt the decline. During the 8th century, the Abbasid caliph Harun al Rashid succeeded in re-opening the water courses of the Babylonians. But the perfect system of dikes with which Harun reclaimed tracts of the Marshes, was destroyed by the Mongols. Arab refugees fleeing from the Mongol hordes sought sanctuary in the marshlands. They were joined by the survivors of the great slave uprising. The black slaves, forced to drain the Marshes, revolted against their inhuman treatment. Led by Ali the Abominable, they rebelled against the caliph, and from the shelter of the reed-beds carried on a guerrilla war of ambushes and night raids. Ali the Abominable captured Basra and came within 30km of Baghdad itself, but his luck ran out in 883, 14 years after the start of the

1950–70	Services improved in the marshlands, land reforms reduced the estates of absentee landlords, clinics and schools opened, and ice factories aided the fishing industry. An earlier scheme to drain saline waters from waterlogged farmland north and west of the marshlands was modified to drain the marshlands themselves, with the construction of Saddam's canal.
2001	Satellite images from the US space agency NASA showed that 90% of the marshlands no longer existed.
Apr 2003	Marsh Arabs began demolishing dams that restricted water flow to the Marshes.
2004	Some 50% of the Marshes have already been re-flooded and the UN Environmental Programme (UNEP) began the extensive marshlands' restoration project. US-led troops raised the level of the river running alongside Al-Jamha village, 110km north of Basra.
24 August 2004	Death of Sir Wilfred Thesiger, legendary British explorer, who lived with the Marsh Arabs for several periods between 1951 and 1958.
2006	The Government of Japan carried out the second phase of support for UNEP's Iraqi Marshlands restoration project.
July 2013	The Central Marshes of Iraq declared the country's first National Park.

rebellion, and his head was sent to the caliph. This insurrection established the Marshes as a place of refuge for political rebels, revolutionaries and criminals. In the 14th century the famous Tunisian explorer and historian Ibn Battuta described the region as 'a waterlogged jungle of reeds, inhabited by Arabs noted for their predatory habits. They are brigands.'

The Turkish Empire After the devastating Mongol invasion, Iraqi history became the history of the struggle between Persia and Turkey. When Baghdad fell to the Turkish sultan Suleiman the Magnificent in 1533, the tribes of the Gharraf and the Central and Hawazia marshes of Basra quickly made obeisance to him. But their rebellious nature could not be subdued until the Turkish expedition of 1546, when 300 ships were sent to the Marshes. In 1549 they were up in arms again. Even after their defeat at the hands of Ali Pasha on the Euphrates, they still threatened the approaches to Basra. Ali Pasha's enlightened rule, however, saw the establishment of a humane and liberal government within the Ottoman Empire. The arts flourished and even the Marsh Arabs were mollified for a time. But Ali Pasha's graceless successor, Hussein, infuriated the Marsh Arabs through the imposition of a buffalo tax. The tribes of southern Iraq developed into a force to be reckoned with. The most powerful confederation was on the lower Euphrates. After a long period of feuds and bloodshed, the main tribes – the Beni Malik, the Ajwad and the Beni Said, in the area between Samawa and the Hor Al-Hammar – were united under the famous grouping known as the Muntafiq Confederation.

In *Return to the Marshes*, Gavin Young comments that during the 16th century, when the tribes in the marshlands paid nominal obeisance to the Turkish sultan, the obscure children of the reeds had grown up: 'What were they originally but peaceful spear-fishers of Sumer, then sanctuary-givers to refugees from Assyrian "kings of the Universe" and from Mongolian horsemen.' Later, the intrusive shahs and khans of Persia found a different sort of population. Centuries of unwelcome arrivals – foreign soldiers, tax-gatherers, cattle-rustlers, and the predatory henchmen of tyrannical over-lords – had bequeathed them an intense suspicion of visitors. Transformed by constant infusions of the fiery blood of the Arabian tribes, the Marsh Arabs still fished, kept buffaloes and grew rice, but they had become fighters, too. Pashas learned to think twice before sending expensive armies to put them in their place. The marsh people had become the Marsh Arabs, with the shrewd will-o'-the-wisp spirit of their desert kinsmen'.

During the four centuries of the Ottoman occupation of Iraq, there was no effective administration of the Marshes region. Only during the last 50 years of Turkish rule, especially from the reign of Midhat Pasha, the Wali of Baghdad (1869–72), onwards, did the Turks establish a few gendarmeries here and there, along with administrative centres in the towns and bigger villages. For the previous seven centuries all of Iraq's tribesmen had lived under feudal sheikdoms, with a tendency towards despotic rule. During the days of the Ottomans hardship and insecurity grew because of the destruction of irrigation works, poor communication and the lack of organised administration and law and order. The tribes lived in a state of constant hostility, which strengthened feudalism. From 1865 the Turks paid increasing attention to the marshlands. They adopted a policy of trying to induce the tribes to settle and cultivate land and their sheiks to become Turkish officials. Under Midhat Pasha, Nasir Pasha Ahl Sadun, the paramount sheikh of the Muntafiq tribal confederation, became the pasha's chosen and willing tool to tame the confederation. Midhat Pasha was even prepared to appoint him governor of Basra. Through the long period of Ottoman rule the majority of the Shia population were dominated by Sunni Turks, so, at first, many welcomed the British occupation in 1918 at the end of World War I.

British rule During the struggle for Iraq between the British and the Ottoman Turks, some of the Marsh tribes fought with the Turks, while others sided with the British. The sheiks were shrewd enough to realise that their status, power and land holdings depended on whoever won and they frequently changed allegiances. The war was a great time for replenishing the supply of rifles – again from both sides. Under the British Mandate (1920–32) and the period of monarchic rule (1932–58), public services began to be introduced into the Marshes, starting with police posts and administrative centres in the 1920s, and a few tiny schools in the 1930s. Frequent contact between the marshlands dwellers and the neighbouring towns and villages began only after World War I, with the penetration of the Marshes by the Iraqi administration and the growth of law and order in the region. The marshlands dwellers began to realise that the markets of the neighbouring villages and towns were profitable places in which to sell their produce. Women began to make daily visits carrying reed mats, usually 2.4m by 1.2m – a major source of income and an essential house covering – buffalo and cattle dung for fuel, dairy products, fish, birds and other produce. When this trade proved profitable, they began to spend some of the money earned on luxury articles such as sugar, tea, tobacco and cloth. Contact increased steadily until eventually townsmen started opening shops in the Marsh region. Later the Marsh Arabs themselves became shopkeepers selling sugar, tea, tobacco and later aspirin, pencils and safety razors. Shops were designated by a white cloth, resembling a flag. Trade at first was by barter, according to the convenience of the shopkeepers. Canoes fitted up as floating shops also began to tour the remote parts of the Marshes. This trade and constant contact between villagers and neighbouring towns encouraged the marshlands dwellers to consider leaving the Marshes temporarily or even permanently. The main inducement was the readiness of the Iraqi government in the early 1920s to enlist an enormous number of young men in its newly formed army and police force. Men and women from the Marshes also worked in towns as porters, night-watchmen, building workers and servants. The slump in cereal prices during the 1920s and early 1930s compelled the government to raise taxes on produce. The sheiks passed these demands on to the peasants. In the marshlands the cruelty of the sheiks coupled with the low prices offered for their crops prompted thousands to leave. After 1931 the difficulty of finding employment in the urban areas checked the migration tide.

Iraqi independence When they first came under the direct rule of the central government in Baghdad, most of the marshlands' tribes welcomed the new regime because of the hope it gave them of throwing off the yoke of many corrupt despots and absentee landlords and of enjoying justice and security. But not all the sheiks were tyrants and the people voted for those who were genuinely concerned about their welfare to remain. In the field of law and order the government accomplished a great deal. Blood feuds were checked, since the wronged party in a dispute was compelled to accept compensation in money and not to take any unlawful action. As the British explorer Wilfred Thesiger, who lived in the Marshes from 1951 until 1958, notes in *The Marsh Arabs*, the settlement of feuds was a complex affair and the truce was only negotiated for a year: 'No sheikh, however powerful, and no *sayyid* (a holy man who claims descent from the Prophet Mohammed), however revered, could finally settle a blood feud. Only the headman (*qalit*) could seal the pact by binding the head cloth round the reed and handing one end to either party.' Compensation in the form of women, a traditional tribal practice, was not paid in disputes settled by the government. S M Salim, author of *Marsh Dwellers of the Euphrates Delta*, commented that during the 1920s, when the government accomplished more than the people expected, the villagers were particularly disposed to co-operate with the new regime, which promised improved living standards and an end to old extortions.

The atmosphere cooled somewhat through three decades of increasing administrative corruption, but the Minority Rights Group points out in its report *The Marsh Arabs of Iraq* that the period from the 1950s to the end of the 1970s was one of gradually improving, state-provided public services and land reforms. More schools were opened, small clinics were established in larger villages, and mobile health services reached into the heart of the Marshes by motor boat. Doctors treated the most common diseases such as dysentery, bilharzia, skin diseases, tuberculosis and trachoma, as well as horrific injuries caused by wild pigs. Explorer Wilfred Thesiger always carried a medicine chest and treated a variety of ailments from cataracts to swollen genitals. Personal charms were also used as a protection against sickness.

The abolition of the sheikhs During the 1950s the abolition of the sheikhs had the most disruptive effect on the traditional marshland social structure. Clan heads, known as *mukhtar*, who acted on behalf of the sheikh, were installed as *sirkals*, appointed by the governor of the province with the approval of the Interior Ministry in Baghdad. As Gavin Young pointed out in *Return to the Marshes*, just as the post-Raj British disappeared, so did the sheikh landlords of the marsh world. After the imposition of the monarchy by the British in 1920, nationalism proliferated in the kingdom like a strong creeper grappling a wall: 'By 1958 the wall collapsed, burying not only the royal family and those close to the palace, but merchants, politicians and land-owners as well.' After depriving the traditional tribal leaders, many of whom were served by slaves, of their power and status, the Iraqi authorities realised that they were having trouble controlling the Marsh tribes. At first they thought they would be able to rely on the *sirkals*, but these government surrogates did not have the same authority as the traditional, well-respected tribal leaders. The government tried to provide public services for the marshlands' inhabitants but it remained wary and suspicious of the people, realising the difficulty of controlling an intractable area with a history of challenging government authority and providing refuge to dissidents.

The 30 years between 1950 and 1980 were a time of relative prosperity and beneficial land reform. The giant land-holdings of the tyrannical absentee landlords, who lived in stone fortresses on the edges of the marshlands, were broken down into 6,000m^2 plots. The government provided social services such as schools and clinics. The introduction of ice factories during the 1960s made fishing more of a commercially viable proposition and helped change attitudes to the practice of net as opposed to spear fishing, as barbel, carp and binny were eagerly sought as far away as Baghdad. In the 1970s, the boat-building business was booming in Al-Huwayr, a town near the junction of the Tigris and Euphrates, where 200 small *mashufs* were constructed every month.

During the Iran-Iraq War (1980–88) The Marsh Arabs were generally patriotic, although the army made numerous incursions into the marshlands to seek out deserters. The invasion of Kuwait in 1990 and the First Gulf War of 1991 was a terribly difficult time for the Marsh Arabs. Saddam's regime was determined to destroy the marshlands to make military movements easier, to gain access to 50% of Iraq's oil reserves in the area, and to teach the Shias a lesson for using the region as a hideout during the uprising against his regime which followed. Baghdad's plans to quell any remaining opposition seeking sanctuary there resulted in the systematic destruction of the area, which shrank the original marshlands from 15,000–20,000km^2 to 1,500–2,000km^2.

Post Saddam After the toppling of Saddam Hussein's regime the UNEP launched a major restoration project. Rania Dagash of the International Organisation for Migration in Basra, who carried out an assessment of Marsh Arab communities, discovered that they want both worlds: 'those close to town centres have tasted the modern world and they don't really want to let go of it. Their farming is quite stable and it is probably the only stability they have seen. They want their children to know the other world, but at the same time to have the benefits of services in the urban world.'

As in the rest of southern Iraq, opposition to the occupation cast a shadow over developments in the marshlands. Rory Stewart, in *Occupational Hazards: My Time Governing in Iraq*, notes that:

'by the beginning of 2006, the Sadrists, the Dawa Party and the Iranian-linked parties had taken almost all the votes across the south and the majority of seats in the new national parliaments. Southern Iraq was under Coalition occupation but not Coalition control. Most people in the south believed the occupation was illegal. They only tolerated it because they believed the presence of the troops in bases might deter civil war. Iraqis were reluctant to trust us or work with us. Because of this lack of cooperation, it had been difficult for the Coalition to achieve as much as it hoped with its billions of dollars in development aid, and it had received almost no credit for its efforts. Despite thousands of troops and tens of millions invested in essential services, despite a number of impressive reconstruction projects, despite ambitious programmes in police training and in developing "good governance and civil society", the Coalition has had only a minimal political impact in southern Iraq.'

The Marshes today Worldwide interest in the Marshes has encouraged the Iraqi Government to declare the Marshes as the first National Park in Iraq. As the waters slowly return, and the bird life again multiplies, so the future looks brighter for the Madan. Villagers still complain about the toxicity of the waters, and the apparent lack of Government interest in their welfare. There are still many large pockets of real poverty, but there is a general air of optimism, and as usual in the Marshes, cheerfulness. The Madan have always been a cheerful, buoyant people. In October 2013, I was struck by the hum of activity at the usual reed collection points along the road. Near one particular place there also seemed to be a new village, surrounded by water. In contrast, some distance further along on the other side of the road, there were dried-up river beds and poverty-struck housing, with little water and few animals to be seen. Between Chebaish and Querna in particular, however, new dams and weirs are in place, and more are being constructed. The further edges of the Marshes, both in the south and west, do not seem to have been improved much though. This is understandable when you consider the enormity of the undertaking, progress has to move one step at a time.

GETTING THERE There are several routes to the Marshes, depending on your starting point. On Highway 6 it is 456km south from Baghdad or 70km north from Basra via Querna.

GETTING AROUND
By road The Marshes extend for many thousands of square kilometres, most of which is not accessible by road. The best way to view the Marshes is to go west from Querna on the Central Road which cuts across the southern part of the Marshes via Chebaish to Nasiriyah.

By boat Boats can be hired in Chebaish, Querna and Al-Amarah for excursions into the Marshes.

WHERE TO STAY AND EAT As this book is being prepared, there is currently nowhere to stay or eat in the Marshes unless you are invited to stay or dine with a local family. Hotel accommodation is being planned, but there are no dates for when this will be built and operational. Two tourist centres with some accommodation have recently been built but are not yet open.

In his book *Occupational Hazards, My Time Governing in Iraq*, Rory Stewart, the Coalition Provisional Authority's deputy governorate co-ordinator of Maysan and Dhi Qar provinces from 2003–04, provides a penetrating insight into life in a marshlands village.

'Once the old men had shaken hands and seen us depart their day was largely over. They would walk slowly back to huts or small reed shelters in mud courtyards. There they would wait out the day until the evening meal, which might be little more than bread and perhaps rice with no meat or fruit or vegetables. Some would listen to religious sermons and the news on the radio. The older men did not and often could not read and there was no electricity in the village to power a television.

At dusk the water buffalo would return to the compound, thrusting out their hairy lips and loose, bristled necks, lowing for fodder, their horns grey, cracked and mud-caked like ancient pottery. The women would push them towards the corners of the yards and squat beside them, running their fingers down each teat in turn and sometimes dropping a little of the milk on the cow's flat black nose as a reward. Families now had only one or two buffalo each. But that was enough for a glass of the strong sweet milk for dinner.

The women did much of the work: operated a loom if they had one, fetched water, washed, cared for the children and swept the thick layer of sand that accumulated daily in their huts into the street. But they were almost entirely excluded from education and the political life of the village. Often they were not welcome in the mosque. They were frequently the victims of honour killings, forced marriages and domestic violence. I never met them. But when not looking after buffalo they were known for composing and reciting poetry – oral poetry, because almost all the women were illiterate. Shortly after dark it was time to sleep, since everyone would wake early for ablutions and the dawn prayers.

Perhaps a quarter of the province lived in this fashion – though in many cases growing wheat and keeping sheep rather than relying on fish and buffalo. They did not pay taxes and they received little from the state. Legal punishments were meted out by the elders in the *mudhif*: people seldom used courts or the police.

I visited the community in order to learn about their political influence. I concluded they had next to none. They were too poor and too remote.'

Querna, Al-Amarah and Nasiriyah are the nearest places for eating and overnight accommodation.

OTHER PRACTICALITIES Most of the Marsh Arabs have extremely large and semi-wild guard dogs roaming around their houses and property. You should exercise extreme caution if you hear or see a dog. Do not approach unless you are sure that the owner has firmly secured it. Bites from these animals can inflict terrible wounds and rabies treatment is not readily available.

WHAT TO SEE AND DO The best months for taking trips in the Marshes are March and April. The weather then is pleasant and the whole place is chock-full of plants and flowers. Reeds may rise 6m high and papyrus to 3m. In the winter season water birds of all kinds migrate to the Marshes, which then become a birdwatchers' and photographer's paradise. Fish are always plentiful and the local inhabitants catch them with nets or spear them with a five-pronged *fala*, peculiar to the area.

ENDEMIC SPECIES: JEWELS IN THE BIODIVERSITY CROWN

An environmental and ecological study of the Marshlands of Mesopotamia, produced in 1994 by the Wetland Ecosystems Research Group at Exeter University, said the marshlands support a significant number of rare and endemic species. These include mammals such as the long-fingered bat, the bandicoot rat, the smooth-coated otter, Harrison's gerbil and wild boar; amphibians and reptiles such as the tree frog, the Mesopotamian spiny-tailed lizard, and the soft-shell turtle; and a variety of snakes and birds including the Iraqi babbler, the Basra reed warbler, the marbled teal, the African darter, the Goliath heron (*zurgi*), the pigmy heron (*rikhaiwi*) and the sacred ibis. Legend tells us that herons slept in flocks guarded by a sentry that stood on one leg so he would fall over if he was in danger of dozing off. Some 134 species of birds are found in the marshlands, among them the threatened white-headed duck, the red-breasted goose, the black vulture, the brilliantly coloured kingfisher (known as the sheikh's daughter) and the imperial eagle. The wetlands comprise a mosaic of different marshland and lake units, including open water of varying depths, permanently and temporarily flooded marsh, islands, inland deltas and two great rivers, the Tigris and Euphrates, which, before the drainage project, attracted geese from Siberia. One of the most deadly inhabitants of the water world is a snake known as the arbid, whose bite can kill within 20 minutes. Two monsters, the anfish and the afar, are said to live in the heart of the marshlands.

For tourism, this is still early days, as the general security situation in Iraq needs to improve greatly. The government has almost completed two tourist centres, comprising bungalow-style accommodation along the Central Road through the Marshes, from Querna to Nasiriyah and close to Chebaish.

For a short visit to view the Marshes, this road offers the best route to see a little of what the way of life of the Marshes can be really like. For short excursions lasting 1 or 2 hours, hiring boats in Chebaish is the best option. This part of the Marshes offers superb opportunities for photography. Taking these excursions helps the local people and puts money into the local economy. *En route* you will see the wonderful hospitality houses of the Madan, usually one in every village, built by the journeymen craftsmen.

For longer excursions lasting several days, for bird watching, for instance, serious planning needs to be undertaken and local knowledge and expertise sought. Bird watching is a prime reason for visiting the Marshes, but as all enthusiasts will tell you, local knowledge is vital. Accommodation, food and health requirements are of prime importance for such excursions, as no doubt your tour operator will advise you. It is seriously recommended for these longer stays, that you use tour operators in Nasiriyah and Al-Amarah who have the necessary local contacts. Once the tourist complexes are open and operating fully, then this situation may change.

The Marshes have always been a delicate balance of environment and local commerce, while protecting the local people from being over-exploited. I believe that this is very much recognised by all today, after the 30 years of trials that the area has suffered. So many have left the Marshes to seek a more financially rewarding life, especially the young men, but the song of the Marshes never ceases. Many will never return but remain in spirit.

Tourists can be very insensitive, especially where photography is concerned. The Madan of the Marshes are proud people, and like all Arabs, their families are very private. This needs to be respected. Hospitality is second nature to them and visitors should be aware of this and not abuse it. They also have tribal honour, again this needs to be understood and respected.

It is recommended for all visitors to the Marshes to read *The Marsh Arabs* by Wilfred Thesiger and *Return to the Marshes* and *Iraq: Land of the Two Rivers* by Gavin Young. These books will give you a flavour of yesteryear in the Marshes. Once you are deep into the marsh reeds, under a startling, blue sky, with the birds around you and the burbling of your boat, you will understand what drew these writers, and yourself, to the Marshes.

AL-UZAIR (CONTINUING ON THE ROAD NORTH)

Continuing on the road north, the village of Al-Uzair is a little squalid. It consists of one main street, with a small, fairly primitive Islamic mosque, which leads to the River Tigris and the shrine of Ezra.

HISTORY Written history of the village and the shrine is obscure. It is mentioned by Arab and Jewish travellers in their writings from 1050 onwards as possessing the reputed tomb of Ezra and also as a staging post for caravans.

The village and the shrine were much involved in World War I and the fighting between the Turks and the British in the advance up the river towards Baghdad. Heavy fighting took place here over some weeks and both the British and Turkish artillery gunners sited their guns by the dome on Ezra's tomb. Amazingly the tomb, dome and Ezra are still here today. Note the Jewish inhabitants of this mixed community left in the exodus from Iraq in 1951–52. In the past the village has had a reputation for banditry but the people today are curious and pleased to see foreigners. However, being so close to the border and the river means that there is a large presence of armed police in the streets.

GETTING THERE Al-Uzair is on Highway 6, approximately 50km from Querna, on the left bank of the Tigris.

SHOPPING The main street contains an interesting market with fresh fruit and fish. Photography and stopping here is not encouraged by the heavy police presence.

OTHER PRACTICALITIES Female visitors to the tomb must wear one of the *abayahs* from the booth in the courtyard. Photographs are allowed in the tomb.

EZRA

Ezra was a direct descendant of the priestly family that included Zadok and Aaron. He was probably born in Babylon and was living there when he gained the favour of the Persian king Artaxerxes, who granted him a commission to return to Jerusalem (457BC). He was a skilled scribe in the law of Moses, and an expert in the commands of the Lord and his statutes to Israel. He is an important part of the Old Testament Bible and mentioned in Koranic texts. He is said to be buried in Al-Uzair, but also in Tadif, near Aleppo in Syria. Tradition states that he built the synagogue there.

WHAT TO SEE AND DO The Tomb of Ezra, if indeed it is his, has a distinct green-tiled dome and has recently been refurbished with a Shia Islamicisation, including booths in the courtyard for women to don the obligatory *abayah* and for physical checking of all who visit. The shrine is beautifully clean. In the centre of the main chamber is the sarcophagus covered with green cloths. The walls are adorned with inscriptions in Hebrew and there are also tablets or slabs inscribed in Hebrew in the doorway. Attached to the shrine is the mainly 19th-century AD synagogue, which is remarkably well preserved. Its origins can only be surmised. It has a women's balcony and Torah cupboards and Hebrew inscriptions around the walls and cut into the wooden entrance doors. Behind the dome itself are brick walls and an entrance suggesting medieval origins. For many centuries caravans and river traffic halted here to worship at the shrine. Both Jewish and Muslim pilgrims visited Ezra, as is spoken of in the Koranic literature as well as in the Bible.

The views of the River Tigris can be quite stunning here.

AL-AMARAH *Telephone code 43*

Al-Amarah is the capital of the Maysan Province and is situated on the banks of the River Tigris. It is a trade centre for livestock, wool and hides and also known for its weaving and silverware.

HISTORY For some centuries this site was a meeting place and an alternative encampment for the two powerful tribes, the Banu Lam and the Al-Bu Muhammed who fought each other in this province for several hundred years. These formidable tribesmen also made forays as far as Basra and often interrupted trade along the river to Baghdad. Eventually the Ottoman Turks were stirred into action and built the town of Al-Amarah in 1866 and reinforced it with troops. By 1915 it was a respectable size but still ruled by sheikhs who owned large estates in this rice-growing area, both in Iraq and over the border in Iran. These private armies became, and still are, a great source of trouble. Collecting taxes to govern such an area has always been difficult.

During World War I the British army advanced towards Baghdad along the river and took Amarah in 1915. A general hospital was built by the British to deal with the terrible attrition suffered by their troops due to sickness and the hard fighting. After the war in the pre-monarchy years the British attempted to regulate the area and the Marshes, trying to make for ordered government and land reform and taxes. Then came the monarchy and the enhancement of the tribal chiefs with land and allowances, some becoming extremely rich. During the Baathist regime under Saddam Hussein, owing to its turbulent history and proximity to Iran, the town was heavily supervised and allowed little progress, especially when the draining of the Marshes took place.

During the last Gulf War invasion and subsequent unrest the town was a hotbed of opposition and dissension to the regimes. Many of these involved private armies formed by the local sheikhs and the fighting was intense and subject to much brutality. Hopefully this has now been put behind everyone in this region.

Today there is a renewed building programme for the town and a road system which has aspirations to exploit the regeneration of the Marshes and the potential tourist traffic into the Marshes. The town is ideally placed to capitalise on this resource.

GETTING THERE Leaving Al-Uzair and continuing north on Highway 6, Al-Amarah is 186km from Basra.

WHERE TO STAY AND EAT

Janat Adan Tourist Resort and Hotel Near the Al-Sadr general hospital; m 0781 666 6532; www.janatadan.com. This resort has been built recently to explore the tourist potential of the Marshes. It comprises of a new luxury hotel complex with gardens, swimming pool, restaurants, pool table & arcade-style games, & bungalow bedrooms set in picturesque grounds. **$$$$**

OTHER PRACTICALITIES The checkpoints that need to be negotiated prior to entering Al-Amarah can be pedantic and aggressive, particularly if there is the slightest discrepancy with your paperwork (*khittab*).

WHAT TO SEE AND DO Situated just outside the town on the Chahla Road just to the east of the River Tigris, there is a large Commonwealth war cemetery (*www.cwgc. org*) containing more than 4,620 British graves in 31 plots, a memorial stone and a cross. Opposite there are two separate cemeteries for the Muslim and Hindu troops who fought in the British army.

AROUND AL-AMARAH Leaving the town on the newly completed flyover and travelling along the east bank of the Tigris approximately 40km is the small town of **Ali Sharqi**, which has numerous tea stalls and local kebab shops and is handy place to break your journey north. The soil here is very fertile; however, the countryside is very flat and prone to flooding and salinisation. The scenery along this stretch of road is somewhat relieved by the views of the snow-capped Zagros Mountains of Iran in the distance.

AL-KUT

Al-Kut, otherwise known as Kut Al-Amarah ('a bend in the river'), is the largest city and capital of the province of Wasit (formerly the province of Al-Kut), so named because the old town of Kut is situated in a U-bend of the river, almost making it an island. The town was the centre of the carpet trade for many centuries, but unlike Al-Amarah to the south, it developed as a trading centre and then as a Turkish-army base. Kut is now an agricultural trading city, principally dealing in the cereals grown nearby. Some 20–30km away are gas and oil fields. The former Baghdad Nuclear Research Facility, destroyed in 2003, was near Al-Kut.

Now serving as a river port and agricultural centre Al-Kut is a relatively new city. It is also known for the Kut barrage which was constructed on the Tigris river to provide irrigation waters for the surrounding area. Completed in 1939, the Kut barrage diverts water into irrigation channels. Al-Kut's prosperity has always depended on the River Tigris course changes and the city declined and then revived when the present river course became established again. However, the town is mostly famous for the World War I siege when much of the existing town was destroyed.

HISTORY During World War I Turkey was a German ally and thus an enemy of the British. The British campaign against the Turks in Iraq (1914–18) included the siege of Kut. The British advance into central Iraq was delayed for a time by their defeat at Kut, when the garrison under General Townshend surrendered unconditionally to the Turks on 29 April 1916 after a siege lasting 140 days. See box, opposite, for more information on the siege.

GETTING THERE Al-Kut is on Highway 6 approximately 400km from Basra, two-thirds of the way from Basra to Baghdad.

The alternative route from Basra to Al-Kut Leaving Basra and travelling north to Querna and cutting across the Marshes to Nasiriyah via Chebaish and skirting Nasiriyah, you can take the slower and more congested Highway 7 to Kut, a journey of approximately 200km. Then at Al-Kut, re-join Highway 6 to Baghdad. Along the road from Nasiriyah to Al-Kut, there are small towns and villages but few road signs. There are, however, plenty of tea stands, fruit stalls and kebab houses on the way. We are skirting the Marshes through a very fertile part of Iraq, but also on the edge of ancient Sumer as we understand it. The first and major sites on this route are approximately 41km from Nasiriyah and just north of Sayyid Al-Jalil and Al-Shattra, following alongside the Gharraf Canal.

WHERE TO STAY AND EAT

Kut Tourism Hotel Kurneesh St; m 0780 283 8714. Set in its own grounds on the banks of the River Tigris with views of the river, the Kut Tourism Hotel is not a luxury hotel by any means but has water & simple beds. A stay here is a must for military-history buffs. *Single rooms from US$50 per night & doubles from US$90 per night.* **$$**

WHAT TO SEE AND DO At the northern edge of the town, on Cemetery Road at the point where the Baghdad road enters the town, and 800m from the river is the **Kut War Cemetery**. This compact cemetery has 410 identified burials, a war cross and a memorial stone. **Note:** While the current climate of political instability persists, it is not possible for the War Graves Commission to manage or maintain its cemeteries and memorials located within Iraq. Alternative arrangements for commemoration have therefore been implemented and a two-volume Roll of Honour listing all casualties buried and commemorated in Iraq has been produced and is on display at the Commission's head office in Maidenhead, UK.

KUT WAR CEMETERY

In April 1915, the Indian Expeditionary Force 'D', which had landed at Fao the previous November, began its advance inland with the intention of clearing Turkish forces out of southwest Iraq. Amarah was occupied in early June and the advance continued along the line of the Euphrates to Nasiriya, and along the Tigris to Kut, which was taken on 29 September. The advance to Baghdad was resumed on 11 November, but was brought to a standstill against the strong Turkish defences at Ctesiphon on 22–24 November. By 3 December, the force, comprising chiefly the 6th (Poona) Division of the Indian Army, was back in its entrenched camp at Kut, where it was besieged by Turkish forces. Heavy casualties were suffered in desperate but unsuccessful attempts to reach the town and raise the siege in January, March and April. The garrison was forced to capitulate on 29 April 1916 and nearly 12,000 men were taken prisoner, many of whom later died in captivity. The town was re-occupied by Commonwealth forces in February 1917 and at the end of June it became an administrative, railway and hospital centre. Kut War Cemetery was made by the 6th (Poona) Division between October 1915 and May 1916 and was increased in size when graves were brought in from other sites after the Armistice. The cemetery now contains 420 World War I burials.

Following the US invasion in 2003, US marines helped to clear, photograph and re-consecrate the cemetery.

Courtesy of http://www.roll-of-honour.com/Overseas/KutWarCemetery.html

This siege became very famous for its catastrophic defeat of the British army, which showed a startling ineptitude by the general staff, and conduct of the war in Mesopotamia by the Indian Colonial Government (British).

Under the active command of General Charles Townshend of Chitral fame, a relatively small force in comparison to the Turkish troops marched north from Basra and took in succession, after hard fighting, Querna, Al-Amarah and Al-Kut. The troops advanced to Ctesiphon with ambitions to take Baghdad, which would then be only about 30km away. The costly battle of Ctesiphon was probably a draw, with huge numbers of casualties on both sides. The determination and fighting spirit of the Turks had been underestimated, along with the water barriers and terrible conditions.

General Townshend then realised that, combined with the small and diminishing number of his troops and his unsupported position, that he would have to withdraw. A masterly retreat followed and the British forces settled back into Kut. In hindsight they would have fared better had they withdrawn further. Here in Kut, they stayed until 7 December 1915 until the Turkish army, now much reinforced owing to the Allies withdrawal from the Dardanelles and ably commanded by the German Field Marshal Baron Von Der Goltz, advanced to Kut and began the siege. Despite desperate efforts made by the British from Basra and Al-Amarah to relieve the garrison, they failed. But over 23,000 British and Indian troops died in these attempts. At the garrison of Kut, the troops numbering between 10,000 and 12,000, were kept on diminishing rations during the siege. After various attempts to negotiate a ceasefire withdrawal General Townshend simply surrendered on 29 April. His subsequent behaviour and apparent disregard for his captured troops also caused him to lose his reputation and virtually ended his military career. Around 12,000 allied troops were taken prisoner and 70% of the British and 50% of the Indian troops died of disease and the infamous neglect and ill treatment by the Turkish general staff. The captured troops were separated, with officers sent to Turkey and enlisted soldiers held in forced labour conditions. The troops were marched overland to Turkey from Kut and it became known as the death march. The only mitigating circumstance was that the Ottoman government treated its own troops just as brutally.

Townshend was adored by his troops because of his personal approach to them but in Britain the government and general public were scandalised by his three years in luxurious captivity on an island close by Istanbul. They also frowned on his subsequent friendship with leading Turkish army and government officials; he appeared not to have overly concerned himself with the captured troops and did little to amend their treatment. After this historic loss the generals Lake and Gorring were removed from command and General Maude took over as commander. He trained and organised the army and began a successful campaign, recovering Kut on 23 February 1917 and Baghdad on 11 March 1917.

AL-HIBA (LAGASH)

The ancient city state of Lagash comprised three city sites – Lagash itself (modern Al-Hiba), Girsu (modern Telloh) and Nina-Sirare (modern Zirghal).

HISTORY The ancient city of Lagash was founded at the end of the 4th millennium or the beginning of the 3rd millennium BC. A king of Kish, Mesilim (c2700BC) is mentioned on a mace found at Telloh during the construction of a temple dedicated to Ningirsu, when prince Lugal-Shag-Engur was *patesi* of Lagash. The word 'patesi' encompasses not only a chief of state or city but also a religious chief, a high-priest of a city's principal temple. About 2580BC the important dynasty of Ur-Nanshe came to power. It was contemporary with the 1st Ur Dynasty. In his inscriptions Ur-Nanshe proclaims himself King of Lagash and repudiates the suzerainty of Ur. Another king of the same dynasty, Eannatum, represents himself as a great sovereign in the victory stele called the Stele of the Vultures, now in the Louvre museum in Paris. The stele relates Eannatum's resounding victory over the city of Umma and the Akkadian allies of Kish. He captured Ur and allowed a prince descended from the 1st Ur Dynasty to establish himself at Uruk. With the plunder from his wars, Eannatum was able to beautify the temple which his grandfather Ur-Nanshe had dedicated to Ningirsu. The circuit wall of the sanctuary was adorned with a gateway in white cedar wood with guardian lions in acacia wood. About 2425BC Uruk again had to endure a disastrous war against Umma led by Lugalzaggrisi, who for 25 years remained the uncontested king of Mesopotamia before his overthrow at the hands of Sargon of Akkad.

Towards the end of the Guti supremacy over Sumer and Akkad several princes reigned in Lagash, including Ur-Bau and Gudea (about 2130BC). During the reign of Gudea Sumerian sculpture reached its apogee. With the arrival of the 3rd Dynasty in Ur, Lagash moved to playing only a secondary role, with its princes exercising primarily religious functions, and declined in importance accordingly. The site was occupied later, in the 2nd century BC, by Adad-Nadin-Akeh, a king of Sharacene, who built himself a palace amid the ruins of a Sumerian monument attributed to Gudea.

GETTING THERE The site is approximately 41km northwest of Nasiriyah, just north of Sayyid Al-Jalil and Al-Shattra, alongside the Gharraf Canal.

OTHER PRACTICALITIES It isn't possible for tourists to get to the site easily and there are no facilities for tourists here.

WHAT TO SEE AND DO The ancient Sumerian City of Lagash nowadays forms an area of ruins approximately 3km by 1.5km. It has been disturbed by clandestine excavations and has also been partly excavated or investigated by various expeditions. It was first excavated by Robert Koldewey in 1887 and later by French and American teams.

The main structure on the site is the Palace of Gudea, which produced some remarkable diorite statues, which now take pride of place in the Louvre Museum in Paris. Also unearthed here were the Stele of the Vultures (of the Ennatum period), a slab of sculptured stone from the Ur-Nansheh period and a beautiful Entemenea silver vase on a copper plinth. Several thousand Sumerian tablets going back to the 3rd millennium BC were also discovered in the vicinity. The purpose of the building in Gudea's day is disputed; some archaeologists compare it to E-Ninnu, a temple built by Gudea on the site of the E-Ninnu of Ur-Bau.

The building comprises a group of structures, which may not be attributed in their entirety to Gudea. Important alterations were made in the 2nd century BC by an Aramaean prince, Adad-Nadin-Akhed. The façades he constructed have a significant slope, but the constructions of the Sumerian *patesis* have vertical façades characterised by grooving and double-notched projections.

A little further to the south is a second tell where French archaeologists unearthed a building called the House of Fruits, probably a temple dedicated to Ningirsu before the Neo-Sumerian period (22nd–21st century BC).

Around Al-Hiba (Lagash) About 25km to the northwest of Al-Hiba (Lagash), **Girsu (Telloh)** is a separate, but connected city belonging to the state of Lagash. There is some evidence of Ubaid occupation, but the main period of settlement is that of Early Dynastic period III (c2600–2300BC) when Girsu was capital of Lagash State. Many tablets have been discovered here. **Nina-Sirare (Zurghal)** is 10km to the southeast of Lagash, and also dates principally from the Early Dynastic period III and Neo-Sumerian period. Little excavation has been done here. As with Al-Hiba (Lagash), it has not been possible to visit these two sites recently, so their current state is unknown. **Al-Hayy**, 30km east of Wasit, is the largest town on the route to Al-Kut. It manufactures leather goods and woollen rugs. It also has a former Iraqi air force base which was under siege during the Second Gulf War and was destroyed by the American forces.

WASIT *Telephone code 23*

Now completely ruined, Wasit was one of the most important towns in Mesopotamia in the Abbasid period.

HISTORY Wasit was founded by al Hajaj ibn Yusuf al Thaqafi, viceroy of Mesopotamia in the reign of the Umayyad caliph Abd el Malik Wasit in AD694. Known as 'the town of the middle' (because it was situated at equal distances from Kufa, Basra and Ahvaz (now in Iran)), it was, for a time the prosperous capital of the Kaskar district, especially before the foundation of Baghdad. The town was built on both banks of the main arm of the Tigris linked by a pontoon bridge. Al Hajaj built here his famous Green Palace and also a Friday Mosque on the west bank. Two small river harbours accommodated a very prosperous trade. The city was, and is, famous for the founding of the first Islamic mint in Iraq. Al Hajaj died in Wasit in 714. In the 13th century, the buildings on the east bank were the first to fall into ruin. Timur, the Central Asian conqueror, who captured the town at the end of the 14th century, maintained a garrison in it. The Tigris then changed its course during the 15th century and resumed its old direction past Al-Amarah; Wasit in consequence declined and fell into ruin.

GETTING THERE Wasit is 54km from the centre of Al-Kut, along Adejail Road towards the west bank of the Tigris.

OTHER PRACTICALITIES Wasit is very difficult to get to and the roads are bad, therefore it takes a long time to travel there and back and there is no accommodation in the area. Needless to say, the site is not signposted, there are no guards, guides or guidebooks, no admission charges or times. Visitors are free to wander with just their imagination. Ideally travellers should retreat to Al-Kut for bed and food.

WHAT TO SEE AND DO Some excavations have been carried out on the site, beginning in 1936 when archaeologists uncovered a large mosque with a minaret, tombs and a school dating back to the 7th century AD. Later in that decade remains of a residential district were also uncovered. Wasit's most famous monument is the Gateway, so named because in ancient times the town was known as the gateway to

Islamic Iraq. Historically it was the first Islamic city in Iraq. Although the Gateway has been heavily restored, and some preservation work has been carried out on the minaret, no further restoration work has been done at the site to date. Wasit was added to the UNESCO World Heritage Tentative List in 2000.

From Al-Kut it is approximately 200km to Baghdad along Highway 6, bypassing Salman Pak (see pages 161–3). There are small towns and villages *en route* but usually by now the hotel in Baghdad beckons to the weary traveller. **Note:** On reaching, and after, Salman Pak district, traffic becomes constant and heavy. This end of the journey is not helped by the many checkpoints around the city which you have to pass through and they can hold you up for a considerable time.

UPDATES WEBSITE

You can post your comments and recommendations, and read the latest feedback and updates from other readers online at www.bradtupdates.com/iraq.

Part Three

IRAQI KURDISTAN

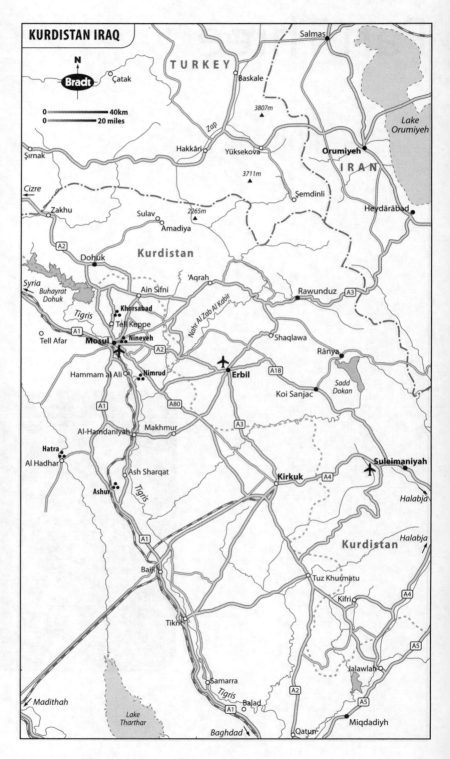

KURDISTAN IRAQ

N
Bradt

0 ————— 40km
0 ————— 20 miles

Çatak

T U R K E Y

Salmas

Baskale

3807m ▲

Lake
Orumiyeh

Zap

Şırnak

Hakkâri

Yüksekova

Orumiyeh

I R A N

Cizre

3711m ▲

Zakhu

Sulav

Amadiya

2265m ▲

Şemdinli

Heydārābād

A2

Dohuk

Kurdistan

'Aqrah

Rawunduz

A3

Syria

Buhayrat
Dohuk

Ain Sifni

Khorsabad

Tell Keppe

Tigris

Mosul

Nineveh

A2

Shaqlawa

Rānya

Nahr Al Zab Al Kabir

Tell Afar

A1

Hammam al Ali

Nimrud

Erbil

A18

Sadd
Dokan

Koi Sanjac

A1

A80

Al-Hamdaniyah

Makhmur

A3

Suleimaniyah

Hatra

Al Hadhar

Ash Sharqat

Kirkuk

A4

Halabja

Ashur

Tigris

Kurdistan

Halabja

A1

Baiji

Tuz Khurmatu

Kifri

A4

Tikrit

A5

Jalawlah

Madithah

Samarra

Tigris

Balad

A2

A5

Lake
Tharthar

A1

Baghdad

Qatun

Miqdadiyh

10

Practicalities in Kurdistan

Nobody should say the Kurds are dead, the Kurds are alive
Our banner shall never be lowered
We are the descendants of the Medes and Key Khasrew
Our homeland is our faith and religion.
We are the heroes of revolution and the colour red
Just look how blood-stained our history is.
The Kurdish people are gallantly standing to attention
Ready to decorate their living crown with blood.
Kurdish youth is ever present and ready
To sacrifice with their lives.

Kurdish National Anthem, translated by M T Ali

For the traveller, Kurdistan Iraq is virgin country. Not yet full of tourists, the people and the country are warm and welcoming and it is a great place to visit. However, the lack of tourist infrastructure does mean that for most of the time travellers have to seek out many of the sites themselves. This guide mentions the main sites of interest, but there are still many out of the way, long-forgotten places full of history waiting to be discovered. Kurdistan also has a lot of caves, whose history we can currently only guess at. The hills and mountains of Kurdistan are part of its character and history, places of refuge in ancient and more modern times. So whether you have a guide, a guide book or just intend striking out to explore as the road takes you, a little knowledge of the area will help you appreciate the treasures you will encounter along the way.

GENERAL INFORMATION

GEOGRAPHY Kurdistan is the northern, mountainous part of the state of Iraq, created by Great Britain after its mandate (League of Nations) in 1921 from the three old Ottoman provinces. A thin crescent around the upper rim of the country extending from Dohuk to Erbil and Suleimaniyah Kurdistan is a traditional area of refuge from the heat of the plains. The mountains of Kurdistan Iraq form a natural barrier between Turkey and Iran and are responsible for the nature and the character of the Kurds. The hidden valleys and traditional village houses have not only been a retreat from outside forces, but have fostered the traditional way of life and sense of community of the Kurds for centuries. Approximately 40,643km² in area, roughly the same size as Switzerland, it is the home of over five million Kurds. There are three governorates: Erbil, Dohuk and Suleimaniyah. The capital of the region is the city of Erbil. Major rivers include the Tigris, Higher Zab, Lower Zab, Sirwan Zab, Khaboor and Kahzir.

CLIMATE The summer months (May–September) are hot and dry, especially in the Erbil plain. Temperatures can reach 45°C or more during the day. It is cooler in the evenings. Temperatures are lower in the mountainous regions around Dohuk and Suleimaniyah. Winters can be cold, with frequent falls of snow.

NATURAL HISTORY AND CONSERVATION In Kurdistan the scenery is magnificent, sometimes wooded and watered by turbulent streams, sometimes gaunt and bare, but always dramatic and often awesome. The bright dazzling colours of tulips, roses, hyacinths, gladioli and daffodils, which appear in spring, are reflected in the costumes of Kurdish women. The men also love flowers and take a special delight in growing roses. Love of nature assumes a spiritual significance: trees and ponds are full of colourful pieces of cloth used as a sign of vigil for a wish. Some 56,000 years ago a Neanderthal man was buried in a flower bed in the area and today flowers are grown on graves to let the soul rest. They are also a constant feature of Kurdish art and decoration. The main crops are wheat and barley grown on the plains of Erbil, and Suleimaniyah is a traditional tobacco-producing region. Fruits such as apples, cherries, plums and pomegranates are also grown in Iraqi Kurdistan.

More than 40 different types of fish are found in the rivers and streams. The mountains were once popular hunting grounds for wild boars, bears, hyenas, ibexes and hares, and the last lion was reportedly killed in around 1910. The mountains also form a natural barrier between Turkey and Iran, and Halgurd is the highest peak in the Hasarost Mountains, 3,607m above sea level. The mountain villages are fascinating places, providing a penetrating flash of insight into rural life and a largely traditional society, centred around land (tribe and village) and blood (family). Traditional village houses are single-storey buildings of mud brick or stone; the flat roofs allow the houses to blend with the terrain. The corrugated iron of 'modernity' has found its way into Iraqi Kurdistan, as has the breeze-block. Life for the local population, however, remains unchanged, and villagers gather firewood and tend to their crops and livestock as they have for centuries. The villages may be only a few kilometres apart but every settlement has its own unique character and a well-developed sense of community.

Tragically, much of the landscape has been devastated by war and the wanton destruction of the woodlands. Since the 1960s, the Iraqi regime had systematically destroyed the forests that provided a cover for the *peshmerga* (Kurdish guerrilla fighters whose name means 'those who face death') and the use of oak beams in houses in Baghdad and Basra has accelerated deforestation. Animals such as goats, which frequently eat saplings, are also a problem. Attempts at reforestation were made between 1970 and 1974 when the Kurds and the Iraqi government were not at loggerheads, although a large part of the forests were cut down between 1991 and 1996, due to a shortage of fuel and petroleum. Current reforestation efforts include the establishment of 10 nurseries producing around 3.5 million seedlings of different types of trees. There are also two fruit tree nurseries. The annual production of seedlings in Erbil and Dohuk alone is 2 million.

HISTORY The history of the Kurds is the history of a proud, rebellious, tribal people who have resisted control by outside forces, and suffered for it throughout the ages. In the words of Teresa Thornhill, author of *Sweet Tea with Cardamom: a Journey Through Iraqi Kurdistan*, 'it is a culture where almost everyone is standing on a mountain of pain and grief.' A popular saying tells us that the Kurds have 'no friends but the mountains'.

The ancient Kurds The Kurds have been living in the Zagros Mountains since the beginning of history, when the first written records appeared in the Sumerian city states in 3000BC. The land of Karda is mentioned on a Sumerian clay tablet from the 3rd millennium BC. In the ancient world they were part of the two-way struggle between the people of the plains and the mountain people of the north. The Babylonians referred to the Kurds as valiant or brave (*garda*), the Akkadians used the term Kuti to denote inhabitants of the eastern Taurus Mountains, while the Persians spoke about the Kurds, a word which was probably derived from the Babylonian word *garda*.

The ancient Kurds waged war with the Assyrian Empire for 700 years. The mountains, the saviours of the Kurdish people from invaders throughout the centuries, were their refuge and prevented their total destruction. In alliance with the Babylonian king Nabopolassar, the Medes and the Elamites, they fought the Assyrian Empire until it crumbled in 612BC.

During the days of the powerful Median Empire (700–553BC) the Kurds coalesced with the Medes and adopted their language. The Median Empire stretched from the southern shore of the Black Sea and Aran province (the modern-day Republic of Azerbaijan) to north and Central Asia and Afghanistan. It included many tributary states, among them that of the Persians, which eventually supplanted and absorbed the Median Empire into the Achaemenid Persian Empire created by Cyrus the Great.

The Achaemenid Empire was followed by the Parthian (247BC–AD226), an arch-enemy of the Roman Empire in the east. At its height the Parthian Empire covered all of Iran proper, as well as regions of the modern countries of Armenia, Iraq, Georgia, eastern Turkey, eastern Syria, Turkmenistan, Afghanistan, Tajikistan, Pakistan, Kuwait, and the Persian Gulf coast of Saudi Arabia, Bahrain, Qatar and the UAE. But the empire was loosely organised and the last king was defeated by one of the empire's vassals of the Sassanid Dynasty. The Sassanid Dynasty defeated the last Parthian king Artabanus. The Sassanid Empire (266–636) witnessed the highest achievement of Persian civilisation and was the largest Iranian empire before the Arab conquest of 641. Persia influenced Roman civilisation considerably during Sassanid times, and the Romans reserved for the Sassanid Persians alone the status of equals, exemplified in the letters written by the Roman Emperor to the Persian Shahanshah (king of kings), which were addressed to 'my brother'. The last Sassanid king Yazdegerd III could not stand up to the Arab conquerors and a new era began in Iraqi and Kurdish history.

The Arab conquest and Saladin David McDowall, author of *A Modern History of the Kurds*, notes that with the Arab conquest the Kurds emerged from historical obscurity, rapidly confirming the longevity of their reputation for political dissidence. They first came into contact with the Arab armies who conquered Mesopotamia in 637.

The pattern of nominal submission to central government, be it Persian, Arab or subsequently Turkic, alongside the assertion of as much local independence as possible, became an enduring theme in Kurdish political life.

One of the most famous Kurds is Saladin, the warrior who effectively took the caliphate and commanded the Muslim forces during the Crusades, Christian-Muslim wars that lasted from 1096 to 1453. His forces fought in the territory of present-day Syria, Lebanon and Israel, and Saladin became the ruler of Egypt in 1169 and Syria in 1186. One of his greatest achievements was the taking of Jerusalem from the Christians in 1187, setting limitations on the Crusader kingdoms and principalities. Saladin was born in Tikrit, also the birthplace of Saddam Hussein, and is buried in Damascus.

During the 11th century a number of Kurdish tribal chiefs (aghas) achieved total autonomy, but most co-existed with the Seljuks. In 1514, after a battle at Chaldrian in present-day northwest Iran between the Safavid Persians and the armies of the Ottoman Empire, most of the Kurds nominally came under the control of the Ottomans, but still managed to preserve some of their autonomy. Four hundred years later, after the break-up of the Ottoman Empire at the end of World War I, the Kurds were promised their own state in the Treaty of Sèvres.

This promise was not kept and the traditional Kurdish homeland now cuts across the national boundaries of Turkey, Iran, Iraq and Syria. These countries have many disagreements but they are united in their rejection of the acceptance of an independent Kurdish state, and have reluctantly conceded to some degree of Kurdish autonomy.

GOVERNMENT AND POLITICS After World War I, Kurdistan Iraq was mandated to the British by the League of Nations (later the United Nations). Britain's attempts to control the region through Sheikh Mahmud Barzinji proved disastrous. He was invited to be the governor, a position he held under the Turks. Barzinji soon came into conflict with Britain as he felt the Kurds should be given greater regional autonomy. He also had differences with the heads of other clans and the long-established Kurdish families settled in Baghdad. In 1931 Sheikh Mahmud revolted, agitating for a united Kurdistan. He was defeated and placed under town arrest in the south of the country. But Kurdish national aspirations could not be arrested.

The establishment of the State of Kurdistan Republic in Mahabad, Iran, in 1945 gave a major impetus to the national aspirations of the Kurdish people. But it collapsed a year later, when Iranian troops marched into Mahabad and ended Kurdish rule in the region.

One of the major nationalist figures to emerge during this time was Mulla Mustafa Barzani, who was appointed commander of the republic's army. After spending 12 years in exile in the Soviet Union, Mulla Mustafa Barzani returned to Iraq when the 1958 coup toppled the monarchy, and formed a friendly alliance with the Prime Minister, Abdul Karim Qasim.

Qasim was the first Iraqi leader to declare that Kurds and Arabs were equal partners. The new Iraqi constitution in fact stated that 'the Kurds and Arabs are partners within this nation and guaranteed their rights within the framework of the Iraqi Republic.' The Kurdish people had great expectations of freedom and democracy, but before long it became apparent that the constitution's fine words could not and would not be translated into actions.

When Qasim could not fulfil the promises he had made to his one-time ally and friend he started arming tribes hostile to Barzani such as the Zibaris, the Baradost, Herki and Surchi. The Kurdistan Democratic Party was banned, the former allies became enemies and the war between the Kurds and the central government continued until Qasim's overthrow in 1963. When the Baathists were firmly in control of the country an 11-point peace agreement was declared on 11 March 1970.

At first the Baathists remained true to the agreement but there was disagreement about three major issues: the demarcation of the Kurdish area; the issue of the oil fields and the Kurds' insistence that Kirkuk must be part of the Kurdish autonomous region; and the central government's Arabisation Programme, which began in 1968. Mistrust between the Kurds and the government increased and fighting started again when the government justified increasing its forces in the Kurdish areas on the grounds of an Iranian threat. The Baathists unilaterally declared an Autonomy Law on 11 March 1974 and gave the KDP 14 days to agree so they could continue their participation in government. The new law was a watered-down version of the 1970 agreement, which the Kurds rejected mainly because of the Kirkuk issue. The KDP insisted on a proportional distribution of revenues from the Kirkuk oil field. The 14-day period expired and a full-scale war began in April 1974. At first the Kurds, aided by the Iranians, inflicted heavy losses on the Iraqi army, but the Kurdish resistance collapsed overnight after the Algiers Agreement of 1975, between Saddam Hussein and the Shah of Iran, in which Iraq gave up its claim to the Shatt Al-Arab waterway (the Tigris/Euphrates outlet south of Basra to the Gulf). Iran cut off its assistance to the Kurds and Barzani departed for America, where he died of cancer in 1979.

The war left 7,000 Iraqi soldiers and more than 2,000 Kurdish fighters dead, and displaced 600,000 people. Apart from the KDP, other parties emerged within the Kurdish movement, namely the Patriotic Union of Kurdistan (PUK) led by Jalal Talabani, and the Kurdistan Socialist Party. In 1987 five main Kurdish nationalist parties set up the Iraqi Kurdistan Front (IKF). Their aim was real autonomy for the Kurds. The end of the Iran-Iraq War in 1988 proved disastrous for the Kurds. They were hoping for an Iranian Kurdish victory and the downfall of Saddam Hussein. But when the Kurds expanded the territory they controlled near the Iranian border to an area almost the size of Lebanon, the regime responded with a chemical weapons attack on Halabja and other areas.

On 22 July 1988 Iran accepted the UNSCR 598 ceasefire resolution and the Iraqi government launched a major offensive against the Kurds using 60,000 troops. Thousands fled across the border to Turkey and Iran but the regime continued to use chemical weapons with impunity as the international community did little more than condemn the attacks. On 6 September 1988 an amnesty was offered to the refugees but few returned.

Towards the end of the First Gulf War, the Kurdistan Front was eager to ally itself with the Iraqi opposition committed to the overthrow of Saddam Hussein. During the popular uprising in March 1991 the Kurds controlled nearly all of Iraqi Kurdistan but the Iraqi army brutally sought to re-establish the government's writ over territory controlled by the Kurds, prompting another refugee exodus. Over 1.5 million Kurdish people fled towards the Turkish and Iranian borders to escape from Saddam's forces.

Turkey refused to let the refugees in. The deaths of 1,000 people a day on the Iranian and Turkish frontier prompted the setting up by Britain and the US of the safe haven, which was officially handed over by the Western allies to the United Nations on 7 June 1991. The refugee crisis was alleviated and at the beginning of 1992 most refugees returned to Iraqi Kurdistan.

The safe haven and autonomy under the Kurdistan Regional Government

From mid-1991 until the 2003 war and invasion, Coalition war planes regularly policed the no-fly zone to prevent the Iraqi regime from launching air attacks against the safe haven which became a de facto autonomous Kurdish entity ruled by the two main Kurdish parties. The Kurdish elections of May 1992, judged as free and fair by more than 50 observers from 12 countries, were a watershed in Kurdish history, which sent shock waves through the dictatorial regimes of the Arab world. There was an overwhelming eagerness among the young and old to vote. A picture of a man carrying his old mother to the polling station was published by many Western newspapers: the Kurdish democratic experiment was one of the rare 'good news' stories to come out of the Middle East.

The PUK gained 49% and the KDP 51% of the votes, while smaller parties, such as the socialists and the Islamic Union Movement in Kurdistan-Iraq, failed to gain the minimum 7% of the vote required to secure a parliamentary seat. Five seats were allocated for the Christians. Women made up 7% of the parliament, compared with 9% in Britain! A Kurdish Regional Government was formed and the Kurdish Assembly started meeting in Erbil.

The 50/50 power-sharing deal to prevent autonomy in the governing of the Kurdish region did not work and the ensuing power struggle resulted in armed clashes between the PUK and KDP militias. In 1994 the PUK seized Erbil and the ambitious, idealistic democratic experiment came to an inglorious end. Attempts by both the USA and Britain to bring the two parties to the negotiating table failed and regional powers entered the conflict: Turkey on the side of the KDP and Iran on the side of the PUK.

In 1996, when Iranian forces entered PUK-controlled territory under the pretext of pursuing members of the Kurdistan Democratic Party (Iran), the KDP first asked the Americans to intervene. When the plea fell on seemingly deaf ears, Baghdad's help was enlisted: 30,000 Iraqi troops entered the city of Erbil and surrounding areas and assisted the KDP in ousting the PUK from the regional capital. The intervention of the Iraqi army dealt a death blow to the activities of a number of anti-Saddam opposition groups based in Iraqi Kurdistan; after the occupation a large number of Iraqi secret police remained in the area to root out Saddam's opponents. Around 1,500 people were arrested and 2,500 Iraqis and Kurds who were working with the INC (Iraqi National Congress, a coalition of opposition parties and groups) were evacuated to Guam and subsequently re-settled in the USA.

America's attempts to reconcile the two main Kurdish parties culminated in the Ankara Accords of October 1996 and the Washington Agreement of September 1998. Under this agreement Barzani and Talabani agreed to set up a coalition administration in preparation for new elections.

When hostilities first broke out between the US-led Coalition and Saddam Hussein in 2003 the northern front was almost forgotten. As Ben Rooney pointed out in *The Daily Telegraph*'s publication *War on Saddam*, an unsteady peace had existed in northern Iraq since the 1991 Gulf War and the establishment of the UN safe haven to protect the Kurdish majority. The Kurds were bitter opponents of Saddam, and in them the American commander General Franks saw a useful ally. When his plans to open up a second front against Baghdad through Turkey were thwarted by Ankara, he hoped to see the Kurdish freedom fighters, the *peshmerga*, take on the Iraqis in the north.

On 29 March 2003 American bombing enabled the *peshmerga* to attack the bases of Ansar al-Islam, an extremist group with suspected links to al-Qaeda. The first major battle on the northern front was fought on 3 April, when the *peshmerga* seized a strategic bridge on the road to Mosul.

Throughout the war the Kurds were unable to seize Mosul and Kirkuk. But after the fall of Saddam's regime the Americans could not restrain them any longer. On 10 April they arrived in Kirkuk to a tumultuous welcome as posters of Saddam were torn down and government shops looted. Refugees who had been forced out of the city during the government's Arabisation programme returned, while the supporters of Saddam fled. Kirkuk is one of the most disputed areas, with the Kurds seeking to integrate the city (which they call 'the Kurdish Jerusalem') into the semi-autonomous Kurdistan Region. The Kurds have a strong historical, cultural and emotional attachment to Kirkuk, which they see as the legitimate capital of an autonomous Kurdistan state. In Mosul the Iraqi garrison surrendered to the Americans *en masse*. A new chapter in the history of Iraqi Kurdistan had begun, characterised by the domination of two main parties.

Kurdistan was referred to by the Kurdistan Development Corporation as 'The Other Iraq' in an advertising campaign on American television to promote investment and trade in the region. The adverts featured humming towns, full of well-patronised cafés and many mobile-phone shops and internet cafés. They went on to say 'liquor is also freely available, sometimes sold by Christians who fled from the troubled south. Neon signs light the streets full of people, including women and girls, who were seldom seen in public before'. Assad Nejmeddin, an English student at the University of Erbil, said: '*I don't know why we're bothering with Baghdad. I and my friends (sic) don't even speak Arabic. We have done very well on our own. Let's continue.*' It seems that most Kurds resident in 'The Other Iraq' agree with her. Peter Galbraith, author of *The End of Iraq*, noted that:

'When the January 2005 elections took place, there were referendum booths just outside, or actually inside, every polling place. Two million Kurds voted in the referendum and 98% chose independence. The outcome put Kurdish and Iraqi leaders on notice that Kurdistan's voters would reject a permanent constitution that required any significant reintegration of the region into Iraq. The permanent constitution institutionalised a virtually independent Kurdistan, the very result Bremer (*the American pro-consul to Iraq*) sought to avoid.'

The KRG has two main priorities: to ensure the autonomy of the Kurdish region of northern Iraq and to encourage investment and development. Following the unification agreement of 21 January 2006, the KRG established the first unified cabinet. Prior to the agreement the governorate of Suleimaniyah was governed by a PUK-led administration, while the governorates of Erbil and Dohuk were governed by a KDP-led administration. The current government, led by Prime Minister Nechirvan Barzani, took office on 5 April 2012. It consists of several political parties, reflecting the ethnic and religious diversity of the region's people: Kurds, Turkmen, Chaldeans, Assyrians, Syriacs, Yezidis and others.

The cabinet is made up of members of the Kurdistani List coalition, which won the region's parliamentary elections in July 2009, together with other parties. The coalition government consists of the Kurdistan Democratic Party (KDP), Patriotic Union of Kurdistan (PUK), Kurdistan Islamic Movement, the Chaldean Assyrian Syriac Council, Turkmen representatives, communists and socialists. The government has 19 ministries.

The region is plagued by five intractable problems: the dispute between Kurdistan and the central government about the region's right to enter into deals with oil companies without Baghdad's consent; the status of Kirkuk which the KRG wants incorporated into its territory; problems with Turkey about the presence of PKK (Kurdistan Workers Party) guerrillas in the region; and care for refugees: displaced Christians who are congregating on the Nineveh Plains and Syrian refugees fleeing the civil war between President Bashar al Assad and the rebels.

The constitution entitles the Kurdistan region to receive 17% of total Iraqi oil revenues but Erbil and Baghdad cannot agree who has the authority to strike exploration contracts with Baghdad, denouncing agreements signed between the KRG and Exxon Mobil Corp as illegal. Oil exports from Iraqi Kurdistan halted in mid 2012 amid a row over contracts with foreign firms, and the Kurds said they would start exporting oil via a new pipeline to the Turkish border in 2013.

The KRG and the central government were on the brink of war at the end of 2012. In November Kurdish forces and the Iraqi army and police sent troops and armoured vehicles to reinforce positions around Kirkuk which has some of the world's largest oil reserves. Iraqi President and Secretary General of the Patriotic Union of Kurdistan Jalal Talabani played a major role in defusing tensions until he suffered a stroke in December 2012 and was flown to Germany for treatment. Kurdistan's President Massoud Barzani, dressed in military uniform and flanked by troops visited Kurdish controlled areas of Kirkuk and said: 'We are against war and we do not like war but if things come to war than all the Kurdish people are ready to fight in order to preserve the Kurdish identity of Kirkuk.' A census to determine whether the city has a Kurdish or Arab majority has long been delayed, as has a referendum on whether Diyala, Kirkuk, Salad ad Din and Nineveh will become part of the Kurdistan region, and the issue of the return of internally displaced Kurds to Kirkuk and Mosul, even though they were forced out of their homes by Saddam's regime, remains unresolved – title deeds to properties notwithstanding.

Guerrillas of the separatist Kurdistan Workers Party (PKK) have camps in Iraqi Kurdistan and Turkish armed forces are engaged in cross-border air operations against the guerrillas who have a major base and training camp in the Zap area. Turkey's feud with the PKK is linked to issues inside Iraq, among them the tug of war between the Kurds, Arabs and Turkmen over Kirkuk. Kurdish political allegiances are complex, with the PUK and KDP backing different Syrian Kurdish parties. The Kurds on either side of the Tigris, which runs between Syria and Iraq are united by kinship and a history of oppression.

All Kurds dream of an independent homeland. In May 2013, Kurdish fighters took up positions on the outskirts of Kirkuk after Iraqi security forces were redeployed elsewhere and in June, following the collapse of the Iraqi army in the face of advances by ISIS, the *peshmerga* took control of the city. The fall of Mosul, the country's second city, to the Islamists in their lightning campaign across northern Iraq, sent shock waves across the Middle East. As this book goes to press American air strikes against ISIS are taking place around the city in an effort to isolate ISIS in Mosul. Kirkuk is now controlled by the *peshmergas*.

ECONOMY Since the establishment of the no-fly zone by the then British Prime Minister John Major in 1991, the Kurdish region underwent an economic boom. Well over half of the villages destroyed by Saddam Hussein have been rebuilt, two new airports have been opened and new roads, schools and hospitals have been built. Many of the Kurdish diaspora have returned to the region to live and enjoy a level of peace and prosperity not yet realised in the rest of Iraq. Among the increasing number of visitors to Kurdistan are international business people who are realising the potential of the area. The Kurdistan Regional Government (KRG) encouraged the participation of foreign investors into the development of the region. In 2011, despite the global economic crisis, Kurdistan registered 8% growth driven by the exploitation of its gas and oil reserves (estimated at 3–6 trillion m³ and 45 billion barrels, respectively). In 2012, growth was 12%, which, according to the International Monetary Fund, made Kurdistan the second fastest-growing economy in the world after Mongolia.

In addition to immense profits in the oil industry, non-oil investment totalled US$12 billion in 2011, according to the Board of Investors of the KRG. The primary source of investment in Kurdistan during 2012 was in local property markets, which saw an increase of US$4.7 billion; the banking sector followed with a US$2.29 billion increase.

The construction boom is being fed by Turkey. Every day hundreds of trucks cross the border with steel, concrete and other raw materials. Investment in tourism has begun for the days when oil will no longer be able to sustain the region's development. The two new airports which opened in Erbil and Suleimaniyah, have over 80 direct flights scheduled each week to and from Dubai, Jordan, Istanbul, Frankfurt, Stockholm, Amsterdam and other destinations.

In 2013 there were approximately 1,600 foreign and 11,000 local companies in Kurdistan. Foreign and domestic investment had been rising annually for the previous six years with more than US$3 billion invested in the first six months alone in 2012. Local investment, foreign direct investment and foreign/local partnerships are impressive. Since 2006 around US$21 billion has been invested in Kurdistan (US$12 billion in Erbil and US$6 billion in Suleimaniyah).

There are 17 consulates and foreign representations, 7 universities and a new road has been built between the two main cities of Erbil and Suleimaniyah. Buying a Rolex watch is no problem in Erbil which is no stranger to Italian pizzerias, Chinese restaurants and sushi bars. There is even a go-kart track at US$20 per lap.

Foreigner investors still have their reservations about investing in Iraqi Kurdistan. Building materials and goods such as processed food products are almost all imported and expensive. Basic services like water and electricity have improved in past years, but the Erbil municipality doesn't yet have constant, reliable electricity, while in the countryside some villages still don't have power at all. Despite the current unrest in the north of Iraq, however, with American airstrikes near Erbil and US personnel located in the city, the economy still continues to be buoyant. In September 2014 Lufthansa resumed flights to Erbil and the KRG is still finding buyers for crude oil despite threats of legal action from Baghdad, with the Kurdish Minister of Natural Resources, Ashti Hawrami, announcing the sale of 7 million barrels of oil on the international market. In 2014 the KRG was producing 300,000 barrels of oil per day with the expectation that the figure would reach 500,000 barrels of oil per day by the end of the year. This increase in oil production has helped to eliminate previous fuel shortages occasioned by offensives by ISIS earlier in the year.

PEOPLE The diversity of ethnicity in modern Kurdistan is due to history, religion and language. Ethnic groups dwelling in the Kurdistan region, including Arabs, Turkmen, Assyrians and Yezidis, plus some smaller minorities such as Armenians and Palestinians, also consider themselves as Kurds. The very large number of

WHO ARE THE KURDS?

A widely held belief among historians, and the Kurds themselves, is that they are the descendants of the Medes of central Asia who helped to bring down the powerful Assyrian Empire. Some Kurdish Jews believe that Solomon sent genies to collect maidens for his harem. They succeeded the year he died, kept the maidens and lived in the desolate mountains. The Kurds are their children. There are also claims that the Kurds are the descendants of the lost tribes of Israel.

The name Kurdistan refers to the place where the Kurds live. Today this region cuts across the national borders of Turkey, Iran, Iraq and Syria. Large numbers of Kurds are also found in the Khanaqin, Diyala and Baghdad provinces of Iraq.

10

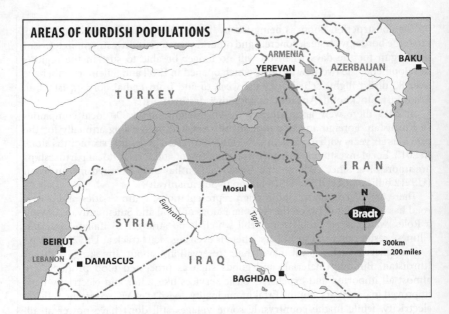

AREAS OF KURDISH POPULATIONS

Syrian refugees (2014/15) will inevitably alter this balance in some areas as they are ethnic Arabs, speaking Arabic as their first language. The sheer diversity of these peoples is what makes Kurdistan such an interesting place to visit.

LANGUAGE There are two dialects of Kurdish spoken in the Kurdish Region, Kurmanji (spoken mainly in Dohuk and environs) and Sorani (spoken mainly in Erbil, Suleimaniyah and environs). Please see opposite and pages 413–14 for basic Kurdish vocabulary.

RELIGION In Iraqi Kurdistan, religion and pagan superstition go hand in hand. Allied to the different ethnic origins from the region's past conflicts, there is a great awareness of the invisible realm in everyday life, and blessings and endearing spontaneous prayers are part of the normal vocabulary. In line with the beliefs of Zoroastrianism, an ancient Persian religion, women are careful when pouring hot liquid into an empty container as a spirit (*jinn*) could be harmed. Angels are seen as God's messengers who can bring rewards or punishments. Amulets for protection against the evil eye are common throughout the area.

Kurdistan, along with the rest of northern Iraq (notably centres such as Mosul and Kirkuk), is a region of total fascination for anyone interested in how religion has changed history and influenced communities right up until the present day.

Kurdistan at present is 80% Sunni Muslims and 15% Shia Muslims. The Kurds embraced Islam during the time of the Arab conquest in the 7th century AD, motivated in part by a desire to avoid paying taxes imposed on non-Muslims.

The remaining 5% are followers of minority religions Yezidis, Zoroastrians, Christians, Jews, as well as Sufi Muslims (members of the Qadiriya and Naqshbandiya brotherhoods) and members of Islamic sects such as Ahl Al-Haqq (People of the Truth).

Today Westerners, along with many modern Muslims in the Muslim world, know little about the historical aspects and practices of these Islamic sects. Although the Kurdish form of Islam contains many mystical elements associated with Sufism,

BASIC KURDISH WORDS

English	Kurdish (phonetically)
How are you?	*Choni?*
Good morning	*Bayane bash*
Good afternoon	*Eware bash*
Good night	*Shaw bash*
Good day	*Roj bash*
Welcome	*Bakher beyt*
How much is this?	*Ava bye chanda?*
Yes	*Bale*
No	*Na*
Please	*Bezahmet*
You're welcome	*Shayane nea*
Excuse me	*Ba yarmateet*
Do you speak English?	*Inglese azani?*
I don't speak Kurdish	*Kurdi nazanm*
Tea without sugar	*Chi be shakir*

this is fractured, with the Suleimaniyah region, for example, heavily influenced by the Qadiriya and Naqshbandiya Islamic brotherhoods. The Qadiriya order is a widespread Sufi order and the Naqshbandi order is a Dervish order founded in the 14th century.

Dr Michiel Leesienberg of the University of Amsterdam has written about and described some of the ethnic groups of Muslims scattered along the fringes of Kurdistan. These include the Shebash, the Bajalon, the Sarli, the Kakais and the Yezidis (although most people would deny that they are Muslims). Some of these communities are hidden away in small valleys, marked out only by their different dialects: Gorani or Maclo. These groups resemble orthodox Sufi orders and all have a hereditary class of religious leaders. Their religious beliefs and practices form a mixture of heterodox Islam with pre-Islamic elements.

Yezidis are found in the town of Sinjar, on the slopes of the Sinjar mountains and the Dohuk region, intermingled with the other religious communities (see page 25).

We should also briefly mention the Cult of Angels, Alevism, Nusayrim and Yarsanism, all of which are small religious communities that make no attempt to be Muslim and are, therefore, ready targets for abuse by their Muslim neighbours today. It says much for past community tolerance that they still exist at all. Zoroastrianism as an organised faith probably dates from 1700BC. It rose to prominence when Kurdistan was part of the Persian, Parthian and Sassanian empires. There are still a small number of followers in the region today.

Kurdistan was also an early home of Christianity. According to Dr Sebastian Brock of the Oriental Institute, Oxford University, 'most people are unaware that Christianity was already in Iraq well before it reached Britain and that it continued to be a significant cultural and religious influence in the country right up to the present day'. The scattered churches and monasteries of Kurdistan, many still with monks and priests, reflect this. Despite the day-to-day difficulties in the face of persecution, and despite the mass exodus of many Christians, there is now a reverse flow of Christians settling in Kurdistan, refugees from Baghdad and the south, but also from neighbouring areas such as Mosul, seeking religious comfort and safety. Assyrian Christians are found mainly in Dohuk and Chaldean Christians are concentrated in Shaqlawa and Erbil. The Christian quarter of Suleimaniyah (in the eastern part of the city) has three churches and most Christians in Suleimaniyah belong to the Chaldean Church, which is linked to the Church of Rome. (See page 15.)

There were many communities of Jews in the various cities of Kurdistan, and small villages and farmsteads in the country had Jewish inhabitants, who are, alas, very few or no more. The origin of Judaism in the country is a debatable subject. Traditionally it is said that the Tribe of Benjamin was first settled in Kurdistan after the Assyrian conquest of the Kingdom of Israel during the 8th century BC. In the following centuries there was a history of Jews emigrating from surrounding countries to form settlements in Kurdistan. In Zakhu, for example, there are still traditional Jewish songs and verse, a relic of their now lost Jewish community. The majority of Kurdish Jews, along with the Iraqi Jews, were evacuated to Israel in 1950–51. Today in Israel, many live in enclaves still holding on to their Kurdish heritage and traditions.

EDUCATION In the last 10 years education in Kurdistan has improved at all levels. Numerous educational establishments have been opened all over Kurdistan, including international universities and colleges. Public universities have been founded and the people of Kurdistan have been given opportunities to improve their education. American universities and colleges have greatly assisted in the establishment of courses for students in Kurdistan, particularly in the study of the English language and IT skills, and the American University of Iraq in Suleimaniyah which opened its doors in 2007, now offers a truly comprehensive American-style education. The Kurds have been quick to seize the opportunity to develop a modern educational system and this investment will eventually show great results.

Suleimaniyah is the cultural centre of the Sorani-speaking Kurds. The first school for Kurdish girls was founded here in 1915. The actual University of Suleimaniyah was founded in 1968 and is the oldest institution of higher education in northern Iraq. Currently there are approximately 10,000 students studying there, over half of whom are women.

CULTURE Culture, media, sports and the arts have all been enhanced in Kurdistan through a policy of free press and media. Over 60 publications are issued monthly. Music, art exhibitions, theatrical productions and cinema are all popular pastimes.

Storytelling The long Kurdish winters are ideal times for storytelling and many stories describe how to survive in an inhospitable environment. A rich oral culture has been encouraged by the frequent destruction of Kurdish villages and property, which made it unsafe to commit inspiring traditional tales to paper. Some stories detract from the worries of everyday life. There are plenty of satirical tales. Animal stories with a spiritual moral are common. Sometimes the animals are portrayed as intelligent beings with their own code of conduct. There are also plenty of legends with a supernatural dimension, and historical epics. Tales of Imam Khidir i Zinde (The Immortal) are among the most common. He is an omnipresent, supernatural being who can be called to come to a person's help after elaborate rituals are performed. But he is the master of disguise and often goes unrecognised. There is also the story of the avatar Shah Khushin, conceived when his mother was impregnated by the sun's rays, which entered her throat when she yawned during the ritual of bowing before the rising sun. When her family ordered her death for dishonouring their name, the sword was petrified in the air before it struck and the child was born as a speck of light, which turned into a man-child. The birth occurred after only 21 days, the multiplication of the sacred numbers 3 and 7. Khushin assumed his role as an avatar at the age of 32, one year short of when Christ died on the cross. He disappeared under the waves of the Gamasiyab river aged 61, one year short of when Mohammed died.

Festivals The Kurds like to celebrate. Nowruz, or spring rites (similar to Easter), is the main festival, which welcomes spring on 21 March, the Kurdish New Year. It is also the Kurdish national day. The Kurdish calendar begins in AD380, the fall of the last Kurdish kingdom – the Kavusakan Dynasty – with an extra seven years added on. Spring is a joyous time in contrast to the hardship of winter. It is the most beautiful season, with clear skies, pleasant sunshine and the blossoming of a fascinating range of flowers. Festivities last for more than a week and include breaking pottery for good luck, resolving misunderstandings and giving children presents. A few days before Nowruz, bonfires are lit to signify the end of the dark winter season and the beginning of spring, the season of light. Evil spirits are scared off with fire crackers. According to ancient legend, 21 March is also the day on which the blacksmith Kawa smashed the head of the tyrant Zuhak. Zuhak was suffering from a brain disease and doctors advised him to eat the brains of young people. Kawa offered Zuhak a number of his children but when he wanted to take his last son, Kawa revolted and killed him, emerging as a national hero. Seasonal festivals, such as the first lambing, are also a feature of rural life. At harvest time the first sheaf reaped is offered to a stranger who passes by.

Dance The comment by the late Mulla Mustafa Barzani, the most renowned Kurdish leader of the 20th century, that 'one who cannot dance is not a Kurd', illustrates the importance of dance in Kurdish culture. Traditional dance is often used by *peshmerga*, politicians, as well as villagers, to make a political statement when Kurdish culture is suppressed. The dances resemble the Lebanese *dabka* and consist mainly of handholding group dances round a circle. Musicians who play for the dancers are often also singers. **Kurdish music**, which influenced that of Iran and Turkey, tends to be melancholic, a reflection on the trials and tribulations of life. In Iraq, Kurdish music has been influenced by the fast, joyous tempo of Arabic music. Kurdish folk songs, or story songs with heroic, amorous, religious and political themes, are stories told to the accompaniment of music. Travelling Kurdish balladeers once sang about the achievements of epic heroes.

PRACTICAL INFORMATION

WHEN TO VISIT Summer months (May–September) are very hot and dry, especially on the Erbil Plain, often reaching temperatures of more than 45°C and sometimes as high as 50°C. It is slightly cooler in the evenings and in the mountainous regions around Dohuk and Suleimaniyah. In **autumn**, October and November, the weather is very pleasant and still warm enough to enjoy sightseeing. The **winter** months can be cool with rain and some snowfall. In the mountain regions heavy snow falls during the winter months and the temperature can plummet. The best time to visit Kurdistan is in **spring**, in March when people celebrate Nowruz, the New Year marked by the spring equinox. This is the time for picnics and dancing in the hills and valleys.

HIGHLIGHTS

THE ANCIENT CITY OF ERBIL This is one of the oldest continually inhabited cities in the world. Brimming with history, Erbil stands as a testament to the numerous influences on the region: Turkmen, Safavid, Ottoman and British.

GAUGAMELA Some 90km northwest of Erbil is the site of the famous battle between Alexander the Great and King Darius III in 331BC, which resulted in a decisive victory for the Macedonians and led to the fall of the Persian Empire. Darius chose this flat, open plain deliberately, so that he could deploy his numerically superior forces to their best advantage. Definitely a site for history buffs, using their imagination!

DOHUK A picturesque city situated in a valley surrounded by mountains, Dohuk is traditionally associated with agriculture and is locally famous for its grapes. Once known for its colourful houses, it is now more famous for its fascinating bazaar.

LALISH The temple complex of Lalish is an important pilgrimage site for followers of the Yezidi faith, who are expected to make the trek here at least once during their lifetime. The tomb of Sheikh Adi is located here in a cave which also displays various features of the religion – holy water pools, fire and further tombs of earlier holy men.

AMADIYA Once an almost impenetrable fortress, Amadiya is located northeast of Zakhu on a high promontory above a breathtaking landscape overlooking the Sapna river valley, which is fed by a geothermal spring originating far below the mountain. It is believed by some to be the home of the biblical Three Wise Men, who made a pilgrimage to see Jesus Christ after his birth. The town has ruins from the Assyrian era, the ruins of a synagogue and a church.

HALABJA The town of Halabja is a place of unspeakable horror at the hands of Saddam Hussein's military forces where chemical weapons were used against the Kurds. At the monument of the Halabja Martyrs and the Halabja Cemetery visitors can learn about the brutal legacy of Saddam Hussein's regime.

HAMILTON ROAD In 1928, A M Hamilton was commissioned to build a road that would stretch from northern Iraq, through the mountains and gorges of Kurdistan on to the Iranian border. Hamilton overcame immense obstacles – disease, ferocious brigands, warring tribes and bureaucratic officials – to carve a path through some of the most beautiful but inhospitable landscapes in the world. Even by today's standards it is a considerable feat of engineering.

SUGGESTED ITINERARIES

Kurdistan is not a large region and most sites can be visited quite comfortably within a one-week period. If time is limited, it is best to select one of the three main cities and make this the hub for your excursions. With more time available, a journey taking in all three, with time to enjoy the spectacular scenery *en route*, is quite possible. As previously mentioned, local people are often uncertain of many of the locations of the ancient and historical sites.

At the time of going to press the security situation in northern Iraq, including the Kurdistan Region, was in a state of flux. In August 2015 the Foreign and

Commonwealth Office advised against travel to all areas where fighting has taken place and to the city of Erbil, as well as advising against all but essential travel to the rest of the region. The situation is changing daily, however, so you should check the current situation prior to planning travel to the region.

TWO DAYS As the roads have improved immensely over the previous two years it is possible to pack a lot into a two-day trip, basing yourself in Erbil. **Day one** in Erbil will give you a chance to soak up the flavour of the city, with time to explore the citadel, the Museum of Civilisation, the Church of St Joseph, the Muzzafariya Minaret, the covered markets and the parks. Enjoy the friendly atmosphere everywhere and experience Kurdish food in one of the cafés in the bazaar area at the foot of the citadel. **Day two** begins with an early-morning departure to Ain Sifni, the Yezidi village, to visit the tombs and the home of the sheikh. Travel on to Lalish and the Yezidi Temple, the Church of St Ith Llath and cave, via the Assyrian reliefs at Khinnis. The next stop is Amadiya, the walled town perched on a bluff, which is a scenic delight seen from the almost encircling main road. The gateway at one end of the walls is superb. A late lunch can be taken at one of the many wayside eating places. **Note:** An alternative day's schedule is to travel to the Syrian Orthodox Monastery of Der Mar Behnam, followed by a visit to the 8th-century BC Assyrian site of Nimrud and finally Der Mar Matte Monastery, also Syrian Orthodox. However, it is not possible in 2015 to do this without a full Iraq visa and a guide as these sites are on and around the Kurdish Regional Government (KRG) / Iraq border areas. In future it should be possible to visit these sites, although at the time this book goes to print Mar Behnam is under ISIS control.

ONE WEEK See pages 85–6 for a one-week itinerary.

TWO WEEKS For those with time and energy, consider the following route which will mean that you are nearly always in sight of magnificent mountains and the real undisturbed countryside. In times past this would have been the wildest route to take, only for the most intrepid traveller. Bandits, wild and domestic sheep dogs and possible difficult weather conditions would have come your way. Before you start, you need to search out a car and driver, discuss with him the route and work out how far he will take you. You will find that local taxi and car drivers will hesitate to stray beyond their usual route and latest knowledge. In any case you will want the freedom to stop and go at the pace that suits you. I suggest breaking the journey up as follows:

Zakhu to Amadiya You will want to stop here just north of the Christian village of Kani and the monastery of Mar Odisu, before travelling on to Barzan, the ancestral home of the Barzani family. Then travel on to Akri, which has a castle and caves. From here to Rawanduz, passing Shanidar and its famous Neolithic burial cave *en route*. It is possible to park near the cave. Next, travel along part of the famous Hamilton Road to Rawanduz. This town's history is full of tribal and old conflicts. Close to Rawanduz you will find the Pank Resort, perched high on the hill with magnificent views of the mountains. Then traverse one or other of the hill and mountain routes to Dokan Lake and Dokan town resort. This resort is growing constantly and has many pleasant tourist chalets by the river (Little Zab). The next stage of the journey is the 2-hour drive to Kurdistan's second city, Suleimaniyah. Another rapidly growing city, it is slightly different from Erbil, more influenced by its relative proximity to Iran. Suleimaniyah is not so ancient, but is lively in a modern way. It also has a modern airport with international flights. A 3-hour excursion will take you to Halabja and back.

Leaving Suleimaniyah for Erbil, you will find taxi and car drivers reluctant to take you via Kirkuk. A disputed city, Kirkuk is on the edge of the Kurdistan area and has continual security problems with its mixed ethnic population. Instead, you will be taken on a meandering drive through some more diverse countryside before reaching Erbil. The seat of the Kurdistan Regional Government, Erbil claims to be the oldest-inhabited city in the world. It has an extensive choice of hotels, restaurants and a fast night life. The ancient citadel dominates the town and the archaeological world is most anxious to dig and explore the remains underneath it. Two hours further on is Dohuk, a quiet town and the third city of Kurdistan, which also has ambitions for modernity. The airport is under construction. From Dohuk it is possible to encounter adherents of the Yezidi religion. The Sheik of the religion lives in Ain Sifni, an interesting village. Not so far away is Lalish, with the temple complex which every Yezidi has to visit at least once in their lifetime. It is a fascinating, unique place. Close by Dohuk is one of the oldest church buildings in the region, the Church of St Ith Llaha. Return to Zakhu and Turkey.

TOUR OPERATORS

Although it is possible to travel independently within Kurdistan, many first-time visitors choose to go with a recognised tour operator as this generally reduces the hassles of checkpoints, arranging internal transport and the language barrier. The companies listed below, all of which offer specialist, small group tours, also provide knowledgeable and sometimes specialist guides who can help you get the most out of your visit. For contact details and descriptions of the types of tours available, see pages 87–9.

Kurdistan Adventures, Iraq **Robert Broad Travel**, UK
Hinterland Travel, UK **Wild Frontiers**, UK
Undiscovered Destinations, UK **The Other Iraq Tours**, USA

RED TAPE

All visitors to Kurdistan will require a visa, usually obtained on arrival at the land border or at the airport. Some nationalities, however, require a visa prior to arrival in Kurdistan. Check with your local Kurdistan Regional Office before you travel.

VISAS Although the Kurdistan Regional Government (KRG) is part of Iraq, this autonomous region insists on its own visa. For most nationalities this is granted readily on arrival at the airports and at the land border between Turkey and Kurdistan Iraq. However, this visa is valid only in Kurdistan Iraq and does not apply to the rest of Iraq.

In order to maintain the level of peace in Kurdistan there are checkpoints on the borders and the perimeters of the cities. It is illegal to travel outside the Kurdistan Regional Area without a valid Iraq tourist visa. The Iraq tourist visa granted by Iraqi embassies abroad or by the Baghdad authorities covers all of Iraq, including Kurdistan Iraq. However, at a KRG border you will be forced to obtain a KRG visa even if you have the full Iraq visa.

Note: In common with most Arab countries, you will probably be refused a visa if your passport contains an Israeli stamp or that of any crossing point with Israel including Araba border, Sheikh Hussein border, Rafah border and Taba border.

POLICE AND MILITARY It is strongly advised not to attempt to leave Kurdistan Iraq without a full Iraqi visa (2015). See page 89.

Note: If returning by road via Turkey at the end of your trip you should avoid bringing out any items which refer to the Greater Kurdistan area such as maps, magazines, flags, or souvenirs bearing the word 'Kurdistan', etc. If discovered these can lead to long delays at the border and the items will be confiscated and destroyed.

EMBASSIES AND OTHER REPRESENTATION

Affairs of the Kurdistan Regional Government abroad are dealt with by the Iraqi embassies (see page 91) and KRG offices.

For a list of all consulates and foreign offices in Iraqi Kurdistan visit the website of the KRG: www.krg.org and click on the Department of Foreign Relations link.

FOREIGN EMBASSIES IN KURDISTAN

France 33 Salahaddin St, Erbil; ✆ (0) 66 257 3583; e consulat.erbil-fslt@diplomatie.gouv.fr
Germany Kirkuk Rd (opp Salahaddin University), Erbil; m 0750 790 7909; e info@erbi.diplo.de; www.erbil.diplo.de

UK Khanzad Hotel, Shaqlawa Main Rd, Erbil; m 0750 823 7415; ◷ 9.30–11.00 & 14.00–15.30 Sun–Thu (exc public hols); e enquiries.erbil@fco. gov.uk; www.ukiniraq.fco.gov.uk
USA Ainkawa, Erbil; ✆ +1 240 553 0590; e erbilpublicaffairs@state.gov; www.iraq. usembassy.gov/

GETTING THERE AND AWAY

At this time (2015) most foreign visitors will travel to Kurdistan either by land from Turkey through the one border, Habur, which is currently open but subject to closure without warning, or by air to Erbil or Suleimaniyah. Most flights operating from Europe and the Middle East fly directly to Kurdistan without going via Baghdad. **Note:** Border closures and flight suspensions can happen at short notice during the current conflict, so although this information is accurate at the time of going to press, it is as well to check before you set off.

BY AIR The Kurdistan region has two international airports: Erbil International Airport and Suleimaniyah International Airport. A new international airport is under construction in Dohuk. Most flights operating from Europe and the Middle East fly directly to Erbil, without going via Baghdad. Several IATA scheduled carriers already fly to Erbil, and more IATA airlines are expected to start flights there. Several charter companies also operate flights to Erbil or Suleimaniyah. Both airports post fairly current flight schedules on their websites: www.erbilairport.net and www.sul-airport.com.

The national airline, **Iraqi Airways** (✆ +964 750 423 5555, +964 750 466 6444; e iq_erbil@yahoo.com, iraqairwayssul@yahoo.com; www.iq-airways.com; see ad in colour section), flies direct between Gatwick and Suleimaniyah via Malmo. See website for full details. Bookings can be made online. Other operators who fly directly to Kurdistan include **Emirates** (www.emirates.com), **FlyDubai** (www. Flydubai.com) and **Turkish Airlines** (www.turkishairlines.com).

BY LAND Overland entry into the Kurdistan Region is possible through **Turkey.** The suggested route is to fly to Istanbul Ataturk Airport and then take a 2-hour domestic flight to Diyarbakir. Turkish visas can be obtained on arrival at Istanbul

Airport. Baggage may have to be retrieved from the international terminal and checked in at the domestic terminal.

For those arriving in the morning at Diyarbakir Airport taxis can be hired to drive to the Ibrahim Khalil/Habur border crossing point, Turkey's border with the Kurdistan Region in Iraq that day. Many drivers do this journey frequently and are familiar with the route. It is advisable to settle the price beforehand. A guide price is US$150. Check that the driver has the necessary paperwork to take passengers over the border. Because of the journey time it is advisable for those arriving later in the day to stay overnight in Diyarbakir and start the overland journey the following morning.

Land borders can be a trial wherever you are, and Habur is no exception, whether on foot or with your own vehicle. Most important if arriving by car: all your vehicle documents should be up to date. The Carnet de Passage needs to be valid and insurance documents relevant. Be prepared for insurance to be levied again if your documents are not approved by customs, etc. You can, of course, check all the requirements with motoring agencies in your own country. In the UK, the RAC is the best authority. Always carry spare fuel and water, plus any vital spare parts.

Having crossed into Iraqi Kurdistan and had your passport stamped, you then go to the transport yard/taxi rank where you will find a number of different taxis for individuals or groups available. It is about 10km from the border to Zakhu, so for the lone traveller stopping in Zakhu is a reasonable proposition. It will enable you to orient yourself, talk to the local warm, friendly people and prepare for your travels. For others, the 1-hour drive from Zakhu to Dohuk is worth it as it gets you nearer the hub of the road system. Alternatively, the drive to Erbil takes 4 hours and to Suleimaniyah 6 hours.

After crossing the border at Ibrahim Khalil, you can take another taxi to your destination in the Kurdistan Region. The approximate journey time from Diyarbakir to the border is 4 hours; then from the border to Dohuk is 1.5 hours; to Erbil 4 hours; and to Suleimaniyah 6 hours. This is currently the only overland crossing from Turkey to Iraqi Kurdistan for international travellers. All other land routes are for locals only. There are alternative routes via Iran but these are less frequently used and travellers may be turned back due to a lack of facilities for processing international passports. The Kurdistan/Iran border crossing at Piranshah is for local traffic only, as are those at Mawat and Penjewin. At present there is no direct border crossing between Syria and Iraqi Kurdistan.

HEALTH

Comprehensive travel insurance is generally available for travel to Kurdistan Iraq as long as the British foreign office does not advise against travel to this region.

Local health care in Kurdistan is largely funded by the government, and while services may not quite meet the standards of some thoroughly developed and established systems, care is available in all major cities and towns. Private medical treatment is readily available to foreign nationals for example, medical examinations and lab diagnostics are easily obtainable and require only a small payment of a few thousand IQDs (usually not more than US$5–10).

The number for the ambulance service in Kurdistan is 122.

For other health information that applies to the whole of Iraq, see pages 94–8.

SAFETY

The security situation in Kurdistan is very different from the rest of Iraq, a fact which has been recognised by most Western governments who, until the recent offensives launched by ISIS, did not advise against travel to Kurdistan. Travel and tourism to the region has also been encouraged as the Kurdistan Regional Government (KRG) visa is available on arrival.

The areas under the control of the KRG have been and still remain virtually free from terrorist attacks and suicide bombings. This is not the case in Mosul and Kirkuk which have historically been outside KRG control (although at the time of going to press the *pershmerga* are currently in control of Kirkuk). Although these areas are not officially in Kurdistan, they are close enough to warrant discussion here. In Kirkuk, great vigilance needs to be exercised, and while some routes skirt the city, it is not advisable to linger there any longer than necessary. Currently (2015) it is impossible to visit Mosul, which is under ISIS control. See page 211 for more details.

The official Regional Guard, the *peshmerga* forces, are highly trained and experienced in providing security. Working in close co-operation with these regional guards are the Asayish (the security police) and the regular police, who provide comprehensive protection against threats and help with routine police matters. To maintain the level of peace in Kurdistan, there are checkpoints on the borders and city perimeters and at the entrance to every village and town.

To enhance security and improve the road systems the Kurdistan Regional Government, has built and is still building many highways and roads throughout the region, to avoid contact with the Arab areas beyond the regional border as much as possible. However, it is now noticeable that the Iraqi police and militia are beginning to work side by side with the Kurdish *peshmerga* to police these road checkpoints. These shared checkpoints are recognisable by the joint national flags flown together.

WOMEN TRAVELLERS

Being traditionally Muslim, Kurdish society is divided along gender lines. Foreign women are often considered 'honorary men' and given the opportunity to share the company of both men and women in a way foreign men cannot. The vast majority of female travellers to Kurdistan experience no adverse treatment because of their gender, and Kurdistan is considered safe for single women to travel in alone. The threats of crime and physical harassment are relatively low and the locals will often go out of their way to help a woman travelling on her own. However, women travelling alone should take the usual common-sense precautions such as travelling with a companion wherever possible; making sure that they are not out alone late at night; dressing modestly and suitably for a Muslim country (especially in conservative, rural areas) and not in a way likely to draw unnecessary attention. If you do feel uncomfortable in a particular situation leave quickly and head for somewhere well populated such as a hotel, café or restaurant.

GAY TRAVELLERS

Under Saddam Hussein, Kurdistan Iraq did not have a law against homosexuality and that remains the case under the Kurdistan Regional Government today. In Kurdistan, like most Middle Eastern societies, homosexuality is generally not approved of – see page 101 for further information. However, as Kurdish society struggles with modernity and the changing gender roles, an acceptance of the open practice of sexual freedom is beginning, albeit in a small way among the younger generation living in the major cities such as Erbil. Erbil has a small gay scene, the T-Bar in Akwara Exit Street and Cool Cafe in Iskar Street, close to the New City Mall are two of the places that gays frequent (see *erbilgaylife.blogspot.com*).

TRAVELLERS WITH DISABILITIES

Many of the new shopping malls and some of the newer hotels, especially those being built with foreign investment, are starting to include disabled access, lifts, etc, but generally speaking Kurdistan is not terribly well equipped for travellers with mobility problems. That said, most of the pavements and roads in the major cities are well paved. The major public transport option, taxis, are rarely able to carry wheelchairs, although as newer vehicles start appearing in the major cities this may change.

TRAVELLING WITH KIDS

Like the rest of Iraq, Kurdistan is a child-friendly place. Don't expect to find a lot of things specifically for children in museums, hotels or restaurants, but they will be made welcome in these places nevertheless.

WHAT TO TAKE

See pages 101–20.

MONEY

The currency used in the Kurdistan Region is the Iraqi Dinar (IQD). See more information about money that is also relevant to Kurdistan on page 102.

GETTING AROUND

Kurdistan is not a big region and the roads are improving rapidly. Although journeys to more rural areas will still take some time, it is best to look at the time spent travelling as part of the experience. Admire the scenery and the views. The Ministry of Construction has prioritised the improvement of roads between the main cities. Estimated travelling times by car between the major cities are: Erbil–Suleimaniyah (170km) 2½ hours; Erbil–Dohuk (245km) 3 hours and Dohuk–Suleimaniyah (340km) 5 hours.

BY CAR Travel by car in the Kurdistan Region is very simple and generally safe. Private cars and drivers are available, but they can often be quite expensive.

Car rental
Only experienced drivers should attempt to hire a self-drive car. The roads are mostly good, but Kurdish drivers are not the best. For car rental try **Europa Car Erbil Rental** (*Bahrka St, Alhaydar Group Bldg, Erbil;* m *0750 77 2288*).

BY BUS Infrequent bus services run between the major cities. See the local city travel agents for details. Some local buses operate within the urban centres but are predominately for the use of locals.

BY TAXI Taxis are a far more economical option, and they are readily available on most major roads in all the cities. A ride to, or from, almost anywhere in the cities normally costs IQD3,000–5,000, and you can get a seat in a shared taxi between any of the major cities for IQD10,000–25,000 depending on the distance – just ask a city taxi driver 'garajee + the name of city/town where you want to go'. There are generally two types of taxis in the cities: some are painted orange and white, while others are painted a light tan colour. The light tan taxis are driven by government-vetted drivers, and they are considered to be safest – these cars are usually newer and cleaner also.

A new local taxi service, the Hello Company has recently begun operations. They can be contacted on m 0750 415 000. Journeys with them within any of the three main cities should cost IQD3,000–5,000, depending on local petrol prices.

BY BICYCLE An adventurous way to travel through Kurdistan, this is only for the hardiest bicycle enthusiasts, who are not easily dismayed by local drivers and the often tough terrain, especially in the east.

MAPS Detailed, up-to-date maps of Kurdistan are best purchased before travelling. Stanfords in London (*www.stanfords.co.uk*) may have maps of Kurdistan, Iraq and the surrounding countries. Maps and city plans can be purchased in the large cities, but few are in English, and as they are not always easy to decipher, they should be used in conjunction with local maps and your GPS.

ACCOMMODATION

Accommodation is generally expensive in Kurdistan in comparison with equivalent accommodation in Europe and the US, and mid-range and even top-end prices can be paid for what would be classed as budget accommodation in other countries. At the **top end** of the market, Erbil has luxury hotels with good restaurants, fitness suites and swimming pools, and all the usual facilities you would expect. These hotels are usually frequented by business people and well-heeled ex-pats and can cost up to US$300 per night. **Mid-range** hotels are a mixed bag, with some charging high prices (US$200+) for the most basic of facilities and amenities. However, there are some which buck the trend, such as Monaco Palace and the Chwar Chra hotels in Erbil. Kurdistan's **budget**-priced accommodation is generally of a very poor standard and not recommended. Backpacker hotels can be found in all cities, but very few advertise internationally on the web or have reliable phone lines. A greater selection of reasonably priced hotels can, however, be found in smaller towns such as Zakhu.

Outside of cities and towns, accommodation is very sparse indeed. **Camping** is potentially a problem due to security issues and is not recommended unless you are on an organised tour. There are no organised campsites such as you might find in Europe, although some are planned.

EATING AND DRINKING

The Kurds are fanatical about fresh food. To share food together is one of the best and most enjoyable ways for people of two cultures to cross boundaries and to establish a friendship. The land of the Kurds, in the northern part of the Fertile Crescent, (the region in the Middle East where the civilisations of the Middle East began) offers abundant resources for wonderful cooking. Wheat grows on the sunny plains, as do apricot, peach and plum trees. Apples, walnuts, cherries, almonds and pears offer bounty in baskets. Pomegranates, figs and grapes of all varieties delight any guest who is fortunate enough to visit Kurdistan in late summer. Large flocks of sheep and goats, fattened on the tastiest grass of the mountain pastures, are raised for meat as well as for their milk, which is transformed by skilled Kurdish housewives into creamy cheese, white butter and chilled buttermilk. Grape syrup and honey-sweetened bowls of thick yogurt, are delicious, while wild herbs and mushrooms add their delicate flavours to grilled wild partridge and quail.

Kurdish cuisine, which has been influenced by Turkish and Iranian dishes, is rich and varied. Before urbanisation, a cooked breakfast and dinner were the main meals as people worked in the fields and did not return home for lunch. Today lunch is the main meal, eaten after 14.00 when offices have shut for the day. Meat, lamb or chicken, in the form of kebabs, are nearly always served during the midday and evening meals. Legendary Arab hospitality is also a Kurdish characteristic and foreigners are often invited to stay with families. During the mass exodus of Kurds to the Turkish and Iranian borders after the failed uprising of 1991 the starving refugees were worried about not having any tea to share with personnel from international aid agencies.

EATING OUT All the hotels in Kurdistan have restaurants of varying quality. The very best hotels in the major cities have excellent restaurants, with a Kurdish flavour among the international cuisine. In Erbil and Suleimaniyah there is a selection of foreign restaurants, notably Italian and Chinese, and fast-food restaurants and takeaways serving wraps, burgers and pizza. There are many foreign-food restaurants, for example Italian. Local restaurants tend to be small and scattered around the cities. It can be difficult to find places with varied menus, as despite their often elaborate (and badly translated) descriptions, you will usually find they serve little more than chicken, rice and kebabs with maybe soup and a side dish of beans or aubergine. Do try some of the Kurdish delicacies if they are available. Local breads, which vary slightly from town to town, are excellent. Most of the food

A TYPICAL KURDISH MENU

Shish kebab	Minced lamb
Mreshk kebab	Marinated chicken breast
Gosht kebab	Seasoned lamb
Baly Menshka	Crispy chicken wings marinated in lemon, oil and tomato paste
Mushakal kebab	Skewers of chicken wings, minced lamb and chicken breast
Qozy Gosht	Braised lamb on the bone with rice
Qozy Mreshk	Half a chicken with rice
Qozy Mahicheh	Lamb shank with rice
Lamb Tashreeb	Braised lamb on the bone with onions, peppers and tomato
Kebab Ba Sada	Minced lamb with rice
Mreshk Ba Sada	Chicken breast with rice
Bal Ba Sada	Chicken wings with rice
Gosht Ba Sada	Lamb fillet with rice
Biryani	Rice, chicken breast, green peas, sultanas and almonds
Nawashifi Mreshk	Half a chicken cooked with onion and spices
Nawashifi Gosht	Lamb on the bone with rice

Water, salad and nan (bread) are usually served with every meal and you will often receive a complimentary soft drink as well. Prices for the above range from IQD5,000 for the Biryani, to IQD8,000/10,000 for the kebabs.

produced locally in Kurdistan is still organic. The bazaars are the perfect place to find authentic, local food. Seek recommendations from the locals, taxi drivers and hotel staff – as in all cities restaurants come and go and standards fluctuate.

There are, of course, local variations; for example, the locally caught fresh fish is excellent in the mountain regions. At a roadside restaurant near Rawanduz several years ago, a couple of travellers who ordered the local speciality were amazed at the size of the fish they were presented with; eventually the whole group had to help them consume this delicious monster. Masgouf, which is the traditional fish of Baghdad, can be found on the menu of more upmarket hotels, such as the International in Erbil.

The price of a three-course meal in a local city restaurant will cost about US$10–12 per person, however in hotels the price will probably be double that.

WHAT TO DRINK It is not advisable to drink the tap water. If you wish to purchase alcohol then it is available in some upmarket restaurants and hotels and can also be purchased in shops. There are alcohol shops in the major cities such as Erbil and Suleimaniyah, and a few in Dohuk mainly run by Christians or Yezidis. Alcohol may also be served with meals or in the bar in certain upmarket restaurants and hotels in those cities, but you are unlikely to find it in local restaurants.

Kurdistan has very few clubs and bars, apart from just a few in Erbil which tend to be frequented by foreigners, business people and army personnel.

PUBLIC HOLIDAYS

Nowruz or Kurdish New Year falls on 21 March and is a celebration of the first day of spring and the beginning of a new cycle. Visitors to Kurdistan during Nowruz will experience the warmth and fun of a traditional Kurdish celebration. Government offices can be closed for up to a week during this period.

Dates for Ramadan vary as the month begins with the new moon. During Ramadan Muslims are obliged to abstain from all food and drink during daylight hours. Ramadan ends with a three-day celebration, Eid. Often during the fasting period government offices are only open for half a day and they are closed over Eid.

Public holidays in Kurdistan are as follows:

1 January	New Year's Day
3 January	Mouloud (Prophet Mohammed's birthday)*
5 March	Uprising Day (Rebellion Anniversary)
11 March	Liberation of Erbil City
14 March	Mustafa Barzani's birthday
21–23 March	Nowruz (Kurdish New Year / Spring Equinox)
9 April	Baghdad Liberation Day (fall of Saddam Hussein's regime)
1 May	Labour Day
14 July	Republic Day
18 June	Ramadan starts*
18 July	Eid ul Fitr starts (end of Ramadan)*
23 September	Eid Al-Adha*
13 October	Al-Hijra/Muharram (Islamic New Year)*
23 October	Ashura*
25 November	Christmas Day
31 December	Iraq Day

*The lunar calendar dictates the days of these festivals which change every year

On public holidays ministries and government offices are closed. Businesses may also close. If the holiday falls at the weekend (Friday or Saturday) then the next working day is taken as the holiday.

SHOPPING

The best place to shop for crafts is in Erbil where new shops are being constructed, and also by and in the citadel. The famous market opposite the citadel has the usual wares which can be found in most Middle Eastern bazaars. Suleimaniyah has an extensive network of shopping streets, to meet the needs of local customers. In both cities **mobile-phone** shops abound and there are shops selling the latest technology. There is plenty of **gold jewellery** to be found in both cities.

Kurdistan is disappointing for **carpet** purchases. The traditional carpets of the area are very difficult to find. There are few carpet shops with traditional, handmade carpets, and older carpets are not so easy to find either. Attempts are being made to produce carpets in Erbil. In Suleimaniyah there are some carpet dealers, but mostly stock imported, Iranian-made carpets.

Postcards can be purchased in Erbil and there is a post office near the Erbil Tower Hotel (see page 384). Postcards can be left with hotel receptions, but caution is advised as experience shows they often get no further than this.

There is little in the way of tourist-type **souvenirs**, though locally made soap, spices and sugar cones make acceptable and unusual gifts. Small rugs and carpets can be purchased featuring the Kurdish flag or pictures of local heroes, but caution should be taken before purchasing these if leaving Kurdistan via Turkey (see pages 367–8).

ARTS AND ENTERTAINMENT

Art exhibitions, theatrical productions, musical events and cinema are all popular pastimes in Kurdistan. **Kurdish art** has influences dating back to the Halaf period (6000–5000BC). It is characterised by decorative motifs on painted pottery fired in two-chamber kilns. Some decorative motifs are based on geometric forms found in nature, while others have no connection with natural forms. Flower designs are still used in textiles and decorations. The unique Kurdish colour-madness also runs through Kurdish art, which ranges from a modern abstract to Cubist style to the traditional miniature painting style of the East. Artwork varies from socially committed nationalist themes popular with painters Gara Rasul and Rebwar, to the freestyle of still-life scenes, a favourite of Manoor Ahmed. Other traditional artefacts include works in stone, metal and pottery. Riotous and gaudy colours, many of them thrown together seemingly haphazardly with absolutely no control or care to match them, is a trademark of Kurdish taste. Mehrdad Izady notes, for example, that unusual dress makes a Kurd stand out in any crowd of conventionally dressed people, in ancient times as now. In days gone by Kurdish men and women wore large amounts of jewellery. Today it is worn mainly by women and is regarded as a source of family wealth and savings, often used to buy land or finance education.

Rugs and carpets also have a long history. Pile rugs were introduced by the nomads from the cold, northern Eurasian steppes. The obelisk of the Assyrian king Shalmaneser III (858–824BC) shows his tribute, which included a pile of rugs. Clay impressions at the site of Jarmo near Suleimaniyah dating back to 8500–7000BC (see page 206) contain the world's oldest records of cloth weaving. Woven products were given as royal presents to the Assyrian court, and as Mehrdad Izady, author of *The Kurds: A Concise Handbook*, notes, 'the tradition of fine weaving continued in Kurdistan until at least the end of the medieval period in the 15th century.' The Kurdish economy stagnated after the 15th century due to the decline in international trade and the 'best and handsomest carpets in the world', as described by Marco Polo, became a thing of the past, giving way to more rustic products.

Village **theatre**, a natural progression from storytelling, appeared as a form of entertainment during the Hellenistic period (4th–2nd century BC) when the Greeks established city states in the Zagros Mountains. Some plays have a simple plot and are easy to stage: an old man is played by a miller who powders his beard with flour; a boy with a scarf around his head represents a female character. In two-actor plays the characters abuse each other in a form of slapstick comedy resembling that of Charlie Chaplin. In other plays the lines are all in verse.

Gymnasia were another Greek influence adopted by the Kurds, who were keen on **wrestling** matches. **Games** such as backgammon and chess are also popular. So is *ganem ganieh*, a game of chance played with wheat grains.

MEDIA AND COMMUNICATIONS

CNN International and BBC World broadcast in Kurdistan and both are available in most hotels. The *Hewler Globe* is a weekly English-language magazine covering a variety of international, national and regional news.

Currently (2015) international mobiles work only intermittently in Kurdistan. To remain in contact we advise purchasing a local SIM card. Top-up vouchers are available in some hotels and local shops for US$10, US$20 and US$50. To contact a local Kurdish number from the UK you need to use the prefix 0032 48 or 00 964 750.

Internet connections are available in all the international and upmarket hotels, usually high speed and free. This is how the majority of visitors get on line. Many

ERBIL INTERNATIONAL POST CENTRE

The post centre was recognised by the International Post Union in 2008, meaning that, based on international regulations and principles, items can be received and sent through post offices in the region. The Kurdistan Regional Government (KRG) is in the process of correcting and modernising the postal code system using a comprehensive postal code numbering system, including street names or delivery addresses, along with postal areas. In the suggested system, each family and house will have its own number to help get mail delivered quickly and accurately. A major benefit of using such a system would be an increase in security of the mail due to the reduction in hand sorting and a faster, more accurate delivery to the customer. Unfortunately, this attempt to change the system comes at a time when few people use the mail system because of a lack of trust in it.

Historically, few people use Kurdistan post offices; the main job of the offices has been delivering business items and official government mail. During the past three years, however, according to Omed Muhammad Salih, director of the Erbil Post Office, the volume of mail has increased. During the first six months of 2010, for example, 22 tonnes of items were posted while in the first six months of 2011 about 44 tonnes of items were sent, showing a 100% increase.

10

of the better quality hotels also have conference facilities catering for the influx of business people to Kurdistan and so have well-equipped business centres. Internet cafés are plentiful and can be found in the main shopping and bazaar areas of Erbil, Dohuk and Suleimaniyah as well as in some smaller towns.

Kurdistan is 3 hours ahead of Greenwich Mean Time (GMT).

BUSINESS

Erbil is one of the fastest growing cities in Iraq and the Middle East. It is modernising and developing as it seeks to emulate Dubai with its ability to attract wealth, patronage and more power. Witness to this is the terminal constructed at the international airport opened in 2004, which has attracted a growing number of airlines to the city. The relatively stable security situation also helps its ambitions, and its access to oil and crucial investment from worldwide sources helps it to satisfy these ambitions. The city has transformed itself since 2009 and sets an example to the rest of Iraq with its cleanliness and modernity. New apartments, new shopping centres, stores and hotels continue to spring up. The first phase of the 1 million m^2 Nishtiman complex, with 8,000 shops and 4,000 offices, has been completed. It is the brainchild of Nizar Hana, who describes his complex as 'the biggest single development in the Middle East'. Elsewhere in Erbil, the Kurdistan Company For Real Estate is planning a US$120 million mall with a hotel, offices, market, shopping centre, apartments and a recreational area. The Park Kempinski Hotel is one of the first major foreign investment projects in the region. Byblos Bank, Lebanon's third largest lender, has opened a branch in Erbil in the hope of heralding a new financial era in a region where banking services are underdeveloped and people buy houses with piles of cash.

BUYING A PROPERTY

As Kurdistan is generally more secure and more open to international investors than many other parts of Iraq there are more and more people climbing onto the property ownership ladder. Locals are enjoying a property boom, as demand outstrips supply, and one of the latest trends in the property market is buying off-the-plan properties from a larger development. These are very much in demand and often popular projects sell out almost immediately. Even before a property development is completed, buyers may have been able to cash in on up to a 40% increase in the property's value. Although theoretically it is possible for foreigners to buy property in Kurdistan without a Kurdish partner, as with many things in Kurdistan this can be a time-, money- and bureaucracy-intensive process for which you will require specialist legal advice as well as local assistance.

CULTURAL ETIQUETTE

Kurdistan is progressive, pluralistic and relatively open; however, Middle Eastern etiquette in business, dress and behaviour is still adhered to. Behaviour is governed by a strict code of ethics; marriage and family are essential and adultery or free love is not socially acceptable, as a family's reputation depends on the 'honour' of its members. Kurds place tremendous emphasis on generosity and hospitality, and guests are treated as royalty. Elderly people are respected far more than in Western society and loyalty to the tribe and family is essential. Rumour-mongering is frowned upon and bad-mouthing even one's worst enemies is not acceptable.

In 2015, Iraqi Kurdistan was flooded with 850,000 refugees fleeing ISIS alone. That is in addition to the 551,000 refugees from Syria and other parts of Iraq that came to the region.

'That's the equivalent of Scotland – which like us has a population of about 5 million – taking in 1.4 million refugees,' the representative of the Kurdistan Regional Government in the UK, Bayan Sami Abdul Rahman, pointed out.

'This is beyond our capability alone and we need Britain to help, not just with airdrops of aid but also with running refugee camps, dealing with the vast numbers of people who need sanitation, healthcare and education for their children.

'We also need Britain to provide heavy and advanced arms to our *peshmerga* who are fighting ISIS with light weapons. Even some basic non-lethal equipment is needed, such as night-vision and body armour.'

As this guide went to press Dohuk governorate was hosting close to 400,000 displaced Iraqis, including Yezidis, Christians, Shabak, Kakai, Armenian and Turkmen minorities – some of whom have endured repeated displacement. Many are now in the towns of Khanke, Shariya, Zakho, Shekhan and in and around Dohuk town. They are scattered across hundreds of sites. Some are staying with relatives, others are in schools, churches, mosques, parks and shells of apartment buildings without water or electricity. UNHCR is distributing mattresses, blankets, emergency relief kits, household items and hygiene kits to locations in Dohuk, Zakho, Akre, Shekhan, Khanke and the village of Bajet Kandela.

The local people are providing meals for the refugees and spontaneously handing out aid.

Between 7,000 and 10,000 people are staying at the Bajet Kandela camp – a former reception centre for Syrian refugees, most of whom passed through there two years ago after crossing the border at Peshkhabour. While basic facilities are in place, conditions are crowded and local NGOs have been installing family tents on the site wherever space can be found.

In Erbil refugees live in 'sites' such as abandoned farms and next to mosques.

Hospitality towards visitors is an important part of Kurdish culture. If you are invited to someone's home you should take a small gift for your host. A souvenir item from your home country would be most acceptable, but if you have nothing suitable then flowers or sweetmeats are fine. On entering a house you should normally remove your shoes at the door. In many households you will find that men and women are entertained separately, with the women of the household sitting apart from the men along with the children. Foreign women, however, are usually able to participate in both male and female social groupings and so can get to know all members of the family.

Mosques, shrines and other holy places often have their own sets of rules and you should observe these. If in doubt always ask, rather than being disrespectful, even if unintentionally. Requirements vary, but generally may include removing your shoes, covering your head (especially women) and wearing modest clothing. Shorts and strapless tops will be out of place anywhere in Kurdistan and are definitely unacceptable at religious sites. Sometimes there are separate entrances for men and women or only one gender or members of a particular religion will be allowed to enter certain places. Whatever your personal opinion you should be respectful of this.

TRAVELLING POSITIVELY

Many charities operate in Kurdistan. Kurdistan Save the Children is the international, non-political agency based in Suleimaniyah. It supports social and educational projects all over Iraq. Save the Children UK (*www.savethechildren. org.uk*) has been active in Iraq for many years. It was a leading humanitarian agency in the aftermath of the 2003 Coalition invasion, remaining operational throughout the conflict, transporting children to school and rebuilding schools, paediatric hospitals and primary health centres throughout Iraq. Today it also works to alleviate the suffering of refugees and displaced people from Syria, as does **UNHCR** (*www.unhcr.org*) who have erected shelters, established water and food distribution at crossing points and, in conjunction with the International Organization for Migration and the Kurdistan Regional Government (KRG), provided buses and trucks to move the thousands of people from the border zone deeper into Iraq.

The **Kurdistan Emergency Appeal** is raising money and collecting goods to help the 1.5 million refugees and displaced people who have fled to the safety of the Kurdistan region in Iraq (*http://kurdistanemergency.org*) and **The Kurdish Aid Foundation** is a small UK-based registered charity run solely by volunteers to provide assistance to those in need in the Kurdistan region (*http://kurdishaid.help*).

There are currently four permanent camps for Syrian refugees in Erbil – Kawergosk Camp; Qushatefa Camp; Darashakran Camp and Basirma. In September 2014 there were thought to be approximately 84,000 refugees in the Erbil area, many of them living outside the established camps and since then the numbers have increased. Their number is expected to change as the situation waxes and wanes, and they are joined by increasing numbers of Kurdish refugees from the persecuted minority Yezidi and Christian communities from both within and outside Kurdistan.

There are two animal charities in the region founded to work with the Coalition forces. Operation Baghdad Pups (*www.spcai.org*) was founded at the behest of US military personnel serving in Iraq. Providing veterinary care as well as clearance and transport for the animals that service personnel came to love during deployment in the area, it does more than just save the lives of these animals, it also brings comfort and peace of mind to soldiers serving overseas and helps them cope when they return home. To date, SPCA International has helped hundreds of soldiers transport their animals out of war zones. Nowzad (*www.nowzad.com*) a UK-based charity operated a similar scheme for British soldiers and still does so in Afghanistan (see pages 115–16).

11

Erbil and Environs

Telephone code 66

Erbil (known in Kurdish as Hewler, seat of the Gods) and today the home of one million people is one of the fastest growing cities in Iraq and the Middle East. The seat of government and power in Kurdistan, it is modernising and developing as a regional capital. The city has transformed itself since 2009 and sets an example to the rest of Iraq with its cleanliness and modernity. New apartments, new shopping centres, stores and hotels continue to spring up. Ein Kawa, a Christian suburb of the city, is the place for restaurants, entertainment and an amusement park. Among the recent additions is a mosque: a replica of the blue mosque in Istanbul.

As always, there is a price to pay. The cost of living is very high – rents, fuel supplies and so on, and there are ever-increasing traffic jams. Not everyone is keen to preserve Kurdish heritage, which is threatened by the new wave of modernisation. The amazing covered market selling everything from fabrics and jewellery to cheese made from sheep's milk was described as 'full of rubbish' by Nizar Hana, who is convinced stall-holders should move into his giant mall. The freedom of movement in the city is, at first, a tonic after the wearying security restrictions which prevail in the rest of Iraq. But travellers have to decide for themselves whether the attraction of a large, modern city is what they are looking for in Kurdistan.

Since the 1970s, the city has been the home of the Kurdish parliament. The first parliament of the Kurdish Autonomous Region was set up by Saddam and housed in an impressive building. It was, however, under the control of the central government. After the uprising at the end of the 1991 Gulf War, the Kurds held elections and set up a parliament, which functioned until 1996, when fighting broke out between the KDP and the PUK. The PUK set up an alternative government in Suleimaniyah. The parliament reconvened again in Erbil after a peace agreement was signed in 1997. The KRG was officially recognised in the 2005 constitution and the KDP and PUK set up a unitary government in May 2006. Since the overthrow of Saddam there has been little violence in Erbil.

Attempts are being made to promote Erbil as a major tourist attraction and Kurdish cultural centre. The ancient citadel, recognised as an historic site by UNESCO, is being renovated and, for the first time in its history, is uninhabited. Three large houses from the 19th century have been turned into museums, with displays from the Sumerian to the Abbasid period, handicrafts and an art gallery.

HISTORY

After the downfall of the Assyrian Kingdom in 612BC the city fell, consecutively, under the control of the Medes (possibly the ancestors of the Kurds), the Persians, and the Greeks under Alexander the Great (who defeated the Persian King Darius III in the Battle of Gaugamela in 331BC), fought 100km west of the city. The Parthians ruled from 126BC to AD226.

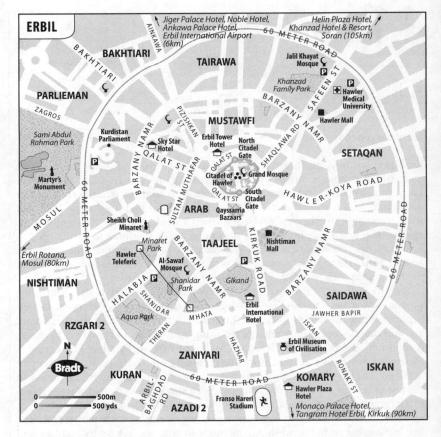

ERBIL

Jiger Palace Hotel, Noble Hotel,
Ankawa Palace Hotel,
Erbil International Airport
(6km)

Helin Plaza Hotel,
Khanzad Hotel & Resort,
Soran (105km)

BAKHTIARI

BAKHTIARI

TAIRAWA

60 METER ROAD

AINKAWA

Jalil Khayat
Mosque

SAFEEN ST

PARLIEMAN

ZAGROS

Khanzad
Family Park

BARZANY NAMR

Hawler
Medical
University

Sami Abdul
Rahman Park

Kurdistan
Parliament

PIZISHKAN ST

MUSTAWFI

SHAQLAWA RD NAMR

Hawler Mall

Sky Star
Hotel

QALAT ST

Erbil Tower
Hotel

QALAT ST

North
Citadel
Gate

SETAQAN

Martyr's
Monument

BARZANY NAMR

SULTAN MUTHAFAR

Citadel of
Hawler

Grand Mosque

South
Citadel
Gate

QALAT ST

HAWLER-KOYA ROAD

MOSUL

Erbil Rotana,
Mosul (80km)

Sheikh Choli
Minaret

ARAB

Qayssarria
Bazaars

60 METER ROAD

Minaret
Park

BARZANY NAMR

TAAJEEL

KIRKUK ROAD

Nishtiman
Mall

60 METER ROAD

Hawler
Teleferic

Al-Sawaf
Mosque

HALABJA

SHANIDAR

Shanidar
Park

Glkand

BARZANY NAMR

SAIDAWA

NISHTIMAN

Aqua Park

THERAN

MHATA

Erbil
International
Hotel

JAWHER BAPIR

RZGARI 2

ZANIYARI

HAZNAR

ISKAN

Erbil Museum
of Civilisation

60 METER ROAD

RONAKY ST

Bradt

KURAN

ARBIL-BAGHDAD RD

60 METER ROAD

KOMARY

ISKAN

0 ——— 500m
0 ——— 500yds

AZADI 2

Franso Hareri
Stadium

Hawler Plaza
Hotel

Monaco Palace Hotel,
Tangram Hotel Erbil, Kirkuk (90km)

During the Parthian era Erbil was the centre of the Hidyab region, where a kingdom was established. It was invaded by both the Armenians and the Romans and was an important Christian centre in the early centuries after Christ's death. In the Sassanian era (226–642) it was an administrative centre.

The Muslims arrived in 642 and established the Atakakian principality. In Abbasid times (1128–1232) the city was an Islamic social and cultural meeting place, and leading Muslim scientists and men of letters made it their home. The Mongol occupation, which destroyed the Abbasid Empire, lasted from 1258 until 1410.

The city was ruled by the Turkmen between 1410 and 1508 and the Persian Safavids between 1508 and 1514. They were ousted by the Ottomans who remained in control until 1918 when the British army entered. The governorate of Erbil was then established. Throughout its history Erbil has been a major trading centre on the route between Baghdad and Mosul.

GETTING THERE AND AWAY

BY AIR Most flights operating from Europe and the Middle East fly directly to Erbil International Airport. The site was an airfield and military base for the Baath regime; in 1993 the Kurdistan Regional Government (KRG) decided to build a civil airport to be the gateway towards the world. On 1 July 2003 the construction of the airport began and on 15 December of the same year the first aircraft landed.

Although this part of Iraq is one of the most important places in the world for the study of the culture of Neanderthal man (55,000–70,000 years ago) evidence of his presence in Erbil still awaits the archaeologist's spade. Sumerian cuneiform inscriptions suggest that Erbil was already established by the end of the 3rd millennium BC. Syrian inscriptions from the 2nd millennium BC refer to it as 'Urbilum' or 'Erbilum'. In late Assyrian and Babylonian texts it is called 'Arballum' (the four Gods).

During the Assyrian period Erbil was a centre for the worship of Ishtar, whose temple was called E-kshan-klama, or House of the Lady of the Regions. There was also a temple devoted to the god Assur. A stele (a stone slab with inscriptions) of Ashur-banipal (668–627BC) was unearthed here, together with images of other Assyrian kings.

Sennacherib (705–681BC) built an irrigation canal that carried water down to the city from the Bastura valley, 20km away. At Bastura where the canal starts there is a well-built stone wall with a cuneiform transcription that reads: 'I, Sennacherib, King of Assyria, have dug three rivers in the Khani mountains above Erbil, home of the venerated Lady Goddess Ishtar, and made their courses straight.'

Initially, flights were between the Kurdistan region and its neighbouring countries, but from 2005 onwards direct flights from Kurdistan to Europe were started by the now defunct Kurdistan Airlines.

You will find Erbil airport a model for the rest of the Middle East: clean, efficient and with smooth visa facilities for a quick entry. Security is very tight here. If arriving alone you will need to navigate your way through the immigration and security procedures, including taking the official bus or an official taxi from the airport, which will cost you approximately US$25. The airport is 7km northeast of Erbil.

Airlines Several IATA scheduled carriers already fly to Erbil, and more IATA airlines are expected to start flights in the near future. **Austrian Airlines** launched flights between Vienna and Erbil twice weekly in December 2006, increasing these to four flights a week to/from Vienna from 2007. At the time of writing, regular flights to Erbil are also available weekly from Dubai, Amman, Istanbul and very recently, Tehran. **Egypt Air** flies four times per week from Cairo to Erbil, and three times per week from Erbil to Cairo. **Lufthansa** has recently restarted four-weekly roundtrip flights from Frankfurt. **Qatar Airways** flies four times a week between Erbil and Doha. **Fly Hellas** flies to Erbil from Athens (Eleftherios Venizelos International Airport) and Stockholm. **MEA** flies to Erbil from Lebanon on six flights per week. **Atlas Jet**, **Turkish Airlines** and **Pegasus** have flights to Istanbul. **FlyDubai** has flights to Dubai. **Etihad Airlines** flies from Erbil to Abu Dhabi with connecting flights onwards. Several charter companies also operate flights to Erbil and post fairly current flight schedules on their websites (*www.erbilairport.net*). For further information on airlines and routes, see page 367.

Citizens of the EU, the US, Canada, Japan and Australia are given a free stamp for 10 days on arrival. After that you must visit the residency office to extend your visa. Other nationalities must have an Iraqi visa before arrival. This situation is subject to change in the future.

11

BY ROAD Recently bus companies have been running services between Erbil and Diyabakir (10–15 hours) and Erbil and Istanbul (36–48 hours). Cizre Nuh Buses (m *0750 340 4773*) run every day at 15.30 from the New City Mall, 60 Meter Street, to Istanbul (*US$100*) via Silopi (*US$40*), Diyabakir and other cities in between. Tickets can be bought at the New City Mall, Flyaway on Barzani Namir and at Phone Shop on Shekhi Choli, close to the bazaar. Can Diyabakir Buses (m *0750 895 6217/18/19*) leave daily from Family Mall on 100 Meter Road to Istanbul via Diyabakir, There are at least two other Turkish companies running buses from Erbil to cities in Europe currently (look around for flyers on Iskan Road): Best Van, running from Ainkawa Road in Erbil to Istanbul via Adana, Aksaray, Ankara and Diyabakir, and the Federal Company (✆ *066 224 6999*; e *federal_col@yahoo.com*), who run daily services from Erbil to Istanbul. Arrival times depend on border formalities (around 2 hours from Turkey to Iraq and 5–8 hours back to Turkey). See page 367 for information on border restrictions.

GETTING AROUND

Erbil is small enough to explore almost everywhere on foot, although if time is at a premium it may be worth getting a cab. Pavements are usually in decent condition, and the citadel makes a good landmark to orientate yourself by. Public transport is available in the form of taxis and some bus routes.

BY TAXI This is the usual form of transport for city travel and also excursions outside of the city. For travelling further afield shared taxis are popular. In terms of taxis there are essentially two choices. **Hello Taxis** are Erbil's branded taxi company and they employ English-speaking drivers, but at highly inflated rates. They will accept payment in US$. From the airport to central Erbil the rate is about US$60. **Street Taxis** are generic, independent taxis and will take you to most places in Erbil. Rates are negotiable; for a drive across town of 15–20 minutes duration expect to pay around IQD6,000. Make sure your driver knows where you want to go and agree a price beforehand. It is always useful to get a business card or leaflet from your hotel and carry it with you to ensure you can get back there if you encounter language problems.

BY BUS There are some bus routes in Erbil; however, if you don't know your way around or don't have a guide with local knowledge and language with you, it is not advisable to try it alone. There is no bus station as such in the city at this time.

TOURIST INFORMATION

Although there are no official tourist information offices in Erbil as yet, enquiries can be made to the Board of Tourism (✆ *1 537 2870/69*), the National Bureau of Tourism (✆ *1 537 0454*) or the Common Bureau of Tourism (✆ *1 537 2522*).

WHERE TO STAY

The last few years have seen a dramatic increase in both the number and standard of accommodation in Erbil, with international hotel chains opening. Accommodation prices are significantly higher than you would expect to pay for similar accommodation elsewhere, due in part to the influx of business travellers and NGOs travelling on expense accounts. It is always worth trying to negotiate the price or asking for a discount.

It is very difficult to find anywhere desirable to stay anywhere in Erbil for under US$40 a night. Cheap hotels come and go and don't advertise, so can be difficult to find. Advice for travellers on a budget is to book into one of the mid-range hotels for a night and then head to the bazaar area or the university area and look around. See page 105 for accommodation price codes.

It is virtually impossible to pre-arrange your stay anywhere in Erbil for less than US$50 a night. The best way to arrange budget accommodation is either to pre-book your first night in a mid-range hotel or to just take a taxi from the airport to the bazaar area below the citadel. On the main road there you will find the **Shahan (or Shakhan) Hotel**, which offers basic but clean and comfortable rooms at good rates. Single rooms cost IQD40,000 and double rooms IQD50,000 (*US$40*) per night. Have a look at the rooms & if you don't like them, walk out of the hotel, turn right and you'll run into plenty of other hotels to check out within a 5-minute walk. Across the street the **Samira Miss Hotel** (*Bata St;* m *0770 468 6337, 0750 468 6337*), is a mid-range option (*around IQD20,000*) and has a very friendly, English-speaking owner with good rooms. **Hotel Peace Pigeon,** also in the bazaar area is a negotiable US$60 for a single or US$75 for a clean double room, hot water, Wi-Fi, breakfast and a friendly owner.

Bear in mind there is currently redevelopment work going on around the citadel and bazaar. A lot of older property has been demolished recently and more is due to be demolished as work progresses. Inevitably, some of the smaller, cheaper hotels have been casualties of this and will continue to be so.

Virtually all of the hotels in the luxury and upmarket range can arrange airport pickups – just ask (and ask the price, if any) at the time of booking.

LUXURY

⌂ **Erbil International Hotel** (167 rooms) 30 Metre St; ☏ 223 4460/70; e info@erbilinthotel. com; www.erbilinthotel.com. The Erbil International Hotel is located on one of Erbil's main roads, overlooking the Gelgand Park, 2km from the city centre & 15-mins' drive from the airport. Sister hotel to the Khanzad Hotel & Resort (see below), its facilities include free Wi-Fi, indoor & outdoor swimming pools, a gym, a tennis court & sauna. The hotel has 5 restaurants, inc one in the grounds serving freshly caught masgouf fish (from a tank) & excellent, though expensive, Lebanese wine. **$$$$**

⌂ **Erbil Rotana** (201 rooms) Gulan St; ☏ 210 5555/56; www.rotana.com/ rotanahotelandresorts/iraq/erbil/erbilrotana. Erbil Rotana is located adjacent to the English Village & less than 10-mins' drive from the airport. The property is opposite Park Sami Abdulahman, the largest park in Iraq. It is a great hotel for a few days' stay, security is excellent but discreet. The price of rooms is high, but they are comfortable, spacious, well maintained & clean with internet, tea- & coffee-making facilities & minibar. The hotel has 3 restaurants, inc Lebanese & Italian, a pool bar & a coffee bar in the lobby. The food is good,

though on the pricey side, with a wide choice of dishes & a more than adequate wine list. The outside dining area, amid water pools & beautiful gardens is especially pleasant in summer. The hotel staff are friendly & those who are from the Kurdistan region are knowledgeable about the area & more than willing to provide advice. As well as a pool, the hotel has a spa with massage, steam room & sauna. The hotel is conveniently located, a taxi ride to the centre of the city is about IQD5,000, & there is a standard charge of US$25 from or to the airport. **$$$$**

⌂ **Khanzad Hotel & Resort** (80 rooms) Salahaddin Rd; ☏ 224 5273/74/76/77; e info@ khanzadresort.com; www.khanzadresort.com. Situated 15km north of Erbil, this impressive hotel overlooks the Bastora countryside, about 25-mins' drive from the city centre. It has luxurious rooms & suites, all of which are equipped with direct telephone lines, internet connection, safe-deposit boxes, minibar, hair dryer, TV with international channels, wake-up calls & 24-hour room service. **$$$$**

UPMARKET

⌂ **Chwar Chra Hotel** (64 rooms) Shekh Abdulsalam, Barzani St; ☏ 223 1508; e info@

chwarchrahotel.com; www.chwarchrahotel.com. If you want to stay in a hotel with some real character, then this is your choice. There are comfortable beds, fridges in the bedrooms & free, reliable Wi-Fi. The lobby & restaurant have the most amazing glass mosaics on the pillars & there are some odd stuffed animals around as well as a crazy 'Tiffany' lamp. The entrance path has white lions with red tongues that light up a night & there is a huge lantern light in the entrance porch – all great fun. Breakfasts are good with plenty of choice, & the hotel has 3 good restaurants as well as outdoor dining on the enclosed lawn, where a famous Kurdish lunchtime buffet is served. It even has its own 'library' with foreign-language books for guests to borrow. It is near the Museum of Civilisation about 15–20 mins' walk from the citadel and bazaar. **$$$**

🏠 **Hawler Plaza Hotel** (50 rooms) Kirkuk Rd (nr Fransoa Hariri Football Stadium); ☎ 222 8890; e hawler_plaza@yahoo.com. Centred in the heart of Erbil, the hotel is proud of its Kurdish hospitality & friendly staff, although it is somewhat overpriced for what it offers. The spacious rooms have free Wi-Fi & satellite TV & are tastefully furnished with parquet floors & a sitting area. Breakfast is included in the room rate. Alcohol is available in the restaurant. There is a business centre with a good internet connection & which also sells wireless cards. Rooms have satellite TV, minibar, good working fridge & AC. The management is Lebanese, very friendly & most of them speak French. **$$$**

🏠 **Helin Plaza Hotel** (40 rooms) Ankawa St; m 0750 444 2891/7412; www.helinplazahotel. com. Just 15 mins away from the airport & 10 mins from the citadel & the centre of Erbil, this hotel is furnished simply. Facilities include rooms with AC, a minibar & seating area, and free Wi-Fi. Guests can enjoy a buffet for breakfast & dine at the on-site restaurant. **$$$**

🏠 **Jiger Palace Hotel** (49 rooms) Ankawa St; ☎ 225 3006; m 0750 349 4242; e reservation. jiger@yahoo.com; www.jigerhotel.com. Located in the centre of Erbil, the Jiger Palace Hotel is a modern hotel established in 2010 with comfortable & well-furnished basic single, double & deluxe suite rooms, a street-side cafeteria, an open-air restaurant, a gift shop, a news-stand & free Wi-Fi. **$$$**

🏠 **Noble Hotel** (80 rooms) Peshawa Qazi St (100 Meter St), Ankawa; ☎ 225 2630, 225 2620;

m 0750 431 2244, 0771 193 6300; www.noble-hotel.com. Located in the historical Ankawa district of Erbil, the Noble Hotel is a professionally run, well-managed hotel very close to the airport. Facilities include a fitness centre with spa & wellness centre, massage, Turkish/steam bath & indoor pool. The rooms are very well appointed (even single rooms have a king-sized bed) with 24-hour room service, free high-speed Wi-Fi, satellite TV & minibars. The hotel has 2 restaurants, one à la carte & one buffet-style offering a variety of cuisines, & room service is very efficient. Buffet b/fast is inc. The hotel has multi-lingual staff. **$$$**

🏠 **Tangram Erbil** (118 rooms) Kirkuk Rd; ☎ 229 6900; e info.erbil@tangramhotels.com; www.erbil.tangramhotels.com. Conveniently located in the Rasti area in the southern part of the city, the hotel is next to the Naza Shopping Mall. Rooms are well equipped, quiet & spacious with comfortable beds, a flat-screen TV, a working desk & a large shower. Internet & buffet b/fast are inc in the room rate. The hotel also features a large gym with a sauna, a buffet-style restaurant, a lounge bar with outdoor terrace where you can enjoy nargile pipes & local music, & a roof-top nightclub with live music & karaoke. **$$$**

MID-RANGE

🏠 **Ankawa Palace Hotel** (33 rooms) Shlama St, Ankawa (near Residency Office) ☎ 225 3030; m 0750 486 3030; e info@ankawapalace-hotel. com; www.ankawapalace-hotel.com. Located in the heart of the Ankawa district, this hotel was the first hotel in Ankawa. Opened in 2009, it is 3km from the airport & 5km from Erbil. The hotel has a luxury restaurant with an afternoon & night open buffet & bar. The rooms are basic, but all have AC, free Wi-Fi & satellite TV. **$$**

🏠 **Erbil Tower Hotel** (66 rooms) Citadel Rd (facing Old Judgment); m 0770 888 8533; erbiltower.com. Well-located, central hotel right at the northern gate of the citadel so really handy for sightseeing & right next to the bazaar. It is one of Erbil's oldest hotels, so rooms are dated & simply furnished, but have AC, satellite TV & mini-fridge. Wireless internet is available. B/fast is inc in the restaurant & a coffee shop provides light meals, but there are also several restaurants within walking distance. Staff are friendly & helpful, though speak only limited English. **$$**

Monaco Palace Hotel (19 rooms) Kirkuk Rd; ☎ 229 5555; m 0770 642 5555; www. monacopalacehotel.com. Some 30 mins' drive from the airport & close to Saladin University & shopping centre, rooms here are spacious, clean & the beds are very comfortable. Rooms have tea- & coffee-making facilities provided & complimentary newspapers. The hotel has 24-hour internet, free Wi-Fi, a business centre with computer, internet & printer available for use of guests, a currency exchange, laundry facilities & luggage store. This is a clean, child-friendly hotel with welcoming English-speaking staff. Restaurant has good choice of food with a varied & delicious open-buffet b/fast & in the evening a choice of national or international food. Alcohol is available & is reasonably priced. **$$**

Sky Star Hotel (41 rooms) 30 Metric Av (opposite Council of Ministers); ☎ 223 0074; e info@skystarhotel.net. Located in the centre of Erbil, about 2km from the airport & opened in 2008, this hotel has 6 main floors. Rooms have free Wi-Fi & satellite TV. The hotel has an international restaurant, coffee shop & bar, sauna & sports hall. **$$**

✗ WHERE TO EAT AND DRINK

With all the reconstruction and development going on in Erbil, new restaurants and eateries are opening all the time, and older ones being taken over, changing or closing. What follows is a cross section of restaurants and café bars currently in operation, aimed at the short-term visitor. Most hotels in Erbil offer acceptable food, and some of the better hotels have a superb choice of restaurants serving both local and international cuisine to a very high standard, so if you prefer to eat wherever you are staying, you won't necessarily miss out. If you don't want a full-blown meal, Erbil is a city of coffee bars, most of which also serve delicious snacks.

Be aware though that Erbil is an expensive city and that is reflected in the cost of eating out. Expect to pay around US$40 per head for a meal in a good restaurant, excluding drinks, and a similar amount for a bottle of wine. Local snack bars are more economical: you can usually get a snack and a soft drink/coffee for US$15.

Unless stated otherwise, the restaurants below are open for both lunch and dinner. Telephone numbers are given only where there is one advertised and there is likelihood that the phone will be answered. It is advisable to check opening days and times by email or on the website, as these do change, especially during Ramadan and other religious holidays.

RESTAURANTS

✗ **Bakery & More** Shoresh St; m 0750 747 2000; e info@bakeryandmore.com. This is one of the city's longest-standing haunts of the expat community. On the ground floor is the Lebanese bakery, which also serves traditional Italian pizzas, & an attractive, richly stocked deli counter brimming with sweetmeats, caviar, smoked salmon & speciality cheeses from around the world. On the 1st floor is the spacious, laid-back café-style eatery serving up a range of mouth-watering snacks & Oriental & international dishes, from fish & chips to fajitas. They also offer free delivery, m 0750 747 1000.

✗ **Basilico Italian Restaurant** Mezzanine floor, Erbil Rotana Hotel, Gulan St. Basilico is the first Italian restaurant in Erbil offering authentic Italian cuisine in a modern setting. Also visit the Aquarius Pool Bar in the hotel for lighter snacks & sandwiches.

✗ **Chili House Erbil** Ankawa Rd; www. chilihouse.com. Established in Jordan in 1985, the Chili House chain has proved a popular hit across the Middle East. It serves quality American-style burgers, hot dogs & grills with an Oriental twist that offer value for money.

✗ **Hawler Restaurant** Ankawa Rd; m 0750 448 2564; e sirwan2564@yahoo.com. One of the oldest venues for fine dining on the Erbil scene, Hawler Restaurant has long been a firm favourite of the local business community. There is a fully licensed bar & it serves a plethora of classic Oriental dishes until the early hours.

✗ **Iraqi Touch Restaurant** Family Mall, 100

Meter Rd; www.iraqitouch.com. The restaurant's upbeat, monochrome interior & friendly staff provide an elegant yet laid-back setting serving some of the best Iraqi food on offer in the Kurdish capital.

✗ **Kahve Keyfi** Roof Floor, Majidi Mall; ☎ 258 4141. Kahve Keyfi is one of the most elegant restaurants in Erbil with cheerful & knowledgeable staff & retro-style decoration. It serves Turkish & Ottoman cuisine & you can finish off your meal with a nargile pipe while enjoying the views from the huge panoramic windows.

✗ **Qi21 Shushi and Grill Bar** 21st floor of the Divan Erbil Hotel; ⊕ 19.00–midnight Sat–Thu. Carefully designed interiors & soothing colours, the vast windows & outdoor balconies give you 360° panoramic views of Erbil while enjoying sushi or grills from the à la carte menu.

✗ **Samad Restaurant** 60 Meter St, near White Mosque; ☎ 264 1161. One of the best-known restaurants in Erbil, Samad Restaurant is Erbil's luxury branch. It serves Eastern & Western meals for lunch & dinner.

✗ **Seasons Restaurant** Divan Erbil Hotel Inner Lobby. The Divan Erbil also houses the Chopin Piano Bar & the Saray Lounge. Seasons is open for breakfast, lunch & dinner. It serves international cuisine & seasonal Kurdish food in a vast outdoor garden, with pools & water fountains.

✗ **Sultan Restaurant** Shoresh St (next to the Shoresh petrol station). An unassuming eatery, perfect for those who have savoured the delicious, bone-warming soups & other Turkish culinary delights in Istanbul's plethora of eating houses.

✗ **Tarin Restaurant** Just after the checkpoint on the Massif-Salahaddin Rd (leaving Erbil); www.tarinrestaurant.com. The rolling lawns & sophisticated dining rooms of this high-standing restaurant provide a peaceful retreat from the madding crowds of the city centre. Tarin's menu offers a choice selection of Oriental & Occidental dishes & there are live concerts by international singers every evening.

COFFEE BARS

☕ **American Bar Coffee** American Village on the road to Massif; ☎ 258 5382. Far from the hustle & bustle of downtown Erbil (& in the arid summer months a precious degree or two cooler), the American Bar Coffee is an authentic & relaxing US bistro/bar/café-experience. It serves a good range of pizzas, steaks, salads, ice creams, shakes & smoothies as well as beers, wines & spirits. Watch football on the big-screen TVs or smoke a nargile pipe. Self-billed as the 'Ibiza experience in Erbil', it's the place to party.

☕ **Barista Coffee** Ankawa main st (close to Ankawa Police Station; m 0750 398 9131; www.baristacoffeeshop.com. Ankawa Barista's laid back atmosphere, friendly staff & great range of quality coffees have made it one of the most popular cafés in Erbil. The café's house breakfast is a lavish treat rivalling anything you might find in a luxury hotel & their great range of panini & thin-crust pizzas, served all through the day, offer a taste of continental Europe in Kurdistan.

☕ **Saquella Expresso Club** Family Mall, 100 Meter St; m 0750 720 0055; ⊕ 10.00–midnight. Saquella has a long history, being founded by Clemente Saquella in 1856. Saquella was the first pioneer to start trading colonial spices of different quality & origins in Abruzzo, including tea, barley & cocoa. This tradition has been handed down the 3 successive generations & now Saquella is one of the most established coffee-makers in Italy.

ENTERTAINMENT

As you would expect in a Muslim country, Erbil is not known for its nightlife. It does not have a swathe of nightclubs or discos, although this is slowly changing. Shar Garden Square below the citadel, with its nargile cafés and tea shops, is a favourite evening haunt of Erbilites of all ages. During the summer months it is alive with tourists from the southern provinces. Fountains feature heavily in this square. The main fountain draws a lot of attention at night as it is lit up and changes colour every few seconds. Photographers are on hand to take your portrait as the fountain does its best to soak you through, while onlookers eat ice cream and munch their way through packets of nuts and seeds. On three sides, you have the bazaar, the Nishtiman Mall, and a new mosque with attractive brick archways, while on the fourth, towering above you, you have the citadel. The American Bar Coffee (see opposite) is a favourite hangout for locals and tourists alike. Most of the new shopping malls have cinemas and food courts, as well as amusement-arcade-style games. The bigger hotels (such as the Tangram Erbil) have late-night bars and clubs, which are open to non-residents. The Computer Game Centre, near Raperin and Brayeti streets, is popular with children.

SHOPPING

Nishtiman Mall is one of the largest shopping malls in Erbil city. The mall is divided into several sections: clothes shops are in one area, while electrical and electronics stores are in another part. There is a video arcade in the basement and restaurants and cafés can be found in the corners of the open areas.

Erbil's famous bazaar lies at the foot of the citadel, next to the square. At its entrance you will see men sitting on chairs and exchanging currency. Inside there are avenues of women's clothes, men's tailors, fabrics, accessories, shoes, perfumes, spices, cheeses, nuts, henna, nargile pipes (hookahs) and even some very traditional decorations for your home. The one product that thrives in the bazaar is gold. Displays are filled with pure 18-, 22- or 24-carat gold; you really can't find anything less than that. In Erbil, when a couple get married it is traditional for their families to go to these stores to pick out the ring, necklace and bracelet for the bride. In the bazaar the locals still conform to the old tradition of closing their shops around 1pm to go for lunch or when it is their time to pray, rest and nap because of the high temperatures in the summer months.

There are also many new shopping malls springing up. The Majidi Mall on Koya Road out of Erbil (if going by taxi, just ask for the clock tower on the highway and the driver will know the direction) sells the usual branded fashion and sportswear, designer sunglasses, footwear and jewellery. There is also a fast-food floor with a range of restaurants and cafés, including the unappealingly named Fatburger, and a selection of arcade-style games for children.

Erbil is disappointing for **carpet** purchases. The traditional carpets of the area are very difficult to find. A carpet and textiles shop can be found at the foot of the ramp leading up to the citadel, but most of the stock is modern, machine-made items featuring local Kurdish and religious characters. There is little in the way of tourist-type **souvenirs**, though locally made soap, spices, sugar cones, etc, make acceptable and unusual gifts.

SPORTS/FITNESS

Erbil's top-end hotels typically have their own pools and fitness facilities, and these are probably the most modern and high-quality sports venues in the city. Some may be open to non-residents for a daily fee; it is always worth enquiring.

Erbil's Qazi Mohammed Sports Centre is in Arbil Road. Please be aware it is usual in Muslim countries to have separate public bathing and facilities for men and women/children, or for the facilities to be open at different times to each of these groups. Times can change regularly, so it is always worth enquiring ahead.

In Sami Abdul Rahman Park there is a newly opened health club complete with open-air swimming pools, a gym and a sauna, which is open to the public during daylight hours. The park is situated at the west side of Erbil, neighboured by the 60 Meter Road in the east, opposite Kurdistan's Parliament and Council of Ministers buildings. Near its southern entrance is the main road between Erbil and Mosul. The park also has a running track, football pitches and a children's playground.

OTHER PRACTICALITIES

MEDICAL FACILITIES The largest hospitals are:

Emergency Hospital Baxtyaree area, close to 60 Meter St; ☎222 4911. Specialities: trauma centre
Nanekaly Private Hospital 60 Meter St, close to Azadi Centre; ☎254 8301. Specialties: general medicine

Rojawa 100 Meter St; ☎250 9843. Specialties: medical, surgery, trauma & burns
Rojhalat 100 Meter St; ☎227 3883. Specialties: emergencies, general surgery & medical centre

WHAT TO SEE AND DO

THE CITADEL OF ERBIL Known as Qelay Hewler in Kurdish, the citadel is located in the centre of the city. It is a round construction, which dominates the old city, and has been built upon many layers of civilisation. These layers are the historical settlements built in ancient times. The total area of the citadel is 102,000m² and the tell has a height of 26m from ground level. The first village was established here around the 6th millennium BC and has been continually inhabited since its founding. The citadel has seen the reign of many historic civilisations, including Sumerian, Akkadian, Babylonian and Assyrian. Other ancient powers, including the Achaemenian Persian, Greek, Iranian Parthian, Seljuks and Sassanians, also dominated the citadel before being finally conquered by the Ottoman Turk Muslims. The Citadel of Erbil consists of three main quarters: Topkhana, Saray and Taki.

Sitting at the main entrance to the citadel is an imposing **statue of Mubarak Ahmad Ibn al Mustawfi** (1167–1239), a former minister and historian from Erbil who rose to fame chronicling the history of this ancient city. From here there is an impressive view over Shar Garden Square and the roof tops of the covered bazaar below. Until 2006, the interior of the citadel contained more than 600 houses and the area was abuzz with daily life. Today, with restoration work by the Kurdistan Regional Government (KRG) in co-operation with UNESCO going on, an eerie silence reigns. The main gate overlooking the town, which was rebuilt by Saddam Hussein, is now being removed and a fresh gate is being built, more in keeping with the original one. The walls of the citadel are slowly being repaired and the houses are also being reconstructed. This work is scheduled to last for many years. Because of this on-going rehabilitation, the citadel with its internal alley ways and dwellings is currently out of bounds to visitors, but it is not difficult to imagine its former glory and a way of life that had changed little across the millennia.

KURDISH TEXTILE MUSEUM Located just inside the gate of the citadel, this museum of Kurdish weaving (*www.kurdishtextilemuseum.com;* ⏀ *09.00–17.00*) offers the visitor a glimpse of the beauty and intricacy of this handicraft art, as well as insight into the cultural heritage of the Kurdish people themselves. It includes numerous woven arts from both settled and nomadic tribes in the area. Here the art of Kurdish weaving is such an integral part of life that it reflects the Kurds' social situations, unique cultural influences and their very lifestyle. This craft has a rich tradition, peculiar to the Kurdish people and, therefore, plays an extremely important role in ethnological research. Weaving is widely used by the Kurdish tribes to provide for their daily needs, so it includes all kinds of goods, clothing and hats. This ingenuity has resulted in self-sustained communities that are not dependent on imported goods for their economic survival. Unfortunately, due to its location, the museum is also currently inaccessible to visitors during renovations to the citadel, but hopefully will be open again in 2015.

ERBIL MUSEUM OF CIVILISATION The Museum of Civilisation (*1km south of the citadel;* ⊕ *09.00–16.00 most days; free*) houses a small but interesting collection. Of particular note is the pottery from Erbil and the surrounding regions. The **Mound of Qalich Agha** lies within the grounds of the museum. An excavation in 1996 found tools from the Halaf, the Sumerian Ubaid and Uruk periods.

THE QAYSSARRIA BAZAARS While touring Erbil you should visit the colourful bazaars. The main bazaar is a covered market and is located in the city centre to the south of the citadel. You enter the bazaar through a number of alleys surrounding it, and walk through the maze of narrow paths between the shops. Many of the alleys contain similar products: clothing, shoes, jewellery, cloth. In the northeast corner of the bazaar you will find a north–south alley selling a variety of honey and dairy products like yoghurt and cheeses. This bazaar, with its maze of intricate little booths and shops, is now surrounded by a newly constructed wall and fresh pavements.

SHAR GARDEN SQUARE Shar Garden Square is a recently constructed public square and esplanade just below the citadel, complete with fountains, brick arcades and a clock tower modelled on London's Big Ben. A favourite haunt of Erbilites with its nargile cafés and tea shops, the square attracts locals of all ages and during the summer months is alive with tourists from the southern provinces. Part of Erbil's urban redevelopment plan, the square offers a great view of the citadel and its many fountains cool the arid air, offering a refreshing respite from the bustling bazaar.

MINARET PARK AND THE MUZZAFARIYA MINARET A short walk or taxi ride south from the citadel, this is without a doubt the most architectural of Erbil's green spaces. **Minaret Park** offers up an eclectic fare of circular terraces, Etruscan columns and cascading fountains. Lit up like an urban wonderland on summer evenings, the park is a popular destination for the city's youth and young families taking in the cool evening air. Well-planted walkways and shaded groves provide a romantic backdrop for promenading couples and a raised-terrace café offers nargiles and welcome refreshments.

Tucked away in a quiet corner of the park is the 36m high **Muzzafariya Minaret**, dating back to the reign of King Muzzafar al Din Abu Saeed al Kawkaboori (brother-in-law to the crusader-battling Saladin) in the late 12th/early 13th century. The ornate brick minaret has an octagonal base decorated with two tiers of niches, which are separated from the main shaft by a small balcony, which is also decorated. It is all that now remains of the city's medieval growth beyond the confines of the citadel. On the other side of the street, and connected to the Minaret Park via a cable car is the **Shanidar Park and Art Gallery** (⊕ *daylight hours; free*), Erbil's oldest permanent exhibition space. Although much of the artwork on display in the gallery's regularly rotating exhibitions doesn't stray too far from what you might expect from a provincial art space showcasing mainly student works, there are occasional treasures to be discovered. A visit to the gallery can also provide an opportunity to meet local artists who, language-permitting, will be delighted to talk about their work and experiences. Don't be surprised to find queues after sunset in the summer months when locals turn out in hoards to take in the cool evening air and do a little people-watching of their own. The park has a labyrinth of stone paths winding between the planted areas around a small central lake. There is an ample selection of garden terrace cafés offering welcome refreshments. At the heart of the park is an unusual edifice, half-cave and half-fortress, complete with cascading waterfalls and stalactites.

SAMI ABDUL RAHMAN PARK The biggest and greenest of Erbil's parks, Sami Abdul Rahman is situated at the west side of Erbil on 60 Meter Street, opposite Kurdistan's Parliament and Council of Ministers buildings. To the south is the main road between Erbil and Mosul. It is a favourite spot among the residents of Erbil for family picnics and a welcome refuge from the hustle and bustle of the city. It is divided into well-mapped sections with leafy walkways, rolling lawns and flower gardens, a small amphitheatre, and a newly opened health club complete with open-air swimming pools, a gym and a sauna. During the summer months, the park stays open long after sunset and this is when it is busiest. It has several well-equipped play areas for children, lakes, cafés, planted walks, boat rides, fountains and a garden restaurant offering a basic but well-prepared selection of local culinary delights. Formerly a large military complex, the park stretches over hundreds of acres. It takes its name from a former prime minister who was killed in a 2004 suicide bomb attack that claimed around a hundred lives. A large monument in the park dedicated to the victims of the blast provides a solemn reminder of Iraq's bloody history and Kurdistan's struggle for autonomy. A poignant inscription on the monument reads simply: 'Freedom is not free'. If you're curious to know what the citizens of Erbil get up to of an evening, a trip to Sami Abdul Rahman Park is sure to offer you a privileged insight.

WALKING TOUR OF ERBIL Any stroll around Erbil should always start at the citadel. The views from the ramparts are spectacular and the on-going restoration work is interesting to observe. In time it will also be possible to visit the museums located within the walls. Descending from the citadel, you have time for a tea or coffee in one of the traditional tea houses at its foot, sitting at the original old tables or benches while watching the world go by. Then cross the road to visit the newly built city square with its fountains and clock tower or maybe wander to the neighbouring bazaar with its narrow alleyways and crowded stalls selling local food, jewellery and clothing. Walk south towards the Minaret Park and the Muzzafariya Minaret and you will pass the Museum of Civilisation. Stop and take some time to browse its interesting and eclectic collection before arriving at the park. After viewing the minaret, take lunch in one of the park's cafés, before catching the cable car to the art gallery. Round off your day with a visit the Sami Abdul Rahman Park and enjoy an early evening stroll among local families.

AROUND ERBIL

Although it is the capital city of Kurdistan, there isn't a great deal more than one day's sightseeing to be done. However, Kurdistan is famed for its natural beauty and so it is worth getting out of the city and visiting some of the pleasant locations in its environs. The following sites are all within a short distance of the capital and make for either a pleasant day trip or a stop *en route* to Dohuk or Suleimaniyah.

SALAHADDIN Only 19km from Erbil, this is a popular mountain village close to Mount Pirman. Khanazad Castle is nearby. This 40m-high fortress built over a hill in the period of Suleiman Beg, prince of Soran, was reconstructed in 2005. The site is a popular place for day visitors from Erbil. There are tea houses and refreshments are available.

SHAQLAWA The town of Shaqlawa is about 50km (90 minutes' drive) east of Erbil. Built at the base of Mount Safeen (which is nearly 2,000m at its peak), Shaqlawa has luscious springs and trees, several fruit orchards, a food market, restaurants and hotels. Scenic, but under-developed, the city is not well kept but people are buying land, so change is in the air. The Iraqi Communist Party has a massive building in the town. Opposite the city, close by the main highway, is the Raban Boya Shrine (Sheikh wso Rahman). It is a curious place, quite a strenuous climb to reach, famous for its fertility blessings. Muslims and Christian women alike visit here to take advantage of its legend which says that if a women slides down a natural, rocky slide she will become pregnant! It was home to Sheikh Rahman, a hermit.

RAWANDUZ Located 107km northeast of Erbil, the town is perched 150m above sea level, surrounded by huge mountains, Korek, Zozil and Brandasot, and spectacular valleys. It is famous for its Kurdish tribal blood feuds and as a centre of resistance to whichever government was in power. It was a base for British troops and Assyrian militia co-opted by the British in the 1920s to control the area. The town is also well known as the base for Sir A M Hamilton, who built the Hamilton Road and its famous bridges across the Rawanduz river. This road opened up the region and promoted access to the Iranian border. Today travellers and commerce travel on this road through this magnificent country.

Pank Resort, **Rawanduz** just above the town is the main place to stay. It offers 74 small holiday villas in a park with funfair rides and attractions, and a fine restaurant, surrounded by stunning mountain views. Rawanduz has a roller-coaster ride, known as 'shinglbana', found only in four other countries and consisting of 50 cabins moving on a railway. It is 1,475m long and 300m high. The cabins move down to the valley at 55kph. Along this journey one can view the Rawanduz Valley and the Bechal and Ali Bag Falls.

HAJI OMRAN Right on the Iranian border 180km east from Erbil is where you will find the Kurdistan Region's highest mountains. The local spa water is renowned for treating ailments and the highlands usually remain green through summer, boasting spectacular scenery. In the future it has great potential for winter sports. It is also a haven for the illicit transfer of goods between the two countries. As of 2014 this border is not open to international travellers.

BEKHAL RESORT This small resort 140km east from Erbil is a short drive from the ravine of Gali Ali Berg. It is the place for restaurants and popular cafés visited by large numbers of tourists from early spring until the end of autumn, although maximum temperatures here reach 32°C in summer. Just a 10km drive away can be found the **Gali Ali Berg Waterfall**. Hailed as the highest waterfall in the Middle East, Gali Ali Berg, is a mountain resort located on the intersection of two mountain ranges (the Korek chain in the north and the Baradost chain in the west) and two rivers, the Rawanduz Sidakan and the Khalifan. The breathtaking scenery around the waterfalls has long since assured the site's popularity as a picnic spot, and the resort today, complete with a waterside souk and its host of terrace cafés and eateries, offers a warm, authentic welcome. During the long summer months, tourists from all over Iraq can be found at these popular waterfalls, famous for their outstanding natural beauty. The dramatic mountain scenery in the second half of the 3-hour drive makes the excursion well worth the effort. There are food stalls here serving wraps, sandwiches and tea; however, there is currently no overnight accommodation.

SHANIDAR CAVE A famous large cave with deep sediments, Shanidar was first occupied 100,000 years ago. It is of particular archaeological importance as the first adult Neanderthal skeletons found in Iraq were discovered here during excavations which took place between 1957 and 1961. A team from Columbia University, USA unearthed nine Neanderthal skeletons dating from 60–80,000 years ago. The cave is on the south face of the Baradost Mountain overlooking the Shanidar Valley at an elevation of 822m. There is a car park nearby, but no other facilities for tourists at the moment. In 2014 further excavations and a reappraisal by Manchester University in association with Iraqi archaeologists were planned. Following this, facilities should improve, opening the site to visitors.

THE PLAIN OF HARIR BATASS Accessible by road from Shaqlawa, the plain is the place for ancient tells (artificial mounds formed by the accumulated remains of ancient settlements) that date back to different ages in the country's history.

RABBAN HORMIZED MONASTERY The ancient Rabban (Monk) Hormized Monastery was founded about 640. It was the official residence of the Patriarchs of the Church of the Middle East. From the 16th to the 18th centuries it became a Chaldean church; however, the turbulence of the area caused it to be abandoned in the 18th century. It was later occupied, and renovated in part, until in 1859 a new monastery was built approximately 1.5km away, near Al-Gosh, which became the principal monastery of the Chaldean Church and remains so today. Rabban Hormized Monastery overlooks Shaqlawa Resort in the valley of the same name, 30 minutes' walk from the public road. There are two large highly engraved cave-like chambers in the locality that date back to the 4th century.

12

Dohuk and Environs

Telephone code 62

Dohuk means 'small village'. It lies in a wide valley with the White Mountain to the north, the great Dakhan (Shinodokha) Mountain to the south and the Mamseen Mountain and Sumeal agricultural plain to the east. Two rivers meet in the southwest of the city and water the fruit farms on their banks. Dohuk Governorate covers the mountainous borderlands with Turkey. It is a region of caves, ancient tombs, castles, woodlands and rivers. It is also the garden of Iraq, rich in fruit and vegetables, and arable crops: wheat, barley, lentils, chickpeas, rice, tomatoes, onions, garlic, tobacco, peas, beans, grapes, peaches, sumac (small trees with red, hairy fruits), apricots, quinces, walnuts, figs, apples and nuts all grow in abundance. The environs of the town are being landscaped and many trees are being planted. Locals will tell you that Saddam Hussein had the original treescape flattened!

Dohuk is a pleasant welcoming city where tourists feel very safe. There is a positive buzz about Dohuk, which is warming after all the problems of this region in the past. Dohuk is the third most important city of Iraqi Kurdistan and is growing fast with an influx of enthusiastic returning ex-pats, who are bringing finance. Although the area suffered severely from the Anfal campaign (see box, page 394) and Saddam Hussein's Arabisation programme, many of the region's residents who were expelled are now returning and reconstruction of the villages has begun. Small industries, such as the canning factory, which stopped operating during Saddam's regime, are coming back. Much building is taking place along with the projected new airport complex and the city is growing quickly. In the east of the city many blocks of apartments and business premises under construction are doubling the size of the town. The investment is immense. The centre of the city is also booming with some new buildings and shops.

Dohuk governorate also contains the only border crossing between Turkey and Iraqi Kurdistan at Ibrahim Khalil/Habur. This is the border-crossing point for trucks that make their way daily from Turkey to northern Iraq and vice versa. The town of Ibrahim Khalil is the first stop after the border and is just one great truck park; such is the on-going trade. The town is named after the prophet Ibrahim Khalil and is a tourist and recreation area for the people of Zakhu.

HISTORY

The city's strategic importance dates back to Assyrian times when the roads passing through it connected the empire with other ancient kingdoms. It was part of the Badinan Emirate, a Kurdish principality like the principalities of Baban and Soran, which contracted or expanded as the powers ruling the area (the Ottoman Empire or Persia) became stronger or weaker. Villagers and farmers who migrated to the city of Dohuk over the years settled mainly in the southern, western and eastern suburbs. The Post and Communications Office now stands on the site of Dohuk Castle, once a place of court intrigues. Only the castle wall, overlooking the river, remains.

THE ANFAL CAMPAIGN

The campaign took its name from Suratal-Anfal in the Koran. Al Anfal literally means the spoils (of war) and was used originally to describe the military campaign of extermination and looting commanded by Ali Hassan al Majid. However, the Baathist regime used it as a code name for a series of systematic attacks carried out against the Kurdish population in the late 1980s during which thousands of men, women and children were executed. The campaign also targeted the villages of minority communities, including Christians.

Historically it could be said that the Kurdish genocide began decades before the Anfal with the arabisation of villages around Kirkuk in 1963; the deportation and disappearances of Faylee Kurds in the 1970s and 1980s, and the murder of male Barzanis in 1983. The term Al Anfal is generally associated with a succession of attacks against the Kurdish population in Iraq during the final stages of the Iran-Iraq War, by Saddam Hussein and his cousin Ali Hassan al Majid (known as 'Chemical Ali'), including the use of chemical weapons in the late 1980s (notably the poison gas attack against Halabja on 16 March 1988 during which approximately 5,000 people were killed, see box, pages 408–9).

Part of the Anfal campaign involved the 'arabisation' or population redistribution of the area, a tactic used by the Baathist regime to drive the pro-insurgent population out of their homes in villages, as well as in oil-rich cities like Kirkuk, and relocate them to the southern parts of Iraq.

In 2006 Saddam Hussein and others were put on trial for offences, including genocide, committed as part of Operation Anfal. The trial for the Anfal campaign was still underway when he was executed for his role in the unrelated Dujail Massacre.

St Thomas the Apostle (Doubting Thomas) is said to have passed through the Dohuk area *en route* to India.

GETTING THERE AND AWAY

BY AIR A new airport is planned for Dohuk which should open in 2017.

BY ROAD Dohuk is located approximately 1 hour's drive from Zakhu and just over an hour from the Ibrahim Khalil/Habur border crossing with Turkey. Shared taxis regularly travel this route and from Dohuk to other parts of Kurdistan.

GETTING AROUND

Dohuk is easy to get around by foot or taxi and it should cost no more than IQD3,000 to travel within the city. Public transport is available in the form of taxis and some bus routes. Dohuk makes an excellent base for exploring the Kurdistan region.

BY TAXI This is the usual form of transport in Dohuk city and its environs. Make sure your driver knows where you want to go and agree a price beforehand. It is always useful to get a business card or leaflet from your hotel and carry it with you to ensure you can get back there if you encounter language problems.

BY BUS Cross city regular bus travel is still in its infancy in Kurdistan and although there are some bus routes in Dohuk, if you don't know your way around or have a guide with local knowledge and language with you it is not advisable to try it alone.

TOURIST INFORMATION

Although there are no official tourist information offices in Dohuk as yet, see page 134 for details of national tourism information centres.

WHERE TO STAY

Dohuk has a good range of centrally based inexpensive hotels, many on the two main roads on either side of the bazaar area – Kawa Road and 11 Ayloul Road, the two main roads close to the central bazaar, as well as newly built luxury hotels catering for the top end of the market.

Single rooms are almost impossible to find in Kurdistan. It is not unusual for a room to have two or three beds and to cost the same regardless of how many people use it, so prices will be cheaper if you have a travelling companion.

In budget hotels, and even some mid-range ones, squat toilets are the norm and showers free range all over the bathroom with a small drain hole in the corner of the room. Hot water, like electricity, is not a constant feature. Most budget hotels do not have email or a webpage. See page 105 for accommodation price codes.

UPMARKET

Dilshad Palace Hotel (96 rooms) Zakhu Way, Shahedan Rd; 722 7601–9; e info@ dilshad-palace.co;m; www.dilshad-palace.com. Located in the heart of the city, this hotel has an outdoor swimming pool, 24-hour room service, laundry service, a Lebanese restaurant & a café. Officially classified as 5 stars, it would not meet this classification according to European standards, despite lots of marble in the lobby! The rooms are huge & equipped with minibar, free Wi-Fi, AC, LCD TV, water boiler, safety-deposit box & hair dryer. There is a supermarket across the street & an amusement park, which is handy for those travelling with children. **$$$$**

Jiyan Hotel (85 rooms) 722 2400; e info@jiyanhotel.com; www.jiyanhotel.com. Well located near Gali Park, in the middle of a quiet green area with nice views of the mountains, this hotel is very close to the shopping centres. It has 2 restaurants, 3 bars, an indoor & an outdoor pool & free Wi-Fi. It was built during Saddam era, & therefore the rooms, restaurant & lobby are now in need of updating. That said, it offers good services at a moderate price, the rooms are clean & it is a good choice for tourists & travellers. English, Arabic, Turkish & Russian are spoken by the staff here. Airport transfer is available at cost. **$$$$**

Parwar Hotel (50 rooms) 25 Barzan St; 724 4554. This hotel, completed in 2013, is just outside the city centre. Its location is a little far from city centre & there are no places of interest close by to walk to, so you need to take a taxi. It is well furnished in a traditional Turkish style & most rooms have a small kitchen. The hotel has a restaurant, internet & laundry service. The staff are very helpful. **$$$$**

MID-RANGE

Hotel Bircin (35 rooms) Cnr Kawa Rd & Cinema Nawrouz St; m 0750 491 9781; e bircin@ yahoo.com. Located in the centre of Dohuk, this hotel is very easy to find & the building itself is a landmark in the Bazaar/Souk area. Officially classified as 4 stars, it would not meet this classification according to European standards; however, it certainly is one of the best choices in town. B/fast is inc in the room rate with a good choice of food, but no coffee. The rooms have European toilets unlike in many other hotels in this price range, but no shower curtain. Most rooms have a view of Dohuk. Luggage can be safely stored at reception. One of the main long-distance taxi stands is conveniently situated just a few yards away from the hotel entrance & here you will find transport to other cities within Kurdistan. **$$**

Rasan Hotel (40 rooms) Gali Roundabout; m 0750 781 8888; e info@rasan-hotel.com. This is a new hotel in the centre of Dohuk with a restaurant & bar. Rooms have AC but no Wi-Fi, although the hotel does have conference facilities. Its website is still in the process of being developed. **$$**

SHOESTRING

Abin Hotel 11 Ayloul Rd. Good-sized rooms with massive beds & beautiful decorations. Bathrooms have European-style toilets. The owner speaks good English. **$**

Dolphin Hotel (55 rooms) Sulav St; m 0750 374 5572; e dolphin1241@yahoo.com. This hotel has a restaurant & a cafeteria for b/fast.

Internet access. *Single US$35, double US$60, triple US$90.* **$**

Duhok Palace Hotel 11 Ayloul Rd. Modern, well-furnished rooms. **$**

Duski Hotel Sulav St; m 0750 717 9335. *Single rooms from US$35; doubles from US$50 & triples from US$75.* **$**

Hotel Perleman Kawa Rd (practically in the market, although the entrance is down a small lane). Budget priced, clean hotel with en-suite rooms which contain a TV, fridge & a heating/AC unit. **$**

Slivan Hotel (19 rooms) 14 Athar St; \722 5683. This hotel has a reputation for being the centre of the backpacker universe in Dohuk. **$**

✖ WHERE TO EAT AND DRINK

With all the development currently taking place in Dohuk, new restaurants and eateries are opening all the time. What follows is a cross section of restaurants and café-bars currently in operation. Most better-class hotels in Dohuk, such as the Jiyan, have restaurants offering a good choice of local and international cuisine so if you are staying at one of these hotels do check out what is on offer. Many hotel restaurants are also open to non-residents. All the new shopping malls which are springing up around Dohuk have food courts, serving mainly international food. There are many restaurants and eating places in the city centre, plus small snack bars, which are mostly congregated in the streets around the central market. A sample meal at an ordinary restaurant (for example, in Sulav Street) consisting of chicken and rice with salad trimmings, and a soft drink, will cost about IQD13,000.

Unless stated otherwise, the restaurants below are open for both lunch and dinner. Opening days and times can and do change, though, especially during Ramadan and other religious holidays.

✖**Al-Azaim** Barzan Rd, Gavarke District. This centrally located spacious restaurant is very clean & has professional, polite staff & swift service. As well as serving well-prepared Kurdish/Iraqi dishes, they also serve masgouf, the grilled fish that is considered the national dish of Iraq & originates from regions near the Tigris-Euphrates Basin. The desserts are good, too. In summer the gardens are pleasant & there is a space for kids to run about and play.

✖**Duhok Paradise** Located in the centre of Dohuk, by the riverside near the waterfalls. The closest thing to nightlife for the young men of the city, this restaurant is packed with tourists coming from Baghdad or Basra at weekends & holidays. Expect to pay around IQD12,000 for a 3-course dinner.

✖**Khan Kabab** Kawa Rd. A recently opened, comfortable restaurant serving tasty grills & kebabs, side plates & dessert. It is popular for serving simple, reasonably priced local food; however, at peak periods you'll need to allow time to be served. It is also very clean. Close to the city centre & handy to visit when shopping or sightseeing.

✖**Shawarma Roj** Zakho Way, Nohadra District. The restaurant serves delicious barbecued lamb or chicken shawarma grilled over coals, accompanied by hummus, two kinds of salads & soup. The staff are very obliging & the service is quite speedy. Overall good value, atmosphere, quality of food & location.

Further afield in Dohuk province at the Sulav Resort there are open-air restaurants providing diners with a view of the nearby ancient town of Amadiya (see page 402).

ENTERTAINMENT

The Dream City Amusement Park, located on the outskirts of Dohuk at the checkpoint entrance to the city behind the Mazi Plus Shopping Centre, is a popular place after dark with local families, teenagers and tourists alike. Admission is free and it is open most of the day, and at weekends and holidays late into the night. It has the usual fairground attractions, including a Ferris wheel, dodgem cars and a roller coaster, as well as go-karting and arcade games such as ping-pong, air hockey, table football and pool tables. There is also a cafeteria-style eatery.

The Azadi Panorama is a brand new park with a stunning view over Dohuk, which in the right light is really quite beautiful. The park isn't fully open yet, but walking around the complex, you can still get a taste of the views, take a closer look at the enormous Kurdish flag, the clock tower, and the unusual sculpture on the viewpoint. Signposts to it can be found all around in Dohuk.

SHOPPING

Dohuk is the first big Kurdish city in Iraq after the Turkish border, so all the trucks full of merchandise arrive here first. Consequently, the city is full of shops and you'll be able to find quite a few traditional neighbourhood markets spread around the city, as well as huge supermarket complexes such as Dream City. Dohuk city centre is, in effect, the main bazaar, with its covered streets radiating around the central bazaar area full of interesting shops and stalls, where you can browse for several hours. Like most Middle Eastern cities, the bazaar in Dohuk is a central part of life, selling almost anything you can imagine. A local favourite is the soft-serve ice cream which seems to be sold everywhere. One cone costs IQD500. The fresh fruit juice stands serve a bewildering array of jewel-coloured offerings. Dohuk bazaar also has several carpet/rug stalls. As well as making purchases, you can get all your travel repairs done here – shoes, clothes and any baggage repairs. Shops can also tailor clothing for you in the typical Middle Eastern fashion. The owner of a well-established souvenir shop with traditional artefacts is happy to expound on the history of the area, as are many of the locals, lacing their narratives with family history, personal experiences, many myths, facts and dreams.

The neighbourhoods on the hills in the east end of Kawa Road can be fun to wander through, getting lost in the maze of living quarters while greeting curious kids. The money exchange centre on the west end of Kawa Road is a good place to change money. Here street dealers sit at cardboard boxes stacked with big wads of cash, a reminder that Iraq is not a budget destination. At the western end of Kawa Road, look out for the **Al-Jazira Bookshop**. Even if you don't speak or read Kurdish or Arabic, you might like to buy a map of the region or a Kurdish flag. If you do read Arabic, then you can pick up a semi-useful Kurdish phrasebook, optimistically entitled *Speak Kurdish Fluently!*, and discover how to read the Kurdish alphabet, which is based on Arabic but joins up differently. It won't teach you how to speak fluently, and you really have to scour the phrases for something you might actually be able to use, but it may give you a head start.

There are also new modern malls currently under construction. At the checkpoint entrance to the city is the **Mazi Plus Shopping Centre**, which opened its doors in the second half of 2013. Here you will find Mazi Supermarket, Iraq's first comprehensive hypermarket, offering an extensive selection of consumer goods, along with a variety of shops including The Mazi Greenhouse, a landscape design and garden centre, a home improvement centre, a toy shop and a spacious home furnishings gallery. The complex boasts that it provides 'the ultimate shopping and family entertainment experience for Kurdistan's growing population'. It also has cafés, restaurants and a cinema.

SPORTS/FITNESS

Owned and operated by two ex-pats from the US, the **Gerdun Recreation and Fitness Centre** has a state-of-the-art indoor swimming pool, sauna, steam room, Jacuzzi and cold pool as well as snooker, 8-ball and 9-ball tables in its billiard hall. The fitness centre has a modern weights studio. Gerdun also offers special women-only opening hours and is the only place in Dohuk where women can exercise in a gym and learn to swim. It also has a restaurant, the 'California Cafe' serving American food, including hamburgers, pizzas, quesadillas, tacos, burritos, hot wings, French fries and chicken fingers.

The **Dream City Amusement Park** complex (see page 397) has a state-of-the-art fitness centre, complete with indoor and outdoor swimming pools. **Dohuk Stadium**, built in 1992, on Raza Road is where Dohuk football club, who are considered one of the best teams in the Iraqi Premier League, play their home games. It is a multi-use stadium, which can hold 25,000 people, making it one of the largest in Iraq.

OTHER PRACTICALITIES

MEDICAL FACILITIES The largest hospitals are:

Azadi (Teaching) Hospital Nakhosh-Khana St, nr Barzan St; ☎ 722 4074. Specialties: general medicine
Hevi Hospital Nakhosh-Khana St; ☎ 724 2612. Specialties: paediatrics

Naoere Public Hospital Shimek Zera; ☎ 722 5555. Specialties: general medicine
Shilan Private Hospital Qazi Mohammed St; m 0750 457 7788. Specialties: general medicine

WHAT TO SEE AND DO

CENTRAL AND GRAND MOSQUE In the centre of the bazaar stands the Azadi Mosque, constructed by Sultan Hussain Wali some 400 years ago. It is one of the oldest mosques in Dohuk with a traditional 16th-century interior. The sultan was famous for collecting many books and manuscripts and built a library to house these, some of which can still be seen in the mosque.

FOLKLORE MUSEUM Situated in the city centre next to the Hotel Bircin there is a folklore and heritage museum (⊕ *Hours vary*). Its focus is on the Kurdish traditions and way of life in ancient Kurdistan. Despite its small size, it covers a big archive of Kurdish heritage and gives a flavour of the Kurdish lifestyle of the past.

DOHUK ZOO This zoo (*Malta district*; ⊕ *daily*; *IQD1,500*) has more than 50 species of animals and birds – everything from chickens to tigers! Highlights include the opportunity to feed or even hold some of the animals. Look out for the boa constrictor near the front of the zoo with a sign that says 'I eat chickens and rabbits'. Worryingly, the zoo is well stocked with both … The zoo is on the road out of **Malta,** an old Assyrian village which is now a family-oriented area with cafés, restaurants and bakeries. A small cemetery on the hill pre-dates the city.

DOHUK UNIVERSITY For those interested in the educational advances in Kurdistan, Dohuk University, established in 1992, and situated on the international highway between Iraq and Turkey, is a shining example of local enthusiasm and what can be done. The building was once an army barracks for Saddam's soldiers. The people of Dohuk are proud of the programme here and the American Development Centre is offering advanced exchange programmes with the opportunity to travel abroad to study English through Dohuk University, as well as other universities in the Kurdistan region.

SAINT ITH LLATH CHURCH Located in the west of Dohuk, close by the presidency building of Dohuk University, this is the oldest still-extant church in the Middle East, believed to have been built in the 6th century. Although the exterior has been renovated in modern times, the church retains its original layout. Regular services are still held here. Next to the church is an ancient cemetery with some interesting early gravestones.

PARASTAGA ZARDASHT This site is home to a recently discovered ancient Zoroastrian/Mithradate temple cave with early artefacts dating from 500BC, to the Mithras temple dating from the 2nd to 3rd century AD. It consists of three parts with underground pillars and temple remains, and a bench facing the sun, which is significant in the Mithras religion for prayer. This site is on the road out of Dohuk, towards the Dohuk dam. The entry to the cave is on the right-hand side when walking towards the dam and costs IQD11,000 to enter. **Dohuk Dam** just north of the city was completed in 1988 for irrigation water and has a 60m high wall. Close by is a spectacular waterfall with a recreation area and restaurants.

MALTAI RELIEFS These Assyrian sculptured bas-reliefs carved into bare rock are approximately 3,000 years old. They are just a 30-minute walk, via a narrow bridge path and a footbridge, from Dohuk. They consist of three pictures, which together form a long sequence of nine personages. The character appearing on both sides of the sacred cortege seems to be the Assyrian king Sennacherib (705–681BC) son of Sargon and the others, from right to left are: Assur, Ninlil, Enlil, Sin, Shamash, Adada and Ishtar. They represented in some way a final blessing from the Gods on the Assyrian troops marching against Uratu, a powerful rival of Assyria (based in the Van area of Turkey). Sadly, excavations of anchorite cells have mutilated the pictures.

ZAKHU Zakhu is the most northerly city in Iraq. The stone bridge across the Khabour river, dividing the city in two and dating back to Abbasid times, is still in use and the main architectural feature. Many of the townspeople are engaged in trade. The traditional clothing industry, which specialised in fine woollen clothes, including shawls, is a shadow of its former self because the men have adopted other fabrics. In the past Zakhu was known for its ancient Aramaic-speaking Jewish community and was called as the 'Jerusalem of Assyria'. The Jewish population was attacked in 1891 and one of their synagogues burnt down. The troubles continued in the following years with heavy taxes being imposed and Jews being arrested, tortured and ransomed. Many emigrated, first to Palestine after 1920 and finally to Israel in the 1950s. While the Jews of Zakhu may have been among the least literate in the Jewish diaspora, they had a unique and rich oral tradition, and were known for their legends, epics and ballads, whose heroes came from both Jewish and Muslim traditions. Zakhu was also a diocese of the Chaldean Christian Church from the second half of the 19th century and for most of the 20th century. It merged with the Chaldean diocese of Amadiya in 1987. In December 2001 a new bishop was consecrated.

The city is a little run down but many structural road improvements are being made. With the upsurge of business between Turkey and Iraqi Kurdistan traffic is increasing all the time and traffic jams are now common in the town.

Getting there From the Turkish border it is 30 minutes by taxi to Zakhu. Zakhu to Dohuk takes one hour by taxi.

Where to stay

Tanahi Hotel Main St; m 0750 325 5400. This hotel has single rooms for US$46 & double rooms for US$60.

Bazaz Hotel Next to the bazaar; m 0750 418 7190. A basic but good hotel, with single rooms for US$30 & doubles for US$50, inc b/fast. It has Western-style toilets, AC & satellite TV.

Hotel Sinor Near Der Masseh church by the river. Hotel Sinor has single/twin rooms from US$10. The room are modern & good value with a big bed. This hotel is in a quiet location, but at night the street to the hotel is not well lit. The hotel staff aren't used to foreigners & don't speak any foreign languages. In the neighbourhood you can find several other similar hotels.

Hotel Zozek Reka Barzan/Baderkhan St, near Hotel Bazaz; m 0750 450 2781. The Zozek has welcoming staff & an owner who speaks some English & is very honoured to have foreign guests. The price includes a large b/fast. The rooms are quiet & modern with sparkling toilets. Rooms cost US$31 for a single and US$45 for a double.

Hotel Arya Reka Barzan/Baderkhan St, at the opp end to Hotel Zozek. This hotel is handy for what nightlife there is in Zakhu, with several late-night restaurants & a cyber café nearby. It is a good location for single, female travellers. Some rooms have a balcony facing a rather busy street. The rooms without balconies face a quieter alley. Double rooms start at US$25.

✗ Where to eat and drink

✗The Batman Main St, west of the roundabout, opposite the souk. Known locally for its tasty kebabs, they have a separate oven where they prepare pizza Kurdish style with the layer of dough crisp & thin. Portions are generous & service is friendly & efficient. Good value.

✗Solav Restaurant Next to the Dalal Bridge. The Solav Restaurant is located in pleasant surroundings, near the water of the Khabur river with a nice view of the bridge, this large restaurant serves average food at over-inflated prices.

What to see and do Located over Khabour river, **Delal Bridge** is a unique stone bridge considered to be the oldest of its kind in the Middle East. There are different theories about its construction. Some historians say it is Roman, others Greek. One of the generals of Alexander the Great could have ordered its construction. According to the Iraqi General Directorate of Archaeology it might have been erected by one of the Badinan rulers on the remains of a more ancient bridge; the Badinan princes just renovated and repaired the bridge. There is a famous epic in the form of a song in Kurdish about the construction of the bridge, which is about 114m long, nearly 5m wide, and 15.5m above the water's surface. It was built from carved stones and consists of a wide and high curve in the middle and other smaller curves on the sides. The walls are built from blocks of carved limestone and are put together in a beautiful and decorative way by using lime for plastering the walls.

Zakhu Castle, Qubad Pasha's hexagonal-shaped structure lies in Zakho cemetery on the western bank of Khabour river. Built on the ruins of an older castle, it has six windows and a gate as an entrance. It is constructed from large pebbles coated with gypsum, and earthenware and lime were used in building and plastering the castle, with writings and pictures. It dates from the beginning of the Kurdish Badinan Emirate (1376–1843), serving initially as the governor's house before being extended by prince Ali Khan. Today only the tower remains.

AIN SIFNI Less than 1 hour's drive southeast from Dohuk, is the Yezidi village of Ain Sifni where the sheikh of the religion lives. This is a fascinating village with one or two monuments overlooking it. It is interesting to meet the sheikh as a matter of courtesy before continuing with your visit to Lalish. The Yezidis welcome support as they are persecuted by the Muslims of the area and feel isolated in their own homeland.

LALISH The temple complex of Lalish is an important pilgrimage site for Yezidis, who are expected to make the trek to the tomb and temple here at least once during their lifetime. Located in a narrow valley is the tomb of Sheikh Adi, the central figure of the Yezidi faith. The tomb is in a cave dating back to 500BC and has various features of the religion – holy water pools, fire and further tombs of earlier holy men, as well as the tomb of Sheikh Adi himself. Outside the temple complex are various holy places, mostly based on water legends. During festival times many people come to stay in the various houses in the valley or camp on the slopes. This is one of the most esoteric mysterious places in the Middle East. Respectful visitors are very welcome.

JERWAN This Yezidi hamlet is 10km from Ain Sifni. It is the site of the canal and aqueduct built by King Sennacherib in the 6th century BC to bring water from the Gomil river to Nineveh. A stone statue with carvings of winged oxen remains. Charwana Viaduct is one of 18 canals in Sennacherib's canal construction project in which two million stones were used. An archaeological team from Chicago University visited the area in the 1930s and discovered Sennacherib's chamber and details about the construction of the viaduct.

THE BAVIAN GORGE (KHINNIS) One hour from Ain Sifni, the river Nahr Gormel has hollowed out a gorge where you can see 11 panels of bas-reliefs inscribed by Sennacherib. This Assyrian site is now being looked after and gives an idea of the immense engineering developments during the king's reign. Its purpose was to harness water for the fruit orchards supplying Nineveh. This is a delightful spot with pools where the local children often swim while picnicking here.

AMADIYA About 90km northeast and a 2-hour drive from Dohuk, this is a 4,000-year-old town dating back to the Assyrian period. It has city walls and an interesting gate. It is also impressively located atop a mountain plateau, with stunning views of the surrounding mountains and valleys. Muslims and Christians once lived alongside each other for centuries in this small town, and it was also home to a thriving Jewish community. Amadiya offers a wonderful view of the nearby valleys and gorges. It is surrounded by many natural beauty spots, waterfalls, orchards and vegetable-growing areas. **The citadel** is located on the eastern side of Amadiya city. The huge western marble gate has four carvings of smaller-than-life-size figures, perhaps Parthian kings who fought the Romans in AD226. Little remains of the cemetery of the Amadiyan princes in the east of the town except two marble domes. It is possible to climb the steps inside the **Amadiya Mosque** minaret built by Sultan Hussein Wali in the 14th century. The minaret is 30m high, with views from the top of the nearby mountains and valleys. On Hussein Wali's coffin there is a carved quotation from the Koran which reads 'everything is fatal except His face'.

An ancient religious school which flourished during the reign of the Badinan princes (1376–1843) and which closed to students only in the 1920s is nearby, close to the **Amadiya river**. Also not far from Amadiya is **Dergani** village, famous for its vessel pottery. Just north of Amadiya is the Christian village of **Kani** and the **Monastery of Mar Odisu**. Shared taxis travel regularly between here and Dohuk, departing from the Amadiya garage.

SULAV RESORT
At the end of the road from Dohuk, 5km away from Amadiya, Sulav Resort is an entertainment complex with cafés, shops and restaurants. It can easily be seen from Amadiya and has great views of the surrounding countryside. A visit here provides an excellent photo opportunity. Sulav has a freshwater spring that runs down the valley and it is from here that the water for Amadiya comes. You can walk along the road and enjoy the perfect views to Amadiya on top of the mountain. You can also climb up the stairs along the river until you reach the stone bridge and waterfalls. On your way you will pass several nargile- and coffee-houses overlooking the river where you can sit and relax at the end of the day. If you like to hike there are several hiking trails into the valley.

Sulav attracts lots of tourists from all over Iraq and during the summer months Arabs from Baghdad come north to enjoy a little bit of peace and have a good time with their families. It is a popular place with locals and tourists at weekends. There are several cheap eating places here, and the open-air restaurants provide a view up to the nearby ancient town of Amadiya and over the nearby valleys and gorges.

AKRI CASTLE
Akri Castle sits on the top of the mountain to the northwest of Akri town. In the castle there are the remains of monasteries, and there are carved caves in the face of the mountain itself. One of these, **Gondik Cave**, has stone carvings, dating back to 3000BC, including a number of animals and a sitting man, a hunter killing a mountain goat, and scenes from a feast. To the northeast of Akri Town lies **Showsh Castle**. Higher than Akri Castle, it contains the great mosque built by Sultan Hussein Wali, which houses a collection of ancient texts.

MALATHAYA
Known as Malta Hill, Malathaya lies on the Dohuk–Mosul road and is believed to be the site of an important Assyrian castle. Assyrian earthenware has been discovered here.

HALAMATA CAVE
The historic Halamata Cave is 7km east of Dohuk at the foot of Shindokhan Mountain in front of Kifrki village. It contains four pictures carved into the walls of the cave depicting a procession of six gods (Ashur, Anilil, Seen, Sun, Ishtar and Adid) riding on sacred animals led by the king. It is thought that these pictures are to commemorate Assyrian triumphant military battles.

13

Suleimaniyah and Environs

Telephone code 53

Like Erbil, Suleimaniyah is a rapidly developing metropolis in Kurdistan. It is getting larger and larger, the traffic is horrendous and there are an enormous number of new cars on the road. The international airport opened in July 2006. Owing to its prosperity and natural beauty, local Iraqis and Middle Easterners are coming to the city as tourists. Suleimaniyah has strong economic ties with Iran and is a major business and commercial centre. Overlooking the city is Asmar Mountain and the views from here of Suleimaniyah and its surroundings are breathtaking. Few cities can be seen as completely in the round as Suleimaniyah. On the top of the mountain is the Hotel Asmar. A number of small shops and restaurants can be found on the winding road leading up to it.

Suleimaniyah is becoming an important commercial centre for Kurdistan. The supporting investment laws and the quiet and peaceful nature of the city generally makes it a good base for business and makes for steady growth and expansion.

Great attention is paid to the promotion of Kurdish culture. The university has a Kurdish language faculty and Kurdish poetry festivals are held here amid much fanfare. The university's Cultural Centre is accommodated in one of Suleimaniyah's oldest houses. It is host to a collection of traditional Kurdish artworks and folklore. Nearby, Serchnsar, a suburb with coffee shops and restaurants, has been developed into a tourist area, and has the appearance of a local Coney Island, with fairy lights illuminating the restaurants.

HISTORY

Suleimaniyah does not have the ancient history of Erbil or Dohuk. It was founded in 1784 by Suleiman Pasha, King of the Emirate of Baban. At that time the area was divided into small emirate-like states, each with its own ruler. Legend says that one day the king went hunting on Asmar Mountain and on the plain below saw a woman called Malaka Khan. After falling in love with her he started building the foundations of Suleimaniyah. The principality played an active role in the Ottoman-Persian conflict. The last Baban prince left Suleimaniyah in 1850, after fighting a long and brave battle against the Turks for the independence of southern Kurdistan.

The Baban rulers encouraged cultural and literary activities within their domain. In the first half of 19th century, a poetry school was established under Baban's patronage. The famous classical Kurdish poet Nali (also known as Mullah Xidir Ehmed Sawaysi Mikayali) (1800–73) became the central figure.

Much of Suleimaniyah's historical architecture, such as the Palace of Hamid Beg the last Baban prince, was destroyed during the 1958 Iraqi revolution. The palace of Adila Khanem, chief of the Jaf tribe and the last relic of traditional princely architecture, was destroyed in 1988 in Halabja.

GETTING THERE AND AWAY

BY AIR The international 'Suleimaniya Airport' is near Bakrajo, with regular direct flights from Dusseldorf in Germany, Dubai in UAE, Amman in Jordan and Istanbul in Turkey.

BY ROAD From Erbil to Suleimaniyah via Kirkuk is a 3-hour journey. At Kirkuk it is possible to take the ring road around the town to travel on to Erbil. **Note:** Passports are often checked at this bypass to ensure that they contain the proper visas, etc. Iraq and KRG police jointly administer this checkpoint.

GETTING AROUND

Suleimaniyah is a big sprawling city, so apart from the actual city centre, where the main shopping streets are fairly close together, it is not easy to get around on foot. Taxi is the most usual form of transport. Public transport is available in the form of buses.

BY TAXI A taxi should cost no more than IQD5,000 to travel within the city. Make sure your driver knows where you want to go and agree a price beforehand. It is always useful to get a business card or leaflet from your hotel and carry it with you to ensure you can get back there if you encounter language problems.

BY BUS Cross-city regular bus travel is still in its infancy in Kurdistan. There are some bus routes in Suleimaniyah; however, if you don't have a guide with local knowledge and language with you it is not advisable to try it alone.

WHERE TO STAY

Tourism is still in its infancy in Suleimaniyah, with both Iraqi and international hotel chains opening up in the city. However, technology still lags behind and few of the smaller, cheaper hotels advertise or have websites or email addresses and their phone numbers are often mobiles and change frequently. There are cheap hotels to be found in addition to those listed, but as they don't advertise, they can be difficult to find. Advice for travellers on a budget is to head to Pyramid Street in the bazaar area and look around. There are also quite a few cheap hotels on Kawa Street, near the bazaar. Don't be frightened to ask for a discount and barter. Check out the room before you strike a deal. See page 105 for accommodation price codes.

LUXURY

🏠 **Highcrest Hotel** (92 rooms) Bakrajo Main Rd, opp Majidi Mall; m 0770 818 1336/7/8; e reservations@highcresthotel.com; www.highcresthotel.com. Located close to the city centre & only 5 mins' drive from the airport, this top-range hotel has clean & spacious elegant rooms with local & international TV channels, high-speed wireless internet, minibar, AC, tea- & coffee-making facilities & a balcony. The Atoussa Restaurant serves delicious international food, & the hotel also has a piano bar, shisha terrace & lobby lounge bar for beverages & snacks. There is a spa, gym & swimming pool with poolside bar, all of which are very clean & tidy. The staff are very friendly & attentive, fluent in English & make you feel more than welcome. **$$$$**

UPMARKET

🏠 **Areen Hotel** (19 rooms) 87 Peramagroon St; ☎ 320 9103/04; m 0770 155 9150; e info@ areenhotel.com; www.areenhotel.com. Situated

404

in the Shorish Quarter next to Azadi Park, the Areen Hotel & Restaurant is located at the heart of Suleimaniyah, overlooking the scenic Azadi Park & Shari Yari Amusement Park. The rooms are clean & spacious with internet, satellite TV, minibar, refrigerator and king-size beds. On the 9th floor there is a bar & restaurant with open-air dining on the terrace affording good views of the city. **$$$**

🏠 **Copthorne Hotel Baranan** (78 rooms) Sarchnsar Main St; 📱 0770 600 0000; www. millenniumhotels.com/copthornebaranan. Ultra-spacious rooms with all the modern amenities inc a TV with USB connection. The bathrooms are well appointed & clean with a conveniently placed concave mirror, although the showers can be a little temperamental. The food quality is excellent: delicious & meticulously cooked & the chefs are happy to cater for individual dietary requirements. The restaurant staff are very hospitable & friendly. B/fast has a variety of Middle Eastern, Continental & American options. **$$$**

🏠 **Lalezar Hotel** (14 rooms) Sarchinar Hill; 📞 319 2601; 📧 info@lale-zar.com; www.lale-zar. com. The hotel is extremely clean as are the rooms, which have comfortable beds, a small table with two chairs, tea- & coffee-making facilities, minibar, LCD screen TV & free Wi-Fi or wireline web access. Every room has a terrace, but the view is overlooking the roofs of the nearby buildings. The view from the restaurant is great however, & although b/fast is nothing special, they do serve good grills in the evenings. Taxis can be found everywhere outside. Friendly & helpful staff. **$$$**

🏠 **Ramada Hotel** (71 rooms) Salim St; 📞 320 9515; www.ramadasulaymaniya-salimstreet.com. Situated within walking distance of the main bazaar & opposite City Star Mall, this hotel has clean, comfortable & well-equipped rooms with free Wi-Fi. Some rooms have a little balcony. B/fast with a wide variety of choice, inc more Iraqi-style fare than is found in most hotels. The staff are friendly, obliging & speak good English. There is a beautiful aquarium in the lobby & lovely cakes are available in the little café. The pool & spa/fitness centre are very good, too, but the opening times (to maintain a male/female separation) are a little restrictive. The restaurant has wonderful views over the city & a good variety of food to choose from. **$$$**

MID-RANGE

🏠 **Alborz Hotel** (35 rooms) New Rezgari, close by Khasraw Khai Bridge on western outskirts of city; 📞 319 3751; 📱 0770 152 0041; 📧 alborz_Hotel@yajhoo.com. This hotel is recommended as the best value for your money. It is a good, but modest hotel with a nice restaurant. The average meal costs between IQD15,000 & IQD20,000. The rooms are clean & comfortable. *A single room costs US$60 per night, a double US$75. There are plenty of restaurants nearby.* **$$**

🏠 **Mihrako Hotel** (53 rooms) Salim St; 📞 66 314 305. Situated in a popular & busy area, which is buzzing until late at night. Plenty of eateries around the location of the hotel within walking distance. It is about a 15-min bus ride to the central bazaar & 5 mins by taxi to the nearest mall with a cinema. The hotel has 5 floors in total. The rooms are standard, with TV & en-suite bathroom with a separate shower area. Free Wi-Fi & LAN access with a good signal & plenty of access points. The reception staff are friendly with basic English. Staying on the lower floors may be advisable as the lift can sometimes be a little slow. **$$**

🏠 **Sleman (Sulaimani) Palace Hotel** (57 rooms) Salem St; 📞 313 4141; 📧 sulaimanipalace@yahoo.com. Very clean & comfortable with good food, excellent service & polite staff. The business centre & internet facilities are free to residents. The views from the room windows are amazing; huge panoramas across the city to the foothills of the nearby mountain range. B/fast inc. **$$**

🏠 **Yadi Hotel** (40 rooms) Saalam St, opp the general library; 📱 0770 217 9294. Located near the museum in the old town & within easy walking distance of the bazaar area, this hotel is well situated with various restaurants & shops close by. It is economical, friendly & clean, & although the standards may not be up to those in better European-style hotels, it is a comfortable place to stay. The manager speaks good English. The only meal available is b/fast, which is very good & there are excellent views from the b/fast room. For dining, the nearby Star City store has excellent restaurants on the top floor, & the ice cream there is not to be missed! **$$**

BUDGET

🏠 **Bukan Motel** Pyramid St. Large, rather old-fashioned rooms with shared bathrooms. *Dbl US$30, though cheaper rooms are available.* **$**

Hiwa Hotel Kawa St. Basic rooms with shared bathrooms. Friendly, obliging staff. *Sgl US$20.* **$**

Hotel Chrakhan Salim St, next to Ashti Hotel. One of the cheaper hotels in this part of Suleimaniyah. A little tired looking but still passable. The hotel has en-suite bathrooms (unlike many budget hotels) & some of the rooms even have a balcony, though not the quieter rooms at the back of the hotel. Hot water & electricity are fairly reliable & there is a nice, though modest restaurant attached. *Dbl room around US$35.* **$**

Mewan Hotel Pyramid St. Very basic but reasonable considering the price. One bathroom is shared between two rooms. The staff are friendly & speak a little English. Plenty of cheap eating places nearby. *Trpl room US$12.* **$**

Parezh Hotel Baban St; 210 7185; m 0770 366 8888, 0750 102 1666; mahmud_sirwan@yahoo.com. A modest hotel, but one which is good value for the price. **$**

Hotel Tara Pyramid St. Single rooms are basic but acceptable, though they have seen better days. If you pay a few dollars more you can get a dbl for one person. Bathrooms are shared between 3 rooms. *US$20 sgl.* **$**

✖ WHERE TO EAT AND DRINK

For those on a budget, there are many restaurants serving Italian and foreign food. The upper floors of the Kawa Shopping Mall have a selection of Chinese restaurants and other Chinese shops and businesses, mostly catering for the migrant Chinese workforce. Local restaurants tend to be small and scattered around the city. Seek recommendations from the locals or hotel staff; as in all cities restaurants come and go and standards fluctuate. If you like a good coffee, try **Pasha's Coffee House** in the bazaar area. Walk through the gate opposite the Sulaimani Palace Hotel and up the street to the first circle with the booksellers, go around them, take the shallow right and look for Pasha's on the left.

✖Chalak's Place Salim St; m 0770 151 2976. Housed in a beautiful classic, old building is one of the most beautiful locations to dine in the whole of Kurdistan. It is an excellent choice for both youngsters & adults, with authentic pizza, grills & espressos. Not cheap, but with delicious food, friendly & professional service, & a romantic atmosphere, if you want a special dining experience, this is the place. There is also a nice veranda & a bar on the 2nd floor.

✖Copthorne Hotel Barnaman m 0770 600 0000. With 3 restaurants and a patisserie, the Copthorne Hotel Barnaman (see page 405) is a good place for drinking & dining. They have an excellent Italian restaurant **Salute** (🕐 noon–16.00, 19.00–23.30) just beside the lobby, an international cuisine buffet restaurant called **Downtown** (🕐 06.30–10.30, noon–15.00, 18.00–22.00) where you can get a good steak & amazing mojitos, & **Uptown** (🕐 19.00–01.00), an Asian Fusion restaurant over 2 stories, which also has a late-night lounge bar overlooking the skyline of Suleimaniyah. There is a little café beside the main lobby Cakes & Bakes (🕐 10.00–22.00) with a Western-style bakery serving Danish pastries, croissants & great coffee.

✖Lazelar Restaurant Sarchinar Hill; 319 2602. On the 5th floor of the Lazelar Hotel (see page 405) this restaurant has good views overlooking the city, as well as absolutely delicious food. The lamb shank comes well recommended, as does their famous 'Lalezar Steak' presented on a wooden plate with vegetables & mashed potato. Lazelar's has good service & a solid selection of drinks.

ENTERTAINMENT

The **Zamoa Gallery** has a cinema which screens Kurdish and foreign films. There is a touristy feel in the neighbourhood of Sarchinar which is dotted with clubs and restaurants and the Nowroz Amusement Park, with a zoo, a cinema-complex and a water park.

SHOPPING

During much of the week the central streets of the city, close by the major mosques, are one huge market, selling everything that is modern: top-of-the-range electrical goods, mobile phones, clothes and local produce. Scattered through the streets are many little cafés and tea stalls. The 21st century also makes its presence felt in the form of three large supermarkets, the most popular being Altun. The riverside walk is a pleasant way to spend an afternoon, and the riverside market is the place for rugs at bargain prices and other interesting souvenirs. There is also a bird market and a craft market with bowls and pots made of wood

SPORTS/FITNESS

Suleimaniyah's top-end hotels typically have their own pools and fitness facilities. Some may be open to non-residents for a daily fee; it is always worth enquiring. The Hawary Shar Park development, a 100ha leisure and entertainment park currently under construction, will include a shopping mall, a golf course and zoological gardens and is due to open in 2017.

OTHER PRACTICALITIES

MEDICAL FACILITIES The largest hospitals are:

Emergency Hospital Girdi Joga Centre; ☏327 0570. Specialties: general medicine and trauma (car accidents)
Shahid Dr Aso Hospital Qirga City Centre; ☏326 6714. Specialties: general medicine and ophthalmology

Suleimaniah Maternity Hospital City Centre; ☏320 0068. Specialties: obstetrics and gynecology
Suleimaniah Paediatrics Hospital Qanat Street; ☏320 2953. Specialties: paediatrics
Suleimaniah (Teaching) Hospital Girdi Joga Centre; ☏327 0565. Specialties: general medicine and trauma

WHAT TO SEE AND DO

SULEIMANIYAH MUSEUM The Suleimaniyah Museum in Salim Street is home to a collection of Kurdish artefacts from around the region, many of which are several thousand years old. It is the second-largest museum in Iraq after the National Museum in Baghdad, but is still undergoing restoration and refurbishment.

AMNA SURAKA (THE RED HOUSE) MUSEUM Notoriously known as the 'red house' owing to the red colour of the security buildings used by Saddam Hussein's regime, this former detention centre is now preserved as a memorial and museum (⊕ 08.00–17.00 daily), showing how its detainees lived. The museum provides information about the genocide campaigns against the Kurds in Iraq. Shattered building still standing at the site poignantly reflect these atrocities as do sketches and pictures scratched on the walls of former cells. In the grounds there is also a small ethnological display showing a typical Kurdish home, a hall of mirrors and a display of taxidermy. A children's play area situated in the centre lightens the atmosphere. Some of the bullet-scarred buildings here also show the last stand of Saddam's police and troops in the city when it was reclaimed by the Kurds.

JEWLAKAN This is the old Jewish quarter of Suleimaniyah on the eastern outskirts of the city. The neighbourhood consists of narrow alleys and mud-walled homes, with a few synagogues that have been recently renovated by the government. Most of the once-large Jewish population emigrated *en masse* to Israel in 1951.

GALLERIES The **Zamoa Gallery** in Qaesari Naqeeb Bazaar is open year round and displays the works of the city's artists. It is run by Rostam Aghala, a well-known, modern Kurdish artist.

Aram Gallery (*Sequami Bexud, off Khak St*) is another place for artistic activities. It started the night-cinema project screening Kurdish and foreign films.

JAFF TOWERS Situated on Serchnsar Road, Jaff Towers is a major residential and retail skyscraper. It is in the same area as Chavy Tourism City, the Nowroz Amusement Park and zoo, a bowling alley, City Star Games Centre and the main city cinema.

AROUND SULEIMANIYAH

DOKAN About 65km northwest of Suleimaniyah is the picturesque Dokan Lake lined with cabins for visitors to enjoy boating or swimming. A place of natural beauty, the lake is at the meeting point of two rivers, the Tanjarow and Sirwan, and was formed as a result of hydro-electric power dams built decades

HALABJA: TRAGIC PAST, UNCERTAIN FUTURE

Just over an hour's drive from Suleimaniyah and relatively close to the Iranian border is the town of Halabja. It was brought from obscurity by the horrific poisonous gas attack on its inhabitants during the Anfal, the anti-Kurdish campaign led by Saddam's regime between 1986 and 1987, during the Iran-Iraq War. Altogether, there were 180,000 victims of the Anfal, civilians killed by chemical and conventional bombardments. Hundreds of villages were destroyed.

In Halabja more than 5,000 inhabitants, mostly women, children and old men, were killed in about 20 minutes on 16 March 1988. This brutal and inhuman retaliation to the possession of the town by the Iranians and Kurdish *peshmerga* was perpetrated by Saddam's cousin, Ali Hassan al Majid (Chemical Ali). Unbeknown to the Iraqi command there was an Iranian news team in Halabja at the time who filmed the attack and subsequent grotesque deaths. Images of children's corpses shocked the world. This one attack played a significant role in changing the attitudes of many, particularly those from Europe, about Saddam Hussein's Iraq.

The dead were gathered by the *peshmerga* and Iranians and hurriedly buried in five large pits scattered around the outskirts of the town. The long-term effects of the poisonous gas were not known then and few of the bodies were identified individually. Today, the pits are marked and simply enclosed. The town cemetery, whose gate has a sign 'Baathists should not enter here' in English, has an area set aside for headstones marked with each family's name, their only record.

Halabja was effectively abandoned for some time and a 'new' Halabja was built a few kilometres away, although this is now in decline. The original Halabja has recovered and has a busy air with many reconstructed buildings. Families take their children to play in the wooded areas near some of the death pits and life goes on.

ago, which are now an important source of electricity for the whole area. Dokan itself, by the side of the Little Zab river and close by Dokan Lake, was once a sleepy town of 5,000 inhabitants. After the fall of Saddam, business in the town started booming and cabins for tourists were constructed. Visitors feast on fish and marinated apricots, the local specialities. In Dokan is a tourist village owned by the PUK; the local militias get some of the profits from this enterprise. Today, as the village grows and chalets and hotels continue to be constructed, Dokan can claim to be one of Kurdistan's major resorts, experiencing a boom in hotels, restaurants and holiday chalets, and showing just how much the tourist industry is taking off in Kurdistan.

Where to stay and eat

Ashur Hotel (66 rooms) m 0770 154 2159. Located right on the lake with a beautiful view of the mountains, the Ashur Hotel is spacious & welcoming. Rooms are very clean, with en-suite, AC, Wi-Fi & cable TV. There is an outdoor swimming pool. The restaurant has a decent selection of food & b/fast is inc in the room cost. **$$$**

SARCHINAR A mountain resort 5km from Suleimaniyah, Sarchinar is a place of beautiful forests and a pond formed by several springs.

KALAR An hour's drive south from Suleimaniyah after Darbandikan Lake and dam is the town of Kalar, home to the ancient Sherwana Castle, also known as

On the 25th anniversary of the chemical weapons attack a major conference on the genocide in Iraqi Kurdistan was held in London. Nechirvan Barzani, Prime Minister of the KRG, emphasised that: 'In Halabja, we continue to allocate land and provide house-building funds for the families of the victims.'

In February 2013 the British Government officially recognised the Anfal campaign as genocide against the Kurdish People. It has also been recognised as such by the Norwegian and Swedish governments.

But despite encouraging words from the KRG the citizens of Halabja and the victims of the chemical weapons attack feel not enough has been done to assist them with health issues and to develop and modernise Halabja. On the 2006 anniversary of the gas attack, violent demonstrations erupted, with an estimated 7,000 demonstrators protesting against priorities in reconstruction, claiming that officials were not sincerely addressing the problems of the gas-attack victims. The memorial museum was set on fire.

Since those days the memorial has been completely renovated with the plaques inside repaired and restored. The gardens surrounding the memorial were landscaped and are now well maintained. Computer disks and information about the atrocity are readily available for the visitor.

In December 2012 the 'White' organisation was formed for the collection of remnants and memories concerning the gas attacks, including reports, articles and documents. 'All this must be collected and preserved for future generations,' a White Organisation spokesman said in a statement. 'Until today we lack basic services and support, both from the Kurdistan Regional Government and the International Community'. White, which stands for peace and is the colour of the smoke of poison-gas grenades, has not yet been granted official registration by the KRG.

Shirwanah Castle. It was built by King Mohammed Jaff in 1734 and is still the home of the Jaff family today. The castle also houses the Garmiyan Museum. In April 2004, there was an influx of 2,000 Iraqi Kurds into Kalar. They had fled from their homes in Fallujah after being threatened by Arab insurgents for supporting the Coalition and refusing to fight against the US military.

PENJWIN About 35km east of Suleimaniyah, Penjwin is a popular picnic area. A famous Kurdish personality, the writer, politician and philosopher Tawfiq Wahbi, is buried there.

HAMRAN The area of Hamran lies east of Suleimaniyah, on the Iranian border. A region of quaint mountain villages and walnut trees, Hamran is famous for its handmade shoes.

CHAMCHAMAL VALLEY Zarzi Cave in the Chamchamal Valley lies between Suleimaniyah and Kirkuk. In the 1920s Dorothy Garrod excavated the caves and discovered flint tools, stones and scrapers, as well as animal bones dating back at least 15,000 years.

DARBAND KHAN Close to the Iranian border is an interesting place for an excursion *en route* to Halabja. The fine mountain scenery with lakes and reservoir begun by Saddam Hussein make the 2-hour journey to Halabja worth the detour. By the normal route the journey takes no more than 90 minutes.

HALABJA The Halabja Monument (see box, pages 408–9) is being refurbished once again and is closed at the time of writing. The town's cemetery has a moving simplicity, reminiscent of the World War I war graves in northern Europe. The return journey from Halabja to Suleimaniyah by the direct route takes 90 minutes.

KOI SANJAC Located on the road between Erbil and Suleimaniyah, Koi Sanjac was one of the most significant trade centres in Abbasid and Ottoman times. It has a building known as the Great Khan, which was once a bazaar.

JARMO One of the earliest archaeological sites in the Middle East, Jarmo lies a 35-minute drive from Suleimaniyah on the Kirkuk road, and then off-road into the hills. Excavated between 1948 and 1955 to explore the origins of agriculture, the site shows the occupation of 12 building phases and the transition from aceramic to pottery Neolithic (c7500–6500BC) and contemporary with late pre-pottery Neolithic B and the Hassuna cultures. Most of the Jarmo site dates from perhaps one of the first fully fledged mixed-farming economies. A difficult site to find, it is close by the town of Chamchamaland on the main road, but a local guide is needed to locate it.

Appendix 1

Compiled by Henry Stedman with Maria Oleynik

ARABIC
Useful words

aeroplane	طائرة	*tayara*
airport	مطار	*mataar*
bank	بنك	*bank*
baths	حمام	*hammam*
beach	شاطئ	*shatt*
bicycle	دراجة الهوائية	*daraja hawai'ya*
bus	باص	*baas*
café	مقهي	*mak-hah*
church	كنيسة	*kaniisa*
clock tower	برج الساعة	*burj as-sa'a*
embassy	سفارة	*sifaara*
good	طيب	*tayeb*
hill	تل	*tel*
hospital	مستشفى	*mustashfa*
hotel	فندق	*funduk*
laundry	مصبغة	*masbagha*
market	سوق	*souq*
mausoleum	ضريحة	*dariha*
monastery	دير	*der*
mosque	مسجد	*masjid*
museum	متحف	*madhaf*
passport	جواز سفر	*jawaaz safar*
police	شرطة	*buliis*
post office	مكتب البريد	*maktab al-bariid*
restaurant	مطعم	*mata'am*
room	غرفة	*ghurfa*
servis taxi	سرويس	*servees*
shower	دش	*duush*
station	محطة	*mahatta*
street	شارع	*sharia*
synagogue	كنيس	*kanis*
taxi	تاكسي	*taksi*
telephone	تلفن	*talifawn*
ticket	تذكرة	*tadhkara*
toilet	حمام	*hamam*
tourist office	مكتب سيحة	*maktab siyaha*
tower	مجدل، برج	*majdal, burj*

Food and drink

beer	بيرة	*biira*
bread	خبز	*khubz*
breakfast	فطور	*futu'ur*
cheese	جبنة	*jibneh*
chicken	دجاج	*djaj*
coffee	قهوة	*qahwa*
fish	سمك	*samak*
fruit	فاكهة	*fakiha*
ice-cream	بوظة، دندرما	*buuza, dondurma*
juice	عصير	*a'asiir*
lamb	خروف	*kharu'uf*
pork	لحم خنزير	*lahm khanziir*
salad	سلطة	*salata*
soup	حساء	*hass'a*
spicy	حار	*har*
tea	شاي	*shai*
vegetarian	نباتي	*nabati*
water	ماء	*mayy*

Numbers

Unlike the written language, Arabic numerals run from left to right.

1	واحد	*wahid*
2	اثنين	*ithnayn*
3	ثلاثة	*tala'ata*
4	آربع	*arba'a*
5	خمسة	*khamsa*
6	ستة	*sita'a*
7	سبعة	*saba'a*
8	ثمانية	*tamanya*
9	تسعة	*tissa'a*
10	عشرة	*a'ashra*
11	أحد عشر	*ihdashr*
12	أثنا عشر	*itnayshr*
13	ثلاث عشر	*tala'atashr*
14	أربع عشر	*arba'ata'ashr*
20	عشرين	*ishri'in*
21	واحد و عشرين	*wahid wa'ishri'in*
30	ثلاثين	*talathi'in*
40	أربعين	*arba'ati'in*
50	خمسين	*khamsi'in*
60	ستين	*sitti'in*
70	سبعين	*saba'i'in*
80	ثمانين	*tamaani'in*
90	تسعين	*tis'i'in*
100	مائة	*miyya*
200	مائتين	*mittayn*
1,000	ألف	*elf*
2,000	ألفين	*alfayn*
3,000	ثلاثة الآف	*tala'athat aalaaf*
1,000,000	مليون	*malaayin*

Days of the week

Monday	يوم الاثنين	*Yawm al-Ithnayn*
Tuesday	يوم الثلاثاء	*Yawm al-Tala'ata*
Wednesday	ءيوم الآربعا	*Yawm al-Arbaa*
Thursday	يوم الخميس	*Yawm al-Khamis*
Friday	يوم الجمعة	*Yawm al-Juma'a*
Saturday	يوم السبت	*Yawm al-Sabt*
Sunday	يوم الآحد	*Yawm al-Ahad*

Conversation

hello	مرحبا (سلام عليكم)	*maharba*
		(formal: salaam wa'aleikhoom)
goodbye	مع السلامة	*ma assalama*
yes	نعم، ايوه	*na'am, aywa*
no	لا	*la*
please	من فضلك	*min fadlak*
sorry	سامحني	*samahni*
thank you	شكرا	*shukran*
what is your name?	ما اسمك؟	*ma asmak*
I would like	من فضلك	*min fadlak*
how much?	بكم	*beekam?*
cheap	رخيص	*rakhees*
expensive	غالي	*ghaali*
how long (time)?	قديش؟	*gaddaysh*

KURDISH
Greetings

Hello	چۆنی	*Choni*
Goodbye	خوا حافیز	*Khwahafeez*
Pleased to meet you	خۆشحالم به ناسینت	*Khosh'halim be nasinit*
Good morning	به یانیی باش	*Beyane bash*
Good day	رۆژ باش	*Rozh bash*
Good afternoon (or evening)	نئواره باش	*Neware bash*
Good evening	نئواره باش	*Neware bash*
Good night	شه و باش	*Shaw bash*
How are you?	له چییای؟	*Le chiyai?*
I'm fine, tank you.	من باشم، سوپاست ده که م	*Man bashim, spasem dekam.*
What's your name?	ناوت چییه؟	*Nawt chiye?*
Where are you from?	تو خه لکی کوئیت؟	*To khelki kwey?*
Cheers/Good health!	نوش!	*Nosh*
Have a nice day	رۆژ خوش	*Rozh xosh*
Welcome	بهخیربیت	*Bakher beyt*
You're welcome		*Shayane nea*

Basic Phrases

Yes	به لئ	*Baleh*
No	نه	*Na*
I don't understand	من تئ ناگه م	*Man tenagem*
Please say that again		*Tikaye, dîsan bîllêrewe*
Please write it down		*Tikaye, ewe binûse*

English	Kurdish	Transliteration
Do you speak English?	ئایا زمانی ئینگلیزی قسه ده كه يت؟	Aya smani englizi qse dekeyt?
Do you speak Kurdish?	ئایا زمانی كوردی قسه ده كه يت؟	Aya zmani kurdi qse dekeyt?
What is that called in Kurdish?	ئه وه چی پی ده ووترئت به كوردی؟	Awe chi pe dawtret be curdi?
I don't speak Kurdish		Kurdi nazanm
Excuse me	ببووره	Bbuwre
How much is this?	یه مه به چه نده؟	Ame be chande?
Sorry	ببووره	Bbuwre
Please	بئ زه حمه ت	Bezahmet
Thank you	سوپاس	Spaas
Where's the toilet?		Twayleteke li kwê ye?
Okay/good	باش	Bash

Food

English	Kurdish	Transliteration
Yoghurt	مست	Mast
Bread	نان	Nan
Honey	هه نگوین	Hangwin
Banana(s)	مۆز	Moz
Fried eggs		Helke ron
Tea	چايه	Chai
Tea without sugar	چايه به بئ شه كر	Chai bebi shakir
Cheese	په نیر	Penir
Rice	برنج	Birinj
Salad	زه لاته	Zalate
Meat	گۆشت	Gosht
Fish	ماسی	Masi
Chicken	مریشك	Mirishik

Days of the week

Day	Kurdish	Transliteration	Day	Kurdish	Transliteration
Monday	دوو شه مه	Dushama	Friday	جومعه	Juma
Tuesday	سئ شه مه	Seshama	Saturday	شه مه	Shama
Wednesday	چوار شه مه	Chwaarshama	Sunday	يه ك شه مه	Yekshama
Thursday	پینج شه مه	Penshama			

Numbers

Number	Kurdish	Transliteration	Number	Kurdish	Transliteration
1	يه ك	Yek	6	شه ش	Shash
2	دوو	Du	7	حه وت	Hawt
3	سئ	Se	8	هه شت	Hasht
4	چوار	Chwaar	9	نۆ	No
5	پینج	Penj	10	ده	Dah

UPDATES WEBSITE

You can post your comments and recommendations, and read the latest feedback and updates from other readers online at www.bradtupdates.com/iraq.

Appendix 2

FURTHER INFORMATION

BOOKS AND WEBSITES
General introduction

Hunt, Courtney, *The History of Iraq*, Greenwood Press, London (2005).

Nakash, Yitzak, *Reaching For Power: The Shia In The Modern Arab World*, Princeton University Press, New Jersey (2006).

Polk, William, *Understanding Iraq*, I B Tauris, London (2006).

Stansfield, Gareth, *Iraq*, Polity Press, Cambridge (2007).

Thabit, Abdullan, *A Short History Of Iraq*, Harlow Pearson Education, Harlow (2003).

Tripp, Charles, *A History of Iraq*, Cambridge University Press, Cambridge (2002).

Vali, Nasr, *The Shia Revival*, W W Norton & Company, New York (2006).

The ancient kingdoms

Dalley, Stephanie (ed), *The Legacy of Mesopotamia*, Oxford University Press, Oxford (1988).

Leick, Gwendolyn, *The Invention of the City*, Penguin, London (2001).

McCall, Henrietta, *Mesopotamian Myths*, British Museum Press, London (1990).

Reade, Julian, *Mesopotamia*, British Museum Publications, London (2000).

Roux, Georges, *Ancient Iraq*, Penguin Books, Harmondsworth (1966).

Van der Mieropp, M, *A History of the Ancient Near East ca. 3000-323BC*, Blackwell, Oxford (2004).

The Abbasids, Ummayads and Ottomans

Hawting, G R, *The First Dynasty of Islam*, Croom Helm, London (1986).

Kennedy, Hugh, *The Prophet and the Age of the Caliphates*, Longman, London (1986).

Kennedy, Hugh, *The Court of the Caliphs: When Baghdad ruled the Muslim World*, Phoenix, London (2005).

Lyons, Malcolm, *Saladin: The Politics of the Holy War*, Cambridge University Press, Cambridge (1982).

20th-century Iraq

Aburish, Said, *Saddam Hussein: The Politics of Revenge*, Bloomsbury, London (2000).

Alsamari, Lewis, *Out of Iraq: The terrifying true story of one man's escape from the harshest regime of the modern era*, Bantam Press, London (2007).

Arnove, Anthony (ed), *Iraq under Siege*, Pluto, London (2000).

Childs, Nick, *The Gulf War*, Wayland, Hove (1988).

Goodman, Susan, *Gertrude Bell*, Berg Women's series, Leamington Spa (1985).

Graves, Robert, *Lawrence and The Arabs*, Jonathan Cape, London (1927).

Hassan, Hamdi, *The Iraqi Invasion of Kuwait: Religion, Identity and Otherness in the Analysis of War and Conflict*, Pluto Press, London (1991).

Jabbar, Faleh, *Why the Intifada Failed in Iraq since the Gulf War: Prospects for Democracy*, CARDRI (Committee Against Repression and for Democratic Rights in Iraq), Zed Books, London (1994).

Al-Khalil, Samir, *Cruelty and Silence*, Penguin Books, London (1994).

Al-Khalil, Samir, *Republic of Fear*, Hutchinson Radius, London (1989).

Al-Khayyat, *Honour and Shame: Women in Modern Iraq*, Al Saqi Books, London (1990).

Simons, Geoff, *Iraq: From Sumer to Saddam*, Macmillan, London (1994).

Sluglett, Peter, *Britain in Iraq: Contriving King & Country*, I B Tauris, London (2007).

Sluglett, Marion and Peter, *Iraq since 1958: From Revolution to Dictatorship*, I B Tauris, revised paperback, London (2001).

The 2003 war and the Battle of Fallujah

Bellavia, David (with Bruning, John) *House to House: An Epic of Urban Warfare*, Simon & Schuster, London (2007).

Buzzell, Colby, *My War: Killing Time in Iraq*, G P Putman's Sons, USA (2007).

Cushman, Thomas, *A Matter of Principle: Humanitarian Arguments for War in Iraq*, University of California Press, California (2005).

Fawn, Rick and Hinnebusch, Raymond (eds) *The Iraq War: Causes & Consequences*, Lynne Rienner Publishers, Colorado (2006).

Hiro, Dilip, *Secrets & Lies: The True Story of the Iraq War*, Nation Books, New York (2004).

Pauly Jr, Robert, *Strategic Pre-emption: US Foreign Policy and the Second Iraq War*, Ashgate Publishing, Aldershot (2005).

Rai, Milan, *Regime Unchanged: Why the War on Iraq Changed Nothing*, Pluto Press, London (2003).

Ramesh, Randeep (ed), *The War We Could Not Stop: The Real Story for the Battle of Iraq*, Faber & Faber, London (2003).

Simpson, John, *The Wars Against Saddam: Taking the Hard Road to Baghdad*, MacMillan, London (2003).

Useful website
www.mnf-iraq.com

Post-Saddam Iraq

Ajami, Fouad, *The Foreigners' Gift: The Americans, the Arabs and the Iraqis in Iraq*, Free Press, New York (2005).

Alawi, Ali, *The Occupation of Iraq: Winning the War, Losing the Peace*, Yale University Press, Yale (2007).

Ali, Tariq, *Bush in Babylon: The Recolonisation of Iraq*, Verso, London (2003).

Baer, Robert, *See No Evil: The True Story of a Ground Soldier in the CIA's War on Terrorism*, Crown Publishers, New York (2002).

Bremer III, Paul (with McConnell, Malcolm), *My Year in Iraq: The Struggle to Build a Future of Hope*, Threshold Editions, New York (2006).

Byman, Daniel and Pollack, Kenneth, *Things Fall Apart: Containing the Spillover from an Iraqi Civil War*, Brookings Institution Press, Washington (2007).

Chehab, Zaki, *Iraq Ablaze: Inside the Insurgency*, I B Tauris, London (2006).

Cockburn, Patrick, *The Jihadis Return: ISIS and the New Sunni Uprising*, Or Books, London (2014)

Cockburn, Patrick, *The Occupation: War and Resistance in Iraq*, Verso, London (2006).

Ferner, Mike, *Inside the Red Zone*, Prager Publishers, Westport (2006).

Foulk, Vincent, *The Battle for Fallujah: Occupation, Resistance and Stalemate in the War in Iraq*, McFarland & Company Inc, North Carolina (2007).

Galbraith, Peter, *The End of Iraq: How American Incompetence Created a War Without End*, Simon & Schuster, London (2006).

Hiro, Dilip, *Secrets and Lies: Operation 'Iraqi Freedom' and After*, Nation Books, New York (2004).

Jamail, Dahr, *Beyond the Green Zone: Dispatches from an Unembedded Journalist in Occupied Iraq*, Haymarket Books, Chicago (2007).

Kember, Norman, *Hostage in Iraq*, Darton, Longman and Todd, London (2007).

McCarthy, Rory, *Nobody Told Us We Are Defeated: Stories from the New Iraq*, Chatto & Windus, London (2006).

Packer, George, *The Assassins' Gate: America in Iraq*, Farrar, Straus and Giroux, New York (2005).

Parenti, Christian, *The Freedom: Shadows and Hallucinations in Occupied Iraq*, The New Press, New York (2004).

Phillips, David, *Losing Iraq: Inside the Post-war Reconstruction Fiasco*, Westview Press, New York (2005).

Al-Rehaief, Mohammed Odeh, *Because Each Life is Precious: Why an Iraqi Man Risked Everything for Private Jessica Lynch*, Harper Collins, New York (2003).

Ricks, Thomas, *Fiasco: The American Military Adventure in Iraq*, Penguin Press, New York (2006).

Riverbend, *Baghdad Burning: Girl Blog From Iraq Vols I and II*, Marion Boyars Publishers Ltd, London (2006).

White, Andrew, *Iraq: Searching for Hope*, Continuum, New York (2005).

Wilding, Jo, *Don't Shoot the Clowns: Taking a Circus to the Children of Iraq*, New Internationalist Publications, Oxford (2006).

Useful websites

www.iraqupdates.com
www.einews.com
www.uruknet.info Anti-occupation website
www.zaman.com
www.iraqrevenuewatch.org
www.idao.org Iraqi Democrats Against Occupation
www.iraqigovernment.org
www.anotherIraq.com Good news website about Iraq

Archaeological sites

Bogdanos, Matthew and Patrick William, *Thieves of Baghdad*, Bloomsbury, New York (2005).

Curtis, John and Reade, Julian E, *Art and Empire: Treasures from Assyria in the British Museum*, British Museum Press, London (2005).

Polk, Milbry and Schuster, Angela (eds), *The Looting of the Iraq Museum, Baghdad: The Lost Legacy of Ancient Mesopotamia*, Harry N Abrams Inc, New York (2005).

Al-Radi, Nuha, *Baghdad Diaries*, Al Saqi Books, London (1998).

Russell, John, *The Final Sack of Nineveh*, Yale University Press, New Haven (1998).

Useful websites

www.thebritishmuseum.ac.uk
http://oi.uchicago.edu/OI/IRAQ/iraq.html Lost Treasures from Iraq, at the Oriental Institute, University of Chicago

www.britac.ac.uk/institutes/iraq British School of Archaeology in Iraq
www.baghdadmuseum.org

Travels in Iraq

Arnold, Catherine, *Baghdad City Guide*, Bradt Travel Guides, Chalfont St Peter (2004). Out of print.

Blunt, Anne, *Bedouin Tribes of the Euphrates*, Cass, London (1968).

Dabrowska, Karen, *Iraq: the Bradt Travel Guide*, Bradt Travel Guides, Chalfont St Peter (2002).

Heude, Lieutenant William, *A Voyage up the Persian Gulf in 1817*, Longman, London (1819).

Niebuhr, Carsten, *Travels Through Arabia and Other Countries in the East*, R Morison and Son, Edinburgh (1792).

Thesiger, Wilfred, *Arabian Sands*, Collins, London (1959).

Useful website
www.hinterlandtravel.com

Art and culture

Baram, Amatzia, *Culture, History and Ideology in the Formation of Ba'thist Iraq*, MacMillan, London (1991).

Faraj, Maysaloun, *Strokes of Genius: Contemporary Iraqi Art*, Al Saqi Books, London (2001).

Al Hashimi, Miriam, *Traditional Arabic Cooking*, Garnet Publishing, Reading (1993).

Al-Janub, Tariq, *Studies in Medieval Iraqi Architecture*, Ministry of Culture, Baghdad (1982).

Al-Khalil, Samir, *The Monument*, Andre Deutsch, London (1991).

Stevens, E S, *Folk-tales of Iraq*, Oxford University Press, Oxford (1931).

Tatchell, Jo, *Nabeel's Song: The story of the Poet of Baghdad*, Sceptre, London (2006).

Baghdad

Chandrasekaran, Rajiv, *Imperial Life in the Emerald City: Inside Baghdad's Green Zone*, Bloomsbury, London (2007).

Coke, Richard, *Baghdad: The City of Peace*, Butterworth, London (1927).

Eames, Andrew, *The 8.55 to Baghdad*, Bantam, London (2004).

Gunning, Heyrick Bons, *Baghdad Business School*, Eye Books, London (2004).

Pax, Salam, *The Baghdad Blog*, Atlantic Books, London (2003).

Roberts, Paul William, *The Demonic Comedy: The Baghdad of Saddam Hussein*, Mainstream Publishing, Edinburgh (1999).

Wiet, Gaston, *Baghdad: Metropolis of the Abbasid Caliphate*, University of Oklahoma Press, Oklahoma (1971).

Useful website
http://riverbendblog.blogspot.com Weblog of an Iraqi woman

The north

Ahmed, Mohammed and Gunter, Michael, *The Kurdish Question and the 2003 Iraq War*, Mazda Publishers Inc, California (2005).

Astarjian, Henry, *The Struggle for Kirkuk: The Rise of Hussein, Oil and the Death of Tolerance in Iraq*, Greenwood Publishing Group, Westport (2007).

Bird, Christiane, *A Thousand Sighs, A Thousand Revolts: Journeys in Kurdistan*, Random House (2004).

Bowen, Wayne, *Undoing Saddam: From Occupation to Sovereignty in Northern Iraq*, Potomac Books, Dulles (2007).

Bruinessen, Martin van, *Agha, Shaikh and State*, Utrecht University, Utrecht (1978).

Chaliand, Gerald, *The Kurdish Tragedy*, Zed Books, London (1994).

Cook, Helen, *The Safe Haven in Northern Iraq*, Human Rights Centre, University of Essex, Kurdistan Human Rights Project, Exeter (1995).

Hamilton, A M, *Road through Kurdistan*, Faber & Faber, London (1937).

Hiltermann, Joost, *A Poisonous Affair: America, Iraq and the Gassing of Halabja*, Cambridge University Press, Cambridge (2007).

Izady, Mehrdad, *The Kurds: A Concise Handbook*, Taylor and Francis Inc, Washington (1992).

McDowall, David, *A Modern History of the Kurds*, I B Tauris, London (1996).

Meiselas, Susan, *Kurdistan in the Shadow of History*, Random House, London (1997).

Middle East Watch, *Genocide in Iraq: the Anfal Campaign Against the Kurds*, Human Rights Watch, New York (1993).

O'Leary, Brendan, McGarry, John and Salih, Khaled (eds), *The Future of Kurdistan in Iraq*, University of Pennsylvania Press, Pennsylvania (2005).

Parry, Oswald, *Six Months in a Syrian Monastery*, London (1895).

Solecki, R, *Shanidar: The First Flower People*, Alfred Knopf, New York (1971).

Thornhill, Teresa, *Sweet Tea with Cardamom: A Journey Through Iraqi Kurdistan*, Pandora, London (1997).

Yildiz, Kerim, *The Kurds in Iraq: The Past, Present & Future*, Pluto Press, London (2007).

Useful websites
www.kurdmedia.com
www.kurdishart.net
www.kurdistanobserver.com
www.krg.org Kurdistan Regional Government
www.kdp.pp.se Kurdistan Democratic Party
www.puk.org Patriotic Union of Kurdistan
www.kurdistancorporation.com Kurdistan Development Corporation
www.theotheriraq.com

The south
Alderson, Andrew, *Bankrolling Basra: The Incredible Story of a Part-time Soldier, $1bn and the Collapse of Iraq*, Constable & Robinson, London (2007).

Chesney, General Francis Rawdon, *The Expedition for the Survey of the Rivers Euphrates and Tigris in 1835, 1836 and 1837*, Longman Green and Co, London (1850).

Maxwell, Gavin, *A Reed Shaken by the Wind*, Longman, London (1957).

Middle East Watch, *Endless Torment: The 1991 Uprising in Iraq and its Aftermath*, Human Rights Watch, New York (1992).

Nakash, Yitzhak, *The Shi'is of Iraq*, Princeton University Press, Princeton, New Jersey (1994).

Salim, S M, *Marsh Dwellers of the Euphrates Delta*, Athlone Press, London (1962).

Stewart, Rory, *Occupational Hazards: My Time Governing in Iraq*, Picador, London (2006).

Thesiger, Wilfred, *The Marsh Arabs*, Penguin, London (1964).

Wetlands Ecosystems Research Group, *An Environmental and Ecological Study of the Marshlands of Mesopotamia*, Amar Appeal Trust, London (1994).

Wiley, Joyce, *The Islamic Movement of Iraqi Shi'as*, Lynne Rienner, Boulder, Colorado (1992).

Useful websites

www.albasrah.net

www.sistani.org

www.iraqiparty.com Iraqi Islamic Party

www.islamicdawaparty.org

Minorities

Benjamin, Marina, *Last Days in Babylon: The story of the Jews of Baghdad*, Bloomsbury, London (2007).

Betts, R B, *Christians in the Arab East: A Political Study*, John Knox Press, Atlanta, Georgia (1978).

Al-Rashid, Madawi, *Iraqi Assyrian Christians in London*, Edwin Mellen Press, Lewiston, New York (1998).

Rejwan, Nissim, *The Last Jews of Baghdad: Remembering a Lost Homeland*, University of Texas Press, Texas (2004).

Shibblak, Abbas, *The Lure of Zion: the Case of Iraqi Jews*, Al Saqi Books, London (1986).

Tapper, Richard, *Some Minorities in the Middle East*, Centre of Near and Middle Eastern Studies, School of Oriental & African Studies, London University, London (1992).

Useful websites

http://members.tripod.lycos.nl/Kerkuk Kirkuk and Turcomans

www.themesopotamian.org

www.zowaa.org Assyrian Democratic Movement

Appendix 3

BIBLIOGRAPHY

Anthony, Lawrence, *Babylon's Ark: The Incredible Wartime Rescue of the Baghdad Zoo*, Thomas Dunne Books/St Martin's Press, New York (2007).

Bates, Daniel and Rassam, Amal, *Peoples and Cultures of the Middle East*, Prentice Hall, New Jersey (1963).

Bowen, Wayne, *Undoing Saddam: From Occupation to Sovereignty in Northern Iraq*, Potomac Books, Dulles (2007).

Dodge, Toby, *Inventing Iraq: The Failure of Nation Building and a History Denied*, C Hurst & Co. London (2003).

Gibb, H A R, Kramers, J H, Levi-Provencal, E and Schacht, J (eds), *Encyclopedia of Islam*, Luzac and Co, London (1960).

Gunter, Michael and Ahmed, Mohammed, *The Kurdish Question and the 2003 Iraqi War*, Mazda Publishers, California (2004).

Haj, Samira, *The Making of Iraq, 1900–1963*, State University of New York Press, New York (1997).

Hayden, Tom, *Ending the War in Iraq*, Akashic Books, New York (2007).

Hitti, P K, *History of the Arabs*, Macmillan, London (1937).

Hunter, Erica, *The Dictionary of Religions*

Keegan, John, *The Daily Telegraph, War On Saddam: The Complete Story of the Iraq Campaign*, Daily Telegraph, London (2003).

Kenneth Kattan, *Mine was the last Generation in Babylon*

Al-Khalil, Samir, *The Monument*, Andre Deutsch, London (1991).

Kimball, Lorenzo, *The Changing Pattern of Political Power in Iraq, 1958–1971*, Robert Speller and Sons, New York (1972).

Kjeilen, Tore, *Encyclopaedia of the Orient* (Online Encyclopaedia http://lexicorient.com/e.o/index.htm).

Kramer, Samuel Noah and The Editors of Life Books, *Cradle of Civilisation*, New York (1967).

Lloyd, Seton, *Twin Rivers*, Oxford University Press, Oxford (1943).

Longrigg, Stephen and Stoakes, Frank, *Iraq*, Ernest Benn Ltd, London (1958).

Longrigg, Stephen, *The Middle East, a Social Geography*, Duckworth, London (1963).

Lovejoy, Bahija, *The Land and People of Iraq*, J B Lippincott Company, New York (1964).

Metz, Helen, *Iraq: A Country Study*, Library of Congress, Washington (1988).

Penrose, Edith and Penrose, E F, *Iraq: International Relations and National Development*, E Benn, London (1978).

Polk, Milbry and Schuster, Angela (editors), *The Looting of the Iraq Museum, Baghdad: the Lost Legacy of Ancient Mesopotamia*, Harry N Abrams, Inc, New York (2005).

Sayyid, Fayyaz Mahmud, *A Short History of Islam*, Oxford University Press, Oxford (1960).

Schoenbaum, Thomas, *International Relations: the Path not Taken – using international law to promote world peace and security*, Cambridge University Press, Cambridge (2006).

Stark, Freya, *Baghdad Sketches*, Murray, London (1947).

Sweetman, Denise, *Kurdish Culture, a Cross-Cultural Guide*, Verlag fur Kultur und Wissenschaft, Bonn (1994).

Tatchell, Jo, *Nabeel's Song*, Doubleday Books, New York (2007).

Totton, Michael, *Where Kurdistan Meets The Red Zone*, Internet blog www.windsof change.net

Tsimhoni, Daphine, *Nationalism, Minorities and Diasporas: identities and rights in the Middle East*, Tauris Academic Series, London (1996).

Warren, John and Fethi, Ihsan, *Traditional Houses in Baghdad*, Coach Publishing House, Horsham, UK (1982).

Whitehead, K J, *Iraq The Irremediable: a Time of Treachery, Intrigue and Murder*, K J Whitehead, London (1989).

Young, Gavin, *Iraq: Land of Two Rivers*, Collins, London (1980).

Young, Gavin, *Return to the Marshes*, Penguin, London (1989).

Index

Page numbers in **bold** indicate major entries; those in *italic* indicate maps

INDEX OF ADVERTISERS